The New York
Botanical Garden
Illustrated Encyclopedia
of Horticulture

The New York Botanical Garden Illustrated Encyclopedia of Horticulture

Thomas H. Everett

Volume 2
Be-Cha

Garland Publishing, Inc.
New York & London

15 14 13 12 11 10 9 8 7 6 5 4 3 2 1

Library of Congress Cataloging in Publication Data

Everett, Thomas H
    The New York Botanical Garden illustrated encyclopedia of horticulture.

    1. Horticulture—Dictionaries. 2. Gardening—Dictionaries. 3. Plants, Ornamental—Dictionaries. 4. Plants, Cultivated—Dictionaries. I. New York (City). Botanical Garden. II. Title.
SB317.58.E94   635.9'03'21   80-65941
ISBN 0-8240-7232-4

PHOTO CREDITS

Black and White

Agriculture Canada: Dominion Arboretum and Botanic Garden, p. 468. W. Atlee Burpee Company: *Browallia viscosa* 'Sapphire', p. 501. Evan's Gardens: *Buddleia salviifolia*, p. 514. Fairchild Tropical Garden: Fairchild Tropical Garden, p. 463. A. B. Graf: *Boea hygroscopica*, p. 438; *Bolbitis heteroclita*, p. 443; *Bolusanthus speciosus*, p. 445; *Bowenia spectabilis*, p. 475; *Brownea coccinea*, p. 502; *Canistrum lindenii*, p. 603; *Carruanthus ringens*, p. 629; *Catopsis morreniana*, p. 650. Logee's Greenhouses: *Begonia pustulata argentea*, p. 374; *Begonia speculata*, p. 375; *Begonia boweri*, p. 376; *Begonia hemsleyana*, p. 379; *Begonia involucrata*, p. 383. Longwood Gardens: Longwood Gardens (2 pictures), p. 466. Los Angeles State and County Arboretum: *Bellis perennis*, p. 396. Missouri Botanical Garden: Missouri Botanical Garden, p. 464. Montreal Botanical Garden: Montreal Botanical Garden (2 pictures), p. 468. Norfolk Botanic Garden: Norfolk Botanic Garden, p. 467; *Camellia japonica* (d), p. 583; *Camellia sasanqua*, p. 583; *Camellia granthamiana* (a), p. 585. Rancho Santa Ana Botanic Garden: Rancho Santa Ana Botanic Garden, p. 461. *Southport Visiter:* Southport Flower Show, p. 537. The New York Botanical Garden: *Beaumontia grandiflora* (b), p. 361; Beets, the harvest, p. 365; Typical female flowers of begonia, p. 367; *Begonia tuberhybrida* varieties, p. 368; *Begonia hiemalis* 'Clibran's Pink', p. 370; *Begonia socotrana* (bulbs), p. 371; *Begonia froebelii*, p. 371; *Begonia pearcei* (a, b), p. 372; *Begonia dregei macbethii*, p. 373; *Begonia suffruticosa*, p. 373; *Begonia sutherlandii*, p. 373; *Begonia goegoensis*, p. 374; *Begonia imperialis*, p. 374; *Begonia imperialis smaragdina*, p. 374; *Begonia ludicra*, p. 375; *Begonia acida*, p. 376; *Begonia glabra*, p. 379; *Begonia aconitifolia*, p. 379; *Begonia luxurians*, p. 380; *Begonia dichotoma*, p. 381; *Begonia foliosa*, p. 383; *Begonia gigantea*, p. 383; *Begonia isoptera hirsuta*, p. 383; *Begonia lobulata*, p. 384; *Begonia maculata wightii*, p. 384; *Begonia manicata aureo-maculata*, p. 385; *Begonia olbia*, p. 385; *Begonia poggei*, p. 386; *Begonia sanguinea*, p. 386; *Begonia ulmifolia*, p. 387; *Begonia undulata*, p. 387; *Begonia venosa*, p. 387; *Begonia* 'Abel Carriere', p. 388; *Begonia argenteo-guttata*, p. 388; *Begonia* 'Corbeille de Feu', p. 388; *Begonia erythrophylla*, p. 389; *Begonia erythrophylla bunchii*, p. 389; *Begonia gilsonii*, p. 389; *Begonia heracleicotyle*, p. 389; *Begonia thurstonii*, p. 390; *Begonia verschaffeltii*, p. 390; Covering newly sown begonia seeds with glass, p. 391; Begonia seedlings, p. 391; *Billbergia pyramidalis*, p. 421; *Blephilia ciliata*, p. 432; *Brassia gireoudiana*, p. 486; *Brodiaea coronaria*, p. 492; *Bruckenthalia spiculifolia*, p. 503; Feeling to test heads, p. 535; An amateur's cactus collection, p. 541; *Calceolaria tripartita*, p. 555; *Camoensia maxima* (a), p. 587; *Campanula cochlearifolia*, p. 593; *Campanula poscharskyane*, p. 594; *Canna generalis* variety, p. 605; *Carludovica palmata* (fruits), p. 619; *Catalpa longissima*, p. 645; *Catalpa hybrida*, p. 655; *Catasetum viridiflavum*, p. 647; *Cattleya mossiae*, p. 651; *Cattleya dowiana*, p. 651; *Cattleya luteola*, p. 653; *Cedrus atlantica glauca*, p. 665; *Celsia arcturus*, p. 672; *Celsia cretica*, p. 672; *Centaurea americana*, p. 674; *Centradenia grandifolia*, p. 677; *Centradenia floribunda* (a), p. 677; *Cephalocereus* species, p. 681; *Cercis chinensis* (b), p. 691; *Cereus hexagonis*, p. 693; *Cereus tetragonus*, p. 695. The Botanic Garden, Smith College: The Botanic Garden of Smith College (2 pictures), p. 464. University of Washington Arboretum: University of Washington Arboretum (2 pictures), p. 467. United States Department of Agriculture, Washington, D.C.: Administrative Building, p. 462.

Color

Harold Frisch: Begonia (female flowers). Krieger's Wholesale Nursery, Inc.: Blueberries. Logee's Greenhouses: *Begonia imperialis* variety; *Begonia rajah*. Netherlands Flower Institute: Hardy bulbs (a, b, c, p). The New York Botanical Garden: *Befaria racemosa*; *Begonia tuberhybrida*; *Begonia rex-cultorum* variety; Hardy bulbs (e); *Calochortus apiculatus*; *Calochortus gunnisonii*; *Calochortus kennedyi*; *Calochortus macrocarpus*; *Calopogon noctiflorus*; *Camellia japonica* variety (3 pictures); *Cattleya* hybrid.

Published by Garland Publishing, Inc.
136 Madison Avenue, New York, New York 10016

Printed in the United States of America

This work is dedicated to the honored memory of the distinguished horticulturists and botanists who most profoundly influenced my professional career: Allan Falconer of Cheadle Royal Gardens, Cheshire, England; William Jackson Bean, William Dallimore, and John Coutts of the Royal Botanic Gardens, Kew, England; and Dr. Elmer D. Merrill and Dr. Henry A. Gleason of The New York Botanical Garden.

Foreword

According to Webster, an encyclopedia is a book or set of books giving information on all or many branches of knowledge generally in articles alphabetically arranged. To the horticulturist or grower of plants, such a work is indispensable and one to be kept close at hand for frequent reference.

The appearance of *The New York Botanical Garden Illustrated Encyclopedia of Horticulture* by Thomas H. Everett is therefore welcomed as an important addition to the library of horticultural literature. Since horticulture is a living, growing subject, these volumes contain an immense amount of information not heretofore readily available. In addition to detailed descriptions of many thousands of plants given under their generic names and brief description of the characteristics of the more important plant families, together with lists of their genera known to be in cultivation, this Encyclopedia is replete with well-founded advice on how to use plants effectively in gardens and, where appropriate, indoors. Thoroughly practical directions and suggestions for growing plants are given in considerable detail and in easily understood language. Recommendations about what to do in the garden for all months of the year and in different geographical regions will be helpful to beginners and will serve as reminders to others.

The useful category of special subject entries (as distinct from the taxonomic presentations) consists of a wide variety of topics. It is safe to predict that one of the most popular will be Rock and Alpine Gardens. In this entry the author deals helpfully and adequately with a phase of horticulture that appeals to a growing group of devotees, and in doing so presents a distinctly fresh point of view. Many other examples could be cited.

The author's many years as a horticulturist and teacher well qualify him for the task of preparing this Encyclopedia. Because he has, over a period of more than a dozen years, written the entire text (submitting certain critical sections to specialists for review and suggestions) instead of farming out sections to a score or more specialists to write, the result is remarkably homogeneous and cohesive. The Encyclopedia is fully cross referenced so that one may locate a plant by either its scientific or common name.

If, as has been said, an encyclopedia should be all things to all people, then the present volumes richly deserve that accolade. Among the many who call it "friend" will be not only horticulturists ("gardeners," as our author likes to refer to them), but growers, breeders, writers, lecturers, arborists, ecologists, and professional botanists who are frequently called upon to answer questions to which only such a work can provide answers. It seems safe to predict that it will be many years before lovers and growers of plants will have at their command another reference work as authoritative and comprehensive as T. H. Everett's Encyclopedia.

John M. Fogg, Jr.
Director Emeritus, Arboretum of the Barnes Foundation
Emeritus Professor of Botany, University of Pennsylvania

Preface

The primary objective of *The New York Botanical Garden Illustrated Encyclopedia of Horticulture* is a comprehensive description and evaluation of horticulture as it is known and practiced in the United States and Canada by amateurs and by professionals, including those responsible for botanical gardens, public parks, and industrial landscapes. Although large-scale commercial methods of cultivating plants are not stressed, much of the content of the Encyclopedia is as basic to such operations as it is to other horticultural enterprises. Similarly, although landscape design is not treated on a professional level, landscape architects will find in the Encyclopedia a great deal of importance and interest to them. Emphasis throughout is placed on the appropriate employment of plants both outdoors and indoors, and particular attention is given to explaining in considerable detail the how-and when-to-do-it aspects of plant growing.

It may be useful to assess the meanings of two words I have used. Horticulture is simply gardening. It derives from the Latin *hortus*, garden, and *cultura*, culture, and alludes to the intensive cultivation in gardens and nurseries of flowers, fruits, vegetables, shrubs, trees, and other plants. The term is not applicable to the extensive field practices that characterize agriculture and forestry. Amateur, as employed by me, retains its classic meaning of a lover from the Latin *amator*, it refers to those who garden for pleasure rather than for financial gain or professional status. It carries no implication of lack of knowledge or skills and is not to be equated with novice, tyro, or dabbler. In truth, amateurs provide the solid basis upon which American horticulture rests; without them the importance of professionals would diminish. Numbered in millions, amateur gardeners are devotees of the most widespread avocation in the United States. This avocation is serviced by a great complex of nurseries, garden centers, and other suppliers; by landscape architects and landscape contractors; and by garden writers, garden lecturers, Cooperative Extension Agents, librarians, and others who dispense horticultural information. Numerous horticultural societies, garden clubs, and botanical gardens inspire and promote interest in America's greatest hobby and stand ready to help its enthusiasts.

Horticulture as a vocation presents a wide range of opportunities which appeal equally to women and men. It is a field in which excellent prospects still exist for capable entrepreneurs. Opportunities at professional levels occur too in nurseries and greenhouses, in the management of landscaped grounds of many types, and in teaching horticulture.

Some people confuse horticulture with botany. They are not the same. The distinction becomes more apparent if the word gardening is substituted for horticulture. Botany is the science that encompasses all systematized factual knowledge about plants, both wild and cultivated. It is only one of the several disciplines upon which horticulture is based. To become a capable gardener or a knowledgeable plantsman or plantswoman (I like these designations for gardeners who have a wide, intimate, and discerning knowledge of plants in addition to skill in growing them) it is not necessary to study botany formally, although such study is likely to add greatly to one's pleasure. In the practice of gardening many botanical truths are learned from experience. I have known highly competent gardeners without formal training in botany and able and indeed distinguished botanists possessed of minimal horticultural knowledge and skills.

Horticulture is primarily an art and a craft, based upon science, and at some levels perhaps justly regarded as a science in its own right. As an art it calls for an appreciation of beauty and form as expressed in three-dimensional spatial relationships and an ability to translate aesthetic concepts into reality. The chief materials used to create gardens are living plants, most of which change in size and form with the passing of time and often show differences in color and texture and in other ways from season to season. Thus it is important that designers of gardens have a wide familiarity with the sorts of plants that lend themselves to their purposes and with plants' adaptability to the regions and to the sites where it is proposed to plant them.

As a craft, horticulture involves special skills often derived from ancient practices passed from generation to generation by word of mouth and apprenticeship-like contacts. As a technology it relies on this backlog of empirical knowledge supplemented by that acquired by scientific experiment and investigation, the results of which often serve to explain rather than supplant old beliefs and practices but sometimes point the way to more expeditious methods of attaining similar results. And from time to time new techniques are developed that add dimensions to horticultural practice; among such of fairly recent years that come to mind are the manipulation of blooming season by artificial day-length, the propagation of orchids and some other plants by meristem tissue culture, and the development of soilless growing mixes as substitutes for soil.

One of the most significant developments in American horticulture in recent decades is the tremendous increase in the number of different kinds of plants that are cultivated by many more people than formerly. This is particularly true of indoor plants or house-plants, the sorts grown in homes, offices, and other interiors, but is by no means confined to that group. The relative affluence of our society and the freedom and frequency of travel both at home and abroad has contributed to this expansion, a phenomenon that will surely continue as avid collectors of the unusual bring into cultivation new plants from the wild and promote wider interest in sorts presently rare. Our garden flora is also constantly and beneficially expanded as a result of the work of both amateur and professional plant breeders.

It is impracticable in even the most comprehensive encyclopedia to describe or even list all plants that somewhere within a territory as large as the United States and Canada are grown in gardens. In this Encyclopedia the majority of genera known to be in cultivation are described, and descriptions and often other pertinent information about a complete or substantial number of their species and lesser categories are given. Sorts likely to be found only in collections of botanical gardens or in those of specialists may be omitted.

The vexing matter of plant nomenclature inevitably presents itself when an encyclopedia of horticulture is contemplated. Conflicts arise chiefly between the very understandable desire of gardeners and others who deal with cultivated plants to retain long-familiar names and the need to reflect up-to-date botanical interpretations. These points of view are basically irreconcilable and so accommodations must be reached.

As has been well demonstrated in the past, it is unrealistic to attempt to standardize the horticultural usage of plant names by decree or edict. To do so would negate scientific progress. But it is just as impracticable to expect gardeners, nurserymen, arborists, seedsmen, dealers in bulbs, and other amateur and professional horticulturists to keep current with the interpretations and recommendations of plant taxonomists; particularly as these sometimes fail to gain the acceptance even of other botanists and it is not unusual for scientists of equal stature and competence to prefer different names for the same plant.

In practice time is the great leveler. Newly proposed plant names accepted in botanical literature are likely to filter gradually into horticultural usage and eventually gain currency value, but this sometimes takes several years. The complete up-to-dateness and niceties of botanical naming are less likely to bedevil horticulturists than uncertainties concerned with correct plant identification. This is of prime importance. Whether a tree is labeled *Pseudotsuga douglasii, P. taxifolia,* or *P. menziesii* is of less concern than that the specimen so identified is indeed a Douglas-fir and not some other conifer.

After reflection I decided that the most sensible course to follow in *The New York Botanical Garden Illustrated Encyclopedia of Horticulture* was to accept almost in its entirety the nomenclature adopted in *Hortus Third* published in 1976. By doing so, much of the confusion that would result from two major comprehensive horticultural works of the late twentieth century using different names for the same plant is avoided, and it is hoped that for a period of years a degree of stability will be attained. Always those deeply concerned with critical groups of plants can adopt the recommendations of the latest monographers. Exceptions to the parallelism in nomenclature in this Encyclopedia and *Hortus Third* are to be found in the CACTACEAE for which, with certain reservations but for practical purposes, as explained in the Encyclopedia entry Cactuses, the nomenclature of Curt Backeburg's *Die Cactaceae,* published in 1958–62, is followed; and the ferns, where I mostly accepted the guidance of Dr. John T. Mickel of The New York Botanical Garden. The common or colloquial names employed are those deemed to have general acceptance. Cross references and synonomy are freely provided.

The convention of indicating typographically whether or not plants of status lesser than species represent entities that propagate and persist in the wild or are sorts that persist only in cultivation is not followed. Instead, as explained in the Encyclopedia entry Plant Names, the word variety is employed for all entities below specific rank and if in Latin form the name is written in italic, if in English or other modern language, in Roman type, with initial capital letter, and enclosed in single quotation marks.

Thomas H. Everett
Senior Horticulture Specialist
The New York Botanical Garden

Acknowledgments

I am indebted to many people for help and support generously given over the period of more than twelve years it has taken to bring this Encyclopedia to fruition. Chief credit belongs to four ladies. They are Lillian M. Weber and Nancy Callaghan, who besides accepting responsibility for the formidable task of filing and retrieving information, typing manuscript, proofreading, and the management of a vast collection of photographs, provided much wise council; Elizabeth C. Hall, librarian extraordinary, whose superb knowledge of horticultural and botanical literature was freely at my disposal; and Ellen, my wife, who displayed a deep understanding of the demands on time called for by an undertaking of this magnitude, and with rare patience accepted inevitable inconvenience. I am also obliged to my sister, Hette Everett, for the valuable help she freely gave on many occasions.

Of the botanists I repeatedly called upon for opinions and advice and from whom I sought elucidation of many details of their science abstruse to me, the most heavily burdened have been my friends and colleagues at The New York Botanical Garden, Dr. Rupert C. Barnaby, Dr. Arthur Cronquist, and Dr. John T. Mickel. Other botanists and horticulturists with whom I held discussions or corresponded about matters pertinent to my text include Dr. Theodore M. Barkley, Dr. Lyman Benson, Dr. Ben Blackburn, Professor Harold Davidson, Dr. Otto Degener, Harold Epstein, Dr. John M. Fogg, Jr., Dr. Alwyn H. Gentry, Dr. Alfred B. Graf, Brian Halliwell, Dr. David R. Hunt. Dr. John P. Jessop, Dr. Tetsuo Koyama, Dr. Bassett Maguire, Dr. Roy A. Mecklenberg, Everitt L. Miller, Dr. Harold N. Moldenke, Dr. Dan H. Nicolson, Dr. Pascal P. Pirone, Dr. Ghillean Prance, Don Richardson, Stanley J. Smith, Ralph L. Snodsmith, Marco Polo Stufano, Dr. Bernard Verdcourt, Dr. Edgar T. Wherry, Dr. Trevor Whiffin, Dr. Richard P. Wunderlin, Dr. John J. Wurdack, Yuji Yoshimura, and Rudolf Ziesenhenne.

Without either exception or stint these conferees and correspondents shared with me their knowledge, thoughts, and judgments. Much of the bounty so gleaned is reflected in the text of the Encyclopedia but none other than I am responsible for interpretations and opinions that appear there. To all who have helped, my special thanks are due and are gratefully proferred.

I acknowledge with much pleasure the excellent cooperation I have received from the Garland Publishing Company and most particularly from its President, Gavin Borden. To Ruth Adams, Nancy Isaac, Carol Miller, and Melinda Wirkus, I say thank you for working so understandingly and effectively with me and for shepherding my raw typescript through the necessary stages.

How to Use This Encyclopedia

A vast amount of information about how to use, propagate, and care for plants both indoors and outdoors is contained in the thousands of entries that compose the *New York Botanical Garden Illustrated Encyclopedia of Horticulture*. Some understanding of the Encyclopedia's organization is necessary in order to find what you want to know.

Arrangement of the Entries

Genera

The entries are arranged in alphabetical order. Most numerous are those that deal with taxonomic groups of plants. Here belong approximately 3,500 items entered under the genus name, such as ABIES, DIEFFENBACHIA, and JUGLANS. If instead of referring to these names you consult their common name equivalents of FIR, DUMB CANE, and WALNUT, you will find cross references to the genus names.

Bigeneric Hybrids & Chimeras

Hybrids between genera that have names equivalent to genus names—most of these belonging in the orchid family—are accorded separate entries. The same is true for the few chimeras or graft hybrids with names of similar status. Because bigeneric hybrids frequently have characteristics similar to those of their parents and require similar care, the entries for them are often briefer than the regular genus entries.

Families

Plant families are described under their botanical names, with their common name equivalents also given. Each description is followed by a list of the genera accorded separate entries in this Encyclopedia.

Vegetables, Fruits, Herbs, & Ornamentals

Vegetables and fruits that are commonly cultivated, such as broccoli, cabbage, potato, tomato, apple, peach, and raspberry; most culinary herbs, including basil, chives, parsley, sage, and tarragon; and a few popular ornamentals, such as azaleas, carnations, pansies, and poinsettias, are treated under their familiar names, with cross references to their genera. Discussions of a few herbs and some lesser known vegetables and fruits are given under their Latin scientific names with cross references to the common names.

Other Entries

The remaining entries in the Encyclopedia are cross references, definitions, and more substantial discussions of many subjects of interest to gardeners and others concerned with plants. For example, a calendar of gardening activity, by geographical area, is given under the names of the months and a glossary of frequently applied species names (technically, specific epithets) is provided in the entry Plant Names. A list of these general topics, which may provide additional information about a particular plant, is provided at the beginning of each volume of the Encyclopedia (see pp. xvii–xx).

Cross References & Definitions

The cross references are of two chief types: those that give specific information, which may be all you wish to know at the moment:
Boojam Tree is *Idria columnaris*.
Cobra plant is *Darlingtonia californica*.
and those that refer to entries where fuller explanations are to be found:
Adhatoda. See Justicia.
Clubmoss. See Lycopodium and Selaginella.

Additional information about entries of the former type can, of course, be found by looking up the genus to which the plant belongs—*Idria* in the case of the boojam tree and *Darlingtonia* for the cobra plant.

ORGANIZATION OF THE GENUS ENTRIES

Pronunciation

Each genus name is followed by its pronunciation in parentheses. The stressed syllable is indicated by the diacritical mark ´ if the vowel sound is short as in man, pet, pink, hot, and up; or by ` if the vowel sound is long as in mane, pete, pine, home, and fluke.

Genus Common Names
Family Common Names
General Characteristics

Following the pronunciation, there may be one or more common names applicable to the genus as a whole or to certain of its kinds. Other names may be introduced later with the descriptions of the species or kinds. Early in the entry you will find the common and botanical names of the plant family to which the genus belongs, the number of species the genus contains, its natural geographical distribution, and the derivation of its name. A description that stresses the general characteristics of the genus follows, and this may be supplemented by historical data, uses of some or all of its members, and other pertinent information.

Identification of Plants

Descriptions of species, hybrids, and varieties appear next. The identification of unrecognized plants is a fairly common objective of gardeners; accordingly, in this Encyclopedia various species have been grouped within entries in ways that make their identification easier. The groupings may bring into proximity sorts that can be adapted for similar landscape uses or that require the same cultural care, or they may emphasize geographical origins of species or such categories as evergreen and deciduous or tall and low members of the same genus. Where the description of a species occurs, its name is designated in *bold italic.* Under this plan, the description of a particular species can be found by referring to the group to which it belongs, scanning the entry for the species name in bold italic, or referring to the opening sentences of paragraphs which have been designed to serve as lead-ins to descriptive groupings.

Gardening & Landscape Uses
Cultivation
Pests & Diseases

At the end of genus entries, subentries giving information on garden and landscape uses, cultivation, and pests or diseases or both are included, or else reference is made to other genera or groupings for which these are similar.

General Subject Listings

The lists below organize some of the encyclopedia entries into topics which may be of particular interest to the reader. They are also an aid in finding information other than Latin or common names of plants.

PLANT ANATOMY AND TERMS USED IN PLANT DESCRIPTIONS

All-America Selections
Alternate
Annual Rings
Anther
Apex
Ascending
Awl-shaped
Axil, Axillary
Berry
Bloom
Bracts
Bud
Bulb
Bulbils
Bulblet
Bur
Burl
Calyx
Cambium Layer
Capsule
Carpel
Catkin
Centrals
Ciliate
Climber
Corm
Cormel
Cotyledon
Crown
Deciduous
Disk or Disc
Double Flowers
Drupe
Florets
Flower
Follicle
Frond
Fruit
Glaucous
Gymnosperms
Head
Hips
Hose-in-Hose

Inflorescence
Lanceolate
Leader
Leaf
Leggy
Linear
Lobe
Midrib
Mycelium
Node
Nut and Nutlet
Oblanceolate
Oblong
Obovate
Offset
Ovate
Palmate
Panicle
Pedate
Peltate
Perianth
Petal
Pinnate
Pip
Pistil
Pit
Pod
Pollen
Pompon
Pseudobulb
Radials
Ray Floret
Rhizome
Runners
Samara
Scion or Cion
Seeds
Sepal
Set
Shoot
Spore
Sprigs
Spur
Stamen
Stigma
Stipule

Stolon
Stool
Style
Subshrub
Taproot
Tepal
Terminal
Whorl

GARDENING TERMS AND INFORMATION

Acid and Alkaline Soils
Adobe
Aeration of the Soil
Air and Air Pollution
Air Drainage
Air Layering
Alpine Greenhouse or Alpine House
Amateur Gardener
April, Gardening Reminders For
Aquarium
Arbor
Arboretum
Arch
Asexual or Vegetative Propagation
Atmosphere
August, Gardening Reminders For
Balled and Burlapped
Banks and Steep Slopes
Bare-Root
Bark Ringing
Baskets, Hanging
Bed
Bedding and Bedding Plants
Bell Jar
Bench, Greenhouse
Blanching
Bleeding
Bog
Bolting
Border
Bottom Heat
Break, Breaking
Broadcast
Budding
Bulbs or Bulb Plants

Gardening Terms and Information
(Continued)

State Agricultural Experimental Stations
Stock or Understock
Straightedge
Strawberry Jars
Strike
Stunt
Succession Cropping
Sundials
Syringing
Thinning or Thinning Out
Tillage
Tilth
Tools
Top-Dressing
Topiary Work
Training Plants
Tree Surgery
Tree Wrapping
Trenching
Trowels
Tubs
Watering
Weeds and Their Control
Window Boxes

FERTILIZERS AND OTHER SUBSTANCES RELATED TO GARDENING

Algicide
Aluminum Sulfate
Ammonium Nitrate
Ammonium Sulfate
Antibiotics
Ashes
Auxins
Basic Slag
Blood Meal
Bonemeal
Bordeaux Mixture
Calcium Carbonate
Calcium Chloride
Calcium Metaphosphate
Calcium Nitrate
Calcium Sulfate
Carbon Disulfide
Chalk
Charcoal
Coal Cinders
Cork Bark
Complete Fertilizer
Compost and Composting
Cottonseed Meal
Creosote
DDT
Dormant Sprays
Dried Blood
Fermate or Ferbam
Fertilizers
Fishmeal
Formaldehyde
Fungicides
Gibberellic Acid
Green Manuring
Growth Retardants
Guano
Herbicides or Weed-Killers
Hoof and Horn Meal

Hormones
Humus
Insecticide
John Innes Composts
Lime and Liming
Liquid Fertilizer
Liquid Manure
Manures
Mulching and Mulches
Muriate of Potash
Nitrate of Ammonia
Nitrate of Lime
Nitrate of Potash
Nitrate of Soda
Nitrogen
Orchid Peat
Organic Matter
Osmunda Fiber or Osmundine
Oyster Shells
Peat
Peat Moss
Permagnate of Potash
Potassium
Potassium Chloride
Potassium-Magnesium Sulfate
Potassium Nitrate
Potassium Permagnate
Potassium Sulfate
Pyrethrum
Rock Phosphate
Rotenone
Salt Hay or Salt Marsh Hay
Sand
Sawdust
Sodium Chloride
Sprays and Spraying
Sulfate
Superphosphate
Trace Elements
Urea
Urea-Form Fertilizers
Vermiculite
Wood Ashes

TECHNICAL TERMS

Acre
Alternate Host
Annuals
Antidessicant or Antitranspirant
Biennals
Binomial
Botany
Chromosome
Climate
Clone
Composite
Conservation
Cross or Crossbred
Cross Fertilization
Cross Pollination
Cultivar
Decumbent
Dicotyledon
Division
Dormant
Endemic
Environment
Family

Fasciation
Fertility
Fertilization
Flocculate
Floriculture
Genus
Germinate
Habitat
Half-Hardy
Half-Ripe
Hardy Annual
Hardy Perennial
Heredity
Hybrid
Indigenous
Juvenile Forms
Juvenility
Legume
Monocotyledon
Monoecious
Mutant or Sport
Mycorrhiza or Mycorhiza
Nitrification
Perennials
pH
Plant Families
Photoperiodism
Photosynthesis
Pollination
Pubescent
Saprophyte
Self-Fertile
Self-Sterile
Species
Standard
Sterile
Strain
Terrestrial
Tetraploid
Transpiration
Variety

TYPES OF GARDENS AND GARDENING

Alpine Garden
Artificial Light Gardening
Backyard Gardens
Biodynamic Gardening
Bog Gardens
Botanic Gardens and Arboretums
Bottle Garden
City Gardening
Colonial Gardens
Conservatory
Container Gardening
Cutting Garden
Desert Gardens
Dish Gardens
Flower Garden
Fluorescent Light Gardening
Formal and Semiformal Gardens
Greenhouses and Conservatories
Heath or Heather Garden
Herb Gardens
Hydroponics or Nutriculture
Indoor Lighting Gardening
Japanese Gardens
Kitchen Garden
Knot Gardens

Types of Gardens and Gardening (Continued)

Miniature Gardens
Native Plant Gardens
Naturalistic Gardens
Nutriculture
Organic Gardening
Rock and Alpine Gardens
Roof and Terrace Gardening
Salads or Salad Plants
Seaside Gardens
Shady Gardens
Sink Gardening
Terrariums
Vegetable Gardens
Water and Waterside Gardens
Wild Gardens

PESTS, DISEASES, AND OTHER TROUBLES

Ants
Aphids
Armyworms
Bagworms
Bees
Beetles
Billbugs
Biological Control of Pests
Birds
Blight
Blindness
Blotch
Borers
Budworms and Bud Moths
Bugs
Butterflies
Canker
Cankerworms or Inchworms
Casebearers
Caterpillars
Cats
Centipede, Garden
Chinch Bugs
Chipmunks
Club Root
Corn Earworm
Crickets
Cutworms
Damping Off
Deer
Die Back
Diseases of Plants
Downy Mildew
Earthworms
Earwigs
Edema
Fairy Rings
Fire Blight
Flies
Fungi or Funguses
Galls
Gas Injury

Gophers
Grasshoppers
Grubs
Gummosis
Hornworms
Inchworms
Insects
Iron Chelates
Iron Deficiency
Lace Bugs
Lantana Bug
Lantern-Flies
Larva
Leaf Blight
Leaf Blister
Leaf Blotch
Leaf Curl
Leaf Cutters
Leaf Hoppers
Leaf Miners
Leaf Mold
Leaf Rollers
Leaf Scorch
Leaf Skeletonizer
Leaf Spot Disease
Leaf Tiers
Lightening Injury
Maggots
Mantis or Mantid
Mealybugs
Mice
Midges
Milky Disease
Millipedes
Mites
Mold
Moles
Mosaic Diseases
Moths
Muskrats
Needle Cast
Nematodes or Nemas
Parasite
Pests of Plants
Plant Hoppers
Plant Lice
Praying Mantis
Psyllids
Rabbits
Red Spider Mite
Rootworms
Rots
Rust
Sawflies
Scab Diseases
Scale Insects
Scorch or Sunscorch
Scurf
Slugs and Snails
Smut and White Smut Diseases
Sowbugs or Pillbugs
Spanworms

Spittlebugs
Springtails
Squirrels
Stunt
Suckers
Sun Scald
Thrips
Tree Hoppers
Virus
Walking-Stick Insects
Wasps
Webworms
Weevils
Wilts
Witches' Brooms
Woodchucks

GROUPINGS OF PLANTS

Accent Plants
Aquatics
Aromatic Plants
Bedding and Bedding Plants
Berried Trees and Shrubs
Bible Plants
Broad-leaved and Narrow-leaved Trees and Shrubs
Bulbs or Bulb Plants
Bush Fruits
Carnivorous or Insectivorous Plants
Dried Flowers, Foliage, and Fruits
Edging Plants
Epiphyte or Air Plant
Evergreens
Everlastings
Fern Allies
Filmy Ferns
Florists' Flowers
Foliage Plants
Fragrant Plants and Flowers
Gift Plants
Graft Hybrids
Grasses, Ornamental
Hard-Wooded Plants
Houseplants or Indoor Plants
Japanese Dwarfed Trees
Medicinal or Drug Plants
Night-Blooming Plants
Ornamental-Fruited Plants
Pitcher Plants
Poisonous Plants
Shrubs
State Flowers
State Trees
Stone Fruits
Stone or Pebble Plants
Stove Plants
Succulents
Tender Plants
Trees
Windowed Plants

The New York
Botanical Garden
Illustrated Encyclopedia
of Horticulture

BEAN. Common beans of vegetable gardens are discussed in the next entry. The name black-bean is applied to *Castanospermum australe* and *Kennedia nigricans*. The castor-bean is *Ricinus communis*. The chickasaw-lima-bean or jack-bean is *Canavalia ensiformis*, the coral-bean or mescal-bean *Sophora secundiflora*, the Florida velvet-bean *Mucuna deeringiana*, the Goa-bean or winged-bean *Psophocarpus tetragonolobus*. The name horse-bean is applied to *Canavalia ensiformis*, *Parkinsonia aculeata*, and *Vicia faba*. Hyacinth-bean is *Dolichos lablab*. Indian-bean is a name of a species of *Catalpa*. Lyon-bean is *Mucuna cochinchinensis*, mung-bean *Vigna radiata*, potato-bean *Apios americana*, red-bean *Kennedia rubicunda*, screw-bean *Prosopis pubescens*. The name wild-bean is used for *Apios americana* and *Strophostyles*. The yam-bean is *Pachyrhizus erosus*, the yard-long-bean or asparagus-bean *Vigna unguiculata sesquipedalis*, the Yokohama-bean is *Muncuna hassjoo*.

BEANS. Beans are among the most important vegetable crops. The scarlet runner string bean is also grown as an ornamental vine for its bright red flowers. Favorites of amateur gardeners, beans are easy to grow and rewarding in their returns. All belong to the pea family LEGUMINOSAE. Most are varieties of New World species of *Phaseolus*, but fava or broad beans are varieties of Old World *Vicia faba*, and soybeans of *Glycine max*, a native of the Orient. We shall consider them separately. Varieties of all types, some better adapted than others to particular regions, are listed in seedsmen's catalogs.

Snap beans, available in numerous varieties, are esteemed for their tender, immature pods, and some varieties such as shell beans, for their mature dry seeds called kidney beans, navy beans, and so on. The immature pods are green or in kinds called wax beans or butter beans, light yellow.

Two main types of these beans are grown, pole or climbing varieties and bush ones that need no supports. The former yield heavier crops, but the latter come into bearing sooner and occupy the ground for a shorter season.

Cultivation of snap beans is simple. They respond best to a fertile, friable soil of a loamy rather than extremely sandy or clayey type, that is slightly acid to slightly alkaline. Prepare it by deep spading, plowing, or rototilling, and incorporating a generous amount of compost, manure, or other partially decayed organic material. Before sowing work in a dressing of superphosphate or of a complete fertilizer with a high phosphate content.

Do not sow too early. These beans are lovers of warmth. Even slight frost kills and cold wet earth is not to their liking. At temperatures under 60°F, the seeds are likely to rot. Sow bush varieties in drills 2

Bush snap beans

to 2½ feet apart at a depth of 1 inch to 1½ inches. Drop the seeds 2 to 3 inches apart for early plantings, 3 to 4 inches for later ones. To assure an uninterrupted succession of harvests, in the north make two or three sowings at intervals of ten days to two weeks. Make an additional one or two, depending upon the length of the growing season, in the south and other mild-climate regions.

Routine care consists primarily of keeping down weeds by repeated shallow cultivation or mulching and of supplying

Harvesting bush snap beans

water in times of drought. Do not walk among the plants when they are wet. To do so encourages the spread of disease.

Pole snap beans and string beans need the same treatment as bush varieties except for wider spacing and the provision of supports. Traditionally the last need has been met by planting a stout rustic wood pole or stake so that it sticks out of the ground for about 7 feet in the center of each hill, but strings stretched tautly between horizontal wires spaced 6 to 7 feet apart or between nails driven into crosspieces of wood spaced similarly, or various types of trellis can also be used. If poles are employed they may be vertical, or three can be inclined and tied near their

Supports set for pole beans

tops to form a teepee. Let the hills be 2 to 3 feet apart in rows 4 to 5 feet apart. Make them by mounding soil about the base of each pole to a height of a few inches. Flatten the top of the mound and plant five or six seeds at a depth of 1 inch to 1½ inches in a circle around the base of the pole. Later thin the seedlings to leave the three strongest at each station. If strings or trellis are to be the supports, sow the seeds 3 to 4 inches apart in rows and thin the seedlings to 6 to 8 inches. Pole beans occupy the ground for the whole season and crop over a long period. There is no need for successional sowings.

A row of young lima beans

Thinning pole beans

Lima beans also come in bush and pole varieties. As with snap beans, the climbers are much the more prolific. Limas are even less tolerant of cold and wet than snap beans. Do not sow them until the ground is warm and the weather settled. Spacing for limas may with advantage be a little more generous than for snap beans, but otherwise their needs are the same. In parts of the south, pole limas are sometimes allowed to trail without supports, but this not recommended for home gardeners. In the north, limas are sometimes started early indoors in pots and the plants set outdoors about the time tomatoes are planted. Because they take longer to come into bearing than bush snap beans fewer successional sowings are possible with bush limas. Soil excessively rich in nitrogen is sometimes responsible for lima beans shedding their blooms without setting pods.

Fava or broad beans are much more commonly grown in Europe than North America. To American taste they are less flavorful than limas. They are a cool-weather crop that does better in moister climates

Pole lima beans

than lima beans. In North America the best regions for their cultivation are the Maritime provinces of Canada, British Columbia, Washington, and Oregon, and, as a winter crop in parts of California and the south. As with limas, the seeds, not the pods, of fava beans are the edible parts. Fava beans grow erectly and, unless pinched, to a height of 3 to 4 feet. They need no supports other than possibly that given by hilling a little soil around their bases. Soil preparation is as for snap beans.

Where summers are hot, as in eastern North America, it is very essential to sow

as early in spring as the ground can be gotten into condition. Fava beans withstand light frosts. In milder regions, winter and early spring crops can be had from fall sowings. A good way of sowing is in double drills 8 inches apart with 3 feet between each pair of drills. Alternatively, single drills may be spaced 2 feet apart. Sow the seeds 8 inches apart in the drills.

Planting out lima beans started early indoors

Fava or broad beans

When the flowers of the lower trusses fade, pinch out the growing tips of the stems to encourage the early development of pods and to discourage infestations of black aphids, which are especially partial to this crop.

Soybeans, of tremendous importance as a commercial crop for oil and flour production and for animal feed and other purposes, find little favor in the United States as a vegetable, but are increasingly employed in health foods. Very occasionally they are grown for eating as green pod or as shell beans. Their cultural needs are those for bush limas.

Pests and Diseases. The chief pests of beans are the Mexican bean beetle, which, adults and fuzzy larvae, feeds chiefly on the undersides of the leaves, bean leaf beetle, which also feeds on the foliage, and aphids. Anthracnose, which causes seriously cankered pods, is transmitted by seed. To control it use only western-grown seeds and avoid working or walking among the plants when wet. The same controls are recommended for bacterial blight. Virus mosaic diseases cause stunt and poorly developed, yellow-mottled foliage. Transmitted by aphids and other insects, these must be controlled to limit the spread of the disease. Other diseases include mildew and rust, the latter wintered over on old bean plant refuse and on poles. Wash old poles that have supported rust-infected plants with formaldehyde diluted one part to five of water before using them again.

BEAR-GRASS. This is a common name of *Dasylirion texanum*, *Xerophyllum tenax*, and *Nolina*. It is also sometimes used for *Yucca glauca* and *Y. smalliana*.

BEARBERRY. This is the common name of *Arctostaphylos uva-ursi* and *Oemleria cerasiformis*. The alpine-bearberry or black-bearberry is *Arctostaphylos alpina*.

BEARD GRASS. See Polypogon.

BEARD TONGUE. See Penstemon.

BEAR'S. This word appears as part of the common names bear's breech (*Acanthus*), bear's foot fern (*Humata tyermannii*), bear's paw fern (*Aglaomorpha*), and Cretan bear's tail (*Celsia arcturus*).

BEAUCARNEA (Beau-càrnea)—Pony Tail. Twelve species belonging to the lily family LILIACEAE constitute *Beaucarnea*, a genus of yucca-like trees endemic to desert and semidesert regions of the southwestern United States and Mexico. The name is of uncertain origin.

Beaucarneas have tall trunks, commonly with their bases conspicuously swollen and crowned with tufts of gracefully displayed, long, slender-linear, evergreen leaves. Their small, whitish flowers, in large, branched panicles, have six perianth segments, commonly called petals, six stamens, and a short style. The fruits are three-winged capsules.

The pony tail (*B. recurvata* syns. *Nolina recurvata*, *N. tuberculata*) attains a height of 30 feet and has a trunk greatly expanded at its base and topped by a head of short

Beaucarnea recurvata

Beaucarnea recurvata (flowers)

Beaucarnea recurvata as a pot plant

branches, each ending in an ample tuft of recurved to pendulous, channeled, smooth-edged, flat leaves 3 to 6 feet long by about ¾ inch wide. The fruits are long-stalked. More commonly cultivated *B. r. intermedia* has leaves up to 3 feet long. Leaves not more than ¼ inch wide and up to about 1½ feet in length are characteristic of *B. gracilis* (syns. *Nolina gracilis*, *Dasylirion gracile*). Up to 20 feet tall or taller, *B. stricta* has straight, glaucous, rough-margined leaves up to about 1½ feet long and keeled on their undersides. Its fruits are short-stalked.

Garden and Landscape Uses and Cultivation. These are as for *Nolina*.

Beaucarnea gracilis

BEAUFORTIA (Beau-fórtia). Named after an early nineteenth-century Duchess of Beaufort, who patronized botany, *Beaufortia* of the myrtle family MYRTACEAE comprises fifteen species. It is endemic to western Australia.

Beaucarnea stricta

Shrubs of heathlike aspect, and often aromatic, beaufortias have small opposite or alternate, stalkless leaves. Their brush-like heads of bright red to purple-magenta flowers, reminiscent of those of *Callistemon*, are of many blooms of which the stamens are the conspicuous elements. The top-shaped calyx is five-lobed. There are five short petals, many long stamens united in bundles opposite the petals, and one long style. The fruits are capsules.

Called gravel bottle brush in its native land where it inhabits peaty swamps, *B. sparsa*, 3 to 6 feet tall, sparingly-branched, and with wandlike stems, has blunt, ovate-

Beaufortia sparsa

elliptic leaves ¼ to nearly ½ inch long. Below the new season's shoots, it has bottle brush-like heads about 3 inches in diameter of bright scarlet, with slightly-drooping flowers.

Garden and Landscape Uses and Cultivation. These are as for Callistemon.

BEAUMONTARA. This is the name of multigeneric hybrid orchids the parents of which include *Brassavola*, *Cattleya*, *Laelia*, and *Schomburgkia*.

BEAUMONTIA (Beau-móntia)—Herald's Trumpet. One of the four or five species of this genus of the dogbane family APOCYNACEAE is cultivated outdoors in the tropics and subtropics, and in greenhouses. The genus is Asian, extending from India to Java. Its name honors Lady Diana Beaumont of England, who died in 1831.

Beaumontias are vigorous, woody, twining vines, with opposite, pinnate-veined leaves and terminal clusters of large trumpet- to bell-shaped blooms and conspicuous calyxes. The stamens have very long filaments (stalks) and are attached to the upper part of the corolla tube; they are joined to form a tube around the stigma. The woody, cylindrical fruits split into two parts.

The herald's trumpet (*Beaumontia grandiflora*) is a favorite. A high climber, it has short-stalked, short-pointed, elliptic to ovate, wavy-edged leaves, 4 to 8 inches long, slightly pubescent on their undersides and hairless above. The fragrant blooms, about 5 inches long, have sepals 1 inch to 1½ inches long and five flaring corolla lobes. A rarer species, *B. jerdoniana*, differs in having slenderer, more trumpet-shaped flowers with narrowly-lanceolate calyx lobes. It is a native of northern India.

Garden and Landscape Uses. These magnificent vines are of breath-taking beauty when in bloom. From a little distance they appear to be garlanded with Easter lilies, pure white and deliciously fragrant, and a large specimen may produce thousands. In size of flower they are equaled by few cultivated plants. The angel's trumpet (*Datura*) comes to mind as a rival in this respect, and indeed it is, but its more slender blooms lack the fat opulence of those of *Beaumontia grandiflora*; they are more trumpet- and less bell-shaped. Among vines, the chalice vine (*Solandra*) has flowers as big or bigger, but they lack the pristine whiteness of those of *Beaumontia*, and run, rather, to creamy-whites and banana-yellows. Beaumontias need ample space and a support such as a pergola for their twining stems. If somewhat checked by pruning, they may be allowed to climb trees as they are wont to in their native forests, where in their efforts to reach the light they attain great heights. Only when their heads are in sun will beaumontias bloom, and then only after they have attained a certain size and stability so that root and top growth are in balance. As young specimens they grow vigorously, but are unlikely to produce flowers. As greenhouse plants beaumontias are adapted only to large structures such as display conservatories. They should be planted in ground beds; they rarely bloom satisfactorily in pots or other containers.

Beaumontia grandiflora

Beaumontia grandiflora (flowers)

Cultivation. Beaumontias are easily raised from seeds sown in a temperature of 70 to 75°F and in porous soil kept moderately moist. They are more difficult, but by no means impossible, to grow from cuttings; the percentage of these that root is often rather small. Air-layering affords a sure way of securing increase. As young plants they prefer some shade, but later full sun is needed. Fertile soil well supplied with organic matter is essential for the best growth of these vines. It should be well-drained and neither dry nor excessively wet. As soon as the flowering season is over these vines should be pruned severely to contain them to acceptable size and induce good flowering the following year.

BEAUTY-BERRY. See Callicarpa.

BEAUTY BUSH is *Kolkwitzia amabilis*.

BED. As used by gardeners this term is applied to well-defined areas of small to moderate size planted with one or more kinds of compatable plants. Most commonly the occupants are ornamentals, but the term is also sometimes used for plantings of other kinds. Thus reference may be made to onion beds, asparagus beds, and mint beds. Seedbeds and hotbeds are treated in this Encyclopedia under Seeds, Propagation By, and Hotbeds.

The essential qualities of a bed are that it have discrete, well-marked boundaries and that its immediate surroundings on all or most sides be low, such as lawn, pavement, paths, or low groundcovers. Beds may be geometrical or informal. If very long in relation to their widths they may be called borders, although that term more properly applies to long beds with a wall, fence, hedge, grouping of shrubs, or such-like feature as a background.

Ornamentals planted in beds may be shrubs, herbaceous perennials, or for temporary effects, bulbs such as tulips, hyacinths, or daffodils, bedding plants such as geraniums, begonias, or lantanas, annuals, or combinations of these various types.

The placement of beds is important. They should never be dotted about indiscriminately, but always in sympathetic relationship to the surrounding landscape, as an integral part of the garden design. The imposition of incongruously-placed, variously-shaped flower beds on lawns is one of the commonest tasteless expressions of unskilled designers. See also Flower Beds and Borders, and Bedding and Bedding Plants.

BEDDING AND BEDDING PLANTS. A style of gardening much less practiced since World War II than formerly, bedding consists of filling formal beds, usually cut in lawns, with plants that make gay displays for one season only. The objective, to keep the beds colorful for as many months as climate permits, is usually achieved by making successional plantings.

In regions where winter freezing occurs, this generally involves two changes each year, summer bedding or the planting (bedding out) of annuals and plants treated as annuals for summer bloom, and spring bedding, the planting of hardy bulbs, biennials, and plants treated as biennials, and perhaps some herbaceous perennials for spring display. In frostless or nearly frostless regions annuals and plants grown as such are bedded out in fall for winter bloom.

An essential feature of bedding is that the plants used are grown to blooming or near-blooming size elsewhere before they are transferred to the display areas. With many sorts suitable for summer bedding this necessitates the use of greenhouses or hotbeds. Cold frames and nursery beds are needed to raise plants favored for spring bedding, and for fine, uniform results, new bulbs must be purchased yearly.

A great vogue for bedding existed during the late nineteenth, and early twentieth, century. Vast efforts and much money were expended on extravagant, often ostentatious displays. Wealthy estate owners, city park departments, and others with horticultural aspirations vied to outdo each other in decorating, and not infrequently desecrating, lawns and other areas. Something of a record must have been established in the 1920s at the Greystone Estate, Yonkers, New York, where between fifty and sixty gardeners were employed, much of their efforts directed toward raising, planting, and caring each year for the hundreds of thousands of bedding plants in vast variety that were used in the formal

Spring bedding with tulips

Spring bedding with tulips

Spring bedding with tulips

gardens. Continuous replacement was practiced from spring to fall, some plants being removed after only two to four weeks in the beds.

In Europe, particularly in the British Isles, extremes were reached earlier. Garden books up to World War I and sometimes later included unbelievably elaborate and intricate geometrical designs, and directions for laying out and planting beds.

The decline of bedding, at least on an extravagant scale, chiefly resulted from its high cost in money and labor. But it also reflected a disenchantment with stylized, formal flower gardening in favor of freer-style landscape expressions such as can be achieved with beds of mixed herbaceous perennials and annuals, and by naturalistic gardening. Beside being less costly, such plantings have the great advantage of maintaining interest by exhibiting change and successions of bloom throughout the entire season instead of the beds being cast in one pattern that remains essentially unchanged during the time the plants occupy them.

The set character of formal bedding is less of a disadvantage in public places, where the same people are not obliged to view the same plants daily, than in private gardens. Because of this, bedding on anything approaching a grand scale survives only in such places as public parks and large-scale, commercially inspired garden developments. It is most extravagantly practiced, not infrequently rather tastelessly, in city parks in Europe, especially in Great Britain, to a lesser extent in similar places in America.

Yet bedding on a much more modest scale is viable in present-day gardening. Small beds with simple outlines, advantageously placed, can bring welcome color and gaiety to otherwise drabbish, uninteresting landscapes. But like pictures in a room, they must be appropriately related to their surroundings, display pleasing colors, and not be too numerous. In this manner in the late twentieth century, bedding can be employed advantageously and with reasonable economy.

Spring bedding may involve the use of such hardy bulbs as hyacinths, narcissuses, and tulips, sometimes crocuses and grape-hyacinths, as well as plants raised as biennials, such as arabis, aubretias, *Aurinia saxatilis*, English daisies, English and Siberian wallflowers, forget-me-nots, pansies, polyanthus primroses, and violas. In addition, a few low-growing perennials, including *Phlox divaricata, P. subulata,* and *Polemonium reptans*, are suitable for spring bedding.

Spring bedding with hyacinths

Spring bedding with hyacinths

The hardy bulbs are planted in fall after the beds are cleared of summer plants. Depending upon the severity of the climate, the biennials and perennials are set in the beds in fall or are wintered in protected nursery beds or in cold frames and set out in spring.

The plants used for spring displays are taken out of the beds in late spring, usually shortly after tulips are through blooming, to make room for the summer bedding. The spring-flowering biennials are discarded, the perennials may be planted elsewhere or be divided and grown on in nursery beds for use in the following year's spring bedding. The hardy bulbs may be heeled-in in a suitable place to mature, then be stored for the summer and replanted in fall in other parts of the garden. They will not give sufficiently uni-

form results in their second year to be suitable for spring bedding.

Summer bedding is installed in late spring after the weather is warm and settled, as soon as the spring bedding display wanes and shortly after it is safe to plant toma-

Summer beddings: (a) Marigolds, sweet alyssum, and lobelia

Spring bedding with various biennials

(b) Snapdragons

(c) Cannas

toes. Plants usable for summer bedding are available in great variety. Among the most popular flowering sorts are ageratums, cannas, celosias, China-asters, dwarf dahlias, dwarf marigolds, fuchsias, gazanias, geraniums (zonal kinds), globe-amaranths, heliotropes, impatiens, lantanas, Mexican tulip-poppy, petunias, *Salvia splendens*, snapdragons, stocks, sweet-alyssum, tuberous begonias, verbenas, wax begonias, and zinnias. Of these, fuchsias, geraniums, heliotropes, and lantanas, and some other nonhardy shrubs such as angel's trumpets (*Brugmansia*) and *Plumbago auriculata* are sometimes grown as standards (tree-form specimens) to be dotted among lower plants.

Foliage plants suitable for summer bedding, sometimes used exclusively or nearly exclusively to create subtropical effects, are variegated-leaved abutilons, Abyssinian

Subtropical bedding

Subtropical bedding

banana (*Ensete*), acalyphas, *Albizia distachya*, varieties of *Amaranthus*, caladiums, castor bean, dusty miller centaureas, coleuses, variegated-leaved corn, crotons (*Codiaeum*), dracaenas, elephant's ear (*Colocasia antiquorum*), *Eucalyptus globulus*, *Grevillea robusta*, pandanuses, perillas, and *Setcreasea pallida* 'Purple Heart'. These are few of many. Where summers are warm

a great variety of ornamental-leaved plants are available for subtropical bedding. Some, such as crotons, dracaenas, and pandanuses, will not increase much in size during their brief stay in the beds, but many grow vigorously and allowance must be made for this in spacing them.

Carpet bedding is a special type of summer bedding in which colorful foliage plants, dwarf by nature or kept so by shearing, are used to produce well-defined carpet-like groundcovers with more or less intricate color patterns. Good examples, rarely seen in America, are more common in Europe, where the coat of arms of a city, a welcome to visitors, or other such conceits are not infrequently displayed in public places. Floral clocks, one of the best known in Edinburgh, Scotland, are examples of carpet bedding. Plants appropriate for this use include alternantheras, *Calocephalus brownii*, echeverias, *Herniaria glabra*, iresines, *Lysimachia nummularia aurea*, *Sagina subulata aurea*, *Santolina chamaecyparissus* and *S. virens*, sempervivums, and dwarf sedums.

Winter bedding, which carries its displays into spring, is practicable only in essentially frostless climates and is best adapted to such regions as California where the climate is distinctly Mediterranean. Good winter bedding plants include cinerarias, cyclamens, Paris-daisies, nonhardy primulas, and other plants grown elsewhere for winter display in cool greenhouses.

BEDSTRAW. See Galium.

BEE BALM is *Melissa*. The hyphenated form bee-balm is applied to *Monarda*.

BEE BRUSH is *Aloysia gratissima*.

BEECH. See Fagus. Australian-beech is *Eucalyptus polyanthemus*, blue-beech or water-beech is *Carpinus cardiniana*, southern-beech is *Nothofagus*. The broad beech fern is *Thelypteris hexagonoptera*.

BEEFWOOD. See Casuarina.

BEES. The good wrought by helpful bees, especially honeybees but including bumblebees and solitary bees, far outweighs the damage done by the few destructive kinds, such as carpenter bees, which bore deep tunnels into wood. Bees are the chief insect agents in effecting cross-pollination between plants. This is often desirable and with kinds not fertile or fertile to only a limited degree to their own pollen is practically essential for fruit formation. Unless they are cross-pollinated, such plants, which include many orchard trees, fruit poorly or not at all.

Despite this, in thickly populated areas and ornamental gardens bees generally are undesirable. Close encounters with them are unpleasant and may result in being stung. Stings are painful and to those allergic to them can be a serious hazard. Except in relatively sparsely populated areas beekeeping is impracticable. For pollinating fruits, home gardeners normally rely upon the native bee population. Orchardists sometimes keep bees or arrange for beekeepers to place hives in their orchards when the fruit trees are in bloom.

Flowers especially attractive to bees as sources of nectar, from which honey is made, or pollen, which at certain times the bees consume as food, include alfalfa, buckwheat, buttonbush, clovers, fireweed, goldenrods, lima beans, lindens, mesquite, milkweeds, oranges, salvias, sweet-clovers, toyon, tulip trees, and wisterias.

BEET. Beets or beetroots are varieties of *Beta vulgaris*, a plant of European origin of the goosefoot family CHENOPODIACEAE.

Carpet bedding

(a) Beets before harvesting

(c) Beets, the harvest

They are grown for their turnip-like, usually red, swollen roots, which are cooked and eaten as a vegetable or pickled, and for their foliage, or greens, which is also used as a vegetable. Selected varieties with richly colored red leaves, called ornamental beets, are planted as decoratives in flower gardens. The uses and cultivation of ornamental beets are discussed under Beta. Sugar beets, an agricultural rather than a horticultural crop, are a commercial source of sugar. Mangle beets or mangles are grown for stock feed.

Table or garden beets succeed in a wide variety of climates and soils and are well suited for home gardens. Since they give of their best during comparatively cool weather they are cultivated in the southern one-third of the United States as fall, winter, and spring crops, in the middle one-third for spring and fall use, in the remainder of the country and Canada for harvesting in summer and early fall. For the best results the soil should be ade-

(b) Harvesting beets

quately drained, deep, fertile, crumbly, and well supplied with organic matter. Stiff, clayey earths and those that dry excessively or are deficient in nutrients will not give good results unless modified to bring them nearer to the ideal. Best success

is had with soils slightly acid to neutral, those that have a pH of 6.0 to 7.0, but in some localities somewhat alkaline conditions are tolerated.

When preparing the soil for beets avoid using fresh manure. Land manured heavily for such previous crops as cabbage, broccoli, or peas is ideal. Or the organic content of the soil can be increased by turning under prior to sowing a green manure crop or compost. If the pH of the soil is below 6.0, mix in sufficient ground limestone to raise it to that figure.

The amount and kind of fertilizer to apply depends upon the natural fertility of the soil and the treatment it received for the previous crop. In fertilizing avoid the excessive use of nitrogen, make sure that potash is not in short supply. For average soils the application before planting of a 5-10-5 or 10-10-10 fertilizer at rates up to 4½ pounds to each 100 square feet is appropriate. On soils low in potash substitute like amounts of 8-16-16 or 5-10-30 fertilizer or supplement a 5-10-5 or 10-10-10 one by applying sulfate of potash.

The first sowing may be made three to four weeks before the average date of the last spring frost, the last six to eight weeks before the average date of the first fall frost. To maintain a succession of young, tender roots make sowings, except during very hot weather, at intervals of two to three weeks. Beet seeds germinate when the soil temperature is between 40 and 85°F, most effectively between 65 and 75°F.

In hand-worked home gardens sow in rows 1 foot apart. Where mechanical cultivators are used allow 1½ to 2 feet between rows. What we know as beet seeds are technically fruits, each a conglomerate of several seeds commonly giving rise to several plants. It is important not to sow too thickly. Five or six of these compound seeds to 1 foot of row are enough. Recently monogerm varieties, such as 'Explorer', 'Monogerm', 'Mono King', and 'Pacemaker', have been developed. These produce only one plant from each seed and consequently may be sown a little more thickly. In sandy soils cover the seeds to a depth of 1 inch, in sandy loams to ¾ inch, and in finer, heavier earth to ½ inch.

Prevent overcrowding by pulling out surplus seedlings as soon as they are big enough to handle and certainly before they are 2 inches high. Allow only one of each cluster of seedlings from multigerm seeds to remain. Thin to achieve a final spacing of about 3 inches, 4 or 5 inches for long-rooted varieties grown for winter storage. Routine care consists chiefly of keeping down weeds and watering in dry weather. In home gardens weed destruction is best effected by frequent shallow surface cultivation between the rows and hand pulling in the rows. When needed, soak the ground deeply with water at five- to seven-day intervals. On sandy soils and others of low fertility, apply a light dressing of nitrate of soda or urea when the beets are half grown. This effects rapid growth, necessary to the production of tender beets. Remember, however, that excessive nitrogen results in lush foliage at the expense of root development.

Harvest when the roots are 1½ to 2 inches in diameter. Larger beets become tough and woody. Late fall crops can be stored for up to five months. To do this, pull them before hard freezing (light frosts and mild freezes are tolerated), cut off the tops close to the roots, discard diseased or damaged roots, store the others in baskets or slatted crates where they will not freeze, but where the temperature is as close to 32°F as possible and the relative humidity is 95 to 98 percent.

Varieties differ in the shape of the roots and time needed to attain harvesting size. Long-rooted kinds such as 'Long Dark Blood' and 'Long Smooth Blood' are comparatively slow to develop and are suitable for deep soils only. They are most used as late crops for winter storage. On shallower soils grow varieties with spherical or flattish roots. Early maturing varieties of this type are 'Crosby's Egyptian   Early Wonder', and 'Ruby Queen . Medium early varieties include 'Detroit Dark Red' and 'Perfected Detroit'. For greens 'Crosby Green Top', 'Lutz Green Leaf', and 'Burpee White', the last with white flesh, are specially recommended, but the leaves of all kinds can be used.

Diseases and pests of beets vary in different regions. Consult your Cooperative Extension Agent about these and their controls. The most frequent disease, cercospora leaf spot, causes circular spots with reddish or purplish margins, the centers of which drop out to give a shot-hole effect. Crop rotation, sanitation, and application of fungicides are recommended controls. Pests include aphids, flea beetles, leaf miners, and webworms.

BEETLES. Comprising approximately 40 percent of all known kinds of insects for a total of 250,000 or more described species, beetles, which include curculios and weevils, are the largest group of the entomologists' class *Insecta*. They are distinguished from other insects by their first pair of wings being represented by rigid, horny sheaths called wing covers that except when the creature is in flight, generally meet down the center of its back. In flight they point outward, but play no part in propelling the insect.

Not all beetles harm plants, but many do by feeding on them and in some cases by transmitting diseases. Among the most familiar destructive ones are Asiatic beetle, asparagus beetles, blister beetles, click beetles, the larvae of which are wireworms, Colorado potato beetle, cucumber beetles, elm leaf beetle, flea beetles, Japanese beetle, June beetles, Mexican bean beetle, rose bug or rose chafer, and squash beetle.

Some beetles are beneficial. Best known among these are the lady beetles or ladybugs, which feed on aphids, mealybugs, and scale insects. Less familiar is the red spider mite destroyer, a tiny kind that preys on mites of various kinds. Most ground beetles, fast-moving kinds that cannot fly, must also be respected as destroyers of other insects and as friends of gardeners. Carrion beetles are scavengers and thus are beneficial.

The larvae of beetles are soft grubs that after complete metamorphosis become mature beetles. Both grubs and adults feed, often voraciously, on the same or different kinds of food.

Methods of controlling harmful beetles vary greatly according to kind and with the plants attacked. For advice in specific instances consult your Cooperative Extension Agent, your State Agricultural Experiment Station, or a recent, definitive book on pest control.

BEFARIA (Be-fària)—Tar Flower or Fly Catcher. Sometimes spelled *Bejaria*, the name of this genus of about thirty species memorializes an eighteenth-century Spanish botanist, Dr. Bejar. It belongs to a group of evergreen trees and shrubs of the heath family ERICACEAE and is found in the wild from southern Georgia and Florida to Central and South America. None of its members is hardy in the north.

Befarias have undivided, toothless, leathery leaves, and racemes or clusters of flowers, with seven-lobed calyxes, and very deeply-seven-lobed corollas, with the lobes spreading. There are fourteen stamens and a stout style. The fruits are capsules containing long-winged seeds.

Tar flower (**B. racemosa**), is endemic to sandy pinelands in southern Georgia and Florida. About 6 feet tall, it has conspicuous blooms in summer. It has hairy branches, and broad-elliptic to oblong leaves up to 2 inches long. The slightly fragrant, pinkish-tipped white blooms, about 2 inches across, are in showy racemes up to 8 inches long. Because of their slender petals they have a somewhat spidery look. The sticky calyxes and the flower buds entrap small insects, hence the vernacular name fly catcher.

Garden and Landscape Uses and Cultivation. In the deep south, *B. racemosa* is sometimes planted as an ornamental, for which purpose it could with advantage be more often used. Its natural geographical range indicates the climatic conditions it needs, but it probably can be cultivated somewhat north of its native area. Its soil should be sandy, contain a fair proportion of decayed organic matter, and have an acid reaction. No regular pruning is needed. Propagation is by seeds. Cut blooms of this shrub last well in water, the buds opening freely in succession.

BEGGAR'S LICE is *Hackelia*.

BEGONIA (Be-gònia). There can be few gardeners unacquainted with one sort or more of this tremendously important group of plants. Important horticulturally, that is, for despite the vastness and popularity of the genus, *Begonia* has few uses other than as a rich source of ornamentals. In Africa, Asia, and South America, the leaves of some native kinds are eaten, in the last region to prevent scurvy; in South America, the rhizomes of certain sorts are employed medicinally. The name commemorates Michel Begon, patron of botany and Governor of French Canada. He died in 1710.

By far the most important genus of the begonia family BEGONIACEAE, and consisting of some thousands of horticultural hybrids and varieties in addition to an estimated 1,000 natural species, *Begonia* is widely distributed through the tropics and subtropics, especially in the Americas, but is absent from the native floras of Australia and most islands of the Pacific Ocean.

Begonias exhibit great diversity in habit, foliage, flowers, and other characteristics. Most are small- to moderate-sized herbaceous perennials, often with thick rhizomes or perennial or more rarely annual tubers or, in one species, scaly bulbs. Others become somewhat woody, at least in their older parts, and range from small to as large as 20 feet tall. Some are vining or climbing plants, some are annuals. The leaves of begonias are asymmetrical with one side, to a greater or lesser extent, bigger than the other. In some kinds the leaves are all basal, in others alternate on the stems. They may be undivided or cleft palmately (in hand-fashion) into separate leaflets. Their margins may be lobed or toothed or smooth. Typically the leaves on one side of the stem are oriented with their larger sides faced in one direction, those on the other side, mirror images as it were, with their larger sides in the opposite direction. At the bases of the leafstalks are a pair of prominent appendages (stipules). Some kinds produce tiny tubers in the leaf axils, others plantlets on the stems and leaves.

The flowers are unisexual, with individual plants usually producing both sexes. Because the sepals are petal-like, sepals and petals together are correctly called tepals, but gardeners commonly refer to them all as petals and for simplicity that is done here. Male blooms commonly have two to four petals, more rarely up to eight, and numerous free or united stamens. Female blooms have two to five, less commonly up to ten, petals. There are generally three, more rarely two, four, five, or six two-lobed styles. The ovary is inferior (behind the petals), is usually prominently winged, and is often attractively colored.

Typical male flowers of begonia

Typical female flowers of begonia

The fruits, usually three-winged capsules containing very many minute seeds, rarely have four wings or are wingless, and much more rarely, berry-like.

The history of begonias in cultivation outside their native lands dates to the introduction in 1777 into England from Jamaica of *B. minor*. Other sorts soon followed. In 1798 *B. acutifolia* was brought from Jamaica to England and by the middle of the next century a considerable number of species from the West Indies, Mexico, South America, and other parts were being grown in European gardens, among them *B. acida*, *B. castaneaefolia*, *B. cinnabarina*, *B. coccinea*, *B. cucullata hookeri*, *B. dregei*, *B. grandis*, *B. heracleifolia*, *B. hydrocotylifolia*, *B. incana*, *B. incarnata*, *B. ingramii*, *B. maculata*, *B. malabarica*, *B. manicata*, *B. peponifolia*, and *B. sanguinea*. Dates of early begonia introductions into the United States are less well recorded, but there is little doubt that many reached these shores within a very few years of their appearance in Europe. So far as is known the earliest hybrid begonia to be raised, in England in 1847, was *B. ricinifolia*, its parents *B. heracleifolia* and *B. peponifolia*.

From 1850 until the beginning of World War I, a scarcely interrupted stream of new species was brought into cultivation chiefly by European collectors. Many of the newcomers were grown in the United States soon after their introduction in Europe. Notable was the introduction from the Himalayan region of *B. rex* in 1858. This, hybridized with related species, soon gave rise to a wealth of attractive foliage varieties. Hybridizers were also busy in the second half of the nineteenth century with tuberous Andean species, establishing the beginnings of lines leading to the magnificent *B. tuberhybrida* varieties of today. Another important milestone was the discovery and introduction into Scotland in 1880 of remarkable *B. socotrana* from the island of Socotra off the northeast coast of Africa.

This, if not the most, became certainly one of the most important parent species of hybrids; it was soon crossed with *B. dregei* of South Africa to found the vast Christmas begonia complex designated *B. cheimantha* and with hybrids of Andean tuberous species to establish the Elatior or Winter-flowering varieties, *B. hiemalis*.

Before the end of the nineteenth century there was much interest in begonias in the United States, and especially in California, where the mild climate makes permanent outdoor and lath house cultivation of begonias practicable, and many hybrids were raised here. It was not until after World War I, however, that lead in the introduction of new species, especially from Mexico, the West Indies, and South America, passed definitely to America. The establishment in 1932 of the American Begonia Society gave impetus and direction to collecting and growing begonias, not only in the West, but in the Northeast and other regions as well. One of the most active special plant societies in North America, through its meetings, publications, flower shows, sponsorship of plant collecting expeditions, and other promotions, it has been extremely successful in stimulating interest in begonias and meeting the needs of fanciers. Begonia Society members and other growers probably have in cultivation more species, as distinct from horticultural varieties, of its name genus than has any other plant society of its specialty.

Horticulturally begonias are separated into a number of reasonably distinct groups based on growth habits and the most popular employments of the various kinds. Such groups are not always mutually exclusive. Wax begonias, for example, are often included in permanent collections in addition to their more frequent use as bedding plants for temporary summer display. The term fibrous-rooted is not uncommonly reserved for begonias without tubers or thick rhizomes, but the roots of all begonias are fibrous. Tubers and rhizomes

are swollen or thickened stems. A further complication arises in that some sorts, the stems of which are thick and usually erect, are often referred to as rhizomatous, although by definition rhizomes are horizontal stems at or about ground level. Despite the fact that completely sharp lines cannot be drawn and overlapping occurs, it is useful to group cultivated begonias and that is done here.

Because of their great popularity as summer bedding plants as well as for other uses wax begonias and hybrid tuberous begonias are dealt with first. Then the choice hybrid derivatives of *B. socotrana*, called Christmas begonias, and Elatior or Winter-flowering begonias are considered, followed by the beautiful foliage begonias classed as *B. rex-cultorum* hybrids. Finally our attention will center on species and other hybrids.

Wax begonias, among the easiest to grow and freest-flowering of garden plants, are horticultural derivatives of Brazilian *B. cucullata hookeri* (syn. *B. semperflorens*). They exist in vast variety and for convenience are identified as **B. semperflorens-cultorum.** Characteristically they are essentially

Begonia semperflorens-cultorum

hairless and have somewhat succulent stems that branch freely from their bases, but not much above, to form bushy, leafy, compact specimens 6 inches to 1½ feet tall that when in full bloom are so covered with flowers that their foliage may scarcely be visible. In most the leaves are green, but some varieties have bronze-red to nearly black-red foliage; that of green-leaved sorts grown in full sun is likely to assume bronzy or reddish tones. In a group of varieties known as calla-lily begonias, the younger leaves are completely white; fan-

A variety of calla-lily begonia

cifully they resemble the spathes of miniature calla-lilies. The older ones are patched with white. Typically the leaves are ovate to broadly-oval, blunt-ended, lustrous, and 2 to 4 inches long or somewhat longer. Their margins are finely-toothed and furnished with hairs. In color the flowers range from white to deep crimson, with various beautiful shades of pink being most common. There are double- as well as the more frequent single-flowered varieties. The male blooms of the latter are generally ¾ to 1½ inches in diameter. The females, commonly smaller than the males, have five petals and a green ovary with

three prominent red-tinged wings. One or two varieties which have leaves variegated with pale yellow are occasionally grown.

A variegated-leaved variety of *Begonia semperflorens-cultorum*

Tuberous begonias of hybrid origin to which the group name **B. tuberhybrida** is applied are among the greatest triumphs of skilled breeders of ornamental plants. Their ancestors are tuberous species that inhabit the Andes of South America. Modern kinds exhibit tremendous diversity in plant form, foliage, and blooms. They include erect and pendulous sorts. Their flowers vary in diameter from about 2 to 8 inches; they are single, partially double, or double; they may have plain or frilled petals; and they range in color from pure white through cream, yellow, orange, and practically all shades of pink, apricot-pink, and salmon-pink to brilliant red, purplish-red, and deepest crimson.

These begonias characteristically have large, flattish perennial tubers depressed

at their tops, and semisucculent, more or less hairy stems generally 6 inches to about 1 foot long. The leaves are pointed-ovate-heart-shaped with a deep sinus (cleft) at the base of the blade. Their angled and toothed margins are fringed with hairs. The veins on their under surfaces are hairy.

Groups of hybrid tuberous begonias are based on the forms of their flowers. The Single-flowered group consists of varieties with plain single flowers. The Marginata group has single, sometimes crested or crisped blooms with petals of one color margined with a contrasting hue. Double-flowered varieties with this color pattern are called Picotees. The Camellia-flowered group has double blooms. The Marmorata group is of varieties that have usually double, red, pink, or orange blooms blotched or marbled with white. The Crispa group consists of varieties with single flowers with frilled petals. The Fimbriata or Carnation-flowered group has full double blooms with petals much toothed and frilled. The Cristata group has single flowers with petals decorated with a conspicuous frilled crest. The Narcissiflora group is characterized by its male flowers having the two outer petals spreading widely, the others united, standing nearly erect and with flared and ruffled apexes so that they suggest the trumpet of a daffodil. The Pendula group, as the name suggests, consists of varieties with more or less pendulous or hanging stems and drooping flowers. Varieties of this group are splendid for growing in hanging baskets. Those known in gardens as *B. lloydii* belong here. The Rosebud group, sometimes misnamed *B. rosaeflora*, is a collection of varieties with double, roselike flowers. They are quite different from the Peruvian species *B. rosaeflora*. The Intermedia group, or as it is

Double-flowered *Begonia semperflorens-cultorum* 'Gustav Lind'

Begonia tuberhybrida varieties

Hybrid tuberous begonias: (a) Single-flowered

(b) Camellia-flowered

(c) Carnation-flowered

often called the Multiflora or Bertinii group, consists of varieties that produce small flowers in great abundance.

Christmas begonias (**B. cheimantha**) are hybrids between bulbous *B. socotrana* and semituberous South African *B. dregei* suited only for greenhouse cultivation and grown by florists, although in lesser numbers than formerly, as gift plants. They bloom in midwinter with an abandon scarcely equaled by other kinds. Under favorable conditions the display remains in good condition for several weeks. The first of these, pink-flowered *B. c.* 'Gloire de Lorraine', raised in France by Lemoine in 1892, is still cultivated. Later varieties, unless otherwise noted all with pink flowers, are 'Caledonia' (white-flowered), 'Christmas White' (white-flowered), 'Genesee Beauty', 'Glory of Cincinnati', 'Lady Mac', 'Lonsdale', 'Lucille' (red-flowered), 'Marjory Gibbs', 'Melior', 'Mrs. Petersen', and 'Turnford Hall' (white tinged with pink). Variety 'Mrs. Petersen' has bronze-colored foliage.

In contrast to one of their parent species, Christmas begonias are not bulbous or semibulbous. From a crown of clustered buds and fibrous roots they annually develop slender, semisucculent, branched stems. Their thinnish leaves have slender stalks and roundish, toothed blades with much the aspect of those of *B. socotrana*, but without the deep cuplike central depression; they are usually cleft to the top of the leafstalk at their bases. The flowers, except the last ones produced in each loose cluster, are all males and carried above the foliage. The branches of the inflorescences (flower clusters) are usually pink or pinkish.

A group of larger-flowered hybrids of *B. socotrana*, quite different from Christmas begonias and known as Elatior or Winter-flowering hybrid begonias, is properly identified as **B. hiemalis.** Many of these originated from a cross made at the famous Veitch's nurseries in England about 1883 between *B. socotrana* and an early hybrid of tuberous Andean species, a vermilion-red-flowered *B. tuberhybrida* variety named 'Viscountess Doneraile'. The first *B. hiemalis* sorts were named 'Mrs. John Heal', after the wife of the hybridizer, 'Adonis', and 'Winter Gem'. About 1912 the nursery firm of Clibrans in England began devoting attention to raising new varieties and introduced such kinds as 'Altringham Pink', 'Clibrans' Pink', 'Elatior', 'Emily Clibran', 'Fascination', 'Lucy Clibran', and 'Optima'. These and others raised by Clibrans were great improvements over earlier varieties. They had more vigor, came in a wide range of beautiful shades of pink and red and white, and included some with perfectly double flowers. The name *B. hiemalis* not having been given at that time, these plants were generally referred to as Clibran hybrids. Later, initiative in introducing new varieties passed to Holland and between World War I and World War II new varieties, freer-flowering and in an even wider range of colors, were marketed by the nursery firm of Baardse. Among these introductions were 'Baardse's Wonder', 'Baardse's Favorite', 'Exquisite', 'J. F. Ch. Dix', 'Mevrouw Baardse', and 'Oranjezon'.

Magnificent though the Clibran and Baardse varieties were, they were challenging plants to grow and only highly skilled greenhouse gradeners could count on success with them. The chief difficulties stemmed from the uncertainty of successfully bringing them through their rest period (they inherited from their tuberous ancestor a tendency to die back after flowering, but unlike it possessed no tubers and thus if allowed to do so died). On the other hand if kept a mite too wet they also died. A delicate balance had to be preserved to maintain stocks. Because of this, young plants were very expensive and many who attempted the cultivation of these fine plants knew only disappointment.

Begonia cheimantha

Begonia cheimantha (flowers)

Begonia hiemalis 'Clibran's Pink'

Begonia rex-cultorum: (a) 'Her Majesty'

xanthina. The embracing name for these hybrids is **B. rex-cultorum.** Remarkable for their highly-ornamental, beautifully-colored leaves, they are usually grown primarily as foliage plants, even though many have decidedly attractive, sometimes fragrant flowers.

Begonia hiemalis (flowers)

It was 1972 before Rieger hybrids became available in the United States. Soon the varieties 'Aphrodite', 'Cherry Red', 'Aphrodite Pink', 'Schwabenland Pink', and 'Schwabenland Red' were being offered commercially. The great advantage of the newcomers is the greater ease with which they can be propagated and grown as compared with earlier sorts. Some amateur growers have reported considerable success with them as window plants.

Rex-cultorum or rex begonias as they are often less precisely called comprise a group of more or less complex hybrids of *B. rex* and one or more of several related species including *B. annulata, B. decora, B. diadema, B. laciniata, B. robusta, B. tenuifolia,* and *B.*

(b) 'Merry Christmas'

Elatior or Winter-flowering hybrid begonias attained a new era of popularity with the introduction in the 1950s of a group of varieties bred by O. Rieger in Germany. Although the raiser failed to divulge their parentage, and it has been stated that no tuberous begonia played a part in their ancestry, this seems extremely unlikely and there is no real doubt that they are correctly classified as varieties of *B. hiemalis.* Whereas earlier sorts raised in Holland originated as bud sports from English varieties, the Rieger introductions apparently resulted from new crosses between *B. socotrana* and probably *B. bertinii.*

A Rieger hybrid begonia

(c) 'Mikado'

As a result of their mixed parentage and selection by hybridists, rex-cultorum begonias exhibit remarkable variation in size, leaf forms, and colorings. Most are distinctly rhizomatous and have short thick stems that extend along the surface of the soil and root into it, but a few have thinner, erect, leafy stems. The leaves commonly have decidedly asymmetrically-heart-shaped to elephant-earlike blades that may be more or less sharply-lobed or lobeless. Their margins are toothed, their surfaces often more or less puckered and hairy to a greater or lesser degree. In some kinds their basal lobes are spirally twisted. There are sorts with leaf blades 6 to 9 inches long as well as miniatures with much smaller foliage. Leaf colors and patterns are various and striking. In some silvery hues predominate. Others are chiefly green, gray-green, or slaty-green. There are brilliant-leaved sorts in which the leaves or parts of the leaves become bright pink, red, maroon, chocolate-brown, or nearly black. These kinds are offered in a great profusion of varieties by specialist dealers.

The only species with bulbs is *B. socotrana*, an endemic of the island of Socotra.

Begonia socotrana

Even this has not very well-developed bulbs and is perhaps best described as semibulbous. Nevertheless, its swollen food storage organs, unlike tubers, are not solid and covered with a thin outer skin, but as is true of all bulbs are composed of separate fleshy scales. Those of *B. socotrana* are arranged loosely, the bulbs are very small and clustered. This species has played a remarkable part in the ancestry of the important groups of hybrid begonias identified as *B. cheimantha* and *B. hiemalis*. From 6 to 9 inches tall, it is deciduous and has succulent stems and glossy, circular, toothed leaves 4 to 7 inches wide, which are considerably depressed at their centers, with rolled-back margins, and with stalks united to the blades nearly at their centers. The rose-pink flowers, borne in winter in loose, branched, terminal clusters of few are 1½ to 2 inches wide. Only the terminal one of each cluster is female, the others are males.

Tuberous begonia species that are stemless or almost so include these: *B. cyclophylla*, a native of China, has broadly-heart-shaped, fine-toothed, bluntish leaves with overlapping basal lobes. Its rose-pink, fragrant blooms, the males 1 inch to 1½ inches wide, are in groups of few on slender stalks up to 6 inches tall. *B. davisii* is stemless or has very short, erect stems and short-pointed, broad-ovate, round-toothed leaves with a fringe of hairs where the nearly 3½-inch-long blades join their stalks. The blades, green above, have red undersides. Carried just above the foliage, the 1½-inch-wide flowers have bright orange-scarlet petals with yellowish-pink backs. *B. josephii* of India is variable. Usually stemless, it has long-stalked leaves, those of young plants with stalks joined to the blades well in from the margins. The blades, ovate to broad-ovate in outline, up to 1 foot long or longer by one-half to

nearly as broad as long, sometimes have few to several triangular, pointed lobes. The small rose-pink flowers are in clusters of few on stems not longer than the leaves. *B. veitchii*, of Andean Peru, has very short thick stems and lobed and toothed, asymmetrically-heart-shaped leaves with a bright red spot where blade and stalk join. About 2¾ inches across, the cinnabar-red flowers are carried in pairs on erect stalks up to 1 foot long. This is one of the parents of *B. tuberhybrida*.

Tuberous begonia species that have obvious, often long stems include these: *B. boliviensis*, of Bolivia, is parent of a group of horticultural *B. tuberhybrida* varieties with pendulous stems, popular for growing in hanging baskets. The species is 1½ to 3 feet tall, has slender stems at first erect, later sprawling to drooping, and pointed, lanceolate to ovate-lanceolate, toothed leaves 3 to 5 inches long. The cinnabar-red flowers, the males 2 inches long, the females about 1 inch long, are in pendulous panicles and do not spread their petals widely. The plant known in gardens as *B. bertinii*, which has more upright, bigger, light red blooms, is a horticultural selection of a hybrid between *B. boliviensis* and *B. veitchii* named *B. intermedia*. For the selection, *B. i. bertinii* is the correct name. *B. cinnabarina*, of the Bolivian Andes, is slightly downy with erect, zigzagged stems. The tall flowering stalks carry compact clusters of 2-inch-wide, cinnabar-red blooms. This sort is important as a parent of *B. tuberhybrida* varieties. *B. froebelii*, of Ecuador, has erect stems 4 inches to 1 foot

Begonia froebelii

tall and long-stalked, asymmetrically-heart-shaped, roundish-toothed, bright green leaves reddish on their undersides and 4 to 5 inches long by three-quarters as wide as long. Stems and leaves are densely clothed with soft hairs. The brilliant scarlet-crimson blooms 1¼ to 2 inches across in fork-branched clusters, are softly-hairy on the backs of their outer petals. The anthers are red, edged with yellow. *B. f. strobelii* has smaller leaves and blooms, pink rather than red, with white centers. It

Begonia socotrana (bulbs)

Begonia grandis

Begonia grandis (flowers)

withstands warm summers better than the species. **B. gracilis,** a native of Mexico, is a hairless species with small tubers and slender, erect, often branchless stems up to 1½ feet tall with distantly-spaced leaves becoming successively smaller and shorter-stalked above. They are asymmetrically-pointed-ovate and irregularly-lobed and toothed, or the lower leaves are rounder. The flowers, one, two, or sometimes four on short stalks from the axils of the upper leaves or bracts are pink and 1 inch to 1¼ inches wide. **B. grandis** (syn. *B. evansiana*) of China is the hardiest begonia. In sheltered places, such as the base of a wall, it survives outdoors in the vicinity of New York City. It has small tubers and erect, branched, hairless stems 1 foot to 2 feet tall. Tiny tubers develop in the leaf axils of their lower parts. The thin, pointed-ovate leaves, 4 to 5½ inches in length and about two-thirds as long as wide, with scattered bristly hairs, have heart-shaped bases and toothed, hair-fringed margins. Their stalks and under surfaces are red. The light pink, fragrant blooms in loose clusters on branched stalks from the leaf axils are about 1½ inches in diameter. *B. g. alba* has white blooms. **B. martiana** (syn. *B. gracilis martiana*) is Mexican and is sometimes called hollyhock begonia. It has cream, thin-skinned tubers and erect, rarely-branched stems. The leaves are nearly heart-shaped, the upper ones more pointed than those below. Small tubers develop in their axils. The short-stalked, rose-pink flowers are in slender spires above the leafy parts of the stems. **B. micranthera hieronymii,** of Argentina and Bolivia, has

slender, erect stems and long-stalked, irregularly-lobed and toothed, pointed-ovate to nearly round, more or less hairy leaves. Its white to pink flowers are about 2 inches in diameter. *B. m. fimbriata* differs in the floral bracts being hair-fringed. **B. pearcei,** of the Bolivian Andes, has been important in the development of the magnificent horticultural *B. tuberhybrida* varieties with yellow, buff-yellow, orange-yellow, and similarly-colored blooms. This variable species has finely-hairy, branched stems 6 inches to 1 foot tall and broad-ovate to nearly heart-shaped, strongly-veined, toothed leaves, green and hairless above, short-

hairy and light red on their undersides. The bright yellow flowers, in loose clusters, are 1 inch to 1¼ inches across. **B. pedata** is Mexican. From each tuber develops one or more slender stems up to 2½ feet tall each of which at the end of the season develops a new tuber at its base. The three- to five-lobed leaves are white-hairy on their undersides. The flowers are pink. **B. sandtii**, of Mexico, is allied to *B. viscida* from which it is distinguishable by its leaves being more abruptly pointed and with wavier margins. It produces slender, branchless stems about 8 inches tall and, like the foliage, densely clothed with glan-

Begonia pearcei

Begonia pearcei (flowers)

dular hairs. Small tubers develop in the axils of the lower leaves. The leaves' light green, asymmetrically-heart-shaped, double-toothed blades fringed with fine hairs, are approximately 4 inches long by 3 inches wide. The flowers are in clusters of few. Males, over 1 inch across, have few petals, the somewhat smaller females, five. **B. viscida** is a Mexican with tubers that last for one year only; they are renewed annually. Its parts are clammy or sticky because of slender glandular hairs. Individual plants are unisexual. The branchless stems are erect and up to 3 feet long. The leaves are thin, light green with brownish centers and veins. They are asymmetrically-ovate, slender-pointed, toothed, up to nearly 6 inches long and somewhat wider than long. The flowers, about ¾ inch wide, are white.

Semituberous begonias with, in cultivation but perhaps not always in their natural habitats, permanent stems and evergreen foliage, form a distinctive group of African natives. Their tuberous parts, the much-swollen knobby bases of the stems, are usually partly above the soil surface. Included here are these: **B. dregei,** notable as being a parent of the first Christmas begonia (*B.* 'Gloire de Lorraine') and other important horticultural varieties, is South African. It has brown tubers and much-branched stems 1 foot to 2 feet tall. Its leaves are thin, ovate, shallowly-angled and toothed, 2 to 3 inches long with red-purple veins and reddish undersides. The white flowers, ⅝ inch wide, are in clusters of about five. *B. d. caffra* differs in tending to be larger and in having angular instead of rounded indentations between the teeth along the leaf margins. Its flowers are white to delicate pink. *B. d. macbethii* differs in its smaller leaves, lobed from one-half to three-fifths their diameters and sparingly-coarsely-saw-toothed, be-

Begonia dregei macbethii

ing without red veins. Its blooms are pink or white. A variant cultivated as *B. d. macbethii-obtusa* is more compact and has purple-veined leaves. **B. morelii,** of South Africa, has tubers much like those of *B. dregei,* but they are clear flesh-pink. Its comparatively-long-stalked, asymmetrically-heart-shaped leaves, with slightly-toothed blades about 2 inches long, are at first coppery-brown and hairy, later glossy green spotted and edged with silver and with mottled red under surfaces. Carried a little above the foliage, the flowers are pink. **B. natalensis** is a South African 1 foot to 2 feet tall, hairless and with irregularly-angular-lobed, toothed leaves with those of the main stem up to 2¾ inches long by 1⅓ inches wide and considerably bigger than the leaves of the branches. The 1-inch-wide blooms are white or pale pink, the females even on the same plant with variously-shaped and -sized wings. **B. partita** is much like *B. suffruticosa,* but has at least some hairs or short white bristles on the upper surfaces of its leaves. Also, its lower leaves are merely bluntly lobed instead of being deeply cleft as are its upper ones and all those of *B. suffruticosa.* The flowers are white. **B. sanderana,** although botanically not belonging with the other African semituberous sorts here discussed, is much like them except that its male blooms have four instead of two petals. In this sort the lobing of the leaves is confined chiefly to the lower halves of the blades, the upper halves being long-triangular. **B. suffruticosa** (syn. *B. richardsiana*) is a hairless South African of great elegance. It has

Begonia suffruticosa

thin, markedly unequal-sided leaves dissected in lacy fashion, with one major cleft reaching nearly to the leafstalk and the lobes again deeply cut. The flowers are white. A popular intermediate hybrid between *B. dregei* and *B. sutherlandii* is **B. weltoniensis.** This kind has white or pink blooms, the males usually with four petals. **B. sutherlandii,** of South Africa, very pretty, but somewhat variable, has arching and

Begonia sutherlandii

pendulous, branched, slender stems 1 foot to 2 feet long and ovate-lanceolate leaves 3 to 6 inches in length, deeply indented at their bases. Bright green and toothed, they sometimes have red veins. The flowers are orange- to coppery-red. *B. s. latior* has larger leaves than the typical species. The species and its variety are charming for hanging baskets.

Rhizomatous begonias notable for their beautifully-colored leaves and grown primarily as foliage plants are next considered. Of necessity the selection is arbitrary. Some species, such as *B. bowerae* and *B. ricinifolia,* discussed in the next group of rhizomatous species, have handsomely-ornamented leaves, but in general are esteemed as much for their blooms or for their interest as collectors' items as for their foliage. With some misgivings then as to the completeness of the selection the following are offered as rhizomatous sorts especially attractive as foliage plants. **B. cathayana** is Chinese. From 1 foot to 2 feet tall, it has erect, red or reddish-brown stems clothed with soft, white or pinkish hairs. The long-pointed, asymmetrical, softly-hairy leaves 6 to 8 inches long by 3 to 5½ inches wide are more or less lobed, finely-toothed, and fringed with hairs. They are olive-green with a silvery band paralleling the margins. The veins and undersides of the blades are red. The orange-vermilion flowers are approximately 1 inch in diameter. This sort needs warmth, shade, and high humidity. **B. decora,** of Malaya and Indochina, is a beautiful species related to *B. rex.* It has hairy rhizomes and pointed-ovate to heart-shaped, finely-toothed, green leaves 3 to 4 inches long, with pimply surfaces thickly clothed with short, white hairs. Their upper surfaces are reddish-brown with yellowish-green veins, their undersides red. The blooms are pink. **B. goegoensis,** of Sumatra, is compact, with creeping rhizomes. Its very beautiful, nearly-circular leaves have four-angled stalks that join the puckered-surfaced blades near their centers. The hairless blades, 5 to 9 inches in diameter, are dark olive-green

Begonia goegoensis

Begonia masoniana

Begonia pustulata argentea

with paler veins and reddish undersides. The small, rose-pink flowers are in loose clusters carried scarcely higher than the foliage. **B. imperialis,** one of the loveliest foliage begonias, is native to Mexico. Low, hairy, and rhizomatous, it has small, heart-

Begonia imperialis

shaped, pebble-surfaced, velvety, brownish leaves with pale green veins, and inconsequential clusters of small white flowers. The leaves of B. i. smaragdina are bright emerald-green. B. i. 'Gruss an Erfurt' has sparsely-hairy, silvery-green leaves marked along their margins with greenish-brown. B. i. 'Otto Forster' has brownish leaves with pale green veins. These sorts need much warmth, high humidity, and considerable shade. **B. masoniana,** the iron cross begonia, is a very distinctive rhizomatous sort, native probably of China. Vigorous,

it has medium-large, puckered, round-heart-shaped, hairy leaves, nile-green with, in strong contrast, a German iron-cross-like pattern of dark reddish-brown. The waxy, greenish-white flowers are hairy on their outsides. This kind needs high temperatures and high humidity. **B. pustulata** is Mexican and has beautifully-colored, heart-shaped, pebbly-surfaced, silvery-veined green leaves with red or deep pink under surfaces. The flowers are small and greenish-white. B. p. argentea has leaves nicely variegated with silver along their

Begonia imperialis smaragdina

Begonia rajah

midribs and in smaller patches elsewhere over their upper surfaces. **B. rajah**, of Malaya, is a low, compact, rhizomatous begonia with very beautiful, roundish, slightly-angular, puckered, reddish-green leaves of silky aspect with a contrasting network of yellow-green veins. About 2 inches in diameter, they have dull red undersides. The small pink flowers are in clusters scarcely exceeding the foliage in height. **B. rex** is less commonly cultivated than its hybrid offspring. Its influence as a parent of the popular hybrid group *B. rex-cultorum* and of some other hybrids has been immense. Native to Assam, this species has thick, fleshy rhizomes from which come broad-heart-shaped, crinkly or pebbly-surfaced, hairy leaves with red, hairy stalks and blades 8 inches to 1 foot long. Dark olive-green, and with a wide silvery band paralleling the margin about 1 inch in from it, they have a metallic sheen. The delicate pink flowers, the males 2 inches in diameter, are in clusters on erect, branched stalks. **B. speculata** is perhaps of hybrid origin. Low and durable, it has short, thick rhizomes and crowded, pebbly-surfaced, gray-green, ovate leaves with small green areas between the veins. Their

seven or nine shallow lobes are coarsely-toothed. The white to pinkish flowers, hairy on their outsides, hang from long, erect, hairy stalks. The females have associated with them persistent, red-edged, green bracts. **B. versicolor** is a charming miniature native of China. It has small rhizomes and thick, puckered-surfaced, broad-heart-shaped leaves about 3 inches in diameter clothed with thick red hairs. They are emerald- to apple-green splashed with silvery-white and have maroon veins. The pink blooms are in hairy-stalked clusters of three or four. This sort needs considerable warmth and high humidity and is suitable for terrariums. **B. xanthina**, of India, has much in common with *B. rex*. Its large, fleshy, lustrous leaves are pointed-ovate-heart-shaped, green above, purplish on their undersides. The bright butter-yellow flowers are 1½ inches across. The leaves of *B. x. pictifolia* are decorated with rows of white spots.

Species with horizontal rhizomes and leaves prominently lobed or of several separate leaflets include these: **B. acerifolia**, of Ecuador, is low, with long-stalked leaves. Their blades, up to 8 inches across, have several unequal-sized lobes and on both surfaces short hairs. About 1¼ inches wide, the flowers are frilled and white, or when young pink. **B. circumlobata** is Chinese. It has long-stalked pebbly-surfaced leaves, with stalks shaggy with white hairs when young and blades lustrous above, paler beneath, and nearly hairless, 6 to 9 inches across, deeply cleft into up to seven more or less pointed, toothed lobes. The flowers, few together atop stalks 4 to 6 inches long, are pink and about 1 inch wide. **B. corzoensis**, of Mexico, has subterranean rhizomes and pointed-broad-ovate, seven-lobed leaves. Their stalks, up to 1 foot in length, join the up to 10-inch-long, thin, short-hair blades a little distance in from their margins. The flowers, in clusters of few, are pink, the males about 1½ inches wide, the females smaller. **B. heracleifolia**, the star begonia, is Mexican. Its long-stalked leaves, 6 to 10 inches wide,

are deeply cleft palmately (in hand-fashion) into seven to nine sharp-toothed lobes. They are bristly-hairy, green with bronzy-green veins. The pink blooms, in handsome one-sided, many-flowered panicles 1½ to 2 feet tall, are carried on erect stalks well above the foliage. They are 1 inch to 1½ inches across. The leaves of *B. h. nigricans* are black-green with pale green veins. **B. ludicra** (syn. *B. liebmannii*), native from Mexico to Panama is low and some-

Begonia ludicra

what hairy. Its nearly-circular, sharply-lobed leaves blotched with silvery-white have reddish under surfaces. The flowers are in clusters shorter than the foliage. Males are about 1½ inches across, females smaller. **B. macdougallii** is Mexican, has long-stalked leaves the blades of which are of seven to

Begonia macdougallii

ten shortly-stalked, bronzy-green, toothed, narrow-elliptic leaflets, red on their undersides, the outer ones sickle shaped. A plant grown as **B. purpurea** and reported to be a native of Brazil appears to be a form of *B. macdougallii*. This sort has glossy leaves up to 2 feet wide, with stalks 3 feet long. Its flowers are chartreuse. **B. philodendroides** is a Mexican related to *B. heracleifolia*, but with less deeply-lobed, long-stalked leaves and white flowers. The glossy leaves have heart-shaped blades 8 to 10 inches across and usually wider than

Begonia speculata

Begonia heracleifolia

long. They are deeply cleft into seven lobes, which are sometimes again lobed and are toothed. The blooms, in few-flowered clusters atop stems about 9 inches long, are about 1 inch in diameter. *B. p. multiloba* has bigger leaves, with lobes that have more pronounced secondary lobes. *B. pringlei* (syn. *B. kraussiantha*), of Mexico, sometimes misidentified as *B. schulziana*, has long-stalked leaves with broad-ovate, pointed-lobed and toothed blades 2 to 3 inches long. The flowering stalks, erect and about as long as the leafstalks, are topped with clusters of few ¾-inch-wide pink blooms.

Species with horizontal rhizomes, and leaves not of separate leaflets, but sometimes slightly-lobed or angled, include these: *B. acida,* of Brazil, has creeping rhizomes and bright green, wrinkled-sur-

Begonia acida

faced leaves not or at most slightly lobed. Finely-toothed, bristly-hairy, they are up to 9 inches wide. Their stalks and undersides are furnished with thick, white or pinkish, curved hairs. Small, white or greenish, and atop tall stalks, the flowers are in clusters that are held erect only after the bud stage. This kind needs warm, humid conditions. *B. aridicaulis,* of Mexico, a miniature, has long-pointed, ovate to broad-lanceolate, pale-veined, glossy leaves with translucent panels of pale green between the veins. It produces an abundance of quite large white blooms and is well suited for terrariums. *B. attenuata,* of Brazil, is closely similar to and possibly not specifically distinct from *B. herbacea.* The chief apparent difference is that its smaller leaves have short, wingless leafstalks. *B. barbana* (syn. *B. squamosa*), of Costa Rica, is low, has strongly asymmetrical, pointed-ovate, toothed leaves about 4 inches long,

Begonia aridicaulis

two-thirds as broad as their lengths, with veins toward their bases paler and on their undersides hairy. The flowers are in clusters on erect stalks that branch near their tops. *B. boweri,* sometimes called eyelash begonia, is a native of Mexico that has

Begonia boweri

been freely used in hybridizing. Small and low, it has pointed-ovate leaves 1 inch to 2 inches long, with stitchlike black marks, and eyelashed with erect hairs along their margins. The little pink flowers are carried with airy grace in loose clusters well above the foliage. *B. b. major* has leaves up to 4½ inches long by 2¼ inches wide, without or with only faint marginal markings. *B. b. nigromarga* is distinguished by the main veins of its leaves being banded with black. Also, the teeth of the leaves are more numerous and sharper, their hairs longer. *B. b. rosaeflora* has more angular, longer-pointed leaves than *B. b. major*; they are up to 5 inches long by 3 inches wide. Its flowers are pink. *B. conchaefolia* is Costa Rican. Its fleshy leaves have stalks 3 to 6 inches long and blades sometimes as wide, but often smaller. They are nearly circular, somewhat pointed, and slightly-irregularly-toothed and usually have the stalk attached to the blade some little way in from the margin. The veins on the un-

Begonia conchaefolia

dersides of the blades are densely furnished with brownish, woolly hairs. Rising to twice the height of the foliage, the hairy flower stalks branch to bear sprays of many clear pink, ½-inch-wide blooms. *B. crispula,* of southern China, has roundish, deeply-puckered or corrugated leaves 5 to 6 inches across. The flowering stalks, about 6 inches tall, carry a few white blooms pink-tinged on their outsides, the males are a little more than ½ inch wide, the females smaller. *B. cristobalensis* is Mexican and has seldom-branched rhizomes and leaves with 2-inch-long stalks and short-pointed, broad-ovate blades some 4 inches long by 1¾ inches wide, marbled with irregular small patches and oxblood-red lines. The flowers, in clusters of few and pink, are about ¾ inch across. *B. ficicola,* of West Africa, is a dwarf that in the wild grows as an epiphyte on trees. It has pebbly-surfaced, broad-ovate leaves up to 5 inches long and, scarcely rising above them, small bright yellow flowers tinged on the backs of the petals with orange. This sort needs warmth, high humidity, and considerable shade. *B. friburgensis,* a Brazilian, is low and has lustrous, pointed-broad-ovate, thick, leathery leaves that when quite young are red and crinkled in cockscomb fashion. The clusters of white to light pink flowers are on tall, erect stalks. *B. fusca* is Mexican and has long-stalked, irregularly-scalloped, velvety leaves nearly circular in outline. They have blades up to 2½ feet in diameter with a basal white eye from which spreads a star of pale veins. The little whitish flowers are in erect panicles. *B. herbacea* is most un-begonia-like. Brazilian, in the wild it grows as an epiphyte (perched on trees). It has thick, fiber-coated rhizomes and nearly symmetrical, obovate-lanceolate, finely-toothed leaves, perhaps sometimes spotted with white, that narrow to stalkless bases. The blooms are white, ½ inch or so wide, the males in clusters with a pair of large, fringed, green bracts, the females with ovaries sitting almost directly on the rhizomes. *B. h. ellipticifolia* has oblong-el-

Begonia herbacea

liptic leaves. **B. hidalgensis,** of Mexico, has leaves with long stalks furnished with fine hairs and very asymmetrical, broad-ovate, slightly-angled blades 3 to 4½ inches long, hairless above, with short hairs on their undersides. The flowering stalks, up to 1½ feet long or longer, fork at their ends into clusters of many little yellowish-white blooms. **B. hispidavillosa,** of Mexico, has long-stalked, abruptly-pointed, broad-ovate, minutely-toothed, satiny leaves up to about 7 inches long by two-thirds as wide, moderately furnished with shortish, stiff hairs. Its much-branched flower clustered on stalks about 1½ feet long have many 1-inch-wide light red blooms. **B. hydrocotylifolia,** of Mexico, has circular, thick leaves of waxy appearance, 3 inches or so

Begonia hydrocotylifolia

in diameter, light olive-green with paler veins. The panicles of pink flowers top tall, erect stalks. **B. nelumbiifolia** is a Mexican of imposing aspect. It has long-stalked leaves with ovate-circular blades up to 1 foot wide, the leafstalks joined to the blades well in from their margins. The white or pink-tinged, ½-inch-wide flowers

are many together in crowded, much-branched clusters lifted well above the foliage on long, erect stalks. **B. olsoniae,** of Brazil, up to 1 foot high, has asymmetrical-broad-ovate to nearly-round leaves tapered to slender points. From 5 to 8 inches long and up to about 4½ inches broad, they are bristly-hairy on both surfaces.

Begonia olsoniae

Above they are green strikingly ornamented with ivory-white veins. Their undersides are often reddish. The white flowers, their outsides sometimes flushed with pink, are in erect-stalked clusters. **B. paulensis,** of Brazil, is a striking sort with large, nearly circular, lustrous leaves the stalks of which join the blades near their centers. They are shiny, puckered, and fresh green, with a central star of ivory-white, white hairs, and cross-veins linking in spiderweb fashion those that radiate from the center. The veins and hairs on the undersides of the leaves are red. White with conspicuous red beards on the backs of the petals, the 1½- to 2-inch-wide flowers are in one-sided clusters atop tall, erect stems. **B. peponifolia,** of Mexico and Jamaica, has big, long-stalked, almost circular leaves fringed along their wavy margins with fine hairs. Its clusters of small, pale pink flowers are lifted on long stalks well above the foliage. **B. pinetorum,** Mexican, has large, very asymmetrical, long-stalked, ovate leaves, with a flannel of rusty hairs on their undersides that is easily removed by rubbing and a fuzz of white hairs on their upper surfaces. The tall, erect flowering stalks terminate in quite dense clusters of pale pink blooms, the females with delicate pink ovaries. **B. popenoei,** a hairy, impressively-handsome native of Honduras, is remarkable and possibly unique in having long stolons or runners with nodes up to 4 inches apart. Its leaf

Begonia pinetorum

Begonia popenoei

blades are pointed-broad-ovate, up to 9 inches long, toothed and reddish at their edges. The flowers are in large trusses lifted well above the foliage. The females are 1 inch wide or wider and white, the males smaller and pinkish. **B. prismatocarpa,** a charming miniature, is native to Fernando Po, a small island near the coast

Begonia prismatocarpa

of equatorial West Africa. Its slender rhizomes spread over and near the ground surface. The leaves have long stalks for a plant of its size and asymmetrical, heart-shaped-ovate to somewhat palmately-lobed, toothed blades. The flowers are unusual. They have two yellow petals and an elongated, four-sided ovary without wings. **B. rhizocarpa,** of Brazil, is closely related to and perhaps not specifically distinct from

Begonia rhizocarpa

B. herbacea. It has pointed-elliptic, nearly-symmetrical, finely-toothed leaves, with narrow red margins and short, wingless stalks. Two to three together atop slender stalks shorter than the leaves, the flowers are white. **B. rotundifolia** is an attractive low rhizomatous native of Haiti. Its leaves have comparatively long, slender stalks that unite with the approximately circular, round-toothed blades well in from their margins. The blades are 1½ to 3 inches wide. Lifted on slender stalks to heights of 6 to 9 inches, the small white to pink blooms about 1¼ inches wide are in clusters of few. **B. rupicola,** of Java, is small, with asymmetrically-heart-shaped, irregularly-toothed, 3-inch-long leaves, brownish-green relieved by yellowish areas. The flowers are small and light pink. **B. sar-**

Begonia sarmentacea

mentacea is a Brazilian, with much the aspect of *B. olsoniae,* but more softly-hairy and the light red undersides of its short-stalked, pale-veined leaves paler. The moderately-sized, white flowers are in clusters of few atop erect stalks. **B. staudtii dispersipilosa,** of West Africa, is low and has beautiful, broad-ovate to nearly round, crinkly-surfaced leaves and quite big, deep yellow flowers just showing above the foliage. The males have two large petals. **B. stigmosa,** of Mexico to Colombia, is low, with small, pointed-broad ovate, often slightly-angled leaves mottled with brown and long stalks thickly clothed with papery scales. The small white to pinkish flowers are in long-stalked clusters. **B. strigillosa,** of Guatemala and Costa Rica, has long-stalked, heart-shaped, toothed leaves with hairy margins and veins at first hairy. The long flowering stalks terminate in a cluster of few, red-edged, white to pink, 1-inch-wide blooms. **B. subnummularifolia,** a low native of Banguey Island, North Borneo,

Begonia subnummularifolia

has slender rhizomes and thin, nearly-round, short-stalked, toothless leaves 1 inch to 2 inches in diameter, with slightly-heart-shaped bases. Except for the margins and to a slight degree the veins, they are hairless. The male flowers of the longish-stalked clusters are ¼ inch wide. **B. sudjanae,** of Sumatra, has short, thick rhizomes and pointed-ovate, light green leaves the stalks of which join the wrinkled blades toward their centers. Stalks and blades are densely-hairy. The rather small, white to pinkish flowers have varying numbers of petals, the males two to four, the females two or three. The yellow stamens of the males are united. **B. tacana,** of Mexico, is very similar to *B. cristobalensis,* but has white flowers, the females conspicuously narrower than those of that species. **B. villipetiola** has large broad-ovate leaves. The tall, erect flowering stalks branch at their tops into flattish clusters of white flowers.

Trailing or climbing stems, often under ideal conditions of great length, but likely to be considerably shorter on plants culti-

vated in pots or hanging baskets, and frequently if in contact with moist surfaces rooting from the nodes, are generally characteristic of these species: **B. alnifolia,** of Colombia, has pinnately-veined leaves reminiscent of those of an alder. It has somewhat vining stems and strongly-asymmetrical, irregularly-toothed, pointed-ovate, hairless or nearly hairless leaves 3 to 5 inches long and up to 2½ inches wide. The ½-inch-wide, white flowers are in loose, fork-branched clusters 6 inches or more across. **B. carpinifolia,** of Costa Rica, somewhat straggling, in the wild is often epiphytic or may grow in the ground among bushes that offer support. Up to about 5 feet tall, it has slender stems that may root from the nodes. The leaves have somewhat the aspect of those of beeches and hornbeams and are obliquely-ovate, abruptly-pointed, mostly 2 to 3½ inches long up to nearly 2 inches wide, and hairless or nearly so. The flowers 1 inch to 1½ inches across are white, the petals often tipped with pink. **B. convolvulacea** is a robust native of Brazil. Up to about 6 feet in height, it has fleshy stems with swollen nodes from which in moist environments roots develop. Its pointed-heart-shaped, glossy leaves, broader than wide, are 4 to 6 inches across, with five to seven lobes; the small white flowers are in forked-branched panicles of many. **B. estrellensis,** of Costa Rica, has slender, vining stems

Begonia estrellensis

and short-stalked, slightly-toothed, elliptic to ovate leaves, 3 inches long, that taper to slender points. They have depressed pinnate veins and arch backward from base to tip. The ¾-inch-wide white flowers, the females with green ovaries, are in loose clusters 3 to 5 inches across. **B. francisae,** of Mexico, has slender, trailing, hairy, rooting stems becoming erect toward their ends. The leaves have hairy stalks 3 to 5 inches long attached to ovate-spoon-shaped blades well in from their margins. The blades are about 3 inches long by 2 inches wide, hairless and glossy above, their undersides more or less red with hairs along the veins. The flowering stalks, about 4 inches long, bear clusters of few whitish blooms approximately 1 inch in diameter. **B. fruticosa,** of Brazil, is a much-branched, hairless species of more or less vining habit that often grows as an epiphyte. It has coarsely-irregularly-toothed, very short-stalked, pointed-elliptic leaves 1 inch to 3 inches long by up to 1 inch wide. The white-petaled flowers, about ½ inch wide, are in loose, slender-stalked clusters up to perhaps 4 inches across. **B. glabra,** sometimes misnamed B.

Begonia glabra

scandens, native from Mexico to South America and the West Indies, is hairless, has trailing or climbing stems that root from the nodes, and it is said, in the wild reaches heights of up to 25 feet. The glossy leaves, sometimes with hair-fringed margins, but otherwise hairless, have stalks ½ inch to 3 inches long and nearly symmetrical, broadly-ovate, short-pointed blades 2 to 6 inches long. The small white flowers are many together in fork-stalked, loose clusters. *B. g. amplifolia* has leaves up to 8 inches long by 6 inches wide or sometimes wider. **B. holtensis,** of Colombia and Ecuador, has much-branched, scrambling or climbing stems up to several feet long, and very short-stalked, hairless, red-edged, ovate leaves 2 to 3 inches long, ending in short points. The small to minute flowers in large fork-branched clusters are white, sometimes flushed with pink. *B. h. macrophylla* has bigger leaves. **B. limmingheiana** (syns. *B. glaucophylla, B. g. scandens, B. procumbens*) is a hairless Brazilian with slender, trailing, or pendulous, flattish stems that attain lengths of several feet and under moist conditions root from the nodes. Its wavy, glossy green, ovate-wedge-shaped leaves, some 3 inches long by 1¾ inches wide, are reddish beneath. The flowers, in drooping clusters, are coral-pink to brick-red. The males are about 1 inch across. Much bigger and more intensely colored, the female blooms open after the males. *B. l. purpurea* has bronze-tinged foliage and white flowers with purplish-red centers.

Begonia limmingheiana

The species has been much used in hybridizing. **B. mariae,** of Venezuela, is hairless, has slender, creeping stems, short-stalked, markedly asymmetrical-heart-shaped, bristle-toothed leaves 2 to 4 inches long by 1 inch to 2 inches wide and rose-pink blooms 1½ to 2 inches wide, the males in small clusters, the females solitary. **B. purpusii,** of Mexico, has trailing or climbing stems that may branch and that produce roots freely if in contact with a moist medium. The longish-stalked, thinnish leaves 4 to 5 inches across are roundish to kidney-shaped in outline, have four or five prominent, triangular-pointed lobes with smaller teeth between. The white flowers are in clusters on stalks about 6 inches long.

Species with upright stems and deeply-lobed leaves or several separate leaflets are now considered. Some authorities list certain thick-stemmed sorts, for example, *B. carolinaefolia,* as rhizomatous, but since in cultivation at least their stems are never horizontal it seems more appropriate to include them here. **B. aconitifolia** (syn. *B. faureana*) is Brazilian. From 3 to 4 feet tall and hairless, it has few-branched stems, deeply-lobed leaves with the lobes again lobed and finely-toothed, with narrow red margins. Silvery blotches on the upper surfaces are especially evident on young foliage. The 2-inch-wide male flowers, in slightly drooping panicles, are pinkish in bud, then white. **B. carolinaefolia** is a Mexican of distinctive appearance. It has very thick, erect, rarely-branched, fleshy stems and fairly long-stalked leaves of six to eight glossy, fleshy, elliptic-ovate, coarsely-toothed leaflets up to 4 inches long, with deeply-impressed veins and wavy margins. The pink blooms are in long, weak-stalked, often drooping clusters. **B. deliciosa,** of Borneo, is 2 to 3 feet tall, bushy, and essentially hairless. It has deep olive-green, toothless, conspicuously-pointed-lobed, large leaves, ovate-heart-shaped in outline clearly spotted above with silvery-gray, red on their undersides. The pink, fragrant flowers a little

Begonia aconitifolia

over ½ inch wide are in long-stalked, dense clusters. **B. diadema,** 2 to 4 feet tall and native to Borneo, has stems that come from a swollen base, which are erect, branched, and bear lustrous leaves deeply- and irregularly-lobed in hand-fashion. They are dark green with paler veins, spotted, blotched, or streaked with silvery-gray. The small pink flowers are in drooping clusters, the males about 2 inches across, the females about 1¼ inches. **B. hemsleyana** is a handsome, somewhat hairy native of China. It has thinnish, erect, freely-

Begonia hemsleyana

branched stems 1 foot to 1½ feet tall and shining green, long-stalked leaves with reddish undersides, separated into six to twelve toothed, narrow-elliptic leaflets arranged like the ribs of an umbrella. The rose-pink flowers 1 inch to 1½ inches in diameter are in clusters of few. **B. kenworthyi,** a slow-growing Mexican, has thick, erect, gnarled, fleshy stems and obovate,

Begonia kenworthyi

sharply-five-lobed, ivy-leaf-shaped leaves with blades from 5 to 10 inches long by ¾ inch wide. They are red masked with a waxy bloom that gives a bluish-gray, slaty effect and have gray veins. The flowers are pale pink. **B. laciniata** (syn. *B. bowringiana*), of India and southern China, up to 2 feet tall or sometimes taller, has broad-heart-shaped-ovate, sharply-lobed or deeply-cleft leaves 4 to 8 inches long, nearly hairless except at their margins, blackish-green with a paler zone on their upper sides, and reddish beneath. The 2-inch-wide, white blooms are in long-stalked clusters of few. **B. ludwigii,** of Ecuador, sometimes misidentified as *B. rigida,* has stout stems up to 3 feet tall and olive-green leaves, broad-ovate in outline, about 7 inches across, deeply slashed into about seven coarsely-toothed, pointed lobes, with red veins and whitish markings. The flowering stalks, up to 3 feet long and fork-branched above, carry many 1¼-inch-wide, pink-tinged, white flowers. **B. luxurians** is Chilean.

Begonia luxurians

From 2 to 5 feet tall, it has erect, hairy stems and large leaves hairy on their upper sides, divided in umbrella-fashion into nine to seventeen arching, short-stalked, narrow-elliptic, toothed, green or bronzy-green leaflets 5 to 7 inches long by up to 1½ inches wide. Of little decorative importance, the clusters of ¼-inch-wide, creamy-white flowers top erect stalks. **B. megaptera,** of the Himalayan region, is up to about 1½ feet tall. It has asymmetrical

Begonia megaptera

leaves 5 to 7 inches long, with irregular sharp lobes and teeth. Above they are bright green, on their undersides red-veined. The 2-inch-wide, apple-blossom-pink blooms, mostly in panicles of up to ten, are carried just above the foliage. **B. platanifolia** is a bushy Brazilian 5 to 6 feet tall, with erect stems and kidney-shaped, bristly-hairy leaves 8 to 10 inches wide, cleft halfway to their bases into five pointed lobes toothed and fringed with hairs. They are green with a silvery overlay. The flowers, in forked-stemmed clusters from the leaf axils, are large and white tinged with pink. **B. wollnyi,** of Bolivia, erect and bushy, has leaves deeply cleft palmately (in hand-fashion) and conspicuously marked between the lateral veins with splashes of white. The flowers are greenish-white with pink petals.

Erect-stemmed species with leaves not of separate leaflets and not more than shallowly-lobed are most numerous. Among them are a few, such as *B. manicata,* with very thick stems that some authorities regard as rhizomatous, but since their stems, in cultivation at least, are upright it seems more appropriate to include them here. **B. acetosa,** of Brazil, is compact, with nearly-round, broad-heart-shaped, velvety white-hairy, coppery leaves, reddish on their undersides and with a pale spot where the stalk joins the blade. The flowers are in branched, long-stalked panicles. **B. acutifolia** (syn. *B. acuminata*), of Jamaica, is 1 foot to 2 feet tall. It has lax stems and asymmetrically-ovate, toothed leaves 2 to 3½ inches long that taper to pointed apexes

Begonia acutifolia

and, except for their margins and veins on the undersides, hairless. Almost 1 inch wide, the profusely-produced white flowers are in clusters of up to five. **B. albopicta** is Brazilian. Bushy, compact, much-branched, and 2 to 3 feet tall, it has cane-like, branched stems and asymmetrically-ovate leaves, with short red stalks and glossy blades about 4 inches long with slightly wavy margins and small silvery spots or blotches. Pale pink at first, white or greenish-white at maturity, the flowers, approximately ¾ inch wide, are in small, pendulous clusters. *B. a. rosea* has pink blooms. **B. andina** is a medium-sized native of Bolivia. It has erect stems and fleshy, pointed-ovate leaves up to 4½ inches long; their margins are shallowly-irregularly-toothed, their undersides reddish. Stems, foliage, and flowering stalks are brown-scurfy. The approximately 1-inch-wide white blooms are in flat clusters about 3 inches across. **B. arborescens confertiflora** (syn. *B. confertiflora*), of Brazil

Begonia arborescens confertiflora

and Peru, 3 to 4 feet tall, has short-stalked, pinnately-veined, finely-toothed, hairless leaves with blades up to 9 inches long by 3½ inches wide. The small white flowers are many together in fork-branched clusters 3 to 5 inches across. **B. asplenifolia,** of

Bauhinia punctata

Spring bedding featuring tulips

Spring bedding featuring white pansies and blue forget-me-nots

Summer bedding with purple verbenas, pink, white, and red petunias, pale yellow cannas, and orange rudbeckias

Spring bedding at Hampton Court Palace, England

Summer bedding at the Royal Botanic Gardens, Kew, England, featuring yellow calceolarias, red verbenas, yellow marigolds, and silvery *Senecio vira-vira*

Begonia tuberhybrida varieties at a flower show

Befaria racemosa

Begonia (female flowers)

Begonia tuberhybrida, a picotee variety

tropical West Africa, has erect, slender, forking, rigid stems up to 1½ feet tall. Its short-stalked, pinnately-lobed, toothed leaves are oblong-lanceolate, 1 inch to 1½ inches long. The flowers are in small clusters or the females solitary. **B. bettinae,** of Mexico, has erect, rarely-branched stems about 1 foot tall. Its thin, dull green leaves, confined to near the tops of the stems, are moderately furnished with matted, reddish-brown hairs. They are ovate to lanceolate-oblong, long-pointed, markedly sharply-lobed, and approximately 3¼ inches long by 2¼ inches wide. The flower clusters are of few approximately ½-inch-wide pink blooms. **B. bradei,** of Brazil, low and velvety-hairy, has arching stems and

Begonia coccinea variety

Begonia 'Veitch's Carmine'

Begonia bradei

very asymmetrical, pointed-oblong-elliptic, red-margined, toothed, olive-green leaves, reddish on their undersides, up to 7½ inches long by about one-third wide as long. The comparatively large, pinkish-white flowers are red-hairy on the backs of the petals. **B. caraguatatubensis,** of Brazil, is 2 feet tall and has broad-ovate leaves up to 1 foot in diameter with red undersides. The panicles are of numerous small white blooms. **B. castaneaefolia** is Brazilian. Up to about 2 feet tall, it has hairless, oblongish, short-stalked, pinnately-veined leaves that terminate in short points, which are up to about 9 inches long by 4 inches wide. The small white or pink-tinged flowers are in fork-branched clusters of up to eight. **B. coccinea,** of Brazil, is parent to numerous hybrids sometimes mistakenly identified as *B. rubra* hybrids, although *B. rubra* is a quite separate species not in cultivation. Like *B. coccinea,* these varieties are commonly called angel-wing begonias. The species, usually not more than 1 foot to 1½ feet tall, has branched stems swollen at the joints and very asymmetrical, thickish, short-pointed, ovate to asymmetrically-oblong, hairless leaves with somewhat concave upper surfaces covered with a waxy, gray bloom and somewhat reddish undersides. They have stalks barely 1 inch long and blades 3 to 4 inches long with

wavy, toothed margins edged with red. The coral-red flowers are in large, red-stalked, drooping panicles. They are long lasting, the males 1 inch to 1½ inches wide, the females larger and with an ovary with three nearly equal wings. The name *B. coccinea* is not uncommonly misapplied to *B. corallina* and its derivatives. **B. corallina** attains heights of 6 to 10 feet and is more vigorous than *B. coccinea.* This sort has canelike stems, swollen at the nodes and branched. Its hairless glossy leaves 3 to 8 inches long have markedly asymmetrical, lanceolate blades, sometimes with concave upper surfaces and marked with silvery spots. Their undersides are reddish. The flowers resemble those of *B. coccinea,* but are larger and in bigger clusters. Popular varieties and hybrids of *B. corallina* include *B. c. fragrans, B. c. odorata* (syn. *B. rubra odorata*), *B.* 'Lucerna', *B.* 'President

Begonia 'Lucerna'

Carnot', and *B.* 'Veitch's Carmine'. **B. cucullata** and its variety *B. c. hookeri* (syn. *B. semperflorens*), both of tropical South America, are probably not in cultivation, but derivatives and hybrids of the last are the commonly grown wax begonias of gar-

dens. Although frequently referred to as *B. semperflorens,* they are more correctly named *B. semperflorens-cultorum.* **B. decandra** is an upright, bushy, slender-stemmed native of Costa Rica and Puerto Rico. It has small, ovate, toothed leaves, with impressed, reddish veins, and pinkish flowers. **B. dichotoma,** a rather coarse native of Venezuela, up to 8 feet tall, has semisuc-

Begonia dichotoma

culent, short-hairy stems and shallowly-angled and toothed, oblique-ovate, long-stalked, pubescent leaves up to 10 inches long by 8 inches wide, with heart-shaped bases. Its white blooms, the males about ⅝ inch across, females somewhat smaller, are hairy on their outsides. They are many together in clusters 6 to 7 inches wide on tall, forked, erect stalks. **B. dichroa,** a slow-growing Brazilian is usually broad and not more than 1½ feet tall, but sometimes is higher. Typically it has spreading stems and pointed, shallowly-angled, oblong-elliptic to broad-ovate, short-stalked, hairless, glossy, frequently silver-spotted leaves. Its more or less pendulous flower clusters are of large, showy, tangerine-orange blooms, the males almost or quite 2 inches across, the females smaller. *B. dipetala,* formerly known as *B.* 'Mrs. W. S. Kimball', is a medium-sized, stiffly-erect, sparsely-branched native of India. It has very asymmetrical, pointed-ovate, toothed, grass-green leaves, with scattered bristly hairs on both surfaces and short, few-bloomed, drooping clusters of light pink flowers, the males nearly circular. *B. domingensis* is a miniature sometimes called peanut brittle begonia. Native of Hispaniola, this sort is bushy, with very crinkled, fleshy, pointed-ovate leaves about 1 inch long, hairless above, hairy on their undersides, and white or light pink smallish blooms freely produced in close clusters. *B. dominicalis,* of Dominica, about 3 feet tall, has rather weak stems and ovate-heart-shaped, glossy, somewhat cupped leaves up to 4½ inches long, with slightly-toothed margins, the lowermost somewhat drooping. The flower trusses are of numerous, very small, greenish-white blooms. *B. echinosepala* is a beautiful, medium-sized, bushy Brazilian, hairy throughout, with erect, much-branched, succulent, reddish stems and glossy, short-stalked, coarsely-toothed, pointed-ovate leaves, with darker veins and purple undersides. The white to delicate pink blooms, pink-bearded on the outsides of the petals, are in large trusses. *B. egregia* (syn. *B. quadrilocularis*) is Brazilian. It has light green, rather narrow, oblong-lanceolate, concave, puckered-surfaced leaves and large clusters of fragrant white flowers, the females with four-winged ovaries. *B. eminii* is an attractive native of West Africa, often grown under the name *B. mannii.* Of stiffish, branched habit, it has erect stems and asymmetrically-ovate, irregularly-toothed, red-edged leaves up to 4½ inches long and little more than one-half as wide as long, with pinnately-arranged, brown-hairy veins. The very short flower clusters from the leaf axils are watermelon pink. Male clusters are about seven-flowered. Females, about 1½ inches across, have slender, cylindrical, wingless, usually curved ovaries. *B. engleri,* of tropical Africa, has usually only one succulent, sparingly-branched, purple-spotted stem up to about 5 feet tall. Its thin, coarsely-toothed, asymmetrical-ovate-oblong leaves 3 to 6 inches long have very short, stiffish hairs and purplish veins. The clear pink flowers are in long, flat, arching to pendulous panicles. This kind needs tropical conditions. *B. epipsila* is a subshrub, native of Brazil, 1 foot to 1½ feet tall. It has glossy, short-pointed, asymmetrically-ovate, toothless, shiny, dark olive-green leaves 2 to about 4 inches long by nearly as wide, densely clothed beneath with reddish-brown, woolly hairs. Scarcely longer than the leaves, the red-woolly flowering stalks carry many small white blooms. *B. fernandoi-costae* is Brazilian. It has large, velvety-hairy, pointed-broad-ovate, olive-green

Begonia eminii

Begonia eminii (flowers), showing wingless ovaries

leaves, with red undersides, and white flowers in compact clusters carried well above the foliage atop longish, hairy stalks. *B. foliosa* is a distinctive native of Colombia and Venezuela. Up to 3 feet tall or taller, it has arching to pendulous stems clothed with foliage of fernlike aspect. The many slightly-three-lobed, glossy, ovate leaves ½ inch to 1½ inches long are bronzy-green to dark green. The ½-inch-wide, white blooms of *B. f. miniata* (syn. *B. fuch-*

sioides) of Venezuela has smooth, freely-branched stems 2 to 3 feet tall and abundant foliage. Its leaves are ¾ inch to 2 inches long. The drooping, deep rose-pink to crimson-scarlet, very decorative blooms ½ inch to 1¼ inch across and in twos or threes contrast pleasingly with the foliage. *B. gigantea,* of the Himalayan region, develops a thickish woody base from which spring to heights of 1½ to 2 feet or more erect, thin stems, with a few hairs. The

Begonia manicata

erect panicles are of numerous pale pink, nodding, small blooms. The foliage of B. m. aureo-maculata is blotched with yellow. That of B. m. a. crispa is similar, but the

Begonia manicata aureo-maculata

leaves have frilled margins. The plain green leaves of B. m. crispa are also frilled. B. malabarica, of southern India, 1 foot to 2½ feet tall, bushy, and hairy, has asymmetrically-ovate, irregularly-toothed leaves with blades 4 to 4½ inches long and one-half as wide as long. Its blush-pink to white flowers droop in short clusters. B. mazae, a Mexican, has thin, woody stems, erect, but not self-supporting after they attain a length of about 1 foot. The smallish, satiny-surfaced, pale-veined leaves are roundish with heart-shaped bases. They display a mixture of greens, with a conspicuous pale patch at the base of the blade. The pink flowers are carried high above the foliage on erect, forked stalks. B. m. nigricans has darker leaves, with an overlay of blackish-bronze. In B. m. viridis 'Stitchleaf' the mar-

gins of the leaf are decorated with stitch-like purple marks. B. metallica is Brazilian. Bushy and 3 to 4 feet tall, it has succulent stems and 4 to 6 inches long, shallowly-lobed, toothed, pointed-ovate, hairy, olive-green, and highly glossy leaves, with depressed, metallic-purple veins and red under surfaces. The pale pink blooms, up to 1½ inches across, are hairy on the outsides of their petals. The plant grown as B. cypraea is a variant of this sort. B. minor (syn. B. nitida), of Jamaica, attains a height

Begonia minor

of 4 feet or more, is a vigorous grower with thickish, freely-branched stems, and has glossy, asymmetrically-pointed-ovate leaves that, like the stems, are hairless. They are approximately 4½ inches long by 2½ inches wide, with convex upper surfaces and red or partly red stalks. Their undersides are pale frosty-green with the veins greener. From 1½ to 1¾ inches across, the pink blooms, the males somewhat bigger than the females, are in long-stalked clusters without persistent bracts. B. mollicaulis (syn. B. 'Scotch Luxurians'), of Brazil, has been confused with B. subvillosa. About 1 foot tall, it has more or less woody stems clothed with persistent stipules. Its asymmetrically-heart-shaped, unevenly-double-toothed leaves are about 4½ inches long by slightly more than twice as wide. They are hairy, but the hairs are not matted. The flowers are white. B. odorata (syns. B. odorata alba, B. nitida odorata-alba) has been confused with B. minor, but is distinct. Of uncertain provenance, but probably a native of the West Indies or South America, it is broad, bushy, and up to 4 feet tall. It has slender, erect, much-branched stems that, like the leafstalks, are sparingly furnished with fine, outward-pointing hairs. The leaf blades are asymmetrically-pointed-ovate, finely-toothed, 4 to 7 inches long by 2½ to 4 inches wide, with conspicuously depressed veins. The white or pink-tinged flowers are in long-ish-stalked, loose clusters of many. The males are ½ inch wide or slightly wider,

the females 1 inch wide or wider. The latter have a pair of fairly persistent conspicuous bracts at the bottom of the ovary, but these are often absent from herbarium (dried) botanical specimens. B. olbia is a Brazilian with short, mostly branched stems

Begonia olbia

and thin, white-spotted, bronzy-green, ovate, angled and toothed leaves with scattered white hairs and red undersides. They are up to 5 inches long. The large greenish-white flowers are in short, drooping clusters. B. oxyphylla, a vigorous Brazilian, has stems covered with a felt of red

Begonia oxyphylla

hairs and pointed-oblong, pinnately-veined, slightly rough-hairy leaves 6 to 7 inches long. The numerous tiny white flowers, the males with four strongly-reflexed petals, two of which are cupped like shells, are in clusters about 4½ inches wide. B. paranaensis is Brazilian, with thick stems and large, distinctly-lobed, toothed leaves, broadly-ovate and with pale veins. Its flowers are white, in huge clusters. B. parilis, also Brazilian, has fuzzy-hairy stems and foliage. Its nearly stalkless, narrow-elliptic leaves, olive-green with reddish edges and flushed with red on their undersides, are about 6 inches long by approximately

1 inch wide. The flowers, pink to white and nearly 1 inch wide, are many together in large flattish clusters. *B. peltata* (syn. *B. incana*) is a very distinctive, semisucculent native of Mexico, with thick, erect stems without the conspicuous membranous stipules of *B. venosa*, and closely-spaced, densely-white-scurfy, fleshy, pointed, nearly-circular leaves, with blades 5 to 9 inches long and stalks that join the blade well in from the margin. The small white flowers are in long-stalked, drooping trusses. *B. plebeja,* of Nicaragua, has long-stalked leaves with pointed-broad-ovate, angled or toothed blades 4 to 10 inches long, which are sometimes red. The white to pinkish blooms are in long-stalked clusters. Variety *B. p. kennedyi,* of Panama, differs from the typical species in its leaves being broader, with longer lobes and finer teeth, and its flowers having elliptic instead of round petals. *B. plumieri,* native to Hispaniola, has been cultivated as *B. p. barahonensis.* It is 2 to 4 feet tall, with slender stems and short-stalked, pointed-ovate, few-toothed leaves 2 to 3 inches long. Its white and reddish flowers are on erect, branched stalks. *B. poggei,* of tropical Africa, is distinctive and low, with pointed-ovate, pinnately-veined, dull green leaves and very short-stalked clusters of small greenish blooms from the leaf axils, the females with stalklike, cylindrical, wingless, red ovaries. The young foliage of this sort is reported to be edible. *B. reniformis* (syns. *B. longipes, B. longipes petiolata*), of Colombia, is 3 feet tall or taller. It has erect, stout, succulent stems ridged longitudinally and round-ovate, red-stalked,

glossy, irregularly-toothed leaves up to about 5½ inches long, with scattered bristly hairs. The small white flowers are in clusters atop arching stalks 6 to 8 inches long. *B. roezlii* (syn. *B. bracteosa*), of Peru, was long known as *B.* 'Machu Picchu'. It is hairless, up to about 3 feet tall, with branched, erect stems and lustrous, broad-ovate leaves 5 to 7 inches long by 3 to 4½ inches wide. The pink or lavender-pink blooms, in longish-stalked clusters, are from a little less to a little more than 1 inch wide. *B. roxburghii,* of the Himalayan region, is 1½ to 2 feet tall, bushy, and sparsely hairy. It has many slender, erect, branched stems that sprout from a thickened, knobby base, and broad-ovate, lobeless, but toothed and hair-fringed leaves with blades about 8½ inches long by 6½ inches wide. Their upper surfaces are convex and bright glossy green. The undersides are paler. In short-stalked clusters of few, the flowers are white and fragrant. The females have four-winged, green ovaries. *B. rubro-venia* is a low native of the Himalayas. It has short, thick, sometimes somewhat erect rhizomes and asymmetrical, pointed, narrowly-ovate, glossy, green leaves 3 to 6 inches long by 1½ to 3 inches wide, with shallowly-scalloped or toothed edges, red veins, and red or green undersides that like the leafstalks have a fuzz of brown hairs. The few-bloomed, short-stalked clusters are of pink-tinged, greenish-white flowers ¾ to 1 inch wide. *B. sanguinea* is a popular Brazilian of medium size. Loosely-branched and hairless or sometimes hairy on the veins of the undersides of the leaves, it has red stems and

Begonia sanguinea

fleshy, ovate leaves 4 to 6 inches long, up to 3½ inches wide, with the stalks fixed to the blades a little in from the slightly round-toothed margins. Olive-green above, they have rich blood-red undersides. The flowers are white or tinged pink, the males ¾ inch to a little more than 1 inch wide. *B. scabrida,* of Venezuela, rather coarse and rank, is 3 to 5 feet tall and wide. It has hairy stems and leaves, the latter 6 inches to 1 foot in diameter, asymmetrically-pointed-ovate to circular-heart-shaped, irregularly-toothed. The clusters of white flowers that sometimes exceed 1 foot in diameter are on long stalks that divide repeatedly. Male blooms are ¾ inch across, the females less. *B. scharffiana,* of Brazil, is 1½ to 3 feet tall, bushy, compact, and softly-hairy. It has broad-ovate, long-pointed, thickish, olive-green leaves 4 to 8 inches long, with bright red under surfaces. The large white blooms in long-stalked clusters from the leaf axils have petals clothed on their outsides with red hairs. *B. scharffii* (syn. *B. haageana*) is a full-foliaged, softly-hairy Brazilian 3 feet or so tall and bushy. It has many erect stems and large, ovate, light olive-green leaves, red on their undersides and, unlike those of *B. scharffiana,* not ending in long points. The flowers are in large, heavy, drooping trusses. Pale pink, they are conspicuously bearded on the outsides of their petals. *B. s. drostii,* a distinct variety, is bushy and the entire plant is densely clothed with white hairs. Its very dark green leaves have blades up to 9 inches long by 5½ inches wide, with strongly concave upper surfaces, nearly toothless margins, and brownish-red undersides. The flowers are large, pale pink, and red-bearded on their outsides. *B. schmidtiana* is a low, hairy native of Brazil, much-branched and with slender stems. Its asymmetrically-heart-shaped, toothed leaves have stalks and blades each 1½ to 3 inches long or a little longer, reddish on their undersides and

Begonia poggei

Begonia schmidtiana

dull green. Its freely-produced blooms are white on their insides, pale pink on their outsides, or all pink. Females, slightly smaller than males, have two small hairy bracts at their bases. *B. seretii* (syn. *B. secreta*), of West Africa, and bushy, has arching to pendulous, branched stems and narrow-oblong-elliptic, pointed, sparsely-hairy, glossy, toothed, olive-green leaves. The flowers are white tinged with pink. *B. serratipetala,* a handsome native of New Guinea, forms a 2-foot-tall and -wide mass of erect to drooping branches and narrow sharply-toothed, pink-spotted, bronze-green leaves, which are reddish on their undersides. Its flowers are blush-pink to claret-red, the females with red-toothed petals. This sort is excellent for hanging baskets. *B. seychellensis,* an endemic of the Seychelles Islands, is 3 to 4 feet tall, bushy and hairless with thick, branching stems. Its long-stalked leaves have roundish-elliptic, shallowly-lobed, finely-toothed blades up to nearly 1 foot wide, but on flowering branches considerably smaller, sometimes with red undersides. The rather few flowers are in clusters shorter than the leaves. *B. sikkimensis,* of India, has a thick, woody rootstock, stems over 1 foot tall, leaves with roundish lobes that are again lobed, toothed, and fringed with hairs along their margins. The bright red flowers have bright red stalks. Variety *B. s. gigantea* is larger. The leaves of *B. s. maculata* (syn. *B. s. variegata*) are blotched irregularly with yellow. *B. stipulacea,* of Brazil, is up to 8 feet tall, but often considerably lower. Hairless, it has pointed-oblong-ovate leaves 4 to 6 inches long by 1 inch to 3 inches wide, with distinct grayish-white veins and reddish undersides. In clusters 5 or 6 inches across, the white or pink flowers are about ⅝ inch wide. Variety *B. s. angulata* (syn. *B. angulata*) has more-deeply-grooved stems and bigger leaves and flowers. *B. subvillosa,* of Brazil, erect, bushy, and up to 1 foot tall or sometimes taller, is densely covered with long, matted, white hairs. Its markedly asymmetrical, broad-ovate to kidney-shaped

leaves are slightly angled and round-toothed. The flowers, the backs of their sepals covered with white to reddish hairs, are ¾ to 1 inch wide. They are in somewhat pendulous clusters. *B. sulcata*, of Colombia, is hairless and has erect stems 3 to 4½ feet tall and long-stalked leaves, with very asymmetrical, pointed-round-ovate, irregularly-toothed blades 3 to 5 inches in diameter. Its flowers are in fairly long-stalked clusters from the leaf axils. *B. teuscheri,* of Malaya, has erect stems, which are swollen at their bases and 4 to 6 feet tall. Its fleshy, shallowly-lobed, pointed-ovate to ovate-lanceolate, toothed, olive-green leaves are variously marked with silver. Their undersides are red. The flowers, in clusters from the leaf axils, are deep pink to bright red. *B. ulmifolia,* a tall native of Colombia, has erect, brown-scurfy,

Begonia ulmifolia

four-angled stems grooved lengthway and sharp-toothed, elmlike, pinnately-veined leaves about 4½ inches long by 2 inches wide. The white flowers, about ½ inch in diameter, are in crowded, rounded heads. *B. undulata* (syn. *B. alba-perfecta*) is a Brazilian, bushy and 2 to 3 feet tall, with cane-like stems. Its two-ranked, wavy-surfaced, glossy, essentially hairless leaves are oblong-lanceolate, 3 to 5 inches long and up to 2 inches wide. The small white or whitish flowers are in short-stalked, pendulous clusters from the leaf axils. *B. valdensium* is Brazilian. Sometimes called philodendron-leaved begonia because of its foliage, this sort is erect, with asymmetrical, broad-heart-shaped leaves with shallowly-lobed, toothed, undulated edges. They are satiny grass-green with a clear pattern of pale veins. The flowers are white, sometimes pink-tinged at the petal edges. *B. venosa,* of Brazil, has thick, erect

Begonia undulata

Begonia venosa

stems clothed with big, brownish, papery stipules. Its white-scurfy, nearly-circular to kidney-shaped leaves differ from those of *B. peltata* in that their stalks join the blades at, instead of well in from, their margins. The flowers are white. *B. wadei* is a low native of the Philippine Islands. It has rigid, erect stems foliaged mostly toward their apexes. The leaves, green, fleshy, and oblong-ovate, have convex upper surfaces. The rather few, loosely-arranged flowers are pink.

Hybrid begonias derived from rhizomatous or upright-stemmed fibrous-rooted species, without admixture of tuberous species, bulbous *B. socotrana,* or *B. rex,* and without considering the *B. semperflorens-cultorum* complex, all of which have been dealt with earlier in this entry, exist in great array and their numbers increase yearly and in all probability will continue to do so. In the main, hybrids between species are intermediate between their parents. Here are just a few of classic impor-

Begonia 'Abel Carriere'

Begonia 'Corbeille de Feu'

tance. Others are listed in the catalogs of specialist dealers. Parentage is indicated in the parentheses. B. 'Abel Carriere' (*B. rex* × *B. cucullata hookeri*) develops from a swollen base several erect, branched stems, the branches with age developing at their bases egg-shaped tubers. The hair-fringed leaves are ovate, about 5 inches long by 3 inches wide, and have short, bristly hairs. Their upper surfaces are silvery-leaden with narrow bands of green along the veins, beneath they are red. The flowers are deep pink. **B. alleryi** (believed to be *B. metallica* × *B. gigantea*) is 3 to 6 feet tall, freely-branched, bushy, and hairy. It has pointed-ovate, shallowly-lobed, irregularly-toothed, dark metallic-green leaves 5 to 7 inches long, with purplish veins and paler, purple-veined undersides. The clustered, pale pink flowers have petals hairy on the outsides. Males are 1¾ inches wide, the females smaller. **B. argenteo-guttata** (*B. albo-picta* × *B. olbia*), 2½ to 4½ feet tall by two-thirds as wide, has many erect, canelike stems with weaker branches. The shallowly-lobed, toothed, pointed-ovate leaves are 4 to 6½ inches long and a little more than one-half as wide. They have satiny, rich green upper surfaces decorated

Begonia argenteo-guttata

with many silvery spots of various sizes. Their undersides are light wine-red, with green veins. More or less hidden among the foliage, the short-stalked flower clusters are of greenish or pinkish blooms 1 inch wide or a little wider. B. 'Corbeille de Feu' (*B. fuchsioides* × *B. cucullata hookeri*) is 3 to 4 feet tall or taller, much-branched, and bushy. It has slender stems and lus-

trous, hairless, broad-ovate leaves not notched at their bases, with blades up to 3 inches long by 2 inches wide, but mostly smaller, with round-toothed edges. Borne profusely, the bright coral-red flowers 1¼ to 1½ inches across are in panicles that droop from the leaf axils. **B. credneri** (*B. metallica* × *B. scharffiana*) is bushy, 2 to 5 feet tall, and softly-hairy. It has longish-stalked, asymmetrically-ovate, toothed, olive-green leaves 4 to 6½ inches long, very hairy, metallic-green above, and reddish on their undersides. The pink flowers, hairy on the outsides of the petals, are in large, partly pendulous clusters from the leaf axils. **B. digswelliana** (presumably *B. foliosa miniata* × *B. odorata*) is 2 to 3 feet tall and has erect or arching, freely-branched stems and closely-set, double-toothed, hair-fringed, asymmetrical, ovate to elliptic, glossy leaves up to 2½ inches in length. The bright coral-red flowers, about 1 inch across, are in drooping, red-stalked clusters. **B. duchartrei** (*B. echinosepala* × *B. scharffiana*) is hairy, much-branched, and erect. It has long-pointed, ovate-lanceolate, toothed leaves 5 to 8 inches long and reddish on their undersides. The quite big, waxy-white flowers are red-hairy on the outsides of the petals. **B. erythrophylla** (syn. *B. feastii*) (*B. manicata* × *B. hydrocotylifolia*), the beefsteak begonia, has creeping rhizomes and nearly-circular, thick leaves up to about 8 inches wide; their upper surfaces are lustrous dark green with paler veins, their undersides red with green veins. There is a collar of hairs where the leafstalk joins the blade. The pink flowers, about ¾ inch wide, are gracefully displayed in tall, erect, pyramidal panicles. *B. e. bunchii* has leaves conspicuously frilled at their edges. **B. fuscomaculata** (probably *B. heracleifolia* × *B. strigillosa*) has stout rhizomes and asymmetrically-heart-shaped leaves, with shal-

Begonia erythrophylla

Begonia erythrophylla bunchii

low, triangular, toothed lobes. They are smooth above, hairy on the veins on their reddish undersides. The upper surfaces of the blades are decorated with olive-brown to rust-red or chocolate-brown spots. The pink flowers are in long-stalked, erect panicles. **B. gigantea-rosea** (syn. *B. rosea-gigantea*) (*B. cucullata hookeri* × *B. lynchiana*) somewhat resembles *B. roezlii*. From 2 to 3 feet tall, it has smooth, erect, branched, succulent stems and fleshy, somewhat kidney-shaped, lustrous leaves with a conspicuous red spot where the stalk joins the blade. The flowers are numerous and bright coral-red. **B. gilsonii** originated in New York about 1880 from an unrecorded source and possibly is not a hybrid. It is remarkable for probably being, except for varieties of *B. semperflorens-cultorum*, the only nontuberous begonia with double flowers. This sort has stout, erect, branched stems and pointed-ovate shallowly-lobed, toothed, lustrous plain green leaves, with stalks and undersides hairy. The many smallish white and pink flowers, the males

Begonia gilsonii

double, are in erect panicles. **B. heracleicotyle** (*B. heracleifolia* × *B. hydrocotylifolia*) in habit resembles *B. erythrophylla*, but its leaves, up to 7½ inches long by 6½ inches wide, have seven distinct lobes extending less than one-quarter of the way to the base of the blade. The flowers, in more

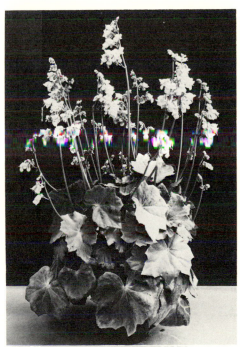

Begonia heracleicotyle

densely crowded, stiffer panicles than those of *B. erythrophylla*, are pink. **B. ingramii** (*B. minor* × *B. foliosa miniata*) attains a height of 3 feet, an even greater breadth. It has many horizontal branches and pointed, oblong-ovate, coarsely-toothed, hairfringed, glossy, olive-green leaves up to 2¾ inches long by 1¼ inches wide, although usually much smaller, with scattered bristly hairs and reddish undersides. The nodding flower clusters are of rose-

pink blooms 1½ to 2 inches wide. **B. kewensis** (*B. undulata* × *B. coccinea*) has slender, spreading or pendulous stems and heart-shaped to ovate-heart-shaped lustrous leaves 4 to 6 inches long. The white or creamy-white flowers are in large clusters. This sort is splendid for hanging baskets. **B. lettonica** (*B. heracleifolia* × *B. nelumbiifolia*) has medium-stout rhizomes and large ovate-heart-shaped, shallowly-lobed, brownish-hairy leaves reddish on their undersides. The clear pink flowers are in tall pyramidal panicles. **B. 'Madame de Lesseps'** (*B. argenteo-guttata* × *B. olbia*) has tall, stoutish, freely-branched stems and big, asymmetrically-ovate, shallowly-lobed, toothed, silvery-spotted, olive-green leaves with red undersides. In clusters from the leaf axils, its flowers are greenish flushed with pink. **B. 'Marjorie Daw'** (*B. rubra* × *B. procumbens*) has spreading to pendulous, freely-branched, smooth stems and bright green, slightly wavy-edged, triangular-ovate leaves. Its many-flowered clusters of quite large pink blooms droop. This is a good hanging basket variety. **B. 'Perle Lorraine'** (*B. polyantha* × *B. strigillosa*) is low and bushy. It has erect, branched, slender stems and pointed-ovate leaves freely marbled with chocolate-brown. Its soft pink flowers, abundantly produced in loose clusters, are paler when open than in the bud stage. **B. phyllomaniaca** (*B. incarnata* × *B. manicata*) has stout, erect stems 1 foot to 2 feet tall that, like the longish-stalked pointed-ovate, glossy leaves with blades up to 7 inches long, develop abundant small plantlets. The leaf margins are wavy and toothed. Small and numerous, the pink blooms are in erect panicles. *B. p. templinii* (syn. *B. templinii*) has yellow-blotched foliage. **B. 'President Carnot'** (*B. corallina* × *B. olbia*) is a tall, vigorous sort, with erect, canelike stems and weaker branches. It has asymmetrically-long-ovate, somewhat lobed, coarsely-toothed, crinkled leaves, with faint silvery spots and reddish undersides. The large carmine-pink flowers are in big pendulous clusters. **B. ricinifolia** (*B. heracleifolia* × *B. peponifolia*) is vigorous, of imposing aspect. It has thick rhizomes and long-stalked leaves

Begonia ricinifolia

with hairy, bronzy-green blades 9 inches to 1 foot or more across, nearly round in outline with five to seven toothed lobes extending one-quarter of the way in from the margin. The pink flowers are in ample panicles with erect stalks 1½ to 2½ feet tall. *B. r. sunderbruckii* (*B. heracleifolia* × *B. ricinifolia*), often mispelled *B. r. sunderbruchii*, has rhizomes and bronzy-green, lobed, toothed leaves, with silvery bands along the veins and reddish-purple undersides. The pink flowers are in erect panicles. *B. rubra*, a name that properly belongs to a species not in cultivation, is also used for variants and hybrids, commonly known as angel-wing begonias, of Brazilian *B. coccinea*. Tall and essentially hairless, they have slender, canelike stems with weaker branches and large asymmetrically-narrowly-ovate to pointed-lanceolate toothless, essentially hairless leaves, reddish on their undersides. In large clusters, the showy flowers, the females with prominently-winged ovaries, are from bright red to shades of pink or almost white. *B. thurstonii* (*B. metallica* × *B. sanguinea*) much resembles *B. credneri*. A vigorous hybrid 2 to 4 feet tall or taller, it has many branched, white-hairy stems and glossy, lopsided, broad-ovate, round-toothed, olive-green, red-stalked leaves up to 7 inches long by 3 inches wide, wine-red on their undersides. The rather small pink blooms, hairy on the outsides of the petals, are in erect clusters. *B. verschaffeltii* (*B. caroliniaefolia* × *B. manicata*) has very robust, thick, erect, succulent stems, with hairs on their younger parts, and long-stalked, somewhat drooping, glossy leaves that are roughly circular in outline, lobed, toothed, hair-fringed, and with hairs along the veins of the undersides. The long-stalked

Begonia verschaffeltii

panicles are of numerous pink flowers ¾ inch or over in diameter.

Garden and Landscape Uses. The horticultural employments of begonias as ornamentals are many and various. In mild, essentially frost-free climates a goodly number are excellent permanent landscape furnishings, enjoyable for their handsome foliage, and most sorts for their beautiful floral displays. Even in climates as harsh as that of the environs of New York City, one species, *B. grandis*, succeeds in sheltered locations as a hardy perennial, but it is unique in this. As a group begonias are not hardy. Where winters are too harsh for their permanent outdoor cultivation some kinds, chiefly wax begonias (*B. semperflorens-cultorum*) and hybrid tuberous sorts (*B. tuberhybrida*), are used with excellent effects as summer adornments for beds, and window boxes and other outdoor containers.

In planning outdoor uses remember the vast majority of begonias demand or at least appreciate some shade. Only the ubiquitous wax begonia revels in full sun. Most sorts prosper in moderately warm and humid climates, some few, notably *B. rex-cultorum* and its allies, are at their best only where constantly high temperatures prevail and where the atmosphere is decidedly humid. Tuberous begonias of Andean provenance and their glorious hybrid offspring (*B. tuberhybrida* varieties) do best where days are medium warm, nights relatively cool, and fairly humid, but not in dank and oppressive atmospheres.

As indoor plants begonias are superb. They lend themselves well to pot cultivation and some can be displayed to excellent advantage in hanging baskets. Sorts that flourish in windows are abundant. Especially satisfactory are wax begonias, as well as Mexican and Central American rhizomatous species and their hybrids. There are numerous others. Low kinds are ideal for terrariums and indoor light gardens. Among such are the many varieties of *B. rex-cultorum* and such jewels as *B. imperialis* and its variants, *B. goegoensis*, *B. herbacea*, and *B. rajah*. Where the climate favors their growth tuberous begonias are splendid window and porch plants.

The great wealth of varieties of begonias makes it practicable for anyone to enjoy some as houseplants and avid begonia fans succeed in growing an amazing array of kinds in their homes.

In greenhouses all begonias succeed, the vast majority without difficulty. Many sorts bloom continuously over periods of many weeks or months. Others have shorter seasons, but even so display blooms for at least a few weeks. The majority of begonias retain their foliage throughout the year, others, notably tuberous and some rhizomatous sorts, are deciduous.

Cultivation. As is to be expected of such a large and diverse group, the cultural needs of begonias differ to some extent according to kind and to a lesser degree according to the particular purpose or purposes for which the plants are grown. Thus, we shall review cultivation under paragraphs beginning Wax begonias, Tuberous begonias, Christmas begonias, Elatior begonias, Rex-cultorum varieties, and

Begonia thurstonii

Other species, varieties, and hybrids. But before doing this let us consider the various ways these plants are propagated.

Seeds afford ready means of obtaining stocks of some begonias. Species raised in this way normally reproduce true to type and with remarkable constancy as do horticultural varieties of wax begonias and, somewhat less reliably, those of tuberous hybrids. But seedlings of the vast majority of hybrids are likely to vary considerably and cannot be relied upon to duplicate the mother plant. For them other methods are necessary to maintain stocks true to name.

Begonia seeds are dust fine. Ordinarily highly viable if sown under reasonable conditions, they yield a very high percentage of germination. Sandy soil containing a considerable amount of leaf mold, peat moss, or other suitable organic material, all passed through a ½-inch-mesh sieve, sand, or milled sphagnum moss are excellent mediums upon which to sow. If soil or sand is used, sterilize it by baking or some other procedure as a precaution against damping off disease. Do this also with the pots, pans, or flats used.

Make sure the containers are adequately drained. Fill them with the sowing medium so that when pressed moderately firmly and made quite level it is ½ inch below the rim. Top off with a ⅛-inch layer of sowing medium passed through a screen as fine as mosquito netting.

Next, water thoroughly with a very fine spray or by immersing the container nearly to its rim in water so that moisture from below reaches the surface. Scatter the seed thinly. Press it lightly into the surface, but do not cover with any sowing medium. Place a sheet of glass or plastic over the container, shade it, and allow to germinate in temperatures of 60 to 70°F.

Covering newly sown begonia seeds with glass

Watch closely for the first evidence of germination. When this occurs expose to good light, but not direct sun. As soon as tiny leaves can be seen take off the glass

or plastic cover and allow the plants to become accustomed to fairly humid air. When the first pair of true leaves (those that succeed the original cotyledon or seed leaves) have developed to a size so that the baby plants can be separated fairly easily, transplant the seedlings an inch or two apart into other containers in porous soil with an abundance of organic matter. From then on grow under conditions appropriate for adult plants of the sorts of begonias being propagated.

Vegetative propagation is easily achieved by stem cuttings, leaf cuttings, and division, the method selected depending upon its appropriateness for the particular kind of begonia. The first is satisfactory for all begonias that develop stems, and such cuttings generally root with great ease. With tuberous sorts to be multiplied in this way it is advisable to use as cuttings young shoots that sprout from the tubers and to take with them to serve as the base of the cutting a heel (thin sliver) of the tuber itself.

Leaf cuttings are most frequently employed for *B. rex-cultorum* varieties and Christmas begonias, but many other sorts

Stem cuttings of begonias: (a) Making the cuttings

(c) Rooted cuttings ready for transplanting

Begonia seedlings are transplanted while still tiny

can be increased in this way. With Christmas begonias, it is usual to use entire mature leaves with a short piece of stalk attached and to plant them with the base of the stalk 1 inch to 1½ inches deep in a mixture of sand and peat moss, sand, vermiculite, or perlite in a greenhouse propagating bench, preferably with a little bottom heat. Mature leaves of varieties of

(b) Planting the cuttings

(d) Covering with a glass jar to conserve humidity

Planting leaf cuttings of Christmas begonia

Leaf cuttings of Christmas begonia planted in greenhouse propagating bench

ing five to fifteen degrees by day, seedlings make good specimens in 2½- or 3-inch pots suitable for planting in outdoor beds, window boxes, etc., in four to six months. This necessitates sowing in January to be sure of having good plants by bedding-out time.

An alternative procedure, often more practicable for those without a greenhouse, is to raise plants for bedding from cuttings taken in March. To obtain these, dig plants from the garden before killing frost in fall, cut them back about halfway and pot in sandy soil in containers just big enough to hold their roots. Grow through the winter in a sunny window or similar place where the temperature will not drop below 50°F. Water rather sparingly. To encourage growth of strong shoots suitable for cuttings, fertilize lightly in February.

As window and greenhouse plants, wax begonias are extremely satisfactory and very easy to satisfy. They thrive in more airy, less humid environments than many begonias, and although they tolerate some shade, they revel in full sun and except for the calla-lily sorts high summer temperatures. The original calla-lily variety was successful only in regions, such as New England, of cool summers, but newer varieties are more heat-tolerant.

Tuberous begonias, hybrids and species, give of their best in fairly humid climates where nights are relatively cool. They will not thrive under hot, arid conditions. In parts of California they are superb and can also be grown to great perfection in many areas of northeastern North America. Propagation can be by seeds, cuttings, or division as detailed earlier, or plants can be grown from purchased tubers. The latter is most practicable unless a greenhouse is available in which to nurture the young plants. December or January sowings give plants that will bloom freely the first summer. Sow the seeds and care for the young plants as recommended for wax begonias, except that the night temperature should

B. rex-cultorum can be used to generate new plants by slicing across the veins of their undersides at junctions where branch veins meet, then laying the leaves undersides down on one of the rooting mediums previously mentioned and either weighting them with three or four pebbles or pinning them down with hairpin-like wires. New plants develop from the cuts. Alternatively, cut leaves into wedges each with a vein junction as its pointed base and plant these ½ inch deep, point downward, as is done with stem cuttings.

Division, splitting a plant into two or more pieces and planting each separately as a new individual, is most often done with begonias with horizontal, rooting rhizomes. To accomplish this, cut through the rhizomes with a sharp knife so that each division has a fair amount of roots as well as a portion of rhizome and some foliage, and plant the divisions in sandy soil in pots just big enough to accommodate them. Tuberous begonias also lend themselves to increase by division, but the manner of doing it is a little different from that employed with rhizomatous sorts. In late winter or spring plant large tubers very

shallowly in a mixture of peat moss and sand or similar material kept damp but not soaking wet. Maintain a temperature of 70 to 75°F. When new shoots ½ to 1 inch long have developed take a sharp knife and cut the tuber into pie-slice-shaped segments, each with at least one shoot. Dust the cut surfaces with powdered sulfer or other fungicide and plant each in a small pot of sandy peaty soil. Put where the temperature is 60 to 70°F and the atmospheric humidity fairly high. Be careful not to water excessively. Division of the bulb clusters of *B. socotrana* is easily accomplished at the start of a new season of growth.

Wax begonias (*B. semperflorens-cultorum* varieties) are very easily raised from cuttings, and this is the only practicable way of raising double-flowered and calla-lily sorts true to kind. But single-flowered varieties come so true from seeds that when large numbers are needed, as for commercial purposes and extensive plantings outdoors, that method of propagation is most commonly employed. Sown in a temperature of 60°F, seeds take ten days to two weeks to germinate and in a greenhouse with a night temperature of 55 to 60°F ris-

Preparing leaf cutting of *Begonia rex-cultorum* by slicing across veins

Pegging prepared leaf cutting onto sand

New plants developing from leaf cutting of *Begonia rex-cultorum*

be 60°F, the atmosphere somewhat more humid, and light shade from strong sun is necessary.

Start tubers purchased or taken from storage in late winter as soon as the buds in their hollow apexes begin to plump up and show signs of beginning to grow. To do this set them closely together, hollow side (top side) down in flats of leaf mold or peat moss mixed with sand in a shaded place where the temperature of 70 to 80°F and the atmosphere is humid. Let most of the bulk of the tubers be above the surface. The purpose of so placing them is so water cannot collect in the hollow tops and cause rotting. After the first week or so inspect the tubers every two or three days by lifting and reversing them to see how the buds are developing. When they are about ½ inch long, plant the tubers right side (hollow side) up with their tops just covered in the same leaf mold or peat moss mixture. Maintain the same warm, humid conditions, and when the tubers have roots about 1½ inches long, pot them individually.

The potting mix should be loose and contain much organic matter such as leaf mold or peat moss and coarse sand or perlite. A few growers prefer to pot directly into the pots in which the plants are to bloom (containers 6 or 7 inches in diameter), but most prefer to use 4-inch pots at first and later repot into larger ones. Do not press the soil mixture more than lightly. Tuberous begonias revel in a loose, open root run.

With large-flowered varieties decide at potting time whether you prefer a few monster blooms or more smaller ones. The first choice necessitates removing all but the strongest growth bud from each tuber, the second removing all except the two strongest. More buds can be left on tubers of naturally small-flowered sorts.

Keep the plants growing where the night temperature approximates 60 to 65°F and that by day a few degrees higher. See that the atmosphere is humid, but not dank and oppressive. Shade from strong sun is necessary, but avoid too much shade. Early morning and evening sun, and sun filtered through leafy branches is beneficial.

The plants may be grown in pots throughout or be transferred from the pots to garden beds, window boxes, or porch boxes. If kept in pots they must be transferred to successively larger ones as their growth requires, and after their final pots are filled with roots, they should be given weekly applications of dilute liquid fertilizer. Delay planting outdoors until the weather is reasonably warm, about the time it is safe to set out tomatoes. Be sure the location is sheltered from strong winds. These can cause much damage. Also be sure that the soil is well-drained, fertile, fairly loose, and contains an abundance of compost, leaf mold, or peat moss. A mulch of organic material over the soil surface, by keeping the ground evenly moist and cool, promotes good growth. If the weather is dry regular watering will be necessary.

After the first touch of frost take potted plants indoors and dig up those in beds without removing their tops and lay them in an airy, dry place in shade indoors. After the tops are thoroughly dry remove them and store the tubers in shallow trays or suspended in net sacks or old stockings where the temperature is about 50°F. Mice and other rodents enjoy begonia tubers; unless they are suspended, protect them from these by covering or enclosing them in metal hardware cloth. During storage inspect the tubers from time to time and promptly discard any that become soft or show signs of decay.

Christmas begonias (B. cheimantha varieties) are best adapted for greenhouses. Occasionally an enthusiast able to provide just the right environment succeeds in a house, but this is exceptional. For medium- to large-sized plants propagate by whole-leaf cuttings taken from November to February, selecting mature leaves with sturdy stalks. Set them at an angle of 45 degrees with the bases of their stalks ½ to 1 inch deep in sand, perlite, or other propagating medium and spaced in rows so each leaf is fully exposed to light and the rooting medium can be moistened as needed by dribbling tepid water from the spout of a watering can between the rows without wetting the leaves. Water thoroughly with a fine spray immediately after the cuttings are planted, but avoid overhead watering afterward. For best results maintain the propagating medium at 70 to 75°F. Air temperatures of 60 to 65°F at night, a few degrees higher by day, are satisfactory. Maintain fairly high humidity, but it should not be so high that condensed water collects on the leaves or on sheets of glass or polyethylene plastic film used to cover the cuttings. Shade lightly from direct sun. Small specimens to flower in 4-inch pots can be had from stem cuttings in July.

In about a month from planting, enough roots will have developed from the bases of the stalks of the leaf cuttings to warrant potting them individually in small pots in a mixture of sand or perlite and leaf mold or peat moss. Sink the newly potted plants to the rims of their containers in peat moss or sand and maintain an environment similar to that in which the cuttings were rooted. In about another month shoots will develop. From then on grow the plants in a humid, lightly-shaded greenhouse where the minimum night temperature is 58°F, that by day five to fifteen degrees higher.

Never allow the plants to become potbound until they are in their final containers, which may be from 6 to 10 inches in diameter depending upon when the cuttings were taken. Before the roots become crowded repot successively into 4-inch, 6-inch, 7-inch, and 8-inch pots or pans (shallow pots), or from the 4- or 6-inch size, transfer to hanging baskets.

Started tuber of begonia ready for potting

Care through the growing season involves maintaining a humid atmosphere, keeping the soil damp without being consistently wet, providing shade from strong sun, and seeing that the temperature at night does not drop below 55°F and by day that it is at least five to fifteen degrees higher. Also needed is an occasional pinching out of the tips of the stems to induce branching, but do not do this later than August. Neat staking and tying so that shapely specimens result is also important. After the final pots are filled with roots, weekly applications of dilute liquid fertilizer are of benefit. If you want plants in full bloom for Christmas, pick off all flower buds that appear before November. The display season of plants in bloom is prolonged if they are kept where the temperature at night is 50°F.

For potting use a comparatively coarse, fertile mix containing an abundance of decayed organic matter. One composed of equal parts of good topsoil, leaf mold or peat moss, and well-decayed manure with a generous sprinkling of coarse sand or perlite and a dash of bonemeal is satisfactory. Pack it rather lightly instead of firmly about the roots. Very large specimens can be had by growing plants on for a second year. To do this manage the plants after flowering as advised for second-year specimens of Elatior begonias.

Elatior begonias (B. hiemalis), including the older winter-flowering hybrids and the newer Rieger ones that bloom at other seasons are best propagated from stem cuttings, can be had less surely from leaf cuttings. To achieve large specimens in pots 8 inches in diameter, those of winter-flowering kinds are best taken in the first half of November. Smaller plants result from later propagations. Cuttings of Rieger varieties taken in late winter or spring give satisfactory results. Subsequent treatment is as for Christmas begonias. With these begonias, as with Christmas begonias it is possible to produce immense specimens by growing them on for a second year. If you intend to do this, after flowering is through keep the plants in a greenhouse where the air is fairly moist and the night temperature is 50°F. Avoid frequent watering, but do not allow the soil to dry completely. In late March shake the roots free of as much old soil as easily possible, cut the stems back lightly, repot in containers just big enough to accommodate the roots, and start the plants into growth again by affording them the same conditions as young, newly-propagated ones. If well cared for, such second-year specimens will be up to 3½ feet across when in bloom.

Rex-cultorum begonias (hybrids of B. rex) are most commonly increased by division and leaf cuttings, both simple procedures. They are also readily had from seeds, but plants so raised exhibit considerable variation in leaf colorings, in patterns, and in other ways. Most are likely to be inferior to the best-named varieties, but among batches of seedlings many good and an occasional quite stunning individual are likely to occur.

The needs of Rex-cultorum begonias are shade from all but the very weakest sun (they stand more shade than the vast majority of begonias), a decidedly humid atmosphere, and temperatures of 60°F or higher. They respond to well-drained fertile soil containing generous proportions of organic matter and throughout the spring-to-fall growing season kept evenly moist.

Watering in winter must be adjusted to the needs of individuals. Some varieties retain their foliage through winter and must be watered moderately, but less abundantly than in summer, others become semidormant or dormant, lose much or all of their foliage, and must be kept nearly dry until new growth in late winter or spring indicates the start of a new growing season.

Repotting is necessary when new growth begins. Remove plants from their containers, cut off any damaged leaves (these can be used for propagation), with a pointed stick prick from the root ball some old soil, if the plant is too large divide it, and then repot in new soil.

Rex-cultorum begonias growing in ground beds, outdoors in the tropics, under greenhouse benches, and in terrariums, for which purposes they are well suited, benefit from having some surface soil removed in spring and replaced with fresh, or if this is not done, from being fertilized then.

Repotting *Begonia rex-cultorum*

Species, varieties, and hybrids other than those discussed in the groups dealt with separately above are somewhat varied in their needs, but also have much in common. For their best performance all must be lightly shaded from strong sun and have at least a moderately humid atmosphere. For most, temperatures at night in winter should be in the neighborhood of 55°F, those by day five to fifteen degrees higher depending upon the brightness of the day. Some do better in the warmer, more humid, more heavily shaded environments that suit the Rex-cultorum hybrids. Here belong B. decora, B. herbacea, B. imperialis and its varieties, B. masoniana, and B. rajah.

Best for somewhat dryish atmospheres and so among the most adaptable as houseplants are sorts with thick rhizomes or upright stems and more or less fleshy leaves. Examples are B. carolinaefolia, B. erythrophylla, B. heracleifolia, B. manicata, B. phyllomaniaca, B. ricinifolia, and B. venosa. These and others that are similar prosper in rather heavier, more loamy soils, achieved by increasing the proportion of topsoil in the mix, than do thinner-stemmed, thinner-leaved kinds.

Soils for the latter should be nourishing mixes of equal parts fertile, loamy topsoil, good leaf mold, compost, or peat moss, and coarse sand or perlite. If the topsoil is on the heavy (clayey) side, increase the proportion of organic materials. To these basic ingredients add about one-eighth part by bulk of dried cow manure and a pint of bonemeal to each bushel. For newly-rooted cuttings omit from the mix the bonemeal and cow manure and increase the proportion of sand considerably.

Propagation of stemless sorts and those with creeping rhizomes is chiefly by division, increase of sorts with other types of stems by cuttings. Leaf cuttings are successful with some, and species are easily reproduced from seeds. In the main, late winter and spring are favored seasons for propagation, but with most begonias this can be carried out successfully at any time.

Routine culture includes watering regularly to keep the soil evenly damp without being constantly saturated. A few rhizomatous sorts that lose their leaves in winter should be kept dry then and until new growth is about to begin naturally. Another that needs such treatment during its rather long season of rest is B. socotrana. Throughout its growing season treat this like its hybrid offspring, the Christmas begonias.

Other care called for involves repotting from time to time, young specimens two times or more a year perhaps, bigger ones annually in late winter or spring or possibly at longer intervals. Pinching the tips out of the stems, especially of young specimens, to induce branching is often desirable, and many sorts need staking and tying neatly. From spring to fall, and vigorously-growing specimens to a lesser extent in winter, weekly or biweekly applications of dilute liquid fertilizer is beneficial. In late winter or early spring prune old specimens to size and shape and look to their need for repotting or top dressing.

Pests and Diseases. Although subject to many pests and diseases, begonias grown under reasonably favorable conditions are generally relatively trouble free. Most infections result from the soil being poorly drained with consequent excessive wetness and poor aeration and from allowing the foliage to remain wet for long periods, especially at night. The most serious of pests are root and leaf nematodes, which can only be controlled by discarding affected plants, using only clean stock for propagation, and sterilizing the soil and pots. Root nematodes are most troublesome in ground beds. Other pests are aphids, black vine weevils, mealybugs, mites, red spider mites, scales, slugs, thrips, and whiteflies. The most prevalent diseases are aster yellows, botrytis or gray mold, crown gall, damping off, bacterial and fungus leaf spots, root rot, stem rot, and spotted wilt disease.

BEGONIACEAE—Begonia Family. The number of species in this family of five genera of dicotyledons is uncertain, but probably exceeds 900. All except about twenty are in *Begonia*. They are tropical or subtropical, a large percentage natives of the Americas. The genus *Hillebrandia* is endemic to Hawaii. The family, rich in ornamentals, is practically without other value.

The species of the begonia family are mostly herbaceous perennials with succulent or sometimes somewhat woody stems, less commonly annuals. Many have tubers or creeping rhizomes. The stems are more or less jointed. The leaves, commonly markedly asymmetrical with one side much larger than the other, and often two-ranked, are undivided and lobeless, palmately-lobed, or are of separate leaflets that spread finger-like from the tops of the leafstalks. The symmetrical or asymmetrical flowers are unisexual with both sexes on the same plant. The males have two petal-like sepals, two usually smaller petals, and numerous stamens. Female blooms have two to many similar perianth parts usually called petals, but more correctly identified as tepals, and one pistil with an often colored inferior (behind the petals) or half inferior, winged or angled ovary. They have two to five, most commonly three, styles and often twisted stigmas. The fruits are capsules containing numerous minute seeds or are seldom berries. The only genera likely to be cultivated are *Begonia* and *Hillebrandia*.

BEILSCHMIEDIA (Beil-schmièdia). Related to *Cryptocarya*, this genus of the laurel family LAURACEAE consists of over 200 species of trees and shrubs of the tropics of the Old World and New World. Its members have leathery, undivided leaves and small blooms in axillary panicles or in panicles grouped near the branch ends. The flowers have six-lobed perianths with short tubes. There are nine stamens, three staminodes (nonfertile stamens), and one style. The fruits are berries, when mature not com-

pletely or nearly completely enclosed by the perianth tube. The name honors the Silesian botanist Carl T. Beilschmied, who died in 1848.

Planted to some extent as an ornamental in southern California and other warm regions, *Beilschmiedia miersii* (syn. *Cryptocarya miersii*) is native to Chile. A tree up to 80 feet tall, it has nearly opposite, broad-ovate to ovate leaves up to 4½ inches long by 2½ inches wide. They are pale green to glaucous on their undersides. The tiny, greenish-yellow flowers are in downy-stalked, broadly-pyramidal panicles. The fruits are small and woody.

Garden and Landscape Uses and Cultivation. In warm climates this sort is occasionally planted for ornament. Little information is available about its cultural needs. It can be propagated by seeds, perhaps by cuttings.

BEJARIA. See Befaria.

BELAMCANDA (Belam-cánda) — Blackberry-Lily. One of the two Chinese and Japanese species that constitute this genus of the iris family IRIDACEAE is the blackberry-lily, a fairly common garden plant, naturalized in parts of North America. The name *Belamcanda* is a modification of a native one of eastern Asia.

These are hardy herbaceous perennials with fans of deciduous, sword-shaped, iris-like leaves from thick, short rhizomes and flowers on forked erect stems 2 to 4 feet in height. The blooms, 1½ to 2 inches in diameter, have six spreading petals (more correctly tepals) united at their bases into a short tube that sits on top of the ovary, three stamens, and a three-branched style. The three inner petals are somewhat shorter than the outer ones. The fruits are capsules that open to reveal close clusters of shining black, fleshy seeds somewhat blackberry-like in appearance, which accounts for the common name.

The common blackberry-lily (*B. chinensis*) has orange flowers with many red or

purple spots. They open for but a single day and as they fade the petals twist. Very similar *B. flabellata* has blooms, which behave in the same way, but are yellow and spotless or only faintly spotted.

Belamcanda flabellata

Garden Uses and Cultivation. Blackberry-lilies are among the easiest of plants to grow. They add color to summer flower beds and borders and may be planted informally under seminatural conditions to brighten less formal areas. Full sun and well-drained soil are essential. Earth of a sandy character suits them well, if it is enriched with compost, peat moss, or other organic matter and is made reasonably fertile. In dry weather watering is desirable and in cold climates a winter covering of branches of evergreens, salt hay, or other

Belamcanda chinensis

Belamcanda chinensis (fruits)

protection is advisable. Seeds form a very ready means of increase and plants normally bloom well in their second year. Division in spring or early fall is also a satisfactory method of propagation.

BELL JAR. Since the advent of polyethylene plastic film, bell jars are less used than formerly. They are bell-shaped glass covers used to put over cuttings to be rooted, newly-sown seeds of plants needing high humidity, and small ferns and other delicate plants needing protection. Their purpose is to ensure a high degree of humidity in the immediate vicinity of the cuttings or plants covered. Bags or other coverings of transparent polyethylene serve the same purposes and are lighter and much less expensive.

BELLADONNA-LILY is *Amaryllis belladonna.*

BELLE ISLE CRESS is *Barbarea verna.*

BELLEVALIA (Bel-levàlia). The name *Bellevalia* honors Pierre Riche de Belleval, founder of the Montpellier Botanic Garden, who died in 1632. More or less intermediate between *Muscari* and *Hyacinthus* and many of its forty-five species in the past classified at one time or another in one or both of those genera or in *Scilla*, the genus *Bellevalia* belongs to the lily family LILIACEAE. Native to the Mediterranean region and western Asia, it is separated from the other genera mentioned on the basis of the forms of the flowers and technical details of their anthers.

Bellevalias are small, spring-blooming bulb plants, with foliage like that of grape-hyacinths, and leafless, erect stalks terminating in racemes of little flowers with bell-shaped perianths that have wide-open throats and six lobes (petals), six stamens, and a single style. The fruits are capsules.

Widely dispersed as a native throughout the Mediterranean region, *B. romana* (syns. *Hyacinthus romanus, Scilla romana*) has comparatively large bulbs and four to eight somewhat fleshy, more or less erect, pointed-linear to sometimes sickle-shaped, smooth-margined leaves 1 foot to 1½ feet in length and longer than the flower stalks and racemes. The racemes are of twenty to thirty moderately-densely-arranged, greenish-white, cylindrical-tubed blooms, ¼ inch long or slightly longer, shaded blue at their bases and becoming white as they age. Their blue anthers, at maturity are dusted with greenish-yellow pollen.

Others sometimes cultivated are *B. ciliata* (syn. *Hyacinthus ciliatus*), which is a native of lands surrounding the Mediterranean basin, and *B. saviczii* (syn. *Hyacinthus saviczii*), which is indigenous from east of the Caspian sea to Iran and Afghanistan. Up to 1½ feet high, *B. ciliata* has three to five lanceolate, hair-fringed leaves and in loose, conical racemes, thirty

to fifty ½-inch-long, lilac-colored flowers that have greenish petals and purple anthers. A little taller, *B. saviczii* develops three to six oblong-lanceolate leaves with hair-fringed or slightly bristly margins. Up to 10 inches long, they have glaucous upper surfaces. About ⅜ inch long and white changing to grayish-brown, the flowers, which have violet-colored anthers, are in conical racemes. Rare *B. tabriziana* (syn. *Hyacinthus tabrizianus*) of Iran is up to about 1 foot tall. It has slender, erect, strongly-channeled leaves, and terminating a stalk shorter than leaves, a crowded raceme of blue-white flowers about ³⁄₁₆ inch long and wide with a green central stripe on the back of each petal. The anthers are black-purple.

Garden Uses and Cultivation. These are as for grape-hyacinths and scilla.

BELLFLOWER. This is the common name for plants of the genus Campanula. Chilean-bellflower applies to *Nolana paradoxa* and *Lapageria rosea*. The giant-bellflower is *Ostrowskia magnifica.*

BELLIS (Béll-is)—Daisy, English Daisy. Of the several genera to which the name daisy is applied, this is most deserving of the name, since the English daisy was the original "day's eye," so called because its flower heads open early in the morning and close at nightfall. It is the kind that, much to the consternation of European gardeners who regard it as a pernicious weed, whitens lawns in the British Isles and other parts of northern Europe with its pretty flowers and smothers desirable grasses with its ground-hugging rosettes of foliage. The English daisy has naturalized itself to some extent in lawns and grassy places in parts of North America, including the northeastern states and California. From this cheerful sprite horticulturists have developed the large-flowered and sometimes monstrous forms (one is called 'monstrosa') grown in America as English daisies, sometimes as bachelor's buttons. But the genus *Bellis* includes more kinds than the English daisy, in all fifteen species, natives of Europe or North Africa. The North American plant previously called *B. integrifolia* is *Astranthium integrifolium.*

A member of the daisy family COMPOSITAE, this genus has a name derived from the Latin *bellus*, pretty, that refers to the flowers. Small, rosette-forming or tufted, the annuals and herbaceous perennials that constitute *Bellis* have solitary flower heads with white, pink, or purplish ray florets and a center eye composed of yellow or greenish-yellow disk florets. The fruits are seedlike achenes.

The English daisy (*B. perennis*) in its wild form is a fibrous-rooted, moderately-hairy perennial with toothed, broadly-ovate or obovate leaves up to 3 inches long that

Bellis perennis

taper to more or less winged stalks. The flower stalks, 3 to 6 inches tall, are unbranched and carry solitary heads, ¾ to 1 inch in diameter, the ray florets of which are white or white tipped with pink. The disk florets are yellow.

Horticultural varieties of the English daisy are the only ones cultivated in gardens. They commonly have very much bigger double or semidouble flower heads

Horticultural variety of English daisy

than the wild type and may have their ray florets attractively quilled, incurved, or reflexed. They are listed in seedsmen's catalogs under varietal names. One especially interesting, called hen-and-chickens, produces secondary stalked flower heads from the leafy collar (involucre) beneath each head of bloom. These spread from the flower head like spokes of a wheel. English daisies, the double-flowered varieties sometimes called bachelor's buttons, are grown as spring bedding plants.

Another species sometimes cultivated is *B. rotundifolia,* native in the Atlas Mountains of North Africa. This sort differs from the English daisy in having round or broadly-ovate leaves with slender stalks 1 inch to 3 inches long. The flower heads of its variety, *B. r. caerulescens,* have blue

Bellis rotundifolia

rays. Native to southern Europe, **B. sylvestris** grows more loosely, is taller than the English daisy, and has leaves that are more toothed. Its flower heads, often drooping, have crimson-tipped white ray florets.

Garden and Landscape Uses. Almost the only use to which English daisies are put is as temporary plants for spring display, that is as spring bedding plants. Often they are interplanted with other spring bloomers, especially with bulbs such as tulips and hyacinths. They are also used for early flowering in window and porch boxes. The variety called hen-and-chickens is suitable for rock gardens and elsewhere where it is not likely to be overgrown by stronger neighbors. Other species of *Bellis* are appropriate for similar locations.

Cultivation. English daisies are usually discarded after they are through blooming, and new plants are raised each year as biennials. An alternative method, applicable when it is desirable to increase an especially fine form, is to divide the plants carefully as soon as their main flower display is over and plant the divisions about 4 inches apart in a nursery bed or in cold frames, and treat them as advised for seedlings. To have plants for spring bloom, sow seeds outdoors or in cold frames in May or June. As soon as the young plants are big enough to handle, transplant them about 4 inches apart to outdoor nursery beds or in very cold climates to cold frames. If possible locate the beds or frames where they receive a little shade from the strongest summer sun. Make sure the soil is moderately fertile and sufficiently porous to drain freely. Stir the surface soil occasionally to promote growth and keep down weeds. Water in dry weather. Where winters are cold it is advantageous to cover the plants in fall with branches of evergreens, a thin layer of salt hay, or some similar protection against winter sun and wind. If grown in cold frames, the sashes should be kept on during the winter to protect against excessive cold and wetness, but on all favorable occasions they should be opened to admit air and to prevent excessive humidity or too high temperatures from building up inside the frame. The objective is not to promote growth, but to hold the plants in good condition until they are ready to be planted out in spring. Before this is done, gradually harden the plants in frames by removing the sashes entirely for a period of a week or more. In mild climates transplanting from nursery beds to flowering quarters may be done in fall.

English daisies wintering in a cold frame

In rock gardens the hen-and-chickens variety of the English daisy as well as *B. rotundifolia*, its variety *B. r. caerulescens*, and *B. sylvestris*, are usually cultivated as perennials and are increased by division. They need porous, well-drained soil, and a location where they receive slight shade from the most brilliant sun of summer.

BELLIUM (Béll-ium). This genus is very like the true daisy (*Bellis*), from which it differs in its ovaries and seedlike fruits (achenes) having a crown of hairs called a pappus. These are absent from *Bellis*. More obvious, belliums are smaller plants. Their flower heads are up to ½ inch in diameter. There are six species of *Bellium*, all natives of the Mediterranean region and all small, tufted, annual or perennial herbaceous plants with solitary flower heads on comparatively long stalks. They belong in the daisy family COMPOSITAE. The name is a modification of *Bellis*.

Most commonly cultivated is **B. bellidioides,** a hardy perennial that spreads rather slowly by stolons and looks like a miniature English daisy (*Bellis perennis*). Its more or less spatula-shaped leaves have blades up to ¼ inch across and long, pubescent stalks. The pinkish or white-rayed flower heads, up to ½ inch in diameter, are on stalks 2 to 5 inches tall. Variety *B. b. nivale* has very short stems. A somewhat hairy or hairless annual up to 3 inches in height, **B. minutum** has narrowly-spatula-shaped, long-stalked leaves, and flower heads approximately ½ inch in diameter, with purplish tips to their white ray florets. The plant grown in gardens as *B. minutum* is often *B. bellidioides*.

Garden Uses and Cultivation. Belliums are charming plants for rock gardens. They prosper with slight shade from the fiercest summer sun or in full sun where summer temperatures are not extraordinarily high provided they are not allowed to suffer for want of reasonable amounts of water. They are best suited with a porous gritty or sandy soil that contains sufficient organic matter to encourage good root development and is sharply drained. They are easily propagated by seeds sown in light sandy soil and the perennial kinds by offsets. These plants are less hardy than the English daisy (*Bellis*). Where cold winters prevail they benefit from the protection afforded by branches of evergreens laid over them in late fall or early winter or from other forms of protection from sun and wind that do not unduly impede air circulation.

Bellium minutum

BELLONIA (Bel-lònia). Two species constitute this genus of the gesneria family GESNERIACEAE, both natives of Hispaniola and perhaps elsewhere in the West Indies. The name commemorates the French naturalist Pierre Belon, who died in 1564. Low shrubs with sprawling stems and opposite, holly-like leaves, bellonias are botanical allies of *Niphaea* and *Phinaea*. Their slightly asymmetrical flowers have corollas with but a suggestion of tube and five to eight spreading petals. The calyx is five lobed, and there are four stamens. The fruits are capsules.

Unique in being the only thorny member of its family, **Bellonia spinosa** is up to 3 feet tall and has stems 4 to 5 feet in length. Its needle-like spines, from the leaf axils, are 1 inch long. The leaves, sandpapery with short, rough hairs, are at first bright green, but later grayish-green. They are elliptic, up to about 1 inch long, and blunt-toothed. White, sometimes with the undersides of the five petals tinged pink, the flowers are about ¾ inch in diameter. It is reported that plants with pink or lilac blooms occur in the wild.

From the last, *B. aspera* differs in being without thorns and in having broader, sharper-toothed, even rougher hairy leaves about 1½ inches long. Its flowers, 1 inch in diameter, have five to eight petals. They are white with yellow at the bases of the petals.

Garden Uses. Collectors of gesneriads find these plants of interest for growing outdoors and in lath houses in the tropics and subtropics, and in greenhouses. They are more tolerant of dryish atmospheres than most of the gesneria family and so accommodate better than many as houseplants.

Cultivation. In the wild bellonias inhabit rocky, somewhat arid areas where, at least seasonally, the soil is dry or dryish. In cultivation sharp drainage and fairly nourishing, porous earth is to their liking. Water moderately at all times, and with particular caution when they are not in active growth. Then the soil may become nearly dry between soakings. Indoors winter night temperatures of 60°F with daytime increases of five to fifteen degrees are satisfactory. Good light with shade from strong sun is needed. Propagation is by seeds and cuttings, the latter made from young, vigorously growing shoots set in a propagating bed with mild bottom heat. Cuttings of hard, woody stems root slowly or not at all. Old plants are refurbished by pruning to shape and repotting in early spring.

BELLS OF IRELAND is Molucella laevis

BELLWORT. See Uvularia.

BELOPERONE. See Justicia.

BELVEDERE. See Kochia.

BENCH, GREENHOUSE. Tables in greenhouses on which potted plants are stood or tables that are designed to hold soil in which planting is done are called benches. They should be of a height convenient for working. Usually they consist of a framework of metal pipes, but sometimes masonry or wooden supports, and tops of rot-resistant wood, asbestos composition, or slate. If they are to hold soil the tops are surrounded by rims about 6 inches deep. Bench is also used as a verb to designate the operation of setting out plants in benches; thus greenhouse gardeners speak of benching carnations or snapdragons.

BENINCASA (Beninca-sa)—Wax Gourd or White Gourd or Chinese Watermelon or Preserving-Melon. A vigorous annual vine of the gourd family CUCURBITACEAE, and a native of tropical Asia, is the only member

Benincasa hispida (flower)

Benincasa hispida (fruits)

of the genus *Benincasa*. Its name is that of an Italian nobleman and botanist, Count Giuseppe Benincasa, who died in 1596.

A softly-hairy, melon-like plant with long-running stems and branched tendrils,

B. hispida (syn. *B. cerifera*) has broadly-heart-shaped to kidney-shaped, shallowly-lobed leaves up to 1 foot in diameter. Its flowers are solitary, wheel-shaped, yellow, and 3 to 4 inches wide. They have five-lobed calyxes. The females are succeeded by bristly-hairy fruits, resembling melons, which are coated with a white wax. They are oblong to nearly globose and up to 1¼ feet long, with solid flesh that contains many small seeds. They are used for preserves, pickles, and curries. Cultivation is as for melons and cucumbers. The wax gourd is sometimes mistakenly called cassabanana, which name properly belongs to *Sicana odorifera*.

BENSONIA. See Bensoniella.

BENSONIELLA (Benson-iélla). The only species of this genus of the saxifrage family SAXIFRAGACEAE is a herbaceous perennial, native to mountains in Oregon and northern California. Closely resembling *Mitella*, it is distinguished from that genus on the basis of technical differences of its flowers, which have much longer stamens and styles than those of *Mitella*. The name commemorates Gilbert Thereon Benson, Californian librarian and botanist, who died in 1928.

Its branching rootstocks horizontal and scaly, ***Bensoniella oregona*** (syn. *Bensonia oregona*) has chiefly basal leaves, and erect, slender, hairy, nonbranching flower stalks approximately 1 foot tall, their upper parts narrow spikes of tiny, slender-petaled, white blooms. The leaves, mostly basal, have long, hairy stalks, and hairless to sparsely-hairy blades. They are 1½ to 3 inches across, deeply-heart-shaped at their bases, shallowly five- to seven-lobed, and toothed. The fruits are capsules.

Garden and Landscape Uses and Cultivation. These are as for *Mitella*.

BENT GRASS. See Agrostis.

BENZOIN. See Lindera.

BERBERIDACEAE—Barberry Family. Here belong fourteen genera and about 575 species of dicotyledons of the north temperate zone, temperate South America, and mountains in the tropics. They include deciduous and evergreen shrubs and herbaceous perennials sometimes creeping by stolons or rhizomes, with alternate or all basal, often spiny, undivided, pinnate, twice-pinnate, or thrice-pinnate leaves. The small, symmetrical flowers are in racemes or branched or branchless clusters. Mostly they have four to six each sepals and similar or different petals, four to eighteen stamens, a short, stout style or none, and one stigma. The fruits are berries. Cultivated genera are *Achlys, Berberis, Bongardia, Caulophyllum, Diphylleia, Epimedium, Jeffersonia, Leontice, Mahoberberis, Mahonia, Nandina, Podophyllum, Ranzania*, and *Vancouveria*.

BERBERIDOPSIS (Berberid-ópsis)—Coral Plant. The choice Chilean evergreen, semi-climbing shrub *Berberidopsis corallina* is the only species of its genus. Its name is from that of the genus *Berberis* and the Greek *opsis*, similar to, and refers to the general aspect of the plant. Botanists have been somewhat puzzled as to its precise botanical status, but now allocate it to the flacourtia family FLACOURTIACEAE. It is a tender species suitable only for greenhouses and for outdoor cultivation in areas of mild climates, such as southern California.

Called coral plant, **B. corallina** attains a height of up to 20 feet and has alternate, firm, ovate to heart-shaped, prickly-toothed leaves, dark green on their upper sides and glaucous beneath, and 1½ to 4 inches long. Produced in late summer and fall, in racemes terminal to the shoots and from the axils of the upper leaves, the pendent, globose, bisexual flowers, ⅓ to ½ inch in diameter, are very showy and attractive. They and their 1½- to 2-inch-long stalks are deep coral-red. Each flower has nine to fifteen petal-like parts consisting of sepals and petals between which there is no sharp distinction. The inner ones are concave and larger than the spreading outer ones. The stamens number seven to ten. The stigma is three-lobed. The fruits are berries.

Berberidopsis corallina (flowers)

Berberidopsis corallina (fruits)

Garden and Landscape Uses. The coral plant forms lovely cover for training against walls, posts, and other supports. In greenhouses it may be used effectively to clothe pillars or be tied to wires stretched a few inches beneath the roof glass. There, its pendent blooms are displayed to good advantage. It needs a sunny location and well-drained, sandy-peaty, slightly acid soil.

Cultivation. In greenhouses this species does best when planted in ground beds rather than in pots or other containers. Both outdoors and indoors the most favorable season for planting is spring. Indoors, cool, airy conditions are needed. A winter night temperature of 40 to 45°F is adequate, and this should not rise more than five or ten degrees by day at that season. In summer, as cool and as airy conditions as possible should be maintained. Watering should be done to keep the soil moderately moist, but somewhat drier in winter than at other seasons. Pruning consists of thinning out older branches when they become crowded. This is done in winter or early spring. Propagation is usually by layering in late summer or fall or by cuttings inserted, preferably under mist, in summer.

BERBERIS (Bér-beris)—Barberry. The presentation of this vast group of species, varieties, and hybrids is less lengthy than otherwise would be the case because a large proportion of its members are alternate hosts to the dread black stem rust disease of wheat and other cereals, and it is unlawful to grow them over large areas of North America. For practical purposes the kinds discussed here are limited to those approved by the U. S. Department of Agriculture as being strongly rust-resistant. The genus *Berberis* of the barberry family BERBERIDACEAE comprises about 450 species. Its name is a modification of an Arabic one for the fruits. Other plants in gardens called *Berberis* belong in *Mahonia*, a related genus that differs in having leaves of three or more leaflets.

Barberries include deciduous and evergreen, hardy and nonhardy, mostly spring- and early summer-flowering shrubs of North and South America, Europe, North Africa, and Asia. They have stems, in all except less than twenty kinds with spines, that like the roots have yellow inner bark and wood. The spines are most commonly three-branched, but sometimes have more branches or are branchless. Usually they are ½ to 1 inch long, but may be longer. The alternate, undivided leaves have smooth or spiny edges and often occur in clusters. The yellow to orange flowers, small but frequently quite showy, are solitary or in drooping racemes or umbel-like clusters. The stalk of each bloom bears two or three bractlets. There are six sepals, six petals, six stamens, and a solitary pistil. The stamens are sensitive; if their stalks

Berberis thunbergii

Berberis thunbergii (flowers)

Berberis thunbergii (fruits)

are touched with a pin or similar object they at once move inward and touch the stigma. The fruits are small berries, red, bluish-black, or dark purple, and often covered with a thin layer of wax.

The most popular deciduous species, ubiquitous in much of temperate North America, and naturalized in parts, is the Japanese barberry (*B. thunbergii*). This is one of the very few barberries that when growing with other kinds can be generally relied upon not to hybridize but to produce seeds that will give plants true to type. Native to Japan, **B. thunbergii** is hardy throughout most of New England. Fairly compact, much-branched, 2 to 5 feet tall, and hairless, it has deeply-grooved, spreading branches and green young shoots. Its obovate to spoon-shaped, toothless leaves, crowded in tufts along the branches, are ½ inch to 1¼ inches long. They narrow gradually to their bases and have whitish-gray undersides. In fall the foliage turns bright red. Sometimes solitary, but usually in umbel-like clusters of two to five, or rarely more, the flowers are borne profusely all along the stems. They have red sepals, pale yellow petals flushed with red, and are ⅓ inch wide or a little wider. Shining, bright red berries about ⅓ inch long, and less wide, decorate the branches in fall and remain plump and attractive until new leaves appear in spring. There are several distinct varieties of this barberry, some with green leaves, some with other colored foliage. Truehedge columnberry (*B. t. erecta*) is a green-leaved variety distinguished by its upright growth. Unsheared, it eventually attains a height of about 5 feet and may be twice as broad as tall. Another excellent green-leaved variety is *B. t. minor*. Ordinarily not more than 1 foot to 1½ feet in height, a 75-year-old specimen is recorded as being 3½ feet tall and 5 feet wide. This variety is smaller in all its parts than the typical species and forms a compact, rounded bush. Another dwarf is green-leaved *B. t.* 'Globe', shaped as its name suggests. At the Arnold Arboretum near Boston, Massachusetts, a

specimen over thirty years old is a little more than 2 feet in height and about 4 feet in width. Unusual because it is without spines or at most has very few is *B. t.* 'Thornless'.

Japanese barberries with colored foliage include *B. t. atropurpurea*, distinguished by its purplish-red leaves. Their color develops most intensely in full sun. Plants grown in shade are an unattractive reddish-green. A more erect habit distinguishes *B. t. atropurpurea erecta*. Also with purplish-red foliage is *B. t.* 'Crimson Pygmy', a dwarf, compact kind not more than about 2 feet in height. Foliage that on plants grown in full sun is bright yellow distinguishes *B. t. aurea*. The leaves of *B. t. variegata* are variously speckled with yellow, pale gray, and white. The leaves on young shoots of *B. t. argenteo-marginata* are margined with white. Narrower purple leaves with green undersurfaces distinguish variety *B. t. maximowiczii*. Handsomely-colored, *B. t.* 'Rose Glow' has purple leaves lavishly variegated with pink and white.

The Korean barberry (**B. koreana**) is an excellent deciduous kind that adequately substitutes for common barberry (*B. vul-*

Berberis thunbergii 'Rose Glow'

garis), in areas where the latter is generally prohibited. A native of Korea, this hairless species attains a height of 5 or 6 feet, and has grooved shoots with mostly flattened, lobed spines that look like leafy appendages to the leaves. The leaves, 1 inch to 2½ inches long, broad-elliptic to obovate and with tapering short stalks, are finely-spine-toothed and paler on their strongly-veined undersides than above. In drooping racemes up to 2¼ inches long with stalks up to ⅓ inch long, the ¼-inch-wide flowers are borne, and are succeeded by egg-shaped, bright red fruits that remain attractive for a long period. The Korean barberry is hardy in southern New England.

Especially handsome in fruit, **B. gilgiana** is a deciduous native of China, hardy in southern New England, that attains a height of about 6 feet and has foliage that turns brilliant red in autumn. It has shortly-hairy, grooved stems. The elliptic or elliptic-ovate, toothless or distantly-toothed leaves, dull green and sometimes slightly-hairy on their upper surfaces and grayish-green and pubescent beneath, are ¾ inch to 1½ inches long. About ¼ inch across, the bright yellow flowers are in pendulous, crowded, spikelike racemes, including their hairy stalks 1½ to 2¼ inches long. The slightly waxy-coated, dark red fruits, ⅓ inch long or slightly longer, are egg-shaped.

Other deciduous barberries worth cultivating include *B. circumserrata* and *B. beaniana*, both Chinese. The former is hardy in southern New England, the latter about as far north as New York City. Upright in growth, and some 3 feet tall, **B. circumserrata** has very stout, rigid, furrowed stems. Its oblongish-rounded to obovate leaves, which in fall turn brilliant red, are ¾ inch to 1½ inches long and have usually densely-spiny-toothed margins. Their undersides are waxy-whitish-gray. The yellow flowers, in clusters of two to five, are ½ inch wide and have stalks up to 1 inch long or slightly longer. Yellowish-red, the oblongish fruits are approximately ½ inch long. Varieties *B. c. occidentalior* and *B. c. subar-*

mata have petals notched at the apexes. The spines of the latter, shorter than those of the species, are less than ½ inch long. At its maximum 6 to 8 feet tall, and fairly densely-branched, **B. beaniana** has hairless young shoots. Its narrowly-elliptic to ovate-elliptic leaves, ¾ inch to 2 inches long, are spiny-toothed, dark green above and waxy-grayish and finely-hairy beneath. The flowers, ¼ inch across, are in broad, loose panicles of ten to twenty, ¾ inch to 1½ inches long on stalks up to ½ inch long. The dark red berries have dense, waxy, mauve coatings. This species retains its foliage late into the fall. It is hardy about as far north as New York City.

A deciduous barberry not hardy in the north, but worth cultivating in milder climates, is **B. potaninii**. This Chinese has stalkless, narrowly-obovate leaves up to 1¼ inches long, with few spiny teeth, and paler on their undersides than above, that become purplish in fall. It reaches a height of 5 to 8 feet, and bears ⅓-inch-wide flowers in racemes. The roundish fruits are bright red.

Deciduous in some regions, semievergreen in other, milder ones, **B. concinna** is hardy about as far north as New York City. Native to the Himalayas, it is compact and ordinarily is 1 foot to 3 feet tall, but a form that attains 5 to 7 feet is described. This species has stout hairless stems. Its oblong-ovate leaves are up to 1¼ inches in length and have a few marginal spiny teeth. They are slightly lustrous and dark green above, very waxy-white on their undersides. In fall the foliage turns red. The globose flowers are solitary, bright yellow, and ½ inch in diameter. The oblongish berries are red and ⅙ to ¾ inch long.

Evergreen barberries are choice landscape furnishings, but unfortunately few are as thoroughly hardy in the north as could be wished. Several, however, succeed in reasonably sheltered locations in southern New England, among them *B. wisleyensis*, a kind commonly misidentified as *B. triacanthophora*, which name properly belongs to a species not known to be in

Berberis sargentiana

cultivation. About 4 feet in height, **B. wisleyensis** has grooved stems and linear-lanceolate leaves up to 2¼ inches long by ⅓ inch wide with a few spiny teeth. Above they are dullish gray-green. Their undersides are bluish-gray. The longish-stalked, whitish-tinged-red blooms are in clusters of two to six. The blue-black, ellipsoid berries are coated with wax. The origin of *B. wisleyensis* is uncertain. It quite possibly is a chance hybrid between *B. triacanthophora* and *B. gagnepainii*.

Almost, perhaps quite as cold-resistant, **B. julianae** is a vigorous species from central China 6 to 7 feet tall and of dense habit. It has stems with stout, three-parted spines, and oblanceolate to obovate, spine-toothed leaves 2 to 3 or rarely 4 inches long, dark green above, paler on their lower sides. In clusters of fifteen to twenty, the ⅓-inch-wide flowers are succeeded by ⅓-inch-long, bluish-black, oblongish berries heavily coated with whitish wax. Similar and sometimes confused with *B. ju-*

lianae, Chinese **B. sargentiana** may be distinguished by its young shoots being red or reddish and not angled, its flowers being in clusters of usually not more than eight and not having a conspicuous style, and by its fruits having little or no waxy coating. The hardiest evergreen barberry, this survives at the Arnold Arboretum near Boston, Massachusetts.

Three other evergreen natives of China are *B. gagnepainii*, *B. verruculosa*, and *B. candidula*. All are hardy in southern New England. Erect-branched and 4 to 6 feet in height, **B. gagnepainii** is hairless, and has narrowly-ovate leaves 2 to 4 inches long. In the wild, variations in the leaves occur and botanists recognize varieties based on this and other features. Commonly cultivated as *B. gagnepainii* is **B. g. lanceifolia,** which differs from the typical species in having narrower leaves and slightly larger flowers. The leaves are up to 2 inches long and have wavy, spiny-toothed margins. Their upper sides are dullish gray-green,

Berberis julianae

Berberis julianae (flowers)

Berberis julianae (fruits)

their undersides yellowish-green. The bright yellow flowers, nearly ½ inch across, are in clusters of three to seven. Oblongish, bluish-black, and covered with a heavy grayish-white waxy coating, the berries are about ⅓ inch long. Densely-warty stems are a characteristic of very beautiful **B. verruculosa,** which is up to 5 feet tall and has rigid, arching branches and shining dark green leaves with a glaucous waxy coating on their undersides that may disappear as the leaf ages. The leaves are pointed-obovate-elliptic and ½ to 1 inch long. The golden-yellow flowers never open fully. They are nearly globular, occur singly or in pairs, and are more than ½ inch across. The fruits are egg-shaped, glaucous violet-black, and ⅓ inch long. Closely related **B. candidula** differs in having narrower leaves with very strongly revolute margins and a whiter coating on their undersides that remains throughout the life of the leaf. Also, the fruits are slightly smaller. This species, 2 to 3 feet tall, forms attractive, dense, rounded bushes, with arching stems and leaves up to 1½ inches long. Its solitary, bright yellow blooms, slightly more than ½ inch across, are succeeded by waxy, pale gray berries about ⅓ inch long.

Berberis candidula

Nearly unique in being an evergreen shrub from south of the equator that is hardy in southern New England, **B. buxifolia** is a variable species native to southern South America. It is most commonly represented in cultivation by variety **B. b. nana,** which differs from the typical species in being compact and about 2 feet in height and width, rather than of looser growth and 6 feet tall and wide. It has grooved stems, arching and pubescent, and obovate to elliptic leaves, ⅓ to 1 inch long, that are toothless but spine-tipped. The flowers, usually solitary and orange-yellow, are followed by dark purple, waxy berries. In cultivation the dwarf variety rarely flowers or fruits.

Another lovely southern South American, unfortunately not hardy in the north, **B. darwinii** was discovered by Charles

Berberis darwinii

Darwin in 1835 while on the famous voyage of the *Beagle.* It is represented by several varieties. Typically it is densely-branched and 5 to 10 feet tall. Its young stems are hairy. The small, holly-like leaves are obovate, up to ¾ inch long, more or less six-sided, with usually three-pointed apexes, and spiny-toothed, with rich glossy green upper surfaces and much paler yellow-green lower ones. In pendulous racemes, 2 to 4 inches long, of generally ten to thirty, the orange-yellow flowers are succeeded by dark blue-purple waxy berries ¼ inch long.

A few hybrids among barberries that retain their foliage throughout the year are deserving of attention. One, *B. stenophylla,* is the offspring of *B. darwinii* and *B. empetrifolia.* Although this graceful shrub will live outdoors in sheltered locations in southern New England it does not prosper north of Washington, D.C. Very beautiful and up to 10 feet tall, **B. stenophylla** has long, slender, arching branches, the younger parts of which have short hairs, and clusters of linear-elliptic, spine-tipped leaves up to 1 inch long, with markedly revolute margins. Their upper surfaces are glossy dark green, beneath they are a much lighter yellow-green. In short racemes or clusters of seven to fourteen along shoots of the previous year's growth are borne the golden-yellow flowers ⅓ inch in diameter. The blue-black globular fruits have a waxy coating and are ¼ inch across. As a parent *B. stenophylla* has produced a group of barberries known as stenophylla hybrids, which are generally intermediate between *B. darwinii* and *B. empetrifolia,* but in some cases show the influence of another, unknown parent.

A most excellent evergreen, hardy in southern New England, and about 4 feet tall, **B. chenaultii** is a hybrid between *B. verruculosa* and *B. gagnepainii.* It has less warted stems than *B. verruculosa* and more arching stems and shorter, glossier leaves than *B. gagnepainii.* Its stems are slightly black-warted. The leaves are narrowly-oblong, ¾ inch to 1½ inches in length, and

spiny-toothed. They are glossy above, glaucous on their undersides, and distantly spiny-toothed. Solitary or in groups of up to three, the flowers are about ½ inch across. The fruits, borne sparingly, are dark blue.

Semievergreen, the vigorous hybrid **B. mentorensis** withstands dry hot summers and cold as low as −20°F. Its parents are evergreen *B. julianae* and deciduous *B. thunbergii,* both outstanding species. The hybrid was raised in Ohio. About 7 feet in height, it has grooved stems, and elliptic-

Berberis stenophylla

Berberis stenophylla (flowers)

Hedge of *Berberis stenophylla*

ovate leaves ¾ inch to 1¾ inches long and slightly spiny-toothed. They are paler beneath than on their upper surfaces. The yellow flowers, solitary or in pairs, are followed by dull red, ellipsoid fruits.

Garden and Landscape Uses. Both deciduous and evergreen barberries are deserving of attention from gardeners, not only because of their beauty, but because they are employable in exceedingly practical ways. All except the lowest form barriers unbroachable with impunity. For such purpose they may be planted as informal or formal hedges or in narrow belts or groups as circumstances permit and fancy dictates. Another use, for which *B. thunbergii* is especially adaptable, is to hold and furnish slopes and banks. Dwarf *B. t. minor* can be clipped to form a hedge only a few inches high to surround flower beds and other areas. In addition to such utilitarian placements, barberries can be employed as ornamentals in shrub borders and foundation plantings, grouped in beds, and as single specimens. The low kinds make neat additions to rock gardens.

The evergreens are generally most valued for their habits of growth and handsome foliage, and some, such as *B. darwinii* and *B. stenophylla*, for the beauty of their blooms. Their fruits are less showy than those of many deciduous kinds. For the most part they are not brilliantly colored and generally are eaten by birds or soon drop. Deciduous barberries are esteemed for their good forms, for the fresh green of their young foliage and for the rich colors the leaves of many assume in fall. The displays of bloom of some are pleasing, although in this feature they cannot compete with such showy shrubs as forsythias, mock-oranges, and azaleas. In fruit, deciduous barberries are often very attractive and the berries of some remain for extended periods. This is especially true of *B. thunbergii*.

To give of their best barberries need a soil of at least moderate fertility and moisture. This is especially true of the evergreens. Although some deciduous kinds, such as *B. thunbergii*, persist under less favorable conditions they have a tendency to look unhappy when so located. In coldish climates it is important that the evergreens be afforded shelter from winter winds, otherwise they are likely to become bedraggled and perhaps partly killed back by spring. Barberries are sun-lovers, but will stand at least part-day shade.

Cultivation. To keep them in good condition it may be necessary to prune barberries to shape and to thin out overcrowded branches from time to time, immediately after flowering or in late winter. Yet, except with formal hedges that need shearing one or more times a year, pruning should as a rule be kept to a minimum. Bushes that through neglect are overgrown or ungainly may be recondi-

tioned and revitalized by cutting them back very severely, even to within a foot or so of the ground, in late winter and, if necessary, thinning out crowded branches, and by following this drastic treatment by fertilization and making sure that they are well watered during dry periods in the summer that follows.

Propagation is easily accomplished by seeds sown outdoors, in cold frames, or in greenhouses. But because of the enthusiasm with which many kinds hybridize, seeds gathered from plants growing in barberry collections are extremely likely to result in plants not true to the seed parent type. The surest plan is to multiply these shrubs vegetatively, by summer cuttings under mist or in cold frames or greenhouse propagating benches, by layering, or with a few kinds, by taking off rooted suckers.

Diseases and Pests. Barberries are not commonly seriously affected by diseases although they are occasionally subject to anthracnose, rust, root rots, wilt, and a virus mosaic. Among insect and like pests aphids, scales, nematodes, and the barberry webworm, a small black caterpillar with white spots that ties together the leaves and stout tips, sometimes infest them. The last is controlled by spraying with a stomach poison insecticide.

BERCHEMIA (Berch-èmia)—Supple Jack. About twelve species of this genus of the buckthorn family RHAMNACEAE are recognized. They are deciduous, twining, woody vines, natives of North America, Asia, and Africa. Their leaves are opposite, their small, greenish-white flowers in terminal and axillary clusters. The generic name is believed to honor the eighteenth-century botanist Count von Berchem.

Berchemias have bisexual flowers with a calyx of five triangular lobes and five petals narrower than the sepals and with their edges incurved around the filaments (stalks) of the stamens. The style is short and not divided. The berry-like fruits consist of a hard stone surrounded by leathery flesh. None is reliably hardy far north, but the native American supple jack persists outdoors in a sheltered location at The New York Botanical Garden, and the Asian *Berchemia racemosa* lives outdoors in southern New England.

The supple jack (**B. scandens**) inhabits wet woodlands and swamps from Virginia to southern Illinois, Florida, and Texas. It is a high climber with strong, flexible stems and ovate to oblong, stalked leaves, up to 2½ inches in length, rounded or wedge-shaped at their bases, that have nine to twelve pairs of conspicuous, ascending, parallel veins. The leaves are hairless and often have wavy, but toothless margins. The pyramidal clusters of tiny blooms are up to 2 inches long, the bluish-black fruits ¼ inch long or slightly longer.

Asian kinds cultivated are **B. kulingensis**, of China, a greenish, flowered, 10-foot-tall vine with pointed, ovate to broadly-lanceolate leaves about 2 inches long, and flower clusters 3 to 8 inches long, and **B. racemosa**, of Japan and Taiwan, which tends to be a sprawling, tangled, lax shrub rather than a pronounced vine. It has ovate leaves with seven to nine pairs of veins, somewhat heart-shaped bases, and rather glaucous undersides. The leaves are up to 2½ inches long. The flowers are greenish and in clusters up to 6 inches long. The fruits, at first green, then red, become black when ripe; they are ¼ inch long and quite attractive. Variety *B. r. variegata*, with its younger leaves marked with creamy white, is known.

Garden and Landscape Uses and Cultivation. As foliage vines, berchemias are graceful and attractive, but cannot compete as display plants with the many vines that have showier flowers or fruits. Their flowers make little or no display, but the fruits have some ornamental value. These vines should be afforded supports around which their slender stems can twine and for their best development need a sunny location. Any ordinary garden soil is appropriate; best results are had in moist soils. Berchemias are easily raised from seeds, cuttings of semimature shoots in late summer or early fall, root cuttings, and by layering. Established specimens need no particular care other than pruning to keep them tidy and shapely.

BERGAMOT is *Citrus aurantium bergamia*. Wild-bergamot is *Monarda fistulosa*. Bergamot mint is *Mentha piperita citrata*.

BERGENIA (Bergèn-ia). There are only six species of *Bergenia*, but there are many hybrids, and in gardens, kinds are often misidentified. The genus belongs in the saxifrage family SAXIFRAGACEAE and is sometimes grown under its now outmoded names of *Saxifraga* and *Megasea*. The name commemorates Karl August von Bergen, a German botanist, who died in 1760. Bergenias are natives of vast territories in temperate Asia from the Himalayas northward into Siberia, Mongolia, China, and North Korea. In their homelands, individual kinds, notably *B. crassifolia*, grow in immense numbers, covering areas of up to tens of square miles. Some grow up to altitudes of 15,000 feet or over. They occupy evergreen and deciduous woodlands, rocky slopes, screes, stream beds, and alpine meadows, in dry and wet soils.

Bergenias are stout herbaceous perennials with thick rhizomes or rootstocks covered with the remains of dead foliage. They have alternate, large, undivided, lobeless, thick, smooth leaves that in regions of fairly mild winters are more or less evergreen. The leaves may have gland-tipped teeth or be smooth-edged. Their

Bergenia cordifolia

stalks are short and expanded at their bases to form sheaths. The flowers are in showy clusters on stout, erect stalks with curved branches that do not rise high above the foliage. They are pink, red, or white and have five sepals, five broad petals, ten stamens, and two pistils. The fruits are capsules. In their native lands some bergenias, including B. purpurascens and B. ciliata, are used medicinally, and teas are made from B. crassifolia, B. cordifolia, B. stracheyi, and B. ciliata. The roots of B. ciliata are the source of a spirit and a dye, and B. crassifolia is used for tanning.

Among the species, **B. cordifolia** and **B. crassifolia** are so similar that they perhaps should be regarded as variants of one spe-

Bergenia crassifolia

cies. They are vigorous plants up to about 1½ feet tall and have smooth, shining leaves without hairs fringing their edges. The leaves of the first-named are orbicular with rounded or heart-shaped bases, those of the latter are proportionately longer, ovate to obovate, and at their bases rounded to wedge-shaped. The leaves of B. cordifolia

are usually green, those of B. crassifolia mostly reddish or purplish and more upright. These kinds also differ somewhat in their flowers. The blooms of B. cordifolia are on spreading branches and are held horizontally or erect, those of B. crassifolia are more or less nodding and form more compact clusters on shorter branches. The blooms of B. crassifolia usually have narrower, less spreading, and deeper colored petals than those of the first. Variety B. crassifolia pacifica, has broader leaves than typical B. crassifolia, sometimes they are nearly as broad as long. Also, its blooms are more intensely colored and usually have longer petals. A distinct horticultural variety of B. cordifolia is B. c. purpurea, which has thick leaves, redder than those of the typical species, and larger, deep purplish-red flowers nearly circular in outline and with orbicular, overlapping petals. The stalks of its flower clusters, which are carried above the foliage, are intensely red. Intermediates between this variety and B. cordifolia are cultivated.

Another commonly cultivated species, **B. purpurascens** differs from B. crassifolia in having larger and redder flowers that expand later than those of most bergenias. Often its petals are dark purplish-red, but pink-flowered forms are known. The blooms are nodding. The elliptic to ovate-elliptic leaves are up to 10 inches long, often obscurely-toothed and frequently have their margins, especially at their bases, fringed with hairs. They are glossy, commonly conspicuously suffused with purplish-red, and have upper surfaces mostly convex. The plant known as B. delavayi belongs here. The species B. ugamica is very similar to and is likely botanically identical with B. purpurascens. Other kinds that belong here are those that have been known in gardens as B. beesiana, B. pauciflora, and B. yunnanensis.

More dwarf than other bergenias and with wedge-shaped to obovate, erect leaves, ordinarily less than 8 inches long and about 4 inches wide, with rounded or acute bases, **B. stracheyi** is distinct from all other species except B. ciliata. Its leaf margins are usually hairy and finely-toothed. The flower clusters are compact and may or may not extend beyond the leaves. They have few branches. The blooms are fragrant and mostly nodding. They are white, yellowish, pinkish, or pink, and normally expand as late as those of B. purpurascens, although an earlier blooming form is known.

Similar to B. stracheyi, but differing in having spreading, orbicular, obovate or elliptic leaves that are hairy, often densely and coarsely so, broader than they are long, and 1 foot long or longer, is **B. ciliata**. Its leaf margins are toothed and fringed with hairs. Most of its leaves live for only one season; overwintering leaves are always very small. The flower clusters are loose and have spreading branches. The erect or horizontally spreading flowers are slightly fragrant and white or sometimes tinged pink. This sort is the earliest species to bloom. The variety B. c. ligulata (syn. B. ligulata), differs from typical B. ciliata in having no hairs on the surfaces of its leaves, but their margins are fringed with hairs.

Hybrid bergenias, which are numerous and difficult to identify, include many splendid garden plants. Hybrids of B. cordifolia and B. crassifolia have been given the names B. media and B. aemula. They are often low plants, intermediate between the parents, with compact flower clusters displayed above the leaves. Also, B. crassifolia has been hybridized with B. purpurascens to produce intermediate progeny. Offspring of B. cordifolia and B. purpurascens are named **B. smithii.** They bloom late and have smaller, relatively broader-petaled and often paler-colored flowers and broader leaves than B. purpurascens. The commonest hybrid cultivated is **B. schmidtii,** the parents of which are B. ciliata and B. cras-

Bergenia schmidtii

sifolia. This fine sort has large evergreen, broadly-obovate leaves fringed with hairs, and ample clusters of rather large, erect, rose-pink flowers produced in early spring and sometimes also in fall. The flower clusters may slightly exceed or be a little shorter than the leaves. A hybrid of *B. ciliata* and *B. stracheyi* is **B. spathulata**. It differs from the first-named parent in having narrower leaves and glandular hairs on the stalks of the flower clusters and from *B. stracheyi* in its longer leafstalks and more erect flowers. Hybrids of *B. ciliata* have also been obtained with *B. purpurascens* and *B. cordifolia*. The progeny of the first-mentioned cross have white or pink flowers, glandular branches to the flower clusters, and narrower leaves than *B. schmidtii*. The hybrids of *B. ciliata* and *B. cordifolia* have usually white flowers carried on tall stalks well above the foliage and short-stalked, orbicular leaves fringed with hairs. Among the best hybrid bergenias that have been given fancy horticultural names are *B.* 'Abendglut' with rich purple-pink blooms, *B.* 'Bressingham Bountiful' with flowers of fuchsia pink and dark green foliage, *B.* 'Morgenrote' with red-pink blooms, and *B.* 'Silberlicht', one of the best white-flowered kinds and one that blooms later than most.

Garden and Landscape Uses. Bergenias are grand plants for use as large-scale groundcovers and in clumps where bold foliage effects are desirable. They are beautiful both in leaf and flower and are among the easiest of plants to grow. They are splendid for rocky slopes where the soil is not unduly shallow and can be appropriately placed by watersides if the ground is sufficiently high so their roots are not in constantly saturated soil. They associate well with masonry, thrive under city conditions, and are long-lived. Their foliage and flowers are effective for flower arrangements. Bergenias thrive best in light shade, but grow well in full sun if the soil is never allowed to dry out completely. Most kinds are perfectly hardy, but some, such as the Himalayan *B. ligulata* and *B. stracheyi*, are not reliably so in a climate harsher than that of southern New England.

Cultivation. Bergenias thrive in any ordinary garden soil but attain their finest dimensions only when afforded a deep, fertile one that is never excessively dry. They are easily increased by division, in spring, immediately after flowering, or in early fall. They also can be readily propagated by seeds but, because they hybridize so freely, seeds are likely to give rise to variable progeny. Individual clones of these plants are often sterile to their own pollen, they set seeds only if pollinated by another clone of the same kind or if they receive pollen from a different sort. The seeds ripen in early summer and may be sown immediately or later. They retain the power

to germinate for at least a year. Once established, the plants may be undisturbed for many years. Only when they show signs of exhaustion by their foliage being less robust and smaller and their flowers being fewer and of inferior size, is it necessary to dig them up, divide and replant them in soil that has been improved by spading, mixing in organic matter such as compost or peat moss, and fertilizing. Established clumps benefit from an application of fertilizer each spring, but care should be taken not to use one that provides too great an amount of nitrogen. To do so encourages lush foliage growth with few blooms.

BERGERANTHUS (Berger-ánthus). Berger's flower is the literal meaning of the name of this genus of low South African succulents. It is composed of the name of the distinguished German botanist Alwin Berger and the Greek *anthos*, a flower. Bergeranthuses are *Mesembryanthemum* relatives belonging in the carpetweed family AIZOACEAE. Not hardy, there are a few more than twenty species.

Bergeranthuses are stemless or nearly stemless and have fleshy roots. Their densely-crowded, smooth, gray-green, opposite leaves are somewhat joined at their bases. Alternate pairs are at right angles to each other. The leaves may be unmarked or have minute dark dots. The flowers, which open in late afternoon, have the characteristic daisy-like aspect of *Mesem-*

bryanthemum, but unlike daisies are single blooms rather than compound heads of many florets. They are ¾ inch to 2 inches in diameter, solitary or few on usually longish stalks. Each bloom has usually five stigmas. The fruits are capsules. Bergeranthuses much resemble *Hereroa*, but the latter has rough-surfaced leaves and differs in technical details of the flowers.

Forming cushions up to 2 inches high, **Bergeranthus jamesii** has slender, somewhat sword-shaped, tapered, bluish-green or glaucous, incurved leaves ¾ to 1 inch long with flat upper surfaces and keeled lower ones. Its lavender-pink flowers are about ¾ inch wide. Attractive, free-flowering *B. multiceps* suckers freely, forming clumps of rosettes each with six or eight spreading, often slightly recurved, three-angled, pointed leaves ¾ inch to 2 inches long and ⅓ inch wide or slightly wider. They are bluish-green and without obvious dots. The yellow blooms, tinged reddish on their undersides, are on stalks up to 1½ inches long, and are about 1¼ inches wide. Similar in habit, **B. scapiger** has dark green leaves 2½ to 4½ inches long and ⅓ to nearly ¾ inch wide. One of each pair of leaves, which are marked with fine dots and have thin, horny edges, is shorter than the other. Up to 2 inches in diameter, the golden-yellow blooms, red-tinged on their outsides, are up to three or four together on flattened stalks about 1½ inches in length. Resembling the last and with three-angled, pointed leaves, keeled

Bergeranthus jamesii

toward their ends and rarely scarcely more than 2 inches in length and ¼ inch wide, **B. vespertinus** bears its yellow flowers three to five together on stalks up to 1 inch long or slightly longer. They are yellow and about 1 inch wide.

Garden Uses and Cultivation. Attractive, easy to grow, and generous of bloom, bergeranthuses are suitable for collections of succulent plants. During their winter season of rest they should be kept dry, at other times watered moderately, never excessively. As with all plants of the *Mesembryanthemum* society they resent poor drainage, and excesses of moisture either in the soil or the atmosphere. Full sun is required. Propagation is easy by division and seeds. For further information see Succulents.

BERGEROCACTUS (Bergero-cáctus). The only species of *Bergerocactus* of the cactus family CACTACEAE is by conservative botanists included in *Cereus*. Endemic to southern California, its coastal islands, and Baja California, the name of this genus pays tribute to a distinguished student of cactuses and other succulents, Alwin Berger, Superintendent of the famous La Mortola Gardens at Ventimiglia, Italy. He died in 1931.

Forming dense clumps of ascending and sprawling, branched stems 1 foot to 2 feet tall and several feet in diameter, **B. emoryi** (syns. *Cereus emoryi*, *Echinocereus emoryi*) is bushy and spreading. Its stems 1¼ to 2½

inches thick are 8 inches to 2 feet long and semiprostrate to erect; they have fifteen to twenty-five very low, slightly lumpy ribs with closely-spaced clusters of ten to thirty needle-like, golden-yellow to brownish spines of which the central ones, up to four in number, are the longer, up to nearly 1½ inches. Pale yellow and about ¾ inch long and wide, the flowers have short tubes furnished with scales with wool in their axils. The spherical, very spiny fruits are a little over 1 inch in diameter.

Garden Uses and Cultivation. This is a collectors' plant. It thrives in sandy soil under conditions that suit *Echinocactus*. For other details see Cactuses.

BERLANDIERA (Berland-ièra). Native to the United States and Mexico, this genus of the daisy family COMPOSITAE consists of about six species. Its name commemorates the Swiss botanist Jean Louis Berlandier, who died in 1851. Berlandieras are hirsute, perennial herbaceous plants with alternate, toothed or pinnately-lobed leaves, and daisy-type, hemispherical, yellow flower heads each usually with five to twelve rays. The ray florets are fertile, those of the disk sterile.

Native from Kansas to Mexico, **B. lyrata** has white-hairy, pinnately-lobed leaves and attains a height of about 8 inches. Its flower heads are solitary and about 1 inch in diameter. Of little horticultural importance, this and other species of *Berlandiera*

are occasionally transferred to gardens and may be grown in collections of native plants. They accommodate easily to conditions that approximate those under which they grow naturally, and may be propagated by seeds.

BERMUDA. As part of the names of plants the word Bermuda appears in the following: Bermuda-buttercup (*Oxalis pes-caprae*), Bermuda-cedar (*Juniperus bermudiana*), Bermuda grass (*Cynodon dactylon*), Bermuda lily (*Lilium longiflorum*), Bermuda olive-wood bark (*Cassine laneana*), and Bermuda palmetto (*Sabal bermudiana*).

BERRIED TREES AND SHRUBS. See Ornamental-Fruited Plants.

BERRISFORDIA (Berris-fòrdia). Named in honor of G. Berrisford, who discovered it in 1931, this genus of one South African species belongs to the carpetweed family AIZOACEAE.

A small perennial of the *Mesembryanthemum* relationship so numerous in its homeland, **Berrisfordia khamiesbergensis** forms mats or clusters of pebble-like plant bodies. Each is of two pairs of opposite, fat leaves the inner pair nearly hidden, the outer approximately ½ inch long, united for one-half or more of their lengths, gray-green and conspicuously roughened with little knoblike warts or teeth especially toward their flattish apexes, and with limy incrustations there. The very short-stalked,

Bergerocactus emoryi

Bergerocactus emoryi (flowers)

bright pink flowers, daisy-like in aspect, but unlike daisies single blooms instead of heads of many florets, protrude but slightly from between the leaves. About ¾ inch across, they open late in the day. The fruits are capsules.

Garden Uses and Cultivation. These are as for closely similar *Conophytum,* from which *Berrisfordia* differs in the warts or little teeth on its leaves. For further information see Succulents.

BERRY. Botanically, a berry is a fleshy or pulpy fruit containing one or more seeds, but unlike drupes no true stone or stones, that results from the development of a single pistil and does not split to disperse its seeds. Typical berries are thin-skinned. They include blueberries, currants, gooseberries, grapes, and tomatoes. Other berries with thicker, hard rinds, are identified as pepos. Here belongs cucumbers, squash, and watermelons. Yet a third group, distinguished as hesperidiums, are citrus fruits. These have interiors separated into distinct segments and easily peelable, soft leathery rinds.

Some fruits colloquially called berries, notably blackberries, loganberries, mulberries, raspberries, and strawberries, are not berries in the botanical sense. Those mentioned are multiple fruits consisting of more or less coherent aggregations of druplets (small drupes). Many plants commonly referred to as berried trees and shrubs have fruits that are not berries. Such include cotoneasters, hawthorns, hollies, pyracanthas, and viburnums.

BERTEROA (Bert-eròa). One of the eight species of this Old World close relative of *Alyssum* is naturalized in North America and occasionally cultivated. As a garden plant it is of minor importance. The genus was named in honor of the Italian physician and botanist Giuseppe Bertero, who died in 1831. It belongs in the mustard family CRUCIFERAE and differs from *Alyssum* in having deeply-notched petals.

A hardy annual or biennial, *Berteroa incana* is up to 2 feet in height and has stiffly erect stems that, like the oblanceolate to lanceolate leaves, are hoary-gray with stellate (star-shaped) hairs. The small, white flowers have four very deeply two-lobed petals and are in terminal, elongating racemes. The fruits are flattened elliptic, pubescent pods.

Garden Uses and Cultivation. To provide variety in semiwild parts of the garden and flower beds, *B. incana* has limited use. It is easily raised from seeds sown in fall or spring where the plants are to bloom. The seedlings are thinned to 4 to 6 inches apart. This plant succeeds in ordinary soil, but it is most attractive when it grows dwarf and compact in soil of poorish fertility. It needs full sun.

BERTHOLLETIA (Berthol-lètia)—Brazil Nut. Brazil nuts, well known in northern markets, are the product of *Bertholletia excelsa,* one of the largest trees native to northern South America. The genus, variously considered as consisting of one or two species, belongs in the lecythis family LECYTHIDACEAE. It is confined to South America and the West Indies. It was named in honor of the French chemist Louis Claude Berthollet. It is of no horticultural importance except insofar as specimens are sometimes grown in educational collections of plants useful to man.

The Brazil nut tree (*B. excelsa*) is up to 100 feet in height and has oblong, leathery, wavy-margined leaves that may be 2 feet long and spikelike racemes of yellow flowers, each with a calyx that divides into two parts as the bloom opens, six petals, and a hooded, massed group of many stamens, the upper ones sterile. The seeds (nuts) are packed, twelve to twenty-four together, as compactly as the segments of an orange, inside a hard, thick-shelled, cannonball-like fruit 6 inches in diameter. They ripen about fourteen months after the flowers fade. The fruits are harvested after they have dropped to the ground, and collecting them entails some danger. Serious injury can result from being hit by a falling fruit. The nuts are released from the fruits by slicing off the tops of the fruit with a machete. A single tree may yield more than one-half ton of nuts.

Garden Uses and Cultivation. In tropical greenhouses small plants may be grown in pots or tubs of well-drained, fertile soil. A minimum temperature of 60 to 65°F, high humidity, and shade from strong summer sun are the chief requirements. Pruning, needed to restrict them to size, and repotting are done in late winter.

Propagation is by fresh seeds sown in a temperature of 70 to 80°F in porous soil kept evenly moist.

BERTOLONIA (Bertolón-ia). Ten species of low herbaceous plants of the rain forests of Brazil and Venezuela belonging to the melastoma family MELASTOMATAEAE constitute *Bertolonia.* The name commemorates the Italian botanist Antonio Bertoloni, who died in 1869. The cultivated kinds are esteemed for their beautifully-colored foliage.

Bertolonias have short, somewhat succulent stems, and opposite, often toothed, ovate-heart-shaped or pointed-elliptic leaves with five to eleven prominent veins. Their white, pink, or purple-red flowers are in terminal clusters. Each has an inflated three-winged or three-angled calyx, five petals, ten stamens, and one style. The fruits are capsules. The genus is closely related to *Sonerila* of tropical Asia and hybrids, named *Bertonerila,* have been raised between the two genera. It is also closely allied to the New World genus *Triolena* from which it differs in its flowers having a minute appendage to the rear at the base of each anther but no forward-pointing projections.

Bertolonias in cultivation include *B. houtteana,* a sort of horticultural origin that does not produce viable seeds. Stemless or nearly so, it has ovate to elliptic, rich olive-green leaves narrowly-striped with rose-pink along the chief veins and spotted or cross-veined with the same color. The flowers are pink. Brazilian *B. maculata* has leaves with white-bristly hairs. They are dark olive-green suffused with lighter green and marked with silvery-green along the center in a continuous or broken stripe. Its flowers are rose-

Bertolonias in a tropical garden

Bertolonia houtteana

Bertolonia maculata

nor is pinching required. When the pots or pans are filled with healthy roots the application of dilute liquid fertilizer at weekly intervals is highly beneficial. Cuttings rooted in late winter or early spring and kept growing without check make good specimen plants by fall. Bertolonias are also easily raised from seeds sown in pots of sandy peaty soil in a temperature of 75°F. The seeds should be scarcely covered with soil. Ideal growing conditions are provided if the relative humidity is above 75 percent and the temperature range 70 to 90°F. Good light, with shade from strong, direct sun is required.

pink. Another native of Brazil, **B. marmorata** has handsome, quilted, dark green leaves suffused with moss-green and with a clear white stripe marking each of the five longitudinal veins. Its flowers are pink. A variety, *B. m. aenea,* has bronzy-reddish-green leaves without stripes. The

bell jar. They can be successfully cultivated in terrariums in warm rooms. When so grown they benefit from being lighted artificially; the lighting is also of great help in displaying the plants effectively. Bertolonias revel in loose, lumpy soil that contains an abundance of organic matter such as rough leaf mold and coarse peat moss. The pots or pans (shallow pots) in which they are planted must be well drained, for although constantly moist soil is necessary, if it is compacted to the extent that air is not freely admitted the roots do not penetrate it freely and are likely to die. For the most effective display bertolonias should be planted 3 or 4 inches apart in fairly shallow containers 6 to 8 inches in diameter. They can also be grown singly in 3- or 4-inch pots. They usually need no staking,

Bertolonia lowii

Bertolonia marmorata

kind cultivated under the apparently botanically unacceptable name *B. mosaica* has broader white stripes along its veins than *B. marmorata* and may be a variant of that species. Very attractive **B. sanguinea,** also a native of Brazil, has bronzy leaves, red on their undersides, with a central silver band. Kinds with names apparently without botanical validity are cultivated as *B. wentii* and *B. lowii.* With corrugated blackish-green leaves suffused with copper and scattered silver markings and white hairs, **B. wentii** has purple undersides. In **B. lowii** the foliage is bronze and the flowers pink. Other plants sometimes cultivated as *Bertolonia* belong in *Bertonerila, Monolena,* and *Triolena.*

Garden Uses and Cultivation. Bertolonias can be grown only in high temperatures under very humid conditions. Even in tropical greenhouses they usually benefit from the additional protection afforded by being grown in a glass case or under a

Bertolonia marmorata aenea

BERTONERILA (Bertoneríl-a). This genus consists of hybrids between *Bertolonia* and *Sonerila*, both members of the melastoma family MELASTOMATACEAE. Its name is composed of parts of the names of its parent genera.

Bertonerilas are pretty foliage plants, in aspect intermediate between their parents. Best-known **Bertonerila houtteana**, often called *Bertolonia houtteana,* has large, ovate, moss-green leaves, with carmine-red veins and spots. The undersides of the leaves are wine-purple. Named hybrids of European origin that may be cultivated are 'Comte de Kerchove', 'Madame de Brezetz', 'Madame Cahuzae', 'Madame Pynaert', and 'Madame Treyeran'. The uses and cultivation of these plants are as for *Bertolonia,* but because viable seeds are not produced, *B. houtteana* is propagated by cuttings.

BERZELIA (Ber-zélia). The brunia family BRUNIACEAE, to which *Berzelia* belongs, is endemic to South Africa. It consists of a dozen genera and some seventy-five species of heathlike shrubs, eleven of which are berzelias. The name honors the famous Swedish chemist Jöns J. Berzelius, who died in 1848.

Berzelias have small, closely-set, spirally-arranged, spreading or erect leaves, and crowded spherical or ovoid heads of small flowers. The blooms have four- or five-lobed calyxes, the same number of petals and protruding stamens as calyx lobes, and one awl-shaped style. The fruits are small and do not split to release the seeds.

An erect shrub, 3 feet tall or sometimes taller in gardens, with softly-hairy young shoots and leaves, **B. lanuginosa** is of rather feathery appearance. Its slender

Berzelia lanuginosa

branchlets are clothed with up-pointing, threadlike leaves, triangular in section, and ¼ inch long. The flower heads, about ⅕ inch across, are many together in flattish to longer panicles that face upward. They are cream in color when at their best in spring, but before midsummer begin to

change to dull brown, and from then until they drop are somewhat unsightly. This species attracts dogs and cats. With creamy-white flower heads about ½ inch in diameter **B. abrotanoides** is more showy than the last. Its stalkless leaves, up to ¼ inch long, are narrowly-ovate, and hairy or hairless.

Garden and Landscape Uses and Cultivation. As interesting ornamentals for gardens and landscapes in California and other warm, dryish regions, the species described have merit. They thrive under conditions that suit heaths (*Erica*), and blend well with them. Well-drained, somewhat acid soil and full sun are to their liking. Any pruning needed to keep the plants shapely is done as soon as blooming is through. Unless seeds are to be collected, faded flower heads should be removed as a measure of tidiness. Propagation is by seeds and cuttings.

BESCHORNERIA (Beschorn-èria). The ten species of Mexican herbaceous and subshrubby plants that constitute *Beschorneria* belong in the amaryllis family AMARYLLIDACEAE. They are related to *Yucca, Furcraea,* and *Agave.* The name commemorates Friedrich Wilhelm Christian Beschorner, a German botanist, who died in 1873.

Beschornerias have big tuberous rootstocks and basal rosettes of narrow-linear to lanceolate leaves, with prominent midribs. The leaves are thickish, but less succulent than those of agaves and furcraeas. Tough and pliable, and with very finely-toothed margins, they are without spines or prickles. The nodding, individually-stalked, tubular, cylindrical flowers are in tall panicles or racemes, the main stalks of which are decorated with large, showy, membranous, red or reddish bracts. The reddish or greenish corollas of the flowers have very short tubes and six petals (properly tepals) that spread but slightly. There are six stamens, shorter than the petals, and one style. The fruits are capsules. Beschornerias are often difficult to identify as to species.

The hardiest, and one of the best known species, **B. yuccoides** is essentially stemless. It has rosettes of about twenty gray-green, lanceolate leaves 1 foot to 1½ feet long by 2 inches wide, with rough undersides. The branchless flower stalks, 3 to 4 feet in height, have pendulous red branches and bright green blooms tinged with yellow, about 2 inches long. Other kinds that may be cultivated include **B. bracteata,** a stemless plant with twenty to thirty 1½- to 2-foot-long, gray-green leaves in each rosette. Above their broadened bases the leaves are about 1 inch wide. The reddish-brown flower stalks, 4 to 5 feet long, have blooms 1½ inches long that change from green to yellowish-red. Each rosette of **B. dekosteriana** (syn. *B. argyrophylla*) has fifteen to twenty leaves 2 to 2½ feet long and

Beschorneria yuccoides

2 to 2½ inches wide. They narrow gradually in both directions from their centers. The green flowers, 1½ inches long, are in broadly-pyramidal panicles.

Garden and Landscape Uses and Cultivation. Beschornerias are dry-country plants, with landscape uses similar to those of yuccas. They associate well with succulent plants and are quite impressive when in bloom. They are also appropriate for inclusion in succulent collections in large greenhouses and conservatories. They have the same cultural needs as *Agave,* but prefer a somewhat more fertile soil. None is hardy in the north, but *B. yuccoides* stands light frosts and is cultivated outdoors in the warmer parts of Great Britain. Specimens accommodated in large pots or tubs should be supplied with dilute liquid fertilizer during spring and summer. Propagation is by seeds. These plants do not form plantlets on their flowering stems as do many furcraeas and some agaves.

BESLERIA (Bes-lèria). This genus of the gesneria family GESNERIACEAE consists of 150 species, the majority subshrubs, but including some shrubs and some herbaceous perennials. In the wild it is confined to warm parts of the Americas and the West Indies. Its name commemorates Basilius Besler, apothecary of Nuremberg, Germany, who died in 1629.

Beslerias have sometimes partly vining stems and usually hairy shoots and foliage. Their opposite, stalked, undivided leaves are commonly elliptic to oblanceolate, but sometimes lanceolate to oblanceolate. They are toothed or practically toothless. The flowers are in racemes sometimes so contracted that they resemble umbels. Usually they have colored calyxes cleft almost to their bases into five sepals, but sometimes united for more than one-half their lengths from their bases. Tubular, the corolla is white, yellow, orange, red, or spotted. There are five small corolla lobes (petals), four stamens, and often one staminode (rudimentary stamen). There is one style. The fruits are fleshy, white, orange, red, or purple berries.

Native to the West Indies, *Besleria lutea* is a variable low shrub, a tree up to 20 feet tall, or a vining plant, with stems hairless when mature and lustrous. The short-stalked, toothed leaves, ovate to elliptic-oblong, are practically hairless above, but hairy, at least on the veins, on their undersides. They are up to 9 inches long by 4½ inches wide. The yellow to white flowers, ½ to ¾ inch long, appear to be in umbels or clusters without an evident common stalk. The fruits are red berries.

Besleria lutea

Garden and Landscape Uses and Cultivation. The species described is chiefly of interest to fanciers of gesneriads (plants of the gesneria family). For successful cultivation, a humid, warm environment, with shade from strong sun, is needed. In greenhouses a minimum night temperature in winter of 60°F is satisfactory, with an increase of ten to fifteen degrees by day. The soil should be well drained, fertile, and contain generous amounts of peat moss, leaf mold, or other decomposed organic matter. It must be kept evenly moist, but not soggy. Increase is easy by cuttings, leaf cuttings, and seeds.

BESSERA (Bés-sera)—Coral Drops. Only one species of these three North American bulb plants of the lily family LILIACEAE appears to be in cultivation. The generic name commemorates a professor of botany, Dr. W. S. J. G. von Besser, who died in 1842. These plants have all-basal foliage and flower stalks that terminate in umbels of nodding, individually slender-stalked, somewhat bell-shaped, red and white or rose-purple and white blooms. There are six perianth segments (petals or more properly tepals) and six stamens joined at their bases for more than one-half their length into a staminal cup or corona. The free parts of the stalks of the stamens are hairy. The slender style is capped by a small, slightly three-lobed stigma. Bes-

seras are closely allied to *Brodiaea* from which they differ in having red or reddish flowers with protruding stamens.

Each bulb of *Bessera elegans* produces two or three leaves up to 2 feet in length, and usually several flower stalks. The latter are slender, about 2 feet tall, and carry a cluster of up to twelve loosely-arranged blooms that are about 1 inch long and bright red, with green keels centered along the outsides of the petals. Rarely, an individual with all-white flowers occurs. The stamens have gray-blue anthers, yellow pollen, and are considerably longer than the petals, the staminal cup is whitish and about ⅓ inch high. The style is red. This species is Mexican.

Bessera elegans

Garden and Landscape Uses. Although coral drops is not accounted hardy outdoors in the north, it has wintered successfully, well protected, at the base of a south-facing greenhouse wall at The New York Botanical Garden and bloomed in late summer. Generally it must be considered hardy only in climates considerably milder than that of New York City. It is a handsome and graceful plant for summer display, useful for sunny flower beds and borders where the soil is agreeably porous and fertile. It is also attractive for pot culture in greenhouses and window gardens.

Cultivation. Where hardy, the bulbs of coral drops may remain in the ground all year. Elsewhere they may be dug after the first fall frost and stored over winter in a dry place where the temperature is about 50°F. They are planted in spring about 3 inches deep and 3 or 4 inches apart. No special aftercare is needed. For pot culture the bulbs may be planted about 3 inches apart in 6-inch containers in February or March. Fertile, porous soil is needed, and careful watering until the pots are well filled with roots. Then, more generous supplies may be given as well as occasional applications of dilute liquid fertilizer. A

night temperature of 50°F with a daytime rise, depending upon the brightness of the day, of five to fifteen degrees, are suitable. After flowering, watering is continued as long as the foliage is green, then is gradually tapered off, and finally discontinued. During their dormant season the bulbs are kept quite dry.

BE-STILL TREE is *Thevetia peruviana*.

BETA (Bè-ta)—Beet, Swiss Chard. One of the six species of this Mediterranean region group of the goosefoot family CHENOPODIACEAE is the ancestor of cultivated edible beets, ornamental beets, sugar beets, Swiss chard, and mangles (used as stock feed). It is *Beta vulgaris*. The genus, the name of which is the Latin one, *beta*, for the beet, includes annuals, biennials, and perennial herbaceous plants. They are hairless and have alternate, undivided or nearly undivided leaves and spikeform panicled flower clusters. The urn-shaped blooms are not showy. They have five perianth lobes and five stamens. They are usually in clusters of two or more and wither to form corky balls that contain two to several seeds.

The wild beet (**B. vulgaris**), an annual or a perennial, is a native of the coasts of Europe. It has swollen roots and leaves up to 8 inches long. Its erect flower stems rise to a height of up to 6 feet. Variety *B. v. maritima* is lower, has smaller foliage, and its roots are usually not swollen.

Varieties of beets and Swiss chard with highly colored, usually red foliage are sometimes grown in flower gardens as ornamentals. For this purpose they are treated as annuals, either by sowing the seeds in spring where the plants are to remain and thinning the seedlings to 9 inches to 1 foot apart, or by sowing six weeks or so earlier indoors and transplanting the seedlings to flats or individual small pots and from these to the garden. These plants need well-drained, fertile soil, full sun, and sufficient water to keep the soil always moderately moist. They provide colorful displays of foliage throughout the summer and are useful for ornamental bedding, grouping at the fronts of flower borders, and for using in porch and window boxes. For the cultivation of vegetable crops belonging in this genus see Beet, and Chard or Swiss Chard.

BETEL NUT PALM or BETLE NUT PALM is *Areca catechu*.

BETEL PEPPER is *Piper betle*.

BETHLEHEM-SAGE is *Pulmonaria saccharata*.

BETONICA. See Stachys.

BETONY. See Stachys. For wood-betony see Pedicularis.

BETULA (Bétu-la)—Birch. The genus *Betula* consists of sixty species of deciduous trees and a few shrubs of the north temperate and arctic regions. They belong to the birch family BETULACEAE. The name is the classical Latin one. Members of this genus are elegant, fast growers, but are not long lived. They are admired for their grace, for their often handsome barks, and for the lively beauty of their foliage. For long men have recognized a kind of feminine quality about birch trees in contrast to the masculinity associated, for example, with oaks.

Birches have alternate, usually ovate or rhomboidal, conspicuously-stalked, toothed and sometimes lobed leaves. The minute male and female flowers are borne on the same tree, the former in pendulous catkins developed in early spring from large buds formed at the ends of the twigs the previous fall, the latter in conelike, erect catkins called strobiles that originate further back on leafy twigs. This mode of flowering demonstrates the close relationship of birches and alders (*Alnus*), which belong in the same family. From alders, birches differ in the scales of their female catkins being thin and three-lobed and falling early. Those of alders are five-lobed, woody, persistent. In both genera the tiny flowers are petal-less. Birch flowers are wind pollinated. As soon as the seeds (tiny nuts) ripen the strobiles disintegrate, and the light, winged seeds are blown for long distances thus encouraging wide dispersal of the species.

In addition to admiring the aesthetic qualities of birch trees, man has made more practical uses of these "ladies of the woods." Every schoolboy knows that the Indians of North America constructed their canoes, covered their wigwams, and made utensils of birch bark, also that they used it as writing paper. The bark employed was that of the canoe or paper birch (*B. papyrifera*), which is tough, durable, and impervious to water. From the bark of local kinds having similar qualities, inhabitants of northern Europe and northern Asia fashion roofing shingles. There, too, good uses are made of the twiggy branches. They are considered prime material for making besoms (brooms) and until fairly recently, the birch-rod was regarded with favor, except by those at the receiving end, as an instrument of chastisement to persuade delinquent and disobedient boys of the error of their ways. Birch wood is one of the finest fuels, but it rots quickly when exposed to moisture unless properly treated with preservatives. Then it may become sufficiently resistant to decay to be used for railroad ties. Birch lumber is much used for flooring, furniture, interior trim, doors, and plywood. From the barks of the cherry birch or sweet birch (*B. lenta*) and Eurasian *B. pubescens* and *P. pendula* essential oils used in medicines and for flavoring are distilled. This oil is also used in the preparation of Russian leather and is responsible for its distinctive odor. From the sugary saps of these kinds and some others an alcoholic beverage called birch beer or birch wine is made.

The canoe or paper birch (*B. papyrifera*) is among the loveliest of the conspicuously white-barked birches. This most obvious and attractive element of North America's northern forests and mountains is native from the Atlantic to the Pacific, from Labrador to Alaska to Pennsylvania and Nebraska. Its stout, creamy-white trunk and spreading branches from which the bark peels in thin strips have a compelling beauty that all admire. Unhappily, in public places vandals often give evidence of their interest by stripping off great bands of bark. But this they do too to other white-barked birches, a sad commentary on the effectiveness of the teaching of conservation. The paper birch, usually not more than 70 feet tall, reaches an extreme height of 125 feet and a maximum trunk diameter of about 3 feet. It has a comparatively small, pyramidal crown, with the branches of older specimens somewhat pendulous.

It is most effective when restricted to a single trunk. The twigs are pubescent when young and often slightly glandular. The strobiles are 1¼ to 2 inches long. Its leaves are squared or slightly heart-shaped at their bases. In fall they become bright yellow. This species is much less susceptible to infestations of bronze birch borer than the European birches. Varieties of the paper birch include these: *B. p. cordifolia*, indigenous from Labrador to Minnesota, is a shrub or small tree with leaves hairy on the veins beneath. *B. p. kenaica*, of coastal Alaska, has orange-tinged bark and shorter strobiles than the typical species. *B. p. neoalaskana*, which ranges from Alaska to Saskatchewan, has densely-resinous-glandular twigs and bark from whitish to reddish-brown. *B. p. occidentalis*, of the northwestern United States, attains a height of 120 feet and has bark from whitish to orange or dark brown.

The gray birch of North America (*B. populifolia*) is not especially aptly named. Its most prominent feature is its chalky-white bark with prominent triangular dark markings where branches join the trunk. Characteristically, it develops a clump of several extraordinarily pliable trunks. These, under snow or ice, may bend without fracturing until their tips touch the ground. When relieved of the burden they usually gradually recover their former positions, but some never do so entirely and crooked trunks are common. The gray birch attains a height of 20 to 40 feet and has glossy, triangular-ovate leaves, which are slightly sticky when young. It is a graceful, but short-lived species that thrives in dry soils, but prospers also in wetter ones. Botani-

Betula papyrifera

Betula papyrifera (trunk)

Betula papyrifera (male catkins)

Betula populifolia

Betula nigra

been segregated and named. Unfortunately this sort and its varieties are very susceptible to infestations of bronze birch borer as a result of which their entire tops are likely to be killed. Native of Europe and Asia Minor, the European white birch is pyramidal and older specimens at least have somewhat pendulous branches. The

Betula pendula

cally it is most closely related to the European white birch from which it differs in being a smaller and usually multi-trunked tree and in having leaves with longer points. Also its bark is chalky-white rather than creamy-white. Gray birch often colonizes abandoned fields and burnt-over areas. Unfortunately it is very susceptible to infestations of the foliage-marring birch leaf miner. Varieties include *B. p. laciniata,* with pinnately-lobed leaves, *B. p. pendula,* with drooping branches, and *B. p. purpurea,* with leaves that become purple when they first unfold, but turn green later.

The river or black birch (**B. nigra**) is a graceful tree with an ovoid crown. It grows by stream and lake sides from Massachusetts to Florida and Kansas. Up to 100 feet in height, and with paper-thin, ragged, flaking, reddish-brown bark, it has oblong-oval leaves up to 5 inches long, heart-shaped at their bases and double-toothed at the margins. Above they are dark green. Their undersides are whitish with hairs on the veins. The strobiles are one-half as long as the leaves. This is a tree for moist or wet soils. It prospers even where the site is inundated for several weeks of the year.

Sweet or cherry birch (**B. lenta**) has common names that refer to two useful identifying features. Its young twigs when chewed have an agreeable, sweetish, aromatic flavor and its dark, reddish-brown bark resembles that of cherry trees. The double-toothed leaves turn golden in fall. They are oblong-oval, up to 5 inches long, heart-shaped at their bases, and tapered at their tips. The strobiles are about one-third as long as the leaves. Sweet birch is very handsome and has the finest fall color of all birches. It attains a height of about 80 feet and at maturity is round-topped. As a young specimen it is pyramidal.

Yellow birch (**B. alleghaniensis** syn. *B. lutea*) has aromatic twigs. It is up to 100 feet in height and may have a trunk 4 feet in diameter. The bark of young specimens is shining yellowish-gray or light orange and peels in plates that remain attached and are rolled at their margins. On older trunks the bark is darker and peels and coils like untidy wood shavings, but remains attached. The leaves of the yellow birch are reddish when they first unfold, more or less oval, and 4 to 7 inches long. They have pale hairs on the veins beneath. The strobiles are one-third as long as the leaves. This is an important timber tree, but has less to recommend it as an ornamental than several other kinds. It is native from Newfoundland to Georgia and Tennessee.

European white birch (**B. pendula**) is almost as lovely as the paper birch, and since it has been in cultivation and observed by plantsmen for many centuries, several distinct horticultural varieties have

white bark of the trunk peels in thin layers. The warty branchlets have resinous glands, but are not pubescent. The leaves, usually wedge-shaped at their bases, turn yellow in fall. The strobiles are not more than 1¼ inches long. These are varieties of European white birch: *B. p. dalecarlica* has deeply-lobed leaves. *B. p. fastigiata* forms a narrow, columnar head of erect branches. *B. p. gracilis* has pendulous branches and finely-dissected leaves. *B. p. purpurea* has purple foliage. *B. p. tristis* has a rounded crown of pendulous branches. *B. p. youngii* has an irregular crown and slender, pendulous branchlets.

Betula alleghaniensis

Betula alleghaniensis (bark)

Begonia, a Rieger hybrid

Begonia imperialis variety

Begonia rex-cultorum variety

Begonia rajah

Betula pendula, in fall

Betula populifolia

Betula populifolia, lower parts of trunks

Popular biennials: (a) Sweet williams

(b) Foxgloves

Billbergia 'Fantasia'

Betula pendula fastigiata

Another Eurasian species, one that extends from northern and central Europe to Siberia, is **B. pubescens.** This differs from *B. pendula* in its young branches being densely-pubescent and entirely without glands and the bark on the lower parts of its trunk being dark, rough, and warty. This kind differs from the canoe birch in having leaves usually wedge-shaped at their bases and strobiles not over 1¼ inches long. The leaves are slightly pubescent beneath, at least when young. Variety *B. p. urticifolia* has leaves more or less lobed or double-toothed, slightly pubescent above, more densely beneath.

Outstanding Oriental white birches are **B. platyphylla** (syn. *B. mandshurica*) and its varieties. The typical species is a native of Manchuria and Korea. It grows 60 to 70 feet in height and has ovate to triangular-ovate leaves usually slightly heart-shaped or squared at their bases. The young twigs are covered with resinous glands and may have tufts of hair in their vein axils be-

Betula pendula gracilis

neath. Japanese white birch (*B. p. japonica*) is similar, but has broader leaves usually with tufts of axillary hairs beneath. Its bark is often pinkish. One of the best varieties is *B. p. szechuanica*, which has bark that is white, silver-gray, or pinkish and leaves that are broadly wedge-shaped to rounded at their bases and densely glandular-dotted beneath. This variety has wide-spreading branches and blue-green foliage that retains its color until late in the fall and then turns yellow.

Of very distinct appearance, the Chinese paper birch (**B. albo-sinensis**) is rather rare. It attains a maximum height of 100 feet and develops a rounded crown. Its most striking feature is its bright orange to orange-red bark that peels in sheets as thin as tissue paper and makes a particularly effective display in winter. Its lustrous branchlets are without pubescence, but are

Betula pubescens

sometimes glandular. The leaves, dark yellow-green above and paler and glandular on their under surfaces, are rounded to squared or more rarely somewhat heart-shaped at their bases. Variety *B. a. septentrionalis,* which attains a height of 100 feet and may have a trunk 5 feet in diameter, has dull yellowish-orange to orange-brown bark, reddish-brown, more densely-glandular branchlets, and tufts of hairs in the leaf axils beneath. The typical species is a native of central and western China, the variety of western China.

Somewhat similar to the American river birch, **B. davurica** thrives in North America and will grow in drier soils than best suits its native American counterpart. Native of northeastern Asia and Japan, it has a wide crown of spreading branches and attains a height of about 80 feet. On the lower parts of the trunks of old specimens the bark is rugged and deeply fissured into irregular blackish squares. Elsewhere it is purplish-brown and peels, but often remains attached in untidy masses of small thin curled flakes. The twigs of this birch

are glandular and pubescent. The leaves are narrow-ovate or rhombic-ovate with wedge-shaped or squared bases. At first the veins on both upper and lower sides are pubescent, but those of the upper side lose most of their hair as the leaves age. Japanese cherry birch (*B. grossa*), although very similar to American cherry birch, is less attractive. It has a more open crown and its trunk often divides into two or three stout secondary trunks. The bark is dark, almost black, and fissured on old specimens. The leaves are ovate to oblong-ovate and usually slightly heart-shaped at their bases. They are coarsely-doubly-serrate and have silky hairs on the veins beneath. The glabrous twigs are aromatic like those of the American cherry birch. In its native forests this is an easy means of identification. It attains a height of about 80 feet.

Monarch birch (**B. maximowicziana**) is a handsome Japanese with large leaves and gray or orange-gray bark that peels in papery flakes. It is considered by some to be the most beautiful of birches. Its reddish-brown, warty twigs are glabrous and its double-toothed, broad-ovate leaves, pubescent on young trees and almost hairless on older ones, and up to 6 inches long, are deeply-heart-shaped at their bases. This birch, which has strobiles 2 to 3 inches long in racemes of two to four, has a maximum height of about 100 feet. It grows rapidly and vigorously in North America. With peeling bark, a white trunk, and slender orange-reddish branches, round-headed, 60-foot-tall **B. ermanii** of northeastern Asia and Japan is decidedly ornamental. It leafs in spring before other kinds and has usually glandular, but not downy twigs and unequally-coarsely-toothed, triangular-ovate leaves up to 4 inches long, slightly heart-shaped at their bases and pubescent on the veins beneath. It has barrel-shaped strobiles 1 inch to 1¼ inches long. Variety *B. e. subcordata* has less glandular branchlets, and leaves commonly more decidedly heart-shaped at their bases. It leafs later in spring than *B. ermanii*. Very graceful **B. costata**, a northeastern Asian species sometimes 100 feet tall, has rather narrow to oblong-ovate, pointed leaves about 3 inches long and grayish-brown bark that peels in papery flakes. Its strobiles are about ¾ inch long.

Other birches include these: **B. fruticosa,** of northeast Asia, is a shrub up to 12 feet tall and rare in cultivation. It is similar to *B. humilis,* but its leaves are more distinctly and more finely serrated. **B. glandulosa** is a shrub 6 feet in height, native from Newfoundland to Alaska and southward to New York and California. It has glandular-resinous twigs and broad-elliptic or orbicular leaves. **B. humilis** is a Eurasian shrub up to 10 feet tall, with glandular-pubescent twigs and ovate to elliptic leaves usually more or less irregularly-toothed. **B. nana** is a shrub not more than 2 feet in height

Betula nana

that has nearly orbicular or obovate leaves usually up to ½ inch long. It is a native of Alaska, northern Asia, and northern Europe. **B. occidentalis** (syn. *B. fontinalis*), the water birch, is native from Alaska to Oregon and Colorado. It is up to 40 feet tall, usually has several trunks and a broad crown and pendulous branches. Its leaves are broad-ovate and up to 2 inches long. **B. pumila**, which ranges from Newfoundland to New Jersey and Minnesota, is a shrub up to 15 feet tall. Its young twigs are densely-tomentose. About 1 inch long, its round to obovate leaves are, when young, densely-pubescent on their undersides.

Garden and Landscape Uses. Birches bring to northern landscapes an elegance unsurpassed by any other tree. Used singly or in groups, they have a light, airy effect and produce a dappled shade that does not impede the growth of many other kinds of plants beneath them. Because of this, they are ideal trees for providing light shade for rhododendrons and other evergreens that benefit from a little protection from the fiercest rays of the sun as well as for other plants, such as primulas, trilliums, and anemones, that flourish better in diffuse sunlight. Many such are rock garden plants, and birches, well located in a rock garden, serve the dual purpose of assuring just the right amount of shade for plants that need it and of adding an illusion of mountain terrain that is an objective of most rock gardeners. This they do effectively because as a group they are characteristic of alpine and boreal regions and the subconscious of even those with no great detailed knowledge of the distribution of Earth's flora sense this. Birches with handsomely-colored barks are seen to best advantage against a background of such evergreens as hemlocks. This is particularly true of the white-trunked kinds, but in planting them ample space should be allowed between the background and the birches for the growth of each, because beautiful birches crowded against lovely evergreens are a disturbing sight to the sensitive gardener. Another excellent landscape use for birch trees is to employ them with discrimination to give shade to lawns and windows that are a little too sunny for comfort. Here, too, sufficient space for the ultimate growth of the tree should be allowed because birches are better and more effective if they do not have to be pruned drastically. For wet soils the river birch (*B. nigra*) is one of the most satisfactory trees. In considering birches as possibilities for planting one must always remember that they are comparatively short-lived. A life-span of fifty years is probably average for most, that of the gray birch (*B. populifolia*) is perhaps not ordinarily over twenty years. Another factor to bear in mind is their susceptibility to insect attack. The destructive bronze birch borer is especially troublesome to the European white birch (*B. pendula*). The gray birch is particularly susceptible to infestations of the birch leaf miner, which can be kept in check only by regular and timely spraying. But as a group birches are hardy. Most sorts thrive in New England. Some, including *B. alleghaniensis*, *B. grossa*, *B. lenta*, *B. nana*, *B. nigra*, *B. occidentalis*, *B. papyrifera*, *B. pendula*, *B. populifolia*, and *B. pubescens* are hardy in just about as severe climates as any tree will survive. Thus, *B. pendula* and *B. pubescens* are the only trees native to Iceland.

Cultivation. All birches thrive in any well-drained soil of moderate fertility and average moisture content, the kind of soil that grows reasonably good vegetables and flowers. Some, such as the gray birch and *B. pendula*, prosper in comparatively infertile, dryish, sandy soils. Yet others, notably the river birch, the cherry birch, and the yellow birch, flourish in moister soils. Birches should be set out as small specimens. When large they do not recover well from transplanting and, as a result of loss of vitality often incident to such moving, they are likely to become infested with borers. Birches require no regular pruning. Any necessitated by storm damage or other reason is better done in early summer than in winter or spring because cuts do not heal quickly and those made before the foliage is fully developed and the spring rise of sap has subsided somewhat are likely to "bleed" (ooze sap) for an indefinite period.

Whenever possible birches should be propagated from seeds, which are freely produced and germinate satisfactorily if sown on the surface of fine sandy peaty soil kept evenly moist. The seed is small and should be covered with soil very shallowly or not at all, merely pressing it into the surface and covering the pot or flat with glass or polyethylene plastic kept shaded until growth begins. Spring is an appropriate sowing time for most kinds, but the seed of the river birch should be sown as soon as it is ripe in July. Birch seed started outdoors should be raked shallowly into the surface and the seed bed covered with brushwood to ensure a little shade and protection. The seeds should be sown rather thickly because the percentage of viable ones is usually fairly small. Grafting rarer kinds onto young potted understocks in the greenhouse in winter is the most satisfactory way of assuring their increase. They can also be budded outdoors in summer. Some kinds can be rooted from leafy cuttings under mist propagation in summer and some by layering outdoors.

Diseases and Pests. Birches are subject to leaf spots, leaf blisters, leaf rust, canker, fungus die-back disease, and wood-decay fungi. Their most serious pests are the bronze birch borer, leaf miner, leaf skeletonizer, aphids including the witch-hazel cone-gall aphid, catkin bug, and seed mite gall.

BETULACEAE—Birch Family. About 150 species of dicotyledons arranged in six genera constitute this family of deciduous trees and shrubs. Some botanists favor splitting the group into three and name the segregate genera *Carpinaceae* and *Corylaceae*. The natural distribution of the birch family is through most temperate and subarctic parts of the northern hemisphere to as far north as trees grow, in tropical mountains, and in South America to as far south as Argentina. The lumber of some kinds is of considerable commercial importance. Oil of betula obtained from twigs of birches smells and tastes like wintergreen and is used in tanning Russian leather. Edible nuts are produced by hazels (*Corylus*).

Members of the birch family have alternate, undivided, toothed leaves with parallel lateral veins, and unisexual blooms with both sexes on the same plant. Male flowers are in slender, pendulous catkins, one to three in the axil of each scale. Each consists of two to ten stamens and a minute, rudimentary perianth or none. Female flowers are pendent or erect, more or less conelike catkins with one to three flowers, with or without minute perianths, and with two styles. The fruits are nuts or nutlets. Cultivated genera are *Alnus*, *Betula*, *Carpinus*, *Corylus*, and *Ostrya*.

BIBLE PLANTS. An understandable interest exists about plants referred to in Holy Scriptures and scholars have given much attention to studying and identifying them. The kinds that are mentioned are not always those to which we give the same names today. When the Bible was first translated into English the translators, theologians unfamiliar with the native vegetation of the Holy Land or of other plants known to ancient peoples there, interpreted the Hebrew and Greek plant names contained in the texts they worked with as those of kinds they knew in England, and so errors of identification occurred. The lilies of the field were almost surely not lilies. They most probably were *Anemone coronaria*. And so, about these and many other plants of the Bible some doubt exists about their identification. Complications arise because the biblical text often employs one name for more than one kind of plant. Nevertheless, many of the plants mentioned can be pinpointed with certainty.

The majority of the plants to which references are made in the Bible are chiefly utilitarian. Trees, spices, and edible vegetables receive more attention than flowers of decorative value only. Yet the latter are not wholly neglected, as witness the lilies of the field. And some ornamentals were surely grown in the gardens of the wealthy and the powerful.

Collections of Bible plants are sometimes made for display and educational purposes. The sorts here listed are fairly available in cultivation. The biblical names used, the titles of the books of the Bible, and the reference chapters and verse numbers are those of the King James Authorized Version. Other translations differ slightly in details. For a very complete account of Bible plants consult "Plants of the Bible" by Harold N. and Alma L. Moldenke.

Almond (Genesis 43: 11. Exodus 25: 33–36. Numbers: 17: 1–8. Jeremiah 1: 11) is the almond. Aloes (John 19: 39) may refer to *Aloe barbadensis* or *A. perryi*. Anise (Matthew 23: 23) is dill (*Anethum graveolens*). Apple (Proverbs 25: 11. Song of Solomon 2: 3 and 5, 7: 8, 8: 5) is probably the apricot. Barley (Exodus 9: 31. Deuteronomy 8: 8. Job 31: 40. John 6: 9 and 13) is barley. Beans (II Samuel 17: 27–28. Ezekiel 4: 9) is the broad bean (*Vicia faba*). Bitter herbs (Exodus 12: 8. Numbers 9: 11), probably this

Plants of the Bible: (a) Bitter herbs, chicory (*Cichorium intybus*)

reference is to chicory, dandelion, endive, lettuce, sorrel, and similar salad plants. Bulrush (Exodus 2: 3 and 5. Isaiah 18: 2. Isaiah 58: 5) is *Cyperus papyrus*. Camphire (Song of Solomon 1: 14 and 4: 13) is *Lawsonia inermis*. Cassia (Exodus 30: 23–24.

Ezekiel 27: 19) is *Cinnamomum cassia*. Cedar tree (II Samuel 5: 11. I. Kings 4: 33. I Chronicles 22: 3–4. Psalms 92: 12. many other references) is cedar of Lebanon (*Cedrus libani*). Chestnut tree (Genesis 30: 37.

(b) Cedar of Lebanon (*Cedrus libani*)

Ezekiel 31: 8. Ecclesiasticus 24: 14) is probably the oriental plane (*Platanus orientalis*). Cinnamon (Exodus 30: 23. Proverbs 7: 17. Revelation 18: 13) is *Cinnamomum verum*. Coriander (Exodus 16: 31. Numbers 11: 7) is *Coriandrum sativum*. Corn (Genesis 42:

(c) Coriander (*Coriandrum sativum*)

1–33. Exodus 22: 6. Mark 2: 23. Acts 7: 12) is wheat. Crown of thorns (Matthew 27: 29. John 19: 2) is probably Christ-thorn (*Paliurus spina-christi*). Cucumbers (Numbers 11: 5. Isaiah 1: 8) are cucumbers. Cummin (Isaiah 28: 25 and 27. Matthew 23: 23) is *Cuminum cyminum*. Dove's dung (11 Kings 6: 25) is probably *Ornithogalum umbellatum*. Ebony (Ezekiel 27: 15) is *Diospyros ebenaster* and *D. melanoxylon*. Fig (Genesis 3: 7. Deuteronomy 8: 8. Matthew 7: 17–20. Mark 11: 13 and 20. Luke 6: 44. Many other references) is the fig (*Ficus carica*). Fir (11 Samuel 6: 5. 1 Kings 5: 8 and 10. Isaiah 60: 13) is probably the Aleppo pine (*Pinus halepensis*). Garlick (Numbers 11: 5) is garlic (*Allium sativum*) or the onion (*A. cepa*). Go-

(d) Dove's dung (*Ornithogalum umbellatum*)

(e) Fig (*Ficus carica*)

pher wood (Genesis 6: 14) is probably *Cupressus sempervirens horizontalis*. Grapes (Genesis 40: 9–11. Deuteronomy 24: 21. Revelation 14: 18–20) are the European vine grapes (*Vitis vinifera*). Green bay tree (Psalms 37: 35) is *Laurus nobilis*. Hazel

(f) Green bay tree (*Laurus nobilis*)

(Genesis 30: 37) is the almond. Husks (Luke 15: 16) are the fruits of the carob (*Ceratonia siliqua*). Ivy (Maccabees 6: 7) is English ivy (*Hedera helix*). Leeks (Numbers 11: 5) are leeks or perhaps fenugreek (*Trigonella foenum-graecum*). Lentiles (Samuel

(g) Lilies *(Anemone coronaria)*

(j) Olive *(Olea europaea)*

23: 11. Ezekiel 4: 9) are lentils. Lilies (Matthew 6: 28–30. Luke 12: 27–28) are probably *Anemone coronaria.* Lilies (Song of Solomon 5: 13) is *Lilium chalcedonicum.* Lily (Hosea 14: 5. Ecclesiasticus 39: 14 and 50: 8) is probably *Iris pseudacorus.* Lily-of-the-valleys (Song of Solomon 2: 1–2 and 16, 4:

ably *Brassica nigra.* Myrtle (Nehemiah 8: 15. Isaiah 41: 19 and 55: 13) is *Myrtus communis.* Nuts (Song of Solomon 6: 11) are English walnuts *(Juglans regia).* Olive (Genesis 8: 11. Deuteronomy 6: 11. Judges 9: 8–9. Luke 19: 29. 21: 37. Romans 11: 17 and 24. many other references) is the olive *(Olea*

europaea). Olive tree (I Kings 6: 23 and 31–33. I Chronicles 27: 28) is probably the Russian-olive *(Elaeagnus angustifolia).* Onions (Numbers 11: 5) are onions. Palm tree (Exodus 15: 27. Leviticus 23: 40. Psalms 92: 12–14. John 12: 13. Revelation 7: 9. many other references) is the date palm *(Phoenix dactylifera).* Paper reeds (Isaiah 19: 6–7) are *Cyperus papyrus.* Pomegranate (Exodus 39: 24–26. Deuteronomy 8: 8. I. Kings 7: 18 and 20. Joel 1: 12) is the pomegranate. Poplar (Genesis 30: 37. Hosea 4: 13) is probably the white poplar *(Populus alba).* Reed (II Kings 18: 21. Isaiah 19: 6. Ezekiel 29: 6–7. Matthew 11: 7) is *Arundo donax.* Rolling thing (Isaiah 17: 13) is *Anastatica hierochuntica.* Rose-of-Sharon (Song of Solomon 2: 1) is probably *Tulipa montana.* Rose plant (Ecclesiasticus 24: 14) is *Anastatica hierochuntica.* Sycamine (Luke 17: 6) is the mul-

(h) Lily-of-the-valley *(Hyacinthus orientalis)*

5, 6: 2–4) are probably hyacinths *(Hyacinthus orientalis).* Linen (Genesis 41: 42. Exodus 28: 5–6, 8, 15, 39, and 42. I. Chronicles 15: 27. Matthew 27: 59. John 19: 40, and many other references) is a produce of flax *(Linum usitatissimum).* Melons (Numbers 11: 5) are muskmelons or watermelons. Mulberries (I. Maccabees 6: 34) are *Morus nigra.* Mustard seed (Matthew 13: 31–32. Mark 4: 31–32. Luke 13: 19) is prob-

(i) Mulberries *(Morus nigra)*

berry (*Morus nigra*). Sycomore (I Kings 10: 27. I Chronicles 27: 28. Psalms 78: 47. Luke 19: 4) is *Ficus sycomorus.* Tree of knowledge (Genesis 2: 9 and 17) conjecturally is the apricot. Vine (Genesis 40: 9–11. Deuteronomy 8: 8. Psalms 80: 8–16. Matthew 26: 27–29. John 15: 1–6. Many other references) is the European grape vine (*Vitis vinifera*). Wheat (Genesis 30: 14. Exodus 29: 2. Deuteronomy 8: 8. John 12: 24) is wheat.

BIDENS (Bí-dens)—Tickseed or Stick-Tight or Bur-Marigold. Most of the 200 or perhaps more species that compose this cosmopolitan genus of the daisy family Compositae are too weedy in appearance to be admitted as ornamentals. A few are sometimes recommended, but in the main, even they cannot compete in attractiveness with the more popular members of the daisy family, such as *Cosmos* and *Coreopsis,* to both of which *Bidens* is so closely related that these genera practically merge. They share with *Coreopsis* the common name tickseed and are also called stick-tights and bur-marigolds. The name, from the Latin *bis,* two and *dens,* a tooth, refers to the bristles on the achenes (seeds).

Bidens are annuals, biennials, and hardy perennial herbaceous plants, with opposite, toothed, deeply-lobed, or variously divided leaves and solitary or clustered flower heads consisting of disk florets only or of disk and ray florets in the fashion of a daisy. The disk florets are yellow, the ray florets yellow or white. The former are fertile and bisexual, the latter sterile.

Inhabiting wet soils from Maine to Minnesota, Virginia, Alabama, and Texas, *B. aristosa* (syn. *Coreopsis aristosa*) is a hairless or slightly hairy annual or biennial 1 to 5 feet tall with pinnate or twice-pinnate leaves up to 6 inches long and with lobed or toothed margins. The flower heads have golden yellow ray florets ¼ inch to 1 inch long.   Native from Arizona to Guatemala,

B. ferulaefolia (syn. *Coreopsis ferulaefolia*) is an erect annual or a biennial 1 foot to 3 feet tall, with deeply-twice-pinnately-lobed leaves consisting of slender, small divisions. The flower heads, in loose clusters, have disk and ray florets and are on slender stems. They are ¾ inch to 1½ inches in diameter and bright yellow. Widely distributed in the American, African, and Asian tropics, *B. pilosa radiata* is a loosely-branched annual about 3 feet tall. Nearly hairless, it has leaves of three leaflets, or pinnate, and flower heads 1 inch to 1½ inches across, with a yellow center and five to nine spreading ray florets toothed at their apexes.

Garden Uses and Cultivation. The species described are suitable for flower beds and naturalistic areas. Like most bidens they succeed in any ordinary soil in sunny locations. They are easily raised from seeds.

BIDI-BIDI or NEW ZEALAND BUR. See Acaena.

BIENNIALS. Plants that are biennials require most of two growing seasons to progress from seeds to flowers. Then they set seeds and die. During the first year they make substantial growth and build up reserves of food in thick roots or in stems and abundant foliage. This to a large extent nourishes the following year's flowering. In addition to true biennials, gardeners find it convenient to grow as such a number of other plants including English daisies, pansies, polyanthus primroses, and sweet williams, which are technically perennials. Because they are generally raised as biennials these are included in this discussion.

Some biennials are completely hardy and may be grown out of doors at all times. Others, in severe climates, need the protection of a cold frame during the win-

ter and a few are suitable only for frost-free climates or greenhouses.

Choice of sowing dates is of great importance with all biennials. These should allow the plants to attain a good size before winter, but not to become so large that they tend to run to flower in the fall, nor to become so leafy and soft that they are likely to be killed in winter.

Sowing dates vary in different parts of the country. Because a week or two one way or the other may make a considerable difference, the best date to sow a particular biennial in your garden may differ by a week or more from the best date for a garden only a few miles away. Find the most favorable dates for your garden by experiment.

Biennials are all sown in the summer months. Sow them either in an outdoor bed or in a bed in a cold frame. Make sure the ground is not likely to wash or erode if heavy rains come. The bed should be level. Take care that it is not under the drip of trees. In any case, prepare the soil very well and scatter the seeds in shallow drills spaced 3 to 4 inches apart.

After sowing, protect the seedbed with lath shades or with burlap tacked to light wooden frames to raise it a few inches above soil level. Such protection is necessary for shade-loving biennials such as foxgloves and forget-me-nots and is desirable for others. Tiny seedlings are easily harmed by fierce summer sun. Do not keep glazed sash on cold frames at this time of the year, shades alone are necessary.

The seedbed must never become dry. Inspect it daily. When the young plants show above ground, gradually accustom them to stronger light if they are sun-loving kinds such as wallflowers. Begin by removing the shades both early and late and putting them in position only during the brightest part of the day. Then, after a few days, take them off altogether.

If the plants are kinds that need shade, leave the shades in place as long as necessary. The important thing is not to shade so heavily that the plants become "drawn," "leggy," or weak. Keep the seedbed weeded and lightly cultivated.

This sowing-in-a-special-seedbed technique is practically essential to success in raising biennials. Inexperienced gardeners sometimes sow their biennials in a patch in the perennial border or in the front of the shrub border or in some other place among other plants. It never works.

Not only must they have a good seedbed but you must also arrange for nursery beds (or cold frames) in which to grow them on. Biennials are grown to almost full size before they are transferred to the locations where they are to bloom. Rarely if ever will they develop satisfactorily if they are set out among other plants when small.

Garden uses of biennials vary according to kind. Low, hardy and near-hardy ones,

Bidens aristosa

Bidens pilosa radiata

Popular biennials: (a) Canterbury bells   (b) Foxgloves   (c) Sweet William

those that winter outdoors or with no more protection than a cold frame, are excellent for spring bedding either alone or in conjunction with spring-flowering bulbs. Taller kinds are useful in flower beds with perennials and perhaps annuals, for planting more informally in naturalistic areas, and as cut flowers. Nearly all the hardier kinds are very useful for late winter and early spring blooms in pots in cool greenhouses. The chimney bellflower, celsias, *Humea elegans,* and skyrocket can be grown from seed to flowering for summer bloom in greenhouses.

Popular biennials, including perennials commonly grown as biennials, are Canterbury bells (*Campanula*), English daisies (*Bellis*), English and Siberian wallflowers, (*Cheiranthus* and *Erysimum*), forget-me-nots (*Myosotis*), foxgloves (*Digitalis*), honesty (*Lunaria*), mulleins (*Verbascum*), pansies (*Viola*), polyanthus primroses (*Primula*), and sweet williams (*Dianthus barbatus*).

Biennials suitable for mild climates or greenhouses only include celsias, chimney bellflower (*Campanula pyramidalis*), *Humea elegans,* and skyrocket or scarlet-gilia (*Ipomopsis*).

BIFRENARIA (Bifren-ària). The Central and South American genus *Bifrenaria* of the orchid family ORCHIDACEAE comprises ten or eleven species of epiphytes (tree-perchers). Its name, from the Latin *bis,* twice, and *frenum,* a bridle, alludes to attachments of the pollen masses.

Bifrenarias form clusters, often large, of strongly-angled pseudobulbs from the apexes of which come the solitary, leathery leaves. The flowers are alone or few together on stalks that originate from the bottoms of the pseudobulbs. They have sepals and petals similar except that the bases of the lateral sepals extend backward to form a prominent spur. The lips, generally three-lobed, have toward their bases ridges or a distinctly callused area.

Blooming in spring and early summer, **B. harrisoniae** (syn. *Lycaste harrisoniae*) has pseudobulbs 2 to 3 inches tall and leaves

up to 1 foot long by 5 inches wide. The richly fragrant flowers, one or two on stalks about 2 inches long, are thick and waxy and approximately 3 inches in diameter. Except for the lip, which is reddish-purple to magenta-red with generally darker veining, the blooms are ivory-white to yellowish or greenish-yellow, sometimes with reddish staining at the apexes of the spreading, elliptic-oblong sepals and petals. The dorsal (back) sepal is smaller than the others and concave. The spur formed by the lateral petals is about 1½ inches long. The lip is three-lobed, with the center lobe very blunt, wavy-edged, notched, and having a hairy callus. The

large, curved, white column is club-shaped. This kind is native to Brazil. Similar in habit and also Brazilian, **B. inodora** (syn. *Lycaste inodora*), and despite its name with blooms that may be fragrant or not, has flowers up to 3 inches across. They have yellow-green or clear green sepals and brighter, but much smaller petals. The lip is white, yellow, or pink, often flushed with a deeper hue. This blooms from winter to summer.

Other kinds cultivated include these: **B. atropurpurea,** of Brazil, which flowers in early summer, has pseudobulbs about 3 inches in height and oblong-lanceolate to linear-lanceolate leaves up to about 10

Bifrenaria harrisoniae

inches in length. The very fragrant flowers, mostly in three- to five-flowered racemes about 3 inches long, have yellow-centered, wine-red sepals and petals and whitish or rose-pink lips. **B. aurantiaca** (syn. *Rudolfiella aurantiaca*) blooms in winter. Native to Guyana and Trinidad, it has slightly four-angled, somewhat flattened, egg-shaped pseudobulbs, in clusters and about 2 inches tall. Each has a solitary, short-stalked, narrow-elliptic leaf up to about 6 inches long by 2 inches wide. The flowers, six to fifteen loosely together on slender, erect or arching stalks that come from the bases of the pseudobulbs, are about 1¼ inches wide. They are orange-yellow spotted with purple, with a brighter yellow patch on the lip. **B. racemosa** (syn. *Stenocoryne racemosa*), a fall-blooming native of Brazil, has clustered, somewhat flattened, evidently-angled pseudobulbs about 2 inches long, each with one pointed-elliptic-lanceolate, lustrous, leathery leaf up to 6 inches long. The flower stalks are erect, up to 10 inches in height, and have four to ten, slightly-scented, yellowish or yellow blooms with red-veined, wavy-edged, white lips. They are about ¾ inch long. **B. tetragona,** of Brazil, has pseudobulbs up to 3½ inches tall and leaves that may attain lengths of 1½ feet. The approximately 3-inch-long racemes have usually three or four 2-inch-wide, richly-fragrant blooms with greenish sepals and petals streaked with purplish-brown or brown, and three-lobed lips, purple toward their bases. **B. vitellina** (syn. *Stenocoryne vitellina*) is a Brazilian similar to the last, but with rather shorter, five- to eight-bloomed stalks with orange-yellow flowers about ¾ inch long that open more widely than those of *B. racemosa*. The blooms have three-lobed, hairy lips blotched at their bases with deep purple.

Garden Uses and Cultivation. Bifrenarias are responsive to cultivation and flower readily. They are esteemed for the beauty, fragrance, and long-lasting qualities of their blooms. They succeed best in intermediate or even warm greenhouse temperatures under conditions that suit the warmth-loving species of *Lycaste*. Good light with shade from strong sun is required. Ample supplies of water and high humidity are needed during the period of active growth, but dank, stagnant atmospheric conditions are detrimental. When the new pseudobulbs have attained full size and maturity the plants are partially rested by removing them to a somewhat cooler and shadier location for several weeks. Root disturbance is abhorrent to bifrenarias. Because of this, repotting should not be done more often than is necessary. For further details see Orchids.

BIFRENLARIA. This is the name of orchid hybrids the parents of which are *Bifrenaria* and *Maxillaria*.

BIG TREE, CALIFORNIA. See Sequoiadendron.

BIGNAY is *Antidesma bunius*.

BIGNONIA (Big-nònia)—Cross Vine. Most of the many species formerly included in *Bignonia* of the bignonia family BIGNONI-ACEAE are now referred to other genera including *Anemopaegma, Campsis, Clytostoma, Cydista, Distictis, Pithecoctenium, Pyrostegia,* and *Saritaea*. The only one remaining is *Bignonia*, as that genus is accepted here, is by some botanists named *Anisostichus*. The name *Bignonia* commemorates Jean Paul Bignon, librarian to Louis XIV, who died in 1743. The name cross vine alludes to a cross-shaped bundle of wood tissue that becomes visible when a stem of this species is sliced through.

The cross vine (**B. capreolata** syn. *Anisostichus capreolata*) is an evergreen, peren-

Bignonia capreolata

nial, woody climber up to 60 feet tall, and a native of rich, moist woodlands from Maryland to Ohio, Missouri, Florida, and Louisiana. Its opposite leaves have a pair of, or rarely only one, ovate to oblong leaflets and a tendril the branches of which terminate in adhesive disks. There are often two stipule-like secondary leaflets. The stalked, trumpet-shaped to somewhat bell-shaped blooms, in clusters of up to five, have toothless or slightly five-toothed calyxes and 2-inch-long corollas with five spreading, rounded lobes (petals). On their outsides the corollas are deep orange to reddish. Inside they are of lighter orange

with reddish coloring in the throat. There are four developed stamens and sometimes a rudimentary one, a staminode. They do not protrude. The single style ends in a two-lipped stigma. The fruits are slender capsules 6 to 8 inches long containing seeds with broadly-winged sides.

Garden and Landscape Uses. Handsome in bloom, the cross vine is a splendid, vigorous ornamental, hardy approximately as far north as as a climber, but surviving as a creeping groundcover into southern New England. It is useful for clothing walls, fences, other supports, and banks.

Cultivation. No difficulties attend the cultivation of the cross vine. It is readily increased by seeds, cuttings, and layering. Pruning necessary to limit its spread and shorten branches that protrude too far from the supports may be done in spring.

BIGNONIACEAE—Bignonia Family. Many showy ornamentals belong in this chiefly tropical and subtropical family of 120 genera and 650 species of dicotyledons, collectively known as bignoniads. Among the best-known sorts are the African-tulip-tree, catalpas, jacarandas, tabebuias, and trumpet vines, and also the calabash tree (*Crescentia*) and sausage tree (*Kigelia*), both remarkable for their large gourdlike fruits. Some members of the family supply excellent lumber. Hardy species occur in the genera *Campsis* and *Catalpa*.

Bignoniads include many twining and stem-rooting woody vines as well as trees and shrubs and a few herbaceous perennials. They have usually opposite undivided or pinnate leaves. If pinnate the terminal leaflet is usually represented by a tendril, and the panicles or racemes by more or less asymmetrical flowers. The blooms sometimes have two-lipped calyxes usually with five teeth or five lobes, those of *Spathodea* spathelike, and tubular or bell-shaped, sometimes two-lipped corollas with five or more lobes or teeth. Most commonly there are four stamens in pairs of different lengths and one nonfunctional stamen or staminode. Less often there are only two stamens and three or no staminodes. There is one style and a two-lobed stigma. The fruits are mostly technically capsules, those of a few sorts, such as the calabash and sausage tree, fleshy. Except in such kinds the seeds are winged. Cultivated genera are *Amphilophium, Anemopaegma, Bignonia, Campsidium, Campsis, Catalpa, Chilopsis, Clytostoma, Crescentia, Cybistax, Cydista, Delostoma, Distictis, Dolichandra, Dolichandrone, Eccremocarpus, Incarvillea, Jacaranda, Kigelia, Macfadyena, Markamia, Oroxylum, Pandorea, Parmentiera, Paulownia, Pithecoctenium, Podranea, Pseudocalymma, Pyrostegia, Radermachia, Rhigozum, Saritaea, Spathodea, Stereospermum, Tabebuia, Tecoma, Tecomanthe, Tecomaria, Tecomella,* and *Tourrettia*.

BIJLIA (Bíj-lia). This is a genus of one non-hardy species. It belongs in the *Mesembryanthemum* group of the carpetweed family AIZOACEAE and is native of South Africa. The name commemorates a Mrs. D. van der Bijl. Considered to be one of the most unusual of the many curious members of the family, *Bijlia* is most closely allied to *Bergeranthus, Hereroa,* and *Ruschia.* A low, suckering, clump-forming species, **B. cana** has rosettes of up to six, three-angled, un-evenly-shaped, thick, firm, fleshy, opposite leaves, the alternate pairs of which are crowded together and set at right angles to each other. Each leaf is 1 inch to 1½ inches long and near its apex about three-quarters as wide as long. The leaves taper to their bases and have rounded undersides keeled toward their tips. Their surfaces are smooth and pale gray-green or are tinged with red or yellow. The yellow or orange-yellow flowers, 1 inch wide or a little wider, arise on very short stalks from between bracts. They are usually solitary, occasionally in twos or threes. There are five stigmas. The fruits are capsules.

Garden Uses and Cultivation. This species begins to grow in fall. It rests in summer. During its dormant season it should be kept dry, at other times water moderately. Environments and care that suit *Lithops, Stomatium,* and other small fleshy plants of the *Mesembryanthemum* group are appropriate. Propagation is by division and seeds. For further information see Succulents.

BILBERRY. See Vaccinium.

BILIMBI is *Averrhoa bilimbi.*

BILLARDIERA (Billardièr-a)—Apple-Berry. Nine species of small, Australian, mostly twining shrubs constitute *Billardiera.* A few are cultivated outdoors in mild climates and sometimes in greenhouses. The group belongs in the pittosporum family PITTOSPORACEAE. Its name commemorates the French botanist and traveler Jacques Julien de la Billardière, who died in 1834.

Billardieras have alternate, toothless, but sometimes sinuate-margined leaves. Their yellow, purple, or blue flowers, solitary or in clusters of usually few, are at the branch ends. They have five each sepals, petals, and stamens and one style. The fruits are fleshy, those of some species edible.

By far the best known and hardiest of the cultivated kinds is **B. longiflora.** It has lanceolate to ovate, evergreen leaves up to 2 inches long, and pendulous flowers, greenish-yellow changing to violet-purple, 1 inch to 1¼ inches long. Of greater decorative value than the blooms are the oblongish fruits that are usually a most wonderful azure-blue or purple-blue, but sometimes are reddish or white, the color varying in different seedling plants. The fruits are borne profusely and are attrac-

Billardiera longiflora (fruits)

tive for about six weeks. They are ½ to ¾ inch long. This kind is a native of Tasmania and southern Australia. Other kinds sometimes cultivated are **B. scandens,** with ovate-lanceolate to linear leaves, recurved at their tips, and yellow, greenish-yellow, violet, or purple, solitary or paired flowers ½ to ¾ inch long, and **B. cymosa,** with oblong or lanceolate, stalkless or nearly stalkless leaves up to 2 inches long. The ½-inch-long, bluish or violet flowers are in clusters.

Garden and Landscape Uses. In the warmer parts of California and in the far south billardieras provide interest for plantings against fences, walls, and in similar locations where the soil is fairly cool and a little shade gives protection against the hottest sun. In their early years these vines grow rather slowly.

Cultivation. These plants are not very choosy as to soil, but they favor a slightly-acid, sandy peaty one that allows water to drain easily. It should always be medium-moist. Trellis, wires, or other suitable supports for the stems to twine around must be provided. Very little pruning is needed, just sufficient to remove straggly, obviously unwanted branches. Propagation presents no difficulty. It may be by seeds, which take several weeks to germinate, by cuttings, or by layering.

BILLBERGIA (Bill-bérgia). This, one of the best known and most popular genera of the pineapple family BROMELIACEAE, comprises more than fifty species and is endemic to tropical and subtropical America. Its members are predominantly epiphytes, that is to say that like many orchids they perch on trees without abstracting nourishment from them, but some kinds are not adverse to substituting rocks for trees or even to growing in the ground. The name of the group commemorates the Swedish botanist J. G. Billberg, who died in 1844.

Billbergias are stemless perennials. They have evergreen, leathery leaves, usually with scurfy scales at least on their under-

sides, and generally toothed margins. Most often they are in tank-type, water-holding rosettes, or rarely are tufted. The rosettes are commonly tubular and mostly of up to eight leaves. The flowers are in bracted spikes or racemes, the flowering stalks usually arched above with the blooms pendulous. More rarely they are erect. Generally the flowering stalks are longer than the leaves. The bracts are frequently brightly colored and showy. Predominantly the blooms are blue or purple, less often greenish-yellow, whitish, or red. They have three each sepals and petals separate to their bases, the petals often coiled backward, at least in newly-opened blooms. Near the bottom of each petal is a pair of frilled or otherwise cut scales or ligules. There are six protruding stamens and, as long or longer, one style ending in a three-branched stigma. The fruits are many-seeded berries. This attractive genus differs from related *Aechmea* in technical details of its pollen grains. Also, the sepals of *Aechmea* flowers are generally prickle-pointed, those of *Billbergia* never. The plant called *Billbergia rhodocyanea* is *Aechmea fasciata.*

The oldest cultivated kind and still highly popular, **B. pyramidalis** (syn. *B. thyrsoidea*) of Brazil has vaselike rosettes of six to fifteen erect to slightly recurved, strap-shaped to strap-shaped-lanceolate leaves 1¼ to 2 feet long by 2 inches wide, broadened at their bases, and with fine teeth along parts of their margins. The flowering stalk is erect, scarcely exceeds the foliage, and has conspicuous, lanceolate to elliptic-lanceolate, rose-pink bracts 2 to 3 inches in length. In crowded, massive, more or less cylindrical, erect spikes 3 to 4 inches long or sometimes longer, the twenty to thirty blooms are about 1¾ inches in length. They have white-scurfy calyxes about one-third of that length and bright rose-red petals tipped with iridescent blue. When they fade the petals twist into tight spirals. Variety *B. p. concolor* has all red petals. The foliage of *B. p. striata* is striped longitudinally with green, blue, and ivory-white.

Another with erect flowering stalks, **B. horrida** belies by its appearance its somewhat repulsive name, which alludes to the large dark-colored spines that occur along its leaf margins. Up to about 1½ feet tall, this native of Brazil has green leaves some 2½ inches broad with obscure, grayish cross-bands. The flowering stalks have showy, rose-red bracts. The flowers, fragrant at night, have blue-tipped green petals. The leaves of *B. h. tigrina* are maroon, heavily cross-banded on their undersides with silvery-white.

An old favorite and one of the most satisfactory bromeliads for growing in windows, **B. nutans,** sometimes called friendship plant, is a native of Brazil, Argentina, and Uruguay. It forms clumps of slender rosettes of erect, arching, olive-green to

Billbergia pyramidalis

Billbergia nutans

bronzy-green, slender leaves. These, 1 foot to 1½ feet long by about ½ inch wide, have small, distantly-spaced teeth along their margins. The gracefully arched slender flowering stalks have decorative, rose-pink to rose-red, narrow bracts. There are up to twelve slender-stalked, pendulous blooms on each flowering stalk. They have a ½-inch-long, salmon-pink calyx with a purplish-blue-edged apex and yellow-green petals margined with rich bluish-purple, 1½ inches long, their upper parts reflexed.

The stamens are conspicuously protruded. Variety *B. n. schimperiana* is more compact. A variant with spotted foliage exists. Almost as common as *B. nutans*, and long in cultivation, Brazilian *B. saundersii* (syns. *B. rubro-cyanea*, *B. chlorostica*) has few-leaved, narrow-tubular rosettes 1 foot to 1½ feet tall. Sometimes lightly suffused with pink, its leaves are freely spotted with cream and maroon. The flowering stalks, with bright rosy-red bracts, end in a large, semidrooping or drooping, loose spike of blooms with blue-tipped, greenish-yellow petals. The anthers are orange-yellow. This kind appears to be closely related to if not identical with *B. brachysiphon*.

Variable *B. amoena* is a Brazilian with many-leaved rosettes varying in its different varieties and forms from sometimes under 1 foot to 3 feet in height. The leaves are strap-shaped, abruptly-pointed, slightly spiny along their margins, and 1 inch to 1½ inches wide. They are green, with obvious silvery cross-bars to bright reddish-bronze and sometimes conspicuously spotted or blotched. The arching flowering stalks with rose-pink bracts terminate in loose spikes or racemes of green flowers 1½ to 2½ inches long, with blue-tipped or blue-margined petals. Variety *B. a. rubra*, up to 3 feet tall, has broad, white- or yellow-spotted, distinctly rosy-red foliage. Variety *B. a. viridis* has green foliage with conspicuous silvery cross-bands and spots of ivory-white. Its flowers have plain green petals. Variety *B. a. minor* is smaller than other variants and has plain green leaves and violet-petaled flowers. Variety *B. a. penduliflora* has narrowly-tubular rosettes

of gray-green foliage and pendulous flowering stalks with bright orange bracts.

Especially showy because of the conspicuous bracts that accompany its flowers, **B. morelii** is native to Brazil. It has rosettes of stiff, sword-shaped leaves up to 2 feet long by 1 inch to 1¾ inches wide. They are plain green with fine-spined margins. About 1 foot in length, the red-bracted flowering stalks terminate in a rather loose, recurved or drooping spike of ten to fifteen blooms 1½ to 2 inches long. They have reddish sepals, green and lilac-blue petals. The stamens protrude conspicuously.

Others with pendulous flower spikes with very colorful bracts are **B. porteana** and *B. zebrina*, of Brazil, and *B. venezuelana*, of Venezuela. The flowers of these have petals strongly coiled backward when the blooms first open so that the stamens are then exposed. On the second day the petals straighten. The first has erect, tubular rosettes of rigid, purple-tinged, grayish-green leaves 3 to 4 feet long and 2½ to 3¼ inches wide. On their undersides they are clearly marked with whitish cross-bands. The mealy-white flowering stalk is decorated with bright rose-red bracts. The blooms, loosely arranged in long, narrow spikes, have green petals 2 to 2½ inches long and violet-colored stamens. The purplish-bronze, spiny-edged leaves of **B. zebrina**, 2 to 3 feet long by 2 to 3 inches wide or exceptionally up to 5 inches wide are

Billbergia zebrina

cross-banded with silvery-white. Up to 1 foot long or longer, the mealy-white flowering stalk is ornamented with big rose-red bracts. The blooms, in long, moderately-crowded spikes, have pink sepals tipped with violet, green to yellow petals, and old-gold stamens. An inhabitant of a hot, quite arid region where it often occurs on cliffs near the ocean, **B. venezuelana** attains a height up to 3 feet, has stiff, channeled, erect, and slightly arching leaves 2 to 3 inches wide. They are cross-banded with deep maroon, mottled with silvery-white. The large, rosy-pink bracts of the 2-foot-long, arching and pendulous flowering stalks are highly decorative. The loosely-arranged blooms have mealy-white sepals and yellow-green petals.

Also of the *B. porteana* relationship, *B. meyeri*, *B. pallidiflora*, and *B. rosea* are attractive Brazilian species with pendulous flowering stalks and flowers with petals curled backward at first; they straighten on the second day. Native of dryish parts of Brazil, *B. meyeri* has tall, slender rosettes of channeled, tapering, mottled, grayish-brown, scaly, spiny-edged leaves up to 3 feet long and approximately 1 inch wide. The long flowering stalks have big bright pink bracts and blooms with blue-tipped, greenish petals. Native to Mexico, Guatemala, and Nicaragua, *B. pallidiflora* has tubular rosettes of about ten arching, silvery-cross-banded, reddish-gray leaves 1½ to 2 feet in length by 1 inch to 1½ inches in width. The arching flowering stalk has pink bracts and green-petaled blooms. Trinidad and Venezuela are the homelands of *B. rosea*, which has tubular rosettes 3 feet tall or taller of boldly-white-spotted, 3-inch-wide, gray-scurfy leaves. The flowering stalks have large rose-pink bracts and many blooms with recurved, yellowish-green petals.

Comparatively small species with rosettes generally up to 1 foot high or sometimes higher include *B. iridifolia*, *B. leptopoda*, and *B. lietzii*, natives of Brazil. Small *B. iridifolia* has short-tubular rosettes of up to six silvery-gray leaves 1 inch to 1½ inches wide, curled outward at their ends, and with conspicuous marginal teeth. These are reported to sometimes attain much greater lengths in the wild. Light pink bracts ornament the pendulous flowering stalk. The loosely-arranged blooms from 2 to 2¾ inches long, have blue-tipped, red sepals and similarly-apexed, yellow-green petals. In variety *B. l. concolor* the petals are wholly yellow. Narrow, tubular rosettes of creamy-white-spotted, 1½-inch-wide leaves that coil backward near their ends and have gray-scaly undersides are characteristic of *B. leptopoda*. Erect and just overtopping the foliage, the flowering stalks have rose-red bracts and blooms with blue-tipped, yellowish-green petals. From six to ten narrow, yellow-spotted, light green leaves form the tubular rosettes of *B. lietzii*. The flowering stem is erect, has rose-pink to red bracts, and terminates in a head of blooms with red sepals and blue-tipped, yellow petals.

Other species in cultivation, all natives of Brazil unless otherwise stated, are *B. alfonsi-joannis*, with leaves 1½ feet long by 4 inches wide and obscurely cross-banded with white and conspicuous brown

Billbergia lietzii

marginal thorns. Much longer than the leaves, the drooping flowering stalk has bright rose-red, showy bracts and large flowers with violet sepals and violet-tipped, greenish-yellow petals. *B. brasiliensis* (syn. *B. leopoldii*) has a tubular rosette up to 3 or 3½ feet tall of eight to ten channeled, horny, fine-toothed leaves cross-banded with silvery-white. The pendulous flowering stalks carry large, rosy-red bracts and a dense, large, cylindrical spike of 2-inch-long violet blooms with protruding stamens. *B. bucholtzii*, a somewhat variable species similar to *B. amoena*, has narrow, funnel-shaped rosettes of faintly-spotted, pale green to bronze-tinged, deep green or purplish leaves barred with gray. They are 1 foot to 1½ feet long, 1 inch to 1¼ inches wide. Its flowering stalks have pink bracts, and blooms with entirely blue or green-tipped-with-blue petals. *B. decora*, of Bolivia, Peru, and Brazil, has tubular rosettes of leaves 1½ to 2 feet long by 2 to 2½ inches wide, grayish-green with irregular mealy-white cross-bands and tiny brown marginal spines. The mealy-white flowering stalk is pendulous and bears showy pink to red bracts up to 6 inches long and a large spike of greenish flowers. *B. distachia* has rosettes of few, minutely-spiny often purplish-tinged, white-scurfy leaves up to 2½ feet long and 1¾ inches wide. Its strongly arching or drooping pink-bracted flowering stalks, as long or slightly longer than the leaves, carry a few 2- to 2½-inch-long blooms with blue-tipped sepals and petals. *B. d. concolor* has plain green sepals and petals. *B. d. straussiana* has blue-tipped sepals, plain green petals. *B. d. maculata* has leaves spotted with ivory-white. *B. elegans*, botanically unrecognized, has a vase-shaped rosette about 1½ feet tall of broad leaves with small, but conspicuous brownish spines. The drooping flower stalk is decorated with rose-pink bracts. The

Bilbergia distachia

loosely-arranged, 2½-inch-long blooms have blue-tipped green petals. Their anthers are blue and golden-yellow. *B. euphemiae* spreads by stolons and has tubular rosettes of leaves about 1 foot long and 2 inches wide, recurved above and with faint cross-bands of silvery-white. The flowering stalks are pendulous and carry small pink bracts and violet-blue flowers 1½ to 1¾ inches long. *B. e. purpurea* has reddish-purple leaves without cross-bands. *B. e. saunderioides* has leaves with pale spots, without cross-bands. *B. fosterana* is a stolon-forming kind with narrow, tubular rosettes up to 3 feet tall of gray-green leaves 1 inch wide or a little wider, with densely-scaly, silvery cross-bands on their undersides. The erect flowering stalk has rose-pink bracts and comparatively few loosely-arranged blooms with lavender sepals and blue-tipped, green petals. *B. macrocalyx* has tubular rosettes of erect or recurved, channeled leaves 2 to 2½ feet long by 1½ to 2 inches wide. They are bright green, banded or spotted with silvery-white and clothed on their undersides with white scales. The bracts on the flowering stalks are rose-red. The flowers have yellowish-green petals tipped with blue. *B. macrolepis*, of Costa Rica, Panama, Venezuela, and Colombia, has dark gray linear leaves extravagently widened toward their bases, up to 4 feet long, and with big white spots on their undersides. The flowering stalks are down-curved and heavily white mealy. The 2-inch-long flowers are bronzy-green. *B. minarum*, 1 foot to 1¼ feet tall, has tubular rosettes of narrow, cream-spotted, gray-green leaves. The pendulous flowering stalk has pink bracts and blooms with green sepals and petals tipped with gun-metal blue. *B. reichardtii* much resembles *B. vittata*. Its tubular rosettes of up to six leaves, up to 2 feet long, have pale, broad cross-bands. The drooping flowering stalk has red bracts and usually up to ten flowers with blue-tipped yellow or green petals. *B. sanderana* has funnel-shaped rosettes of conspicuously black-spined leaves about 1½ feet long by 2 inches wide. The pendulous flowering stalk has big pink bracts and large flowers with violet-blue-tipped green petals. **B. seidelii** has tubular rosettes each of about six clearly white-banded, brown-spined leaves about 1½ feet long. The white-scaly, recurved flowering stalk has rose-red bracts and flowers with petals tipped blue-purple. **B. tweedieana** has tubular rosettes of up to ten white-spotted leaves some 3 feet long, and 2 to 3 inches wide, but considerably wider at their expanded bases. The erect flowering stalk terminates in a loose panicle up to 1 foot long with green floral bracts and flowers with blue-tipped green petals. **B. viridiflora** is indigenous to southern Mexico and Central America. Its rosettes are of twelve or a few more leaves approximately 1½ feet long, sometimes tinged with purple and usually with silvery cross-bands on their undersides. The erect, flowering stalk terminates in a loose panicle with bright red bracts and flowers with green sepals and petals. **B. vittata** exhibits considerable variation. From 2 to 3 feet tall, it has tubular rosettes of olive-green to purplish-brown, spiny-edged leaves with a dusting of grayish scales and sometimes with silvery cross-bands or dots of white. The leaves are 2½ to 3½ inches wide. The long, arching flowering stalk has pink bracts and terminates in an up to 1-foot-long panicle of blooms 1½ to 2 inches long, with reddish and violet sepals, green and violet petals, and orange stamens.

Billbergia vittata

Hybrid billbergias are fairly numerous. Many are very beautiful. Not all have names, nor are the parentages of all known. Among the best and most popular is 'Theodore L. Mead', a free-bloomer with much the aspect of *B. porteana*. Of medium size, it has spreading, soft green leaves and drooping flower spikes with large rose-pink bracts and green and blue flowers. Also very popular, 'Fantasia' is a hybrid of *B. saundersii* and *B. pyramidalis*. It combines the good qualities of both. Its urn-shaped rosettes are of coppery-green

Billbergia 'Fantasia'

leaves heavily blotched and spotted with pink and creamy-white. The arching flowering stalks have scarlet bracts, and blue-petaled blooms. The parents of 'Muriel Waterman' are *B. horrida tigrina* and *B. euphemiae purpurea*. The result is a quite stunning urn-shaped plant with conspicuously-toothed, reddish-purple leaves with prominent silvery-gray cross-bands. The arching flowering stalk has pink bracts and blooms with steely-blue petals. Another urn-shaped beauty, 'Catherine Wilson', the offspring of *B. amoena viridis* and *B. iridifolia*, stiffly erect and up to 1½ feet tall, has leaves with their upper parts recurved. They are green suffused with pink and conspicuously spotted with white. The flowering stalks have rose-pink bracts and flowers with green and blue petals. The parents of 'Henry Teuscher' are *B. pyramidalis* and *B. venezuelana*. This kind has tall rosettes of olive-green leaves purplish on their undersides and with purple spines along the margins. They are marked with silvery-gray lines and cross-bars and ivory-white spots. The flowering stalks have large and showy red bracts. Other hybrids are listed and described in the catalogs of specialists.

Garden and Landscape Uses. Billbergias are among the most satisfactory bromeliads for outdoor cultivation in the tropics and warm subtropics as well as in greenhouses and in favorable locations as houseplants. They are adapted to environments that favor the growth of the majority of warm-climate epiphytes (tree-perchers). Many are well adapted for use as underplantings in lightly shaded ground beds beneath trees and shrubs and around the boles of palms. In Florida and southern California, *B. pyramidalis* is especially esteemed for these uses. Other kinds, especially those that carry their flowers erectly, are equally admirable for these purposes.

Cultivation. Billbergias are among the most accommodating and easy-to-grow of the bromeliads. They tolerate uncomfortable environments and withstand neglect better than most of their kin, but are not

of course better for these. Only favorable conditions and good care produce the finest specimens. They prefer minimum indoor winter night temperatures of 55 to 60°F and for their best growth a fairly humid atmosphere. They are very easily increased from the abundant suckers they produce and from seeds. For preference give these plants a slightly-acid, porous, organic rooting medium, and light shade from the strongest sun. For more information see Bromeliads or Bromels.

BILLBUGS. These are reddish-brown to black beetles with curved, cylindrical snouts. They feed on grasses including corn and some other plants. The larvae are legless, humped, chunky, white grubs with brown or yellow heads. For controls consult a County Cooperative Agent or other local authority.

BILLY BUTTONS. See Craspedia.

BINDWEED. See Convolvulus.

BINGHAMIA. The plants for which this name is sometimes used are treated in this Encyclopedia as *Seticereus*.

BINGLEBERRY. See Blackberry.

BINOMIAL. The name of every species is a binomial consisting of two words, the first that of the genus to which it belongs, the second the specific epithet. Together they form an identifying combination botanically legitimate for only one particular species.

BIODYNAMIC GARDENING. This system of growing plants is akin to organic gardening and like it emphasizes many sound principles that good gardeners without claim to any knowledge of the biodynamic method have long followed. Its practitioners stress the importance of soil improvement through the use of organic materials and advocate the moderate use only of pesticides and then only of those that leave no lasting residues in the soil. They recommend the employment of certain preparations that soil scientists and practical horticulturists generally consider useless, some made from camomile, dandelion, stinging nettle, yarrow, and valerian, for adding to compost piles and for spraying on the ground, and of one made from quartz to be applied to foliage. Although promoting much that is good, the biodynamic gardening movement shows signs of becoming a cult following practices based in part on unsupportable claims.

BIOLOGICAL CONTROL OF PESTS. This embraces all ways of encouraging harmless living organisms, animal and plant, to destroy harmful ones. It is a selective modification of a natural method important in maintaining the balance of nature. Unfortunately, in only a few instances have biological controls proved sufficiently effective to warrant relying upon them exclusively or chiefly.

Among notable achievements is the use in California of an Australian lady beetle to destroy cottony-cushion scale on citrus fruits. Japanese beetle populations can over a period of a few years be decimated by treating lawns at intervals with spores of the bacterium of the milky disease that kills the insects. Another bacterium, *Bacillus thuringiensis*, is employed as a spray to control certain caterpillars. Viruses have been enlisted and in some instances used effectively in the war against pests by distributing the mashed bodies of virus-infected caterpillars among healthy populations.

Future development of biological controls may extend their usefulness, but at present these controls are notably effective against only a few pests. This does not mean that gardeners should neglect to encourage any and all creatures that assist in keeping pests in check. Here belong most birds as well as skunks, snakes, lizards, salamanders, toads, lady beetles, praying mantises, and most ground beetles. Moles destory many noxious creatures, but can effect much harm to lawns in doing so.

BIOPHYTUM (Bio-phỳtum). Some species of this genus, including the only one generally cultivated, are sensitive plants, their leaves being irritable and folding when touched. In this they resemble the common sensitive plant (*Mimosa pudica*), but the two are not closely related. Belonging in the wood-sorrel family OXALIDACEAE, the seventy species of *Biophytum* are tropical, perennial herbaceous plants, differing from closely related *Oxalis* in that their seed capsules split to their bases and the parts spread widely. In *Oxalis* they split only to their middles. The name is from the Greek *bios*, life, and *phyton*, plant, and refers to the sensitive leaves.

The only kind likely to be cultivated is **B. sensitivum**, which is common in the tropics and is often grown in botanical collections in greenhouses to instruct students and as a curiosity. A low plant, it has slender stems and rosettes of leaves, which like those of others of the genus are pinnate. Each leaf has six to fifteen pairs of blunt-oblong leaflets. The small yellow flowers are borne in summer. They have five petals.

Garden Uses and Cultivation. This neat, quite pretty little plant is well worth cultivating as a novelty. Although less sensitive to touch than *Mimosa pudica* and slower to respond, the leaves and leaflets fold downward at visible speed when irritated and recover slowly afterward. The movement is most apparent at high temperatures. This plant needs a humid atmosphere, a minimum temperature of 60°F, and shade from strong sun. Soil that contains an abundance of organic matter and is always fairly moist, but sufficiently drained to avoid stagnation, is appropriate. A good subject for greenhouses, where it may be grown singly in 3-inch pots or three or four together in 6-inch pans, it is also suitable for terrariums. Once a stock is acquired propagation is no problem because this plant is given to producing self-sown seedlings. These spring up in the pots in which mother plants grow and on other nearby soil areas. This because the ripe seeds are ejected explosively from the capsules and may be shot quite a little distance. The young seedlings are easily transplanted. Collected seed sown in pots of sandy peaty soil in a temperature of 60 to 70°F germinates readily.

BIOTA. See Platycladus.

BIRCH. See Betula. West-Indian-birch is *Bursera simaruba*.

BIRD-CATCHING TREE is *Pisonia umbellifera*.

BIRD-OF-PARADISE. See Caesalpinia, and Strelitzia.

BIRD PLANT is *Heterotoma lobelioides*.

BIRDS. In the main birds are attractive and desirable inhabitants of and visitors to gardens. That many are important in keeping down populations of insects and other pests is well known. Yet it cannot be denied that some are generally or on occasion nuisances, sometimes to the extent of becoming pests. This is especially likely in city and suburban areas where sorts such as crows, pigeons, English sparrows, and starlings are numerous and often more or less disturbing or destructive. Many others annoy gardeners from time to time by feeding on newly sown seeds, on seedlings, and on fruit buds and ripening fruits. Soft fruits such as cherries and strawberries are favorites.

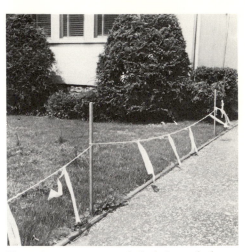

Fluttering streamers of cloth intended to scare birds

Measures to reduce bird damage include protecting seedbeds with fluttering streamers of paper, cloth, or metal foil attached to strings stretched a few inches above the ground between stakes, or more surely, by covering the seedbed with small-mesh netting or chicken wire. They may be discouraged from eating fruit buds, to some extent, by making certain that water and alternative food are available. Protecting ripening fruits from birds is more difficult. Scarecrows have little effect, since birds soon become accustomed to them and then ignore them. In home gardens

Biophytum sensitivum: (a) Normal aspect

(b) Touching leaves causes folding

(c) Plant after leaves have folded

where the number of trees, bushes, or plants is not great the most effective measure is to cover them with netting, cheesecloth, or tobacco cloth (in tobacco growing regions used tobacco cloth is sometimes obtainable at reduced prices). A possibility with cherries is to offer the birds an alternative menu by planting mulberries which ripen fruits at the same time. This is not, however, always effective. In extreme cases trapping or shooting destructive birds may have to be resorted to but be sure to check local laws before employing a gun.

Attracting birds to gardens is more often a concern of gardeners than discouraging them. The chief ways of doing this are by affording shelter and natural nesting sites, by planting trees and shrubbery, by having shallow water available for drinking (deep water with steep instead of gently sloped margins may result in birds, especially young ones, drowning), by supplying natural food by suitable planting, and particularly when this is in short supply or unavailable, by offering supplementary feed and by installing nesting boxes or houses for such kinds as bluebirds, chickadees, martins, nuthatches, wrens, and woodpeckers. Audubon societies are glad to supply suggestions about these and other encouragements for birds, as well as about the desirability or otherwise of attracting them to particular areas.

Anyone who desires to attract birds to gardens should be aware of certain disadvantages that may ensue. A given land area is capable of accommodating just so many of any particular species and over-population results in distress not only for other kinds but also for the too-numerous sort. This is as true of birds as it is of other animals and of man. Surely, once feeding is done to the extent that more birds are attracted to a restricted area than there is natural food to support them, it should be continued without interruption. Unless this is done the results can be disastrous, especially if parent birds are obliged to desert nestlings. Feeding in fall may delay the southward migration of certain kinds until too late and they then may suffer from extreme cold.

Too many birds in an area can increase disease among them, especially if feeding is done in such a way that they must pick the food from ground possibly contaminated by droppings of their own or other kinds including domestic poultry. Feeding stations little likely to admit of such contamination are less hazardous.

Among the worst enemies of birds are cats. Their mere presence has a demoralizing effect and scares birds away. Trap strays and turn them over to appropriate authorities or destroy them humanely. Hang small bells around the necks of pet cats and so far as possible keep them out of gardens. Make sure that bird baths and fountains are fully 3 feet above the ground

Bird baths: (a) Set close to the ground they afford no protection from cats

(b) Raised above the ground they afford better protection

or at least are well away from shrubbery that afford cover for lurking felines. Set birdhouses, nesting boxes, and feeding trays high above the ground in trees or on poles or posts. Cats cannot climb metal poles. If the boxes or trays are on wooden posts or in trees, afford protection by installing below them, 6 feet from the ground, a metal cone, mouth downward, surrounding and extending for 1 foot or a little more outward, or encircle the post or tree trunk with a tightly fitting cylinder 1½ feet long of tin or other smooth metal that affords no hold for claws. Let this be 6 feet above the ground. Other enemies of desirable birds are hawks, jays, and owls. These may be trapped and released at some distant place or if necessary and lawful, shot.

Plants that supply welcome foods for birds include nearly all those that bear succulent fruits and berries. Many are garden ornamentals. Some kinds, not preferred foods when other supplies are available and that hold their berries until well into winter, serve as emergency rations for birds. Among plants that supply food for birds are these: alders (*Alnus*), *Aralia*, arbor-vitaes (*Thuja*), ashes (*Fraxinus*), bearberry and manzanita (*Arctostaphylos*), beauty-berries (*Callicarpa*), beeches (*Fagus*), *Berchemia*, birches (*Betula*), bittersweets (*Celastrus*), blackberries and raspberries (*Rubus*), bloodberry (*Rivina*), blueberries and cranberry (*Vaccinium*), Boston-ivy and Virginia creeper (*Parthenocissus*), buckthorns (*Rhamnus*), buffalo-berry (*Shepherdia*), California-laurel (*Umbellularia*), Carolina moonseed (*Cocculus*), cherries, plums, etc. (*Prunus*), Chinaberry (*Melia*), Chokeberry (*Aronia*), Christmas-berry (*Heteromeles*), *Clintonia*, *Corema*, crowberry (*Empetrum*), dogwoods (*Cornus*), *Ehretia*, elderberries (*Sambucus*), elms (*Ulmus*), *Euonymus*, everglade palm (*Acoelorrhaphe*), false-cypresses (*Chamaecyparis*), false-lily-of-the-valley (*Maianthemum*), false-Solomon's-seal (*Smilacina*), firs (*Abies*), *Forestiera*, fringe trees (*Chionanthus*), *Gaultheria*,

grapes (*Vitis*), greenbrier (*Smilax*), hackberries (*Celtis*), hawthorns (*Crataegus*), hemlocks (*Tsuga*), hickories (*Carya*), inkberry (*Ilex*), honeysuckles (*Lonicera*), hollies (*Ilex*), hop-hornbeam (*Ostrya*), hornbeams (*Carpinus*), huckleberries (*Gaylussacia*), junipers (*Juniperus*), larches (*Larix*), lindens (*Tilia*), locusts (*Robinia*), madroño (*Arbutus*), *Mahonia*, maples (*Acer*), marine-ivy (*Cissus*), matrimony vines (*Lycium*), moonseed (*Menispermum*), mountain-ashes (*Sorbus*), mulberries (*Morus*), *Myrica*, oaks (*Quercus*), *Osmanthus*, osoberry (*Osmaronia*), palmetto (*Sabal*), partridge-berry (*Mitchella*), passion flower (*Passiflora*), pears (*Pyrus*), pepper vine (*Ampelopsis*), persimmon (*Diospyros*), pines (*Pinus*), plane trees (*Platanus*), pokeweed (*Phytolacca*), *Polygonatum*, poplars (*Populus*), red-bay (*Persea*), redbuds (*Cercis*), *Rhus*, roses (*Rosa*), *Sassafras*, shadbush (*Amelanchier*), shittimwood (*Bumelia*), snowberry (*Symphoricarpos*), sour gum (*Nyssa*), spice bush (*Lindera*), spruces (*Picea*), strawberries (*Fragaria*), sweet-fern (*Comptonia*), sweet gum (*Liquidambar*), tulip tree (*Liriodendron*), *Viburnum*, willows (*Salix*), and yews (*Taxus*).

BIRD'S. The word bird's occurs as part of the names of these plants: bird's eyes (*Gilia tricolor*), bird's-foot-trefoil (*Lotus corniculatus*), bird's nest fern (*Asplenium nidus*).

BIRTHWORT. See Aristolochia.

BISCHOFIA (Bischóf-ia)—Toog. In southern Florida, Hawaii, and other warm-climate regions the only species of this genus is cultivated as an ornamental. Long considered as belonging to the spurge family EUPHORBIACEAE, some botanists now segregate it as the only member of the family BISCHOFIACEAE. Its name commemorates Gottlieb Wilhelm Bischoff, professor at the University of Heidelberg, Germany, in the early nineteenth century.

Native of tropical Asia and Indonesia, the toog (**Bischofia javanica**) is an evergreen or partly deciduous tree up to 80 feet tall, but is often much lower in cultivation. It has broad top and alternate, mostly long-stalked leaves of three shallowly-toothed leaflets, the central one the largest, up to 8 inches long, and with a stalk longer than those of the lateral leaflets. Before they drop, the leaves, normally dark green above and paler beneath, turn red. In panicles 2 to 4½ inches long, the male and female flowers are on separate trees. Small, greenish-yellow, petal-less, and fragrant, they are succeeded by reddish to blue-black, berry-like, pea-sized fruits containing three to six seeds.

In its homelands the wood of this tree is used in construction and for furniture, musical instruments, and other purposes. The fruits and other parts of the plants are employed in native medicine. An interesting observation is that tigers are given to cleaning their claws by scratching the bark of the toog.

Garden and Landscape Uses and Cultivation. Suited only for tropical and near tropical climates, the toog grows best in soils that do not lack for moisture. It is reported to prefer some shade, but since it is employed as a nurse tree to supply shade to young coffee and other crops, this is hardly a "must." Propagation is by seed.

BISCUTELLA (Bis-cutélla). The ten species of *Biscutella* belong in the mustard family CRUCIFERAE. Annuals, herbaceous perennials, and subshrubs, they are natives of Europe and adjacent Asia. The name, derived from the Greek *bis*, double, and *scutella*, a shield, refers to the fruits.

Biscutellas are mostly hairy and have smooth-edged, toothed, or pinnately-lobed leaves. Their stalked, yellow flowers are in racemes that lengthen as they pass into fruit. They have four sepals, four petals arranged as a cross, six stamens of which two are shorter than the others, and one style. The fruits are dry pods (technically silicles) that separate into flat, circular, single-seeded parts.

Perennial or perhaps sometimes biennial, *B. frutescens*, of Spain and the Bal-

Biscutella frutescens

earic Islands, is hairy and forms tufted clumps of rosettes of wavy-toothed, ovate to fiddle-shaped, thickish, grayish-felted leaves up to 8 inches long. Its very numerous ¼- to ⅜-inch-wide flowers are in loose-branched panicles up to 1¾ feet high. An annual or biennial, variable *B. laevigata,* of eastern Europe and Asia Minor, has basal rosettes of hairy to hairless, coarsely-toothed, obovate-wedge-shaped to fiddle-shaped leaves 3 to 6 inches long. Slender, branched, and 9 inches to 1½ feet tall, its flowering stalks carry numerous ¼- to ⅜-inch-wide flowers.

Garden Uses and Cultivation. Suitable for mixed flower beds and naturalistic plantings, biscutellas have seed pods that can be used attractively in dried flower arrangements. These plants, easily raised from seeds, succeed in any ordinary well-drained soil and do especially well in soils of a limestone nature. A sunny location is needed.

BISHOP'S CAP. See Mitella. The Bishop's cap cactus is *Astrophytum myriostigma.*

BISHOP'S WEED OR GOUTWEED is *Aegopodium podagraria.*

BISMARCKIA (Bismárck-ia). The only species of *Bismarckia* of the palm family PALMAE, appropriately named *B. nobilis,* is native to Madagascar. Its generic name commemorates the first Chancellor of the German Empire Prince Otto von Bismarck, who died in 1898.

Bismarckia nobilis

With somewhat the aspect of *Latania,* this palm has a solitary, columnar trunk and a majestic, globular crown of massive, blue-green leaves divided into many long segments, some of which droop. At its maximum it attains a height of 200 feet and is thus one of the tallest of palms. In Florida there are specimens with trunks 15 to 20 feet tall. The leaves have blades up to 10 feet in diameter and their stalks, streaked with whitish scurf, are about one-half as

long as the blades. The clusters of flowers, males and females in catkin-like branches on separate trees, arise among the foliage. The male flowers have six stamens, a feature that differentiates *Bismarckia* from *Latania.* The ovoid, about 1½ inches long fruits are dark brown. Each contains a solitary, wrinkled seed.

Garden and Landscape Uses and Cultivation. This magnificent palm is adaptable for cultivation only under humid, tropical conditions. In the United States it can be grown outdoors in Hawaii and southern Florida. It can also be accommodated in large conservatories. Essentially, it is a palm for collectors. Because of the peculiar behavior of its germinating seeds and young seedlings fresh seeds should be sown in the way recommended for *Jubaeopsis.* They germinate in four to six weeks. This palm responds to the cultural conditions recommended for *Veitchia.* For other information see Palms.

BITTER. This forms part of the common names of several plants. Bitter-apple or bitter-cucumber is *Citrullus colocynthis,* bitter-cress is *Cardamine,* bitter-melon is *Momordica charantia,* bitter root is *Lewisia rediviva.*

BITTERNUT is *Carya cordiformis.*

BITTERSWEET. This is a common name of *Solanum dulcamara* and *Celastrus.* The latter is also called false-bittersweet.

BITTERWOOD is *Quassia amara.*

BIXA (Bíx-a)—Annatto or Lipstick Tree. Consisting of one species, or according to some authorities three or four species, *Bixa* is the only genus of the bixa family BIXACEAE. Its name is a modification of a South American native one. Endemic to tropical America, it is the source of annatto, a harmless orange dye esteemed for coloring cheese, butter, margarine, rice, candy, lipsticks, and soap. The dye, extracted from the pulp surrounding the seeds, was used by Carib Indians to decorate their bodies and repel insects. It has been thought to be helpful in treating leprosy. The seeds are said to stimulate fighting bulls.

The annatto or lipstick tree (*B. orellana*) is often a shrub 10 to 12 feet high, but sometimes is a tree up to 30 feet tall. It has alternate, slender-stalked, pointed-heart-shaped leaves 3 to 7 inches long, hairless and with reddish veins, and erect terminal clusters of 2-inch-wide pink flowers, each with five early deciduous sepals and five spreading petals; they look much like the blooms of wild roses or flowers of peach trees and are favorites of honeybees. The fruits are in clusters. They are bright red or brown, ovoid capsules 2 to 4 inches long, densely covered with long soft spines and much resembling the burs of the chestnut tree (*Castanea*). They split into two parts to reveal angular seeds, each enclosed in a layer of orange pulp.

Garden and Landscape Uses and Cultivation. This shrub or small tree is attractive as a single lawn specimen or in borders. It blooms in late summer and fall and carries its colorful fruits in fall and winter. The fruit clusters are esteemed by flower arrangers who use them fresh and dried. This species succeeds in any ordinary soil in sunny locations and is easily raised from seeds. It may also be increased by cuttings. It grows rapidly and blooms and fruits when two years old. The lipstick tree is suitable for frost-free warm climates only.

BIXACEAE—Bixa Family. The only genus belonging here is *Bixa*, a dicotyledonous one described under the previous entry.

BLACK. As part of common names, black is frequently used. Examples are black-alder (*Ilex verticillata*), black bamboo (*Phyllostachys nigra*), black bead (*Pithecellobium unguis-cati*), black-bean (*Castanospermum australe* and *Kennedia nigricans*), black-bearberry (*Arctostaphylos alpina*), black bryony (*Tamus communis*), black-calla (*Arum palaestinum*), black cohosh (*Cimicifuga racemosa*), black-cumin (*Nigella sativa*), black-eyed Susan (*Rudbeckia hirta*), black-eyed-Susan-vine (*Thunbergia alata*), black gum (*Nyssa sylvatica*), black-haw (*Viburnum prunifolium* and *V. lentago*), black hoarhound (*Ballota nigra*), black ironwood (*Olea laurifolia* and *Krugiodendron*), black locust (*Robinia pseudoacacia*), black mustard (*Brassica nigra*), black-olive (*Bucida*), black potherb (*Smyrnium olusatrum*), black salsify (*Scorzonera hispanica*), black-sapote (*Diospyros digyna*), black snakeroot (*Cimicifuga racemosa*), and black swallow-wort (*Cynanchum nigrum*).

BLACK-EYED-PEA, COW-PEA, or SOUTHERN TABLE-PEA. The legume known by the above names is, more realistically, a bean not a pea. Botanically *Vigna unguiculata*, possibly of African origin, it is easily grown. Its pealike seeds are tasty and nutritious.

Black-eyed-peas thrive in any ordinary, fertile, well-drained soil in sunny locations. They are suitable for cultivation only in the south and other places with long, hot, growing seasons. Prepare the soil by spading, rototilling, or plowing. The addition of compost or other decayed organic material is useful, but avoid excessive applications of nitrogenous fertilizers. A 4-12-12 or other fertilizer rather low in nitrogen applied in moderate amounts before sowing is recommended.

Sow in rows 2 to 2½ feet apart after all danger of late frost has passed. Subsequent care consists of keeping down weeds and, in long dry spells, watering. Well-known varieties are 'Brown Crowder', 'Conch', 'Dixilee', 'Louisiana Purchase', and 'Monarch Blackeye'.

BLACKBERRY. Blackberries are delicious, easily grown fruits well suited for home gardens. Selected varieties succeed in most parts of the United States and milder parts of Canada, thriving best in temperate climates. Less hardy than raspberries, they are not suited for the Great Plains and mountain regions where summers are hot and dry and winters severe. Blackberries belong to the genus *Rubus*. They differ from raspberries in that when picked, the central cores come with the fruits, which are solid cones. The central cores of raspberries remain behind when the fruits are picked, leaving them as hollow cones. Cultivated varieties are nearly all developments from native American species. Exceptions are the cut-leaved blackberry (*Rubus laciniatus*), grown and naturalized in the Pacific Coast region, and the Himalaya berry (*R. procerus*), which, despite its common name, is a native of Europe and is cultivated and widely naturalized on the Pacific Coast. Blackberries are of two types, erect and trailing. The latter include kinds called dewberries, boysenberries, loganberries, youngberries, and Himalaya berries. The primary difference between the two chief types of blackberries is the character of the canes (stems). Those of erect kinds are arched and self-supporting, those of trailing kinds essentially prostrate, and when cultivated must be tied to poles, trellises, or other supports. There are other differences. The fruits of trailing blackberries are usually sweeter than, ripen earlier than, and are in looser clusters than, those of erect varieties. Kinds known as semitrailing blackberries have first-year canes that trail; their canes of subsequent years are decidedly more upright. These belong with the erect group.

Blackberries in flower

Choose a location for blackberries protected from the prevailing winds of winter. Particularly in cold areas, these dry the canes and result in winter killing. Avoid frost pockets (low spots surrounded by higher ground, in which cold air collects and remains). A sloping, sunny site is best. A little part-day shade is tolerated. Make sure subsurface drainage is excellent. Blackberries will not stand wet feet, but neither will they prosper in dry soils. Throughout the growing season they need constant supplies of moisture, but the water table (level below which there is standing water) should not be closer than 3 feet to the surface.

The best soil for blackberries is a deep, sandy loam, but success can be had in any good garden or farm soil of agreeable texture, even those of a clayey nature, if well managed. In preparation for planting, spade, rototill, or plow to a depth of 10 inches or more, and mix in generous amounts of compost, rotted manure, or other organic amendment, or the year previous to planting grow on the site and turn under two green manure crops such as cowpeas, vetch, or winter rye.

Plant in early spring or early fall. Space erect varieties 2 to 3 feet apart in rows 8 feet apart to form hedgerows. Set trailing and semitrailing kinds 4 to 6 feet apart with 8 feet between the rows, or very vigorous varieties such as 'Thornless Evergreen', 'Boysen', and 'Young', 8 to 10 feet apart with the same distance between rows. In home gardens where hand cultivation is employed, the rows may be set 2 feet closer than the spacings suggested here. It is often practicable to accommodate a few plants of a trailing variety on an arbor or a fence or along a wall.

Supports must be installed for trailing blackberries and are advisable for erect kinds. They may be posts or trellises, or wires stretched horizontally, one 2½ to 3 feet and another 5 feet above the ground. A single wire about 3 feet from the ground is adequate for erect kinds and sometimes is used for trailers. Tie the canes of erect kinds with soft string where they cross the wire. Train and tie into position those of trailing and semitrailing varieties horizontally along the wires or fan the canes outward and upward and tie them where they cross each wire.

Routine care includes keeping down weeds, and with kinds that make sucker shoots, preventing these developing where they are not wanted and becoming unmanageable tangles. Do this by hoeing or cultivating frequently, but very shallowly, so roots near the surface are not injured. A summer mulch may be beneficial, but is less commonly used for blackberries than other fruits. It discourages weeds and conserves moisture, but does not stop suckers from growing. These must be cut out at intervals through the summer.

Fertilize as soon as flowering is through. Apply five to ten pounds of a 5-10-5 fertilizer, or an equivalent amount of another formulation, to each 50 feet of row, or about 15 pounds to each 1,000 square feet. In the south and in the southcentral states, an additional application of nitrate of soda at 2 to 4 pounds, or of ammonium nitrate at 1 pound to a 50-foot row, made after the fruit is gathered, is recommended.

Pruning and thinning need attention. The canes of most blackberries live only two years. During the first year they grow and branch, in the second short flowering and fruiting shoots develop from the branches. To prune erect varieties cut off the tops of the canes as soon as they are 3 feet long. This encourages the development of strong branches. The following spring remove any weak and broken canes and shorten the branches of those left to 1 foot to 2 feet. Cut out fruiting canes as soon as the berries are picked. At the same time thin out the new canes leaving only three or four of the strongest ones. In parts of the south where anthracnose and rosette diseases are serious, the recommended procedure is to cut out all canes, old and new, following fruiting, then to fertilize and cultivate to encourage the growth of replacement canes that will fruit the next season. Erect varieties produce numerous suckers that, if let to grow unhindered, become thickets. To prevent this, remove all unwanted suckers by pulling them. Taken in this way they do not renew themselves as quickly as when they are cut out.

Trailing blackberries are pruned in much the same way. If on posts, the tips are cut off the canes when they reach a height of about 6 feet, if on horizontal wires, 2 to 3 feet. This allows the development of branches 5 to 10 feet long. These are tied to the stakes and wires, or with prostrate dewberries, they may be allowed to remain on the ground until the following spring and then gathered into ropelike bundles and tied to the supports. In climates in which there is no danger of cold injury in winter, semitrailing varieties may be supported by stretching three or four wires horizontally one above the other and weaving the canes between these in summer when the stems are pliable.

Propagation procedures depend upon the type of blackberry. Tip-layering is practiced with trailing and some semitrailing kinds. To do this, loosen the soil around the plants in fall and bury the tip of a shoot, pointing straight downward, to a depth of about 3 inches. It may be desirable to peg it into position with a forked twig or by a stone placed on the stem. This is the only satisfactory means of multiplying thornless blackberries. If other methods are used the progeny reverts to the thorny types. Propagate erect blackberries by suckers or root cuttings dug from around the parent plant in spring. Take as root cuttings 3-inch-long pieces of root at least ¼ inch in diameter. Plant them 2 to 3 inches deep where the plants are to remain. Whichever method of increase you adopt be sure the parent stock is healthy and free of disease.

Pick blackberry fruits for home use when they are fully ripe. The commercial procedure, to harvest earlier, does not result in as flavorful a fruit. Handle the fruits carefully to avoid crushing or bruising and as soon as a basket or other container is filled put it in the shade. Fruits picked early in the morning keep better than those later in the day.

Protection from winter cold is needed by even the hardiest varieties where temperatures below −20°F are likely and where they may be exposed to cold, drying winds. This is best given by, in fall after warm weather has ended but before the ground freezes, bending the canes along the ground and covering them with soil, straw, littery manure, or similar material. Remove the cover in early spring before new growth begins.

Selection of varieties depends to a considerable extent upon the region where planting is to be done. You will be wise to consult your Cooperative Extension Agent or your State Agricultural Experiment Station about this. Among the more popular erect varieties are 'Bailey', midseason, productive and hardy; 'Dallas', early, less hardy to cold than many varieties; 'Darrow', early, continues fruiting over a long season; 'Eldorado', early to midseason, most resistant to orange-rust disease; 'Lawton', midseason, resistant to orange-rust disease; and 'Nanticoke', very late. Semitrailing and semierect kinds include 'Georgia Thornless', midseason, without thorns; 'Haupt', late, very productive; 'Himalaya', very vigorous, a heavy bearer; 'Jersey-black', midseason, fruiting season long; 'Thornfree', late, thornless, a good bearer; and 'Thornless Evergreen', very late, vigorous and productive. Trailing varieties of note include 'Boysen', late, fruit tart; 'Chehalem', vigorous, productive, berries small; 'Logan', very vigorous and productive, the thornless form most popular; 'Lucretia' (called dewberry, bingleberry), early and productve; 'Olallie', midseason, productive and vigorous; and 'Young', midseason, vigorous, fruits large and sweet.

Diseases and Pests. Blackberries are subject to a number of diseases including verticillium wilt (varieties resistant to this are 'Thornless Evergreen', 'Lawton', and 'Olallie'), crown gall and cane gall bacterial diseases, anthracnose, fungus leaf and cane spot diseases, orange-rust fungus disease, double-blossom (causing enlargement and malformation of the flowers and nonfruiting), fruit rots, and virus-caused sterility. Although a considerable variety of insect and similar pests may attack blackberries, on the whole they are comparatively free from such infestations. Pruning out and burning infested canes, and good general sanitation, is usually all that is necessary. Seek the advice of your Cooperative Extension Agent or your State

Agricultural Experiment Station for the latest and best methods of controlling diseases and pests in your area.

BLACKBERRY-LILY is *Belamcanda chinensis.*

BLACKBOY. See Xanthorrhoea.

BLACKBUTT is *Eucalyptus pilularis.*

BLACKTHORN is *Prunus spinosa.*

BLADDER. This word forms part of the common names of various plants such as bladder campion (*Silene vulgaris*), bladder fern (*Cystopteris*), bladder nut (*Staphylea*), bladder-senna (*Colutea*), and bladder-vetch (*Anthyllis tetraphylla*).

BLADDERPOD. For plants having this as a common name see Alyssoides, Cleome, Lesquerella, and Physaria.

BLADDERWORT. See Utricularia.

BLAKEA (Blà-kea). Belonging to the melastoma family MELASTOMATACEAE, the approximately eighty species of *Blakea* are natives of tropical America. The name honors one Martin Blake of Antigua, described as "a great promoter of human knowledge."

Blakeas are evergreen trees and shrubs with opposite, short-stalked, leathery, undivided, toothless leaves, with three or five main longitudinal veins linked with a hatch of cross-veins, and undersides generally clothed with rust-colored hairs. Solitary or in pairs from the leaf axils, the showy, red, pink, or rarely white flowers have stalks shorter than the leaves. They have a calyx with four or more bracts at its base, six petals, twelve stamens, and one style. The fruits are berries.

A tree sometimes 35 feet tall but frequently much lower, *B. tuberculata,* of Central America, has elliptic to nearly circular leaves, with numerous cross-veins at right angles to the prominent veins that run lengthwise. They are 4½ inches to 1¼ feet long by up to 9 inches wide and hairy

Blakea tuberculata

on their undersides along the veins. Phlox-pink to bright rose-pink the sweetly-scented flowers are 2½ to 2¾ inches wide. From Central America, *B. gracilis* is a shrub usually 2 to 6 feet tall with hairless leaves about 3 inches long and 1½ inches wide. The pink flowers are 2 to 3 inches wide.

Garden and Landscape Uses and Cultivation. In humid, tropical and warm subtropical environments, outdoors or in greenhouses, blakeas thrive in fertile, well-drained soil that contains an abundance of leaf mold or peat moss and is always moderately moist. Some shade from strong sun is needed. Cuttings of firm shoots and seeds afford ready means of increase.

BLANCHING. The eating quality of some vegetables and salads is improved or is considered to be improved by blanching. This consists of subjecting them to darkness. Absence of light causes etiolation by preventing the development of chlorophyll and often results in a more tender, milder-flavored product. Celery and leeks are blanched by hilling soil around them or by wrapping them in heavy, lightproof paper. Forced rhubarb, seakale, and whitloof chicory are grown in darkness under greenhouse benches, in cellars and similar places, or by covering roots in the open ground with large pots, tubs, barrels, or boxes. Endive is also blanched by covering the partly grown plants with pots or boards. Further details are explained under discussions of specific vegetables.

Lightproof paper wrapped around celery to blanch it

BLANDFORDIA (Blandfórd-ia)—Christmas Bells. Four or five species of thick-rooted, nonhardy, evergreen herbaceous perennials compose this eastern Australian and Tasmanian genus of the lily family LILIACEAE. In their homelands they are called Christmas bells. The name commemorates an early nineteenth-century patron of botany, George, Marquis of Blandford.

Blandfordias have mostly basal foliage. Their tough, narrowly-strap-shaped leaves,

triangular in section, are two-ranked and overlap at their bases. The erect flower stalks, 2 to 3½ feet tall, support racemes of pendulous, funnel-shaped to nearly bell-shaped blooms with six short perianth lobes (petals) and six stamens attached to the inside of the perianth tube. The fruits are three-angled capsules containing woolly seeds.

Flowers in loose racemes and leaves up to 2 feet long and not more than ¼ inch wide are characteristics of *Blandfordia grandiflora* (syn. *B. flammea*). Its narrowly-bell-shaped blooms, 1½ to 1¾ inches long, have individual stalks longer than the bracts in the axils of which they grow. They are red with yellow petals. Also with flowers in loose racemes, and each bloom on a stalk longer than the bract at its base, *B. nobilis* differs from *B. grandiflora* in its flowers, three to ten in a raceme, not being more than 1¼ inches long and having narrower perianth tubes that widen suddenly about one-third of the way from their bases.

In crowded racemes of seven to eighteen, the flowers of the most showy species *B. cunninghamii* have individual stalks as long or very slightly longer than the bracts and stamens joined to the perianth tube in its lower one-half. Narrowed below, the red tube, 1¼ to nearly 1¾ inches long, expands above and becomes bell-shaped; the yellow petals are about ½ inch long. Smooth-edged, erect, and spreading, the leaves are up to 3 feet long by up to ⅓ inch wide. From the last, *B. punicea* (syn. *B. marginata*) differs in having leaves with finely-toothed margins, flowers with perianth tubes that broaden gradually upward, petals only ¼ inch long, and stamens joined to the perianth tubes much above their middles. The beautiful orange-red to red-brown blooms are 1¼ to 1½ inches long. The largest leaves, the lowermost, are 1 foot long or longer and up to ¼ inch wide. This species is endemic to Tasmania.

Garden and Landscape Uses. Blandfordias are handsome flower garden ornamentals for warm-temperate to subtropical climates, where little or no frost is experienced, and for cool greenhouses. Their flowers are useful for cutting. Not very well known in America, they are reported to be a little tricky to grow. They need nourishing sandy peaty soil that does not lack for moisture, yet is not saturated, and locations in sun or part-day shade. The species hardiest to cold is *B. punicea*.

Cultivation. Seeds are satisfactory for propagation. They should be sown in summer or early fall as soon as they are ripe in sandy peaty soil kept moderately moist. They are rather slow to germinate, and it is spring before the seedlings are ready for transplanting. As small plants blandfordias make best growth if shaded lightly from the strongest sun. They may be ex-

pected to bloom when about four years old. Increase can also be had by carefully dividing old plants just before new growth begins; such divisions bloom sooner than seedlings. As long as established plants are doing well it is better not to disturb their roots by transplanting. Potted specimens are likely to need repotting every second or third year. This should be done in fall. The pots should not be overlarge, just large enough to accommodate the roots without serious crowding. Following repotting a humid atmosphere is needed and watering must be done with discretion to avoid rotting the roots. As the plants become established the soil is watered more freely, and drier, but never arid atmospheric conditions maintained. Well-rooted specimens during their season of active growth need generous supplies of water and regular applications of dilute liquid fertilizer. The resting season approaches after flowering, and the amount of water supplied is reduced without allowing the soil to become so dry that the roots shrivel. During their summer season of partial dormancy the plants may be kept in a shaded cold frame or lath house. Greenhouse temperatures in winter may be 45 to 50°F at night and five to ten degrees higher by day. A sunny location is needed.

BLANKET FLOWER. See Gaillardia.

BLAZING STAR. See Chamaelirium, Liatris, and Mentzelia.

BLECHNACEAE—Blechnum Family. Some authorities include the eight genera of this family of ferns in the POLYPODIACEAE. Considered separately, the BLECHNACEAE comprises about 250 species; it is cosmopolitan in its natural distribution.

These sorts grow in the ground, not perched on trees. Some have short trunks and are low tree ferns, most have erect or creeping rhizomes. Usually pinnately-lobed or once- or more-times pinnate, less often undivided and lobeless, the fronds (leaves) are mostly large and coarse. The clusters of spore capsules, in continuous or interrupted lines on veins parallel to the midribs of the leaflets, have covers (indusia) that open along the side facing the midrib. Genera in cultivation include *Blechnum*, *Doodia*, *Sadleria*, *Stenochlaena*, and *Woodwardia*.

BLECHNUM (Bléch-num)—Deer Fern. Belonging to the blechnum family BLECHNACEAE, and once named *Lomaria*, this genus of about 200 species of ferns is mostly tropical and chiefly inhabits the southern hemisphere. Its name is from the Greek *blechnon*, a fern. One *Blechnum*, the deer fern, is hardy. Blechnums are mostly stiff, somewhat coarse plants with pinnate or pinnately-lobed fronds (leaves) usually smooth and leathery and with toothed or toothless margins. In most kinds they are arranged in rosettes that, in some species, terminate short trunks. Such kinds are miniature tree ferns. The rhizomes and trunks are covered with stiff, linear, often black scales. The clusters of spore capsules, the arrangement of which is so important in identifying ferns, are in long continuous lines, parallel to and on both sides of the midribs of the leaflets or lobes.

The deer fern (*B. spicant* syns. *Struthiopteris spicant, Lomaria spicant*) is a variable species with erect, often clumped rhizomes and evergreen foliage. It has deeply-pinnately-lobed, sterile (non-sporebearing) fronds up to 3½ feet long by 6 inches wide that form a crown surrounding the fertile, spore-bearing fronds. In North America this species ranges from California to Alaska. It also inhabits northern Europe and northern Asia. Its common name alludes to the fact that deer browse upon it.

Blechnum spicant

Tropical and subtropical kinds most frequently cultivated are *B. brasiliense, B. gibbum*, and *B. occidentale*. As its name indicates, **B. brasiliense** is a native of Brazil. It is also indigenous to Peru. It has a trunk up to 3 feet in height covered with brown scales and crowned with spreading, oblong-lanceolate, fronds, deeply-pinnately-lobed, and up to 3 feet long by 1¼ feet wide. Fertile and sterile fronds are similar. The margins of the fronds are finely-toothed. A variety called *B. b. crispum* (syn. *B. corcovadense crispum*) has smaller fronds with crowded segments that have wavy margins. Its young fronds are bronzy-red. Native to New Caledonia, Isle of Pines, and Aneityum in the South Pacific, **B. gibbum** (syn. *Lomaria gibba*) has a trunk up to 3 feet in height clothed with black scales, as are its leafstalks and the lower parts of its midribs. Its sterile and fertile fronds differ in appearance. The former, about 3 feet long, are deeply divided into narrow segments and spread horizontally. The latter are contracted and much narrower. Variety

Blechnum gibbum

Blechnum moorei

B. g. platyptera is larger and faster growing than the typical kind, and the spores of its many erect, fertile-type fronds are sterile. The plant cultivated as **B. moorei** appears to be a form of this somewhat variable species. It has fewer, more erect fronds divided into a lesser number of broader, conspicuously-toothed segments. Its young leaves are usually reddish-pink. The true *B. moorei* (syn. *Lomaria ciliata*) of botanists, native to New Caledonia, appears not to be in cultivation. Tropical South American **B. occidentale** is quite different. It spreads by creeping rhizomes. Its pointed-ovate leaves, up to 1½ feet long by 4 to 8 inches

wide, are pinnate toward their bases, pinnately-lobed above. Fertile and sterile fronds are similar. Each has twelve to twenty-four segments on each side of the midrib. Rare **B. patersonii,** in its native Australia called the strap water fern, is unusual because of the widely various forms of its leaves. On different plants they vary from deeply pinnately cleft into two to ten lobes to being strap-shaped and lobeless. Up to 1¼ feet long, they are pink when young and later become dark green. The spore-bearing fronds are much narrower than the sterile ones. This species grows natively in wet, fertile soils.

Blechnum occidentale

Blechnum patersonii

Additional kinds include these: **B. auriculatum,** of temperate South America, has a short, scaly rootstock and pinnate, lanceolate, fertile and sterile fronds of similar appearance up to 2 feet long by 8 inches wide. **B. capense,** from South Africa, has a stout, scaly trunk and dissimilar fertile and sterile fronds, the latter ovate, pinnate, up to 3 feet long by 1 foot wide, the leaflets not sickle-shaped. **B. discolor** (syn. *Lomaria discolor*) has oblong-lanceolate sterile fronds up to 3 feet long and 6 inches wide arising from a stout stem and with shiny brown to black leafstalks. **B. fluviatile** (syn. *Lomaria fluviatilis*), an almost or quite trunkless native of New Zealand and Australia, has pinnate, linear fronds with densely-scaly midribs, up to 2¼ feet long by 2 inches wide. The fertile and sterile fronds differ markedly. **B. fraxineum** (syn. *B. longifolium*), of tropical America, has slender, creeping rhizomes and slender-stalked, all-similar, pinnate fronds with large terminal segments and three to six markedly sickle-shaped leaflets on each side of the midrib. The leaf blades are up to 1 foot long. **B. orientale** has a thick trunk 2 feet tall or taller and pinnate fronds, the fertile and sterile of similar appearance, ovate and up to 4½ feet long by 3 feet wide. The leaflets, up to 8 inches long, narrow to long points. This kind is indigenous to Australia, China, Malaysia, and the Himalayas. **B. penna-marina,** of South America, New Zealand, Australia, and Tasmania, has wiry, few-branched rhizomes. Its sterile fronds are erect and have stalks up to 1 foot long and linear to narrow-lanceolate, pinnate or pinnately-lobed blades up to 6 inches long, or rarely longer, by approximately ½ inch wide. Sterile fronds have procumbent to ascending stalks and blades up to 4 inches long by up to ⅓ inch wide. **B. polypodioides,** of tropical America, has long, densely-scaly rhizomes. Its short-stalked sterile fronds have narrowly-lanceolate blades with leaflets not more than 1 inch long by ¼ inch wide or a little wider. Usually with longer stalks, the spore-bearing fronds have linear leaflets 1 inch to 1½ inches long. **B. serrulatum,** the saw fern, of warm parts of the Americas including Florida, and of Asia and Australia, favors wet soils. It has stout, nearly naked, ascending stems up to 1 foot high and pointed-oblong fronds, the sterile and fertile similar, 1 foot to 2 feet long by up to 1 foot wide. The fronds have twelve to twenty-four linear, 5- to 6-inch-long by ½-inch wide, finely-toothed leaflets on each side of the midrib.

Garden Uses. As foliage plants for shaded locations blechnums are attractive and useful. The tree types may be dotted as accents among low-growing ferns or other groundcovers. Displayed in this way they are appropriate in tropical and subtropical rock gardens. They respond well to container cultivation and so accommodated are excellent decoratives for interiors and for greenhouses, patios, and terraces. They withstand dryish atmospheres better than most ferns.

Cultivation. Coarse, thoroughly well-drained, porous soil kept constantly moist, but never waterlogged, is required by most blechnums, but *B. occidentale* prospers in drier, somewhat heavier earth. The soil should contain a generous proportion of leaf mold, peat moss, or other decayed organic material. For container-grown specimens it is well to mix in some broken charcoal. The deer fern (*B. spicant*) is hardy. In mild climates such as that of southern California *B. occidentale* tolerates light frost, but when exposed loses its foliage in winter, replacing it in spring. The other kinds respond best when grown at a minimum night temperature of 55 to 60°F, with an increase by day of five to ten degrees. Shade from strong sun is required, but good light is necessary for best growth. Although dryish atmospheres are tolerated, very arid ones are harmful, and the fullest development of the fronds is possible only when at least moderate humidity is maintained. The soil must never become really dry. Well-rooted specimens in containers are benefited by weekly applications of dilute liquid fertilizer from spring through fall. Those in ground beds should be fertilized each spring and the ground around them kept mulched. Propagation is by spores and of kinds with creeping rhizomes, such as *B. spicant* and *B. occidentale*, by division. Blechnums are subject to a fungus leaf spot disease and may become infested with mealybugs, scale insects, and leaf nematodes. For more information see Ferns.

BLEEDING. Plants, having no blood, cannot in the true meaning of the word bleed. Nevertheless the term is used colloquially to allude to the loss of sap from cuts and wounds resulting from pruning, breakage, disease or insect injury, or other cause. Certain kinds of plants bleed more readily than others. Euphorbias, ficuses, and most sorts with milky sap are likely to do so conspicuously when first cut, but the wounds soon dry and loss of sap ceases.

Blechnum auriculatum

Some deciduous plants bleed profusely from cuts made in spring when they have little or no foliage and the sap is pushed upward from the roots under pressure. Examples are grapes, birches, and maples. Bleeding in such cases is not nearly as harmful as it appears. The loss is chiefly water of which there is an abundance. Nevertheless, it is not pleasant to look upon and most gardeners prefer to avoid it. This is done by pruning grapes in winter instead of spring and by delaying the pruning of maples and other notorious bleeders until well after they are in full leaf. Disease-caused bleeding, of which familiar examples are bleeding cankers, continues over long periods. The only recourse is to control the disease-causing organisms, but unfortunately, no remedy is known for bleeding canker disease, although young, mildly infected trees sometimes recover.

BLEEDING HEART. See Dicentra.

BLEPHILIA (Bleph-ília). To the mint family LABIATAE belong the only two species of the North American genus *Blephilia*. They are deciduous perennial herbaceous plants. The name is from the Greek *blepharis*, an eyelash, in allusion to the bracts being fringed with hairs. Blephilias are square-stemmed and have opposite leaves. They are 1 foot to 2½ feet in height. Their flowers have hairy, two-lipped corollas, with tubes much longer than the lobes. The upper and lower lips are about the same length, the former convex with the two stamens ascending beneath it, the latter spreading, or deflexed, and three-lobed. The stems of blephilias are erect and sparingly-branched. The flowers, crowded in the axils of the upper leaves, are in spike-like clusters. The fruits consist of four seedlike nutlets.

Native of woodlands from Massachusetts to Michigan, Wisconsin, Georgia, Mississippi, and Arkansas, *B. ciliata* has

Blephilia ciliata

pubescent stems and lanceolate to ovate, toothless or few-toothed leaves 1¼ to 2¼ inches long. The purple-spotted, pale blue flowers, up to ½ inch long, form a dense, continuous spike or one in which only the lowermost circle of flowers is separate. The many bracts are about as long as the calyxes. From the above, *B. hirsuta* differs in having its flowers usually in three or four, but sometimes only two, groups or tiers. It has hairy stems and ovate-lanceolate to broadly-ovate, stalked, more or less toothed leaves up to 3 inches long or slightly longer. The flowers are similar to those of *B. ciliata*, but the lobes of the lower lip of the calyx are not long enough to reach the clefts in the upper calyx lip; in *B. ciliata* they extend beyond the clefts. The bracts of *B. hirsuta* are shorter and narrower than those of the other species and soon reflex. This species inhabits woods, usually in moist soil, from Quebec to Minnesota, North Carolina, and Arkansas.

Garden and Landscape Uses. The most appropriate horticultural uses for blephilias are in wild gardens and native plant gardens where they are lightly shaded or in full sun. Provided the soil is not excessively dry, they are more attractive in sun than shade. The soil should be moist for *B. hirsuta*. The other species will grow in moist or fairly dry earth; in the latter plants are stockier and lower than when they are afforded more moisture.

Cultivation. These are very easy plants to grow. They grow readily from seeds sown in spring or fall and in reasonably favorable locations are very permanent. They may also be increased by division in spring.

BLESSED-THISTLE. This is the common name of *Cnicus benedictus* and *Silybum marianum*.

BLETIA (Blèt-ia). Chiefly native of tropical America and the West Indies, this genus, which must not be confused with the Asian orchid genus *Bletilla*, of forty-five species is represented in the native flora of Florida by one or possibly two species. It belongs in the orchid family ORCHIDACEAE. Its name honors Louis Blet, an eighteenth-century Spanish apothecary, who maintained a botanic garden at Algeciras. The first exotic orchid that flowered in England was *Bletia purpurea*; sent to Peter Collinson from the Bahamas, it bloomed in the greenhouse of Sir Charles Wagner in 1755.

Bletias are mostly ground orchids. Rarely they grow on trees as epiphytes (lodgers that take no nourishment from their hosts). They have cormlike pseudobulbs from the tops of which come leafy stems. Their often deciduous, longitudinally-pleated-veined leaves are narrow and grasslike. Terminating slender, leafless stalks, the purple to whitish flowers are in racemes or panicles of racemes. Their sepals and pet-

als, the latter similar to or wider than the former, spread. Joined to the base of the column, the lip has a spreading center lobe, erect side ones, and a disk or palate with several toothed or toothless ridges. It is not spurred.

Native to Florida, the West Indies, and Central America, *B. purpurea* (syns. *B. verecunda*, *B. alta*) has nearly evergreen, linear to elliptic leaves up to 3 feet long and 2 inches wide. The flower stalks are up to 5 feet in length. The rose-purple to pink blooms have yellow-crested lips, with a much crisped and crested middle lobe and large earlike side lobes. The petals, about ¾ inch long, are as broad as the sepals. An epiphytic variant of this species that has blooms that open imperfectly, or not at all, grows on the knees of swamp-cypresses in Florida. Like *B. purpurea*, but its blooms with sepals and petals more than 1 inch long and its column without a distinct foot, *B. patula* (syn. *B. shepherdii*) is a native of the West Indies and perhaps Florida. A white-flowered variant has been named *B. p. alba*.

Garden Uses and Cultivation. These orchids are for collectors, and the indigenous ones for including in assemblages of native plants of Florida, although they have not always proven to be easy to manage there. Bletias succeed in coarse, porous soil that contains an abundance of organic material and is well drained. Throughout the growing season they need abundant water, but little or no water when the plants are dormant. Occasional light applications of fertilizer are of benefit. Diffuse light, neither strong sun nor heavy shade, suits. In greenhouses a minimum night temperature of 60°F during the growing season and 55°F during the dormant season are satisfactory. By day, temperatures should be five to ten degrees higher and more in summer. A humid but not dank atmosphere is favorable. Propagation is by division. For more information see Orchids.

BLETILLA (Blet-ílla). The only species cultivated of about seven of this genus is often wrongly named *Bletia*, the correct title of another genus of the orchid family ORCHIDACEAE. The name, a diminutive of *Bletia*, alludes to similarities in appearance between the two genera.

Bletillas are all Asian. They are indigenous in Japan, Taiwan, China, and adjacent regions and grow in the ground rather than perched on trees like so many orchids. They have tuber-like, subterranean pseudobulbs from which come stalks bearing pleated, sometimes variegated leaves, and terminal racemes of flowers with sepals and petals nearly alike, and more or less spreading. The side lobes of the markedly three-lobed lip partially enclose the small, shortly winged column.

Summer-flowering and native of Japan and China, deciduous *Bletilla striata* (syn.

Bletilla striata

B. *hyacinthina*) is 1 foot to 2 feet tall. It has somewhat flattened, roundish pseudo-bulbs, up to about ¾ inch in diameter, and forms clumps of stiffly erect stems that carry a few leaves up to 1 foot in length. The short-stalked, slightly nodding, ame-thyst-purple blooms, 1 inch to 2 inches across, and never opening widely, are few to up to twelve in each raceme. They have lips darker purple than the petals and se-pals, with their middle lobes with longi-tudinal dark purple ridges, and toothed. Variety B. *s. alba* has pure white blooms, pale yellow at the bottom of the lip.

Garden Uses and Cultivation. Few or-chids are as easy to grow as this kind. Nearly hardy, it can be grown perma-nently outdoors where hard freezing does not occur. For good results fertile, mod-erately moist soil that contains an abun-dance of decayed organic debris, and a lo-cation where they are lightly shaded from the strongest sun, are needed.

Very handsome specimens of B. *striata* can be grown in well-drained pots 7 to 10 inches in diameter. They succeed in coarse, porous soil enriched with liberal amounts of leaf mold or peat moss and a generous dash of dried manure. In regions of frost-less winters, the pots may be kept out-doors all year, elsewhere only from spring to fall, or they may be accommodated in cool greenhouses or cold frames. Light shade from the fiercest sun is necessary. Watering is done freely from the time new growth starts until the foliage dies natu-rally, but in winter the soil is kept nearly dry. Well-rooted specimens benefit from regular applications, during their season of active growth, of dilute liquid fertilizer. Propagation is by natural multiplication of the pseudobulbs. For further information see Orchids.

BLIGHIA (Blīgh-ia)—Akee. The name of this tree commemorates the notorious Captain Bligh of H.M.S. *Bounty.* It was he who in 1793 introduced it from its home in tropical West Africa to the West Indies. As may not be commonly known, this same Bligh brought the breadfruit to the New World, not as a result of the famous *Bounty* voyage, but later.

The akee (*Blighia sapida* syn. *Cupania sapida*) belongs in the soapberry family SAPINDACEAE, and is one of seven species, all African. It is widely cultivated in the tropics and is grown in southern Florida. A tree 25 to 40 feet in height, stiff-branched and usually asymmetrical, the akee has bold pinnate leaves 6 to 10 inches long, each of which most commonly has three to six pairs of elliptic, ovate, or obovate, almost stalkless leaflets that diminish in size from the apex to base of the leaf; the largest leaflets are 4 to 6 inches long. The flowers, small, greenish-white, and ex-ceedingly fragrant, are in axillary racemes, and male, female, and unisexual blooms are on the one tree. They have five petals and eight to ten stamens that in male flow-ers are long-protruding. The somewhat bell-shaped, leathery-rinded fruits, as big as large lemons, are slightly three-lobed and depressed at their ends. They become yellow and red as they ripen and at ma-turity split lengthwise in three places to reveal three large, shining black seeds, each attached to a creamy-white "meat" or aril.

Blighia sapida (fruits)

Eating akee fruits can be dangerous. Un-less they are at just the right stage of de-velopment and are properly prepared they are poisonous. Preparation consists of re-moving the pink membranous skin asso-ciated with the aril (which is the edible part) and discarding the poisonous seeds. The fruits when eaten must be fully ripe and without trace of bitterness, but not soft and overripe; otherwise harm may re-sult. Despite potential dangers, akees are consumed freely as a vegetable in the trop-ics; they are eaten raw and simmered in salted water or fried in butter. They are often grown for home consumption and local markets.

Garden and Landscape Uses and Culti-vation. Adorned with its colorful fruits, the akee is a decidedly ornamental small tree. It grows best in moist, loamy, fertile soil and is propagated by seed.

BLIGHT. This term is sometimes used loosely and indiscriminately for a wide va-riety of afflictions that visibly affect plants. More usefully, it is restricted to a group of diseases the symptoms of which are a usu-ally quite sudden withering and killing of young growing parts, particularly shoots and foliage. No sharp distinction can be drawn between blights and blotch dis-eases, although the former usually affect entire extensive areas, the latter more de-finable patches. Application of the terms is largely determined by usage. Blights are chiefly caused by fungi and bacteria, but a blight of lilacs grafted on privets is a physiological disturbance for which there is no causal organism. Common fungus-induced blights include cane blight of rasp-berries, chestnut blight, botrytis blight of peonies, leaf blight of carrots, petal blight of azaleas, and leaf blight of orchids. Blights caused by bacteria include fire blight of apples, pears, and firethorns (*Pyracantha*) and blights of beans, gladi-oluses, and poppies. Preventive and con-trol measures, depending upon the partic-ular blight and plant affected, include such sanitary measures as the removal of dead wood and plant debris, cutting out af-fected parts, spraying, crop rotation, use of sterilized soil, and the avoidance of propagating by seeds from infected plants. See also Botrytis.

BLINDNESS. Bulbs or shoots that normally would produce flowers but fail to do so are said to be blind. Their failure may be caused by botrytis or other disease, by damage resulting from excessive heating during storage or shipping, by dry soil, or by forcing too early or before adequate root systems have developed.

BLISTER-CRESS. See Erysimum.

BLOOD. The word blood appears as part of the names of these plants: blood flower (*Asclepias currassavica*), blood leaf (*Iresine*), and blood-lily (*Haemanthus*).

BLOOD MEAL See Dried Blood.

BLOODBERRY is *Rivina humilis*.

BLOODROOT is *Sanguinaria canadensis*.

BLOODWOOD TREE is *Haematoxylum cam-pechianum*. The red bloodwood is *Eucalyp-tus gummifera*.

BLOOM. This is another term for a flower. It also describes the thin, waxy, easily re-moved coating that covers the stems and leaves of many cactuses, succulents and other plants and such fruits as grapes and many apples, which is responsible for their glaucous appearance.

BLOOMARA. This is the name of hybrid orchids the parents of which include *Broughtonia, Laeliopsis,* and *Tetramicra.*

BLOOMERIA (Bloom-èria)—Golden Stars. Natives only of California, there are two species of *Bloomeria,* a genus named after the pioneer San Francisco botanist H. B. Bloomer, who died in 1874. They belong in the lily family LILIACEAE and are related to *Brodiaea.* From that genus golden stars differ in not having their petals joined at their bases into a distinct tube and in the filaments (stalks) of the stamens being surrounded at their bases by winged, cup-shaped appendages. The latter characteristic, as well as the possession of corms instead of bulbs, separates them from *Allium.*

Bloomerias have fibrous-coated, flattened corms (called bulbs by the indiscriminating) somewhat like those of crocuses, basal linear leaves, and leafless flower stalks ending in a loose umbel of wheel-shaped yellow blooms each with six petals (more correctly tepals). There are six stamens and a slender, club-shaped style. The fruits are roughly spherical, angular capsules containing angled, wrinkled, black seeds.

Best known in cultivation, *B. crocea* has corms somewhat over ½ inch in diameter. Each produces only one leaf 3 inches to 1 foot long and up to ½ inch wide. The flower stalks are about twice as long as the leaves. The blooms of the umbels have individual stalks ¾ to 2½ inches long. The blooms are about 1 inch wide and are orange-yellow striped with darker lines. This species favors dry, often clayey, soils. Its variety *B. c. aurea* has yellow flowers. Also favoring dry soils, *B. clevelandii* is smaller, less robust, and has several very slender, linear leaves 2½ to 6 inches long and flower stalks up to 6 inches tall. The individual flowers have stalks ¾ inch to 1½ inches long and the blooms, yellow with a greenish stripe to each petal, are ½ to ¾ inch wide.

Garden Uses. Although not hardy in colder parts of North America and unsuited for outdoor cultivation in the East, bloomerias withstand several degrees of frost. They winter outdoors in northern California. For rock gardens, flower borders, and for planting naturalistically in informal landscapes they are pleasing. For satisfactory effects they must be set out in generous numbers; a few make but little show. They are also attractive for growing in greenhouses for late winter and spring bloom.

Cultivation. Golden stars respond best to well-drained, sandy soil of nourishing quality, but not excessively fertilized, and a warm, sunny location. They are not plants for cool, wet climates or for moisture-retentive soils. Where such prevail they may be grown in cold frames and greenhouses. The corms, planted in early fall, are spaced 2 to 3 inches apart and 2 to 3 inches deep. Where the ground is likely to freeze to a depth of more than an inch or so it is good practice to mulch with branches of evergreens, leaves, or other suitable insulating material at the beginning of cold weather. After the foliage has died following blooming, the corms should be taken up and stored in a dry, airy, shady place until fall.

For greenhouse cultivation the corms are planted in pans (shallow pots) in moderately fertile, porous soil. This is done in early fall, setting the corms with a space about equal to their diameters between them, and covering them to a depth of about an inch. Throughout, they are grown in cool, airy conditions. A night temperature of 50°F is adequate. By day it may rise by five or ten degrees. Immediately after planting, the pans are thoroughly watered. To prevent frequent drying it is a good plan to cover them with an inch or two of sphagnum moss. This is removed as soon as growth begins. Watering must always be done with reasonable caution, especially before the roots have taken possession of the soil. Excessive wetness can be disastrous, extreme dryness is to be avoided. After growth begins exposure to full sun is essential. Following blooming, watering is continued until the foliage begins to fade naturally, then intervals between applications are gradually increased, and finally the soil is dried and the corms stored, either in the soil or out of it, until fall planting time. Bloomerias do not increase much by offsets. Seeds sown in late summer or early fall in gritty soil afford the best means of propagation.

BLOSSFELDIA (Bloss-féldia). Probably the smallest of cactuses, the two species of *Blossfeldia,* natives of Argentina, belong to the cactus family CACTACEAE. Their name commemorates Harry Blossfeld, a twentieth-century German nurseryman and collector of cactuses.

Somewhat variable, blossfeldias have solitary or clustered, sunken-disk-shaped or button-shaped plant bodies (stems) up to 1 inch in diameter and even when plump scarcely as high. They are without ribs, tubercles (lumps), or spines, but have woolly areoles (areas from which spines usually come) arranged in spirals. In the wild during the dry season, the plant bodies may become so dehydrated that they are no thicker than a thin sheet of paper. They plump up after the rain. The blooms come from near the centers of the plant bodies. They open by day, very widely in full sun, and are bell-shaped, pale yellow, and ⅕ inch in diameter. The tiny, fleshy fruits contain minute seeds. The species best known in cultivation is *B. liliputana.*

Garden Uses and Cultivation. This delightful collectors' item needs rather special care. Because it apparently can absorb moisture through the above-ground parts as well as the roots it can be kept plump by superficial spraying with water at intervals. This is the best procedure to follow from fall to spring and in dull summer

Bloomeria crocea

weather, but is important not to spray when the plant surfaces are likely to remain wet for long periods. Following spraying, if they seem to remain wet for too long, the plants may be stood in the sun to dry. At other times light shade, with good air circulation, affords the best environment. Only during hot summer weather should top watering occasionally be done. The soil should consist largely of disintegrated rock and fine sand with the admixture of some topsoil. Propagation by seeds and offsets is easy. Increase can also be had from the roots. If pieces of root, attached to the plants or separated from them, are laid along the soil surface so that they are exposed to light they soon sprout new plantlets. For more information see Cactuses.

BLOTCH. There is no clear distinction between the symptoms of plant diseases called blotches and of those called blights. The former term is generally reserved for diseases in which the observable injury is limited to irregularly defined patches, rather than to more extensive areas on leaves or fruits. The chief causes of blotch diseases are fungi. Examples are those affecting apples, avocados, horse-chestnuts, and peonies. Control measures are those suggested for blights.

BLUE. As part of common names, blue finds frequent use. Examples are blue-African-lily (*Agapanthus*), blue-amaryllis (*Worsleya rayneri*), blue-beech (*Carpinus caroliniana*), blue-blossom and blue brush (*Ceanothus*), blue buttons (*Knautia arvensis*), blue calico flower (*Downingia elegans*), blue cohosh (*Caulophyllum thalictroides*), blue curls (*Trichostema*), blue dawn flower (*Ipomoea*

acuminata and *I. a. leari*), blue devil (*Echium vulgare*), blue dicks (*Dichelostemma pulchellum*), blue-eyed-grass (*Sisyrinchium*), blue-eyed Mary (*Collinsia verna* and *Omphalodes verna*), blue-ginger (*Dichorisandra thyrsiflora*), blue grama (*Bouteloua gracilis*), blue grass, Canada and Kentucky (*Poa*), blue gum (*Eucalyptus globulus*), blue lace flower (*Trachymene caerulea*), blue-lily-of-the-Nile (*Agapanthus*), blue lips (*Collinsia grandiflora*), blue-lotus of Egypt (*Nymphaea coerulea*), blue-lotus of India (*Nymphaea stellata*), blue-marguerite (*Felicia amelloides*), blue pincushion (*Brunonia*), blue-poppy (*Meconopsis betonicifolia*), blue-sow-thistle (*Cicerbita alpina*), blue-spirea (*Caryopteris*), blue stonecrop (*Sedum caeruleum*), and blue weed (*Echium vulgare*).

BLUEBEARD. See Caryopteris.

BLUEBELL. This is part of the common name of several plants. The California bluebell is *Phacelia minor*, the Scottish bluebell *Campanula rotundifolia*, the English bluebell *Endymion nonscriptus*, and the Spanish bluebell *E. hispanicus*.

BLUEBELL-CREEPER, AUSTRALIAN is *Sollya heterophylla*.

BLUEBELLS. The Texan bluebells is *Eustoma grandiflorum*, the Virginian bluebells *Mertensia virginica*.

BLUEBERRY. This is the name of a number of North American species of *Vaccinium* of the heath family ERICACEAE. Several grow in their wild state in sufficient numbers and bear fruits of such good eating quality that they are harvested commercially from natural stands and from such stands man-

aged to obtain improved production. But here these are not our special concern. We shall deal chiefly with the improved horticultural varieties of the highbush blueberry (*V. corymbosum*) and of the rabbiteye blueberry (*V. ashei*) that are the result of systematic breeding and domestication for fruit production. These are the kinds upon which the cultivated blueberry industry is based, the kinds most suitable for planting in home gardens for their fruits. Other species of *Vaccinium* from which considerable fruit is gathered from native and managed stands include the lowbush blueberries (*V. angustifolium* and *V. myrtilloides*), the dryland blueberries (*V. pallidum* and *V. alto-montanum*), the Florida evergreen blueberry (*V. myrsinites*), the mountain blueberry or bilberry (*V. membranaceum*), and the Western evergreen blueberry (*V. ovatum*). The highbush blueberry is one of the most recent food crops to be brought into cultivation. Its domestication began in 1906 when Dr. F. V. Coville of the U. S. Department of Agriculture began experiments growing plants collected from the wild. Three years later he initiated a breeding program designed to develop superior varieties. This he continued in close cooperation with Miss Elizabeth White of Whitesbog, New Jersey until his death in 1937. Between 1921 and 1936 Dr. Coville named fifteen varieties. Three others of his raising were named after his death. Other plant breeders have been active in producing new varieties, and hybrids between highbush and lowbush blueberries have been developed in Michigan.

Growing highbush blueberries is not for everyone. To succeed, certain climates are required and exacting soil conditions must be met. Winters must be long enough and

Blueberry

Blueberry (fruit)

cold enough to assure the plants a dormant period during which they are subjected to the approximately 700 hours below 40°F necessary for them to break dormancy satisfactorily and make normal growth. But at no time must the temperature fall below −20°F or, for some varieties, a little lower. If it does the wood is killed. Another requirement is that the growing season be sufficiently long, at least 154 days, for best results 160 to 165 days, between the last frost of spring and the first in fall. The number of hours below 40°F needed and their dislike for excessively high summer temperatures determine the southern climatic limits of highbush blueberry cultivation, their intolerance of temperatures much below −20°F and their need for a minimum-length growing season, its northern ones. Chief commercial production is in New Jersey, Michigan, North Carolina, Washington, and British Columbia, with some in New York, Massachusetts, and Indiana.

Soil for highbush blueberries must be acid, high in organic content, and moist without the water table being nearer the surface than 1½ to 3 feet. Clay land is quite unsuitable. Sandy loams that meet other requirements are ideal. The pH of the soil for good results must be between 4 and 5.2, with 4.5 perhaps the optimum. If azaleas, rhododendrons, mountain laurels, wild blueberries and other acid-soil plants grow well in the area, in all probability the soil is satisfactory, or with a small amount of effort can be made satisfactory, for the home cultivation of blueberries.

The planting site must be sunny, have good air circulation, and free air drainage. Cold air that collects in low frost pockets may injure the bushes in winter or at blooming time. Also, the disease called mummy berry is more likely to be troublesome in such places.

Preparation of the planting site, depending upon its original state, may consist only of spading deeply and incorporating organic matter, or more elaborate procedures may be necessary. Of first importance is the pH of the soil.

Suitable organic additives are peat moss, leaf mold, compost, and sawdust partly decayed or fresh. Use these liberally. Incorporate them very thoroughly throughout the upper 8 or 9 inches of soil. Acidity can be increased by mixing finely-ground sulfur throughout the upper 6 inches. On sandy earths ¾ to 1 pound to 100 square feet will likely lower the pH from 5.5 to 4.5, but twice as much may be needed to achieve the same result on medium-heavy loams. Sulfur works slowly in reducing pH. Apply it a year before you plant. Aluminum sulfate, which increases acidity more quickly than sulfur, is sometimes recommended, but because aluminum in sufficient quantities in the soil can be toxic it is safer to rely upon sulfur.

If your soil is clayey and you still want to try a few blueberries, excavate for each plant a pit 4 feet square and 1½ feet deep. After making sure that their bottoms are sufficiently porous to drain water, fill the pits with a soil mix satisfactory for blueberries. This technique works best when the adjacent soil is acid. If it is alkaline, seepage will gradually raise the pH of the special soil mix. You may be able to counteract this with periodic applications of sulfur as soil tests indicate the need, but it is a tricky business and not always successful. By and large, if you garden on alkaline soil it is better to forgo blueberries.

For planting, two- or three-year-old bushes are usually preferred. If purchased, obtain them from a specialist dealer. It is better that they have unbroken balls of soil around their roots, but if they must come from a considerable distance shipping costs may make this impracticable. Plant in early spring, or if you are willing to provide winter protection, in late fall. The protection consists of mounding sawdust or soil around the newly set plants. This is leveled in spring. If the ground is rather too moist, it is well to plant on low mounds or ridges. Allow 8 to 10 feet between the rows of bushes, 4 to 5 feet between plants in the rows. Make the holes 2 feet or more in diameter and about 6 inches deep. Unless the soil is very rich in organic matter mix equal amounts of peat moss with the soil you pack around the root balls and fill into the holes. Do not use fertilizer at planting time or during the first spring and summer.

Management of established blueberries calls for, if natural soil acidity is not near ideal, checking the pH from time to time and applying sulfur if it must be lowered. Very exceptionally, if acidity is below pH 4, it should be decreased by the cautious application of small amounts of lime to raise the pH.

Fertilizing, chiefly to supply nitrogen, is profitable. Animal manures used in amounts up to 20 tons to the acre or commercial fertilizers that supply ammonium nitrogen in equivalent amounts are satisfactory. An alternative in home gardens is to use a complete garden fertilizer such as a 5-10-5 or 10-10-10 in spring and supplement this about six weeks later with a light dressing of one that supplies readily available nitrogen. Sulfate of ammonia at the rate of one-quarter pound to each large bush is satisfactory. Give smaller bushes less. Weeds are best controlled by mulching with partly decayed or fresh sawdust, peat moss, or oak leaf mold. If surface cultivation is practiced, it must be very shallow because blueberry roots are near the surface. In dry weather periodic deep soakings with water are very beneficial.

Pruning must be done to assure large, high-quality berries, but usually none is needed until the end of the third year following planting. Unpruned bushes produce more fruits than they can bring to fine maturity. Limit each bush to six to eight well-spaced older branches. Occasionally one of these will become so old that it loses vigor to the extent that it is no longer capable of developing moderately-vigorous, fruit-bearing shoots. It then should be removed and a young shoot from the base allowed to take its place. Except when needed for this purpose, cut

Blueberries protected from birds by wire screen cage

out all sucker shoots from the bases of the bushes. Take out too-low, spreading branches, which if left, would have their fruits dirtied. Cut out clusters of thin, twiggy shoots, and with vigorous varieties that produce so many fruit buds (these are fatter and rounder than the flatter, more pointed leaf buds) that if all were left, more fruits would set than the bushes could mature, reduce the number of fruit buds either by shortening the shoots to three to five or by removing some of the spurlike groups from all along the shoots. Commercial growers save labor by pruning with the minimum number of cuts. This involves removing some fair-sized older branches with numerous fruit buds and leaving younger ones with fewer buds. More refined and considerate pruning is practicable for home gardeners. It may be done at any time from fall to flowering.

Protection from birds, squirrels, and rabbits is often necessary where only a few bushes are grown as in home gardens. The first two harvest the berries, the rabbits gnaw the bark. An efficient method of confounding these creatures is to enclose the bushes in cages of 1-inch-mesh chicken wire. These may be individual for each bush or more elaborate, walk-in height cages with frame-works of metal pipes or wood. Simple individual cages are had by driving into the ground around each bush five 1-inch-square, 6- to 7-foot-long wooden stakes and surrounding the bases of these with a cylinder of 2-foot-wide chicken wire attached to the stakes and with the ends overlapped for about 6 inches. The tops of the stakes are joined by a circle of wire or string fastened to them. When birds or squirrels become troublesome, usually shortly after midsummer, complete the cages by completing enclosing the frame of stakes above the chicken wire with mosquito netting, cheesecloth, or similar material. Use this to cover sides and top, overlapping the chicken wire and leaving no access for birds or beasts. Fasten the covering with safety pins, which allows for easy removal and replacement for harvesting.

Harvesting is by making several pickings every five to seven days. Take care not to pick berries before they are ripe. Those of some varieties deceive by changing color before they are sweet and mature.

Propagation of blueberries is more difficult than that of most bush fruits. It is chiefly accomplished by hardwood cuttings 1 foot to 2½ feet long taken in late winter or early spring, but leafy cuttings made in June and planted under mist or in a greenhouse or cold frame propagating bed are also used, and layering is successful. A mixture of three parts peat moss and one part sand is the usual rooting mixture. Hardwood cuttings root more surely if bottom heat of 70°F is supplied.

Varieties of highbush blueberries most suitable for home gardens and even for commercial production differ considerably from region to region, and from time to time new ones are introduced. It is suggested that prospective planters consult local Cooperative Extension Agents or their State Agricultural Extension Station before making selections. Although blueberries crop even when varieties are planted alone, it is thought that superior results are more likely when plantings consist of more than one variety so that cross-pollination is assured.

Rabbiteye blueberries do not require as long a period of winter cold and can stand higher summer temperatures than highbush blueberries and so are well adapted for cultivating in the south. They are grown commercially from North Carolina to Florida and Mississippi. The taming of this species (*Vaccinium ashei*) began in Florida in 1893 when bushes from the wild were planted, but it was not until 1950 that improved varieties became available as a result of systematic breeding. These were developed by the U. S. Department of Agriculture and the Georgia Coastal Plain Experiment Station. Later, crosses between the rabbiteye blueberry and *V. constablaei* resulted in plants hardy as far north as Maryland.

Soil for rabbiteye blueberries does not need to be within such a narrow range of acidity as for highbush blueberries, nor need it be so constantly moist. Because of this, these kinds can be grown in more upland sites. The bushes, larger and more vigorous than highbush kinds, are set out as young plants, spaced about 15 feet apart each way. Planting is in midwinter. General management is as for highbush blueberries, but often pruning is omitted although judicious attention of this kind is undoubtedly helpful. Propagation is by leafy cuttings.

Fruits of rabbiteye blueberries are not as well flavored and have larger seeds than those of highbush blueberries, but these disadvantages are less apparent in the better varieties and may be bred out of them eventually to produce even finer varieties than those now available. The fruits ripen considerably later than those of highbush varieties.

BLUEBONNET is *Lupinus subcarnosus*.

BLUEBOTTLE is *Centaurea cyanus*.

BLUETS. See Hedyotis. Mountain-bluet is *Centaurea montana*.

BLUMENBACHIA (Blumen-báchia). Native to temperate South America, *Blumenbachia* consists of three species of annuals, biennials, or perennials closely related to *Loasa* and *Caiophora* and belonging in the loasa family Loasaceae. Its species are furnished with stinging hairs; one or two kinds are sometimes cultivated for ornament. The name honors Johann Friedrich Blumenbach, a German professor of medicine, who died in 1840.

Blumenbachias have opposite, lobed leaves and solitary flowers of a rather odd shape. The flowers arise from the leaf axils.

The best known species is *B. hieronymii*, a native of Argentina. This annual or bien-

Blumenbachia hieronymii

nial is 1 foot to 2 feet tall and has ovate, palmately five-lobed, toothed leaves and down-facing slender-stalked, white flowers with yellow and red centers. They are about 1½ inches across. In gardens *Loasa vulcanica* is sometimes grown as *Blumenbachia hieronymii*. Less commonly cultivated is *B. insignis*, which has twining stems up to 2 feet long or longer, and

Blumenbachia insignis

deeply-palmately-divided five-lobed leaves up to about 3 inches wide. Its flowers have hooded petals, are 1 inch in diameter and white with crimson and yellow centers. They are succeeded by large, spirally-twisted seed pods that have been described as resembling the top of an oriental mosque. The plant sometimes cultivated as *B. lateritia* is *Caiophora lateritia*.

Garden Uses and Cultivation. Blumenbachias flower freely the first year from seeds and are cultivated as annuals. They add interest and variety to flower beds and borders, but because of their stinging hairs have little appeal as cut flowers. They bloom over a long period. These plants need full sun and succeed in any ordinary well-drained soil. They require no staking. Propagation is by seeds sown outdoors in early spring or earlier indoors to produce plants to be set in the garden after danger of frost is over. When the latter plan is followed, the seeds are sown eight or nine weeks before planting out time and the seedlings are transplanted about 2 inches apart, to flats or individually into small pots. They are sown at a temperature of 60 to 65°F. The young plants are grown in a sunny greenhouse at a temperature of 55 to 60°F. Spacing between plants in the garden may be 6 to 9 inches for *B. hieronymii* and 1 foot to 1½ feet for *B. insignis*. No special summer care is needed.

BLUSHING BRIDE is *Serruria florida*.

BO TREE OF INDIA is *Ficus religiosa*.

BOCCONIA (Boc-cònia). The plants most commonly cultivated in North America under this name do not belong in this genus, but in *Macleaya*. Species of *Bocconia* are sometimes planted in California and other regions where little winter cold is experienced. The genus consists of ten species of trees, shrubs, and subshrubs of the poppy family PAPAVERACEAE. It inhabits warm parts of the Americas from Mexico to tropical South America and differs from the entirely Asian genus *Macleaya* in, among other ways, its seed pods opening from the base upward instead of from the top downward. The name commemorates Paolo Bocconi, a Sicilian botanist and physician, who died in 1703.

Bocconias contain yellowish sap and have alternate, usually large, mostly pinnately-lobed or veined, stalked, grayish leaves, and small, petal-less flowers in branching, terminal panicles. Their seed pods are somewhat fleshy.

A shrub or tree up to 25 feet in height, *B. frutescens,* of the West Indies, and Central and South America, is most likely to be cultivated. It has pinnately-lobed, gray-green leaves up to 1½ feet in length and 4 to 8 inches in width, that are smooth on their upper sides and thickly covered with hairs beneath. The greenish or purplish flowers, in panicles 1 foot long or longer, each have sixteen stamens.

Garden and Landscape Uses and Cultivation. For warm, dry climates bocconias have merit chiefly because of the bold, tropical appearance of their foliage. Their blooms are not colorful or particularly showy. These are plants for sunny, well-drained locations. They can be increased by seeds, and perhaps by cuttings and root cuttings.

BOEA (Bò-ea). Little known horticulturally, this genus of twenty-five species of the gesneria family GESNERIACEAE inhabits tropical Asia, the Seychelles Islands, and Australia. Its name, which has also been spelled *Baea*, commemorates the Reverend Dr. Bau, of Toulon, France. Boeas are blue- or purple-flowered, fibrous-rooted herbaceous plants of diverse habit.

Astonishing *Boea havilandii,* of Malaya, has a leafless woody stem up to 6 feet in length topped by a tuft of leaves from which comes a terminal panicle 3 feet long of light blue blooms. After flowering the plant dies. More typically, plants of this genus are much smaller and have leaves all basal or with small, opposite ones on short stems. The flowers are on stalks from the leaf axils or on leafless stalks arising from the rosettes of foliage. The blooms have five-parted or deeply five-cleft calyxes, and short-tubed corollas with five spreading lobes. There are two fertile stamens and a single style. The fruits are capsules.

Approximately 6 inches in height, *B. hygroscopica* has ovate, short-stalked, coarsely-toothed leaves, with wrinkled-surfaced blades 3 to 4 inches in length by about 2¼ to 3 inches in width, covered with short, white hairs. Its African-violet-like blooms, pale blue to medium purple with a small yellow eye, ¼ to ¾ inch in diameter, are in clusters of several on stalks that carry them a little above the foliage. The two upper corolla lobes are shorter and wider than the three lower. This is native to Australia.

Garden Uses and Cultivation. A plant for collectors of gesneriads (plants of the gesneria family) and warm greenhouses, the species described gives little trouble, responding to the environment and care that suits African-violets, but, unlike those popular plants, appear not to resent having its foliage wetted during watering. If the soil is allowed to become dry the leaves shrink, but they expand again when moisture becomes available, which ability is recognized by the epithet *hygroscopica*. This plant thrives in fairly low light intensities. Propagation is by seeds and leaf cuttings. For additional information see Gesneriads.

BOEHMERIA (Boeh-mèria)—Chinese Silk Plant or Ramie. This is a genus of the nettle family URTICACEAE. It consists of 100 species of herbaceous plants, shrubs, and trees, natives of the tropics, northern subtropics and north-temperate regions, including North America. One kind, the Chinese silk plant, China-grass, rhea, or ramie, contains in its inner bark the longest, strongest, and most silky vegetable fibers known. These are used commercially in the manufacture of fine fabrics for table-cloths, bed linens, clothing, and embroidery threads, and were formerly employed to make the finest gas mantles. The name *Boehmeria* commemorates George Rudolf Boehmer, a German professor of botany, who died in 1803. The plant grown as *B. argentea* is *Myriocarpa stipitata*.

Boehmerias have alternate or opposite, undivided leaves. Their tiny, unisexual or bisexual flowers are in globose clusters or spikes. Male blooms have three to five sepals and as many stamens. The female flowers have tubular calyxes, usually narrowed at their apexes and with two to four teeth and a long, persistent, slender style. The fruits are achenes enveloped by the persistent calyxes.

Boea hygroscopica

The Chinese silk plant (*B. nivea*) is a variable, ornamental subshrub 3 to 6 feet tall, or sometimes sprawling. Its attractions are its pleasing, broad, rounded form, and its wrinkled-surfaced, coarsely-toothed, broad-ovate to practically round leaves mostly 2 to 6 inches long, with densely-snowy-white-hairy undersides. The greenish or whitish flowers are in loose panicles up to 6 inches long. It is a native of Japan, China, and southern Asia. The cultivated variety, called China-grass or ramie, is *B. n. candicans* (syn. *B. utilis*). This kind is larger in its parts than the wild species and has stems about 6 feet tall that branch little or not at all.

Boehmeria nivea

Boehmeria nivea (flowers)

A subshrub or herbaceous perennial of Japan, *B. biloba* inhabits coastal regions and often rocky cliffs near the sea. From 1 foot to 2½ feet tall, it has firm, thickish, opposite, ovate to nearly-round leaves 2½ to 6 inches long by 1¼ to 4 inches wide, two- or three-lobed at their apexes, and finely-toothed. Their bristly-hairy upper sides are roughened with tiny bumps. The flowers are in short, thick spikes. A shrub or small tree of western China, Indochina, and the Himalayas, *B. macrophylla* has opposite, pointed-lanceolate, toothed leaves 4 inches to 1 foot long, with three chief veins, and usually hairy under surfaces. Its flowers are in slender, pendulous racemes

Boehmeria biloba

up to 1 foot long. A variable subshrub or shrub up to 10 feet tall, *B. platyphylla*, of Asia and Africa, has opposite and alternate, coarsely-toothed, usually hairy, broad-ovate leaves 3 to 9 inches long. Its flowers are in long, pendulous spikes.

Native from the eastern portions of Canada and the United States to the West Indies, Mexico, and Brazil, *B. cylindrica* is a herbaceous perennial up to 4 feet tall, with much the aspect of a nettle, but without stinging hairs. Its leaves, opposite on the stems and alternate on the branches, range from narrowly-lanceolate to ovate. They are 2 to 6 inches long and are coarsely-toothed. The flowers are in more or less erect spikes up to 1½ inches long.

Garden and Landscape Uses. North American forms of *B. cylindrica* may occasionally be included in collections of native plants. Beyond that, it scarcely has garden use. The other kinds described are not hardy, but are suitable for outdoors in regions of little or no frost. There, they can be planted for foliage effects. In addition, ramie is appropriate in displays of economic plants (plants useful to man). For that purpose it can be cultivated outdoors in mild climates, and in greenhouses.

Cultivation. Boehmerias respond to fertile earth that never dries excessively. As a group they favor sunny locations, but one form of *B. cylindrica* prefers light shade. In greenhouses ramie succeeds where the night temperature in winter is 45 to 50°F

and that by day is some five to fifteen degrees higher. Propagation is easy by division, cuttings, and seeds.

BOENNINGHAUSENIA (Boenning-hausènia). The rather formidable name of this genus honors a German botanist, C. F. von Boenninghausen, who died in 1864. It belongs in the rue family RUTACEAE and consists of a single species native from eastern Asia to the Himalayas. It is rare in cultivation.

Subshrubby and about 2 feet tall, *Boenninghausenia albiflora* (syn. *Ruta albiflora*) differs from *Ruta* in its blooms having stalked ovaries and in other technical details. This is a hairless, branched plant with two or three times pinnate, glaucous-gray, long-stalked leaves up to 6 inches long. The many leaflets are obovate and ¼ to ¾ inch in length and about one-half as wide as they are long. The numerous, usually-nodding flowers, white and up to ½ inch in diameter, form broad, loose, leafy clusters 1 foot or so long, in summer. When crushed the foliage is ill-scented.

Garden Uses and Cultivation. Chiefly a collectors' item, this plant is appropriate for rock gardens and other special locations. It is not reliably hardy in the north, being more tender than rue (*Ruta*). It thrives in sun in well-drained soils, including alkaline ones, and is propagated by seeds and summer cuttings.

BOERBOON. See Schotia.

BOERHAVIA (Boer-hàvia) — Spiderling, Wine Flower. One of the forty species of this genus of the four o'clock family NYCTAGINACEAE is sometimes cultivated. The group, commonly called spiderlings, consists of tropical and sub-tropical herbaceous plants and is named in honor of H. Boerhaave, a Dutch botanist, who died in 1738. These plants are natives of both the Old World and the New World, some being indigenous to the United States. They are difficult to identify as to species. Their leaves vary greatly in shape and size, and they have minute, five-lobed, bell-shaped or funnel-shaped flowers in spikes, racemes, tight clusters, or solitary. The stamens number one to five. They are related to umbrellawort (*Oxybaphus*), from which they differ in that their flowers are not accompanied by involucres (collars or ruffs of leafy bracts).

The wine flower (*Boerhavia coccinea*) has erect or lax sticky stems 2 to 3 feet in length and stalked, linear-ovate or roundish, wavy-edged leaves, usually white on their undersides. The round heads of tiny red flowers are in panicles. This species, common in the tropics and subtropics, including parts of the southern United States where it is sometimes something of a weed, is probably a native of Ceylon.

Garden and Landscape Uses and Cultivation. Of some use for flower beds and borders and for embellishing informal areas, *B. coccinea* is hardy in mild climates, but not in the north. It succeeds in ordinary garden soil in sun. Propagation is by seed.

BOERLAGIODENDRON (Boerlagio-déndron). New Guinea, the Malay Archipeligo, Taiwan, the Celebes Islands, the Philippines, and Polynesia are homes of this genus of thirty species of the aralia family ARALIACEAE. The name commemorates the Dutch botanist Jacob Gijsbert Boerlage, who died in 1896.

Boerlagiodendrons prevailingly are hairless trees and shrubs, more rarely somewhat woody herbaceous plants. Their alternate leaves have blades with palmately-arranged (in hand-fashion) leaflets, or are palmately-lobed. The leaflets or lobes are lobed or toothed. The flowers are in umbels of three branches, the center one generally shorter than the others and consisting of sterile flowers. The lateral branches bear heads or umbels of small, bisexual blooms with smooth- or wavy-edged calyxes. There are up to eight petals joined at their bases to form a tube, up to about thirty stamens, and a style topped by radiating stigmas. The fleshy fruits are nearly spherical berries containing flattened seeds.

Native to the Philippine Islands, *Boerlagiodendron eminens* is a tree 15 to 30 feet tall. Its glossy leaves, up to 2 feet long, are deeply ten- to fourteen-lobed, the lobes irregularly- and coarsely-toothed. The umbels of five- or six-petaled flowers are usually arranged in larger umbels. A slender tree about 20 feet in height, *B. novo-guineense* of Papua, has leaves 2 to 3 feet long, thorny at the bases of their stalks. The umbels of orange flowers form very large showy panicles. The flowers are succeeded by purple fruits.

Garden and Landscape Uses and Cultivation. Rarely cultivated, these bold-foliaged trees grow well in the humid tropics and may be used in the same manner and managed in the same way as *Trevesia, Tetraplasandra,* and other large-leaved ornamental trees of the aralia family.

BOG. The word bog is incorporated in the common names of such plants as bog-asphodel (*Narthecium*), bog bilberry (*Vaccinium uliginosum*), bog-laurel or bog-kalmia (*Kalmia polifolia*), and bog-rhubarb (*Petasites hybridus*).

BOG GARDENS. An area, natural or contrived, devoted to the cultivation of wet-soil or swamp plants is called a bog garden. Such a feature, usually of small to moderate size, can be attractive at watersides, in rock gardens, and elsewhere when fitted into the landscape naturalistically. Usually it will occupy a low spot, perhaps where the soil is too wet for most garden uses or possibly where it is flooded for part of each year. The plants may include a wide variety of native wet-land species and some exotic (non-native) ones. It is best that the site be sunny.

If the soil is naturally boggy begin by determining the source of the water, whether or not there is an inflow and outflow, whether the ground is kept wet by seepage from a stream, pond, or lake or from an accumulation of surface water where subsurface drainage is inadequate. In the last type of situation make sure the ground can be kept wet throughout the year. It may be necessary to install a supplementary source of water and perhaps, to prevent stagnation, arrange for an outflow. Water may have to be piped in for use when needed.

Follow by clearing away unwanted growth. To facilitate this it may be possible to dry the area temporarily by constructing trenches to carry away surplus water and so make the preparatory work easier. Or this may not be practicable. In any event ruthlessly root out plants you do not want and, except for possibly some large shrubs that are located satisfactorily, dig up kinds you wish to retain and store them packed closely together in flats or a cold frame or heel them in, in a shaded place outdoors. See that their roots are kept wet until they are planted in the bog garden.

Next, attend to contouring the soil and bringing it into condition for planting. The surface of the finished bog cannot depart greatly from the level, but some change of elevation is desirable. In places, an inch or two of free-standing water may show above the soil. Elsewhere the earth may rise from an inch or two to a foot or somewhat more above the water table. Such changes of grade are pleasing to the eye and better accommodate plants needing slightly different environments. If the area is sizable, a meandering, firm path or paths of earth or stepping stones raised 8 to 10 inches above the water surface and underlain with gravel, crushed stone, or other drainage material will facilitate viewing and

A small bog garden

tending. Other features such as a well-placed boulder or two and partially rotted tree stumps or logs may be introduced to add interest and variety.

Preparation of the soil in readiness for planting in naturally wet areas may not involve more than forking, spading, or plowing that already there. Should it be low in organic content, mix in generous amounts of compost, leaf mold, humus, or peat moss. If possible complete preparations well in advance of planting and allow the ground to lie bare for a month or more of growing weather. This gives time for the sprouting and eliminating of weeds and other unwanted vegetation before desirable plants are introduced.

Artificial bog gardens may in good conscience be installed as adjuncts to rock gardens, ponds, and in other appropriate places where the ground is not naturally wet or swampy. They need not be large. A miniature of a few square yards can bring great pleasure. Begin by staking out the area. Excavate it to a depth of 1 foot to 2 feet. Line the basin with a 4- to 6-inch layer of puddled clay, concrete, or with two layers of heavy gauge polyethylene plastic film, with the laps of the layers staggered to minimize water loss. Then fill in with good topsoil mixed with an equal amount, or more, of compost, leaf mold, humus, or peat moss. Pack this firmly and arrange its surface as suggested for bog gardens in naturally wet areas.

A supply of water and an outlet to carry it away after it has flowed slowly through the bog are needed. The flow must be slow. Scarcely more than a trickle is enough for a mini-bog, more will be needed for bigger ones. If the overflow is a pipe, cover its entrance with a grid or a piece of perforated zinc to prevent it becoming clogged with debris.

Planting may be done in spring or fall. Where winters are severe the former season is to be preferred. Seeds of many bog plants may be sown *in situ* as soon as they are ripe or they may be stratified in moist peat moss, vermiculite, or sand in a temperature of 40°F until spring and then sown.

Routine care of bog gardens is not onerous. Neither watering nor staking are needed. The usual garden weeds are not a problem, but some few native wet-soil plants such as Joe Pye weed may stage takeovers by self-sown seedlings. And planted specimens of vigorous habit, such as bogbean and a number of others, are likely to spread with such enthusiasm that they must be curbed from time to time by pulling out the surplus. If in innocence or foolishness you have admitted common cat tail (*Typha latifolia*) or still worse, tall wetland grass *Phragmites communis* into your garden, heaven help you. Once well established, their eradication poses a formidable task likely to defy the efforts of all

A selection of bog plants: (a) Marsh-marigold

(b) Swamp-pink

(c) Forget-me-not

but the most determined gardener. The best chance of success short of back-breaking digging to remove the tough, stout roots entrenched 2 to 3 feet or more below the surface, is to destroy every scrap of shoot that appears before it is 6 inches tall. But you must do that without let-up for two or three years. If you must have these plants, confine their roots in thick-sided containers of concrete, but generally you will be better off without them. There are other less aggressive cat tails and grasses.

Plants suitable for bog gardens, some hardy, some not, include blue lobelia (*Lobelia siphilitica*), bogbean (*Menyanthes trifoliata*, cardinal flower (*Lobelia cardinalis*), flowering-rush (*Butomus*), marsh-marigold (*Caltha*), ostrich fern (*Matteuccia struthiopteris*), rice (*Oryza*), royal fern (*Osmunda regalis*), showy orchis (*Orchis spectabilis*), swamp-pink (*Helonias bullata*), water forget-me-not (*Myosotis palustris*), and willow gentian (*Gentiana asclepiadea*) and species of the following genera: *Acorus, Alisma, Anagallis, Andromeda, Astilbe, Calla, Cardamine, Carex, Chamaedaphne, Colocasia, Cyperus, Cypripedium, Dionaea, Dipidax, Drosera, Echinodorus, Eleocharis, Epilobium, Eriophorum, Gratiola, Hypericum, Iris, Juncus, Lilium, Lysimachia, Lythrum, Marsilea, Mentha, Mimulus, Myrica, Parnassia, Pinguicula, Polygonum, Pontaderia, Primula, Ranunculus, Regnellidium, Rhexia, Sagittaria, Sarracenia, Saururus, Scirpus, Trillium, Xanthosoma, Zantedeschia,* and *Zizania.*

(e) *Calla palustris*

(d) Willow gentian

(f) Japanese iris

(g) *Primula japonica*

(h) *Sagittaria latifolia*

BOG-MOSS. See Mayaca.

BOGBEAN is *Menyanthes trifoliata.*

BOISDUVALIA (Boisduvàl-ia). Eight species, mostly annuals, constitute *Boisduvalia* of the evening-primrose family ONAGRACEAE. They inhibit the west coasts of North and South America and Tasmania. The name honors Jean Baptiste Alphonse Boisduval, French naturalist and physician. He died in 1879.

Boisduvalias have usually alternate, less commonly opposite, undivided, stalkless leaves. Their small, funnel-shaped flowers have four each sepals and petals, eight stamens of which four are shorter than the others, and a two- or four-lobed stigma. The fruits are cylindrical or angled capsules.

Occasionally cultivated, ***B. densiflora*** has erect leafy stems 1 foot to 5 feet tall and branched above. The leaves are narrow, finely-toothed, and pointed. Violet to light purple, the flowers, about ½ inch in diameter, are in clusters arranged in long, leafy, interrupted spikes. This commonly hairy plant of annual duration is native from Idaho to British Columbia, Nevada, and California.

Garden Uses and Cultivation. Of moderate decorative value, *B. densiflora* can be used to add variety to flower beds and borders and, in its native territory, in native plant gardens. Its flowers are not suitable for cutting. It may be grown from seeds sown outdoors in spring or sown indoors earlier, about eight weeks before planting out time, and the young plants, raised in flats, transplanted to the garden after the weather is warm and settled. Space the plants 3 inches apart in the flats, 1½ to 2 feet apart in the garden. This species prefers fairly moist soil, thrives in sun or light shade, and blooms in early summer.

BOKHARA-CLOVER is *Melilotus alba.*

BOLANDRA (Bol-ándra). Named after Dr. Henry N. Bolander, Californian botanist, who died in 1897, this genus of the saxifrage family SAXIFRAGACEAE consists of two western North American species of hardy herbaceous perennials.

Bolandras have very short, bulbiferous rootstocks. Their stems bear long-stalked lower leaves and much shorter-stalked to stalkless upper ones. The thin leaf blades are more or less kidney-shaped and palmately (like the spread fingers of a hand) veined. The blooms, attended by conspicuous leaflike bracts, are borne in terminal, loose, few-flowered panicles. The fruits are capsules.

Inhabiting moist rocks, commonly beside waterfalls, in Oregon, Washington, and Idaho, ***Bolandra oregana*** has stems 8 inches to somewhat over 1¼ feet tall. Its lower leaves have stalks up to 6 inches long and blades 1½ to 3 inches broad. They have nine to thirteen toothed, shallow lobes. The panicles of bloom have a few branches, each with up to seven flowers. The persistent calyx and the corolla are purplish, the former with five linear-lanceolate lobes, and eventually ¾ inch long. The linear petals are about as long as the sepals. The stamens, with stalks one-half as long as the sepals and petals, are reddish-purple.

Similar, but smaller, and confined in the wild to wet rocks in the mountains of California, ***B. californica*** is 6 to 8 inches tall. It has round-ovate leaves with stalks up to 4 inches long, and blades shallowly five- or seven-lobed and toothed, and up to 1½ inches wide. The flowers have purplish-margined, greenish petals about ⅕ inch long.

Garden and Landscape Uses and Cultivation. Bolandras may be grown in gritty, well-drained soil in clefts and crevices of moist or wet cliffs and rocks in shaded wild gardens and rock gardens. They are propagated by seeds and division.

BOLBITIS (Bol-bìtis). This tropical genus of about eighty-five species of ferns belongs in the aspidium family ASPIDIACEAE. Small- to moderate-sized, bolbitises grow in the ground and on rocks, and may climb trees to heights of 2 to 3 feet. They have creeping rhizomes and fronds (leaves) undivided or pinnate, with the leaflets sometimes lobed or toothed. Fertile fronds are considerably smaller than the others. Clusters of spore cases cover their entire under surfaces. The name *Bolbitis,* in allusion to the thickened veinlets of the leaves, is derived from the Greek *bolbos,* a bulb.

Native to Central America and the West Indies, ***B. cladorrhizans*** has clustered fronds 1 foot to 3 feet long, the sterile ones with triangular to ovate blades with their terminal portions deeply-pinnately-lobed, their lower parts separated into many coarsely-round-toothed leaflets. The sporebearing fronds have much narrower, more distantly-spaced leaflets than the fertile ones. Occasionally cultivated, ***B. heteroclita,*** of tropical Asia, has thin, bright green leaves usually in two ranks along slender rhizomes. The stalks of sterile fronds are about 8 inches long, those of the fertile ones up to 1 foot long. The blades may be undivided or have up to four pairs of somewhat-toothed leaflets, with the terminal one 1 foot long or longer and about 2¼ inches wide. Barren fronds generally end in long, slender, tail-like prolongations, with a rooting growth bud near their ends. They have conspicuous, parallel, rather widely-spaced lateral veins at nearly right angles to the mid-vein. Fertile fronds are similar, but smaller and much narrower.

Garden Uses and Cultivation. The species described is suitable for outdoor cultivation in the moist tropics and for humid, shaded greenhouses, where the minimum

Bolbitis heteroclita

winter night temperature is 60 to 65°F and by day five to fifteen degrees higher. At other seasons, substantially more warmth is desirable. These ferns grow well attached to slabs of tree fern trunk and in pots or pans (shallow pots) in a coarse, loose mixture of fir bark of the kind used for growing orchids, peat moss, coarse sand or perlite, and a little crushed charcoal, or some similar mix. The rooting medium must be kept evenly moist without allowing it to be constantly saturated. Propagation is by division and spores. For other information see Ferns.

BOLDEA. See Peumus.

BOLDO is *Peumus boldus.*

BOLIVICEREUS (Bolivi-céreus). Consisting of a few species of the cactus family CACTACEAE, this genus is native to Bolivia and Peru. Its name is a combination of Bolivia and of the cactus genus *Cereus.* Some authorities include *Bolivicereus* in closely-related *Borzicactus.*

Bolivicereuses have ribbed, slender, cylindrical stems with needle-like spines. They branch freely from close to the ground, are more or less erect, and up to 6 feet tall, or prostrate. The markedly-small, s-shaped, funneled, blood-red flowers open by day. They have a very oblique face or lip. The perianth tube, ovary, and fruits are hairy.

A distinct cactus, ***B. samaipatanus*** (syn. *Borzicactus samaipatanus*) has stems with fourteen to sixteen ribs approximately 1½ inches thick. They have rather closely-spaced spine clusters, each of twelve to almost twenty-four spines of uneven length, often not clearly differentiated as radials and centrals. The comparatively short, more or less s-shaped, salmon-red blooms measure about ¾ inch across.

Garden and Landscape Uses and Cultivation. These are as for *Cereus.* For further information see Cactuses.

Bolivicereus samaipatanus

Bolivicereus samaipatanus (flowers)

BOLLEA (Ból-lea). Six or fewer species are included in this charming tropical American genus of the orchid family ORCHIDACEAE. They are evergreen epiphytes; instead of growing in the ground they perch on trees. They differ from *Zygopetalum* in not having pseudobulbs. The name honors Dr. Karl Bolle, a dendrologist of Berlin, Germany, who died in 1909. Bolleas have many, two-ranked leaves with prominently raised veins. The solitary flowers, on stalks shorter than the leaves, have spreading sepals, similar petals, and a lip with a flaring blade with a large, raised, ribbed callus that partly hides the short column.

Its very fragrant, fleshy flowers predominantly violet-blue to nearly clear blue, with the lower portions, edges of sepals, and petals usually yellowish-green to olive-green, and with a large buff-yellow callus on the lip, *Bollea coelestis* (syn. *Zygopetalum coeleste*), is 1 foot to 1½ feet tall. Its oblong-lanceolate leaves 1½ to 2 inches wide, are 1 foot to 1½ feet long. Nodding or semierect, and shorter than the leaves, the flower stems have small bracts. They terminate in a solitary bloom 3 to 4 inches across. From the last, *B. lalindei* (syn. *Zygopetalum lalindei*) differs in having narrower, prominently five-veined leaves and blooms with the top halves of their sepals and petals pink to violet, and often tipped and margined with pale yellow. The lip, large, and bright yellow to orange-yellow, has a recurved apex and edges. The column is pink, sometimes with a white base.

In size and habit very like *B. coelestis*, and by some authorities suggested as being a natural hybrid between that and *Pescatorea klabochorum*, although that is not the prevailing opinion, *B. lawrenceana* has blooms with wide, white sepals and petals, blotched at their apexes with violet-purple, as is the lip. The pale yellow column has a violet anther.

Two other species, *B. patinii* (syn. *Zygopetalum patinii*) and *B. violacea* (syn. *Zygopetalum violacea*, *Huntleya violaceum*), are occasionally cultivated. Both similar in habit to *B. coelestis*, *B. patinii* has blooms about 4 inches wide, with blunt, pale pink sepals and petals, the lateral sepals deeper-colored, and a bright yellow lip with a large flesh-pink crest. The fragrant flowers of *B. violacea* are about 3 inches in diameter, and are rich violet-purple with white edges to the sepals and petals. The dark violet-purple lip has a yellow, thirteen-ridged crest.

Garden Uses and Cultivation. These are as for *Cochleanthes*. For further information see Orchids.

BOLLWYLLER-PEAR is *Sorbopyrus auricularis*.

BOLTING. When plants run prematurely to flower and seed it is called bolting. The term is most often used in reference to such vegetables as lettuce, spinach, radishes, turnips, and onions, which are of little or no use after they begin to run to flower. Bolting frequently results when cool-weather crops experience periods of very hot weather. To avoid this, choose sowing dates that allow for harvesting before high temperatures are likely to occur. Stress caused by damage to the roots during transplanting or by excessive dryness of the soil is also likely to cause bolting.

BOLTONIA (Bol-tònia). Four species are recognized as comprising this American genus. One, and a variety of it, are the only kinds generally cultivated. Asian plants previously included in *Boltonia*, and now separated as *Asteromoea*, do not appear to be cultivated. To the botanically uninitiated, boltonias look very much like tall perennial Michaelmas-daisies or asters, to which they are closely related. Botanically they are differentiated by the pappus of the flower head being composed of short scales or minute bristles and usually two or four longer awns, whereas in *Aster* the pappus consists of more or less hairlike bristles. The genus *Boltonia*, named to commemorate the English eighteenth-century botanist, James Bolton, belongs in the daisy family COMPOSITAE. According to some botanical texts, its members are short-lived perennials. This may be true in the wild, but it certainly does not accurately describe the behavior of *B. asteroides* and *B. a. latisquama* in gardens. In cultivation they are long-lasting, persistent perennials of the easiest culture. The fruits are seedlike achenes.

Boltonias are deciduous, hairless herbaceous plants, with leafy stems, branched above, and smooth-edged or minutely-toothed, stalkless, alternate leaves that are often twisted at their base so that the blade is held vertically. The daisy-like flower heads, in large panicles, have white, pinkish, purplish, or violet ray florets that are female, and bisexual disk florets that form the eye of the flower head.

Native from New Jersey to South Dakota, Florida, and Texas, in dampish soils, *B. asteroides* averages 4 to 5 feet in height, but may be shorter or taller. It has broadly-linear to lanceolate, minutely-toothed leaves 2 to 6 inches long and up to ¾ inch wide. The flower heads, with white, pink, purple, or blue-purple ray florets are ¾ inch across. Variety *B. a. latisquama* (syn. *B. latisquama*) has the bracts of the involucre (collar of green leafy organs surrounding the flower head) spoon-shaped and blunt-ended instead of linear and more or less pointed. Its flower heads are usually 1 inch wide or wider, its ray florets light lavender to blue-violet. A horticultural variant, *B. a. l. nana*, 2 to 3 feet tall, has pinkish ray florets.

Garden and Landscape Uses and Cultivation. Boltonias make little show as single specimens, but when grouped in flower beds, along fences, or colonized in less formal areas, they can be very effective and are especially appreciated because they

Blueberries

Bolivicereus samaipatanus

A bougainvillea variety

Brassaia actinophylla

Bombax ceiba

Brassocattleya 'Albion'

Broccoli, a favorite vegetable

Brunfelsia pauciflora eximia

Hardy bulbs: Tulips and blue grape-hyacinths

bloom in fall. They are also good cut flowers. When used as such it is important to place them with their stems deep in water immediately after they are cut, and keep them in a cool dark place for twenty-four hours, otherwise they are likely to wilt. No difficulty attends their cultivation. They prosper in any ordinary soil in full sun. They are propagated by division in early spring or as soon as they are through blooming. They can also be raised from seeds. They should be spaced 1 foot to 1½ feet apart. Usually they stand well without staking, but where they are exposed to wind some support may be necessary. It is important to divide and replant boltonias fairly frequently, every two or three years. If this is not done they tend to become crowded, leggy, and unkempt.

BOLUSANTHUS (Bolusánth-us)—South African-Wisteria, Rhodesian-Wisteria. This genus of the pea family LEGUMINOSAE consists of one of the most beautiful species of native flowering trees of South Africa, a kind sometimes cultivated in southern California, Hawaii, and other mild lands. The name *Bolusanthus* is a combination of the name of the distinguished South African botanist Dr. Harry Bolus and the Greek *anthos*, a flower; literally it means Bolus's flower.

The South African-wisteria or van wykshout *B. speciosus* (syn. *Lonchocarpus speciosus*), usually 15 to 20 feet tall and occa-

Bolusanthus speciosus

sionally up to 40 feet, has corrugated, brown bark and deciduous, pinnate, lustrous, drooping leaves with usually thirteen lanceolate leaflets. Its violet-blue pealike flowers, in pendulous racemes much like those of *Wisteria*, are succeeded by narrow, grayish pods containing three to five flat seeds. The blooms have an unequally five-toothed calyx with the two upper lobes united high up, five much longer petals, the standard or banner bluntly-ob-

long, and ten stamens free nearly to their bases. There is one style. The fruits are pods. The durable hard wood is esteemed for wheel spokes and yokes.

Garden Uses and Cultivation. Where a small flowering tree is needed, this very attractive species should be seriously considered as such a garden ornamental. Although comparatively slow growing, especially on clayey soils, because of its handsome, shining foliage it is decorative even when quite small. It requires a sunny location and well-drained, preferably sandy soil; one containing lime is advantageous. In its native habitat it withstands several degrees of frost and fairly dry conditions. Because of its straggly root system it does not recover readily from transplanting, and from the seedling stage until they are set in their permanent location the plants should be grown in containers. Seeds germinate readily. The best plan is to sow them individually in small pots and so avoid, from the beginning, disturbing the roots.

BOMAREA (Bo-màrea). Closely related to *Alstroemeria*, but generally more definitely tuberous-rooted, commonly with twining, vining stems, and usually with the outer three petal-like perianth segments of its flowers more or less shorter than the inner three, *Bomarea* belongs in the amaryllis family AMARYLLIDACEAE, or according to those who recognize the segregation, to the alstroemeria family ALSTROEMERIACEAE. It occurs in the wild from Mexico to Chile and the West Indies. There are 150 species. The name commemorates the French botanist Jacques Christophe Valmont de Bomare, who died in 1807.

Bomareas are not extensively cultivated in North America. They are nonhardy, herbaceous perennials with parallel-veined leaves and flowers in pendulous umbels. The blooms have six perianth segments (petals or more properly tepals), six stamens, and one style. The fruits are capsules. The following may be cultivated. From Ecuador and Colombia, *B. caldasii* is up to 6 feet tall or sometimes taller. It has stalked, pointed, ovate-lanceolate leaves 3 to 6 inches long and many-bracted umbels about 5 inches wide of up to thirty blooms. The flowers, on stalks 1 inch to 2 inches long, have bright yellow inner petals and reddish-brown outer ones, the latter about 1½ inches long. Finely-hairy stems furnished with oblongish leaves up to 4 inches long are characteristic of *B. multiflora* of Colombia and Venezuela. From twenty to forty in an umbel, its 1-inch-long flowers have brown-spotted, reddish-yellow inner petals nearly as long as the reddish-tinged outer ones. Native to Peru, *B. oligantha* has pointed-oblong leaves 2 to 4 inches long and 1-inch-long, funnel-shaped blooms, with outer and inner petals nearly equal in length. The inner

Bomarea caldasii

ones are bright yellow spotted with brown. The outer ones are slender, bluntly-oblanceolate, yellow on their insides, reddish without, and are not spotted. Bright red-flowered *B. racemosa,* of Ecuador, sometimes misidentified in gardens as *B. patacocensis*, has oblong-lanceolate leaves up to 6 inches in length, and blooms 2½ to 3 inches long, their inner segments with yellow keels. True *B. patacocensis* has leaves up to 10 inches long and many-flowered umbels nearly 1 foot in diameter. Its flowers, 2½ inches long, are orange-yellow with maroon-red spots. This kind is one of the most magnificent species.

Garden and Landscape Uses and Cultivation. Bomareas are choice and charming vines for outdoors, in mild, nearly frostless climates, and for cool greenhouses. They succeed best where summers are not distressingly hot and are well satisfied with a porous, sandy-loamy, fertile soil that contains a fair amount of organic matter, such as leaf mold or peat moss. Locations that receive just a little shade from the strongest sun are appreciated. Trellises, wires, or other suitable supports around which the stems can twine must be available. A mulch of compost, leaf mold, or peat moss helps maintain uniform soil conditions. In greenhouses a winter night temperature of about 50°F is satisfactory, with a daytime increase of five to fifteen degrees permitted. Whenever the weather allows, the greenhouse should be ventilated freely. During their season of dormancy the soil should be kept almost dry, but from spring through fall it must be evenly moist. Well-rooted specimens benefit from regular applications of dilute liquid fertilizer during the summer. Propagation is easy by seeds that are fresh, and by carefully dividing the underground rhizomes, making sure that each division has some roots attached. The divisions are started in small pots and are grown in these until they are big enough to transfer to larger containers or to plant in beds. In general bomareas do better in ground beds than in pots or tubs.

BOMBACACEAE—Bombax Family. Tropical trees, chiefly natives of the Americas, make up this family of about twenty genera and 180 species of dicotyledons. Balsa wood, lightest of all commercial lumbers, is a product of *Ochroma*, the delicious durian fruit of *Durio*. The baobab (*Adansonia digitata*) is remarkable for its huge, swollen trunk. Other sorts are favored in the tropics as shade and street trees. Many attain great size.

Characteristically, plants of this family have deciduous, alternate leaves, undivided or of several leaflets that spread in finger-fashion from the top of the leafstalk. The prevailingly big, showy, usually symmetrical blooms, often displayed when the trees are without foliage, are solitary or in clusters from the leaf axils or arise from the stems, opposite the leaves. They have calyxes of five lobes or separate sepals, five or less often no petals, five to many separate or united stamens and frequently some staminodes (nonfunctional stamens), one style, and one to five stigmas. The fruits are capsules, pods, or botanically, are berry-like. Cultivated genera include *Adansonia, Bombax, Cavanillesia, Ceiba, Chiranthodendron, Chorisia, Durio, Ochroma, Pachira,* and *Pseudobombax.*

Bombax ceiba

BOMBAX (Bóm-bax) — Red-Silk-Cotton Tree. Closely related to *Pachira,* from which it differs in having its seeds embedded in kapok-like, silky hairs in the fashion of *Ceiba,* this genus of eight species is indigenous to the tropics of the Old World and New World. It belongs in the bombax family BOMBACACEAE and has as its name the Latin one, *bombax,* for cotton. The commonly cultivated *Bombax* is the red-silk-cotton tree (*B. ceiba* syns. *B. malabaricum, Salmalia malabarica*), native of tropical rain forests in India, Malaysia, and Australia. For *B. ellipticum* see *Pseudobombax ellipticum.*

The red-silk-cotton tree (*B. ceiba*) is often confused with the silk-cotton tree (*Ceiba pentandra*), native to tropical America. Like it, it is tall and deciduous and has a conspicuously buttressed trunk. Both species have stout, horizontal, tiered branches, and their trunks and branches have few to many stout, cone-shaped prickles. Both have long-stalked leaves with usually five leaflets that spread from the top of the leafstalk like fingers. From the silk-cotton tree, the red-silk-cotton tree differs in having smaller buttresses, larger, longer-stalked leaves, bigger flowers, usually lustrous red, but sometimes pink or yellowish, and with the column of stamens frayed at its tip into many filaments, and fruits with seeds surrounded by reddish, woolly hair, instead of whitish, silky floss.

Attaining a maximum height of 150 feet, but often not over 75 feet tall, the red-silk-cotton tree is imposing. Its straight trunk tapers only slightly. Its hairless leaves

have stalks only exceptionally over 1½ feet long, and five or seven elliptic to lanceolate leaflets up to 1 foot long. The flowers, in evidence toward the ends of the branches when the trees are leafless, are 4 to 6 inches wide. They have cup-shaped, five-parted calyxes, five velvety, spreading, and somewhat recurved petals 2¾ to 3¾ inches long, and numerous shorter stamens in clusters. The stamens have bright red stalks joined at their bases and purple-black anthers. The nectar contained in the blooms is sought by insects and birds. In Asia the calyxes from newly opened flowers are used in curries. Deer and other animals eat the blooms after they fall to the ground. The woody fruits, 4 to 8 inches long, contain numerous reddish-brown to black seeds and fibers that are inferior to, but are used like those of kapok (*Ceiba pentandra*).

Garden and Landscape Uses and Cultivation. In southern Florida, Hawaii, and other tropical areas, the red-silk-cotton tree is planted for shade and ornament. It grows in a variety of soils and is propagated by seeds.

BONAVIST is *Dolichos lablab.*

BONEMEAL. For long a staple garden fertilizer, bonemeal is probably no better as a source of phosphorus than such fertilizers as superphosphate and basic slag. Nevertheless, many gardeners consider it superior and prefer it. Surely it is safe. It harms neither roots nor foliage. The chief deterrent to its employment is that it costs

considerably more per unit of fertilizer value than superphosphate. For special usages such as potting this is usually of small importance to home gardeners. In addition to phosphorus, bonemeal supplies some nitrogen.

As its name implies, this fertilizer is prepared from bones. The more finely it is ground the more rapidly it is available to plants. Raw (untreated) bonemeal contains 20 to 24 percent phosphoric acid and 3 to 4 percent nitrogen. It is slow-acting. Much more quickly-available, less long-lasting, steamed bonemeal contains 22 to 30 percent phosphoric acid and about 1 percent nitrogen. Apply either in fall or early spring, raw bonemeal at 4 to 8 ounces to 10 square feet, steamed bonemeal at one-half those amounts, or mix them with potting soils at about 1 quart or 1 pint to the bushel, respectively. Bonemeal is slightly alkaline, but in quantities ordinarily used it has no adverse effects except perhaps on very strongly acid-soil plants.

BONESET. See Eupatorium.

BONGARDIA (Bongárd-ia). This unusual member of the barberry family BERBERIDACEAE is named after the German botanist August Gustav Heinrich Bongard, who died in 1839. It consists of one species native to Syria and Iran. Although quite different in appearance, botanically it is akin to the American genus *Caulophyllum,* and like it and *Leontice* is sometimes segregated in the leontice family LEONTICACEAE. A deciduous perennial, ***Bongardia chryso-***

Bongardia chrysogonum

Part of an American collector's bonsai collection

gonum has a woody tuber from the top of which come many glaucous, ovate-oblong, often blue-green, pinnate leaves with stalkless leaflets toothed at their apexes and sometimes purple-spotted at their bases. The flat, upturned, almost buttercup-like, flowers, ⅞ inch wide, have six clear yellow petals and the same number of stamens. They are in loosely-branched, erect panicles 6 inches to 1 foot in height that much overtop the foliage; they bloom in spring.

Garden Uses and Cultivation. Full sun and sandy, well-drained soil of moderate fertility provide suitable growing conditions. Excessive wetness is harmful. This plant cannot be expected to survive severe winters, but it should prosper outdoors in the warmer and drier parts of North America. It is suitable for rock gardens and similar locations and may be grown in a cool, sunny greenhouse. It is increased by offsets and seeds.

BONSAI. The intriguing Japanese art form called bonsai, pronounced bone-sigh, has gained much popularity in North America and Europe since World War II. Before then few collections existed on either continent and Westerners familiar with the training of what were generally referred to as dwarf-trained Japanese trees were few indeed.

Much mystery and many misconceptions surrounded the whole matter. In particular, it was believed that many decades, possibly a century or more of patient care were necessary to develop really fine, mature examples. Now many thousands of American bonsai fanciers know this is not true, that it is possible within a year or two or three to produce from carefully selected plants creditable specimens and that if one begins with just the right plant the basic training may be completed within a few hours. However, many fine specimens of great age are treasured in Japan and some have been imported from there to America and Europe.

The word bonsai (the singular and plural are the same) comes from the Chinese characters for *bon*, a container, and *sai*, to plant. It means a plant in a container, pot, or tray, but not just any plant in any such receptacle is a bonsai. To be such it must be a miniaturized specimen of a normally much larger tree or shrub trained to form an appearance of a considerably older, artistically pleasing specimen. A good test of whether this has been achieved is to photograph the bonsai against a plain background and block out the container. If the picture is apparently that of a full-sized, mature tree of artistic style and proportions it is probably a good bonsai.

The art of bonsai (the same word is used for the art as for the product) owes its origin to the traditional love of the Japanese for their superb mountains, seashores, and countryside and their appreciation of asymmetrical balance as opposed to the symmetry that for long characterized American and European garden art.

Bonsai trained according to classical principles established by the Japanese are of these five basic styles: formal upright, informal upright, slanting, semicascading, and cascading. Many substyles and combinations exist: clump, twin-trunk, multiple-trunk, sinuous, driftwood, windswept, or root-over-rock. All are variations of the five classic forms.

All bonsai are sculptural, three-dimensional objects with well-defined front, back, left, and right sides. When on display they are always viewed from the front, where a sparseness of foliage exposes the graceful or solid trunk line, a feature the Japanese enjoy very much. The back displays fullness, providing necessary depth.

Bonsai are created from seedlings, layerings, cuttings, nursery stock or naturally-dwarfed native plants. From the beginning the tree is grown in a particular style and shaped by drastic pruning and wiring. Refinements in form—again by pruning and wiring—are continued throughout the life of the plant, although a well-proportioned, twiggy tree will develop in a few years' time.

The creation of bonsai follows certain rules of design that dictate the final composition. They have been worked out and refined by the Japanese for generations. The component parts of a finished bonsai are container, surface roots, trunk, branches, twigs, and leaves. The trunk is the focal point and is proportioned into three approximately equal parts. The bottom one-third is completely bare of branches. The middle is free of branches in the front but framed by branches at the sides and in the back. The top one-third shows branches on all four sides.

The branches of a bonsai are arranged in sets of three. Number one branch of the first triad is the lowest of the tree. It is trained to one side and slightly forward. Number two is slightly higher on the trunk. It is inclined to the opposite direction. Number three is often situated between the first two and extends to the back. This patterning is repeated up the trunk in spiraling groups of three. When the top third is reached, small branches are trained forward to cover the trunk. Limbs are always designed in an alternating pattern to avoid monotony. These principles are basic to good design. The beginner in bonsai should strive to follow them, but

Bonsai coniferous trees in American collections imported from Japan: (a) *Chamaecyparis obtusa*, octopus style, 175 years old

(b) *Pinus thunbergiana*, root-above-ground style, 100 years old

(c) *Juniperus chinensis sargentii*, twin-trunk slanting style, 60 years old

(d) *Pinus parviflora*, raft style, 45 years old

nature is not always accommodating and compromises often must be made. Creating the illusion of age is one of the important aspects of bonsai. The shape of the trunk contributes to an aged look, and surface roots add to a venerable appearance. They should radiate around the trunk on all sides, making a solid base on which the tree is supported.

Branch shape must also suggest an old tree. The limbs taper from the trunk slowly out to the end—a network of fine twigs. If the leaves or the needles on these twigs are too large, the illusion is lost. Trees grown as bonsai should have small leaves or needles that are in proportion to the trunk and branches. Large-leaved species with pleasing twig patterns are frequently grown for winter viewing, after the leaves have fallen. The overall composition, in any case, must suggest a large tree reproduced on a miniature scale.

The container is always selected to complement the mood and color of the bonsai. It must help to present the tree and never detract from it.

There are traditional colors that are used with certain species. Muted earth colors, such as darker reds, browns, and grays, are used with evergreens, white or off-white with trees that have red or yellow flowers and fruits. Blue and green serve for plants with brilliant fall foliage. Black is used for trees with white flowers, white berries, or variegated foliage.

Usually the individual bonsai dictates the shape of its container, although there are some general classic rules. Light, feathery, plants are often planted in ornate,

Bonsai broad-leaved trees in American collections imported from Japan: (a) *Acer buergeranum*, informal upright style, 80 years old

(b) Azalea *(Rhododendron)*, root-over-rock style, 75 years old

(c) *Punica granatum*, slanting style, 65 years old

(d) *Elaeagnus pungens*, twin-trunk informal upright, 60 years old

(e) *Carpinus japonica*, informal upright style, 40 years old

(f) *Enkianthus perulatus*, informal upright style, 40 years old

Bonsai trained in America: (a) *Cedrus atlantica glauca*, slanting style, 15 years old

(b) *Chamaecyparis pisifera*, informal upright style, 8 years old

(c) *Juniperus virginiana*, wind-swept style, a collected tree trained for five years

(d) *Pinus mugo mugo*, a nursery-grown specimen trained for four years

(e) *Pinus parviflora*, octopus style

(f) *Juniperus procumbens*, cascade style

(g) Azalea (*Rhododendron*), cascade style

(h) *Juniperus chinensis*, root-over-rock style

(i) *Juniperus*, group-on-rock style

glazed containers that are decorated with designs of flowers and birds. Formal upright bonsai are planted in flat rectangular or oval pots, but heavy-trunked trees, particularly if they have thick foliage, appear to best advantage in bulky, deep, unglazed containers, which give them a stable, settled look. Deep round, octagonal, or square pots enhance the beauty of semicascading or cascading bonsai (and in this style the tree is always planted exactly in the center of the container). Shallow round or oval containers lend an informal feeling to windswept bonsai or group plantings.

A few of the plants commonly used for bonsai are pine, spruce, juniper, maple, hornbeam, flowering quince, and azalea. Some evergreen varieties are most frequently grown because their small leaves or needles are in proportion to the trunk and branches of a bonsai and because they can be viewed throughout the year, at times when other specimens are not at their best. Many deciduous species, however, are grown for their flowers, fruits, or fall foliage.

Bonsai may be created from any woody or semiwoody plant, and there are several ways to obtain good material. Plants may be propagated from seed or cuttings, by layering or any other technique, or they can be found already grown in nurseries or in the woods. The selection of material is important.

Growing bonsai from seed is a lengthy proposition, although frequently it is the only way to include uncommon specimens in a collection. Seedlings are transferred to individual pots or to the open ground until they are fit for training. Those grown directly in the ground produce quicker results, but are less convenient to shape. Cuttings are also handled in the usual way, as nurseries propagate ornamental plant material. Once it has roots, the cutting is placed in a pot, and training is started when the material is woody enough for shaping.

Layering has one advantage that the other propagating methods do not, you can start with a well-developed tree in a short time. The rooted material will have the trunk, branches, and twigs necessary for a fully-formed bonsai. There are several simple methods of layering, all variants of two types, ground layering and air layering. After the roots have formed, the rooted portion of the tree or shrub is severed from its parent and planted in its own container, where it is grown just as any other bonsai. Training can begin as soon as the plant is established.

The most expedient way, however, to obtain material for bonsai is in the form of nursery stock. The plant is fully established with a good fibrous root system, and training can be started immediately. Material that has been nursery-grown in cans is superior for bonsai, since the plant has already become conditioned to its reduced environment, and the procedures of root trimming and training will not cause excessive shock.

Natural dwarfed material collected from fields, mountains, and seashores is excellent for bonsai. Weather and wind have already given the specimen some "training," frequently in remarkable shapes. But collected material tends to have poor roots and must be replanted in the ground for

Bonsai created from nursery-grown plants: (a) Chamaecyparis

(b) Juniper

Seedling pine being trained as bonsai

Step-by-step training of a nursery-grown specimen as a bonsai: (a) Young nursery-grown hemlock

(b) Pruned and branches wired

(c) Close-up view of wiring

(d) Container ready for planting

(e) Specimen installed in container with roots about rock

(f) Close-up of rocks and roots

a year or two until a fine network of roots develops. Then it may be planted in the container and trained.

Select a specimen that has inherent possibilities of becoming a fine bonsai. Set the tree at eye level and turn it slowly around, looking thoughtfully at all sides to deter-

mine which parts to train for the front, the back, and the left and right sides. Now inspect the roots. Take a blunt tool and dig away some of the soil to expose the large, heavy roots near the base of the trunk. They should be of good size and widely spread. After the roots have been exposed,

the style can be settled upon and training can begin.

The traditional arrangement of branches is achieved by drastic pruning and wiring. Remove excess branches, shorten long ones. Then wind annealed copper wire around the trunk and branches, starting at the bottom of the tree with heavy wire and continuing out to the twig ends with lighter gauges. As the wire is applied, gently bend the trunk, branches, and twigs into position. Bending the wire hardens it so that it keeps the branches in place. Select the size of wire according to the thickness of the trunk or branch. Leave it on the tree from six months to one year. If the tree grows quickly, remove the wires before they scar the bark, and then rewire. After six months or so, the woody portions of the branches will retain their shape and the wire can be removed. Wiring is repeated as branches grow out and need positioning.

After the initial pruning and shaping, the tree is ready for planting in its container, which has been selected carefully to frame it. The drainage holes in the bottom of the pot are covered with plastic screen to prevent the soil from falling through. But before the soil is put in, several lengths of copper wire are looped U-shape through the drainage holes with both ends sticking up in the pot. They will eventually hold the plant in its place in the container. If the pot is small and has only one hole, the wire can be looped around a stick slightly larger than the hole. Then the bottom is covered to a shallow depth with very coarse sifted soil to provide good drainage. The main potting soil, which is also sifted, is spread over this—and the container is ready for the tree.

Root pruning is necessary to compensate for the drastic pruning in the upper parts of the plant and to encourage growth of fine, fibrous roots.

Remove one-third of the old soil from the root ball with a blunt tool. Cut back the long, loose roots, but retain fine rootlets that grow out of large roots near the trunk. They will sustain the plant while the new roots form.

Place the tree in its container, and settle it into place with a twisting motion. Pull the wire around the root ball, and twist it tight until the tree is held firmly in position. Cut off excess wire, and push the ends into the soil. Now fill in potting soil around the ball of roots so that no air spaces are left. After the potting soil has settled, brush away any excess and sprinkle sifted topsoil over the surface.

A cover of moss is grown on the topsoil to imitate nature and make the tree look more aged. It also prevents the soil in the container from being washed out during watering. Fresh, wet mosses and lichens give the grower the chance to arrange a natural underplanting with different shades and textures which enhance the composition. Dried, powdered moss, however, can also be sprinkled on and pressed down with a small trowel.

Now that the tree has been planted, it should be watered by placing the container in a basin and spraying from the top with a fine syringe. Be sure that enough water is given so that it flows from the drainage holes. The bonsai should be placed in a protected spot away from wind and strong sun for a period of three weeks until new growth begins to appear. The tree may then be placed in the sunshine and treated as any other.

Throughout its life, a bonsai needs special attention—at times, daily care—and it cannot be overlooked if the tree is to remain healthy and grow steadily more beautiful. A prime need is for fresh air and sunshine, which can best be supplied in the open. Bonsai are usually kept outdoors on tables. This affords free flow of air through the branches and facilitates watering, pruning, and insect control.

Periodic pruning and trimming are extremely important, for treated otherwise, a bonsai quickly loses its shape, and there will be no chance to develop an intricate network of branches. New growth on all bonsai is constantly trimmed. Deciduous trees have their new branchlets shortened, and in some species leaves are cut off healthy trees to promote branching and induce a new set of smaller leaves. Conifers may have their new shoots pinched back so that only four or five needles are left at the base.

A bonsai must be watered daily in spring and fall unless enough rain has fallen to take care of its needs, and in very dry and windy weather it may need water two or three times a day. The tree should never dry out completely, since the damage caused may result in loss of the plant.

There are several ways to water. If the owner has the time, he can use a watering can with a fine nozzle, watering each tree in turn, but a garden hose with a fine spray attachment is easier. In either case, the plant should be checked to see that an excess of water drains out the bottom hole, indicating that the soil has absorbed a sufficient amount.

Bonsai must be fertilized to keep them healthy. The tree needs good foliage color, well-formed flowers or fruits, and an intricate network of healthy branches. The easiest fertilizers to use are the water-soluble chemical compounds that contain trace elements. These are diluted by about one-half the strength recommended for plants grown more conventionally because excessive feeding will encourage the growth of extra-long shoots that spoil the bonsi's shape. Deciduous and flowering trees are fertilized once a week from early spring to late summer, evergreens for three weeks in spring after their new needles have hardened and for three weeks in the early fall before dormancy.

Bonsai are subject to the same pests and diseases as larger trees and shrubs. Because of their diminished surroundings, it is even more necessary to keep them in top condition, healthy and free from pests. They should be inspected frequently. Spray with insecticide at any sign of infestation.

In areas where winters are severe, bonsai need protection not from the cold so much as from high winds that cause the plants to die from parching. The best way to winter them over is in a deep cold frame where they are protected from the wind, alternate freezing and thawing, soil-eroding rains, snow that may crack and break branches, and chewing rodents. The temperature remains fairly constant within a cold frame. If the trees go into shelter well watered, they should pass the winter in good condition.

If a cold frame is not available, the bonsai can be wintered in the ground. The

Watering specimens in a Japanese bonsai nursery

pots are dug into the soil up to their rims, mulch is piled about halfway up the trunk, and a packing case is placed over the entire plant. This solution is particularly helpful to owners of only a few trees.

Frost-free structures adjacent to a heated dwelling, such as a porch or a lean-to plastic greenhouse, can be used if there is a window that can be opened to give heat in the coldest weather. The trees should be checked regularly for dryness and watered when necessary on days when the temperature is above freezing for several hours.

Since a bonsai remains in a container for life, soil becomes a very important matter. The potted tree cannot extend its roots and find moisture or food like a tree grown in the ground. The roots do continue to grow, but they eventually become bound and can no longer absorb moisture or the nutrients that are needed for healthy growth. As a result, bonsai must be repotted whenever they become rootbound. Evergreens, since they are slow-growing in general, can be left in their containers for three to five years. Most deciduous trees need repotting each year or two. Willows and other rapid growers may have to be repotted twice a year. Early spring, when the tree comes out of its dormant period, is the best time for repotting. The tree is taken out of its container, and before replanting in new soil, one-third of the old soil and roots is eliminated. In this way the trees are kept healthy.

The basic ingredients for bonsai soil are subsoil, sand, gravel, garden loam, leaf mold, compost, and peat moss. They are sun-dried, sieved into various sizes, and stored until use.

Subsoil is clay pellets usually obtained from 2 to 3 feet below the soil surface. When first dug, the material is usually crumbly and not sticky. Dried into hard lumps, it is a basic ingredient of potting soil. Coarse sand or gravel is necessary for good drainage and root formation. Local gravel pits or construction companies are the usual sources. Leaf mold, compost, or peat moss give acidity and nutrients. They are used in the proportions that each species requires. Garden loam is used with flowering and fruiting deciduous trees.

The bottom soil is made up of the larger lumps of clay, some leaf mold—each particle ¼ to ½ inch wide—and some coarse sand. The main potting soil is made up of the same ingredients, with each particle about ⅛ inch wide. For topsoil, screen the basic mixture to obtain grains the size of table salt crystals.

Usually bonsai are brought inside only for display. Since they are viewed from the front and at eye level, they must be placed on a stand, shelf, or table. The background should be light, plain muted color without design. Companion pieces such as stones, small containers of grasses, or lacquer boxes may be added to the display. A scroll is frequently hung behind the bonsai and to one side. But other objects are incidental to the tree. They must not be distracting. The display should communicate to the viewer a serene feeling of nature in miniature.

Plants suitable for bonsai include those used traditionally in Japan and related sorts as adaptable. Among those favored in Japan are *Ardisia crispa*, azaleas (various kinds), beech (*Fagus crenata*), black pine (*Pinus thunbergii* and *P. t. corticosa*), boxthorn (*Lycium chinense*), camellias, *Cotoneaster horizontalis*, crab apple (*Malus halleana spontanea*), crape-myrtle (*Lagerstromeria indica*), cryptomerias, dogwood (*Cornus contraversa*), *Elaeagnus pungens*, *Euonymus sieboldiana*, firethorn (*Pyracantha*), five-needle pine (*Pinus pentaphylla himekomatsu*), ginkgo (*Ginkgo biloba*), holly (*Ilex serrata*), hornbeams (*Carpinus japonica* and *C. laxiflora*), jujube (*Zizyphus jujuba inermis*), junipers (*Juniperus chinensis sargentii* and *J. rigida*), katsura (*Cercidiphyllum japonicum*), kumquat (*Fortunella japonica*), lilac (*Syringa vulgaris*), maples (*Acer buergerianum* and *A. palmatum*), pear (*Pyrus serotina*), plum (*Prunus mume*), pomegranate (*Punica granatum*), quinces (*Chaenomeles japonica* and *C. lagenaria*), red pine (*Pinus densiflora*), and spruce (*Picea jezoensis*).

BONTIA (Bón-tia). The only species of this genus of the myoporum family MYOPORACEAE is an inhabitant of the West Indies and northern South America. Its name commemorates the Dutch physician Jacob Bontius, who died in 1631. An evergreen shrub or tree up to 30 feet tall, ***Bontia daphnoides*** has hairless stems and foliage. Its pointed, toothless leaves are alternate, lanceolate to narrowly-oblong, and 2 to 4 inches long. Solitary or clustered in the leaf axils, the stalked flowers have calyxes with five hair-fringed lobes and a strongly two-lipped yellow and purple corolla, very hairy on its inside, and nearly 1 inch long. The lower corolla lip is conspicuously reflexed. Four stamens, in two pairs of different lengths, do not protrude. The egg-shaped, yellow fruits, about ½ inch long, are drupes (fruits structured like plums). They generally have four seeds.

Garden Uses and Cultivation. In frost-free tropical climates *Bontia* is occasionally planted as a general purpose ornamental evergreen. It grows with little difficulty in soil of average garden quality, in sun or part-day shade. It is increased by seeds, and by cuttings under mist or in a cold frame or greenhouse propagating bed. No special care of established specimens is needed. They stand trimming well.

BOOBYALLA is *Myoporum insulare*.

BOOJUM TREE is *Idria columnaris*.

BOOPHONE (Boophòn-e). Rare in cultivation, there are five species of this African genus. They belong in the lily family LILI-ACEAE. Their name is from the Greek *boos*, an ox, and *phone*, slaughter, and alludes to their poisonous properties. From *Boophone disticha* the Hottentots prepared arrow poison. The generic name has also been spelled *Boophane* and *Buphane*.

These plants of dry regions bloom most profusely following grass fires. Their starry flowers, which appear before the new foliage, are numerous and in large, hemispherical to spherical *Haemanthus*-like heads atop leafless stalks. They have perianths with short tubes and six spreading segments (petals) of equal size, six stamens, a threadlike style, and small stigma. The leaves are strap-shaped, the fruits triangular capsules with stalks that lengthen as the fruits develop. When mature the ball-like clusters of dry fruits free themselves and are driven across the ground by the wind like tumble weeds. The Boers call them horse scarers.

Kinds most likely to be cultivated are *B. disticha* and *B. ciliaris,* both South African. They have large bulbs that in the wild sometimes show their tips at the ground surface. They are insulated from the excessive heat of sun and grass fires by dense wads of persistent old foliage. The several to many thick leaves of **B. disticha** are 1 foot to 2 feet long, spring from bulbs up to 1 foot in diameter, and are arranged in a single plane as a wide-spreading fan. They are glaucous and have wavy margins. The flower stalk, up to about 1 foot long, terminates in a head of up to two hundred, but usually fewer, deep pink to red blooms. The four to six leaves of **B. ciliaris** are thick, fringed with hairs, and shorter than those of *B. disticha*. Its flower stalk is about 6 inches long, the blooms dull purple. Another South African, rare **B. haemanthoides** has a spherical or ovoid bulb about 6 inches in diameter and, arranged in two rows, thick strap-shaped leaves 6 inches to 1 foot long by 2 to 4 inches wide. The yellow flowers, which become reddish with age, are in dense umbels of many. They have petals ¾ inch to 1¼ inches long and exerted stamens. This species differs from *B. disticha* in having a shorter perianth tube and petals that do not redden until the flowers age.

Garden Uses and Cultivation. Only in warm climates with a definite dry season is it likely that these collectors' items will prosper outdoors. Elsewhere they must be regarded as indoor plants. They succeed in porous, fertile soil and need repotting at intervals of a few years only. During their dormant period water is withheld completely. As soon as new growth begins the soil is soaked, and copious applications, sufficient to keep it evenly moist, are made until the leaves begin to die naturally and a new season of rest is imminent. Then, watering is gradually reduced and finally abandoned. Applications of dilute liquid fertilizer benefit well-rooted specimens in active growth. Full sun and a minimum

Boophone haemanthoides

winter greenhouse temperature of 50 to 55°F, with a normal daytime increase of five or ten degrees, provide good growing conditions. Propagation is by offsets, which should be sizable before they are removed, and by seeds sown in a temperature of 60 to 70°F. Undoubtedly bulb cuttings could also be used as a means of increase.

BORAGE is *Borago officinalis*.

BORAGINACEAE—Borage Family. Somewhat more than 110 genera and approximately 2,400 species constitute the borage family, a native of tropical, subtropical, and temperate areas and especially abundant as to sorts in the Mediterranean region. Most are annuals, biennials, or herbaceous perennials. Some, removed to the *Ehretiaceae* by those who split the *Boraginaceae* as accepted here into more than one family, are shrubs or trees. A very few are vines. Many beautiful, familiar ornamentals including anchusas, cynoglossums, forget-me-nots, heliotropes, pulmonarias, and Virginia bluebells, as well as the herb borage belong in this family of dicotyledons.

Mostly rough-hairy, but sometimes hairless, plants of the borage family have cylindrical stems and usually alternate, generally undivided leaves, but the lower ones of some sorts are opposite. The flowers are studded along coiled stalks or branches of inflorescences that uncoil as the blooms open in succession from the base upward. Usually bisexual, they have calyxes of five lobes or sepals and a five-lobed corolla that is wheel-shaped and narrowly-tubular, with spreading petals, or funnel- or bell-shaped. There are five often unequal stamens, one style, and one sometimes-lobed stigma. The fruits are of four nutlets. Cultivated genera include *Anchusa, Arnebia, Borago, Brunnera, Buglossoides, Caccinia, Cerinthe, Cordia, Cryptantha, Cynoglossum, Echioides, Echium, Ehretia, Eritrichium, Hackelia, Heliotropium, Lindelofia, Lithodora, Lithospermum, Lobostemon, Mertensia, Messerschmidia, Moltkia, Myosotidium, Myosotis, Omphalodes, Onosma, Pentaglottis, Pulmon-*

aria, Solenanthus, Symphytum, and *Trachystemon.*

BORAGO (Bor-àgo)—Borage. This small group of Mediterranean region annual and perennial herbaceous plants gives name to the assemblage to which it belongs, the borage family BORAGINACEAE. It consists of three species. The name *Borago* is perhaps derived from the Latin *burra*, rough hair, and alludes to the stems and foliage; if so it is appropriately applied to these bristly-hairy plants.

Borages have alternate, lobeless leaves and leafy clusters of long-stalked, rich blue, or more rarely white, starry, wheel-shaped flowers cupped at their centers and carried on curving branches. Their corollas have short tubes with scales or crests of hairs in their throats and five pointed lobes. The five stamens, which may or may not protrude, are erect and joined to form a narrow cone around the slender style. The distinctly four-lobed ovary develops four smooth or rough, top-shaped nutlets, commonly called seeds, but truly fruits.

The common borage (*B. officinalis*) is a good bee plant and a pot herb. In its latter capacity it gives flavor to salads (it has a delicate, cucumber-like taste) and to claret cup. A thirteenth-century Arab writer denizened in Spain claimed that the young leaves and flowers added to wine "made one jolly," but one suspects that any exuberance generated was more the result of the Iberian vintage than of *Borago*. From 1 foot to 2 feet tall, **B. officinalis** has pendulous, blue, purplish, or white flowers about ¾ inch in diameter with protruding stamens. The nutlets (seeds) are rough and wrinkled. The oblong to ovate leaves narrow to stalks that extend down the stems as wings or are stalkless. They are up to 6 inches in length. This plant is naturalized and occurs spontaneously in waste places and along roadsides in many parts of North America.

The most decorative of the race is **B. laxiflora**, a native of Corsica. This rather

Borago officinalis

short-lived perennial easily renewed by seeds, forms tufts of oblong to ovate leaves from among which spread long prostrate stems, covered with backward-pointing hairs, that bear azure blooms over a long period. For *B. orientalis* see Trachystemon orientalis.

Garden Uses. The common borage is rather too weedy in appearance to merit very serious consideration as a flower garden annual; its place is rather in herb gardens and vegetable patches. Were it just a little more refined, judgment might be otherwise. The perennial *B. laxiflora* belongs in rock gardens, but probably is not too tolerant of very cold winters. It is more likely to prosper in the Pacific Northwest than in most other parts of North America. It is so readily raised from seeds, however, that it is surely worth trying.

Cultivation. Common borage grows without difficulty in ordinary garden soil in full sun. To promote the free development of young tender sprigs for picking the soil should be encouragingly nutritious and not excessively dry. The first sowing is made outdoors in early spring, and two or three later seedings are made at intervals to ensure succession. It is a mistake to provide rich soil for *B. laxiflora*. A lean medium that will not support vegetative exuberance is most likely to give flowers of clearest hue as well as neater plants. Full sun (except that, in very hot climates, tempering shade from a nearby rock or evergreen may be beneficial in the afternoon) is needed, and no more water should be provided than essential to keep the foliage from wilting. Seeds are the most practical means of propagation.

BORASSUS (Borás-sus)—Palmyra Palm. The most important of the eight species of *Borassus* of the Old World tropics is the palmyra palm, which according to an ancient Tamil song "Tala Vilasam," has 801 uses. Whether that represents poetic licence is not known, but certainly the natives of regions it inhabits employ it for many purposes. The genus *Borassus* be-

Borago officinalis (flowers)

longs in the palm family PALMAE. Its name derives from the Greek *borassos,* the immature spadix of the date palm.

The palmyra palm (*B. flabellifer*) is native to India, Ceylon, and Malaya. It grows 60 to 70 feet tall or sometimes taller and has a straight, solitary, ringed trunk up to 3 feet or more in diameter, topped with a more or less globose crown of rigid palmate (hand-shaped) leaves with spiny stalks. The leaves are 8 to 10 feet long, broader than they are long, and divided to about their middles into many, slender, sword-shaped segments each notched at its apex. The flower clusters originate in the leaf axils and have catkin-like branches with the small flowers densely packed in pits along them. Male and female blooms are on separate trees, and it is impossible to distinguish the sexes until the first flowers appear, usually when the trees are about fifteen years old. The fruits are subglobose, brown, and up to 6 inches in diameter.

Borassus flabellifer, in Thailand

This species is widely cultivated in tropical Asia. Its fruits are eaten and from its female clusters sap, called toddy, is tapped and used as a beverage. From the sap also is produced jaggery or palm sugar, vinegar, and a potent intoxicating drink called arrack. Seedlings two to three months old are eaten after boiling or are dried and stored for later consumption. The trunk supplies lumber for construction and the leaves are used for thatching and making mats and baskets, the fibers for fabricating into cords and ropes.

Garden and Landscape Uses. This palm grows slowly and retains its lower leaves for a long time so that young specimens have a very different aspect than older

ones. They are clothed with foliage to or almost to the ground. As a single specimen or planted in groups, the palmyra palm lends interest to a landscape. It is appropriate for avenues and withstands seashore conditions well. This palm may be grown in tropical conservatories, especially in those devoted to displaying plants useful to man.

Cultivation. This species succeeds in full sun in any fairly good, not excessively dry soil. Because it has long and deep roots *Borassus* is difficult to transplant successfully when big. Plants should be set in their permanent locations from pots when quite young. Under greenhouse cultivation it responds to a minimum winter temperature of 60 to 65°F with higher temperatures maintained during the day and at other seasons. A humid atmosphere and shade from strong sun are required. The soil should be kept moist at all times, and feeding of container-grown specimens with dilute liquid fertilizer is done at regular in-

Borassus flabellifer, in Florida

tervals from spring through fall. Propagation is by seeds planted in a sandy, peaty soil in a temperature of 80 to 85°F. The seeds are slow to germinate and because they first develop a long, vertical, downgrowing, rootlike structure, called a hypocotyl, it is necessary to plant them in very deep containers such as inverted drainpipes. These should be at least 2½ feet deep. For additional information see Palms.

BORDEAUX MIXTURE. The first effective spray discovered to control a plant disease, bordeaux mixture is still a useful, widely-used protectant. In 1882 in France an alert investigator of downy mildew disease,

then causing serious damage to vineyards, noticed that vines along a road near Bordeaux that had been treated with a poisonous-looking mixture of lime and copper sulfate to discourage pilferage were free or nearly free of the disease. Three years later he published his discovery with directions for preparing bordeaux mixture. There are various formulas. For preparing a standard 4-4-50 mixture, copper sulfate, hydrated lime, and water in the proportions of four pounds each of the two first to fifty gallons of the last are used.

The method of preparation is important. Mix the lime with water at the rate of one pound to a gallon and in a separate container dissolve the copper sulfate in water in the same proportion. Pour the lime water through cheesecloth or a fine wire screen into the sprayer and add water until the amount is such that when the solution of copper sulfate is added the total will be the required amount of bordeaux mixture. Then pour in the copper sulfate solution and mix thoroughly. Small amounts of approximately 4-4-50 bordeaux mixture can be made by mixing four ounces of hydrated lime in two gallons of water, dissolving four ounces of copper sulfate in another gallon of water in a separate container, and then pouring the second into the first. Easier to use but rather less effective, are commercial bordeaux mixture powders and pastes. With these follow the manufacturer's directions.

Use bordeaux mixture as soon as it is made. It soon deteriorates after the lime water and copper sulfate are mixed. By varying the proportions of the ingredients used, bordeaux mixtures containing more lime, better suited for stone fruits such as cherries and plums, and less lime, considered better for azaleas and other acid-soil plants, may be had. Used indiscreetly, bordeaux mixture can harm some plants. Before using it check with your Cooperative Extension Agent or other reliable source for specific information, and do not mix bordeaux mixture with other sprays without checking their compatability. Injury from bordeaux mixture is more likely to occur when it is used in dull, humid weather and does not dry quickly. Bordeaux mixture is visible on plants as a rather unsightly bluish-white deposit.

BORDER. This is a name often used for a bed conspicuously longer than wide planted with shrubs and small trees or with flowering plants, herbs, or vegetables. Usually borders are backed by walls, fences, or hedges and are viewed chiefly from one side. Less commonly they are free-standing island beds. Undoubtedly the term first came into use to designate plantings along the boundaries of properties or of discreet units within properties. The best known employment of the term is probably perennial border, or as it is more com-

Borders of hardy perennials

Border of colored-leaved trees and shrubs

in vigorous condition by watering, fertilizing, pruning, and controlling diseases and pests. The trunks of newly transplanted specimens may be wrapped (see Tree Wrapping). Some trunk borers can be killed by probing with a flexible wire, by carefully cutting out with a sharp knife, or by injecting toxic paste (obtainable from dealers in garden supplies) and then sealing the entrances to the holes with clay, putty or chewing gum. Spraying or painting trunks and branches of susceptible trees and shrubs three or four times at weekly or ten-day intervals during the egg-laying period and before the larvae penetrate is effective with many species of borers. Spraying and pruning out and burning affected parts are recommended to combat root and twig borers. Up-to-date recommendations about sprays to use and other information of local importance in controlling borer damage is available from Cooperative Extension Agents and other authorities.

BORONIA (Bor-ònia). Named in honor of Francesco Borone, a personal servant who lost his life in 1794 collecting a plant desired by his employer, the distinguished botanist John Sibthorp, *Boronia* of the rue family RUTACEAE comprises seventy species endemic to Australia and Tasmania.

Boronias are nonhardy, evergreen shrubs with opposite, undivided or pinnate leaves with a terminal and lateral leaflets. The leaves are sprinkled with tiny translucent dots. The attractive, small, red, purple, or white, often fragrant flowers have four each sepals and petals, the latter spreading or forming a cupped or more or less globose bloom. There are eight stamens, similar or with four small and bearing pollen, the others large and sterile, and four styles. The capsule-like fruits are of two to four carpels.

A leafy, much-branched shrub 3 to 5 feet tall, **B. elatior** has hairy shoots and rather distantly spaced pairs of stalked, pinnate

monly designated in Great Britain, herbaceous border. For more about this see Flower Beds and Borders.

BORECOLE. See Kale or Borecole.

BORERS. These are insects that excavate tunnels or cavities inside roots, tubers, bulbs, trunks, branches, twigs, shoots, stems, or leafstalks and live and feed there. Usually the culprits are the larvae (worm or grub stage) of beetles and moths, but some mature beetles operate in this manner. Infestations originate from eggs laid on the outside of or less often beneath bark or in some cases, as for instance those

of the iris borer, on foliage. They hatch to release minute larvae that immediately bore inward. Many kinds of borers are especially given to invading tissues of trees and shrubs weakened by long periods of drought, or that have recently been transplanted. Some kinds, for example, the peach tree borer, produce masses of sawdust-like frass at the entrances to the tunnels. Others leave no such telltale sign. Many borers restrict their activities to one or a few related hosts. Others are less choosey.

Controls must be tailored to the habits of the kind of borer. Of general importance, maintain susceptible trees and shrubs

Boronia elatior

leaves 1 inch to 1½ inches long, with five to thirteen linear leaflets, hairy or hairless. When brushed against, the foliage gives off a very pleasant, pungent, lemony odor. The short-stalked, deep pink to deep red, ¼-inch-wide, nearly spherical flowers are in cylindrical, leafy spikelike racemes 3 to 6 inches long. Scarcely fragrant, they have two types of stamens and are often of different hues on the same plant. Generally not more than 2 feet tall and hairless, *B. megastigma* has slender, minutely-hairy, wandlike shoots and rather sparse foliage. Its stalkless leaves are of three or five blunt, narrowly-linear, heathlike leaflets ⅓ to ¾ inch in length. The solitary, short-stamened, wonderfully apple-scented, ½-inch-wide blooms have rich brown-purple outsides and yellow interiors. Their stamens are of two kinds. The flowers, along leafy shoots, have a raceme-like effect.

Boronia megastigma

Garden and Landscape Uses. Boronias are elegant shrubs for fronting plantings of taller kinds and for displaying as single specimens and in groups. They are hardy only in dryish, frost-free or essentially frost-free climates that approximate those of their native lands. Sometimes, especially *B. megastigma,* they are grown in pots in greenhouses and windows. In California, where suitable climate conditions prevail, they disappoint a little because they are generally short-lived and for that reason have not attained great popularity. They succeed best where they receive just a little shade, and unlike most Australian plants, they appear to need fairly ample supplies of moisture at all times.

Cultivation. A well-drained soil rich with peat or other organic matter is to their liking. The tendency to die early may in part be overcome by pruning drastically each year as soon as flowering is over.

As indoor pot plants boronias delight in fairly nutritious, sandy-peaty soil. Their containers should be very well drained and

be a little on the small side rather than over-large in comparison to the size of the plants. Flowering shoots are pruned back severely as soon as blooming is through and about one month later, when new shoots begin to show, any repotting needed is done. The soil must never dry out, nor must it remain sodden for long periods. Specimens that have filled their pots with roots benefit from the application of dilute liquid fertilizers. Good light with just a little shade from fierce, summer sun is appropriate. Winter temperatures at night of 45 to 50°F and by day of five to about ten degrees higher are suitable. From spring to fall as much ventilation is as practicable should be given. Propagation of boronias is easy from firm, but not hard cuttings of young shoots planted in a mixture of sand or perlite and peat moss under mist or in a cold frame or greenhouse propagating bed. They are also easily raised from seeds, which generally take three weeks to one month to germinate.

BORZICACTUS (Borzi-cáctus). The genus *Borzicactus* of the cactus family CACTACEAE is variously interpreted by botanists. Those who favor genera and species based on comparatively minute differences recognize four species and refer to other genera closely similar plants the more conservative include in *Borzicactus*. Because cactus collectors and nurseries commonly accept the segregations, as a matter of convenience rather than conviction that it is the soundest botanical procedure they are dealt with separately in this Encyclopedia. Many species that conservatives include in *Borzicactus* are discussed under the entries *Arequipa, Bolivicereus, Loxanthocereus, Maritimocereus, Matucana, Morawetzia, Oreocereus, Seticereus,* and *Submatucana.*

As treated here, *Borzicactus* is a native of Ecuador. Its name commemorates Antonio Borzi, Director of the botanical gardens at Palermo, Italy who died in 1921. Its members are low, bushy, or sometimes prostrate plants with stems with eight to sixteen notched ribs. The spine clusters are of up to twenty spreading radials and one to few down-pointing centrals. The red flowers, open by day, are about 2 inches across and have hairy, cylindrical perianth tubes and a strongly-oblique face or lip with spreading petals. The fruits are about ¾ inch across and hairy.

Typical *B. sepium* has dark green, often prostrate stems up to 4½ feet long by 1½ to 2 inches thick, with eight to eleven or occasionally as many as fourteen ribs. Its spines are red-brown. In each cluster there are eight to ten radials less than ½ inch long and one to three centrals about 1½ inches long. Scarcely distinguishable from the last except that its spines are irregularly twisted and gray, *B. aequatorialis* is by conservative botanists included in *B. sepium* as are *B. websterianus* and *B. morley-*

anus. Light green, fourteen-ribbed stems up to 4 inches thick with clusters of golden-yellow spines consisting of twenty radials and four somewhat stronger centrals, characterize *B. websterianus.* In *B. w. rufispinus* the stems are dark green, the spines stouter and reddish-brown. Of upright, bushy habit, *B. morleyanus* has stems 1½ to 2½ inches thick, with ten to sixteen ribs with closely-spaced large, white areoles (pads from which the spine clusters arise) each with up to twenty down-pointing, thin, bristly, brown spines about 1 inch long.

Garden and Landscape Uses and Cultivation. Attractive for inclusion in cactus collections, borzicactuses succeed in warm, dry climates outdoors along with other desert species reveling in well-drained soil and full sun. Indoors they prefer a winter night temperature of about 55°F. Water moderately in summer, more sparingly in winter. For more information see Cactuses.

BOSSIAEA (Bossi-aèa). Entirely Australian, and consisting of about thirty-five species of shrubs or rarely shrublets of the pea family LEGUMINOSAE, the genus *Bossiaea* has a name that commemorates the French botanist Mons. Boissieu Lamartinière, who lost his life in a shipwreck in 1788.

Bossiaeas are highly variable in appearance. Some kinds are without apparent leaves, but have much flattened, winged stems that function as leaves. Others have wiry stems and alternate or opposite leaves that vary greatly in size and shape according to species. The leaves, undivided, may be toothed or toothless. The yellow, orange, or red, pealike flowers are solitary or in twos or threes from the leaf axils. They have calyxes with the upper pair of their five lobes more or less united into a lip. The standard or banner petal is subspherical, and notched at its apex. The keel is blunt. There are ten united stamens. The fruits are flat pods.

A wiry-stemmed shrub 1 foot to 2 feet tall, *B. aquifolium* has rather distantly spaced, opposite, almost stalkless, prickly-edged, kidney-shaped leaves, broader than their less than 1-inch-long length. Solitary from the leaf axils, the yellow flowers with brown centers and keels are ⅓ to ½ inch long. The shape of the leaves of *B. biloba* give reason for the name. They are alternate, about ½ inch long, narrowly-triangular with the narrow end attached to the stem, and the broad apex deeply notched to form two lobes. The red and yellow flowers, a little more than ½ inch long, come from the axils of the upper leaves and form raceme-like arrangements. Up to 2 feet tall, *B. ornata* has wandlike stems, and alternate, rather distantly spaced, short-stalked, oblong-elliptic to pointed-ovate leaves ¾ inch to 2 inches long. Its clustered, ¾-inch-wide blooms are yellow and red.

Garden and Landscape Uses and Cultivation. Bossiaeas are attractive ornamentals little known to gardeners. They are adapted for outdoor planting in warm, dry climates, such as California, and may be used to add variety to garden and landscape plantings. They need well-drained soil, for most kinds dampish rather than dry, and sunny locations. Propagation is usually by seeds.

BOSTON FERN is correctly *Nephrolepis exaltata bostoniensis.* The name is also applied to other varieties of *N. exaltata.*

BOSTON-IVY is *Parthenocissus tricuspidata.*

BOTANIC GARDENS AND ARBORETUMS.

Botanic or botanical gardens (the terms are interchangeable as to meaning) maintain for display and scientific research permanent collections of a wide variety of living plants of which a large proportion are natural species rather than horticultural varieties and of which comparatively few are likely to be under intensive study by the staff at any one time. In these ways they differ from experimental stations, plant breeding stations, and similar scientific-oriented plantings where ordinarily much larger numbers of many fewer sorts are grown, usually only for the periods, short or long, they are under investigation, and often with the objective of studying or developing horticultural or agricultural varieties. Botanic gardens differ from nature reserves and similar preservations in not limiting their efforts to encouraging spontaneous floras, but in cultivating as well many kinds exotic to their regions.

Botanic gardens differ from the public parks in their primary commitments being to research and education, with passive recreation an important, but secondary function. Provision for active recreation such as ball playing and other games as well as less strenuous public enjoyments are the chief purposes of public parks, with educational features sometimes playing a secondary part. Scientific investigation is usually not undertaken in such places. An arboretum is a botanic garden or a part of a botanic garden devoted exclusively or almost exclusively to trees, shrubs, and woody vines.

A critical requirement of a botanic garden is that it maintains permanent, orderly collections of correctly identified living plants together with appropriate records of their sources of origin and other pertinent data and that these collections be used as the basis of scientific or scholarly observation, investigation, and usually publication. Living plant collections, even extensive ones, labeled or not, the purpose of which are chiefly or only display scarcely qualify within the best meaning of the term as botanic gardens. Nevertheless because of their often great importance to those interested in horticulture some such are included in the selection to be here discussed.

As important as the living plant collections to a well-rounded botanic garden are a herbarium and library. Given these three, with adequate emphasis on each and a technical staff of botanists and botanically-oriented horticulturists who are expert plantsmen and one has a botanic garden. If any one of the three is lacking the result may be an admirable botanic or horticultural institution, but scarcely, in the fullest traditional meaning of the term, a botanic garden.

In addition to the activities necessary to the maintenance and development of the living plant collection, herbarium, and library, and the production and dissemination of information based on these, related spheres of interest, not essential to botanic gardens, but entirely appropriate to them, may be developed. These may include plant breeding, decorative displays, museum exhibits, and programs of public education oriented toward botany, horticulture, and related subject. Botanic gardens have traditionally been active in promoting plant collecting expeditions and introducing new plants to cultivation and in serving as training places for horticulturists and botanists.

Sir Arthur Hill, one-time Director of the Royal Botanic Gardens, Kew, England, pointed out that "There are three things which have stimulated men throughout the ages to travel far and wide over the surface of the globe, and these are gold, spices, and drugs. It is to the two latter of these that we may trace the origin and foundations of botanic gardens." Surely the first such gardens in Europe owed their beginnings to a developing interest in plants with medicinal or presumed medicinal virtues, and certainly more than one botanic garden in the tropics began as an adjunct to the spice trade.

How far back the development of botanic gardens can be traced depends upon one's interpretation of what constitutes a botanic garden. At Alexandria before the great fire, in Assyria, China, and later in Mexico, enclosed gardens in which plants of economic use and ornamental values were cultivated were maintained. The oldest garden of which a representation exists, the Royal Garden of Tholmes III of Egypt, was planned about 1500 B.C. by Nekht, head gardener of the gardens of the temple at Karnak. In all probability the rectangular Royal Garden, planted with palms, grape vines, and lotuses in pools, was primarily for aesthetic enjoyment, whereas that of the temple probably stressed plants useful for healing and in other ways. Aristotle, about 350 B.C., established a botanic garden in Athens that, after his death, was operated by his student, the garden's first director and earliest European botanical author Theophrastus. In Rome, in the first century A.D., Anonius Castor cultivated a garden devoted to medicinal plants, which provided the basis for some of the writings of Dioscorides.

The Chinese Father of Medicine and Husbandry, more or less legendary Shen Nung of 2800 B.C., is said to have investigated the healing powers of herbs. The Han Emperor Wu Ti, who died in 86 B.C. dispatched collectors to distant parts of his empire to bring back for the gardens of his palace rare trees, shrubs, and herbaceous plants. Among those he introduced were alfalfa, bananas, beans, cannas, cinnamon, coriander, cucumbers, grape vines, litchi nuts, sweet oranges, and walnuts.

Aztec gardens, developed quite separately from those of the Old World, contained collections of plants orderly arranged. That at Chalco, continued after the Spanish Conquest of Mexico, as well as those of Atzcapotzalco, Huaxtepec, and Texcoco, provided source materials for the great work on the natural resources of Mexico by Francisco Hernandez, court physician to Philip II of Spain, which was published in 1561. The discovery in 1929 in the Vatican library of the Badianus Manuscript, an Aztec herbal of 1552 by a native physician, more clearly highlighted the high degree of competence in medicine the Indians of Mexico attained before the Conquest, this in part supported by collections of plants that may properly be called botanic.

Modern botanic gardens cannot be directly traced to the gardens so far discussed. Their origin is traceable to monastery and abbey gardens of the ninth century and later. One of the first, that at the Abbey of St. Gall near Lake Constance, Switzerland, maintained a "hortus" of eighteen rectangular beds, and a "herbularius" or physic garden of eight similar beds and surrounding borders. In the sixteenth century the medical schools of universities in Italy and elsewhere established physic gardens for the chief purpose of cultivating medicinal herbs and thus assuring supplies of satisfactory quality.

The earliest of these university botanic gardens were those developed about 1543 at Padua and Pisa in Italy, the Padua garden consisting of geometrically arranged, stone-edged beds. Which was first is not surely known. Both are extant. The movement soon spread. Similar gardens were established at Bologna in 1547, Zurich in 1560, Paris in 1570, Leipzig in 1580, and the Jardin des Plantes, Paris in 1610.

There were several private botanical collections of living plants in England before the first university botanic garden was established there. The Father of English Botany, the Reverend William Turner, who died in 1586, established such a collection in a garden near Kew and later, when he was Dean of the Cathedral at Wells, another there. At what was then fashionable Holborn in London, John Gerard, whose death occurred in 1607, had a physic garden. Of this in 1596 he published the first complete catalog of the kinds of plants contained in one garden. It enumerates 1,030 sorts. Another great English garden was that of the John Tradescants, father and son, at Lambeth. The father, gardener to Queen Elizabeth I and Charles I, died in 1638. A catalog of this garden was published by the son in 1656. Also important was the physic garden of John Parkinson, King's Herbarist to Charles I, at Long Acre in London. Parkinson died in 1650.

The first university botanic garden in England, originally called the Public Physick Garden, was established at Oxford in 1621. It is now the Oxford Botanic Garden. According to Thomas Baskerville, there were in cultivation there by about 1670 "3000 severall sorts of plants for ye honor of our nation and Universtie and service of ye Commonwealth." The first wooden greenhouse ever made was erected in the Oxford garden in 1734, its purpose "to preserve tender plants and trees from the Injury of hard winter." Another early English botanic garden still in existence, the Chelsea Physic Garden in London, occupies land acquired in 1673 to which plants from an earlier garden were transferred in 1676.

The Royal Botanic Gardens, Kew, England, grew in somewhat Topsy-like fashion from an area of nine acres set aside in 1760 by Augusta, Princess Dowager of Wales, as a physic garden, to its present nearly 300 acres that contain by far the largest collection of living plants in cultivation at any one place in the world, as well as a herbarium and library of major importance and other botanical and horticultural facilities. Several acres of greenhouse are maintained. Following the death of the Princess Augusta the garden became the property of George III who added to it adjoining land and placed it under the direction of Sir Joseph Banks who for almost half a century brilliantly administered its development. Eventually Kew became the chief center of botanical enterprise and research for the entire British Empire, with numerous colonial botanic gardens, especially in the tropics, closely associated with it.

The first tropical botanic garden was established at Mauritius in 1735, the next on St. Vincent in the West Indies in 1764. As with nearly all such gardens developed in warm parts of the world, the original objectives of these were to improve the economies of the countries they served and to bring profit to the colonial powers who founded the gardens, by introducing and promoting the planting of useful crops. The Mauritius garden was responsible in bringing into cultivation there, cinnamon, nutmeg, pepper, and sugar cane. The breadfruit trees that Captain Bligh collected on his famous and fateful 1788-89 voyage on the *Bounty* were to have been brought to the botanic garden at St. Vincent to serve as a source of cheap food for slaves. Three years later, Bligh introduced to St. Vincent the first breadfruit trees ever brought to the New World.

Many other tropical botanic gardens and gardens designated as such were founded later, chiefly by the Belgians, British, Dutch, and French, to a lesser extent by the Germans. Others were developed in more temperate regions such as Australia, South Africa, and New Zealand. Some of the smaller tropical gardens, including the one at Mauritius, never became much more than plant introduction and trial stations. Others became the equals of the most important botanic gardens of temperate regions. Greatest of all are those at Bogor, Java, Peradeniya, Ceylon, and Singapore.

The first botanic garden in North America is generally considered to be that of John Bartram. This was preceded, however, by a garden devoted to the cultivation, study, and production of medicinal herbs established in 1694 on the banks of the lower Wissahickon Creek in Pennsylvania by a sect of German Pietists led by Kelpius. Bartram's garden, still in existence and partly restored, is also in Pennsylvania, on a bank of the Schuylkill River at Philadelphia. It was established in 1731 by one of America's most remarkable botanical pioneers. An unlettered farmer, Bartram, well before he was thirty, became so enamored with the study of plants that he gave up farming, hired a school teacher to instruct him in Latin, and plunged into a new career. He journeyed repeatedly through what was the uncharted wilderness of eastern North America from the Canadian border to Florida, following scarcely travelable Indian trails. He discovered and collected numerous new plants for his garden and herbarium, the most noteworthy, the franklin tree (*Franklinia alatamaha*). He conducted a vast correspondence and exchanged plants with botanists abroad and at home. Bartram's home and garden was for long the chief center of botanical culture in North America. In 1765 King George III appointed Bartram, then sixty-six, King's Botanist. In August of that year he discovered the tree he named in honor of Benjamin Franklin. In 1777 Bartram died, but his garden and work were continued by his son William who died in 1823.

The Elgin Botanic Garden in New York City was begun in 1801 by wealthy David Hosack, professor of materia medica at Columbia College. It occupied twenty acres of the land on which Rockefeller Center now stands and included extensive greenhouses. Two thousand kinds of plants are listed as growing there in Hosack's first catalog, published in 1806, more in his 1811 edition. The financial strain of keeping this elaborate establishment strained Hosack's purse to the extent that he had to seek public aid. The garden became the property of the State of New York, by which it was much neglected. In 1814 it was transferred to Columbia College, which considerably later became Columbia University.

The first botanic garden established in North America by a college or university was that of Harvard, founded in 1805 at Cambridge, Massachusetts. Occupying seven acres, this was directed by a succession of prominent botanists and served as an important teaching facility until its abandonment some century and a quarter later.

North American botanic gardens and arboretums extant are numerous. Interpreting the term botanic garden sometimes very generously, here is a selection presented alphabetically according to states and concluded with some in Canada.

ALABAMA
Theodore (near Mobile)—Bellingrath Gardens (75 acres). Specialty: camellias, approximately 1,000 varieties. (Established 1932.)

ARIZONA
Phoenix—Desert Botanical Garden of Arizona (150 acres). Specialty: cactuses and other succulents. (Founded 1948.)

CALIFORNIA
Arcadia—Los Angeles State and County Arboretum (127 acres). Rich collections of subtropical trees, shrubs, and herbaceous plants including orchids, totaling in excess of 1,000 genera, 3,500 species, 1,600 varieties. (Founded 1948.)

Berkeley—Regional Park Botanic Garden (7 acres). Largest collection of species native to California including complete collections of *Arctostaphylos* and *Ceanothus*. (Founded 1940.)

Claremont—Rancho Santa Ana Botanic Garden (87 acres). Extensive collections of plants native to California. (Founded 1927.)

Los Angeles—University of California Botanical Garden (8 acres). Varied collections including a good representation of Australian plants, totaling about 3,500 species and varieties. (Founded 1929.)

San Francisco—Strybing Arboretum and Botanical Gardens (70 acres). Diversified collections of over 6,000 species of trees, shrubs, and herbaceous plants with emphasis on sorts native to South Africa, Australia, and New Zealand. Good collections of camellias, escallonias, lilies. (Founded 1937.)

San Marino—Huntington Botanical Gardens (125 acres surrounding the Huntington Art Gallery and Library). Horticulturally outstanding. Includes one of the most extensive collections of cactuses and other succulents in the world, a fine collection of palms hardy in southern California, many other interesting native and exotic plants. (Founded 1905.)

Aquatic garden, Los Angeles State and County Arboretum

Native plants of California in the Rancho Santa Ana Botanic Garden

View in Strybing Arboretum and Botanical Gardens

Huntington Botanical Gardens (a) Palms (b) Cactuses

Santa Barbara—Santa Barbara Botanical Garden (75 acres). Exclusively devoted to native plants of California of which extensive collections are attractively displayed, mainly in natural settings. (Founded 1926.)

COLORADO

Denver—Denver Botanic Gardens (22 acres). Outdoor plant collections of nearly 150 genera, 1,500 species and varieties. Conservatory collections of more than 600 genera, 2,200 species and varieties. (Founded 1951.)

DISTRICT OF COLUMBIA

Washington—United States National Arboretum (415 acres). Very extensive collections of trees and shrubs including more than 1,000 varieties of azaleas, 300 of crab apples, 1,500 of dwarf conifers, and 700 of hollies. Also collections of daffodils, day-lilies, peonies, and some other herbaceous plants. (Founded 1927.)

FLORIDA

Miami—Fairchild Tropical Garden (80 acres). Unique in displaying outdoors in attractively landscaped grounds larger collections of plants of the humid tropics and subtropics than any other garden in the continental United States. Palms and cycads are especially well represented. (Founded 1938.)

Sarasota—Marie Selby Botanical Gardens (9 acres). This is believed to be the only botanical garden in the world oriented primarily to the cultivation and study of epiphytic plants. These include bromeliads, ferns, gesneriads, orchids, and

Administration Building, United States National Arboretum, Washington, D.C.

Fairchild Tropical Garden: Vista through Bailey Palm Glade

other kinds that grow on trees, rocks, and sometimes other aerial locations instead of in the ground. (Founded 1971.)

GEORGIA

Pine Mountain—Callaway Gardens (2,500 acres, a large part of which is more or less natural, other portions, including a golf course, developed for recreation). There are notable stands and plantings of azaleas, hollies, other trees and shrubs, and herbaceous plants both native and exotic, also greenhouses. (Founded 1952.)

ILLINOIS

Chicago—Garfield Park Conservatory (4½ acres). One of the great conservatories of the world, here are displayed in eight huge compartments magnificent collections of tropical and subtropical flowering and foliage plants in naturalistic and formal arrangements. Many economic plants (sorts that are sources of commercial products) are included. Special seasonal flower displays are held. (Founded 1907.)

Glencoe—Chicago Horticultural Society Botanic Garden (300 acres). A young garden, this is being developed to display a wide variety of plants outdoors and in greenhouses. Its grounds include extensive natural woodlands. (Founded 1965.)

Lisle—Morton Arboretum (1,500 acres including a considerable proportion of woodland and wetland and other natural vegetation). Has as a prime objective the cultivation and display of as many

kinds of trees and shrubs that are hardy in its area as can be obtained. Many sorts are presented in sizable groups instead of singly. (Founded 1922.)

MASSACHUSETTS

Jamaica Plain—The Arnold Arboretum (265 acres plus 125 acres at Weston). This institution has probably had more influence on horticulture than any other American garden, in large measure by supporting plant collecting expeditions to the Orient and raising and distributing desirable kinds so obtained as well as by extensive investigation of and publication, popular as well as scientific, on trees and shrubs, especially those hardy in northeastern North America. One of the outstanding botanic gardens of the world, the Arnold Arboretum is affiliated with Harvard University. Its first Director, John Sprague Sargent, gathered as associates a small, but brilliant team of botanists and horticulturists among the best known to horticulturists Ernest H. Wilson, Alfred Rehder, and William Judd. (Founded 1872.)

Northampton—Botanic Garden of Smith College (100 acres). Collections of hardy trees, shrubs, and herbaceous plants. Greenhouses. (Founded 1893.)

MICHIGAN

Ann Arbor—University of Michigan Botanical Gardens (300 acres, 60 cultivated). Specialties: ferns, native plants, and greenhouse collections of tropical and subtropical sorts. (Founded 1914.)

East Lansing—Beal-Garfield Botanic Garden (8 acres). Collections include over 5,000 sorts of trees, shrubs, and herbaceous plants. (Founded 1873.)

MISSOURI

St. Louis—Missouri Botanical Garden (60 acres plus 2,100 acres at Gray's Summit). Oldest currently active botanic garden in the United States, this, known locally as Shaw's Garden, was established through the munificence of Henry Shaw. Under the wise guidance of a succession of directors of whom Shaw was the first it developed into one of America's foremost horticultural institutions as well as a great center for botanical research. What is believed to be the oldest existing greenhouse in the United States, an orangery called the Linnaean House, strongly contrasts with the Climatron, a conservatory unique in concept, erected in 1960. The Climatron is built as a geodesic dome of aluminum alloy and Plexiglas. Extensive and varied plant collections are maintained outdoors and in greenhouses. (Founded 1859.)

NEW JERSEY

New Brunswick— New Jersey Agricultural Experiment Station Arboretum of Rutgers the State University (123 acres). Trees and shrubs including special collections of azaleas, hollies, and pyracanthas. (Founded 1929.)

NEW YORK

Ithaca—Cornell Plantations (1,200 acres, about ninety horticulturally main-

The Botanic Garden of Smith College: (a) The aquatic garden

(b) In the Lyman Plant Greenhouse

Missouri Botanical Garden: The Climatron

tained). Considerable natural stands of native trees and shrubs, collections of introduced ones and some hardy herbaceous plants. (Founded 1935.)

Millbrook—The Cary Arboretum (2,000 acres), a division of The New York Botanical Garden. The existing flora of this beautiful site is being supplemented to provide extensive collections of native and exotic plants, chiefly trees, shrubs, and woody vines, likely to prove hardy in northeastern North America. (Founded 1971.)

New York City—The Brooklyn Botanic Garden (50 acres). Here are maintained representative collections of a wide variety of outdoor and greenhouse plants including trees, shrubs, and herbaceous sorts displayed with emphasis on the educational needs of an urban public. Scientific research is pursued, but perhaps less than formerly. (Founded 1910.)

New York City—The New York Botanical Garden (250 acres). This institution owes

Brooklyn Botanic Garden: The Cranford Rose Garden

its origin to the foresight and efforts of Dr. Nathaniel Lord Britton, professor of botany at Columbia University and the Garden's first director. Throughout its existence it has maintained an unexcelled position as a center for scientific research. Its grounds possess great natural beauty and include native forest as well as introduced trees, shrubs, and other plants. The Thompson Memorial Rock Garden and the Enid A. Haupt Conservatory are outstanding features of this garden. (Founded 1891.)

Rochester—Highland Park (150 acres) and Durand-Eastman Park (594 acres). Over 1,450 kinds of trees and shrubs representing nearly 250 genera. Specialties: azaleas, crabapples, lilacs, magnolias, pines, and spruces and other conifers. (Founded 1888.)

OHIO

Mentor—Holden Arboretum (2,400 acres). Collections of trees and shrubs. (Founded 1942.)

The New York Botanical Garden: Thompson Memorial Rock Garden

Longwood Gardens: (a) Part of greenhouse display

Newark—Dawes Arboretum (980 acres). Much fine natural woodland and farmland. Representative collections totaling about 200 genera, 5,000 species and varieties, of native and introduced trees and shrubs. (Founded 1929.)

PENNSYLVANIA

Kennett Square—Longwood Gardens (1,000 acres). Magnificent, extensive gardens and conservatories containing large collections of a wide variety of hardy and nonhardy plants beautifully displayed. One of the outstanding show gardens of the world. (Development of the present gardens, partly on land occupied by an early nineteenth-century arboretum, began early in the twentieth century. The Longwood Foundation responsible for operating Longwood Gardens was founded in 1937.)

Lima—John J. Tyler Arboretum (700 acres, a small part developed). About 4,000 species and varieties of trees and shrubs including some exceptional in the Philadelphia region for size and rarity. (Founded about 1830 as the Painter Arboretum.)

Merion—Arboretum of the Barnes Foundation (12 acres). Collections of trees, shrubs, and herbaceous plants. Specialties: cotoneasters, lilacs, magnolias, peonies, and viburnums. (Founded 1922.)

Philadelphia—Morris Arboretum (175 acres). About 3,500 species and varieties, mostly trees, including many old ones, and shrubs. (Opened 1933, tree collections begun much earlier.)

VIRGINIA

Norfolk—Norfolk Botanical Gardens (220 acres). Specialties: azaleas and rhododendrons and camellias. (Founded 1936.)

(b) The fountain garden

Norfolk Botanical Gardens: A view of the plantings

Of the possibly more than 500 botanic gardens in the world about fifty are described and superbly illustrated in Edward Hyams "Great Botanical Gardens of the World," published in 1969. Those most notable as selected by Hyams, his judgments based chiefly on horticultural excellence, interest, and importance, and his choice including some privately owned as well as public establishments, are these:

In North America: Arnold Arboretum (Cambridge, Massachusetts), Brooklyn Botanic Garden (Brooklyn, New York), Fairchild Tropical Garden (Miami, Florida), Huntington Botanic Gardens (San Marino, California), Longwood Gardens (Kennett Square, Pennsylvania), Missouri Botanical Garden (St. Louis, Missouri), Montreal Botanical Garden (Montreal, Canada), and Strybing Arboretum (San Francisco, California).

In Europe: the botanic gardens at Berlin, Germany (Berlin-Dahlem); Edinburgh,

WASHINGTON

Seattle—University of Washington Arboretum (200 acres). Excellent collections, about 4,500 sorts of trees and shrubs. Especially notable, azaleas and rhododendrons, camellias, cherries and other kinds of *Prunus,* mountain ash, and broad- and narrow-leaved evergreens. (Founded 1936.)

WISCONSIN

Hales Corners—Alfred L. Boerner Botanical Gardens (450 acres). Trees, shrubs, roses, and herbaceous plants. (Founded 1939.)

Milwaukee—Mitchell Park Horticultural Conservatory (three huge modern greenhouses). Collections of tropical and subtropical plants and seasonal displays. (Founded 1964.)

CANADA

Hamilton, Ontario—Royal Botanical Gardens (2,000 acres, a large proportion undeveloped horticulturally). Collections of trees and shrubs including an extensive display of lilacs; also herbaceous plants. (Founded 1941.)

Montreal, Quebec—Montreal Botanical Garden (180 acres). Horticulturally one of the finest botanic gardens in North America. Extensive collections of trees, shrubs, and herbaceous plants. Excellent ones of tropical and subtropical plants in an imposing conservatory. (Founded 1936.)

Morden, Manitoba—Canada Agriculture Experimental Farm (700 acres including an arboretum of 30 acres). Many kinds of trees, shrubs, and herbaceous plants. (Founded 1915.)

Ottawa, Ontario—Dominion Arboretum and Botanic Garden, Plant Research Institute, Central Experimental Farm (135 acres). Extensive collections of trees, shrubs, and other plants. (Founded 1897.)

University of Washington Arboretum: (a) Rhododendrons backed by tall trees

(b) Spring-flowering trees and azaleas

Montreal Botanical Garden (a) The main entrance

Scotland (Royal Botanic Gardens); Dublin, Eire (National Botanic Garden); Goteborg, Sweden; and Kew (Royal Botanic Gardens), and Oxford in England.

In the U.S.S.R.: The botanic gardens at Moscow, Minsk, Kiev, Yalta, and Tashkent.

In Japan: The botanic gardens at Kyoto, Nikko, and Tokyo.

In the tropics: The botanic gardens at Bogor, Java; Calcutta, India; Entebbe, Uganda; Peradeniya, Ceylon; Rio de Janeiro, Brazil; and Singapore.

In temperate parts of the southern hemisphere: The botanic gardens at Buenos Aires, Argentina; Cape Town, South Africa (Kirstenbosch); Christchurch, New Zealand; Melbourne, Australia; and Sydney, Australia.

(b) A view in the arboretum

Dominion Arboretum and Botanic Garden, Ottawa, Canada

Hyam's selection is unavoidably subjective and one cannot but wonder why gardens with such interesting collections of plants as those of the Cambridge Botanic Garden in England and the Rancho Santa Ana Botanic Garden in California were omitted; perhaps limitations of space dictated this.

BOTANY. Botany is the branch of the science of biology concerned with plants. As such it is one of the sciences basic to the craft and art of gardening. Whether aware of it or not, all successful growers tailor their procedures to accord with principles explained by botany and, in applying names to plants other than colloquial and horticultural varietal ones, make use of botanical classification. And so it is that people who would deny all acquaintance with botany are likely to be familiar with such botanical names as begonia, chrysanthemum, delphinium, forsythia, petunia, philodendron, rhododendron, salvia, verbena, and zinnia.

An organized study of botany with emphasis on aspects most significant to growers can be decidedly helpful as well as interesting to gardeners. There is no need for this to be of the dry-as-dust kind sometimes envisaged. At its beginning it should as far as possible be confined to learning about familiar plants and about principles underlying common horticultural procedures. Such a study may involve taking popular courses such as are offered by some botanic gardens and other institutions and organizations or depend upon reading and independent study.

Aspects of botany of first importance to gardeners are those concerned with the form and structure of plants and those that explain their life processes and how they grow. The first is called plant morphology, the other plant physiology. Of nearly equal importance are those branches of the science identified as taxonomy and nomenclature. These deal with the classification of plants and the correct application of names to them. But gardeners' studies of botany need by no means end here. Understandings of plant ecology (relationship of plants to their environments), of genetics (basic to plant breeding), of plant geography (concerned with the natural distribution of various kinds of plants over the Earth's surface), and of economic botany (the uses to which plants are put by man) can all be fascinating, helpful to better gardening and enriching life. Books of special value to gardeners interested in botany are *Botany for Gardeners* by H. W. Rickett and *The Living Garden* by E. S. Salisbury.

BOTHRIOCHILUS (Bothrio-chilus). Mexican and Central American species that belong in this genus were formerly accommodated in *Coelia*. They belong to the orchid family ORCHIDACEAE and bear a name derived from the Greek *bothrion*, a small pit, and *cheilos*, a lip, that refers to the small two-lobed sac at the base of the lip in some kinds. There are four species.

Bothriochiluses are summer-blooming, evergreen epiphytes (tree-perchers), with egg-shaped, conical, or more or less spherical pseudobulbs from the tops of which sprout at the end of a short stalk a few, longitudinally ribbed, rather narrow leaves. Their few to many flowers are in spikes, furnished with brown or tan bracts that develop from the bases of the pseudobulbs.

The largest flowered kind, with blooms 2 inches long or longer in spikes of six or fewer, is **Bothriochilus bellus** (syn. *Coelia bella*). Its somewhat flattened, egg-shaped to spherical pseudobulbs, about 2 inches tall, carry several pointed, linear-lanceolate, lustrous leaves from 1 foot to 2 feet long. The bracts of the 6-inch-tall spikes of flowers are tan. Tubular at their bases, becoming funnel-shaped above, the more or less upright blooms have rose-purple apexes to their yellowish-white sepals and petals, and a lip with an orange middle lobe.

Differing in its blooms being white, not more than ½ inch long, and in crowded spikes of up to 100 or 150, and in having slightly smaller pseudobulbs and rather wider leaves, **B. densiflorus** (syn. *Coelia densiflora*) is otherwise similar in aspect to *B. bellus*.

The leaves of **B. macrostachyus** (syn. *Coelia macrostachya*), usually three from each 4-inch-tall, globular to egg-shaped pseudobulb, are up to 3 feet long by 1 inch wide. The densely-sheathed flower stalks, up to 2 feet tall, terminate in 6-inch-long racemes of fragrant, pale to deep pink blooms about ⅛ inch in length, with tiny, slightly two-lobed, spherical lips.

Conical pseudobulbs, about 2 inches tall, and leaves thickish and shorter than those of other species are characteristic of **B. guatemalensis** (syn. *Coelia guatemalensis*). The flowering stems, up to 8 inches in length, have several ¾-inch-long blooms with sepals, petals, and lip white with usually pink apexes.

Garden Uses and Cultivation. For their successful cultivation these orchids need fairly high temperatures and high humidity. They are grown in intermediate and warm orchid greenhouses and are best kept in pots rather small in comparison to their sizes. Because they resent root disturbance repotting is done only when quite necessary. Osmunda or tree fern fiber are suitable rooting mediums. The pots must be well-drained, and their contents kept moist, but not saturated. Light shade from the brightest sun is needed. For additional information see Orchids.

BOTRYCHIUM (Botrých-ium) — Rattlesnake Fern, Grape Fern, Moonwort. Of no great horticultural importance, this genus of about twenty-five species of ferns of the adder's tongue family OPHIOGLOSSACEAE is widely distributed in the wild, chiefly in temperate regions. Its name derives from the Greek *botrys*, a bunch, and alludes to the appearance of the panicles of sporebearing organs.

Botrychiums are mostly small ferns with short subterranean stems, each of which produces, normally one each year, a one- to three-times pinnately-divided and cleft leaf. The sterile leaves may be stalked or not, the fertile ones are stalked and have, in addition to the blade, an erect panicle of globular sporangia (sporebearing organs) with the sporangia forming two rows on the ultimate divisions. Species of *Botrychium* are often highly variable in the degree of dissection of their fronds (leaves).

The rattlesnake fern (**B. virginianum**) is indigenous throughout much of North America from Newfoundland to British Columbia and Mexico, and in Europe and Asia. It is 6 inches to 2½ feet tall, deciduous, and rather fleshy. It has triangular, sparsely-hairy, pale green leaf blades, twice-pinnately-divided, with the final segments pinnately-lobed. The sterile leaves have blades 3 to 8 inches long and wider than their length; those of sporebearing fronds are rather smaller, and have a slender panicle of sporebearing organs sprouting from the bottom of the leafy part; the latter spreads more or less horizontally. This species favors neutral to mildly acid soils in moist and dry woodlands. Unlike many ferns, its new fronds are not of the familiar fiddle-head form; in very early spring they push out of the ground practically fully formed and tightly folded, and expand rapidly as soon as they are above the soil.

Common grape fern (**B. dissectum**) has evergreen leaves that in winter become bronzy. They are triangular, sparsely-hairy, and up to 1½ feet tall, with blades up to 4 inches long and up to 6 inches wide. They are mostly three-times pinnately-divided and have toothed segments. Varieties with less dissected foliage are *B. d. tenuifolium* and *B. d. obliquum*. In one or other of its varieties the common grape fern occurs in dry or moist fields and woodlands from southern Canada to Florida and Texas. Variety *B. d. obliquum* is also a native of Jamaica.

Another evergreen, **B. multifidum** inhabits moist sandy soils in open locations from Labrador to British Columbia, Pennsylvania, and Minnesota, as well as Europe and Asia. From 2 or 3 inches up to 1½ feet in height, this very variable species has twice- or thrice-divided leaf blades generally not more than 2 inches long and wide, with the segments of the fronds more rounded than in *B. dissectum*. Varieties of this are *B. m. oneidense*, *B. m. intermedium*, and *B. m. silaifolium*. These differ in technical details.

Moonwort (**B. lunaria**) occurs from Labrador to Alaska, Maine, Michigan, and California, and in Europe and Asia. Up to about 10 inches tall, it has pinnate leaves with seven to fifteen more or less moon-shaped leaflets, which may or may not be toothed. This species occurs in fields and meadows. It is deciduous. Variety *B. l. minganense* is the common California kind.

Garden Uses and Cultivation. Except for inclusion in native plant gardens and among fern collections, botrychiums are rarely grown. They succeed with little trouble in loose woodland-type soil, which is not too dry, with a considerable organic content. They are well adapted for lightly shaded places and for planting on north sides of walls. Increase is had by spores and by careful division. For additional information see Ferns.

BOTRYSTEGE. See Tripetaleia.

BOTRYTIS. Also called gray mold blight, this is common on a wide variety of flowers, foliage, fruits, and vegetables. Under humid conditions it develops as a visible grayish fungal growth, causing rotting of underlying tissues. It is familiar on overripe soft fruits such as raspberries and strawberries. Controls include avoidance of crowding, warm, humid conditions, and poor air circulation; good sanitation and the prompt removal of affected parts are essential. Diseases attributable to this fungus include lily blight, peony blight, and tulip fire.

BOTTLE. This word is included in the common names of such plants as bottle gourd (*Lagenaria*), bottle palm (*Colpothrinax wrightii* and *Mascarena lagenicaulis*), and bottle tree (*Adansonia gregori* and *Brachychiton rupestris*). Brandy bottle is a common name of *Nuphar*.

BOTTLE BRUSH. This is the common name of *Callistemon*, *Melaleuca*, and *Metrosideros*. The bottle brush buckeye is *Aesculus parviflora*, the bottle brush grass *Hystrix patula*, the Natal-bottle-brush *Greyia*, and the one-sided-bottle-brush *Calothamnus*.

BOTTLE GARDEN. A bottle garden is a decorative and highly interesting feature consisting of a bottle or carboy in which living plants are growing. In effect it is a very special kind of terrarium. Bottle gardens have something of the appeal, but because their contents are alive a more dramatic one, of the model ships sailors were fond of constructing and displaying in such containers. And like the little ships, they can be interesting conversation pieces in living room, dining room, den, or office. They are easily cared for and not difficult to make.

To begin, secure a suitable bottle of plain, not colored glass. For preference let it be fairly large. A quart container may be taken as about the general minimum, although it is possible to use smaller containers. A half-gallon, one-gallon, or two-gallon size gives greater scope. Large carboys are splendid. It is not essential that there be drainage holes, but they help. A glazier can drill a few in what is to be the underside of the finished garden. (Some bottles lend themselves to being lain on their sides and planted in this position.) If there are drainage holes, a tray should be kept under the bottle to collect seepage if this would mar furniture, paintwork, or some other surface.

Having obtained your container, assemble the other supplies. These include gravel, chips of charcoal or other material to be used as under drainage, suitable soil, and tools. Use soil appropriate for terrariums (see Terrariums).

The tools you must largely contrive. They are a slender paper funnel through which drainage material and soil is poured into the container, a "spade" for digging

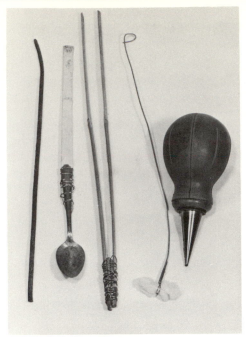
Tools for bottle gardens

holes, a slender pair of long-handled tongs or tweezers and a wire hook for lowering the plants into place, a tamper for firming soil about the roots, a swab for cleaning the glass, and for maintenance later, a pruner. The "spade" can be a small teaspoon securely wired or in other way fixed to the end of a piece of bamboo cane or a not-easily-broken, slender stick. Tongs can be purchased from dealers in aquarium supplies or from sources of medical supplies, and you can fashion tweezers by splitting a longish piece of a fairly slender bamboo cane nearly to its upper end, inserting in the top of the split a small piece of rubber and binding the end to prevent further splitting with fine wire or strong adhesive tape. It is easy to fashion a hook from a wire clothes hanger or other piece of wire. Just bend its end to form an incomplete circle. For a tamper impale a cork or a piece of wood similarly shaped on a piece of bamboo cane or wooden dowel. The swab consists of cotton attached to the

Planting a bottle garden

end of a stick or wire. A sharp razor blade fixed to the end of a cane or stick is the pruner. Tool size must be in proportion to the size of the container.

The plants can be almost any of the kinds ordinarily used in terrariums with the exception of cactuses and succulents, which are generally not suitable. Those desert inhabitants need a drier atmosphere and freer air circulation than bottle gardens provide. The plants must be of sizes that can be passed through the neck of the bottle. If the leaves are flexible, plants with tops large in comparison to the opening can be maneuvered through it. Root balls are less tractable. Sometimes it is possible to reduce these in size or wash away much of the soil and plant bare-rooted.

Planting bottle gardens calls for a certain amount of imagination, and dexterity. If the container is small one plant may be adequate. More often a few to several are used, and their arrangement is important. It should be pleasing and natural. In large bottles miniature landscapes can be contrived with varied elevations and slopes. It is even possible to introduce small rocks or pieces of rough cork bark to serve as naturalistic features or to fashion such, as well as tiny pools and rivulets out of moist cement.

In preparation for planting, pour into the bottle through the funnel enough gravel, perlite, or charcoal chips to form a drainage layer an inch or two deep as a base, then sufficient soil to cover this to a depth of 2 to 4 inches. If the soil surface is to slope, keep the bottle tilted while drainage and soil are being installed. Take care not to spill these against the sides of the bottle or else the glass will be dirtied. Firm the soil with the tamper.

Planting can now begin. Take each plant in turn, beginning with the larger ones that are to be features of the arrangement, remove them from their pots, and tease as much soil as practicable from their roots. Then with the "spade" dig a hole large enough to accommodate the roots, fit the loop of the hook around the neck of the plant and lower it through the bottle neck into place. Carefully slide the hook from around the plant and withdraw it. Now a two-handed job; with the tweezers hold the plant in place and with the spade fill soil around the roots. Still holding the plants with the tweezers firm the soil with the tamper. When planting is finished swab away any soil (it is hoped that there will be none) that has inadvertently spilled on the inside of the container and spray the plants with a fine mist of water but not enough to flood the drainage.

Routine care of bottle gardens is minimal. Keep them in good light, out of direct sun. They do well under fluorescent light but placement too close to incandescent (Mazda type) bulbs may cause the temperature inside the bottle to rise to uncom-

Planted bottle garden: (a) Vertical

(b) Horizontal

fortable or even fatal levels. Because moisture loss is minimal watering is very rarely needed, and no fertilization—please. Only when the earth begins to show a definitely approaching dryness should watering be done, and then with circumspection and in the form of a fine spray. From time to time a little housekeeping or tidying will be needed. Remove any leaves that die. It may be necessary to first cut these off with the pruner and the same tool may from time to time be employed to shorten overvigorous shoots. If an entire plant dies or becomes too big, take it out by cutting it to pieces with the pruner and removing the debris with the tongs or tweezers. If you can remove some of the old soil from around the old roots and, when a new plant is positioned in the hole pack some new about it, that is to the good. The needs for these simple attentions are likely to be months apart. Betweentimes you can enjoy your bottle gardens. Eventually, but probably not for a couple of years or considerably longer, it will become necessary to redo and replant the entire garden, removing all the contents of the bottle and beginning again.

BOTTOM HEAT. Many cuttings root more surely and quicker and some plants grow more rapidly if the temperature of the medium in which they are planted is kept five to ten degrees warmer than the air above them. This is done by supplying bottom heat. As a gardening term this means warming, from beneath, the soil, sand, vermiculite, or other growing or rooting medium in a greenhouse bench or hotbed. In the past this was commonly achieved in hotbeds by the laborious method of building under the soil a thick, carefully made and managed layer of fermenting horse manure. In greenhouses hot water pipes usually supplied bottom heat to propagating benches. This last is still often done, but the fermenting manure hotbed is nearly a thing of the past. Certainly it is impracticable for the vast majority of gardeners. The common practice today is to equip hotbeds and indoor propagating benches with electric heating cables, thermostatically controlled to maintain the desired temperature. Sets of such equipment are sold by dealers in garden supplies. In managing benches or beds equipped with bottom heat, care must be taken that the rooting medium just above the source of heat does not dry out.

BOUGAINVILLEA (Bougain-víllea). This genus of tropical and subtropical woody vines is well known and much appreciated by gardeners, especially by those who practice their art in warm climates where these plants are so effective in outdoor landscaping; elsewhere their cultivation is confined to greenhouses. Belonging to the four-o'clock family NYCTAGINACEAE, the genus *Bougainvillea*, the name of which honors L. A. de Bougainville, a French navigator, who died in 1811, consists of eighteen species. Only three are of any considerable horticultural importance, but many hybrids are also cultivated.

Bougainvilleas have somewhat thorny stems and alternate, stalked, ovate to elliptic-lanceolate leaves that vary considerably in size, shape, and other characteristics within the species and sometimes on the same plant. The thorns are in the leaf axils. As with the poinsettia, the showiness of bougainvilleas is not due to their flowers, but to the large, colorful, petal-like bracts that accompany them. The flowers themselves are small and tubular, narrowed at about their middles and broadening toward their bases. Five ridges run the length of the tube and the five or six tiny corolla lobes spread like the points of a star. There are no petals; both tube and lobes represent the calyx. The seven or eight stamens, of different lengths, do not ordinarily protrude. The flowers are borne in threes and each group is surrounded by three bracts. The fruits are five-ribbed achenes.

The first bougainvillea known was *B. spectabilis*. Although not described botanically until 1789, this species was discovered more than twenty years earlier in Brazil, but was not introduced to cultivation until some years after the published ac-count of it appeared. It is still important horticulturally. From other cultivated species very vigorous, tall-growing **B. spectabilis,** with thorny stems, differs in having its stems, leaves, and the outsides of the flower tubes densely covered with comparatively long hairs; other kinds are hairless or have very short hairs. The bracts of its very large flower trusses are 2 to 2¼ inches long. In the typical species they are bright rosy-purple, but varieties with bracts of other colors exist. In *B. s. lateritia* they are brick-red and smaller than in the typical species; those of *B. s. thomasii* are pink. Remarkable *B. s.* 'Mary Palmer' has carmine- and white-bracted flowers on the same plant.

A less rampant grower, **B. glabra** differs in having its stems, foliage, and outsides of its flower tubes more or less sparsely furnished with extremely short hairs, producing an effect botanists term puberulent rather than pubescent. The leaves are elliptic, up to 5 inches in length, and about 2½ inches in diameter. Their under surfaces are paler than their upper surfaces. The floral bracts are typically rosy-purple and distinctly veined, but in cultivated varieties range from amaranth-purple through coral-red and pink to white. Of the many named varieties, *B. g. sanderiana* is one of the most widely grown; a prolific and reliable bloomer, its large bracts are rosy-purple. Another splendid variety is *B. g. cypheri*, with bright rose-pink or mallow-purple bracts. Having pompeian-red bracts, *B. g.* 'Mrs. Leano', is extremely beautiful. The white-bracted *B. g.* 'Snow White' is an unusual, easily recognized variety. One with its leaves variegated with creamy-white is *B. g. variegata*.

The third cultivated species **B. peruviana** inhabits the Pacific coast of northern South America and differs from *B. spectabilis* and *B. glabra* in being hairless and in its flower tubes being very slender. Its broadly-ovate

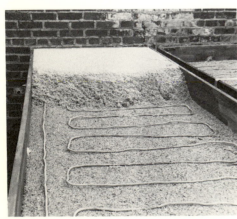

Propagating bench wired for bottom heat

Bougainvillea, as a greenhouse vine

Bougainvillea (flowers)

Bougainvillea glabra 'Snow White'

Espaliered bougainvillea

leaves are up to 4 inches long and 3 inches wide and its bracts, with more or less crinkled margins, are light magenta-pink. This species is cultivated under the names 'Ecuador Pink', 'Lady Hudson', and 'Princess Margaret Rose'. In many places it does not flower as freely as other kinds.

Hybrid bougainvilleas resulting from crossing *B. glabra* and *B. peruviana* are grouped under the name **B. butteana.** They are numerous and often difficult to identify as to variety, particularly since the same kind is likely to be grown under different names in different parts of the world. The typical variety of this hybrid complex is *B. b.* 'Mrs. Butt' (syn. *B. b.* 'Crimson Lake'), which has rich crimson bracts; others have bracts of red, carmine, scarlet, rosy-purple, orange, and yellow; the margins of the bracts are much crinkled. Varieties of *B. butteana* are sturdy climbers with broadly-ovate leaves up to 5 inches long by two-thirds as wide; their lower surfaces are paler than their upper surfaces and are hairless except for the midribs, which are short-hairy (puberulent), as also are the veins of the bracts and the outsides of the flower tubes. Good varieties are *B. b.* 'Mrs. McLean', with orange bracts; *B. b.* 'Golden Glow', with yellow and pinkish bracts; *B. b.* 'Miss Manila', with carmine bracts, and *B. b.* 'Pigeon Blood', with bracts of oxblood-red.

Garden and Landscape Uses. Bougainvilleas are among the most gorgeous flowering vines for landscape use in the tropics and subtropics and are greatly esteemed for clothing walls, pergolas, borders, fences, and other surfaces and supports. They climb or clamber by means of the strong thorns on their stems, but these cannot attach themselves to flat vertical surfaces and so wires, trellises or other supports to which the stems can be tied must be provided. In constantly humid climates bougainvilleas are evergreen, but where dry and wet seasons alternate they lose their foliage for part of each year. Where they do this they are apt to bloom most profusely. Probably no more brilliant sight is to be seen in warm countries than a big old red or rosy-purple bougainvillea in full bloom. The display lasts for a very long time since the bracts, unlike the flowers of many plants, do not soon fade or drop.

Bougainvilleas are also excellent ornamentals for conservatories and greenhouses, either planted in ground beds or in tubs or pots. When grown in such containers they are also useful as terrace and patio plants. For container cultivation *B. glabra* and its varieties and varieties of *B. butteana* are better adapted than the more rampant *B. spectabilis*. A rather unusual use for pot-grown bougainvilleas is as summer bedding plants; well-grown specimens so displayed are brilliant additions to such more commonly used items as lantanas, acalyphas, abutilons, and begonias.

Cultivation. Bougainvilleas need full sun at all times. Outdoors they thrive in any well-drained garden soil; in containers they need fertile, loamy earth. Most kinds are readily propagated by cuttings in a temperature of 65 to 70°F, those of *B. s. lateritia* are often difficult to root. Treatment with a hormone rooting powder before insertion and the employment of mild bottom heat (so that the sand or other propagating medium in which the cuttings are planted is about five degrees warmer than the air temperature) stimulates rooting. Air layering is an easy means of securing increase. When grown indoors a winter night temperature of about 50°F is satisfactory for most kinds, but 55 to 60°F is more agreeable to *B. spectabilis*; day temperature may be five to ten degrees higher than those maintained at night. As spring approaches, both day and night temperatures may be increased by five to ten degrees and then the atmosphere should be kept more humid and water supplied more abundantly. To develop pot or tub specimens, cuttings are rooted in late winter and potted individually in 3- or 4-inch pots as soon as they are rooted. Later they are transferred to pots 6 or 7 inches in diameter. In mid-May, the tips of the shoots are pinched out to encourage branching. If kept growing without check, by midsummer the plants will be ready for 8- or 9-inch pots. Four or five stakes 4 feet long should be stuck firmly into the soil just inside the rims of these pots and the shoots tied loosely around and to them. From first potting until fall, the plants are grown in a sunny greenhouse in a minimum temperature of 70°F or, during warm summer weather, say from about mid-June to early or mid-September, they are kept outdoors with their pots plunged to their rims in sand or sandy soil. In either case enough water should be given to keep the soil uniformly moist. From October on the soil should be allowed to become drier between waterings and after the middle of November no more is needed than is necessary to keep the shoots from shriveling. Then begins a period of dormancy in a night temperature of 50 to 55°F, with a day temperature not more than five degrees or so higher. Depending upon when blooms are wanted, plants are started into growth from January to March. This is done by removing the plants from their pots and picking away with a pointed stick all soil not occupied with healthy roots, soaking the root balls in water for an hour or two, and after allowing them to dry for about a day, repotting them in pots or tubs 3 or 4 inches more in diameter than those they previously occupied. They remain in the new containers throughout the season. At potting time all weak shoots not stout enough to produce lateral flowering branches are pruned away. Following repotting, the plants are placed in full sun in a greenhouse with a night temperature of 65 to 70°F and day temperatures five to ten degrees higher. On sunny days they are sprayed with water and the soil is always kept moist. When the bracts are half formed the plants should be removed to a somewhat cooler, more airy location. Under these conditions the bracts become firmer and last longer.

The treatment of specimens over one year old is the same as that described above for younger plants except that the winter or spring pruning involves shortening severely (spur pruning) the lateral branches that bloomed the previous year (the faded flower clusters of these are, of course, snipped off the previous fall as soon as they cease to be decorative) as well as cutting out weak, unwanted shoots. Also, if accommodated in large containers, it may not be practical to transfer the plants to bigger receptacles; in that case they are simply top dressed with rich soil and are fed regularly with dilute liquid fertilizer.

The pruning of permanently planted out specimens, outdoors or indoors, consists of removing all weak and unwanted shoots and cutting all subsidiary lateral shoots back close to their bases (spur pruning them) at the beginning of their season of growth.

BOUNCING BET is *Saponaria officinalis.*

BOUSSINGAULTIA. See Anredera.

BOUTELOUA (Boutél-oua)—Grama Grass. Up to fifty species of annual and perennial grasses, natives chiefly of semiarid and arid parts of the Americas including the United States, constitute *Bouteloua* of the grass family GRAMINEAE. They supply valuable forage. This name commemorates the brothers Claudius and Esteban Boutelou, professors, respectively, of botany and agriculture in Spain. Esteban died in 1813, Claudius in 1842.

Grama grasses are tufted or spread by stolons. They have rigid, slender stems and flat or rolled narrow leaves. The flowers are in few to many, dense, one-sided spikes or spikelike racemes of stalkless or nearly stalkless spikelets. The spikelets are arranged in two rows along one side of the axis that carries them. Each has one bisexual flower and rudiments of others.

Blue grama (**B. gracilis** syn. *B. oligostachya*) inhabits the central and western United States and Mexico. A tufted perennial 9 inches to 1½ feet tall or sometimes taller, it has flat or rolled leaves less than ¹⁄₁₀ inch wide. The stems carry two, or more rarely one or three, slender, bristly flower spikes, held horizontally or recurved, and 1 inch to 2 inches long.

Bouteloua gracilis

Garden Uses and Cultivation. Blue grama is occasionally cultivated as an ornamental at the fronts of flower beds and in native plant gardens. Fresh or dried, its flowers are useful for indoor decoration. Where winters are not excessively cold it is perennial, but it may be grown as an annual by sowing seeds early outdoors where the plants are to remain or by sowing early indoors and transplanting the young plants to the garden later. Ordinary soil, preferably dryish, and a location in full sun suits. Propagation is by seeds and division.

BOUVARDIA (Bouvàrd-ia). Named in honor of Charles Bouvard, seventeenth-century Superintendent of the Jardin du Roi, Paris, France, *Bouvardia* comprises fifty species of the madder family RUBIACEAE. Native from Texas and Arizona to subtropical South America, it is most abundantly represented as to species in Mexico and Central America. At one time bouvardias were popular with florists as cut flowers, but are now much less commonly grown for that purpose.

Bouvardias are evergreen shrubs or much less often herbaceous perennials. Their undivided leaves are opposite or in whorls (circles of three or more). Their tubular flowers are usually in flattish clusters at the termination of the branches. Each white, yellow, pink, or red flower has a four-lobed calyx, four spreading corolla lobes, four stamens that may or may not protrude from the corolla, and two stigmas. The fruits are capsules.

Native to Texas and Mexico, **B. ternifolia** (syn. *B. triphylla*) is a shrub up to 6

Bouvardia ternifolia

feet high, with lanceolate-ovate leaves about 2 inches long in whorls of three or four, and typically with red flowers pubescent on their outsides and ¾ to 1¼ inches long. There are varieties with pink and coral-pink blooms. Dark red-flowered **B. leiantha**, native to Mexico and Central America, is much like *B. ternifolia*, but bushier. It has ovate leaves up to 3 inches long in whorls of three to five and pubescent on their undersides. Its flowers are not hairy on their outsides and are ½ to ¾ inch long. Mexican **B. laevis** is up to 3 feet in height, hairless or nearly so, and has slender branches and short-stalked ovate to lanceolate leaves 1¾ to 5 inches long. Its red or yellow flowers, not pubescent on their outsides, are 1 inch to 1½ inches long with a tube that tapers to a narrow base. Also Mexican, **B. longiflora** (syn. *B. humboldtii*), up to 5 feet tall, has opposite, ovate to lanceolate leaves up to 2 inches long and solitary and fragrant flowers 2 to 3½ inches long by up to 1¾ inches across, and hairless on their outsides. Variety *B. l.* 'Albatross' is 2 to 3 feet

Bouvardia laevis

tall. Formerly, other named varieties were popular for cultivating in greenhouses, but these are little grown now and it is possible that at least some may be lost to cultivation. Favorites included 'Hogarth', with brilliant scarlet flowers; 'Christmas Red' or 'Fire Chief', with red flowers; 'Maiden's

Bouvardia ternifolia (flowers)

Blush', with pink blooms; and 'Alfred Neuner', a white or pale pink double-flowered variety. None of these is fragrant.

Garden Uses. In frost-free and nearly frost-free climates bouvardias are attractive

Bouvardia longiflora

Bouvardia 'Fire Chief'

for shrub beds and borders. Elsewhere they may be grown in greenhouses as decorative specimens and for cut flowers.

Cultivation. Outdoors bouvardias grow in any fairly good garden soil not subject to drought, and in full sun. They may be pruned by thinning out weak and crowded stems and shortening others at the beginning of the growing season. Indoors they are grown in sunny greenhouses at a minimum night temperature of 50 to 55°F. Daytime temperatures, before the greenhouse ventilators are opened, may be permitted to exceed the minimum night temperature by five or ten degrees. Except in large conservatories where they are planted in ground beds permanently and are treated in the same way as if they were growing outdoors, bouvardias are usually kept for one or two years only. They are raised from cuttings taken from plants kept nearly dry from the time they cease blooming until late January or February and then cut back and watered and encouraged to produce new growth by keeping them at a temperature of 52 to 55°F and spraying them lightly with water two or three times on sunny days. Bouvardias can also be raised from seeds, but this is only practicable with natural species, not with garden varieties. The seeds, sown in sandy peaty soil, germinate at a temperature of 55 to 60°F.

Cuttings, made from the young shoots, root most surely in a propagating bench supplied with a little bottom heat. An alternative method is to prepare root cuttings in February by cutting the stouter roots into pieces about 1 inch long. These are scattered over a layer of sandy, peaty soil, covered with one-half an inch or so of the same, watered, and placed in a warm greenhouse over mild bottom heat. The root cutting method is surer for most kinds, but *B. longiflora* roots satisfactorily from stem cuttings. As soon as they have rooted they are potted in 2½-inch pots in sandy peaty soil, and after they are established in these and are about 4 inches tall,

they are pinched to promote branching. If they are to be grown in benches or beds for cut flowers, they are planted in them directly from the pots or are planted, after the weather is warm and settled, in a nursery bed in a sunny location outdoors and are dug up, with root balls as intact as possible, and transferred to the greenhouse beds or benches in late August. If the later plan is followed the plants should be kept shaded and lightly sprayed with water at frequent intervals for a week or two after being transferred to the greenhouse to aid their rapid reestablishment without excessive wilting or loss of foliage. In any case all branches should be pinched occasionally during the summer, the last pinch being given in late August. If the plants are to be kept a second year they can be lifted from the beds or benches after they are through blooming in December and stored dry under the benches or elsewhere until the end of January when they are shaken free of soil, cut back, potted into 5- or 6-inch pots, and started into growth again. When grown as pot plants the details of cultivation do not differ from when they are planted in greenhouse beds or benches except that they must be transferred to successively larger pots, the final potting being in late August or early September. Once they have filled their final containers with roots they are kept in thrifty condition by weekly or semiweekly applications of dilute liquid fertilizer. Pot-grown bouvardias succeed best when they are kept outdoors through the summer plunged to the rims of their pots in a bed of sand or ashes.

BOWENIA (Bow-enia). This Australian genus of the cycad family CYCADACEAE, or according to those who acknowledge the separation, the zamia family ZAMIACEAE, consists of two species. Its name commemorates a nineteenth-century Governor of Queensland, George F. Bowen.

From all other cycads *Bowenia* differs in having twice-pinnate leaves. Its species have thick, underground stems each topped with up to three or rarely five stubby branches bearing crowns of foliage. The leaves are 3 to 6 feet long. No flowers are borne. Male and female elements are in separate cones. The species are *B. spectabilis* and *B. serrulata.* The latter differs from the former in having a nearly spherical rather than an elongated underground stem and in its leaflets being regularly rather than irregularly toothed or toothless.

Garden Uses and Cultivation. These are choice, rare, and beautiful collectors' items. They respond to the same conditions and care that suit *Macrozamia.* For more information see Cycads.

BOWER PLANT is *Pandorea jasminoides.* The name glory bower is a common name for *Clerodendrum.*

Bowenia spectabilis

BOWIEA (Bowiè-a). A word of thanks to the botanists who through their *nomina conservanda* preserved for this strange South African the name used here rather than the more tongue-twisting *Schizobasopsis* sometimes used. Its conserved name commemorates a plant explorer from Kew Gardens, England, James Bowie, who collected in southern Africa and died in 1869. There is only one species, *Bowiea volubilis.* It belongs in the lily family LILIACEAE.

A striking feature of *B. volubilis* is that it has no leaves other than two tiny bracts, at the base of the flower stalk, which soon

Bowiea volubilis (bulbs)

Bowiea volubilis, in bloom

wither and die. From large, fleshy, above-ground bulbs it develops to a length of 6 to 8 feet slender, green, branching flower stalks, which carry on photosynthesis and the other functions of the leaves of more usual plants. These stalks twine in the manner of the stems of some vines, and in the wild, scramble among bushes or other available supports. The starlike, green to whitish flowers are about ⅓ inch wide and each has six persistent petals (strictly tepals), six stamens, and a short pistil. They are comparatively long-stalked. The fruits are capsules containing several seeds.

Garden Uses. Although undoubtedly a curiosity and as such usually grown, *B. volubilis* (syn. *Schizobasopsis volubilis*) is not freakish. Its globose bulbs, the largest 7 inches in diameter, are silvery-green. They sit on top of the ground and develop offsets freely so that older specimens consist of a cluster of these in various sizes, nudging and pushing each other to one side or the other to accommodate to the available growing space. And that is all there is for several months of each year. But in fall some recondite factor triggers new growth as if the plant were stirred by a memory of the South African spring. Then, slender growths appear from the bulb tips and develop with astonishing rapidity, in due time presenting flowers. The frail stalks remain until late spring and then gradually fade and die and the bulbs enter summer dormancy. In mild, nearly frost-free climates, and especially those that know dry summers, this strange plant can be grown outdoors. It is not uncommonly grown in greenhouses and is a good window garden specimen.

Cultivation. Few plants make as little demand on gardeners' time or are as tolerant of neglect as this. It survives long periods without water, even when in an actively growing condition, although then it is better if provided with a constant supply, and even longer periods without fertilization, although applications of very dilute liquid fertilizer during the growing period are in order. When grown in containers, it will live for years without repotting. It will not survive in poorly drained soil, nor if kept wet during its resting season. As soon as new shoots begin to grow, supports around which they can twine must be put in place and regular watering should be instituted. Moderate supplies are afforded until the stalks begin to yellow and die down naturally, when applications are gradually reduced in frequency and finally withheld. For the best results *Bowiea* should be grown in full sun and in a dryish atmosphere. A winter night temperature of about 50°F is satisfactory with a few degrees increase in the day permitted, but it is fairly adaptable in this respect and will do well at higher temperatures if it receives full sun. Propagation is most usually by offsets. Seeds, sown in well-

drained containers of sandy soil, also give good results.

BOWKERIA (Bow-kèria). One representative of this group of eight species of the figwort family SCROPHULARIACEAE is cultivated in California and elsewhere where winters are mild. The genus, endemic to South Africa, consists of evergreen shrubs or trees. Its name honors two nineteenth-century South African botanists, James Henry Bowker, and his sister, Mrs. F. W. Barber.

Bowkerias have short-stalked or stalkless leaves usually in whorls (circles) of three, but sometimes paired. Their asymmetrical, two-lipped flowers are in axillary or approximately terminal clusters. They have five-cleft, persistent calyxes. The corollas have a short, pouched tube, a shortly two-toothed upper lip, and a lower inflated one with three brief teeth. There are four stamens, two shorter than the others, and sometimes a nonfertile one (a staminode). The style is small and branchless, the fruits many-seeded capsules.

Clear yellow-flowered *Bowkeria citrina* is the only known member of the genus with blooms other than white. First discovered in 1929, it apparently was not brought into cultivation until 1968. It promises to be a good ornamental, but probably is not yet in cultivation in North America. Lemon-scented, it is a shrub about 10 feet tall with narrow-elliptic leaves 1½ to 2½ inches long in circles of three.

Up to about 10 feet tall, *B. gerrardiana* has gray-hairy stems, and stalkless, long-

Bowkeria gerrardiana

pointed, ovate-lanceolate, finely-toothed, somewhat hairy leaves 4 to 7 inches long. The hairy-stalked flowers are in loose, clammy clusters of up to ten from the leaf axils. The calceolaria-like, white blooms, about ¾ inch wide, are spotted red inside. Their upper lips are flat, two-lobed, and about ½ inch long by ⅓ inch wide, their lower ones shorter and three-lobed. Another species, perhaps cultivated, although its name is sometimes misapplied

to *B. gerrardiana*, is *B. triphylla.* This differs from *B. gerrardiana* in having flowers with narrower upper lips.

Garden and Landscape Uses and Cultivation. The species described are beautiful foliage and flowering shrubs for general purpose use where little or no frost is experienced. They may be grown in California and places with similarly mild climates, and sometimes in conservatories. Their needs are simple. They succeed in sun or part-day shade in ordinary, well-drained, fertile soil. No systematic pruning is needed. Propagation is by seeds, cuttings, and air layering.

BOWMAN'S ROOT is *Gillenia trifoliata.*

BOWSTRING-HEMP. See Sansevieria.

BOX. This is a common name for *Buxus.* Box-elder is *Acer negundo.* Box huckleberry is *Gaylussacia brachycera.* Brisbane-box is *Tristania conferta.* Marmalade-box is *Genipa americana.* Rattle-box is *Ludwigia alternifolia.* Red-box is *Eucalyptus polyanthemos.* Victorian-box is *Pittosporum undulatum.* Yellow-box is *Eucalyptus melliodora.*

BOXTHORN. See Lycium.

BOXWOOD. See Buxus. African-boxwood is *Myrsine africana.* Oregon-boxwood is *Paxistima myrsinites.*

BOYKINIA (Boy-kínia). As now interpreted, *Boykinia* of the saxifrage family SAXIFRAGACEAE comprises eight species of North America and Japan. The plant previously named *B. jamesii* is *Telesonix jamesii,* *B. tellimoides* is *Peltoboykinia tellimoides.* The name commemorates Dr. Samuel Boykin, an early nineteenth-century resident of Georgia.

Boykinias are hardy herbaceous perennials of the *Heuchera* relationship, with branchless stems from scaly root-stocks and alternate, undivided, kidney-shaped to round-heart-shaped, toothed and often lobed leaves. Their flowers, in branched or panicle-type clusters, are small. They have five each sepals, spatula-shaped to obovate, soon-deciduous petals, and short-stalked stamens. There are two styles. The fruits are capsules containing many minute seeds.

From 1 foot to 3 feet in height, *B. major,* a native of moist places in evergreen forests from Montana to Washington and California, is more or less clothed with brown glandular hairs. Its stems are erect and stout. Long-stalked, five- to seven-cleft, with the lobes again cleft and toothed, the lower leaves are 4 to 8 inches across. The stem ones are smaller and have large green basal appendages (stipules). Densely crowded, the tiny flowers have well-protruded white petals ⅕ inch long or slightly longer. From this species, *B. elata,* a native

(c) *Brodiaea versicolor*

Hardy bulbs: (a) Blue grape-hyacinths, red hyacinths, and pale yellow narcissuses

(d) Spring-flowering crocuses

(b) Narcissuses

Hardy bulbs: (a) A hybrid Lily (*Lilium*)   (b) Tulips

Non-hardy bulb plants: (a) Canna,
a garden variety

(b) Crocuses, tulips, and daffodils forced for winter flowers

(c) *Crinum powellii*   (d) *Alstroemeria aurantiaca* variety

of moist, shaded places from Washington to California, differs in being from 9 inches to 2 feet tall, in its erect stems being more slender, in the stipules of the upper leaves often being represented by bristles, and in its white flowers being smaller. The longish- to long-stalked lower leaves, ¾ inch to 3½ inches wide and kidney-shaped to heart-shaped, are somewhat five- to seven-lobed. They have bristle-pointed teeth. White flowers with petals not conspicuously longer than the sepals are characteristic of **B. rotundifolia.** This densely-hairy endemic of California inhabits wet places in canyons. It has stout stems 1 foot to 2½ feet tall. Its long-stalked lower leaves, with shallow, rounded lobes and rounded teeth, have round-heart-shaped blades 2 to 5 inches wide. Native to moist mountain woodlands and streamsides from Virginia to Kentucky, Georgia, and Alabama, **B. aconitifolia** is 1 foot to 3 feet tall. It has five- to nine-lobed, toothed, kidney-shaped to nearly-circular basal leaves 2 to 5 inches wide and, carried well above the foliage in graceful, glandular-pubescent, loose sprays, numerous tiny white flowers.

Garden and Landscape Uses and Cultivation. Boykinias are appropriate for planting in naturalistic fashion in wild gardens, woodland gardens, and other lightly shaded locations in rock gardens and similar places. They adapt readily to moist woodland-type soils and are easily increased by seeds and division.

BOYSENBERRY. See Blackberry.

BRACHYCARPAEA (Brachy-carpaea). The only species of *Brachycarpaea* of the mustard family CRUCIFERAE is native to South Africa. Its name, alluding to the fruits, derives from the Greek *brachys*, short, and *karpos*, fruit.

A subshrub 1 foot to 2 feet tall or less often somewhat taller, **B. juncea** (syn. *J. varians*) has much the aspect of closely related *Heliophila*. Its slender, cylindrical stems, which branch from near their bases, are sparingly furnished with soft, narrow-linear, stalkless, pointed leaves mostly ½ to ¾ inch long. The sweetly-scented flowers, an inch or a little more wide, are in erect racemes. They have four persistent sepals, four wide-spreading, deep violet, bright blue, mauve, or white petals, six stamens two of which are shorter than the others, and one stout style. The fruits are short capsules.

Garden Uses and Cultivation. This lovely crucifer, perhaps not in cultivation in North America, makes a delightful garden plant. It is adapted to well-drained sandy soils and sunny locations in regions where Mediterranean-type climates prevail, such as California and parts of the southwestern United States. Propagation is by seeds, and perhaps by cuttings.

Bowkinia aconitifolia

BRACHYCHILUM (Brachy-chilum). Two species of the ginger family ZINGIBERACEAE constitute *Brachychilum*, the name of which is derived from the Greek *brachys*, short, and *cheilos*, a lip, and was given in allusion to the very short lips of the blooms. This feature and the fact that the spikes are few-flowered, serve to distinguish these plants from the nearly related ginger-lilies (*Hedychium*). They are hairless and form clumps of leafy stems that look very much like those of other plants of the ginger relationship.

One species, **B. horsfieldii,** a native of Java, has been cultivated under the name *Alpinia calcarata.* In its native state it grows as an epiphyte (it perches on trees, but does not abstract nourishment from them as do parasites and saprophytes). In cultivation it succeeds in soil. About 2 feet in height, it has slender-pointed, lanceolate to linear-lanceolate leaves up to 1 foot long, with short stalks. Its blooms are in few-flowered loose spikes, about 3 inches long. The blooms are white or greenish-white marked with yellow and red. The

Brachycarpaea juncea

Brachychilum horsfieldii

most attractive feature is the fruits. These are fleshy and split to reveal brilliant orange interiors and three rows of bright crimson, berry-like seeds. They remain attractive for long periods. Native to the Moluccas, **B. tenellus,** is smaller in all its parts and more slender.

Garden Uses and Cultivation. These are lower plants than ginger-lilies (*Hedychium*) and so can be accommodated in less space whether planted outdoors in warm climates or in tropical greenhouses. Their culture is the same as for *Hedychium.*

BRACHYCHITON (Brachy-chiton)—Flame Tree, Kurrajong, Bottle Tree. This genus of eleven species is confined in the wild to Australia. It is closely related to, and has been included in, *Sterculia*, which has a very much wider natural distribution. From *Sterculia* it differs in technical details, such as the placement of the radicle in relation to the hilum in the seeds and in the seeds being usually hairy. The name comes from the Greek *brachys*, short, and *chiton*, a tunic, and alludes to the scales and short hairs possessed by some kinds.

Brachychitons are evergreen or more or less deciduous trees of the sterculia family STERCULIACEAE. They have alternate, undivided, sometimes lobed leaves and unisexual or bisexual flowers, often on the same plant. The blooms, usually axillary and in panicles, racemes, or clusters, have generally bell-shaped calyxes with four or five spreading lobes. There are no petals. The ten to fifteen stamens form a column. The five styles are united. The fruits are woody, and each consists of five podlike sections. Their insides and the seeds are usually hairy.

The flame tree or laceback tree (**Brachychiton acerifolius** syn. *Sterculia acerifolia*) is a beautiful species. Partly or wholly deciduous, and oval-crowned, it ordinarily is 50 to 60 feet tall, but sometimes considerably taller. Its leaves, thick-textured, and hairless at maturity, vary considerably in shape. Basically they are three- to seven-lobed; sometimes the lobing is very deep and

Brachychiton *acerifolius*

sometimes the lobes are again lobed thus creating highly decorative and interesting leaf patterns. The largest leaves have blades 10 inches in diameter on stalks as long. When in flower, the flame tree is quite dazzling. Its blooms and their stalks are brilliant red. The flowers come in summer, are about ½ inch long by over ½ inch wide, and are in long, erect loose panicles. The podlike sections of the 4-inch-long fruits are boat-shaped and contain numerous, slightly-hairy seeds about ½ inch long. The Australian name lacebark tree alludes to the lacelike fiber or bast of the bark, which is used for making baskets, mats, and cordage, and for similar purposes.

The kurrajong (*B. populneus* syn. *Sterculia diversifolia*) grows up to 60 feet tall and

ened near their bases. The often brown- or purple-spotted blooms, ¾ inch in diameter, are reddish inside. They are in axillary panicles. The seed pods are boat-shaped and 1½ to 3 inches long. This evergreen tree makes islands of green even when the rest of the landscape is parched and brown. In its native land, the kurrajong supplies excellent, nutritious fodder for sheep and cattle, which is especially esteemed in times of drought.

An unusual species of distinctive appearance, the bottle tree or barrel tree (*B. rupestris*) favors dryish soils in the wild. This curious kind has a trunk much swollen above its usually constricted base, which then gradually tapers above to a long flagon-like neck. The name bottle tree seems particularly appropriate not only because of the shape of the trunk, but because it serves as a reservoir of water that is stored between the inside of the inner bark, and contains a sweet, edible juice-like jelly. The soft, pithy interior of the trunk, as well as the foliage, serves as food for livestock. The bottle tree is 30 to 50 feet tall. Its massive trunk is crowned by a dense head of foliage. The leaves are hairless, undivided and lobeless, 3 to 6 inches long and up to ¾ inch wide, or divided in hand-fashion into five to nine linear-lanceolate leaflets up to 7 inches long by slightly more than ½ inch wide. They are often smaller. Both types of leaves are produced on the same tree. In downy panicles 1 inch to 2 inches long from the leaf axils, the ½-inch-long, deeply-lobed, bell-shaped flowers are borne. The fruits are 1 inch long.

Pink blooms are characteristic of *B. discolor* (syns. *B. luridus*, *Sterculia discolor*),

A shrub or tree up to about 20 feet in height, *B. bidwillii* (syn. *Sterculia bidwillii*) is softly-downy throughout. Its deeply-three-lobed leaves, with heart-shaped bases, are 3 to 6 inches long and wide, and have stalks approximately equaling their blades in length. The light red, nearly stalkless blooms, 1¼ inches across and bell-shaped with recurved lobes, are clustered in the leaf axils.

Garden and Landscape Uses and Cultivation. Brachychitons are planted as ornamentals in warm, frostless or essentially frostless climates. They stand dry conditions well and thrive in a variety of soils. The kurrajong is especially resistant to drought, and so is the bottle tree. The former is used in California as a windbreak. Brachychitons are easily raised from seeds and transplant well even when large. Their rates of growth vary considerably with the fertility of the soil and the availability of moisture. Under favorable conditions they develop rapidly, especially in their early years.

BRACHYCOME (Brachý-come) — Swan-River-Daisy. One annual species of *Brachycome* of the seventy-five that inhabit North America, Australia, New Zealand, and Africa is cultivated. The genus belongs in the daisy family COMPOSITAE and consists of annuals and herbaceous perennials. Its name is derived from the Greek *brachys*, short, and *kome*, hair, alluding to the hairs attached to the ovaries and seeds.

Brachycomes have branched or branchless stems and basal or alternate, lobeless and toothless or lobed or toothed leaves. The flower heads, of the daisy type and solitary or clustered, have yellow disks and one or two rows of white, pink, lavender, or blue ray florets. The fruits are seedlike achenes.

The Swan-River-daisy (*B. iberidifolia*) is a charming Australian, 1 foot to 1½ feet tall and much-branched. Its stems are slender, its alternate leaves deeply divided into slender segments. The brightly colored,

Brachychiton populneus

Brachychiton discolor

Brachycome iberidifolia

develops a shapely broad-oval crown. It has glossy, hairless, ovate to ovate-lanceolate, poplar-like leaves that are three- or five-lobed or lobeless. They resemble those of the portia tree (*Thespesia populnea*). They have pointed blades 2 to 3 inches long and 1- to 2-inch-long stalks decidedly thick-

which is 40 to 100 feet tall, has larger flowers, and grows more quickly than *B. acerifolius*. From 4 to 6 inches across, its maple-like leaves are 5- to 7-lobed or angled, and white-woolly on their undersides. The bell-shaped flowers, displayed in summer, and the fruits are clothed with rusty hairs.

Brachycome iberidifolia

cineraria-like flower heads, 1 inch to 1½ inches in diameter and fragrant, are produced in great profusion. Their ray florets are usually clear blue, more rarely pink or white.

Garden Uses. The Swan-River-daisy is a beautiful plant for flower gardens, in areas where summers are not excessively torrid and humid, and is delightful for growing in pots as a decorative greenhouse plant for late winter and spring display. In the outdoor garden it serves well for edgings and may be used effectively in patches at the fronts of flower borders and in rock gardens.

Cultivation. Best results with this plant are usually had when the seeds are sown indoors in a temperature of 60 to 65°F in spring and the resulting plants are grown, spaced 2 inches apart, in flats in porous, well-drained soil, in a sunny greenhouse, for six to eight weeks before being transplanted to the garden. This latter move may be made about the time it is safe to plant corn and lima beans, after all danger of frost has passed. While they are in the flats, excessive watering must be avoided. A constantly wet soil is likely to destroy the plants through rotting. Young plants may be pinched once to encourage bushiness. Outdoors, a deep, fertile soil that is well drained and a location in full sun best suit the Swan-River-daisy. The plants may be set 4 to 6 inches apart. An alternative methods of cultivation is to sow the seeds outdoors in early spring, rake them into the surface soil, and thin the resulting seedlings so that they stand 4 inches apart. Outdoor care is minimal. It consists of keeping down weeds, watering if the weather is dry, and perhaps a little discreet staking with brushwood or other unobtrusive supports.

To have pot plants in bloom in greenhouses in late winter and spring, seeds are sown in September, October, or January and the young plants transplanted singly to 2½-inch pots. Later, fall-sown plants are potted three together in 6-inch containers

or four or five in 7-inch pots. Those sown in January may be transferred individually to 5-inch pots. They are kept in a sunny greenhouse where the night temperature is 50°F and the day temperature rises five to ten degrees above the night minimum. Until the plants are well rooted careful watering is required so that the soil does not remain wet for long periods. Later more generous watering is appropriate. After the plants are thoroughly and well rooted in their final containers, occasional applications of dilute liquid fertilizer are beneficial. Indoors, the atmosphere should be dryish, but not arid. To achieve this, the greenhouse must be ventilated freely on all favorable occasions. Excessive humidity and too-high temperatures are particularly harmful. Plants from fall-sown seeds attain a height of about 2 feet. They need to be neatly staked so that their stems are supported without the means by which that is accomplished being obvious or detracting from the beauty of the plants.

BRACHYGLOTTIS (Brachy-glóttis). Very closely related to *Senecio*, this genus of a single species is endemic to New Zealand. It belongs in the daisy family COMPOSITAE. Its name comes from the Greek *brachys*, short, and *glossa*, a tongue, in allusion to the short, tongue-shaped corollas of the ray florets.

An evergreen shrub or tree up to about 20 feet tall, *Brachyglottis repanda* has stout, spreading branches, and young shoots heavily felted with whitish hairs. Its firm, alternate, oblong to ovate-oblong leaves have grooved stalks up to 4 inches long, and dull green blades 4 to 10 inches long by 4 to 8 inches wide, with edges scalloped into prominent shallow lobes or teeth. They are densely-whitish-hairy on their undersides. The tiny heads of greenish to creamy-white blooms, fragrant with a scent somewhat like that of mignonette, are in terminal, freely-branching panicles, up to 1 foot long and wider than long. Each flower head is about ⅕ inch in diameter and consists of about twelve tiny disk and ray florets. The fruits are seedlike achenes. Variety *B. r. rangiora* (syn. *B. rangiora*) differs in having glossy, more leathery leaves, and in the bracts of the flower heads being purplish. In *B. r. arborescens* (syn. *B. arborescens*) the trunk attains 1 foot in diameter, and the leaves are highly glossy and obovate.

Garden and Landscape Uses and Cultivation. Not hardy in the north, these spring-blooming shrubs or small trees are appropriate for general garden planting in mild climates and are most esteemed for their handsome foliage, but their branches are brittle. They succeed in sun in ordinary soils and are grateful for some decayed organic material mixed in. They are propagated by seeds and by cuttings taken in late summer and planted under mist or in a greenhouse propagating bench.

BRACHYPODIUM (Brachy-pòdium). Sixteen species, chiefly native of temperate parts of the northern hemisphere, and occurring in Mexico and Central America, constitute this genus of the grass family GRAMINEAE. They include annuals and perennials, some of which are ornamental. The name, from the Greek *brachys*, short, and *podion*, a foot, alludes to the brief stalks of the spikelets of flowers.

Brachypodiums, sometimes called false brome grass, form tufts of erect, slender stems and flat or rolled leaves. Their narrow, spikelike racemes of flowers, nodding or upright, are unbranched. Each flattened spikelet contains five flowers or more.

A fairly attractive annual, *Brachypodium distachyon*, up to 1½ feet tall, has branched or branchless stems and slightly hairy, slender leaves up to 4 inches long by up to ⅛ inch wide. The racemes of blooms, about 3 inches long and consisting of up to six spikelets, have awns (bristles) up to ¾ inch long. This species is native to the Mediterranean region. Also from that area, but extending into other parts of Europe and into Asia, comes *B. sylvaticum*, a perennial that inhabits woodlands and other shady places. This species attains a height of 3 feet and has erect or lax, branchless stems, linear-lanceolate, hairy leaves up to 1 foot long by ⅛ to ½ inch wide, and nodding spikes of usually more than six spikelets, 2 to 8 inches long. The awns of the spikelets are about ½ inch long.

Garden and Landscape Uses and Cultivation. The species first described can be accommodated in beds and other places where annual grasses are appropriate. It requires full sun and well-drained soil and is raised from seeds sown in spring where the plants are to remain. The seedlings are thinned to 5 or 6 inches apart. The perennial species described is suitable for woodland gardens and other partly shaded locations. It thrives in ordinary soil and may be increased by division and seeds.

BRACHYSEMA (Brachy-sèma)—Swan-River-Pea. Australia is home to the fifteen species of procumbent and vining shrubs of the genus *Brachysema*. The name, alluding to the short standard or banner petal of the pealike flowers, is from the Greek *brachys*, short, and *sema*, a standard. The genus belongs in the pea family LEGUMINOSAE. It has alternate or opposite, ovate to ovate-lanceolate, toothless leaves, silky-hairy on their undersides, and with a tiny sharp point at their tips. The flowers are few together in axillary and terminal racemes. The fruits are pods.

Long grown in California and elsewhere in mild, dryish climates, the Swan-River-pea (*B. lanceolatum*) is a shrub about 3 feet high in its homeland, but in California often 5 or 6 feet tall. It has wandlike branches, and usually opposite, ovate or ovate-lanceolate leaves 2 to 4 inches long and up to 1 inch wide, silvery-white when young, but becoming darker later. Rich, but not brilliant red, the slender, 1-inch-long flowers, which do not open widely, are in axillary clusters close to the branches. They are abundant. In gardens near San Francisco, this species blooms almost continuously.

Garden and Landscape Uses and Cultivation. Suitable for outdoor cultivation only in warm dry climates, the Swan-River-pea is sometimes grown in greenhouses and conservatories. It is adapted for massing and for planting as single specimens. A sandy somewhat peaty soil and a sunny location is to its liking. Propagation is by seeds, and by summer cuttings. In greenhouses a winter night temperature of 45 to 50°F is adequate. Day temperatures may be five to ten degrees higher. On all favorable occasions the greenhouse must be ventilated freely. Water to keep the soil moderately moist.

BRACHYSTELMA (Brachy-stélma). A genus of thirty species restricted in the wild to Central and South Africa, *Brachystelma* belongs in the milkweed family ASCLEPIADACEAE. Its name, from the Greek *brachys*, short, and *stelma*, a belt or girdle, refers to the coronas of the blooms. The tubers of some kinds, edible when cooked, were used as native foods.

Brachystelmas are low succulents, usually with an underground tuber or cluster of thick, fleshy roots from which come slender, occasionally twining, erect or prostrate stems bearing opposite, deciduous, lanceolate to ovate leaves in pairs. The blooms, often ill-scented and much like those of *Stapelia*, are solitary or in few- to many-flowered umbels from the leaf axils or terminal. They have a five-lobed calyx, a five-lobed corolla, the lobes free and spreading or reflexed to form a starlike bloom or joined at their tips to form a sort of cage. The stamen column bears a corona or crown of a double row, sometimes appearing to be a single row, of parts. The fruits are smooth, paired, podlike follicles.

A few kinds are grown by fanciers of succulents: **B. barberiae,** about 6 inches

Brachystelma barberiae

tall, has linear-oblong, pointed leaves, umbels of yellow-speckled, dull purple blooms; **B. tuberosum,** up to 1½ feet tall, has linear-lanceolate, hair-fringed leaves. Its flowers, in clusters of three or four, are green, dotted with red on their outsides, on their insides purple streaked at their centers with yellow.

Garden Uses and Cultivation. These rare and interesting *Stapelia* relatives require about the same conditions and care as members of that genus. A porous soil containing a respectable proportion of humus suits. It should be kept moist during the season of growth, dry during the dormant period. Propagation is by seeds and cuttings. For more information see Stapelia, and also Succulents.

BRACKEN or BRAKE is *Pteridium aquilinum.*

BRACTS. Bracts are modified leaves associated with the flowering parts of plants or on the stalks below the flowering parts. They may be small, green, and leaflike in texture, colorless, papery, or horny, or white or brightly colored and petal-like. In some kinds of plants they form the chief attraction. This is true of the red, pink, or white bracts of poinsettias, the white or pink ones of flowering dogwoods and of those of many aroids and bromeliads. The bracts of aroids are called spathes. Those of the common calla-lily are white. Those of anthuriums are generally bright red or pink.

BRAHEA (Bra-hèa)—Rock Palm, Hesper Palm, Soyal Palm. Plants that some authorities treat separately as *Erythea* are in this Encyclopedia included in *Brahea*. When this is done the genus consists of a dozen species of the palm family PALMAE, natives of Mexico and Central America. The name honors Tycho Brahe, a Danish astronomer, who died in 1601. Plants cultivated in the United States as *Brahea* are often misidentified.

Braheas are small- to medium-sized fan-leaved trees with erect or reclined trunks and globular crowns of deeply-cleft, rigid, often bluish leaves. The flower clusters arise among the foliage and equal or exceed the leaves in length. The flowers, tiny and solitary or in clusters of three, have three each sepals and petals and six stamens. The brown or blackish fruits are usually flattened somewhat on one side.

Best known, **B. dulcis,** of southern Mexico and Guatemala, has a solitary, erect, leaning, or decumbent trunk up to 20 feet in length, and nearly round, dull, bluish leaves cut to more than one-half their depth into thirty to sixty narrow, pointed, slightly two-cleft segments that stand out stiffly from the undivided portion of the leaf and have threadlike filaments along their margins. When the trunk is prostrate or semiprostrate, suckers or secondary trunks arise from its base. The flower clus-

ters are 6 to 9 feet long and much-branched. The fruits, called miche or michire, have thin, edible flesh and are about ¾ inch long. The leaves of this palm are used for thatching and the trunks for framing houses. Often taller than the last, **B. nitida,** ranging from Mexico to Guatemala, is often misnamed *B. calcarea,* which name is properly a synonym of *B. dulcis.* Its leaves, usually without filaments, have stalks without teeth along their edges. Its clusters of solitary flowers are up to 10 feet long. The fruits are about ¾ inch long.

The Mexican blue palm or big blue hesper palm (**B. armata** syn. *Erythea armata*) is stout and up to 40 feet tall. Unless cut

(a) *Brahea armata,* as a native in Baja California

(b) In cultivation in California

or burnt off, its trunk is clothed in a skirt of persistent old leaves in the manner of *Washingtonia.* Typically the foliage is very glaucous-blue, but there is some variation between individual specimens. The very beautiful, plume-like flower clusters, 12 to 15 feet long and much exceeding the leaves in length, arch gracefully downward well outside the heavy crown of foliage and make a pretty display. The fleshy, globose fruits, about ¾ inch long, are variegated with brown. The leaves, 3 to 6 feet in diameter, are divided into about fifty segments.

The Guadalupe palm (**B. edulis** syn. *Erythea edulis*), one of the most distinctive of the genus, takes its common name from the island off the coast of Baja California where it is native. It received its botanical appellation *edulis* in recognition of the fact that its discoverer found that "the fruit is eaten by man, goats, birds, and mice." This stout-trunked tree, up to 35 feet in height, has leaves green on both sides, 3 to 6 feet in diameter, with mostly nearly spineless stalks with their bases enveloped in cloth-like fibrous sheaths. The blades are dissected one-third to one-half their depth into seventy to eighty segments. The flower clusters are shorter than the leaves. The pulp of the black fruits is sweet.

Brahea brandegeei

Brahea edulis

Other species cultivated include these: **B. brandegeei** (syn. *Erythea brandegeei*), the San Jose hesper palm, is native to Baja California. This kind has a slender trunk up to 40 feet tall, leaves with long, spiny stalks, and blades up to 3 feet wide or wider, with glaucous undersides. Each has fifty to sixty deeply-two-cleft segments. The flowers, in groups of three, are in clusters up to as long as the leaves. **B. elegans** (syn. *Erythea elegans*), the Franceschi palm, believed to be a native of Mexico, is of small to medium size. Its leaves, more or less glaucous on both surfaces, have spiny stalks. The flowers, in groups of three, are in clusters longer than the leaves. **B. pimo** is Mexican. Up to about 15 feet high, it has leaves with spiny stalks that when young

Brahea elegans

are densely-hairy. Its bright green leaf blades are divided into fifty or more shortly-two-cleft segments. In clusters exceeding the leaves in length, the flowers are in groups of three. **B. salvadorensis**, of Central America, is up to 20 feet tall. Not long-persistent, its leaves have spiny stalks, when young hairy, and green blades of about seventy shortly-two-cleft segments. The clusters of flowers, composed of groups of three, are as long as the leaves.

Garden and Landscape Uses. Braheas are generally satisfactory garden and landscape plants well suited for cultivation in dry climates such as that of the warmer parts of California. They are primarily sun-lovers, although they stand part-shade. Characteristically of rather massive appearance, although comparatively low, they are attractive as solitary specimens or in

groups, and they associate effectively with architectural features such as buildings, steps, and terraces. In their native habitats, at least some sorts show distinct preference for limestone soils, which may be worth considering when selecting planting sites.

Cultivation. These palms thrive in any ordinary garden soil that never becomes excessively dry and are propagated by sowing fresh seeds in a sandy, peaty soil in a temperature of 75 to 85°F. Under greenhouse conditions they need a minimum winter night temperature of 55 to 60°F, with a rise of five or ten degrees in the daytime permitted. At other seasons both night and day temperatures may be considerably higher. Water freely from spring through fall, less freely in winter. Well-established plants benefit from dilute liquid fertilizer applied biweekly from spring through fall. A humid atmosphere and light shade from strong summer sun are necessary. For further information see Palms.

BRAKE. This is the common name of ferns of the genera *Pteridium* and *Pteris*. Cliffbrake is *Onychium*.

BRAMBLE. See Rubus.

BRANDY BOTTLE. See Nuphar.

BRAPASIA. This is the name of orchid hybrids the parents of which are *Brassia* and *Aspasia*.

BRASENIA (Bras-ènia)—Water Shield. The only species of this genus is a widely distributed aquatic that is part of the natural floras of North America, Cuba, Asia, Africa, and Australia. Its name is of unknown origin. It belongs in the water-lily family NYMPHAEACEAE. In North America the water shield (**Brasenia schreberi**) is indigenous in quiet waters from Nova Scotia to British Columbia, Florida, Texas, and California. It has creeping rootstocks and slender, branching stems up to 6 feet long. Like the undersides of the leaves, they are covered with a thick coating of jelly. The leaves, alternate and mostly crowded at the ends of the stems, have long stalks to which the blades are attached at their centers. They float. The bright green blades are elliptic and 2 to 5 inches in length; they often have purplish undersides. The solitary, dull purple flowers are on stout stems up to 6 inches long. They are ½ to ¾ inch wide and have similar sepals and petals, usually three but occasionally four, of each. There are twelve to eighteen stamens. The leathery, one- to two-seeded, beaked fruits are about ⅓ inch long.

Garden Uses and Cultivation. The water shield is one of the less showy cultivated aquatics. Unlike its relatives, the water-lilies and spatterdocks, it makes no appreciable display of bloom. Nevertheless it is useful for adding variety to pool plantings and is appropriate for inclusion in collections of native plants. It grows satisfactorily in quiet water from 1 foot to 6 feet deep. Although it succeeds in slightly brackish water, it does not thrive if the water is alkaline. It is easily propagated by seeds and by division in spring. It requires the same conditions and care as hardy water-lilies (*Nymphaea*).

BRASILICACTUS (Brasíli-cactus). By some authorities *Brasilicactus* of the cactus family CACTACEAE is included in *Notocactus* to which it is clearly closely related. It comprises three species, natives of southern Brazil and Uruguay. The name is a modification of that of the country Brazil joined to the suffix cactus.

Brasilicactuses are small, short-spined, spherical or flattish plants with ribs of rounded tubercles. They have short, funnel-shaped flowers that open by day. The fruits are spiny.

Beautiful *B. haselbergii* (syns. *Notocactus haselbergii*, *Malacocarpus haselbergii*) is nearly spherical, about 3 inches in diameter, and has thirty ribs or more. The spine clusters are of about twenty white, bristly radials and three to five pale yellow centrals. About 1 inch across, the blooms are red. About 4 inches wide and shorter and flatter than the last, *B. graessneri* (syns. *Notocactus graessneri*, *Malacocarpus graessneri*) usually has in excess of sixty spiraled ribs. The spines are greenish-yellow to bright yellow, about ¾ inch long. They are numerous and each cluster includes three to six centrals. The blooms are small and yellowish-green. *B. g. albisetus* has white hairs among the spines.

Garden Uses and Cultivation. These cactuses are choice collectors' items. They need decidedly sandy, fairly nutritious, thoroughly-drained soil and a little shade from the strongest sun. For more information see Cactuses.

BRASS BUTTONS is *Cotula coronopifolia*.

BRASSAIA (Brass-àia)—Queensland Umbrella Tree or Octopus Tree. Depending upon the interpretations of individual botanists, *Brassaia* of the aralia family ARALIACEAE consists of forty species, of only one species, or is included in *Schefflera*. If recognized it includes the popular sort, commonly known as schefflera, described here. The name honors Samuel von Brassai, a Hungarian botanist, who died in 1897.

Accepted broadly, *Brassaia* occurs natively from Hawaii to the Philippine Islands, Malay Peninsula, and Australia. Its kinds are trees and shrubs with crowded terminal clusters of long-stalked leaves with blades divided into several leaflets joined to the top of the leafstalk. The flowers are small and in more or less spherical umbels assembled in panicles or racemes. Each bloom has five early deciduous sepals, the same number or more petals, and as many stamens as petals. The fruits are berry-like drupes.

The Queensland umbrella tree or octopus tree (*B. actinophylla* syn. *Schefflera actinophylla*) is a handsome evergreen that attains a maximum height of about 40 feet.

Brassaia actinophylla

Brassaia actinophylla (flowers)

Brassaia actinophylla, young specimen

In its homeland it sometimes grows as an epiphyte, that is, it inhabits the crowns of other trees without sending its roots to the ground, but does not derive nourishment directly from its hosts. Instead, it satisfies its needs from the vegetable and animal debris that collects in crotches and crevices and from rainwater. From the apexes of the long leafstalks of the Queensland umbrella tree spread seven to sixteen, or in young specimens fewer, stalked, oblong to obovate-oblong, shiny, leathery leaflets up to 1 foot long, and with a few irregularly-spaced teeth. The small wine-red flowers

Brasilicactus haselbergii

are in compact umbels strung along stiff, spike-like stalks up to 2 feet long that radiate like the arms of an octopus to provide a decidedly modernistic display. The purplish-black fruits contain about a dozen seeds. This species is a native of Australia.

Garden and Landscape Uses. The sort described is of distinctive, bold aspect and is highly satisfactory in Florida, Hawaii, and other places with warm climates, with little or no frost. It may be used to good advantage as a solitary lawn specimen, to frame a house or other building or a view, or as a screen. It succeeds in any ordinary well-drained soil in sun or part-shade. This species is also a first-class ornamental foliage plant for pots, tubs, and other containers. It is especially esteemed as a change from palms, rubber plants, and philodendrons in locations where bold-foliaged plants of massive appearance are needed.

Cultivation. Seeds provide a ready means of securing young brassaias. They germinate well and quickly in a temperature of 60 to 70°F in sandy peaty soil kept moist, but not saturated. Cuttings, sectional stem cuttings, and air layering are also satisfactory means of propagation. In suitable outdoor locations in warm climates these plants require no special care. When grown in containers they succeed in fertile porous soil, with good light, but not necessarily direct sun, and a moderately moist atmosphere. A minimum temperature of 55°F is appropriate, ten or even fifteen degrees higher is satisfactory. The containers must be well drained and care must be taken not to keep the soil too wet. Failure to attend to this is one of the commonest causes of disaster with container-grown Queensland umbrella trees. If the roots are long in saturated soil the leaves soon yellow and drop, and the plants look bedraggled. The approved procedure is to soak the soil very thoroughly when water is given, then apply no more until the earth becomes dry, almost, but not quite, to the point where the leaves wilt. The application of dilute liquid fertilizer about once a month aids specimens that have filled their pots with roots. The leaves should be kept free of dust by sponging them occasionally with soapy water. Spraying the foliage with a fine mist of water two or three times a day is beneficial. When specimens become too tall for their locations they may be cut back quite severely, and by repotting into as small containers as will hold their roots or by removing an inch or two of surface soil and replacing it with rich earth to which some fertilizer has been added, encouraged to make new growth. Following drastic pruning, greater care than ever must be exercised to prevent the soil from being constantly saturated for long periods.

BRASSAVOLA (Brass-ávola). Fifteen species related to *Laelia* constitute this genus, which inhabits a natural range extending from Mexico to South America and the West Indies. It belongs in the orchid family ORCHIDACEAE and has a name that commemorates the Venetian botanist, Antonio Musa Brassavola (or Brasavola), who died in 1555.

Brassavolas are showy-flowered evergreen orchids that in the wild generally perch on trees, more rarely on rocks. Their pseudobulbs are slender and cylindrical like the single or rarely paired fleshy leaves that terminate them. From the point of attachment of pseudobulb and leaf, except in one species, the flower stems, carrying solitary blooms or in some kinds several in a raceme, arise. The flowers of *B. acaulis* are on separate, leafless shoots from the rhizomes.

Popular *B. nodosa,* wild from Mexico to Venezuela and Peru, is highly variable. Its pseudobulbs are about 6 inches long. Its pointed, linear to linear-elliptic, usually erect leaves are mostly 1 foot long or longer and up to 1 inch wide. They are deeply-channeled along their upper sides. Very fragrant at night, the long-lasting flowers, up to 3½ inches in diameter, are in racemes that may be 8 inches long. Up to six to a raceme, they have slender, pale green, yellowish, or nearly white sepals and petals and a broad, white lip, with a pointed-heart-shaped, scooplike blade longer than its up to 1-inch-long stem, and sometimes spotted with purple near its base. This species blooms chiefly in fall and winter, sometimes in summer. Somewhat like *B. nodosa,* but commonly with smaller pseudobulbs and leaves, *B. martiana,* of northeastern South America, has yellowish to greenish flowers up to about

Brassavola martiana

3 inches wide that have a white or yellowish-white, fringed lip, and usually a green or yellow blotch in their throats. This kind blooms in summer.

Native from Mexico to South America and the West Indies, summer- to fall-blooming *B. cucullata* has pseudobulbs up to 5 inches tall and cylindrical, usually arching or drooping, whiplike leaves 1½ feet long or longer. The fragrant, long-slender-tubed flowers, mostly solitary, but sometimes in twos or threes, have tail-like, drooping sepals and petals up to 3½ inches long. White, yellowish, or greenish-white, sometimes tinted red toward their tips, they are tapered-linear and end in long points. The cream-tinted lip is fringed.

Endemic to the West Indies is summer-, fall-, or winter-blooming *B. cordata.* It has slender, recurved or pendulous, channeled leaves, grooved along their upper

Brassavola nodosa

Brassavola cucullata

Brassavola flagellaris

Brassavola cordata

sides, and about 1 foot long. Flowers, about 1¾ inches wide, are in racemes of few to many. Fragrant, they have greenish, lanceolate-linear, yellow to green sepals and petals and a large heart-shaped, white lip, with a purple-marked, toothed basal part that encloses the column and has a blade scarcely as long as its stem.

Very slender pseudobulbs up to 1 foot long are characteristic of *B. flagellaris,* of Brazil. Its sharply-pointed, very slender, recurved leaves are cylindrical, grooved along their upper sides, and up to 1½ feet long. From 2½ to 3 inches across, the blooms have wide-spreading or recurving, pointed-linear to narrowly-elliptic, pale yellowish or greenish sepals and petals and a large, white lip, with a green or yellow-green blotch at its base. Similar, but with smaller pseudobulbs and leaves, spring-blooming *B. perrinii,* a Brazilian native, has blooms up to 3 inches wide that do not always open fully. Much like it, but with more flowers, each about 2 inches across, *B. cebolleta* is also Brazilian. Yet a third of this origin and aspect, *B. tuberculata* is distinguished by having sepals and petals spotted with red.

Brassavola flagellaris (flowers)

Brassavola acaulis

Beautiful **B. acaulis** has slender stemlike pseudobulbs and long, often purplish, narrow leaves that droop for up to 2½ feet. Unlike those of other species, the flowers of this, in racemes of up to four or sometimes solitary, come not from the pseudobulbs but from the ground. Very fragrant, and up to 5 inches across, they have narrow, greenish, pale brownish, or whitish sepals and petals, generally purplish-brown on their undersides, and a large, creamy-white to pure white lip that narrows into a funnel-shaped tube toward its base. This species is a native of Costa Rica and Panama.

Native from Mexico to Guatemala, **B. digbyana** (syns. *Rhyncholaelia digbyana, Laelia digbyana*) has flattened, club-shaped pseudobulbs 6 inches tall or somewhat taller. The leaves are glaucous, linear to elliptic, 5 to 8 inches in length, and over 2 inches wide. The flowers, exceedingly fragrant especially at night, are 4 to over 6 inches wide, with pale yellow-green, spreading, oblong sepals and petals, or the latter may be suffused with purple. There is often an emerald-green patch in the throat. The sepals are elliptic-lanceolate to strap-shaped, the petals elliptic-lanceolate and somewhat wavy. The large, heart-shaped, cream or white, much-fringed lip encloses the column. In *B. d. fimbripetala* the petals as well as the lip are fringed.

Endemic from Mexico to Panama, **B. glauca** (syns. *Rhyncholaelia glauca, Laelia glauca*) has glaucous, spindle-shaped pseu-

dobulbs up to 4 or 5 inches long and blunt, oblong-elliptic, stiff, leathery, glaucous leaves up to nearly 5 inches long by 1¼ inches wide. The long-lived blooms, 4 and 5 inches wide, are of substantial texture. The spreading, linear-elliptic to oblong-lanceolate sepals and petals, the former are olive-green to lavender or white, the petals

Brassavola glauca

commonly lighter colored than the sepals. The lower part of the lip surrounds the column. Its large, expanded part is rounded, slightly three-lobed, not fringed.

Garden Uses and Cultivation. These are satisfying plants for collectors of orchids and in the main are easy to manage. They respond to environments suitable for cattleyas and may be accommodated in pots or baskets or on slabs of tree fern. For kinds with pendulous foliage, the containers or slabs should be suspended. Bright light is important. No more shade than is needed to prevent scorching of the foliage should be given. Water must be provided liberally except for a rest period of two or three weeks following completion of the growth of the new pseudobulbs. For additional information see Orchids.

BRASSIA (Brás-sia)—Spider Orchid. Ranging in the wild from southern Florida to Mexico, tropical America, and the West Indies, *Brassia* consists of about fifty species of the orchid family ORCHIDACEAE, related to *Odontoglossum*. The name honors William Brass, a botanical collector in Africa, who died in 1783.

Brassias are evergreen epiphytes (they perch on trees without extracting nourishment from their hosts), or they sometimes grow on rocks. They have creeping rhizomes and usually, crowded, rather flattened pseudobulbs with one to three leaves. From the bottoms of the pseudobulbs, or in some kinds from the leaf axils of young growths, the flower spikes, which are often very long, develop. They have few to many, generally large, attractive, and often oddly-shaped blooms. In many kinds the sepals, and in some, other flower parts, are extraordinarily long and slender, and because of their appearance are responsible for the name spider orchid. Not all are of this appearance, however. Hybrids of *Brassia* and *Aspasia* are offered under the name *Brapasia*.

Occurring from southern Florida to Mexico, northern South America, and the West Indies in the wild, very variable *B. caudata* has flattened, oblong-elliptic, generally glossy pseudobulbs up to 6 inches long, each with two or three leathery, oblong-elliptic to oblong-lanceolate leaves that may be 1 foot or more in length and 2½ inches in width. In racemes of three to fifteen, the decidedly fragrant blooms have yellowish to greenish sepals and petals, barred and spotted with chocolate or paler brown. The lip, similarly marked near its base, is yellowish and has a fuzzy callus. From *B. caudata,* Central American *B. gireoudiana* differs mainly in being more robust, and in having less floppy, larger, and more beautiful blooms sometimes fully 1 foot long. Another robust species with much the habit of *B. caudata,* and with sometimes solitary leaves bigger and broader than those of other kinds, is *B. maculata,* of Central America, northern South America, and the West Indies. The 5- to 8-inch-long flowers of this kind have rigid, greenish to greenish-yellow sepals and petals, cross-barred and spotted with reddish-brown or purple as is the yellowish lip, which has a brighter yellow or orange callus.

Brassia gireoudiana

Pseudobulbs flatter than those of *B. caudata,* with occasionally two leaves, but more often one leaf, are typical of *B. longissima* (syn. *B. lawrenceana longissima*), of Central and South America. The leaves are up to 2 feet long by 2½ to 3 inches wide. The erect or arching flower stalks, 1½ to 2 feet long, have racemes of up to fifteen fragrant blooms that have bright yellow, buff-yellow, or greenish-yellow sepals and petals, blotched and spotted toward their bases with reddish-brown. The pale yellow to cream lip is similarly marked. The threadlike sepals, longer than the petals, may be 1 foot long or longer. Similar to *B. longissima,* but with two leaves to each pseudobulb, and with erect, white projec-

Brassia longissima

Brassia caudata

tions in front of the crest of the lip, is *B. chloroleuca,* of Costa Rica and Panama.

Vigorous *B. verrucosa* (syn. *B. brachiata*), which in the wild is found from Mexico to Venezuela, has flattened, generally somewhat furrowed, narrowly-egg-shaped pseudobulbs 3 to 4 inches long, with leaflike sheaths at their bases in addition to two oblong-elliptic to lanceolate leaves, up to 1¼ feet long by 2 inches wide at their tops. The racemes of up to eight or more blooms are on stalks sometimes more than 2 feet in length. The flowers, pale green with dark green or reddish spots, have whitish lips, with the lower portions with conspicuous black-green warts, and a yellow callus. The largest-flowered variants have blooms 6 to 8 inches long.

Strongly-flattened, clustered pseudobulbs 3 to 5 inches long are characteristic of *B. lanceana,* of Surinam and Venezuela. Each has one to three, usually two, lanceolate-oblong leaves up to 1 foot long. Erect, angled, or spreading horizontally and 1 foot to 2 feet in length, the inflorescences are of up to a dozen blooms. The sepals, about 2½ inches long, and petals, one-half as long as the sepals, are yellow, greenish-yellow, or orange with brown

Brassia lanceana

Ornamental kale

markings. The pointed-oblong-fiddle-shaped lip is yellowish-white flecked with brown.

Very different from others in being without pseudobulbs, **B. allenii,** of Panama, has fans of narrowly-strap-shaped to lanceolate leaves up to 1½ feet long by about 1½ inches wide, with overlapping bases. From the upper leaf axils come erect or arching stalks bearing up to eight crowded, approximately 3-inch-long, honey-scented blooms. The not extraordinarily long sepals and the petals are cinnabar-red to tannish, with greenish-yellow bases. The squarish, yellow lip, spotted with brown, has a white callus.

Garden Uses and Cultivation. Long-lasting, fragrant blooms of much charm and often curious aspect are responsible for the appeal of these generally-easy-to-manage orchids. They bloom at various seasons depending upon kind, and to some extent local conditions. It is not unusual for some to flower twice a year. Environments suitable for cattleyas are appropriate for brassias. They grow best potted in osmunda or tree fern fiber or attached to slabs of tree fern. Fir and red-wood bark as potting mediums have usually proved less satisfactory. Stagnant conditions about the roots are not tolerated by brassias. As soon as the fiber in which they grow shows definite signs of deterioration, they must be repotted. Except during a resting period of two or three weeks following the maturing of the new pseudobulbs, water to keep the roots always moist, and apply fertilizer regularly to well-rooted individuals. Good light,

with only sufficient shade to forestall scorching of the foliage, is needed. For additional information see Orchids.

BRASSICA (Bráss-ica). Because it is the source of several important vegetables, *Brassica* (syn. *Sinapsis*) of the mustard family CRUCIFERAE is known to almost everyone. It is also the source of the condiment mustard and of mustard, rape, and colza oils. It contains about forty species, some, such as charlock or California rape (*B. kaber* syn. *Sinapsis arvensis*), pestiferous weeds. The name is the classical Latin one for cabbage.

Mostly annuals and biennials, but including a few herbaceous perennials and shrubs, this genus is native only in the Old World. Several of its sorts, however, have been cultivated for so many centuries that it is impossible to pinpoint more accurately their precise provenance, and some are now naturalized extensively in parts of the world, including North America, other than where they are native. Chiefly hairless and more or less glaucous, the species of *Brassica* are generally erect and often branched. They have alternate leaves, the lower ones mostly pinnately-lobed or coarsely-toothed. In terminal racemes, the smallish, prevailing yellow, yellowish-white, or less commonly white flowers have four sepals, four petals spread to form a cross and with much-narrowed bases, two stamens two of which are shorter than the others, and one style. The fruits, technically siliquas, are slender and podlike.

No wild species of *Brassica* is ordinarily cultivated for ornament, but rape and mustard are occasionally sown as cover crops to be turned under while still green to improve the soil by adding organic matter. Certain varieties of kale, called ornamental kale or sometimes ornamental cabbage, with center rosettes of crinkled, colorful, pink, purple, or white leaves, are grown as decorations.

Vegetables that belong in *Brassica* discussed in this Encyclopedia under their common names are broccoli, broccoli raab (turnip broccoli, or Italian turnip), brussels sprouts, cabbage, Chinese cabbage (pakchoi, or pe-tsai), collards, kale, kohlrabi, mustard greens, rutabaga, and turnip. In Europe, and less commonly in America, seeds of black mustard (*B. nigra*) are sprouted and the young seedlings used as salad greens.

BRASSIDIUM. This is the name of bigeneric orchids the parents of which are *Brassia* and *Oncidium.*

BRASSIOPHOENIX (Brassio-phoènix). Named in honor of its discoverer, Leonard John Brass, American botanist and plant collector, who died in 1971, *Brassiophoenix* of the palm family PALMAE has a name combining his with that of the palm genus *Phoenix*. Native of New Guinea, it was first found and introduced to the United States in 1953. There is one species.

As described by its discoverer, **B. schumannii** is 30 feet high. It has a slender trunk and long pinnate leaves with broad, wedge-shaped leaflets. Borne in clusters below the crown of leaves, the fruits are large, yellow, and decorative.

Garden and Landscape Uses and Cultivation. As yet uncommon in cultivation, this palm has proven very satisfactory at the Fairchild Tropical Garden, Miami, Florida. It does best in partial shade, but needs much water. For more information see Palms.

Brassocattleya heatonensis

BRASSOCATTLEYA. This is the name of bigeneric orchids the parents of which are *Brassavola* and *Cattleya*.

BRASSODIACRIUM. This is the name of bigeneric orchid hybrids the parents of which are *Brassavola* and *Diacrium*.

BRASSOEPIDENDRUM. This is the name of bigeneric orchids the parents of which are *Brassavola* and *Epidendrum*.

Brassoepidendrum 'Phoenix'

BRASSOLAELIA. This is the name of bigeneric orchids the parents of which are *Brassavola* and *Laelia*.

BRASSOLAELIOCATTLEYA. This is the name of trigeneric orchid hybrids the parents of which are *Brassavola, Cattleya,* and *Laelia*.

BRASSOPHRONITIS. This is the name of bigeneric orchid hybrids the parents of which are *Brassavola* and *Sophronitis*.

BRASSOTONIA. This is the name of bigeneric orchids the parents of which are *Brassavola* and *Broughtonia*.

BRAUNSIA (Braún-sia). This is the correct name of a genus previously named *Echinus* of the carpetweed family AIZOACEAE. The name commemorates Dr. Hans Heinrich Justus Carl Ernst Brauns, a South African entomologist, who died in 1929. There are seven species, all South African. They are low, more or less creeping, succulent shrublets allied to *Mesembryanthemum* and having curious short, thick, opposite, three-angled, keeled leaves, with each pair united for one-half or more of its length. Terminal and nearly stalkless, the flowers, like others of the *Mesembryanthemum* group, give the impression that they are of the daisy type. They are not. The flower heads of daisies are composed of numerous florets, the blooms of *Braunsia* are single flowers. The fruits are capsules containing seeds roughened with small appendages.

Sometimes cultivated, *B. apiculata* (syn. *Echinus apiculatus*) attains a height up to 8 inches and has stems clothed with remnants of old foliage. Its velvety-hairy leaves are ½ inch to 1¼ inches long by ¼ to ⅓ inch broad and thick. The pink blooms are about ¾ inch wide.

Garden Uses and Cultivation. The plant described, as well as others of the genus, is appropriate for inclusion in collections of nonhardy succulents. Its needs are those of its other lower *Mesembryanthemum* relatives, such as *Stomatium*. For further information see Succulents.

BRAVOA. See Polianthes.

BRAZIL and BRAZILIAN. Words used as part of the common names of certain plants such as Brazil-cress (*Spilanthes oleracea*), Brazilian guava (*Psidium guineense*), Brazilian monkey pot (*Lecythis pisonis*), Brazilian pepper tree (*Schinus terebinthifolius*), and Brazil nut (*Bertholletia excelsa*).

BRAZILETTE is *Haematoxylum brasiletto*.

BREADFRUIT is *Artocarpus altilis*. Nicobar-breadfruit is *Pandanus leram*.

BREADNUT. See Brosimum and Artocarpus.

BREAK, BREAKING. As commonly used, breaking into leaf and breaking into bloom allude to the expansion after a period of dormancy of buds into leaves and shoots or flowers. As a noun, break is used by gardeners to denote a new young shoot that starts spontaneously or in response to pruning from dormant or growing stems. It is also employed to describe mutants or sports (genetical deviations) markedly different in appearance from the parent plant. Thus, if a branch bearing yellow blooms is borne on a normally red-flowered rose it is termed a break.

BREDIA (Bréd-ia). Belonging to the melastoma family MELASTOMATACEAE, the thirty species of *Bredia* are natives of eastern and southeastern Asia and India. Their name commemorates a Professor, Jacob Gijsbertus Samuel van Breda, who died in 1867.

Bredias are nonhardy, hairy or hairless shrubs and subshrubs with unequal pairs of opposite, stalked, pointed, ovate to more or less heart-shaped or lanceolate, toothed leaves with five or seven prominent, longitudinal veins. In terminal panicles, the flowers have persistent, four-lobed calyxes, four petals, eight stamens of two types, and one style. The fruits are capsules.

Sometimes cultivated in choice collections of greenhouse plants, *B. hirsuta* is a low, shrubby native of Japan and the Ryukyu Islands. Its stems and foliage are clothed with spreading hairs. The leaves,

Bredia hirsuta

1½ to 4 inches long by up to 2 inches wide, have five or seven veins. About ½ inch across, the clear pink flowers are in loose clusters up to 4½ inches long. They have broad, spreading petals and shorter, not long-exserted stamens. Chinese *B. tuberculata* has red stems. Its leaves are similar, but rather more acutely-pointed than those of *B. hirsuta* and are reddish on their undersides. Its ¾-inch-wide, pink flowers have long protruding, curiously-curved, creamy-white stamens that are responsible for their spidery appearance.

Garden and Landscape Uses and Cultivation. These are as for centradenias and many begonias.

Bredia tuberculata

BREVOORTIA. See Dichelostemma.

BREXIA (Bréx-ia). The little known genus *Brexia* of the saxifrage family SAXIFRAGACEAE, or according to those who favor splitting that group, to the brexia family BREXIACEAE, inhabits lowlands in tropical Africa, Madagascar, and the Seychelles Islands. It comprises nine species. The name, alluding to the shelter some kinds of these trees afford from rain, derives from the Greek *brexis*, rain.

Brexias are shrubs and small trees with alternate, undivided leaves and green or

greenish blooms in bracted umbels. As its name suggests, a native of Madagascar, *B. madagascariensis* attains a height of 20 to 30 feet, has oblong to obovate leaves 4 to 5 inches long by up to 2½ inches wide, and clusters of pale green blooms with protruding stamens tipped with orange anthers. The fruits are capsules.

Brexia madagascariensis

Garden Uses and Cultivation. Brexias revel in humid, tropical environments and well-drained, always reasonably moist, fertile soil. Increase may be by seeds, cuttings, and leaf-bud cuttings. The species described here is cultivated in Hawaii and in some places there self-sows.

BREYNIA (Brèy-nia)—Snow Bush. The one cultivated species of this genus of twenty-five was well known to previous generations of gardeners as *Phyllanthus nivosus*. It is still sometimes grown under that synonym. Its correct designation is *Breynia disticha*. Breynias belong in the spurge family EUPHORBIACEAE. The name commemorates the German botanist Johann Philipp Breyne, who died in 1764. From *Phyllanthus* the genus *Breynia* differs in having alternate, comparatively broad leaves not arranged in two opposite rows on slender side shoots to give the impression that they are leaflets of a pinnate leaf. The genus is native to Southeast Asia, islands of the Pacific, and Australia.

The snow bush (*B. disticha*), so called because its foliage is freely variegated with white, which shows to excellent advantage against the green background, is a native of the South Sea Islands, and naturalized in Florida and the West Indies. A loosely-branched shrub 3 to 5 feet tall, it has slender, slightly zigzagged green stems and alternate, short-stalked, broadly-elliptic to ovate thin leaves 1 inch to 2 inches long. The long-stalked, greenish flowers, unisexual, but with both sexes on the same plant, are without petals and tiny. Solitary, or the males few together in the leaf axils, they are without ornamental importance. The fruits are berries up to ½ inch in di-

ameter. In *B. d. roseo-picta* the stems are red and the leaves are beautifully mottled with pink, white, and green.

Breynia disticha

Breynia disticha (foliage)

Garden and Landscape Uses. In the tropics and subtropics the snow bush and its variety are useful shrubs for providing color in landscape plantings and for hedges. They thrive in sun or light shade in any moderately good soil. They are well adapted for growing as foliage plants in pots in tropical greenhouses and in the north can be buried to the rims of their pots in outdoor beds in summer. They are not practical as houseplants.

Cultivation. When grown outdoors in warm humid climates breynias pose no particular problems to the gardener. They respond to the moderate use of fertilizer and should be watered to keep the soil from becoming excessively dry. Whatever pruning is needed to keep them shapely and of reasonable size may be done at the commencement of a new season of growth. Hedges are trimmed as often as needed, more frequently if they are formal rather than informal.

In greenhouses these plants require a winter minimum temperature of 60°F, with a daytime rise of five to fifteen degrees according to weather; on sunny days the higher temperatures should prevail. From spring through fall, minimum night temperatures should be in the region of 70°F and correspondingly higher during the day. The atmosphere at all times should be humid. Very light shade from strong sun is beneficial. The soil should be fertile, sandy, peaty loam, sufficiently porous for water to drain through it freely. The containers must be well drained. At potting time the soil is packed moderately firmly. Water to keep the roots fairly moist; saturation for long periods rots them and is disastrous. For the best results breynias are kept growing without check from late winter or early spring until early fall. To ensure this, environmental conditions must be uniformly favorable, and after the pots are well filled with roots, weekly applications of dilute liquid fertilizer are given. In winter the plants are less active, but never dormant. At the conclusion of that season they are overhauled by pruning them fairly severely to encourage fresh new growth, which has the most colorful leaves, and repotted. At this potting, because the tops have been reduced by pruning, a fair amount of old soil can be picked or shaken from the roots, and plants in quite large containers can be returned to them and new soil packed around their roots. Smaller specimens may need transferring to bigger pots. Following potting, the plants are kept shaded, in a very humid warm atmosphere, and sprayed lightly several times on bright days with a fine mist of water. This encourages root growth and the production of new shoots. Propagation is usually by cuttings and root cuttings. Seeds may also be used. Breynias grown in greenhouses are rather subject to infestations of red spider mites.

BRICKELLIA (Brick-éllia)—Tassel Flower. This genus of the daisy family COMPOSITAE, contains nearly 100 species, natives of North and South America, and mostly of warm parts. As cultivated plants its members are little known. The name commemorates an early American physician and botanist, Dr. John Brickell of Georgia, who died in 1809.

Brickellias are closely allied to *Eupatorium*, differing in technical details of the achenes (fruits), those of *Brickellia* being ten-ribbed. They include annuals and perennials, sometimes more or less woody and shrublike. Their alternate or opposite, undivided, veiny leaves are usually sprinkled with resinous dots. White to pinkish-purple, the bisexual florets that form the small flower heads are all of the disk type; there are no ray florets. The flower heads are assembled in clusters or panicles.

The tassel flower (**B. grandiflora**), native of dry, rocky, mountain slopes in western North America, is sometimes cultivated. A deep-rooted herbaceous plant, it has stems 1 foot to 2½ feet tall, usually branched only near their tops. The mostly opposite, triangular-ovate leaves, up to 4 inches in length, have very short hairs that often give a grayish appearance to the foliage. Greenish, yellowish-white, or pinkish, the flower heads are about ½ inch wide and drooping. They are in large panicles.

Brickellia grandiflora

Garden Uses and Cultivation. This is a candidate for gardens of native plants where its inclusion is geographically appropriate. It is also grown in flower borders. Moist, fertile soil and shade favor it. It may be raised from seeds and from cuttings planted in a greenhouse propagating bench or in a cold frame.

BRIDAL WREATH. This is a common name of *Spiraea prunifolia* and *Francoa appendiculata*. Korean bridal wreath is *Spiraea trichocarpa*.

BRIDE'S BONNET is *Clintonia uniflora*.

BRIER or BRIAR. Certain prickly-stemmed roses, particularly the sweetbrier (*Rosa eglanteria*) and Austrian brier (*R. foetida*), are called briers as are certain kinds of *Smilax*. The sensitive-briers are species of *Shrankia*. Brier wood of which tobacco pipes are made is the root of *Erica arborea*.

BRIGGSIA (Brígg-sia). Named in honor of botanist Munro Briggs Scott of the Royal Botanic Gardens, Kew, England, who was killed in the battle of Arras in 1917, *Briggsia* belongs to the gesneria family GESNERIACEAE. It consists of fourteen species from the Himalayan region and China.

Briggsias are herbaceous perennials, stemless and with leaves in basal rosettes or with stems foliaged near their tops in which case the leaves are opposite. The flowers, solitary or several on a stem, have obviously inflated corolla tubes. The calyx is of five sepals. The corolla has one two-lobed and one three-lobed lip. There are four nonprotruding fertile stamens and one style. The fruits are capsules containing minute seeds.

Delightful **B. agnesiae,** of Yunnan, has basal rosettes of densely-gray-hairy, flat-stalked, ovate leaves up to 2 inches long by about ½ inch wide and margined with rounded teeth. The solitary, nodding, widely-tubular blooms atop slender, erect, 4- to 6-inch-long stalks, rose-pink to crimson, are minutely-glandular on their outsides. Their petals are pointed. Tibetan **B. aurantiaca** has basal rosettes of crinkled green leaves clothed with red-brown hairs. Mostly solitary or in pairs, the up to ¾-inch-long blunt-petaled blooms are golden-yellow, with their insides spotted and lined with reddish-brown.

Native of Sikkum, **B. kurzii** has short stems and crowded, opposite to alternate, coarsely-toothed, elliptic leaves up to 8 inches long by about 4 inches wide. The long flowering stalks carry several yellow blooms with orange-brown spots in their throats. Stemless **B. muscicola** ranges in the wild from Bhutan and Tibet to western China. In dense rosettes, its white-hairy leaves have stalks 1 inch to 1½ inches long and narrowly-elliptic-lanceolate, round-toothed blades up to 2½ inches long. The about ½-inch-long flowers, greenish-yellow on their outsides and golden-yellow variegated and spotted with purple within, are in branched clusters of two to six on stalks up to 2 inches in length.

Garden Uses and Cultivation. Briggsias are choice for collectors of rare and unusual plants. Little is reported about their cultural needs, but it is to be expected that a cool, humid greenhouse or possibly a cold frame protected from frost would be likely to afford the most suitable accommodation. They need moist but not wet, humus-rich soil and shade from strong sun. Propagation is by seeds. It probably can also be effected by leaf cuttings.

BRIMEURA (Brim-eùra). Previously included in *Hyacinthus*, the genus *Brimeura* of the lily family LILIACEAE is native in southern Europe. It consists of two species. Its name commemorates Marie de Brimeur, an ardent French flower gardener of the sixteenth century.

Brimeuras are hardy deciduous bulb plants with up to eight basal leaves and leafless flowering stalks terminating in a raceme of bell-shaped blue, pink, or white flowers, with perianths of six lobes (petals), six stamens, and one style. The fruits are capsules containing black seeds. From *Hyacinthus* the sorts of this genus differ in having bulbs that replace themselves with new ones annually.

A pretty sprite that blooms in late spring, **B. amethystina** (syns. *Hyacinthus amethystinus*, *Scilla amethystina*) is native to Spain. It has smallish bulbs covered with the remnants of the basal parts of old leaves and six to eight channeled, narrowly-linear, bright green leaves 6 to 8 inches long. The slender flowering stalk, up to 10 inches tall, displays in a loose raceme six to twelve or more nodding, nearly ½-inch-long bells on very slender stalks. Typically soft china-blue with a paler streak down each perianth lobe, they are without fragrance. Those of *H. a. alba* are white.

Garden and Landscape Uses and Cultivation. These are as for grape-hyacinths (*Muscari*) and hardy squills (*Scilla*).

Brimeura amethystina

BRISBANE-BOX is *Tristania conferta*.

BRISBANE-LILY is *Eurycles cunninghamii*.

BRISTLY-SARSAPARILLA is *Aralia hispida*.

BRITOA. See Psidium.

BRITTLE BUSH is *Encelia farinosa*.

BRITTLE FERN is *Cystopteris fragilis*.

BRITTONIASTRUM. See Agastache.

BRIZA (Brì-za)—Quaking Grass. A few of the two score species of this genus of the grass family GRAMINEAE are cultivated as ornamentals. The genus, the name of which is an ancient Greek one for some kind of grass, probably rye, inhabits temperate parts of the northern hemisphere and extends into South America. It includes both annuals and perennials, with loose flower panicles, the spikelets of which are flat and suggestive of tiny hops. In the cultivated kinds they are showy. The glumes (bracts that protect the petal-less flowers) are boat-shaped and without awns (bristle tips). Because their stems are scarcely thicker than threads the spikelets are set in motion by even a light breeze; this is the reason for the common name quaking grass.

Kinds most commonly grown, all natives of the Old World, but naturalized in North America, are the annuals *Briza max-*

ima and *B. minor* and the perennial *B. media*. Native of the Mediterranean region and the Canary Islands, **B. maxima** is a tufted plant 1 foot to 2 feet in height, with smooth stems, and leaves up to ⅓ inch wide with rough upper surfaces and smooth sheathing bases. The nodding flower panicles are about 4 inches long and consist of about eight ovate, slender-stalked spikelets each about 1 inch long. Variety *B. m. rubra* has glumes bright red margined with white. As its name suggests, **B. minor** is usually a lower plant, 6 inches to 1¼ feet in height, but sometimes taller, and growing in tufts. Its leaves are about ⅓ inch wide and rough on both sides, and its erect, broadly-pyramidal flower panicles up to 8 inches long with three-angled, ovate, greenish-white spikelets ⅛ inch long. It is native to the Mediterranean region and western Europe. The perennial **B. media** has short creeping rhizomes and smooth stems up to 2 feet tall. Its very slender rough-edged leaves have smooth sheaths. The flower panicles, about 6 inches long, are composed of nodding, heart-shaped, usually purplish spikelets, ¼ inch long.

Garden Uses and Cultivation. These slender grasses are decidedly attractive in the garden and for cutting for indoor decoration. For the latter purpose they are useful fresh or dried. Their cultural needs are simple. They do well in any fertile, well-drained garden soil in full sun. The perennial is usually increased by division in early spring, the others are raised from seeds sown in early spring or early fall where the plants are to remain. The seedlings are thinned to 3 or 4 inches apart.

BROAD-LEAVED and **NARROW-LEAVED TREES AND SHRUBS.** As used in this context, broad-leaved means belonging to the botanical group called angiosperms, which is further separated into monocotyledons and dicotyledons. It contrasts with narrow-leaved, an inclusive term for trees and shrubs botanically identified as gymnosperms. It is important to note that although the leaves of most broad-leaved sorts are proportionately wider than those of the narrow-leaved group, this is by no means universally true. As one example, those of heathers and heaths (of the broad-leaved group) are markedly narrower than those of ginkgos and plum-yews and some podocarpuses (all of the narrow-leaved group).

Broad-leaved trees and shrubs include vast numbers of both deciduous and evergreen sorts, the latter commonly known as broad-leaved evergreens. By contrast the many fewer kinds of narrow-leaved trees and shrubs are, with few exceptions, evergreens, generally called narrow-leaved evergreens. The only deciduous sorts belong in the genera *Ginkgo*, *Glyptostrobus*, *Larix*, *Metasequoia*, *Pseudolarix*, and *Taxodium*.

BROAD-LEAVED PEPPERMINT GUM is *Eucalyptus dives*.

BROAD-LEAVED PINCUSHION. is *Leucospermum nutans*.

BROADCAST. Sowing broadcast means scattering seed evenly over the area to be sown and then raking it into the surface or, less commonly, sifting soil over it. In general, broadcasting is much less economical of seeds than sowing in drills or hills. Its most common use is in sowing seeds of lawn grasses and of inexpensive small annuals such as portulaca and sweet alyssum.

BROCCOLI. There are two types of broccoli, the Calabrese or Italian, which has also been known as sprouting broccoli and asparagus broccoli, and the cauliflower-heading. Although the latter is popular in Great Britain and other parts of northern Europe, only the first is widely grown in North America. As its name implies, cauliflower-heading broccoli produces large, tight, white heads scarcely distinguishable from those of cauliflower, but because the plants are hardier, harvestable in winter in climates not harsher than that of Great Britain. In the United States it is suitable for cultivation only in the Pacific Northwest and parts of the south.

Both broccolis are members of the brassica group of vegetables belonging to the mustard family CRUCIFERAE. Botanically identified as *Brassica oleracea botrytis*, cauliflower-heading broccoli is in fact a winter cauliflower. Italian broccoli, botanically *Brassica oleracea italica*, differs in its heads being smaller, looser, more branchy, and green to purplish.

The best soil for broccoli is a deep, fertile one such as suits the majority of vegetables, but if manure is used, it should be applied for the previous crop rather than immediately in advance of planting the broccoli. This places broccoli in the rotation of vegetable garden crops as a good follower of such crops as peas, celery, and potatoes. For best results the ground should be relatively cool and moist, but not poorly drained and wet. On hot, dry sites broccoli plants develop poorly, the heads being small and soon opening into flowers.

Prepare the ground by deep spading, rototilling, or plowing, turning under in the process added organic materials such as good compost, but not manure. Instead, apply and fork or harrow into the upper few inches a dressing of complete vegetable fertilizer such as a 5-10-5. If the soil is more acid than pH 6.5 apply lime to bring it to within that level and pH 7, and work this also into the upper 4 or 5 inches.

Raise young plants of Italian broccoli from seeds exactly as you would cabbages. Be sure to obtain the finest quality seeds. Inferior strains give very disappointing results, the heads being small and too loose.

Good strains of the varieties 'Calabrese' and 'DeCicco' are recommended.

The first planting is made by setting out young plants from a greenhouse or hotbed as soon as danger from killing frost is past. Allow a minimum of 2 feet between plants; more is better. In most regions, and certainly where hot summers prevail, it is advisable to treat this broccoli as a two-season crop, the first to be chiefly harvested before high summer, the other in the cooler weather of late summer and fall. For this latter crop, sow seeds outdoors or in a cold frame in June or July and transplant, preferably during cloudy, humid weather, the young plants as soon as they are of convenient size to where they are to mature.

Routine care is directed toward encouraging rapid, unchecked growth. To this end weed control by repeated shallow surface cultivation or mulching is important. In dry weather, deep watering at intervals of five to seven days is beneficial as is the application of a dressing of fertilizer made about the time the first heads are ready to cut.

Harvest the heads by cutting them with a sharp knife while they are still fairly tight and before any flowers are in evidence. At this stage the succulent branches are green, not whitish or yellowish. Italian broccoli is a cut-and-come-again crop. Harvesting the first heads, which are the biggest, stimulates the development of somewhat smaller, lateral ones. Cutting these in turn encourages the production of successively smaller heads. Do not allow any heads to develop to the flowering stage. Cut them off earlier even if they are not needed for kitchen use.

Cauliflower-heading broccoli is raised from seeds sown from April to June and is grown in the manner of cauliflower. It needs a longer season of growth than cauliflower, however, and is not ready for harvest before the following winter or spring.

Pests and Diseases. These are as for Cabbage.

BROCCOLI RAAB or TURNIP BROCCOLI.
Also called ruvo kale and Italian turnip, this little known leaf vegetable is cooked and eaten like broccoli or kale. Formerly *Brassica ruvo* and now accepted as a variety of *B. rapa*, it attains a height of 2½ to 3 feet. The leaves are dark green, and often glossy. It responds to conditions and care that suit kale and may be harvested in its first year from seeds sown in spring or in mild climates in spring from fall-sown seeds.

BRODIAEA (Brodi-aèa).
According to modern botanical interpretation, *Brodiaea* comprises fifteen species and is endemic from British Columbia to northern Baja California. Other plants previously included are segregated as *Dichelostemma, Ipheion,* and

Triteleia. Belonging in the lily family LILIACEAE, the genus has a name that commemorates the Scottish botanist James Brodie, who died in 1824.

Brodiaeas have underground, fibrous-coated, dark brown, bulblike organs called corms. As with crocuses and gladioluses, individual corms last only one year. They are replaced by new ones developed during the growing season, which extends from late summer until late spring. The few, all basal, linear leaves have flat or longitudinally-channeled upper surfaces and rounded undersides without keels. Slim, rigid, and erect, the flowering stalks are topped by an umbel of blooms with at its base several small, papery bracts. Each bloom, on a jointed individual stalk, has six spreading perianth segments (petals or more properly tepals), their bases united to form a tube. Generally the three outer are narrower than the others. There are usually three stamens with arrow-shaped anthers attached by their bases to the stamen stalks and pressed against the style. Except in *B. orcuttii,* in addition to the stamens there are three staminodes (rudimentary, nonfertile stamens) that have something of the appearance of additional small petals. The stout style has spreading or recurved lobes. The fruits are capsules.

Harvest brodiaea (**B. coronaria** syn. *B. grandiflora*) has leaves, in cross section crescent-shaped, 6 inches to 1 foot long, and about ¹⁄₁₂ inch wide. About as long as the leaves, the flowering stalks terminate in umbels of three to twelve rose-purple to lavender or violet blooms with egg-shaped to narrowly-bell-shaped perianth tubes ¼ to ½ inch long and ascending, recurved, lanceolate-oblong petals ½ to 1 inch long. The broad white staminodes, their margins incurved, lean inward to the stamens. Variety *B. c. rosea* is distinguished by its shorter flowering stalks having pale lavender to pink blooms with white to pink staminodes. The stalks that support the umbels of blooms of *B. c. macropoda* (syn. *B. terrestris*) are entirely subterranean or extend not more than 2 inches above the surface, those of the individual flowers are from 1½ to 6 inches long. The rose-violet flowers have bell-shaped perianth tubes under ½ inch long, ascending, recurved petals up to ½ inch long, and staminodes that lean slightly inward, but are not closely folded around the anthers.

Much like the harvest brodiaea and sometimes so called, **B. elegans** differs in having a funnel-shaped perianth tube and in the flat staminodes not leaning toward the stamens. In *B. e. hooveri,* the stami-

Brodiaea coronaria

nodes have from slightly to strongly in-curved margins.

Tall **B. californica** has leaves slightly crescent-shaped in cross section. Up to 2½ feet tall, the flowering stalks carry umbels of up to a dozen, often fewer, lilac to rosy-violet or nearly white blooms 1 inch to 1¾ inches long. They have narrow-funnel-shaped perianth tubes barely one-third as long as the ascending, recurved petals. The narrowly-linear staminodes are erect and have slightly incurved margins.

Other sorts cultivated are these: **B. minor** (syns. *B. grandiflora minor, B. purdyi*), endemic to California, has umbels of ½- to 1-inch-long, violet flowers atop slender stalks up to 1 foot long. The petals are about twice as long as the perianth tube. The staminodes, which curve outward toward their apexes, are folded about the stamens at their bases. **B. orcuttii**, of southern California, carries its umbels of flowers atop stalks up to about 1¼ feet long. The violet blooms are about 1 inch long, with petals about twice as long as the perianth tube. There are no staminodes. As tall as the last, **B. stellaris,** of California, has violet flowers about 1 inch long. Loosely folded about the stamens, the staminodes have inrolled margins and inturned apexes. The anthers have on their backs a pair of broad appendages. Rare **B. versicolor** is a Californian, 1 foot to 2 feet tall, that has umbels of yellow flowers which as they age change to white or purple.

Garden and Landscape Uses. In regions where they are native brodiaeas are suitable for naturalizing, for the fronts of flower beds, and for inclusion in native plant gardens. Elsewhere they are most often grown in rock gardens and in alpine greenhouses and frames. Like many western North American bulb plants, many do not adapt well to gardens in eastern North America, but the ones described here can be expected to succeed and be reasonably permanent in warm, sunny locations in well-drained, gritty soil. Because all or most of the foliage is dead or dying by the time the blooms appear, brodiaeas tend then to look rather naked and forlorn. Perhaps the best way of avoiding this is to sow among them in early spring the seeds of some not-too-vigorous-rooting annuals such as *Leptosiphon*, California-poppies, or sweet alyssum.

Cultivation. Early fall, as soon as the corms can be obtained, is the time to plant brodiaeas. Set the bulbs closely together, a spacing of 2 to 3 inches is enough, at depths, depending upon the size of the corms, of 3 to 5 inches. In cold climates apply a winter covering of branches of evergreens, salt hay, or other protective material. Remove this gradually in early spring. Brodiaeas need plenty of ground moisture while their foliage is in evidence, but during their period of summer dormancy they should be kept as dry as possible.

Brodiaeas are easy to gently force into bloom in cool greenhouses, sunrooms, and in sunny windows in cool rooms. Night temperatures of 45 to 50°F increased by five to fifteen degrees by day are appropriate. Pot the corms in pans (shallow pots) or pots as soon as they can be obtained in late summer or early fall. Make sure the containers are drained well and use a gritty, porous, fertile soil. Set them an inch or two deep and at a distance equal to about twice their diameter. There is no need to put the planted receptacles in the dark, but keep them out of direct sun until the leaves show. It will help to conserve moisture if the surface soil is covered, until growth begins, with a layer of moss or other mulch. The objective is to keep them moderately and uniformly moist, not alternately wet and dry. Throughout their early stages care must be exercised not to overwater. More water is needed as roots take possession and foliage develops. After flowering is over increase the intervals between applications and finally cease watering altogether. Store the corms in the soil until late summer, then either repot them or plant them outdoors.

BROMELIA (Bro-mèlia)—Heart-of-Flame. This, the type genus of the pineapple family BROMELIACEAE, comprises forty species, natives from Mexico to Argentina and the West Indies. The name commemorates the Swedish botanist Olaus Olai Bromelius, who died in 1705.

Unlike many bromeliads (members of the pineapple family), bromelias grow in the ground, not perched on trees. They much resemble pineapples in aspect, but many kinds are considerably larger. The rosette plants, usually without stems, have tough, rigid, long and narrow leaves, recurved to erect. Along their margins are strong, often vicious, hooked spines, commonly some pointing toward the base, others to the apex of the leaf. The flowers are crowded in spherical to elongated panicles that may be stalkless and set low down among the inner, bright red, lacquered-looking leaves, or lifted on a stalk to a lesser or greater height above them. They have three sepals and three usually fleshy petals, joined by their centers to a tube formed by the filaments (stalks) of the six stamens. The style is three-parted. The fruits are berries.

Spectacular heart-of-flame (**Bromelia balansae**) is a viciously spiny native of Brazil, Argentina, and Paraguay. It is often cultivated under the name of a similar species, *B. pinguin*, indigenous to the West Indies, Central America, and Venezuela. The difference is chiefly that the flowers of the latter are in looser, broader heads, and have sepals with needle-like instead of broad tips. Both are planted as fences in the tropics, and in that capacity are more effective than barbed wire, although they

Bromelia balansae

occupy more space. They survive short periods of a few degrees of frost. Six feet or more wide and sometimes 6 feet high, these kinds have leaves up to 5 or 6 feet long by 1½ inches wide, margined with strong, hooked spines. At flowering time the innermost leaves and the long bracts on the 1-foot-long flower stalk are brilliant red, as are the shorter ones among the blooms. The flowers of *B. balansae*, their petals pink with white margins or white, are in dense heads about 2 feet long, covered with white wool. The small orange-yellow fruits have the flavor of pineapples. The flowers of **B. pinguin** are reddish. Smaller than the species described above, **B. serra,** of Argentina, otherwise much resembles *B. balansae* and sometimes its name is misapplied to that species. Its heads of bloom are nearly spherical rather than markedly elongated. Very handsome *B. s. variegata*, to which the name heart-of-flame is also sometimes applied, has grayish-green leaves with cream margins, and if grown in full sun, pink tones. Its maroon flowers are succeeded by orange fruits. Another of this type, **B. antiacantha** of Brazil in cultivation is often misnamed *B. fastuosa*. Up to about 2 feet tall, it has stiff, arching and spreading narrow leaves 3 to 5 feet long, armed along their margins with stout, triangular, curved spines and tapering to sharp points. Crowded in stiffly-erect, narrow panicles the violet flowers are succeeded by ovoid, lemon-yellow fruits approximately ¾ inch long.

Unlike the kinds discussed above, *B. karatas* and *B. humilis* have flower heads nested low among the center leaves rather than lifted well above them. Native from Mexico to Brazil and the West Indies, **B. karatas** has rosettes of narrow, brown-spined leaves up to 9 feet in diameter. At blooming time the center leaves are cinnabar-red. The pink flowers are covered with a thick, brown scurf. Not more than about 2 feet in diameter, the flattish rosettes of **B. humilis** consist of numerous narrow, spiny-margined leaves; the center ones are brilliant red at flowering time. The crimson flowers are conspicuously clothed with white wool. This kind is native in Venezuela and Guiana.

Garden and Landscape Uses and Cultivation. Despite their obvious merits as ornamentals, where space is at a premium these larger bromelias scarcely fit. For such places, the comparatively small *B. humilis*, and others of similar dimensions that may be acquired, are better suited. All kinds, but especially the large ones, should be located only where their dangerous spines cannot cause injury. They require the conditions and care that suit the majority of terrestrial bromeliads. For more information see Bromeliads or Bromels.

BROMELIACEAE—Pineapple Family. The pineapple (*Ananas*) and Spanish-moss (*Tillandsia*) are probably the most widely known bromeliads or bromels, as members of this family of monocotyledons are called. Many more are grown as ornamentals by houseplant enthusiasts and specialist collectors. The group totals sixty genera and approximately 1,400 species, all except one West African species of *Pitcairnia* natives of warm parts of the Americas including the West Indies. The majority are epiphytes (tree-perchers); the pineapple and a few others grow in the ground.

Bromeliads include herbaceous perennials and some subshrubs. They have parallel-veined, evergreen or deciduous leaves more or less furnished with scurfy scales and usually spirally arranged in flat to upright tubular rosettes. Generally they are stiff and more or less strap-shaped and have channeled or troughlike upper surfaces. Less frequently they are slender, flexuous but tough, and in aspect suggest coarse grasses. Their margins may be spiny, toothed, or smooth. The mostly rather small, symmetrical or nearly symmetrical flowers, in terminal heads, spikes, or panicles, rarely are solitary. Often they have

Bromelia antiacantha

associated with them brightly colored, long-lasting bracts that are the showiest parts of the inflorescences. Individual blooms have three each sepals and petals, six stamens, one style, and three stigmas. The fruits are capsules or berries, those of *Ananas* united to form the familiar compound fruits called pineapples.

The following genera are dealt with in this Encyclopedia: *Abromeitiella, Acanthostachys, Aechmea, Ananas, Araeococcus, Billbergia, Bromelia, Canistrum, Catopsis, Cryptanthus, Cryptbergia, Deuterocohnia, Dyckia, Fascicularia, Fosterella, Greigia, Guzmania, Hechtia, Hohenbergia, Neoglaziovia, Neoregelia, Nidularium, Ochagavia, Orthohytum, Pitcairnia, Portea, Pseudananas, Puya, Quesnelia, Ronnbergia, Streptocalyx, Tillandsia, Vriesia,* and *Wittrockia.* The name *Cryptbergia* is applied to hybrids between *Cryptanthus* and *Billbergia.*

BROMELIADS OR BROMELS. Just as plants of the orchid family ORCHIDACEAE are called orchids, so plants of the pineapple family BROMELIACEAE are called bromeliads or sometimes bromels. They include many extremely popular ornamentals suitable for cultivation outdoors in the tropics and warm subtropics, for greenhouses, and terrariums, and as houseplants and components of dish gardens and similar arrangements. Two of the most familiar bromeliads are the pineapple and Spanish-moss. These, interestingly, represent the two great life-styles adopted by bromeliads. The former roots into the ground in the manner of most plants and obtains the greater part of the water and nutrients it needs from the soil. Spanish-moss does not live in the ground. It perches on trees, but without taking nourishment from its hosts. It is an epiphyte, not a parasite. So are the majority of bromeliads. Some cling to rocks and cliffs, at least one (*Tillandsia recurvata*) on occasion to telegraph wires. In deserts near the ocean in Peru there is a species that lives without permanent attachment, lying on the ground, being rolled about by wind, and satisfying its need for moisture from fogs and mists that drift in from the sea at night. Desert and semidesert bromeliads are a minority. By far the greater number of kinds are natives of the humid tropics and subtropics. None is hardy. Except for one species of *Pitcairnia* that occurs in West Africa, all bromeliads are endemic to the Americas, where they range from the southern United States to southernmost Argentina and the West Indies.

Bromeliads early attracted the attention of Europeans. The pineapple, then cultivated by the natives, was discovered on the island of Guadeloupe in the West Indies by Columbus on his second voyage to the New World in 1493. He took fruits back to Queen Isabella of Spain. By the end of the next century the pineapple had been

taken to many tropical parts of the globe and was widely cultivated for its delicious fruits. As early as 1690 it and *Bromelia pinguin* were being grown in England and by 1811 sixteen species of bromeliads were in cultivation at Kew Gardens.

In continental Europe especially Belgium, France, Germany, and Holland, great interest has long been shown in bromeliads as ornamentals. From early in the

Humid-climate bromeliads, a variety of sorts on a tree

twentieth century collections were assembled and maintained at botanical gardens in the United States, but it was not until after World War II that popular interest in these truly beautiful, generally easy-to-grow tropicals expanded explosively. This expansion of interest was fostered by the Bromeliad Society and especially by the dedication and work of Dr. Lyman B. Smith, botanist, Mulford and Racine Foster, horticulturists and plant hunters, and other specialists, who engaged in studying, collecting, growing, and breeding bromeliads.

The cultural needs of bromeliads, except desert species, closely parallel those of orchids. In fact for the most part they succeed in identical environments. As with

A dry-climate bromeliad, *Puya berteroniana*

Spanish-moss draping a cypress tree
(*Taxodium*)

Bromeliads on the trunk of a palm

orchids, the needs of individual kinds vary somewhat and must be studied and catered to somewhat if the best results are to be obtained. There is room here for experimentation on the part of the grower. Clues are to be sought in the natural habitats of particular species and careful appraisal of the plants themselves.

Learn all you can about the conditions under which your kinds of plants grow in the wild. Do not assume that all plants from the tropics live in continuously hot, humid environments. Some tropical regions have alternate rainy and dry seasons, others are semideserts and deserts. At high elevations remarkably uniform cool and moist conditions are likely to prevail. One of the most fascinating aspects

of collecting bromeliads, and indeed other plants, is learning about their home environments.

The appearance and structure of bromeliad plants often provide hints as to their cultural needs. Those with richly colored foliage almost surely need considerably more shade than kinds heavily furnished with gray or whitish scales. Such scales are a natural defense against intense light and indicate that their possessors grow in exposed locations in the wild. Many tillandsias are typical of this group. Thin-textured, rather soft, green foliage strongly suggests a preference for shade and high humidity and for the need of keeping the tank or cup formed by the bases of the leaves filled at all times with

water. The absence of well-developed tanks or reservoirs and the presence of harsh, stiff, thick, conspicuously-spiny foliage signals that the species in the wild probably grows under dry conditions, even drought, for part at least of each year and that it is exposed to fairly strong or strong light. Do not keep the roots of plants of this description constantly wet. Allow them to become fairly dry between soakings, just during the period of active new growth water at considerably more frequent intervals than at other periods. Bromeliads of this group benefit greatly from daily mistings with water without wetting the soil, in between more distantly-spaced root soakings. Such mistings to some extent simulate the humidity which many bro-

Hechtia argentea

Tillandsia recurvata on a cactus

Tillandsia recurvata, on telegraph wires

The pineapple, a terrestrial bromeliad

meliads enjoy in the wild and from which they are able through their scales to abstract moisture. Many desert, terrestrial bromeliads are best served with sparse watering and without overhead misting.

Temperatures most agreeable vary according to kind. The vast majority of the epiphytes do well indoors where the minimum at night is 60 to 65°F, that by day five to fifteen degrees higher and in summer even higher. Desert and semidesert terrestrials generally succeed indoors in temperatures about ten degrees lower than those suggested for epiphytes. But none is finicky about exact temperatures. Bromeliads are surprisingly accommodating.

Tank-type bromeliads, those with leaf bases that form definite cups, must have

A tank-type bromeliad (*Aechmea fasciata*)

these tanks filled with nonalkaline water. If they are dry for extended periods the plants suffer, and eventually die. From these tanks the plants absorb the moisture they need and, under natural conditions, nutrients from decayed vegetable and animal debris, such as dead leaves and insects, bird droppings, and the like that collect in them. The accumulation of excessive amounts of foreign materials in the cups of cultivated specimens can cause rotting and similar trouble, or death can ensue if harmful chemicals are present in the water. These include iron, copper, and other metals. Drip from an overhead galvanized or copper pipe or the use of water that has stood for a long time in a metal watering can or other container can seriously injure tank-type bromeliads. An instance is recorded in which a copper tack that accidentally dropped into the leaf cup of a bromeliad "ate" its way through the tissues of several layers of leaves. Never use copper wire to attach labels to bromeliads and never use copper or arsenate of lead insecticide sprays where there is any danger of drift settling on bromeliads. The careful use of fertilizer is helpful. The golden rule is dilute and frequent, not strong and infrequent applications. Any of the fertilizers specially prepared for houseplants at one-half the recommended strength or small amounts of a slow-release, pellet-type fertilizer that will provide nutrients over a fairly long period can be used.

Desert and semidesert bromeliads, most of which are terrestrials, do not form

water-holding tanks. Such kinds are useful for planting in association with cactuses, succulents, and other dry-climate plants outdoors in areas where the climate is mild, such as southern California, and in greenhouses devoted to succulents. The terrestrials succeed in soils suitable for cactuses, desert epiphytes in rooting mediums agreeable to tree-perching kinds from more humid regions. Dry-climate bromeliads include dyckias and hechtias, and in frostless climates pitcairnias. In addition, at the Huntington Botanic Gardens at San Marino, California, *Bromelia fastuosa* and *Deuterocohnia schreiteri* have been grown satisfactorily.

Potting mixes for bromeliads may vary in composition to a fairly considerable extent as long as a few conditions are met. Mixes must drain freely, and for epiphytic kinds, they must contain an abundance of organic matter and be acid rather than alkaline. One highly successful grower recommends, for most kinds, one part of a mixture of coarse peat moss and shredded osmunda fiber or one-half part decayed sawdust or leaf mold, and one part sand or crushed granite, together with a generous dash of dried cow manure. But a variety of mixes give success and many epiphytic bromeliads grow well planted in the fashion of epiphytic orchids in osmunda fiber only, or in bark chips.

Bromeliads in an orchid basket-type container made of slats of wood

Artificial trees constructed of a supporting framework of metal pipes encased in osmunda fiber and suitably sheathed with cork bark to give the illusion of trunk and branches, when suitably planted with bromeliads and perhaps some other epiphytes can be very convincing and decorative. Somewhat more artificial in appearance, but highly practical for such small epiphytic kinds as many tillandsias are cylinders of wire hardware cloth with closed lower ends packed with osmunda or other suitable rooting material and suspended. Rafts or slabs of cork bark or tree fern trunk can be used similarly.

A suspended raft of cork bark planted with bromeliads

to pots or flats containing a peat-moss-sand or other suitable soil mix. If preferred, the seeds may be sown directly on such a mix, but not covered with it, and be managed as for those on blotting paper. Many bromeliads under good conditions will bloom in three years from seeds. Some take longer.

BROMHEADIA (Brom-heàdia). Less than a dozen species, native from Malaya to Sumatra, New Guinea, and Australia, make up this rarely cultivated genus. *Bromheadia* belongs in the orchid family ORCHIDACEAE and includes species that grow in the ground as well as kinds that perch on trees as epiphytes. The name commemorates the English amateur botanist Sir Edward Thomas Bromhead, who died in 1855.

Bromheadias fall into two groups, one with leaves that spread variously and horizontally, and another in which the leaves are flattened laterally and form one plane with the stem. Their short-lived flowers show only minor differences in coloring and size. Chiefly they are yellowish, with markings of yellow and purple.

Terrestrial **B. findlaysoniana** (syn. *B. palustris*, *Grammatophyllum findlaysonianum*), of the Malay Peninsula, Sumatra, and Borneo, has clustered stems 3 to 7 feet tall, their lower parts sheathed with bracts, and their middles having about six pairs of two-ranked leaves. Somewhat higher is a portion of stem also sheathed with bracts. The sometimes branched raceme, about 4 inches long, is of flowers that open in

Flowering of many bromeliads, including pineapples, is induced or accelerated by treatment with various chemicals, notably ethylene, acetylene, and commercial products sold for the purpose. In some cases flowering can be induced by enclosing the plant in a polyethylene plastic bag along with a couple of ripe apples and leaving it tightly closed for about forty-eight hours. The ethylene gas given off by the fruit provides the treatment.

The rosettes of the majority of bromeliads bloom only once, but continue to live for a year or two after the flowers fade. In the meantime, or even before the flowers develop fully, daughter rosettes develop as offshoots from the base of the old plant or from its leaf axils. If these are permitted to grow undistrubed a clump-type specimen of several rosettes results. The offsets may also be cut from the parent and potted as separate individuals. Do not repot until the youngsters have attained a fair size and are firm-textured. Let them grow and develop the characteristic form of the mature plant before detaching them.

Propagation by offsets is the common and generally simple way of increasing bromeliads. These are produced, prolifically or sparingly according to kind, and may hug the parent plant tightly or be less intimately associated with it at the end of a definite shoot or stem. In some kinds of *Cryptanthus*, offshoots develop from the leaf axils; more commonly, they come from the bases of the old rosettes. It is helpful, a few weeks before the sprout is severed from the mother plant, to wrap its stemlike base with sphagnum moss or osmunda fiber; this is kept moist to encourage the development of roots.

Seeds are also used for propagation. An easy way to secure germination is by sprinkling them on a thick sheet of blotting paper placed on a saucer, moistening it, and keeping it constantly moist by inverting a glass cover over it. In a temperature of 70 to 80°F the seeds soon give rise to tiny plantlets, which when large enough, are carefully transplanted an inch or so apart

Bromeliads growing on slabs of cork bark

succession at about ten-day intervals. They may be 3 inches in diameter, or considerably smaller, and have white or creamy-white sepals and petals, sometimes tinged with lilac, and a three-lobed lip veined and spotted with purple with a yellow middle lobe. The clustered 4- to 6-inch-high stems of **B. aporoides,** of Burma and Thailand, have two ranks of fleshy, flattened leaves 3 to 4 inches long and about ¼ inch wide. The solitary flowers, about 1¾ inches wide, creamy-white with pink veining, have a yellow patch on the lip.

Bromheadia aporoides

Garden Uses and Cultivation. Well worth including in collections of fanciers, these orchids respond to conditions and care that suit dendrobiums. For more information see Orchids.

BROMUS (Brò-mus)—Brome Grass, Quake Grass. Few of the more than 100 species of brome grass are ornamental, some are useful forage, several are important elements in the vegetation of North American cattle ranges, and a number are troublesome weeds. The genus belongs in the grass family GRAMINEAE and occurs chiefly in temperate parts of the northern hemisphere and sometimes in the high mountains in the tropics and in South America and South Africa. The generic name is from the Greek *bromos,* oats, signifying food.

Brome grasses are mostly coarse annuals, biennials, and herbaceous perennials. They have erect, often stout stems, with the lower portions of the leaves (sheaths) encircling them. The leaf blades may be flat or rolled. Erect or nodding, the loose or dense flower panicles are terminal and have rather large, often drooping spikelets each of several to many flowers.

A handsome ornamental, the quake grass (**Bromus brizaeformis**) is an annual up to

about 2 feet tall. Native to northern Europe and Asia, it is naturalized in North America. Its stems are solitary or in tufts, its leaves up to about 6 inches long and with softly-hairy basal sheaths. The loose panicles of blooms, 3 to 6 inches long, have pendulous branches each with one, or rarely two, flattened, ovate-oblong, green or purplish spikelets ½ to 1 inch long that are not unlike those of quaking grass (*Briza maxima*). They are without bristles (awns) and hang like pendent earrings.

Two other annuals or biennials worth cultivating are the compact brome grass (*B. madritensis*) and *B. danthoniae* (syn. *B. macrostachys danthoniae*). The former is a native of the Mediterranean region, the latter of southwest and central Asia. Sometimes 2½ feet tall, but mostly lower, *B. madritensis* has stems solitary or in tufts, hairy leaves, and narrow, erect, often dense, green or purplish flower panicles 1½ to 6 inches long and up to 2¼ inches wide. The spikelets, flattened and at maturity wedge-shaped, are 1¼ to 2½ inches long and end in a bristle (awn) ½ to ¾ inch long. Of stiff habit and up to 1½ feet tall, *B. danthoniae* has solitary or tufted stems and narrow, softly-hairy leaves up to 4 inches long. Its panicles of bloom are of one to several lustrous green or purplish spikelets, up to 2 inches long, and erect and slender. They have three bristles (awns), the middle one becoming twisted at maturity.

Garden Uses and Cultivation. The chief horticultural use of brome grasses is for cutting for dried flower arrangements. They are also decorative in groups at the fronts of flower borders. They thrive in any ordinary garden soil in sun or in part-day shade. No special trouble attends their cultivation. Seeds are sown in spring or in early fall where the plants are to remain and the seedlings are thinned to about 3 inches apart. For drying, the panicles should be cut just before they reach full maturity.

BROOM. As a common name this is used for plants of several shrubby genera of the pea family LEGUMINOSAE, particularly *Cytisus* and *Genista* and the related genera *Chamaecytisus, Chamaespartium, Echinospartum, Lembotropis, Lygos, Notospartium, Spartium,* and *Teline.* Common or Scotch broom is *Cytisus scoparius.* The name Spanish broom is used for *Genista hispanica* and *Spartium junceum.* The latter is also called weavers'-broom. Plants with the word broom as parts of their common names, which do not belong to the genera listed above, include broom-corn (*Sorghum bicolor*), broom-corn-millet (*Panicum miliaceum*), broom-crowberry (*Corema*), chapparal-broom (*Baccharis pilularis consanguinea*), butcher's-broom (*Ruscus aculeatus*), climbing-butcher's-broom (*Semele androgyna*), hedgehog-broom (*Erinacea*), and turpentine-broom (*Thamnosma*).

BROSIMUM (Brós-imum)—Cow Tree or Milk Tree, Breadnut. In using the name breadnut care must be taken not to confuse *Brosimum* with the seed-producing type of the breadfruit (*Artocarpus communis*), which is also called breadnut in parts of the West Indies. The genus *Brosimum* belongs in the mulberry family MORACEAE and comprises fifty species of milky-juiced trees indigenous to the warmer parts of the Americas. They have alternate, undivided, leathery leaves and unisexual flowers. The males consist of only one stamen, the females are included in a fleshy receptacle. The name is derived from the Greek *brosimos,* edible, and alludes to the fruit of the breadnut.

The cow tree or milk tree (**B. galacto-dendron**), of Venezuela, produces an abundance of milky sap that natives drink like the milk of animals, which it is said to resemble in taste. The wood, called snakewood, of several species is used for furniture, fine cabinets, umbrella handles, fishing rods, drumsticks, and violin bows.

The breadnut (**B. alicastrum**) is a native of Mexico, Central America, and the West Indies. Under favorable conditions it attains a height of 100 feet and has a broad, dense crown. Its oblongish or ovate leaves, which are used as fodder, are about 7 inches long by 2⅓ inches wide. They are short-stalked, smooth, and leathery. Each globose head of flowers consists of a central female one, which has only its style protruding from the receptacle in which it is buried, and many males. The spherical fruits, about 1 inch in diameter are yellow and contain one large seed. The seeds, after boiling or roasting, are used for human food.

Garden and Landscape Uses and Cultivation. The breadnut is used for outdoor planting in the tropics only. It is sometimes included in botanical collections and grown in greenhouses. It grows in ordinary soil and is propagated by seeds and by cuttings of firm young shoots in a tropical greenhouse propagating bench.

BROUGHTONIA (Brought-ònia). The only species of this genus of the orchid family ORCHIDACEAE is restricted in the wild to Jamaica. The plant sometimes named *Broughtonia domingensis* is *Laeliopsis domingensis.* Charming *B. sanguinea* has been crossed with *Cattleya* to give *Cattleytonia,* and with *Diacrium* to produce *Diabroughtonia.* Its name commemorates the English botanist Arthur Broughton, who died in 1779.

Flowering almost continuously, but mainly from fall to spring, *B. sanguinea* is a tree-perching evergreen, with tight clusters of generally grayish-green, globular to cylindrical or flattened pseudobulbs about 2 inches tall. From the top of each pseudobulb, two stiff, more or less pointed, oblong leaves up to 8 inches long sprout, and in season, slender stalks that, with their panicles of six to fifteen blooms, are up to 2 feet long. The sepals and petals are spreading and range in color from vivid crimson to other shades of red, or rarely, yellow. Commonly the petals have paler mid-veins. Wider than long, the roundish, slightly-toothed lip is yellowish to whitish, veined with brilliant rose-purple.

Garden Uses and Cultivation. An admirable specimen for collections of or-

Broughtonia sanguinea

Broughtonia sanguinea (flowers)

chids, *B. sanguinea* is less satisfactory as a pot plant than attached to slabs of tree fern or planted in tightly packed osmunda fiber mounded on wooden rafts. It needs tropical temperatures, strong light with only slight shade from intense sun, free drainage, and dryish, but not dry, rather than wet conditions about their roots. Because it is intolerant of root disturbance, transplanting should be done as infrequently as practicable. For further information see Orchids.

BROUSSONETIA (Brous-sonètia)—Paper-Mulberry. Seven or eight deciduous trees or large shrubs comprise this genus of the mulberry family MORACEAE. They differ from mulberries in having the sexes on separate trees. Natives of eastern Asia, their name commemorates the French naturalist P. M. A. Broussonet, who died in 1807. Broussonetias are deciduous and have a milky juice. Their toothed and often lobed leaves are stalked and alternate. The flowers have no particular beauty, but are rather curious. They are small, greenish, and without petals, the males in nodding, often curling catkins, the females in dense globular heads. Both sexes have a four-parted calyx and the males four stamens. Long, protruding styles give the heads of

female flowers a pincushion effect. The fruits are dense globose groups of small orange-red, one-seeded, berry-like bodies that protrude from the mass of persistent calyxes and bracts.

The common paper-mulberry (*Broussonetia papyrifera*) has played, and to some extent still does play, an important role in the lives of the peoples of many parts of Polynesia and Asia. This is related to the fact that its inner bark consists of tough interlacing fibers that can be extracted in broad layers. These are the basis of tapa cloth, made by cleaning, soaking, and pounding strips of the bark in such a way that their overlapping edges join and the material is reduced to a desirable thinness. It is often dyed or in other ways ornamented. In earlier times tapa was the chief raiment of many Polynesian and Asian peoples. That made from paper-mulberry was considered the finest kind in Hawaii. The Japanese make very strong paper used for writing and for making lanterns and umbrellas from the inner bark. The Chinese also use this material for papermaking, and in some parts of China the leaves are fed to silkworms.

The only species much planted in North America is the common paper-mulberry (*B. papyrifera*). In some places it has escaped from cultivation and occurs spontaneously. A native of China and Japan, it is 30 to 50 feet tall, or especially toward the northern limits of its hardiness, it may be a wide shrub. It has a gnarled, smooth-barked trunk and hairy shoots. Its broadly-ovate, often lobed leaves, are densely woolly-hairy on their undersides and rough-hairy with the feel of sandpaper above. They are 3 to 8 inches long and have stalks 1 inch to 6 inches long with large basal appendages called stipules. The heads of fruits are ¾ to 1 inch in diameter and are decorative in early summer. Varieties are *B. p. laciniata*, with finely-divided leaves, *B. p. leucocarpa*, with white fruits, and *B. p. variegata*, with its leaves variegated with white or yellow.

Garden and Landscape Uses. Although this kind does not rank as one of the finest deciduous trees, it is by no means a poor one and it has the great advantage of growing well under conditions discouraging to many trees. It is very tolerant of heat, grime, and smoke and thrives on almost sterile soils of a gravelly or sandy character. It also does well under more favorable conditions. It may be used as a shade tree and street tree, and for screening. Some fine old specimens grow at Williamsburg, Virginia.

Cultivation. Paper-mulberries need no special care. Except for horticultural varieties, which cannot be expected to come true when so propagated, they are easily raised from seeds sown in fall or spring. They are also easily propagated by leafy cuttings under mist in summer, by hard-

(a) *Broussonetia papyrifera*, at Williamsburg, Virginia

(b) Trunk

(c) Female flowers

(d) Male flowers

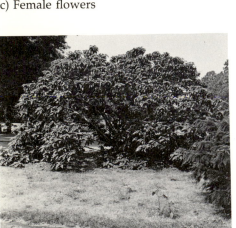

Broussonetia papyrifera, as a tall shrub at New York City

wood cuttings in fall, and by root cuttings started in spring. They may also be layered. Alternative ways, with horticultural varieties, is to graft them in winter in a greenhouse or bud them outdoors in summer, using as understocks seedlings of the common kind.

BROWALLIA (Browál-lia). A genus of six species of annuals, or plants grown as annuals and native to warm parts of South America and the West Indies, *Browallia* belongs in the nightshade family SOLANACEAE. Its name commemorates the Swedish botanist and Bishop of Abo Johan Browall, who died in 1755. The group consists of branching plants with mostly wiry stems and opposite or alternate leaves nearly or quite lobeless. They may be glandular-hairy or hairless. The flowers, either solitary in the leaf axils or in more or less one-sided racemes, are blue, violet, or white and have corollas with long, slender tubes and five spreading, somewhat unequal lobes (petals). There are four fertile stamens joined to the upper inside of the corolla tube, sometimes a fifth rudimentary stamen, and one style. The fruits are dry capsules surrounded by the calyxes.

The most handsome species is *B. speciosa*, which in its native Colombia, attains a height of 5 feet, but as cultivated is ordinarily not more than about 2½ feet tall. From other cultivated kinds this differs in having larger flowers with petals not notched at their ends. It is hairless or nearly so and becomes subshrubby toward its base. Its leaves are opposite or alternate and pointed-ovate. The short-stalked flowers, solitary in the leaf axils, have tubes 1 inch long or longer that are swollen at their tops and are two to three times as long as the calyx. They are blue or violet with paler reverses to their petals or, in variety *B. s. alba*, pure white. The face of the flower is about 1½ inches across. Variety *B. s. major* has blooms 2 inches in diameter. A tropical American species, **B. americana** (syns. *B. demissa*, *B. elata*) is 1 foot to 2 feet tall, pubescent or hairless, and has stalked, ovate to nearly round leaves with wedge-shaped or sometimes heart-shaped bases. In the lower parts of the plant the flowers are solitary in the leaf axils, above they are in racemes. They have hairy calyxes much shorter than the ½-inch-long corolla tubes and short, deeply-cleft petals. The face of the flower is about ½ inch across. This species has violet-blue flowers. Variety *B. a. alba* has white blooms, variety *B. a. caerulea* pale blue. A dwarf variety is *B. a. nana*. From the kinds described above *B. viscosa* (syn. *B. pulchella*) differs in being sticky-hairy, at least on its younger parts and especially on its calyxes. A native of South America, about 1 foot in height and of stiffer habit than *B. americana*, it blooms more profusely. The ovate leaves are roughly-hairy on both surfaces, and the flowers are solitary in the leaf axils in the lower parts of the plant, in racemes above. Their calyxes are shorter than the corolla tubes, which are up to ¾ inch long. The flowers, dark blue with a distinct white eye or center, are about 1 inch in diameter. Their petals are deeply notched. A compact variety is *B. v.* 'Sapphire'.

Garden Uses. Browallias are attractive plants for summer displays outdoors and for blooming in greenhouses throughout the fall, winter, and spring. Separate batches of plants should be raised for these uses. Outdoors they are attractive for beds

Browallia speciosa alba

Browallia viscosa 'Sapphire'

and borders and for ornamenting urns, planters, tubs, and other containers. The smaller-flowered sorts are attractive in rock gardens. The kinds most used outdoors are *B. americana* and *B. viscosa* and their varieties, but *B. speciosa* can also be usefully employed in this way. Kinds most commonly grown for greenhouse decoration are *B. speciosa* and its varieties. These are outstanding for producing winter bloom and excellent for planting in hanging baskets, and as pot plants. The flowers of browallias, especially those of *B. speciosa* and its variants, are quite charming for cutting and last well in water.

Cultivation. A fertile, deep soil suits these plants best, but in rock gardens a leaner earth is preferable because it produces dwarfer, less lush specimens that are more appropriate in such settings. Even in comparatively poor soil browallias grow surprisingly well. Although for outdoor use plants are usually raised from seeds sown early indoors, results can be had by sowing in early spring where the plants are to bloom and thinning the seedlings to about 6 inches apart. This is a good method in rock gardens. Seed indoors eight to ten weeks before the young plants are to be set in the garden. This should not be done until the weather is warm and settled. Seeds germinate well in a temperature of 65 to 70°F, and the seedlings are transplanted 2 inches apart in flats or individually to 2½-inch pots and are kept growing in a sunny greenhouse where the

Browallia speciosa major

Browallia speciosa major (flowers)

Browallia speciosa: (a) As a pot plant

(b) In a hanging basket

night temperature is 55 to 60°F and the day temperature a few degrees higher. The plants should be pinched two or three times to encourage branching, and a week or two before they are to be planted in the garden, they should be transferred to a cold frame or sheltered place outside to harden. Planting distances of 6 inches to 1 foot, depending upon the vigor of the variety and fertility of the soil, are appropriate. No special care, beyond watering in dry weather and keeping weeds pulled or hoed, is necessary.

Winter-flowering specimens are had by sowing seeds in July or August and transplanting the seedlings individually to 2½-inch pots. From these they are planted in baskets or into successively larger pots until containers 4 to 6 inches in diameter are attained. One plant in a 4- or 5-inch pot, or three in a pot or pan 6 inches in diameter, produces a good effect. The soil should be coarse, porous, and fertile, and moderately moist, but not constantly saturated. As the plants develop they should be pinched back two or three times or more. This promotes branching. Pinching consists of nipping out the tips of the young shoots. For good results grow browallias for fall, winter, and spring bloom in a sunny, fairly humid greenhouse where

the temperature is maintained at 55 to 60°F at night and five to ten degrees higher during the day. From the time their final containers become filled with roots, apply dilute liquid fertilizer weekly.

BROWN. This word forms part of the common names of the following plants: brown-apple (*Angophora*), brown mallet (*Eucalyptus astringens*), and brown pine (*Podocarpus elatus*).

BROWN-EYED SUSAN is *Rudbeckia triloba.*

BROWNEA (Brown-ea). To the nonbotanist the flower clusters of *Brownea* do not suggest the pea family LEGUMINOSAE to which these plants belong, but are more reminiscent of those of rhododendrons. The fruits, however, are typically leguminous; they are flat, leathery pods containing compressed seeds. The genus consists of twenty-five species of evergreen trees and tall shrubs, in the wild confined to tropical America. Its name honors Patrick Browne, an Irish physician, who wrote on the history of Jamaica and died in 1790.

Browneas have alternate, pinnate, leathery leaves consisting of one to several pairs of leaflets according to species. A remarkable characteristic is the manner of development of the new foliage, which resembles that of its sister genus *Amherstia* and the unrelated chocolate tree (*Theobroma*). Long leaf buds are formed at the ends of the branches, and these split and let fall limp tassels of nearly full-sized leaves of a pinky-bronze color. These dangle like clusters of soft seaweed and are thin to the point of being almost translucent. They seem as unable to cope with the elements as newly hatched, unfeathered birds, yet within a few days they stiffen and eventually become green and rigid. The tight, almost globular clusters or short racemes of flowers arise from the leaf axils, branch ends, or sometimes directly from the trunk and major branches. The blooms are tubular and commonly red, more rarely rose-pink, and occasionally white.

Fairly commonly planted in the tropics, *B. coccinea* of Venezuela is a low, broad tree with somewhat drooping branches. It has leaves 6 to 8 inches long each with two to five pairs of pointed-ovate oblong leaflets. The scarlet flowers, in drooping heads that come from the shoots and older branches, have petals about 1¼ inches long and stamens almost twice that length.

The rose-of-Venezuela (*Brownea grandiceps*) may attain a height of 50 to 60 feet, but is often lower. It has downy branches and leaf stalks, and leaves with twelve to eighteen pairs of long-pointed, lanceolate-oblong leaflets, each 6 to 7 inches long. The scarlet blooms are packed in globular heads about 9 inches in diameter, which develop from the tips of the branches. It is native to South America. Also South

Brownea coccinea

American and with scarlet blooms, *B. rosa-de-monte* is a shrub that has leaves with only two or three pairs of short-pointed leaflets. A native of Panama and Venezuela, *B. macrophylla* is a partially climbing shrub up to 18 feet tall, commonly occupying dense forest, and in its native habitat usually with hollow trunks inhabited by ants. Its leaves are downy on their undersides. When in bloom this species almost completely hides its trunk and branches with 6-inch heads of red flowers. The clusters of bloom are borne on the trunk and major branches.

Hybrid browneas have been raised and are very decorative. Two are accommodated in the great Palm House in Kew Gardens (England)—*B. crawfordii,* which has as its parents *B. grandiceps* and *B. macrophylla* and bears huge clusters of rosy-red blooms, and a very beautiful unnamed hybrid between *B. coccinea* and *B. latifolia,* which has orange-red flowers.

A hybrid *Brownea,* its parents *B. coccinea* and *B. latifolia*

Garden Uses and Cultivation. Trees and shrubs for strictly humid tropical climates, browneas are sometimes planted in southern Florida and Hawaii, but are not common. They need sheltered locations and, for the best results, fertile, moist soil. They grow slowly and are propagated by seeds, layering, air layering, and cuttings.

BROWNINGIA (Browníng-ia). This genus interpreted narrowly as is done here consists of one species of the cactus family CACTACEAE. Authorities who take a more conservative view include *Azureocereus* and *Gymnocereus*. Named in honor of W. E. Browning, one-time head of the Instituto Ingles in Santiago, Chile, *Browningia* is a native of that country and Peru.

Impressive **B. candelaris** has an erect trunk 10 to 15 feet tall, branched near its top to form a massive head. Its branches are erect and spreading and some pendulous. As much as 1 foot in diameter, they have up to thirty-four, shallow, rounded ribs with areoles (specialized areas from which spines develop) closely spaced, and on older stems conspicuously raised above the surface. Young plants are abundantly armed with spines, the biggest 4 to 6 inches long, many from each areole, and of unequal lengths. As the plants age they become much less spiny, and the flowering branches have either weak spines or sometimes none. The 3½- to 4½-inch, scentless flowers, which open in the evening and fade the following morning, have ovaries and perianth tubes with many large scales. The inner perianth segments (petals) are white to pinkish, the others rose to brown. They are longer than the stamens and style. The slender, cream style ends in a stigma with about a dozen lobes. The yellow fruits, reported to be edible, contain hairy, black seeds.

Garden and Landscape Uses and Cultivation. In warm desert and semidesert climates this cactus is very worthwhile for outdoor landscaping and is appropriate for inclusion in greenhouse collections of succulents. Thriving in full sun and porous, well-drained soil, it is easily raised from cuttings and seeds. For more information see Cactuses.

BRUCKENTHALIA (Brucken-thália)—Spike-Heath. The spike-heath is the only species of the genus *Bruckenthalia*. Native in mountains in eastern Europe and Asia Minor, it belongs in the heath family ERICACEAE and differs from true heaths (*Erica*) in its flowers having minute, inconspicuous disks and the stamens originating at the base of the corolla. Its name honors Samuel von Bruckenthal, an Austrian nobleman, who died in 1803.

The spike-heath (**B. spiculifolia**) is a charming, free-flowering, low evergreen, hardy with a little winter protection in southern New England. It forms broad, compact tufts 4 to 6 inches high, in bloom somewhat higher. Its numerous erect stems, downy when young, are densely clothed with irregularly-spaced, alternate, spreading or erect, linear leaves under ¼ inch

Bruckenthalia spiculifolia

long, slightly hairy and terminating in a bristle. Their undersides, almost hidden by the recurved margins, are white. The flowers, borne over a long period in summer, are in dense terminal racemes up to 1 inch long. About ⅛ inch in length, they are broadly-bell-shaped, with four rounded corolla lobes and eight stamens. Typically, the flower color is pink. A very fine variety, *B. s. alba*, has pure white blooms.

Garden Uses and Cultivation. The spike-heath is a choice and dainty subject for rock gardens and other intimate plantings. It makes an effective groundcover where it can be given an acid, peaty, not-wet soil, and a sunny location. In climates as severe as that of southern New York, it is benefited by a light winter covering of branches of evergreens, salt hay, or other loose material that will temper the coldest winds and strong winter sun, but this is not absolutely necessary. Young plants may be set out in spring, spaced about 6 inches apart. Following planting, mulching with peat moss is good practice. Established plants need no particular care other than lightly trimming after the flowers have faded. Young plants are easily raised from cuttings planted in summer in a mixture of peat moss and sand in a shaded, humid cold frame, or they may be set under mist. Seeds germinate readily in sandy peaty soil kept evenly moist. They are minute and are sown and cared for in the same way as those of heaths (*Erica*) and heathers (*Calluna*).

BRUGMANSIA (Brug-mánsia) — Angel's Trumpet. By some botanists the five species of chiefly Andean shrubs and small trees that constitute *Brugmansia* of the nightshade family SOLANACEAE are included in *Datura*. The name commemorates Sebald Justin Brugmans, a Dutch professor of natural history, who died in 1819.

Brugmansias have alternate, undivided, sometimes coarsely-toothed leaves and big, nodding or pendulous, trumpet-shaped flowers with five spreading or recurved teeth around their margins. There are five stamens, a slender style, and two stigmas. The fruits, technically berries, are fleshy and usually contain large seeds.

Probably most common in cultivation in North America, *B. candida* (syn. *Datura candida*), a hybrid of *B. aurea* and *B. versicolor*, is frequently misidentified as *B. arborea*, a species rarely cultivated and from which **B. candida** differs in having much longer flowers and in rarely fruiting. A tall shrub or tree up to 20 feet high, the hybrid has downy, ovate to oblong-elliptic, smooth-edged to coarsely-toothed leaves and markedly pendulous white or rarely yellow or pink flowers 9 inches to 1 foot long with recurved marginal teeth 2 to 4½ inches long. The fruits 2½ to 4½ inches long are oblong-cylindrical to spindle-shaped. Horticultural variants in which the flowers have double corollas, one nested within the other, are known. The inner corolla may be shorter, as long as, or longer than the outer one.

Brugmansia candida

Brugmansia suaveolens

greenhouses, preferably in ground beds. As pot plants they are less satisfactory, but if kept well watered and fertilized creditable specimens can be had in large tubs. From fall to spring the night temperature in the greenhouse should be 45 to 50°F and that by day only a few degrees higher. Then, water more sparingly than at other times. In late winter or spring the plants are pruned fairly severely and are top-dressed or repotted. Following this, regular watering is resumed. From spring to fall, container specimens benefit greatly from frequent applications of dilute liquid fertilizer.

Another hybrid, **B. insignis** not infrequently passes under the name of its parent, *B. suaveolens*. Its other parent is *B. versicolor*. From *B. suaveolens* this differs in its white or pink flowers having pubescent calyxes and longer corollas with bigger marginal teeth.

Species cultivated include *B. sanguinea*, *B. suaveolens*, and *B. versicolor*. Native of Colombia and Chile, **B. sanguinea** is a shrub or tree up to 35 feet high. Its leaves

a yellow-flowered variety is known. Beautiful **B. versicolor** (syn. *Datura mollis*), of Ecuador, is a tree up to 15 feet tall. It has toothless, hairless to softly-hairy, oblong-elliptic leaves and pendulous flowers 1 foot to 1½ feet long or sometimes longer that typically are white changing with age to apricot or peach-pink. They have long, recurved marginal teeth. The spindle-shaped fruits are up to 1 foot in length.

Brugmansia aurea

Brugmansia sanguinea

Brugmansia versicolor

are downy, those of young specimens coarsely-toothed, those of mature ones nearly toothless. The flowers, 7 to 10 inches long, red or orange-red with yellow corolla tubes, have five marginal teeth not over ¾ inch long. Varieties include *B. s. flava*, with bright yellow blooms, and *B. s.* 'Sangre', which has the portion of the corolla that extends beyond the calyx evenly red, or green in its lower part and red toward its mouth. Brazilian **B. suaveolens** is a hairless or minutely-hairy shrub or small tree, up to 15 feet tall, that has toothless, ovate to narrowly-elliptic leaves. Its more or less bell-shaped flowers 8 inches to 1 foot long and nodding, but not absolutely pendulous, have spreading teeth up to 1½ inches long. Typically they are white, but

Commonly planted in gardens in Colombia and Ecuador, where it is native at high altitudes, **B. aurea** is a tall shrub or tree occasionally 35 feet high. It has hairless or pubescent leaves, with those on young plants sometimes toothed. The more or less pendulous flowers have a two- to five-toothed calyx and a white or golden-yellow corolla 6 to 10 inches long, flared outward at the mouth and with long, recurved teeth. The fruits are 3 to 6 inches in length.

Garden and Landscape Uses and Cultivation. Brugmansias are magnificent lawn specimens and shrub border plants in warm climates where little or no frost is experienced. They bloom nearly continuously. They can also be accommodated in

Where winters are cold success may be had by planting brugmansias outdoors in summer and keeping them indoors over winter. Set them out about the time it is safe to plant tomatoes. Dig them up carefully before frost with as much soil attached to their roots as possible, and store them over winter in a cool, light, frost-proof cellar or shed. Brugmansias need rich, loamy, well-drained soil and full sun or at most a little part-day shade. They root easily from cuttings.

BRUNFELSIA (Brun-félsia)—Yesterday-To-day-and-Tomorrow, Lady-Of-The-Night. Old-time gardeners knew *Brunfelsia* by the now discarded name *Franciscea*. It belongs to the nightshade family SOLANACEAE and comprises forty species. Natives of warm parts of South America, Central America, and the West Indies, these are evergreen shrubs or sometimes small trees. The name commemorates the German monk, physician, and botanist Otto Brunfels, who died in 1534. The common name yesterday-to-day-and-tomorrow is used for some kinds because within a short time of opening their blue-purple blooms change to paler hues and eventually nearly white.

Brunfelsias are chiefly winter-blooming. They have alternate, undivided, toothless, commonly thickish, rather leathery, lustrous leaves, and generally quite large, showy, sometimes fragrant flowers in clusters or solitary at the branch ends. The blooms have a five-toothed or five-lobed, tubular to bell-shaped calyx, a funnel-shaped corolla with five broad, blunt, spreading lobes (petals), four nonprotruding stamens in two pairs, and one style. The fruits are dry or sometimes berry-like capsules.

Brazilian **B. pauciflora,** up to 9 feet high, has oblong to oblong-lanceolate leaves 3 to 6 inches long. In clusters of up to ten, its white-eyed, purple flowers 1¼ to 3 inches across have minutely-hairy calyxes up to 1¼ inches long, at least one-half as long as the corolla tube. Like *B. australis,* called yesterday-today-and-tomorrow and morning-noon-and-night, *B. p. eximia* (syn. *B. calycina eximia*) has larger blooms than the

Brunfelsia pauciflora eximia

typical species. As they age they change from purple to white. Variety *B. p. calycina* (syn. *B. calycina*) is distinguished by the calyxes of its flowers being larger than those of the typical species, and hairless. Variety *B. p. floribunda* (syn. *B. floribunda*), rather low and compact, has flowers with flat or nearly flat petals. Robust *B. p. macrantha* has larger leaves and flowers than typical *B. pauciflora.*

Native of Argentina and southern Brazil, **B. australis** shares with *B. p. eximia* the common names yesterday-today-and-tomorrow and morning-noon-and-night. In cultivation often misidentified as *B. latifolia,* it differs from that species in being larger and having fragrant flowers in clusters of two or three, or sometimes solitary. It has broad, elliptic to ovate leaves 1½ to 5 inches long. Its flowers, 1¼ to 1½ inches wide, fade from purple to white as they age.

Lady-of-the-night (**B. americana** syn. *B. violacea*), usually a shrub up to 10 feet tall,

is sometimes a tree up to 20 feet tall. It has elliptic to ovate leaves 1½ to 5 inches long. The flowers, solitary at the branchlet ends and fragrant at night, yellowish when they first open, soon change to white. Trumpet-shaped, they are 2 to 3 inches long by 1½ to 2½ inches wide. The fruits are orange.

Brunfelsia pauciflora macrantha

Other sorts cultivated include these: **B. grandiflora,** of western South America, up to 12 feet tall, has lanceolate to oblong leaves 2½ to 9 inches long. In clusters of five or more, its white-eyed, purple flowers are approximately 1½ inches long by 2 inches wide. Those of *B. g. schultesii* are about two-thirds as big. Brazilian **B. latifolia,** from 1 foot to 3 feet tall, has elliptic to oblong leaves 1½ to 4 inches long. Its light violet flowers are scentless, have a white eye, and are about ¾ inch long by 1¼ inches wide. **B. nitida,** of Cuba, is about 6 feet tall, with glossy, obovate leaves 2 to 3 inches long. Its flowers, solitary from the leaf axils, are white, fragrant,

Brunfelsia latifolia

Brunfelsia undulata

and from 3½ to 4½ inches long by 2 inches across. **B. undulata,** of Jamaica, is a shrub up to 12 feet high, or less commonly a small tree. It has oblong-lanceolate to elliptic leaves 3 to 5 inches long, and in clusters of up to ten or solitary, white to yellowish flowers. About 3½ to 5 inches long by 2 inches wide, they have wavy petals. The fruits are orange.

Brunfelsia nitida

Garden and Landscape Uses and Cultivation. In warm, humid, essentially frostless climates, brunfelsias are among the most useful flowering shrubs for general landscape use. They are especially lovely in foundation plantings. In greenhouses they thrive in ground beds and containers. They do well in a wide variety of soils, including limy ones, and are easy to grow. Partial shade is an important requisite. In full sun the foliage turns yellow or brown, and may even drop.

In greenhouses brunfelsias give little trouble in ground beds, but good specimens in pots are more difficult to attain. They tend not to grow as vigorously in containers as when they have a free root run. The answer is not to over-pot them. Container specimens seem to bloom more freely when their roots are moderately crowded than in too large pots. Coarse, well-drained, fertile soil that contains a generous proportion of organic matter, but that will not pack as a result of repeated watering to the extent that free aeration is impeded, suits. Because many species are natives of limestone regions it may be that the addition of lime to the soil would be beneficial, but it is not usually added. Experience shows that brunfelsias do best grown under fairly warm conditions until the flower buds begin to open, then they should be kept cooler. During the growing period a night temperature of 65 to 70°F is favorable with a five to fifteen degree increase by day. When they are about to bloom 55 or even 50°F at night is satisfactory, with corresponding reductions by day. Shade from strong sun is essential, as is a humid atmosphere. Too much shade results in soft foliage and few blooms. Propagation is easy by cuttings of firm, but not hard terminal shoots planted in spring in a greenhouse propagating bench where the temperature is about 70°F. When roots are well formed pot the cuttings individually in small pots. As soon as those are filled with roots transfer them to 4-inch pots. When the shoots are 4 to 6 inches tall pinch out their tips and peg the stems into a horizontal position. This allows the production of more branches than if the shoots are left erect. Pinch the tips out of these new shoots when they are 6 inches long. Shortly after midsummer, a move into larger pots is likely to be needed. Water frequently enough to keep the soil moderately moist, more generously from spring through fall than in winter. Give specimens that have filled their containers with roots weekly applications of dilute liquid fertilizer through the summer. In spring, after flowering is over, prune to shape and attend to any needed repotting.

BRUNIA (Brún-ia). Little known in America, *Brunia* of the brunia family BRUNIACEAE consists of seven species of South African shrubs of heathlike aspect. The name honors a Dutch traveler, Corneille de Bruin (Le Brun).

Brunias have whorls (circles of three or more) of erect or spreading branches, with narrow, usually-overlapping leaves. Their blooms are in tight spherical to oblongish, solitary or clustered heads. The tiny flowers have five each sepals, petals, and stamens, and a straight style. The fruits are little leathery capsules.

Up to about 3 feet tall, *B. nodiflora* has awl-shaped, three-edged, tightly-overlap-

Brunia nodiflora

ping, hairless leaves. Its flowers are white. About 8 feet tall, *B. albiflora* has sparsely-hairy, slender-linear leaves about ½ inch long. The heads of white flowers approximately ½ inch wide are in flattish clusters of twenty to forty. The stamens protrude.

Brunia albiflora

Garden Uses and Cultivation. Very little experience with the cultivation of these plants away from their homeland is recorded. They may adapt to outdoor cultivation in southern California and places with similar climates. The cultural care that suits proteas and South African heaths (*Erica*) will probably be successful for brunias.

BRUNIACEAE—Brunia Family. Seventy-five species of a dozen genera of dicotyledons constitute this family of chiefly heathlike, evergreen South African shrubs. They have small, undivided leaves and dense heads or spikes of little, usually symmetrical flowers with calyxes and corollas that have five sepals and petals, respectively, or are five-lobed. Four or five stamens, usually separate, are sometimes united at their bases. The fruits are capsules or nutlets. Genera in cultivation are *Audouinia, Berzelia, Brunia,* and *Brunonia*.

BRUNNERA (Brun-nèra)—Forget-Me-Not-Anchusa. One species of this genus of three is commonly grown in gardens, often under the name *Anchusa*. The group consists of herbaceous perennials, natives of the eastern Mediterranean region and western Siberia. From *Anchusa* it differs in having broad, net-veined leaves and flower clusters without bracts. It belongs in the borage family BORAGINACEAE. The name commemorates the Swiss botanist Samuel Brunner, who died in 1844.

The forget-me-not-anchusa (*Brunnera macrophylla* syn. *Anchusa myosotidiflora*) is

Brunnera macrophylla

a hardy perennial, with abundant, very broadly-heart-shaped, somewhat rough-hairy leaves up to about 8 inches across, and loose clusters of ¼-inch-wide flowers in spring and early summer. They look remarkably like the blooms of forget-me-nots (*Myosotis*). The plant attains a height of about 1½ feet and has slender stems with their upper leaves distinctly narrower, smaller, and shorter-stalked than those below. The flowers are intensely blue; nothing gardens offer is bluer. They have small yellow throats. Their coloring contrasts well with that of the verdant foliage, which when flowering first begins, is only partly developed. Leaves and flowering stems increase in size together; the former continue to enlarge after blooming and eventually form quite massive clumps, too large and lush for the plant to neighbor small, delicate plants. This abundance of coarse foliage discourages weeds and has the advantage of reducing maintenance. Attractive *B. m. variegata* has leaves generously margined with creamy-white.

Brunnera macrophylla variegata

Garden and Landscape Uses. Partial shade and moist soil favor the forget-me-not-anchusa. Given these, it flourishes and, whether represented by a single clump in a rock garden, by colonies along a waterside, by groups of three to five at the fronts of perennial borders, or by greater numbers forming groundcovers, it is of merit. Good combinations are had by locating it near such yellow-flowered plants as forsythias, daffodils, doronicums, and primroses. It is astonishingly hardy and tolerates much neglect. It often propagates by self-sown seeds.

Cultivation. This is simple. Established plants may remain virtually unattended except that, when they show evident deterioration at the centers of the clumps they should be divided and replanted. This is best done in spring. It may also become necessary to remove self-sown seedlings, by transplanting, wielding a hoe, or hand pulling. New plants are readily raised from seeds sown in late summer or early fall outdoors or in cold frames. Pieces of thick root, 1½ to 2 inches long, planted as root cuttings outdoors in early spring, or in a greenhouse in winter, also provide ready means of propagation, but roots taken from the variegated plants produce plain green offspring. Division is the only satisfactory method of propagating the variegated-leaved variety.

BRUNONIA (Brun-ònia)—Blue Pincushion. To the brunia family BRUNIACEAE belongs the blue pincushion **Brunonia australis,** the only species of this entirely Australian genus. Its name commemorates the distinguished eighteenth-century British botanist Robert Brown. The blue pincushion is widely distributed throughout its native land. It is a tufted, stemless herbaceous perennial with much the aspect of *Scabiosa.* Its leaves, all basal, are unlobed and without teeth. Spoon-shaped to oblanceolate or obovate, they are about 3 inches long and downy. The leafless flower stalks, up to 1 foot tall, are topped by solitary, glandular or hemispherical

headlike clusters about ¾ inch across. They consist of numerous blue flowers attended by membranous bracts. The flowers are almost symmetrical and have very small, five-lobed calyxes, five petals, five stamens, and one style. The seedlike fruits, technically nuts, are small, dry, and contain one seed.

Garden Uses and Cultivation. Not hardy where harsh winters prevail, this interesting perennial is appropriate for rock gardens and suchlike locations in California and other areas of mild, dryish climates. It needs good drainage and seems to prefer sandy soils that contain an abundance of decayed manure, compost, or other organic matter. Sunny locations are to its liking. It is propagated by seed and by division just as new growth starts in spring.

BRUNSDONNA. See Amarygia.

BRUNSVIGIA (Bruns-vígia)—Josephine's-Lily. The entirely African genus *Brunsvigia* of the amaryllis family AMARYLLIDACEAE has thirteen species. They are summer- and fall-flowering bulb plants of the belladonna-lily (*Amaryllis*) relationship and are allied to *Crinum* and *Boophone.* Hybrids between *Brunsvigia josephinae* and *Amaryllis belladonna* are named *Amarygia.* The name *Brunsvigia* honors the royal house of Brunswick. Its species have large umbels of asymmetrical, tubular flowers, each with six perianth parts (petals or properly tepals) and six upturned stamens. At flowering time the bulbs are leafless. The stalks of the individual flowers lengthen after the blooms fade. The fruits are capsules.

Josephine's-lily (*B. josephinae*) was named by Redouté in compliment to the Empress Josephine of France, wife of Napoleon, and distinguished patron of botany and horticulture. He beautifully illustrated this species in 1813 in his well-known atlas folio "Liliacees." The picture was of a plant that bloomed in Josephine's garden at Malmaison, which had been bought for that royal garden in France in Holland, whence it had been brought from its homeland, South Africa, in 1789. At its first blooming in 1805 it was described as *Amaryllis gigantea.* So much for the botanical background of this quite astonishing species.

The bulbs of **B. josephinae** are ovoid, and with or without longish necks. They are up to 1 foot long by 8 inches wide and grow with the greater part of their lengths above ground. They are protected from desiccating sun and wind by thick, matted, membranous layers. Investigations of these are the bases for estimates that the bulbs can live for up to a century. The smooth, glaucous leaves of Josephine's-lily angle upward and outward. They are strap-shaped or oblong, toothless, up to 3 feet long by 2 to 8 inches wide and sometimes wavy near their ends. Mostly about 1½ feet in length but sometimes twice that,

the erect, flattened flower stalk is surmounted by a spherical, loose umbel of twenty to sixty flowers. The umbel may be almost 3 feet in diameter. The stalks of the individual blooms are reddish and commonly 6 to 8 inches in length. The flowers are bright red with little yellow streaks and 3 to 3½ inches long. They have short tubes, pointed petals, stamens as long as the petals, and a style that becomes longer. This is perhaps the most handsome species.

Other kinds are *B. orientalis* (syn. *B. gigantea*) and *B. natalensis.* Huge-bulbed **B.**

Brunsvigia orientalis (foliage)

Brunsvigia orientalis (flowers)

orientalis has four to six strap-shaped leaves up to 1½ feet long and 4 to 7 inches wide that develop after the flowers and are minutely-hairy along their margins. They spread widely and are nearly prostrate. The flower stalk, 6 inches to 1 foot long, is topped by a huge umbel, sometimes 2 feet in diameter, of dark crimson, long-stalked flowers that radiate from its apex. The flowers have red stamens equaling in length the 2-inch-long petals, which are reflexed at their ends, and a yellow style that becomes longer than the stamens. The smaller bulbs of *B. natalensis* are subterranean. Up to about 9 inches long, the blunt, broadly-oblong leaves are up to one-half the length of the flower stalks. Over 1 inch in length and deep pink, the blooms have very short perianth tubes and pink stamens slightly longer than the petals.

Garden and Landscape Uses and Cultivation. The outdoor cultivation of these plants is possible only in regions of little or no frost and hot and dry summers. They can also be grown in cool greenhouses and conservatories in large pots or tubs or in deep ground beds, but they have not been proven to be easy to make bloom indoors. They need deep, fertile, sharply-drained soil, full sun, and in greenhouses a winter night temperature of 50 to 55°F, increased by five or ten degrees by day. In summer, high temperatures, ample ventilation, and an atmosphere not excessively humid are required. The roots should not be disturbed by repotting or transplanting unless absolutely necessary. Water is supplied in moderation and dilute liquid fertilizer occasionally, when foliage is in evidence, but the soil is kept dry at other times. Propagation is by offsets that occasionally develop, but are not taken from the parent plant until they have attained a fairly large size, and by seeds. It is likely that bulb cuttings would also prove a successful means of multiplication.

BRUSH-CHERRY, AUSTRALIAN is *Syzygium paniculatum*.

BRUSSELS SPROUTS. One of the cabbage tribe of vegetables, brussels sprouts, or sprouts (botanically *Brassica oleracea gemmifera* of the mustard family CRUCIFERAE), is grown for the miniature-cabbage-like buds that develop all along its erect, 2- to 3-foot tall stems crowned with loosely-arranged bigger leaves. Of European origin, this is primarily a fall and winter crop that succeeds best in temperate and cool climates. It withstands light to moderate freezing, for brief periods temperatures as low as 10°F, and where winters do not bring more cold, the plants may be left outdoors. In severer climates they are lifted in fall and planted in deep cold frames or pits

or other suitable storage. Picked sprouts freeze well. It is important to start with a good strain of seeds. Poor strains give loose, instead of desirably compact, firm sprouts. Good varieties are 'Half Dwarf', 'Jade', and 'Long Island Improved'. Pests and diseases and their controls are as for cabbage.

Soil for brussels sprouts should be well-drained, deep, and hearty. Good results are not had on shallow earths nor those lacking fertility. This crop does best on land that is slightly acid to neutral, in full sun. In preparation for planting, spade, rototill, or plow deeply, turning under liberal amounts of manure, compost, or other humus-forming material such as a green manure crop. Mix in also a dressing of a complete garden fertilizer.

For autumn and winter harvesting, sow seeds ¼ to ½ inch deep in nursery rows outdoors about three and one-half months before the average date of the first fall frost. Transplant the young plants 2 feet apart in rows of 2 to 2½ feet. In regions of cool summers, earlier harvests may be had from seeds sown indoors in spring, the seedlings transplanted to flats, individual pots, or cold frames, and as soon as danger of frost has gone, to their field plots at the spacings suggested above.

Care after planting is similar to that for cabbage. It comprises frequent shallow cultivation or mulching, to prevent weed growth and conserve soil moisture, and deep watering at intervals during spells of dry weather. A dressing of fertilizer may be needed when the plants are about half grown. After the sprouts are partially formed and before they crowd each other, gradually break off the lower leaves over a period of a few weeks, working from the base of the stem upward but never removing the uppermost foliage. This gives the sprouts opportunity to develop without hindrance.

Harvesting is done over a period of several weeks by breaking off the sprouts in succession as they become big enough, from the bottom of the stems upward. Pick

them when they are 1 inch to 2 inches in diameter and quite firm, before they loosen and become soft. In severe climates the plants can be dug up in fall with as large balls of earth as can conveniently be taken and be stood closely together in a deep cold frame, or pits, or in a cool cellar, garage, or similar place with soil packed about the roots and kept moist.

BRYA (Bry-a)—West-Indian-Ebony. Seven species of the pea family LEGUMINOSAE constitute *Brya*. They are shrubs or small trees, endemic to the West Indies. Their leaves have an uneven number (one to many) of leaflets. If more than one, they are arranged pinnately. Pea-shaped, the flowers are in clusters from the leaf axils or near the branch ends. They have calyxes with five lobes, and a roundish standard or banner petal. The stamens are joined into a tube split above. Tipped with a minute stigma, the style is incurved. The fruits are pods with one or two broad, flat joints. The name, from the Greek *bryo*, to swell, alludes to the seeds sometimes germinating while in the pods, or may have been given to honor J. T. de Bry, an engraver who died in 1617.

West-Indian-ebony (*B. ebenus*) is a prickly shrub or tree, evergreen, or deciduous in dry weather, up to 25 feet or sometimes 40 feet in height. Native of Cuba and Jamaica, it has boxwood-like, elliptic to obovate-elliptic leaves, ⅓ to ¾ inch long, in clusters. The fragrant, yellow to orange flowers, solitary or two or three together from the leaf axils, have the standard and wing petals a little more than ⅓ inch long. The broad, rounded pods are up to 1 inch long. Densely-grained, the wood of this species is almost black, exceedingly hard, and is used in the same ways as ebony for carving, inlay work, and cabinetmaking.

Garden and Landscape Uses and Cultivation. Little known in cultivation in North America, West-Indian-ebony is occasionally planted in warm, essentially frost-free regions for interest and ornament. It is propagated by seed.

(a) Brussels sprouts

(b) Young sprouts forming along stems

(c) The harvest

Non-hardy bulb plants: (a) *Watsonia* 'Adelaide'

(b) *Hippeastrum hybridium*

(d) *Lilium longiflorum*

(c) *Lachenalia aloides*

(e) *Ranunculus asiaticus* varieties

Non-hardy bulb plants: (a) *Sinningia speciosa* (gloxinia) variety

(b) *Tigridia pavonia*

Buxus sempervirens suffruticosa edging a formal garden

Hedges of *Buxus sempervirens*

Red cabbage

BRYANTHUS (Bry-ánthus). One species only belongs in this genus of the heath family ERICACEAE. Other plants previously included belong in *Phyllodoce*. The name, from the greek *bryon*, a moss, and *anthos*, a flower, alludes to the aspect of the plant.

Native of dry, rocky and gravelly, high mountain slopes in northern Japan and Kamchatka, **Bryanthus gmelinii** (syn. *B. musciformis*) is a prostrate, carpeting, freely-branched, densely-foliaged, evergreen shrublet, 1 inch to 3 inches tall. It has minutely-hairy shoots, and leathery, lustrous, spreading, linear leaves up to ⅛ inch in length that, when young, have short white hairs on their undersides. Its few-flowered, dense racemes of blooms are ¾ inch to 1½ inches long. The flowers are rose-pink, about ¼ inch wide, and have calyxes and corollas divided almost to their bases into four sepals and four petals. There are eight stamens and a style topped with a four-lobed stigma. The fruits are small capsules.

Garden Uses and Cultivation. Little experience has been had with this plant. A species for the collector of rare and choice alpines, it may be expected to respond to conditions agreeable to *Phyllodoce*. Propagation is by seeds, separation of rooted runners, and summer cuttings.

BRYONIA (Bry-ònia)—Bryony. Belonging to gourd family CUCURBITACEAE, the genus *Bryonia* consists of four species of tendril-climbing, herbaceous perennial, deciduous vines, mostly natives of Europe, some of Asia, North Africa, and the Canary Islands. Two are occasionally cultivated. Bryonias have tuberous or fleshy roots, lobed or angled leaves, and tendrils that may or may not branch. Their flowers are unisexual with the sexes usually on separate plants. The blooms are broadly bell- or wheel-shaped, the males in racemes or clusters, the females clustered or solitary. The name is derived from the Greek *bryo*, I sprout, in allusion to the rapid growth of the stems.

White bryony (**B. alba**), the only representative of the gourd family native of Great Britain, also occurs in continental Europe, North Africa, and western Asia. A tall and rapid climber, it has angular, brittle stems and rough-hairy five-angled leaves, 4 or 5 inches across, with curved stalks. Often both sexes of the greenish, about ½-inch-wide flowers are on the same plant. After pollination, the female blooms develop pea-sized juicy berries, which are decorative when ripe. The berries have an unpleasant odor and are emetic. They are unwholesome to eat and may be poisonous. The large tubers are strongly cathartic and so, to a lesser degree, are other parts of the plant. Both species were important sources of medicine to the old herbalists and to the Romans and Greeks. Red bryony (**B. dioica**), of Europe,

Bryonia dioica (flowers)

North Africa, and Western Asia, is similar to the last, but its male and female flowers are always on separate plants and its fruits are red.

Garden Uses and Cultivation. These quick-growing vines, useful for covering arbors, fences, and other supports, are chiefly esteemed for their foliage. Growing without difficulty in ordinary light shade or sun, they are easily increased by seeds and by root divisions. Where danger exists of children eating the berries it is prudent to grow only male specimens. Sex can be determined at the first flowering.

BRYONOPSIS. See Diplocyclos.

BRYONY. See Bryonia, also Tamus.

BRYOPHYLLUM. See Kalanchoe.

BUCHU. See Agathosma.

BUCIDA (Bu-cìda)—Black-Olive. The combretum family COMBRETACEAE includes *Bucida*, a genus of four species of trees and shrubs that inhabit Florida and the West Indies and extend from Mexico to northern South America. The name is derived from the Greek *bous*, an ox, in allusion to the fruits being hornlike. One species is planted in southern Florida and other warm areas for shade and ornament.

The black-olive (**B. buceras**), native from southern Florida to the West Indies and Panama, and up to 75 feet tall, has a broad head of horizontal branches that tend to droop at their extremeties. The younger branchlets are sometimes furnished with pairs of spines up to ¾ inch long. Elliptic to obovate and with slightly-hairy stalks up to ¾ inch long, the alternate, toothless leaves are 1 inch to 3 inches long. Clustered at the ends of short, erect branchlets, they have green upper surfaces and are yellowish-green beneath. The greenish-white or pale brown, stalkless, petal-less flowers in 1- to 4-inch-long, branchless spikes come from among the leaves. They are ¼ to ½ inch wide and have a five-

Bryonia dioica (fruits)

toothed calyx, ten spreading stamens, and a slender, hairy style. The persistent calyx adheres to the apex of the irregularly five-angled, minutely-hairy, dry or fleshy, one-seeded fruit. Normal fruits are about ¼ inch long, but some fruits enlarge very markedly and develop peculiar hornlike galls as a result of irritation by mites.

Garden and Landscape Uses and Cultivation. The black-olive is adapted only for tropical or near tropical, humid climates. Given a suitable environment it is useful for home grounds, parks and other open spaces, and as a street tree. Very wind resistant, it is particularly suitable for planting near the sea. It thrives in a variety of soils including those of a limestone character. It grows slowly and takes a long time to reach maturity. The black-olive is raised from seeds.

BUCK BRUSH is *Ceanothus cuneatus*.

BUCKBEAN is *Menyanthes trifoliata*.

BUCKBERRY is *Gaylussacia ursina*.

BUCKET ORCHID. See Coryanthes.

BUCKEYE. See Aesculus. Mexican-, Spanish-, or Texan-buckeye is *Ungnadia speciosa*.

BUCKLANDIA. See Exbucklandia.

BUCKLEYA (Búck-leya). Named after the American botanist S. B. Buckley, who died in 1884, this genus of the sandalwood family SANTALACEAE consists of two Asian and one American species of deciduous shrubs, remarkable because they are parasitic on the roots of other plants. The host of the American kind, the only one likely to be cultivated and that rarely, is hemlock (*Tsuga*).

Buckleyas have opposite, short-stalked or stalkless, toothless leaves. Their flowers, the sexes on separate plants, are small and of no decorative merit; they have four-parted perianths. The males, in terminal and sometimes axillary umbels, have four stamens. The females, solitary at the ends of short branchlets, have a short style with a two- to four-parted stigma. The fruits are drupes (fruits structured like plums).

Native of North Carolina and Tennessee, *Buckleya distichophylla* is a graceful, slender-branched shrub up to 12 feet tall. Its stalkless, pointed, narrowly-ovate to ovate-lanceolate, bright green leaves are in two ranks. They are ¾ inch to 1¼ inches long, and are nearly hairless except for their finely-fringed edges. The tiny greenish flowers, borne in spring, are followed by yellowish-green or orange-yellow, ellipsoid fruits approximately ½ inch long.

Garden and Landscape Uses and Cultivation. Gardeners intrigued by unusual rare plants and botanical curiosities occasionally cultivate this interesting American, which despite its southern natural range is hardy as far north as Massachusetts. Success can be had only by making sure that the seedling buckleyas have opportunity to attach themselves firmly to the roots of a hemlock. This is done by sowing the *Buckleya* seeds above the roots of a living specimen of *Tsuga*, either outdoors in fall or, preferentially, after they have been stratified for three months at 40°F, in late winter or spring outdoors, or better still in a greenhouse around the base of a young potted hemlock. Once the buckleya is well established the potted hemlock and its guest are planted outdoors in a lightly-shaded place in well-drained, but not dry, somewhat acid soil.

BUCKTHORN. This is the common name for *Rhamnus* and for *Ziziphus obtusifolia*. False-buckthorn is *Bumelia*, sea-buckthorn *Hippophae rhamnoides*.

BUCKWHEAT. See Fagopyrum. California- or wild-buckwheat is *Eriogonum fasciculatum*. The buckwheat tree is *Cliftonia monophylla*.

BUD. As a noun bud alludes to what is physiologically a very brief stem with attendant closely overlapping immature leaves or equivalent parts. More poetically it represents a promise of a shoot or shoots, a flower or a cluster of flowers, or of leaves and flowers that under favorable conditions will grow from it. Technically, the eyes of potatoes are buds and, although not in common parlance, bulbs such as those of daffodils, hyacinths, onions, and tulips are highly specialized buds.

Shoot or growth buds and flower buds on the same plant often differ markedly in appearance. This is clearly obvious in many fruit trees, such as apples and pears, in which the fruit buds are much fatter and rounder than growth buds, a distinction important to observe when pruning.

Besides evident buds that break into growth when the appropriate season arrives, stems and roots frequently have dormant or latent buds that retain for many years, and perhaps throughout the life of the plant, the capability of growth. It is these that are excited into activity when an old stem, branch, or trunk is cut hard back, to below the region from which under normal conditions new issue would be expected. Bud as a verb refers to the propagating technique, a form of grafting, called budding.

BUDDHA'S BELLY BAMBOO is *Bambusa ventricosa*.

BUDDING. A fairly common method of vegetative propagation, budding is in fact a form of grafting. It involves transplanting a portion of one plant onto another in such a manner and under such circumstances that the tissues unite to form a new individual. The above-ground parts of the new plant, except sometimes for a trunk, are of the sort it is desired to increase, the roots are those of the understock. The essential difference between budding and grafting is that in budding the transplant is a single bud with a small portion of attached tissue, in grafting it consists of a piece of stem with two or more buds. Budding is better adapted to some kinds of plants, notably stone fruits such as cherries, peaches, and plums, than grafting, and because it is more economical of scion wood it permits a greater number of propagations to be obtained from a limited supply, often an important consideration when new or expensive varieties are being increased. It is a favorite method of propagating roses. In budding as with grafting, it is essential that understock and scion be fairly closely related botanically, and compatible. Also the cambium tissues of the two plants must be brought into intimate contact and be firmly held together until union has taken place. The operation must be done deftly with a razor-keen budding knife, a round-ended one for preference, and at the right season. All cuts must be made cleanly, the parts fitted neatly together and tied firmly. Drying must be prevented at all stages, before and after the bud is inserted. Understocks will usually be plants raised for the purpose from seeds or cuttings.

The time to bud is when the bark of the understock can be raised easily from the underlying tissue and when dormant buds of the plants to be increased are available. In practice, with outdoor plants, this means the period in summer, chiefly July and August, after shoots of the current season's growth have mature buds and before the bark of the understock has tightened so that it cannot be lifted readily with the budding knife.

Various forms of budding are named from the patterns of the cuts made. Shield or T budding, chip budding, patch budding, plate budding, H budding, and other variants are employed. The first three are

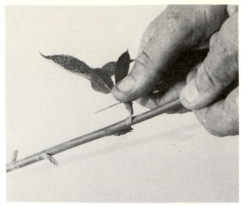

Shield or T budding: (a) Prepare bud stick by removing leaves except for a short piece of stalk

(b) Make a T-shaped cut in the bark of the understock

(c) Ease flaps of bark away from the wood beneath

(d) Cut bud from bud stick

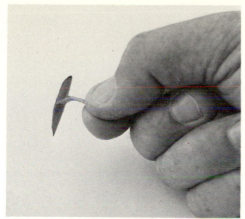

(e) Bud ready for insertion

(f) Slide bud into incision in understock

(g) Trim off bud shield level with cross-cut in understock

(h) Tie the bud securely

most common. To perform shield budding, cut as bud sticks vigorous, firm shoots of the same season's growth with the buds in the leaf axils plump and mature. Snip off all leaves except for about ¼ inch of their stalks left as handles. To prevent the sticks drying, which is fatal, wrap them immediately in damp burlap or put them in polyethylene plastic bags rinsed out with water. At the place on the understock (which generally should not be more than ½ inch in diameter) where the bud is to be inserted, usually low down unless standard (tree-form-trained) specimens are desired, make a T-shaped incision in the bark. The cross stroke is first made with a rocking motion of the knife blade, then the vertical stroke by drawing the end of the blade upward from a point 1 inch to 1½ inches below the cross cut and continued until the cuts meet. Slice through the bark, but not into the wood beneath. As the blade reaches the end of the vertical cut give it a slight twist or flick, left and right, to loosen the bark slightly from the edges of the incision, then if necessary, insert the flat tongue of the budding knife to raise the little flaps further. Now cut the bud from the bud stick by slicing upward from below the bud. Remove the full thickness of bark without taking any underlying wood except for possibly a tiny piece just beneath the bud itself. This may be removed, but only with great care so as not to pick out the bud with it. Grasp the short piece of leafstalk and pull the bud and its attached small shield free without damaging it. Using the leafstalk as a handle, slide the shield downward well into the T incision in the understock. To make a neat fit, trim off any part of the shield that extends above the crossbar of the T. Then tie the bud securely into position with a rubber budding strip (flat bands 2 inches long by ⅜ inch wide sold for the purpose). Raffia, well moistened, can be used, but rubber strips are better because they expand as the stem swells. Pull the tie across the upper end of the bud to prevent it working out, then spiral it downward to the bottom of the vertical slit and back up again, covering all parts operated upon except the bud itself to prevent drying. Wind the tie firmly and smoothly and secure the end by tucking it under a lap of the budding strip or by tying. The tissues of bud and understock will have united sufficiently within three weeks to one month to make cutting the tie necessary, but no shoot will come from the bud until the following spring. Then, cut off the part of the understock that extends above the bud. Do this in two stages a few weeks apart, making the first cut to leave a stub 3 to 6 inches long to which the new shoot can be tied loosely to give it support and direction. Let the final cut remove the stub cleanly and close to the bud. In a variation of shield budding, called inverted or reverse T budding, which is often used in propagating citrus fruits, the horizontal cut is made across the bottom of the vertical one and the bud pushed upward instead of downward.

Patch budding is employed with thick-barked plants, such as mangoes and nut trees. Remove from the understock a rectangle of bark, and cut an identical patch containing a bud from the plant to be propagated. Position it into the exposed area and tie it securely in place. There are special budding knives that, pressed against the bark of understock and scion, cut out identical patches of bark. Plate budding and H budding are essentially similar to patch budding except that the bark lifted from the rectangle on the understock is not removed but remains as flaps to be tied over the bud after it is implanted. In plate budding two vertical cuts and a cross one uniting their tops permit the peeled back bark to hang down until it is brought up to cover the bud. In H budding the cross cut joins the verticals at their middles, producing two flaps, one peeled downward, the other upward to allow insertion of the bud. Then both flaps are pulled over the area of operation and tied in place.

Chip budding is done in late winter or spring while the understock and scion are dormant and before it is practicable to raise the bark as is done in shield or T budding. The procedure consists of removing from the bud stick a "chip" consisting of a single bud and underlying tissue, including a little wood, and mortising this into the understock. To do this, make a slanting cut beginning an inch or less above the bud and continuing a little below it, and a second starting below the bud to meet with the first. Then remove a similarly shaped piece from the understock, and tie the "chip" taken from the bud stick firmly into place and seal it by painting with grafting wax.

BUDDLEIA (Budd-lèia)—Butterfly Bush. Several popular garden shrubs and many lesser known ones, as well as a few herbaceous plants, belong in *Buddleia*. Of the approximately 100 species recognized by botanists, not many are known to gardeners and most are not sufficiently meritorious to be worthy of their attention. Some are very beautiful. As a group buddleias hail from the tropics, subtropics, and warm-temperate regions of the Americas, Asia, and South Africa. Most are not hardy in the north, but there are a few notable exceptions. The genus is variously ascribed to the logania family LOGANIACEAE and to a family named after it, the BUDDLEIACEAE. Its name, sometimes spelled *Buddleja*, commemorates an English botanist, the Reverend Adam Buddle, who died in 1715.

Buddleias have usually angled or winged stems and opposite or alternate, generally woolly or downy, leaves. Their flowers are small and commonly in terminal panicles or axillary racemes, less commonly in globular heads. They have bell-shaped, four- or five-toothed or five-lobed calyxes and tubular corollas with four lobes (petals). The fruits are capsules that open from the top downward.

The identification of buddleias as to species can be confusing, and there is little doubt that at least some plants proudly tagged with name labels in botanical gardens and elsewhere are misidentified. This is partly because they have been raised from seeds obtained from parents growing in mixed collections. Buddleias, notoriously promiscuous in their interspecific relationships, hybridize freely among themselves. Even where this has not occurred and the plants are as pure genetically as in their native haunts, it is not always easy for nonspecialists to assign a particular plant to its species because the differences between them are often based on such recondite characteristics as the comparative length of calyx and corolla tube, position of the stamens, color and density of the hairs, and suchlike botanical niceties. An additional disconcerting factor is that some species vary considerably within themselves.

The common butterfly bush (**B. davidii** syn. *B. variabilis*) is one of the best known

Buddleia davidii

Buddleia davidii (flowers)

and most loved shrubs of American gardens. Its common designation refers to the great attraction its fragrant flowers have for the insects after which it is named. On warm summer days butterflies are to be seen in great numbers flitting around this plant. Unknown in American or European gardens until the closing years of the last century, butterfly bush was then introduced from its native China. As its discarded specific designation, *variabilis*, indicates, in the wild it is a variable species, it includes both horticulturally excellent and poorer forms. Some of the better ones have been given varietal names. The common butterfly bush is a deciduous shrub, not completely shoot-hardy in the north, but with roots that defy considerable cold and send up annual new shoots that bloom the same season. It can be relied upon as far north as southern New England. Where it is not killed back in winter this shrub attains 10 to 15 feet in height. Its branches are widespread and the four-angled shoots are felty-hairy. The leaves, lanceolate to linear-lanceolate, are finely-toothed and taper to long points. Their upper sides are dark green and hairless, beneath they are covered with a felt of white hairs. The flowers, up to ½ inch long and up to ⅓ inch wide, are in roundish clusters arranged in panicles 6 inches to 2½ feet long. They are borne over a long period in late summer and fall. In the wild the flower color varies from lilac to purple, with orange-yellow in the throats of the blooms. The first *B. davidii* brought into cultivation, in 1887 at St. Petersburg, Russia, was very inferior to such later introductions as *B. d. veitchiana*, *B. d. magnifica*, and *B. d. wilsonii*, all stronger growers, and the stocks from which present-day varieties were derived. The first-named variety is more erect than the original introduction and has larger panicles of lilac flowers. Similar, but with violet-purple flowers is *B. d. magnifica*. In *B. d. wilsonii* the flowers are rosy-lilac with orange centers. A good dwarf variety, *B. d. nanhoensis*, does not exceed 4 to 6 feet in height and is very graceful. Its rather small panicles of bluish-lilac flowers with orange throats are borne in great profusion over a long period.

Modern garden varieties of the common butterfly bush are numerous and include some splendid kinds. They are described, and often illustrated, in nursery catalogs. Among the best are 'Charming' with long panicles of pink flowers, 'Dubonnet' with glorious dark purple blooms, 'Empire Blue' with rather short panicles of dark blue flowers, 'Ile de France', a deep-purple-flowered kind, and 'Peace' and 'White Bouquet', both white-flowered.

The hardiest buddleia is distinct from all other cultivated kinds in having alternate leaves, a characteristic recognized by the botanist who named it *B. alternifolia*. This is top-hardy in southern New England and

has been known to stand a temperature of −20°F without damage. It is highly desirable. Quite different from the common butterfly bush, *B. alternifolia* bears in May its lilac-purple blooms, about ¼ inch across,

Buddleia alternifolia

Buddleia alternifolia (flowers)

in 1-inch-wide clusters strung for incredibly long distances along its pendulous, weeping-willow-like shoots of the previous season. They provide a truly elegant cascade of color. Deciduous, and up to 20 feet tall, this kind has lanceolate, toothless leaves 1½ to 4 inches long and not more than ½ inch broad. They are scurfy and glaucous on their undersides. Variety *B. a. argentea* has grayish foliage. A nonhardy, intermediate hybrid between *B. alternifolia* and *B. caryopteridifolia* of China is *B. pikei*.

Other hardy species, less handsome than those discussed above, are *B. albiflora*, *B. nivea*, *B. japonica*, and *B. lindleyana*. The name of **B. albiflora** of China is poorly chosen, its blooms are commonly a rather undistinguished pinkish-lilac, not white as its name suggests. It is very like the common butterfly bush, differing chiefly in having round shoots and smaller flowers, with the stamens attached higher in the corolla tube. Dense silvery-white hairiness of stems and foliage are a pleasing feature of **B. nivea**, but its blooms are disappointing. Purple and ¼ inch long, they are practically

Buddleia pikei

hidden among white woolly hairs. This shrub, 6 to 10 feet tall, a native of China, has long-pointed, ovate-lanceolate, coarsely-toothed leaves up to 8 inches long. There are attractive hybrids between it and *B. japonica*. Except for inclusion in botanical collections, neither *B. japonica* nor *B. lindleyana* are likely to appeal. A deciduous Japanese shrub 4 to 6 feet tall, *B. japonica* has four-angled, winged stems, and lanceolate, slightly-toothed leaves up to 8 inches long, covered with tawny hairs beneath. Its pale lilac flowers are in pendulous panicles up to 8 inches long. The rather similar *B. lindleyana*, of China, has angled, winged stems, and ovate, scarcely-toothed leaves 2 to 4 inches long and nearly hairless. Its panicles of purplish-violet flowers are up to 8 inches in length and erect. This kind is more tender than the others listed here as hardy. It is naturalized in the southeastern United States. A hybrid between *B. japonica* and *B. lindleyana*, rare *B. intermedia* is intermediate in its characteristics.

Bright yellow, fragrant flowers in tight spherical clusters that hang like miniature Christmas tree decorations, and are arranged in loose, terminal panicles, characterize *B. globosa*. This beautiful Peruvian shrub, unfortunately, is not hardy in

the north. It is about 15 feet tall, wide-spreading, rather gaunt, and more or less evergreen. Its shoots are angular, its short-stalked, lanceolate leaves 5 to 8 inches long by about 1¼ to 2 inches wide. Dark green and wrinkled above, their undersides are clothed with felted, tawny hairs. The blooming season is early summer.

Most beautiful of buddleias, *B. colvilei* seems little known in North America, yet surely there are parts of that continent where it would thrive. Native of the Himalayas and not hardy in the north, it is a shrub or tree up to 30 feet in height with shoots and foliage that when young are clothed with reddish-brown hairs. Its ovate-lanceolate, finely-toothed leaves are 3 to 10 inches long. Pink to crimson-maroon, its flowers, largest of any cultivated buddleia, up to 1 inch long and wide in pendulous panicles 6 to 8 inches long, bloom in early summer.

Buddleia colvilei

Another Himalayan summer bloomer, *B. crispa*, is about as hardy as *B. colvilei*. From 6 to 12 feet tall, it has white-woolly shoots and ovate-lanceolate, coarsely-toothed leaves, woolly-hairy on both surfaces, and 2 to 5 inches long. Its delightfully fragrant lilac flowers, each with a white eye and about ⅓ inch across, are in

panicles 3 to 4 inches long and are freely produced over a long period.

Buddleia crispa

Late fall- and winter-blooming buddleias are useful for greenhouses and for outdoor cultivation in frost-free or nearly frost-free climates. Native from China to India, *B. asiatica* is a beautiful and graceful evergreen species with delightfully fragrant white flowers with yellow throats in very slender, drooping spikes up to 9 inches long. This kind is a tall shrub or small tree with round shoots covered with white or faintly yellowish hairs, and narrowly-lanceolate, sometimes toothed leaves, white-downy on their undersides and 4 to 8 inches in length. The flowers are about ¼ inch long.

Native of China, *B. officinalis* is an evergreen or partially evergreen shrub 9 or 10 feet tall with densely-gray-woolly shoots and slender-pointed, narrowly-lanceolate, sometimes toothed leaves up to 2½ inches long and gray-woolly on their undersides. The fragrant, yellow-throated, pale lilac flowers are in terminal panicles up to 1 foot long. A very fine hybrid between the two fall and winter bloomers discussed above and flowering in fall and winter, is *B. farquhari*. It has delicate lavender-pink flowers in broader panicles than those of *B. asiatica*.

Buddleia globosa

Buddleia globosa (flowers)

Buddleia farquhari

A choice South African species, *B. salviifolia*, is beautiful and fragrant-flowered, but adaptable only to climates similar to that it enjoys at home, which means that in North America it can be grown outdoors only in areas such as California, where frost presents no serious problems. It is also a good plant for growing in pots in greenhouses for late winter bloom. This shrub has an extensive natural range and is one of the first elements in the native flora of the southern part of Africa to take possession of burnt-over forest areas. Its wood was employed by the natives for the shafts of spears. An erect shrub of grayish appearance and up to 12 feet in height, **B. salviifolia** has slightly four-angled, woolly-hairy shoots, and nearly sessile, long-elliptic or lanceolate, finely-round-toothed leaves that have much the texture of those of culinary sage. Their upper sides are dark green, beneath they are shortly gray-hairy with the mid-vein very prominent. The opposite pairs of stipules (basal appendages to the leaves) are united, point downward, and hug the stems. Some 5 or 6 inches long and one-half to two-thirds as broad, the erect, dense panicles of bloom, with their branches thickly-hairy, look much like those of lilacs. The corollas are pale lavender tinged pinkish on the outsides of their tubes and bright orange in their throats.

Buddleia salviifolia

Yellow-flowered, winter-blooming **B. madagascariensis** (syn. *Nicodemia madagascariensis*), of Malagasy (Madagascar), belongs to a group of six species segregated by some authorities as the genus *Nicodemia*. This kind is suitable for outdoor cultivation in California and other nearly frost-free areas and can be grown indoors for winter display in greenhouses. An ev-

ergreen up to 20 feet tall, it has dark green leaves white- to yellowish-hairy on their undersides, and bears slender panicles of rather disagreeably-scented, orange-yellow flowers. A hybrid between this and *B. asiatica*, intermediate in its characteristics, is *B. lewisiana*. Another native of Malagasy, **B. indica** (syn. *Nicodemia diversifolia*) is a compact shrub cultivated to some extent as a greenhouse and indoor foliage plant. It has attractive small, coarsely-toothed, oak-like leaves with short, bronzy stalks.

Buddleia indica

Garden and Landscape Uses. Choice varieties of hardy, common butterfly bush are assets to almost any garden. They serve many landscape purposes well. Their chief virtues, in addition to their beauty, are their ease of cultivation and the certainty that they will bloom for several weeks when few shrubs are flowering. They combine well with other summer decoratives and, if pruned well back each spring, can be used to good purpose intermixed with herbaceous perennials and annuals. The other outstanding hardy kind *B. alternifolia* is deserving of being planted more frequently, although not as freely as the common butterfly bush. One, or few, solitary specimens, located where their cascading wands of bloom can be seen to best advantage and their fragrance enjoyed, is likely to suffice. This is excellent espaliered against a wall. Beware of providing *B. alternifolia* too rich a diet. In overfertile earth it blooms reluctantly; comparatively poor, gravely or sandy soil is to its liking. Given that and full sun, it makes a superb display. Tender buddleias are adaptable for planting outdoors only in frostless or nearly frostless, dryish climates. They may be displayed to good advantage as single specimens and in groups. Favorites for greenhouse cultivation are *B. asiatica* and *B. farquhari*, both of which are useful as cut flowers and as decorative specimens in pots or tubs. Also useful as an ornamental pot plant, but of less service

as a cut flower, is *B. salviifolia*. As cut flowers, buddleias tend to wilt too quickly to be rated among the best. But the two suggested are so used and stand up fairly well if most of the foliage is removed from their stems and, before being displayed, they are stood in deep water in a cool, dark place for a few hours. The same treatment helps with cut flowers of common butterfly bush. The variety of the latter that keeps best in water is *B. davidii nanhoensis*.

Cultivation. Growing buddleias presents few problems. They propagate readily from leafy cuttings, hardwood cuttings, and seeds, and are easy to transplant. An understanding of their pruning is important. They fall into two groups, those such as *B. davidii*, *B. albiflora*, *B. japonica*, *B. lindleyana*, *B. asiatica*, *B. farquhari*, and *B. officinalis*, which bloom on shoots of the current season's growth, and those, including *B. alternifolia*, *B. globosa*, and *B. colvilei*, which bear their blooms on shoots of the previous year. Pruning the first group is done in late winter and consists of shortening the shoots to any extent convenient, almost to the ground if desired. The second group needs no more pruning than necessary to keep the plants shapely and free of crowded, weak shoots. It is done immediately after blooming. In regions where the tops are likely to be winter-killed, it is helpful to pile coal ashes, sand, or soil in fall about the lower parts of the stems of the common butterfly bush and of other kinds that bloom on current season's shoots. An annual spring application of a complete fertilizer promotes vigorous growth.

For fall and winter bloom in greenhouses, *B. asiatica*, *B. farquhari*, and *B. salviifolia* are grown in pots or tubs from cuttings taken from March to June. These root readily in sand or other propagating medium in a cool greenhouse. When roots 1 inch to 2 inches long have developed the young plants are potted individually in 2½- or 3-inch pots and, as soon as they have recovered from the disturbance, their tips are pinched out to encourage branching. Successive pottings into larger containers are given whenever the roots become crowded until about mid-August, when the last shift is made. Coarse, fertile, loamy soil of a type suitable for chrysanthemums or geraniums is most satisfactory. To encourage branching the tips of the shoots are pinched out occasionally, the last pinch being given in late July or August. Through the summer the plants may be accommodated in a fully-ventilated greenhouse or stood outdoors in a sunny location. They must be watered generously to avoid checks to growth, and loss of foliage is likely to occur if the leaves wilt. Neat staking and tying to support the stems will be needed. After the final pots are filled with roots, weekly applications of dilute liquid fertilizer are highly desirable. Before frost comes specimens summered outdoors are brought inside. Cool conditions are very important. The greenhouse is ventilated freely whenever weather permits. Night temperatures of 40 to 50°F are adequate, and by day temperatures not more than five or ten degrees higher should be kept on all occasions possible.

A useful outdoor shrub in warm, frost-free climates, *B. diversifolia* is attractive in pots in greenhouses and as a houseplant. It prospers in porous, well-drained, fertile soil kept moderately moist, but not wet, in bright light, but not necessarily strong sun. For best results winter night temperatures should be 60 to 65°F. By day and at other seasons higher temperatures are advantageous. A reasonably moist atmosphere is needed. Propagation is by cuttings. Occasional pinching out of the tips of the shoots promotes bushiness.

BUDWORMS AND BUD MOTHS. These are small caterpillars that feed on or in young buds. See Caterpillars.

BUFFALO-BERRY is *Shepherdia argentea*.

BUFFALO CURRANT is *Ribes odoratum*.

BUFFALO WOOD is *Burchellia capensis*.

BUGBANE. See Cimicifuga.

BUGLE WEED. See Ajuga.

BUGLOSS. See Anchusa. Viper's bugloss is *Echium*.

BUGLOSSOIDES (Bugloss-òides). This name is that of a few species for long included in *Lithospermum*. From that genus, the seven or more species of *Buglossoides* differ in having five definite longitudinal lines of glands or hairs inside their corolla tubes. The group, inhabiting southern Europe, North Africa, and Asia, belongs to the borage family BORAGINACEAE. Its name, a compound of the common name bugloss (*Anchusa*) and the Greek *oides*, similar to, has obvious application.

Included here are annuals, biennials, herbaceous perennials, and subshrubs, hairy plants with alternate leaves and spikes or racemes of flowers each with a five-cleft calyx, a tubular corolla with five spreading lobes (petals), five nonprotruding stamens, and one style. The fruits consist basically of four nutlets, but in cultivated specimens frequently only one develops.

Cultivated sorts are *B. gastonii*, *B. pur-pureo-caeruleum*, and *B. zollingeri* all of which carry the same specific epithets (last parts to their names) when treated under *Lithospermum*. Probably the best known is *B. purpureo-caeruleum*, with densely-branched rhizomes, arching sterile stems that root at their tips, and erect flowering stems 1 foot to 2 feet tall. The lanceolate leaves are 1

inch to 3 inches long, and the flowers, purple at first but changing to rich blue, ½ to ¾ inch across, have anthers twice as long as the filaments on which they are carried and are in paired, flattish clusters. The nutlets are glossy-white. From this *B. gastonii* differs in its unbranched terminal flower clusters and its oval to oblanceolate leaves and in not being more than about 10 inches in height. Its flowers are ½ to ¾ inch in diameter. Distinct by reason of its white-centered, light blue flowers ½ to ⅝ inch across, with anthers as long as the filaments that bear them and yellowish nutlets, is *B. zollingeri*. It has trailing or arching stems that root at their tips and elliptic to oblanceolate leaves.

Garden Uses and Cultivation. These are plants for the fronts of perennial borders and perhaps for larger rock gardens, but they are not especially easy to grow. They need well-drained, reasonably moist soil and full sun or just a little shade from the strongest summer sun. A limestone soil suits them better than one that is acid. They are unlikely to be happily located where summers are extraordinarily hot, nor are excessively cold winters entirely to their liking. They may be increased by seeds, cuttings, and division.

BUGS. The use of this name for nearly all kinds of insects is entomologically improper. It is, however, historically correct for it is a very old English word for beetles and other small, unappealing creatures. Entomologists limit the name bug to sucking insects of the suborder *Heteroptera* of the order *Hemiptera*. These true bugs usually have wings that they fold against the abdomen. Generally the lower parts of the front wings are hard and horny and the outer parts thin and membranous. An overlap forms a crosslike pattern on the back of the insect. Bugs undergo gradual rather than complete metamorphosis. The young, except for size, are much like the adults.

Among true bugs are a goodly number of plant pests including the box-elder bug, chinch bugs, four-lined plant bug and other plant bugs, harlequin bug, various lace bugs and stink bugs, and the squash bug. Neither mealybugs or spittlebugs are true bugs. The first are relatives of scale insects, the second of leaf hoppers.

Control of bugs is various according to kind and the plants they are damaging. Follow up-to-date recommendations of County Cooperative Agents, State Agricultural Experiment Stations, or other authorities.

BULB. In its strict botanical meaning a bulb is a special, well-defined type of organ. In common garden parlance the word is often used with less precision to include other bulblike plant parts. See Bulbs or Bulb Plants.

A true bulb is an apical portion of a stem densely clothed with thick, modified leaves called scales. Structurally it is a fat bud. The scales may, like those of onions and tulips, be in concentric layers each completely covering those beneath, and the whole enclosed in an outer skin or tunic. Such bulbs are called tunicated bulbs. Or there may be no outer tunic so that the

Tunicated bulbs of hyacinth, one sliced through to show scales enclosed in a tunic and at the center a mature flower bud

scales, more or less overlapping like shingles on a roof, are clearly visible. Such bulbs, among the most familiar those of lilies, are scaly bulbs.

Scaly bulbs of lilies, without outer tunics

In the economy of the plant, bulbs serve as storage organs for food materials manufactured in the leaves and other green parts. The food is drawn upon to support the early development of the next growing period. Because of the immediate availability of this food many plants with bulbs flower in late winter or spring, or like most amaryllises and the belladonna-lily, flower before their leaves appear or, like daffodils, hyacinths, tulips, and many other kinds, lend themselves to forcing into early bloom indoors.

There are deciduous and evergreen bulbs, hardy and nonhardy kinds. Occurring in several plant families, they are especially numerous in the amaryllis family AMARYLLIDACEAE; iris family IRIDACEAE; and lily family LILIACEAE. Most, probably all, true bulbs can be propagated by bulb cuttings as well as by other means. Genera with true bulbs include *Albuca, Allium, Amaryllis, Amianthium, Ammocharis, Bellevalia, Bessera, Bloomeria, Boophone, Bowiea, Brodiaea, Brunsdonna, Brunsvigia, Calostemma, Camassia, Chionodoxa, Chionoscilla, Chlidanthus, Chlorogalum, Crinodonna, Crinum, Cyanella, Dichelostemma, Dipcadi, Elisena, Endymion, Erythronium, Eucharis, Eucrosia, Eucomis, Eustephia, Eustylis, Fritillaria, Gagea, Galanthus, Galtonia, Habranthus, Haemanthus, Hippeastrum, Hyacinthus, Hymenocallis, Ipheion, Iris* (some kinds), *Ixiolirion, Lachenalia, Leucocoryne, Leucocrinum, Leucojum, Lilium, Lloydia, Lycoris, Milla, Muscari, Narcissus, Nemastylis, Nerine, Nomocharis, Nothoscordum, Ornithogalum, Oxalis* (some kinds), *Pamianthe, Pancratium, Phaedranassa, Polianthes* (some kinds), *Puschkinia, Rhodohypoxis, Scilla, Sprekelia, Stenomesson, Sternbergia, Tulbaghia, Tulipa, Urginea, Vallota, Veltheimia, Zephyranthes,* and *Zigadenus.*

BULBILS. These are tiny bulbs that develop in the leaf axils or on other above-ground parts of certain plants. They are sometimes called bulblets, a term better reserved for little bulbs that grow from the bases of larger ones.

Bulbils on stem of *Lilium lancifolium*

BULBINE (Bulbìn-e). This name, pronounced in three syllables, is that of a genus of South African and Australian plants of the lily family LILIACEAE, and related to *Anthericum.* It includes both annuals and perennials. The name is from the Greek, *bolbos,* a bulb. These are stemless or short-stemmed plants, sometimes bulbous or tuberous and with linear or broadly-lanceolate leaves. The flowers, in racemes, are starlike and usually yellow. They are smallish and have six spreading petals (more correctly tepals) and six stamens all or some with hairy stalks. There are more than fifty species.

Distinguished by having erect, branched stems about 1 foot long and 2 feet high, **B. caulescens,** native of South Africa, is not uncommonly grown in collections of succulent plants. It has slender, semicylindrical, mostly erect, soft, pale green leaves up to 1 foot in length and ⅓ inch in diameter. Its yellow flowers are in 1-foot-long, erect racemes from the upper leaf axils. This species is perennial.

Bulbine caulescens

Stemless or nearly stemless perennials commonly cultivated are *B. alooides* and *B. bulbosa.* The former is native of South Africa, the latter of Australia. The South African **B. alooides** forms clusters of basal tufts of soft, narrow-triangular to strap-shaped leaves, flat on both sides. They are up to 4 inches long by 1¼ to 2 inches broad at their bases, and pale green with reddish ends. One to several many-flowered racemes, 8 inches to about 1 foot long, of yellow blooms, develop from each tuft of foliage. The Australian **B. bulbosa** has bulblike tubers and all-basal, grooved, fleshy, pointed-linear leaves 5 inches to 1 foot long, and more or less in rosettes. Its racemes of bloom attain a height of 1 foot to 2 feet and have yellow flowers occupying their upper halves.

An annual kind from Australia, *B. semibarbata* often masquerades under the name of *B. annua,* which rightly belongs to a South African annual believed not to be cultivated. The roots of *B. semibarbata* are fibrous rather than tuberous. Its leaves are similar to those of *B. bulbosa,* but it has fewer blooms, and three instead of all six of its stamens have hairy stalks.

Garden Uses and Cultivation. In mild dry climates, such as that of California, bulbines are suitable plants for flower beds and for large rock gardens. They are also appropriate for inclusion in collections of succulents and can be successfully grown in window gardens. They need full sun and sandy, well-drained soil. All are easily raised from seeds sown outdoors in spring or started early indoors and later planted out. The perennials are also easy to multiply by cuttings. When grown in greenhouses they need a dryish, well-ventilated atmosphere and cool conditions. Night temperatures in winter may be 40 to 50°F and day temperatures only a few degrees higher. At other seasons, when there is no danger of frost, normal outdoor temperatures are satisfactory. Water so that the soil becomes nearly dry between thorough soakings.

BULBINELLA (Bulbin-élla). There are fifteen species of *Bulbinella,* mostly natives of South Africa, but also represented in the native floras of New Zealand and the Campbell and Aukland islands. They are fleshy-rooted herbaceous perennials of the lily family LILIACEAE. The name is a diminutive of that of the related genus *Bulbine,* from which bulbinellas differ in not having hairy stamens. The foliage of bulbinellas is all-basal, usually mixed below with the fibrous remains of old leaves. The leaves are linear or cylindrical. Borne in dense cylindrical to conical racemes atop erect, naked stalks, the flowers are bright yellow to orange or whitish. The perianth is tubeless, and consists of six petals, or more properly tepals, of nearly equal size. There are six slender-stalked stamens, and one style. The racemes open from below upward, the lower flowers fading as those above open. The fruits are globose capsules.

South African **B. floribunda** (syns. *B. robusta, B. r. latifolia*) favors swampy soils and is reported to bloom most freely after fires. It attains heights of 1½ to 2½ feet and has tapering, strap-shaped leaves that sheath each other prominently at their bases. They are 1 foot to 2 feet long by 1 inch wide at their bases and deeply grooved down their centers. The little yellow or orange flowers are in dense racemes about 3½ inches long that grow up to 8 inches.

New Zealand **B. hookeri** in its homeland commonly favors moist, peaty soil, but occurs also in drier places. Its narrowly-sword-shaped leaves are up to 1¼ feet long. The stout flower stalks attain heights

Bulbinella floribunda

Narcissus bulb, with bulblet attached

Bulbinella hookeri

of 1 foot to 2½ feet. Each terminates in a raceme 4 inches to 1 foot long of starry, bright yellow blooms a little more than ½ inch wide.

Garden and Landscape Uses and Cultivation. These are excellent plants for regions of mild winters. The South African species described above also does well in pots in greenhouses, blooming from January onward. The New Zealand kind is a summer bloomer. All thrive in fertile, moist, but not wet soil that contains abundant peat moss or other organic matter. They can be accommodated in flower borders and in naturalistic surroundings. The New Zealander is probably hardier than the South African and more grateful for fairly cool summers, but all are grown outdoors in southern England. They are good cut flowers. Propagation is by seed and division.

BULBLET. Small bulbs borne as offsets from larger ones are called bulblets. See also Bulbils.

BULBOCODIUM (Bulbo-còdium). The attractive small bulb plant that bears this name is closely related to *Colchicum* and by some authorities is included there. The differences are that the perianth segments (petals) of *Bulbocodium* narrow markedly below into slender halves as long as the blades, whereas the lower parts of the petals of *Colchicum* are joined into a tube. In *Colchicum* there are three styles, in *Bulbocodium* one, slightly three-branched at its tip. From *Crocus*, which in aspect it somewhat resembles, *Bulbocodium* is readily distinguished by its six instead of three stamens. Belonging in the lily family LILIACEAE, and native of mountain pastures in Europe and the Caucasus, *Bulbocodium* has a name from the Greek *bolbos*, a bulb, and *kodion*, a head. The application is not clear.

The underground, blackish-brown storage organs of **Bulbocodium vernum** are corms, ovoid and almost 1 inch in diameter. From these the blooms arise in early spring, solitary or in twos or threes, together with the leaves. The flowers have narrow, rosy-lilac, or much more rarely white, petals about 2 inches long, that instead of, like those of crocuses and colchicums forming tidy goblets, spread irregularly into casual, informal stars. The leaves, three in number and broadly-lanceolate or strap-shaped, with numerous longitudinal veins, are only partly grown when the flowers are fully developed. Later they attain lengths of 5 or 6 inches. The fruits are capsules.

Garden Uses and Cultivation. A choice, hardy plant for rock gardens, *B. vernum* does not always make itself as thoroughly at home or do as well as could be wished. A theory advanced by some gardeners is that for it to prosper it must be trans-

Bulbocodium vernum

planted every other year into very well-drained, fertile earth, gritty, and with a lacing of leaf mold or other decayed organic matter. Replanting is done in late spring or early summer as soon as the foliage has died. A location in full sun or with very little dappled shade, and where the soil does not become dry during the spring growing season, gives best results. The corms should be planted about 3 inches deep and 3 to 4 inches apart. Propagation is by division at replanting time, and by seed.

BULBOPHYLLUM (Bulbo-phýllum). A remarkable agglomeration of 1,000 or possibly considerably more species constitutes *Bulbophyllum* of the orchid family ORCHIDACEAE. As accepted here, the genus includes kinds by some authorities segregated as *Cirrhopetalum* and *Megaclinium*. Widely distributed in the wild in many tropical and subtropical regions, bulbophyllums are epiphytes, growing on trees without taking nourishment from them. The name, alluding to the pseudobulbs and the leaves that sprout from them, comes from the Greek *bolbos*, a bulb, and *phyllon*, a leaf.

The majority of bulbophyllums are not particularly showy, but some few are, and some have blooms distinctly verging on the bizarre. These appeal to lovers of the curious and unusual. The range of variation in this vast genus is so great that it is not possible to give a short, comprehensive, useful description of it. Cultivated kinds mostly have creeping rhizomes with, clustered or more widely-spaced, usually one-leaved, often angled pseudobulbs. The stalks, carrying one to many flowers, come from the rhizomes, near or some distance from the bases of the pseudobulbs. The blooms, as in all orchids, have three sepals, two petals, a lip (a modified third petal), and a column comprising the male and female elements of the bloom. In *Bulbophyllum* the sizes, shapes, and colors of these organs vary tremendously from species to species. The blooms are from minute to fairly sizable. There is no easily recognizable feature that identifies bulbophyllums as such. A few cultivated kinds are described below. Others are likely to be found in special collections.

Intriguing *B. barbigerum*, of tropical Africa, has flattish, 1- to 1½-inch-long, clustered pseudobulbs each with a blunt, oblong leaf about 3 inches long by 1 inch wide, and spikes of up to fifteen two-ranked blooms. About 1 inch in length, the flowers have greenish-brown sepals and tiny petals and a green and yellow, tongue-shaped lip, with an abundance of long chocolate hairs that quiver in every breeze.

Imaginatively-named *B. medusae* (syn. *Cirrhopetalum medusae*) has rather widely-spaced pseudobulbs 1 inch to 1½ inches in

Bulbophyllum barbigerum

height, each with a single leaf up to 8 inches long by 1½ to 2 inches wide, its blunt apex slightly notched. The creamy-white, frequently pink- or red-spotted flowers are crowded in moplike heads that suggest the hair of Medusa because the two lateral sepals of each flower are prolonged beyond their short, broader basal portions into slender, drooping threads 3 to 5 inches long. This kind is native to southeast Asia and Indonesia.

Very different *B. makoyanum* (syn. *Cirrhopetalum makoyanum*), of Indochina, has 1-inch-tall pseudobulbs not closely clustered. The leaf of each is 3 to 4 inches long. From the tops of the flower stalks radiate, like spokes of a wheel, twelve or more 1½-inch-long flowers. Their lateral sepals, joined for most of their lengths, are their most conspicuous feature. They give to the head of blooms an almost daisy-like appearance. Native of the Molucca Islands, *B. mastersianum* (syn. *Cirrhopetalum mastersianum*) has egg-shaped pseudobulbs about 2 inches long, each with one strap-shaped leaf up to 8 inches long by 3 inches wide. The flowers, in umbels at the ends of long, slender, drooping stalks, usually up to ten, spread in a fanlike semicircle. Yellow, with brownish spots and brown lips, they are about 2 inches long. Hailing from Malaya and Indonesia, *B. macranthum* has pseudobulbs with leaves up to 1 foot long by 4 inches wide, cleft at their apexes. The solitary blooms have a whitish upper sepal and petals and yellow lateral sepals. Both sepals and petals are spotted with purple. The lip is yellowish.

Other kinds cultivated include the following: *B. biflorum*, of Malaya and Indonesia, has pseudobulbs each with one leaf about 3 to 5 inches long by 1¼ inches wide. The paired, fleshy flowers, about 3 inches long, are greenish, striped and spotted with purple. *B. collettii* (syn. *Cirrhopetalum collettii*) has four-lobed pseudobulbs. Its fleshy leaves are up to about

Bulbophyllum mastersianum

6 inches long. The flowers, in umbel-like clusters of about six, are 4 to 5 inches long. They have a conspicuously-fringed upper (dorsal) sepal and petals, and are pale orange with red stripes. The lip is carmine-crimson to magenta. This kind is native of Burma. **B. dearei** (syn. *B. godseffianum*), of Borneo and the Philippine Islands, has one-leaved pseudobulbs, the leaves up to 6 inches long and 1½ inches wide. The solitary flowers, 2 to 3 inches across, have an upper sepal and petals yellow flushed with orange-red, the lateral sepals yellow streaked and suffused with red-purple. The lip is white and purple. **B. lobbii,** of Malaya, Thailand, and Indonesia, some-

Bulbophyllum lobbii

what resembles *B. dearei*. It has pseudobulbs rather widely spaced on the rhizomes, 1 inch to 2 inches long. Each has one leaf up to 10 inches long by 3 inches wide. Solitary, the fragrant, waxy blooms are 3 to 4 inches wide. They are pale yellow to buff-yellow suffused and spotted with rosy-purple to purple. The lip is yellowish to yellow finely spotted with purple, with an orange-colored patch at its base. **B. pachyrhachis,** the only species native in the United States, extends in the wild from Florida to the West Indies, Mexico, and Panama. Not showy, it has 1-inch-long, widely-spaced pseudobulbs each with usually two strap-shaped leaves up to 8 inches long by nearly 1 inch wide. The tiny, usually purple-spotted, greenish-yellow flowers are in erect to drooping, slender racemes 1 foot long or longer. **B. picturatum,** of Burma, has pseudobulbs, with leaves about 6 inches long. The umbel-like fans of about ten green flowers, spotted with red and with red lips, terminate stalks up to about 10 inches long. **B. robustum** (syn. *Cirrhopetalum robustum*), of New Guinea, has clustered, egg-shaped pseudobulbs about 3 inches tall, each with two elliptic-oblong leaves up to 1 foot long and 3 inches wide. The ill-scented flowers, in umbels of up to ten, are arranged in a

circle atop a stalk 2 to 3 inches long. The sepals are yellow suffused at their bases with brownish-red, the much smaller petals are yellowish-brown. The short, thick lip is dark red.

Bulbophyllum robustum

Among less well known species are those now to be described: **B. elatius,** native of Borneo, is without evident pseu-

Bulbophyllum elatius

dobulbs. Up to 1½ feet long, the leathery leaves are oblong-ovate to obovate. The tiny cream flowers are in slender, erect racemes as long or longer than the leaves. **B.**

Bulbophyllum porphyroglossum

porphyroglossum of central Africa is small. It has little, more or less spherical pseudobulbs each with one broad-oblong leaf. The tiny flowers, in wiry-stemmed arching spikes from the base of the pseudobulb, are green. **B. purpureorachis** (syn.

Bulbophyllum purpureorhachis

Megaclinium purpureorhachis) of tropical Africa has long, tapering, flattened pseudobulbs crowned with two oblong-elliptic leaves. Its erect, curiously-twisted, dull purple flowering stalks, about 1¼ feet long by 1¼ inches wide, are of snakeskin-like texture. Disposed along them on both sides of the mid-vein, and in the bud stage concealed by peculiarly shaped bracts, the tiny flowers are yellowish spotted with purple. Together they and the bracts resemble tiny toads. **B. wrightii** of tropical West Africa is a small species with angled

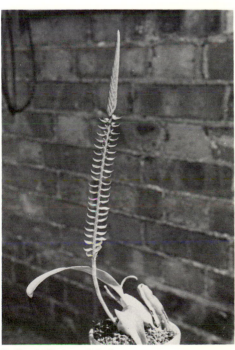

Bulbophyllum wrightii

pseudobulbs each with one oblong leaf up to 5 inches long. Its little lemon-yellow and maroon or brown flowers are in the axils of prominent, persistent, horizontally-spreading bracts, brown above and with gray undersides, arranged in ladder-like fashion along erect flowering stalks which are up to 6 inches long and come from the bases of the pseudobulbs.

Garden Uses and Cultivation. Bulbophyllums have their greatest appeal to enthusiastic fanciers of orchids. Because of their wide natural distribution and great diversity, their cultural needs vary considerably and must be determined by consideration of where individual kinds grow natively, supplemented by trial and error. In general the commonly grown kinds succeed in tightly-packed osmunda or tree fern fiber in pans (shallow pots), filled for the greater part of their depth with crocks, or in hanging baskets. Small, delicate kinds appreciate having sphagnum moss mixed with the fiber. They may also be grown on slabs of tree fern trunk. High humidity and fairly heavy shade are generally needed. Temperatures may vary according to species from about 55 to 65°F minimum on winter nights, with a five to fifteen degree increase by day allowed. Most bulbophyllums need watering regularly throughout the year. Some, hailing from lands of alternate dry and wet seasons, benefit from a period of about one month after the new shoots have attained full maturity during which water is withheld or its amount markedly reduced. For further information see Orchids.

BULBS OR BULB PLANTS. Not all plants commonly called bulbs or bulb plants have parts that fulfill the botanical definition of a bulb. See Bulb. But all possess thickened underground food storage organs that serve essentially the same purposes as bulbs and that are more or less bulblike in appearance. Technically such parts may be corms, tubers, tuberous roots, or rhizomes. As a gardening term bulbs serves usefully to identify a group of plants more closely allied by their life-styles and cultural needs than in other ways. Custom rather than strict definition decides which plants are accepted as bulbs, which not. There are borderline cases for which the decision may go either way. For example, few gardeners consider lily-of-the-valley a bulb yet it is commonly listed in catalogs of bulb dealers. The same is true of foxtail-lilies (*Eremurus*). Agapanthuses and clivias are other examples of plants that may be included or excluded.

Bulbs include sorts with evergreen foliage, such as certain crinums, eucharises, and hippeastrums, but the great majority are without foliage during their seasons of rest. There are hardy and nonhardy bulbs, kinds that are dormant in winter and grow in summer; others that are dormant for a

Some spring-flowering bulb plants: (a) Snowdrops

(b) Crocuses

(c) Narcissuses

(d) Hyacinth

(e) Freesias

(f) Ranunculuses

(g) Calla-lily

period in summer are in active growth, at least so far as their roots are concerned, at other times. Some, such as gladioluses, Spanish irises, and tulips, when dormant lose their roots completely and develop new ones at the beginning of the next growing season. Others, including crinums, eucharises, hippeastrums, and spider-lilies, have permanent roots.

The history of bulbs as garden plants is long. Because several great civilizations had their origins in lands where many sorts of bulbs were natives it was natural that they received attention from those

Some summer- and fall-flowering bulb plants: (a) Belladonna-lily

(b) Tuberous begonia

(c) Gladioluses

(d) Summer-hyacinths

(e) Lily (*Lilium lancifolium splendens*)

(f) Cannas

(g) Dahlias

who practiced the art of healing and those who gardened. An Egyptian papyrus written eighteen centuries before the birth of Christ refers to the employment of colchicums and squills in medicine, and we know that the Pharaohs grew anemones, lilies, and narcissuses in their gardens and that the last two were used by the ancient Egyptians in funeral wreaths. The Greek Theophrastus, who lived three centuries before Christ, wrote about alliums, anemones, crocuses, cyclamens, gladioluses, grape-hyacinths, lilies, and squills, and Dioscorides in his great work on medicinal plants written in the first century A.D. also discussed hyacinths and ornithogalums. A mid-fifteenth-century manuscript mentions candidum lilies, crocuses, and daffodils in cultivation in English gardens. Some one hundred years later, the first book dealing with American plants, the "Badianus Manuscript, an Aztec Herbal," appeared. In it a dahlia, an oxalis, and a *Xanthosoma* are clearly pictured. About that time cannas and dahlias were brought from the New World to Spain.

The first tulips cultivated in Europe came from Turkey about the middle of the sixteenth century. In 1634 an amazing fever of speculation in tulip bulbs, which became known as "tulipmania," erupted in Holland and continued for three years. When the inevitable crash came numerous speculators were bankrupt, but fortunately the tulip growing industry in Holland was not and that country remains to this day the chief commercial source of tulips and many other bulbs. The opening to plant collectors of North America, especially the Pacific region and Mexico, brought a new wealth of bulb plants to gardens as did the botanical exploration of that fantastically rich horticultural collecting ground, South Africa. From North America came brodiaeas, calochortuses, camassias, hymenocallises, tigridias, trilliums, and zephyrlilies (*Zephyranthes*); from South Africa, babianas, calla-lilies (*Zantedeschia*), freesias, ixias, lachenalias, tritonias, and numerous others. Many other regions, notably Central and South America, have contributed their share of bulbs to gardens. Foremost among South American bulbs are alstroemerias, bomarias, caladiums, eucharises, and hippeastrums. Neither Australia nor New Zealand are rich in native bulb plants and few from those regions are cultivated.

Bulbs are useful for many purposes. Many supply excellent cut flowers. Here belong calla-lilies, dahlias, Dutch and Spanish irises, florists' anemones, freesias, gladioluses, lilies, montbretias, narcissuses, ornithogalums, ranunculuses, tuberoses, and tulips. As furnishings for formal beds caladiums, cannas, daffodils, dwarf dahlias, hyacinths, tuberous begonias, and tulips are superb, as are in mild climates, anemones and ranunculuses.

These and numerous other sorts, including all kinds most useful for cut flowers, alliums, alstroemerias, *Amaryllis belladonna*, lilies, and tigridias can be planted effectively in groups in beds and borders. Many small bulbs, anemones, chionodoxas, crocuses, grape-hyacinths, scillas, snowdrops, sternbergias, and winter aconites among them, are splendid for rock gardens and for tucking into bays at the fronts of foundation plantings. Other kinds, including bloodroots, English and Spanish bluebells, erythroniums, jack-in-the-pulpits, spring beauties, and trilliums, are seen to best advantage in woodland or other shady settings.

Forcing indoors for early bloom is easy with such hardy spring-flowering bulbs as crocuses, grape-hyacinths, hyacinths, narcissuses, and tulips. Other kinds for blooming in greenhouses in winter and spring, which must be grown under cool conditions without forcing, are florists' anemones, babianas, baby gladioluses and *Gladiolus tristis*, ixias, ornithogalums, Persian and turban ranunculuses, sparaxises, and tritonias.

Commonly cultivated bulbs, in the main easy to grow, reward handsomely for little care. Plant purchased ones as soon as they are available from dealers, which means for most kinds in fall, somewhat earlier for others. When desirable or necessary lift, separate, and replant hardy bulbs in gardens as soon as their foliage has died naturally; or for those without permanent roots, such as tulips, store after lifting and replant in fall. The foliage of deciduous bulbs must be allowed to die naturally and gradually at the approach of the dormant season. It is the leaves that manufacture the food stored in the bulbs to support the next season's early growth. Removal of the foliage before it is fully ripe results in lesser amounts of food being stored, and this can seriously interfere with the production of flowers the following season. If persisted in it will weaken the plants even to the extent of causing their death. Because of this, it is most important not to mow grass in which crocuses, narcissuses, or other spring-blooming bulbs are naturalized until their foliage has died completely. Fertilizing bulbs as soon as flowering is through and making sure they have adequate supplies of water from then until they begin to go dormant does much to promote vigor.

Popular hardy bulbs, in the main easy to grow, reward handsomely with little care. They generally do best in well-drained, deeply-prepared, fertile, fairly loose, loamy soil in sun or light shade according to kind. A few, such as camassias and zigadenuses, appreciate moister earth at least when they are in foliage. A fair number are woodlanders. These need shade or partial shade and prefer soils that contain generous

amounts of organic matter. Belonging here are American and European wood anemones, amianthiums, bloodroots (*Sanguinaria*), corydalises, dog's-tooth-violets (*Erythronium*), Dutchman's breeches (*Dicentra*), English and Spanish bluebells (*Endymion*), jack-in-the-pulpits (*Arisaema*), rue-anemone (*Anemonella*), spring beauties (*Claytonia*), and trilliums.

Dutch bulbs, so called because they are produced commercially chiefly in Holland and make up the greater part of the offerings in the catalogs of bulb dealers of that country, are among the most popular and easy to grow bulb plants. Most are hardy, poppy anemones and Persian and turban ranunculuses are not. Hardy sorts include colchicums, crocuses, crown imperials (*Fritillaria*), English, Dutch, and Spanish irises, English and Spanish bluebells (*Endymion*), glories-of-the-snow (*Chionodoxa*), hyacinths, narcissuses, snowdrops (*Galanthus*), snowflakes (*Leucojum*), squills (*Scilla*), striped-squills (*Puschkinia*), tulips, and winter aconites (*Eranthis*). Kinds of lesser importance or less familiar are offered in catalogs of specialists.

Certain Dutch bulbs, especially Dutch and Spanish irises, English and Spanish bluebells, hyacinths, narcissuses, tulips, and to a lesser degree crocuses, glories-of-the-snow, snowdrops, squills, and striped-squills are often forced into winter and early spring bloom in greenhouses and windows. For this to be satisfactory it is necessary to pot the bulbs in fall, preferably as early as obtainable, and then to give them opportunity to root for several weeks in temperatures up to 40°F before beginning forcing. The chilling is usually accomplished by putting the potted bulbs in a root cellar or by burying them outdoors or in a cold frame under a few inches of sand, peat moss, sawdust, or similar material.

Other well-known hardy bulbs for temperate-region gardens include brodiaeas, bulbocodiums, calochortuses, cyclamens, flowering onions (*Allium*), fritillarias, lilies (*Lilium*), *Lycoris squamigera*, ornithogalums, spring starflower (*Ipheion*), and sternbergias.

Summer bulbs, nonhardy in temperate regions but planted there after all danger of frost has passed and the soil is warm enough to induce growth, comprise several sorts greatly admired for summer display; these are dug in fall and stored indoors over winter. Chief among these are caladiums, cannas, dahlias, elephant's ear (*Colocasia*), gladioluses, gloriosas, montbretias (*Tritonia*), tigridias, tuberoses (*Polianthes*), and tuberous begonias.

Nonhardy bulbs, some deciduous, some evergreen, suitable for permanent planting outdoors in warm-temperate, subtropical, and tropical climates and for growing in greenhouses and other places indoors in pots and other containers, can conveni-

ently be separated into two groups, those that have permanent roots and should remain for at least two years and usually longer without disturbance, and those that lose all their roots as their foliage ripens after blooming and are generally best managed by repotting or replanting annually. The last are mostly, but not exclusively natives of South Africa.

Especially notable among nonhardy bulbs with permanent roots are albucas, alstroemerias, amaryllises (*Hippeastrum*), Amazon-lily (*Eucharis*), belladonna-lily (*Amaryllis*), *Bowiea volubilis*, calla-lilies (*Zantedeschia*), crindonnas, crinums, elisenas, haemanthuses, Jacobean-lily (*Sprekelia*), lycorises, ornithogalums, pancratiums, phaedranassas, pineapple flowers (*Eucomis*), spider-lilies (*Hymenocallis*), summer-hyacinth (*Galtonia*), tulbaghias, urgineas, veltheimias, and zephyr-lilies (*Zephyranthes*). Practically all of these resent undue disturbance of their roots. If this occurs it usually takes a season or two for them to become sufficiently reestablished to bloom freely. Because of this, it is important to choose suitable sites, prepare the ground deeply and well, and after planting leave them alone until they become so overcrowded with offset bulbs that flower production or quality diminishes and replanting becomes necessary. Repotting container-grown specimens involves less root disturbance than replanting outdoors, but still is necessary only at intervals of a few to several years. In between, an annual top dressing with rich soil at the beginning of the growing season and attention to fertilizing when active foliage growth is being made suffice. When grown indoors deciduous sorts of this group are kept dry during their seasons of dormancy. When semidormant, evergreen kinds are kept somewhat drier than at other times.

Nonhardy bulbs that renew their root systems completely each year and are rootless through their dormant periods, or that for other reason, such as rapid multiplication of their bulb parts, are generally repotted or replanted annually just before new growth begins are managed in this way. After they are through blooming and their foliage has died naturally, they are stored dry either in the soil in which they grew or taken out of the soil and put in trays or openwork sacks (old stockings do well for this) suspended from the ceiling of a dry cellar or similar place. If kept through the dormant period in the soil in which they grew, be sure to attend to repotting or replanting before the start of new growth indicates the beginning of the next period of activity. The chief sorts that belong with this group are achimenes, amorphophalluses, anapalinas, babianas, baby gladioluses and *Gladiolus tristis*, cyclamens, florists' anemones, freesias, gloriosas, gloxinias (*Sinningia*), homerias, ixias, lachenalias, oxalises, Persian and turban ranunculuses, rechsteinerias, sparaxises, tritonias, and watsonias.

BULL-BAY. This name is applied to *Magnolia grandiflora* and *Persea borbonia*.

BULL THISTLE is *Cirsium vulgare*.

BULLACE is *Prunus insititia*.

BULLOCK'S HEART is *Annona reticulata*.

BULNESIA (Bul-nèsia)—Verawood. This South American genus of eight species of shrubs and trees belongs to the caltrop family ZYGOPHYLLACEAE. Its name commemorates General D. Manuel Bulnes, a president of Chile in the nineteenth century.

Bulnesias are mostly natives of dry regions. They have opposite, evergreen or deciduous, pinnate leaves without terminal leaflets, and solitary or clustered flowers, each with five sepals, the same number of yellow petals, twice as many slender-stalked stamens, and a branchless style. The fruits are capsules consisting of five broadly-winged, one-seeded segments. In South America the wood of *Bulnesia sarmientii* is used as incense and from it is distilled an oil employed in perfumery.

A good-looking, slow-growing tree, in cultivation usually of small to medium size, *B. arborea* in its native Colombia and Venezuela becomes 50 to 60 or sometimes

Bulnesia arborea

up to 100 feet tall. In bloom it somewhat resembles *Cassia*. Its leaves, about 3 inches long, rather like those of the powder puff tree (*Calliandra haematocephala*), but smaller, have ten to fifteen leaflets. The chrome-yellow flowers, usually clustered, and 1½ to 2 inches wide, are succeeded by fruits 1½ inches long, with semicircular wings. The wood of this species is called verawood. Extremely hard and heavy, it is used for the same purposes as that of its botanical relative lignum-vitae (*Guaiacum*).

Garden and Landscape Uses and Cultivation. The species described, planted to some extent in the tropics and warm subtropics including Florida, thrives in ordinary soil in sunny places, and is raised from seeds.

BULRUSH. See Scirpus. The bulrush of the Bible is believed to be *Cyperus papyrus*.

BUMBLE BEE ORCHID is *Ophrys bombyliflora*.

BUMELIA (Bum-èlia)—Shittimwood, False-Buckthorn. Bumelias are deciduous and evergreen, often thorny trees and shrubs of the sapodilla family SAPOTACEAE. There are about twenty-three species, all American. The genus *Bumelia* ranges from the United States southward. Its name is an ancient Greek one for the ash tree (*Fraxinus*); why it was applied to the present group is not clear. These trees are not allied to the shittimwood of the Bible, which is a species of *Acacia*. Horticulturally, bumelias have little appeal. They are occasionally planted in botanical collections and where they occur as natives may be transferred to gardens.

Bumelias have very hard wood and contain milky or gummy sap. Their short-stalked leaves are alternate or on short, lateral shoots, clustered. The tiny white flowers are in tight, inconspicuous, axillary clusters. They have five persistent sepals, and five petals, five fertile and five infertile stamens. The latter, called staminodes, are petal-like. The fruits are somewhat plum-like, black and one-seeded. Those of *B. lanuginosa* are eaten by Indians and a chicle-

Bumelia lanuginosa, with young fruits

like substance from its bark is used by them as a kind of chewing gum.

The shittimwood or chittamwood (*B. lanuginosa*) is the most likely sort to be cultivated. As a native it occurs in dry and rocky woods from Georgia to Illinois, Missouri, Kansas, Florida, Arizona, Texas,

and Mexico. At its largest it is a tree 50 feet in height, but usually it is smaller and often does not exceed the dimensions of a large shrub. Its toothless leaves, elliptic, oblanceolate, or ovate, are 1½ to 3 inches long and one-quarter to one-half as wide. They are thickish, and softly-hairy on their undersides. Although deciduous, they remain until late in fall. The flowers are five to forty together in rounded clusters. Their stalks are hairy. The fruits are more or less egg-shaped and about ½ inch long.

A shrub or tree up to 30 feet tall, *B. lycioides* inhabits woods and river banks from Virginia to Texas mostly on the coastal plain. From *B. lanuginosa* it differs in its usually more pointed, elliptic to oblanceolate leaves 2 to 4½ inches long and nearly or quite hairless and in its flowers having hairy stalks.

Garden and Landscape Uses and Cultivation. The horticultural uses of *Bumelia* are suggested at the beginning of this entry. They grow in any ordinary soil and are propagated by seeds. The hardiest are *B. lanuginosa* and *B. lycioides*. These survive in sheltered locations as far north as Boston, Massachusetts.

BUNCH FLOWER. See Melanthium.

BUNCHBERRY is *Cornus canadensis*.

BUNIAS (Bùni-as). Native of the Mediterranean region and western Asia, this genus of about six species is not of much horticultural importance; one kind is sometimes cultivated. The group belongs in the mustard family CRUCIFERAE and consists of yellow- or white-flowered biennials and herbaceous perennials, often rough with forked hairs. The name is a modification of the ancient Greek one *bounias*, applied to some plants of the same family.

Native of southern Europe and naturalized in parts of North America, *Bunias orientalis* is a sparsely-hairy biennial or sometimes perennial. From 2 to 4 feet tall, it branches and has pointed-oblong, dandelion-like leaves, the lower, rosette ones up to 8 inches long and more or less pinnately-lobed; the stem leaves are smaller, lanceolate-elliptic, and the upper ones, toothed instead of lobed. The yellow flowers, ¼ inch across, in crowded, branched racemes, have four petals spreading to form a cross and four long and two short stamens. The fruits are asymmetrically ovoid pods about ¼ inch long, covered with small warty protuberances.

Garden and Landscape Uses and Cultivation. In semiwild landscapes the species described may sometimes be found a place, but it is a little weedy looking and may tend to spread by self-sown seeds beyond its allotted area. It thrives in sunny locations in ordinary soil and is raised from seeds sown in late spring, either where the plants are to remain or in a seedbed from which the young plants are transplanted to their blooming sites.

BUNJONG is *Pimelea spectabilis.*

BUNNY EARS is *Opuntia microdasys.*

BUNYA-BUNYA is *Araucaria bidwillii.*

BUPHTHALMUM (Buph-thálmum)—Ox-Eye. This genus of two species inhabits Europe and Asia Minor. It belongs in the daisy family COMPOSITAE and bears a name derived from the Greek *bous,* an ox, and *ophthalmos,* an eye, that alludes to the flower heads.

Hardy herbaceous perennials, buphthalmums have alternate, undivided leaves and terminating long, leafy stalks, daisy-type flower heads. The disk florets are yellow and bisexual, the ray florets, which are in a single row, are female and also yellow. From nearly related *Telekia* this genus differs in the anthers of the florets being hairy at their bases. Their fruits are seedlike achenes.

Native chiefly of hilly and mountainous parts of central and southern Europe, *B. salicifolium* (syn. *B. grandiflorum*) is 6 inches to 2½ feet tall and more or less hairy. It has blunt, obovate-lanceolate, stalked lower leaves 2 to 7 inches long, and stalkless, usually pointed oblong to linear-lanceolate, upper leaves. The flower heads are up to 2½ inches in diameter.

Garden and Landscape Uses and Cultivation. The species described is useful for flower beds and naturalistic and waterside plantings. It prospers with minimal care in sunny locations in moderately fertile, near neutral, or somewhat alkaline soil. Propagation is easy by seed and by division in spring or early fall.

BUPLEURUM (Bu-pleùrum)—Thoroughwax. Rather unusual for the carrot family UMBELLIFERAE, to which it belongs, the genus *Bupleurum* includes a number of shrubby species. Another feature rare in the family is· that its leaves have parallel veins. The group comprises 150 species of Old World, chiefly Mediterranean region, shrubs, herbaceous perennials, and annuals. The name is derived from an ancient Greek one for an unknown plant of the same family.

One species, the thoroughwax or throw-wax (*B. rotundifolium*) is so called because its ovate upper leaves surround the stems, which appear to grow through them. Thoroughwax is a corruption of through wax, meaning to grow through. This annual species, and to a lesser extent two others, are naturalized in eastern North America. They are of no horticultural significance.

Native of southern Europe, and not hardy in the north, *B. fruticosum,* an ev-

Bupleurum fruticosum

ergreen or partially evergreen, summer-blooming, hairless shrub 4 to 10 feet tall, branches mainly from the base and has slender, purplish stems, and nearly stalkless, obovate to ovate, bluish-green leaves 2 to 3½ inches long by ¾ inch to 1½ inches broad, tipped with short points. Its long-stalked, erect flower clusters, 2 to 4 inches in diameter, are compound umbels that terminate the shoots. Each consists of many tiny yellow or yellowish flowers, with five petals and five stamens. The small, dry, seedlike fruits are brown when ripe. Unlike most kinds of *Bupleurum,* the flower umbels of this species have an involucre (collar) of leafy bracts at their bases.

Garden and Landscape Uses and Cultivation. The species described is useful for exposed locations and poor, dryish, or rocky soils. It grows well by the sea and needs full sun. No special care is required other than occasional light pruning to keep it shapely. It is propagated by summer cuttings and by seeds.

BUR. This word occurs as part of the common names of some plants as in bur-cucumber (*Sicyos angulatus*), bur gherkin (*Cucumis anguria*), bur-marigold (*Bidens*), and New Zealand bur (*Acaena microphylla*).

BURCHELLIA (Burch-éllia)—Buffalo Wood. The only species of *Burchellia* of the madder family RUBIACEAE is endemic to South Africa. Its name commemorates the English traveler and collector of plants William John Burchell, who died in 1863.

The buffalo wood (*B. bubalina* syn. *B. capensis*), 3 to 6 feet tall, is extremely hardwooded. It has opposite, evergreen short-stalked, pointed-broad-elliptic to obovate-oblong, leathery leaves about 4 inches long by 2 inches wide and heads of about seven orange-scarlet, cylindrical-urn-shaped, stalkless flowers approximately 1¼ inches long. They have five each sepals, perianth lobes (petals), and stamens, and a short style. The fruits are many-seeded berries.

Garden and Landscape Uses and Cultivation. Suitable only for frost-free subtrop-

ical climates, this is an attractive ornamental. It prospers in well-drained, sandy, peaty, not excessively dry soil in sun or light shade. Propagation is by seeds and by cuttings of firm, but not hard shoots planted in a greenhouse propagating bench with mild bottom heat.

Burchellia bubalina

BURDEKIN-PLUM is *Pleiogynium cerasiferum.*

BURDOCK. See Arctium.

BURKILLARA. This is the name of hybrid orchids the parents of which include *Aerides, Arachnis,* and *Vanda.*

BURL. Burls are more or less dome-shaped swellings or excrescences that develop naturally on the trunks of certain trees and may attain a diameter of up to about 2 feet. If sawed off and stood with the cut surface in a bowl of water, burls of redwood (*Sequoia sempervirens*) and those of some other trees sprout many young shoots and remain alive and decorative for many months. They do not, however, produce roots and so cannot be used as starts for new trees.

BURNET. See Sanguisorba and Poterium.

BURNING BUSH. As a vernacular name this is applied to *Chaenomeles, Dictamnus, Kochia scoparia trichophylla,* and some species of *Euonymus.*

BURRAGEARA. This is the name of multigeneric orchid hybrids having as parents *Cochlioda, Miltonia, Odontoglossum,* and *Oncidium.*

BURRAWANG is *Macrozamia communis.*

BURRO'S TAIL is *Sedum morganianum.*

BURSARIA (Bur-sària). All three species of shrubs and small trees of this genus of the pittosporum family PITTOSPORACEAE are endemic to Australia. They have spiny stems and alternate or clustered, undivided, small leaves. Their white flowers, in terminal racemes or panicles, are small. They have five each sepals, slender, spreading petals, and spreading stamens. The fruits, many-seeded capsules, are flat and kidney-shaped. The name, from the Latin *bursa*, a pouch, alludes to the fruits.

One species, **Bursaria spinosa** is planted as an ornamental in southern California and in areas with similar warm, dryish climates. A spiny, erect, evergreen shrub or small tree, it has alternate, dark green, oblong leaves ¾ inch to 1½ inches long, by ⅜ inch wide, and pretty, ¼-inch-wide, fragrant blooms profusely borne in summer in broad terminal panicles 4 to 6 inches long. The seed pods are reddish and decorative.

Garden Uses and Cultivation. This shrub is suitable for planting in sunny locations in well-drained soils. It is propagated by seeds and by cuttings of firm young shoots inserted in a greenhouse propagating bench.

BURSERA (Bur-sèra)—Gumbo Limbo or West-Indian-Birch, Elephant Tree or Torote. The genus *Bursera* of the bursera family BURSERACEAE consists of forty species of mostly tall trees containing balsamic resinous sap. Natives of warm parts of the Americas, they have alternate, pinnate, or undivided leaves, and small flowers in racemes or panicles in which bisexual and unisexual blooms are intermixed. Each has four or five sepals and petals. There are twice as many stamens as petals. The style is three-lobed. The fruits, plumlike in structure, are drupes, usually one-seeded. The name commemorates Joachim Burser, German botanist and physician, who died in 1649.

Gumbo limbo or West-Indian-birch (**B. simaruba** syn. **B. gummifera**), of Florida, Mexico, Central America, and the West Indies, is a broad-headed, deciduous tree 50 to 60 feet tall. It has smooth bark, with a coppery metallic sheen, that shreds in papery flakes. Confined to the ends of the branchlets, the pinnate leaves are 6 to 8 inches long and 4 to 8 inches wide. Each has three to five pairs of broad, pointed-ovate leaflets and a terminal one. Small and inconspicuous, the flowers appear before or with the new leaves. They are in racemes. The red rinds of the three-angled fruits enclose one, or rarely two, nutlets. A sweet, aromatic balsam, employed in varnishes, adhesives, and medicines, is a product of this species.

The elephant tree or torote (**B. microphylla**), a native of deserts in Arizona, California, and Mexico, is a shrub or tree 4 to 10 feet tall or sometimes taller. This kind has cherry-red, older branches and pinnate leaves up to 1½ inches in length, with seven to thirty-three about ¼-inch-long, oblong-linear leaflets. Solitary or in twos or threes, its little flowers, which come be-

fore the foliage, have five petals and ten stamens. The bark of this species is used for tanning and dyeing. Another desert species, **B. fagaroides**, of Mexico, is a short-trunked, deciduous, twiggy tree up to 25 feet tall, but frequently lower. This kind has straw-yellow, papery bark. Its leaves are pinnate. From 1 inch to 2½ inches long, they have five or seven elliptic leaflets, which turn yellow before they fall.

Bursera fagaroides

Garden and Landscape Uses and Cultivation. In Florida and other warm-climate regions, gumbo limbo prospers outdoors and succeeds without special attention in ordinary soil. It is propagated by seeds and cuttings and is remarkable because even large limbs employed as truncheon cuttings root readily when planted. The fruits are much appreciated by birds. The elephant tree and *B. fagaroides* are sometimes planted in gardens in warm desert regions and are also occasionally grown as bonsai-type container plants in indoor collections of succulents. They succeed under conditions similar to those under which they grow in the wild and are propagated by seeds.

BURSERACEAE—Bursera Family. Some 500 species of tropical trees and shrubs compose this family of dicotyledons. Some are sources of commercial balsams and resins. They have alternate or rarely opposite, usually pinnate, sometimes undivided leaves. The flowers, small and most often unisexual, have three to five sepals, separate or partly united, the same number of petals commonly separate, but sometimes joined at their bases, as many or more often twice as many stamens as petals, and one style. The fruits are drupes or capsules. Species of *Bursera* are sometimes cultivated for ornament.

BUSH. This word often forms part of colloquial names of plants. Examples are bush chinquapin (*Castanea sempervirens*), bush cinquefoil (*Potentilla fruticosa*), bush-clover (*Lespedeza*), bush-flame-pea (*Chorizema*), bush-honeysuckle (*Diervilla*), bush honeysuckle (*Lonicera*), bush morning glory (*Ipomoea leptophylla*), bush-pea (*Pultenaea*), bush-poppy (*Dendromecon*), and bush-rue (*Cneoridium*).

BUSH FRUITS. This is a collective name for all fruits commonly grown for human consumption and harvested from shrubs. The chief bush fruits are blackberries and other bramble-type fruits, and blueberries, currants, gooseberries, loganberries, and raspberries. They are dealt with in this Encyclopedia under their respective names.

BUSHMAN'S. This word is incorporated as part of the vernacular names of some plants including Bushman's candle (*Sarcocaulon spinosum*), Bushman's poison (*Acokanthera oppositifolia*), and Bushman's red-ash (*Alphitonia*).

BUTCHER'S-BROOM is *Ruscus aculeatus*. Climbing-butcher's-broom is *Semele androgyna*.

BUTEA (Bù-tea) — Flame-of-the-Forest or Bastard-Teak. Most notable of the thirty species of Asian trees and woody vines of the pea family LEGUMINOSAE that constitute *Butea* is the flame-of-the-forest or bastard-teak. In India it is common and in addition to being an ornamental, yields from incisions made in the bark an astringent gum called Bengal kino, used medicinally and for tanning. From its dried blooms a yellow or orange dye is obtained. Its inner bark provides fiber for calking boats and making cordage, and its root fibers are used to make sandals and rope. Its seeds are used in India as a vermifuge. It is one of the most important of the several trees on which the lac insect is cultivated for the production of shellac. The Hindus hold the flame-of-the-forest sacred to Brahma, and its wood is used for sacred utensils and in religious ceremonies. The genus name honors the Earl of Bute, who died in 1792.

The flame of the forest (**B. monosperma** syn. **B. frondosa**) is deciduous, upright, and usually 30 to 40 feet tall. Its trunk and branches characteristically are crooked. Its long-stalked leaves, of three leathery, blunt, somewhat lopsided, ovate or obovate leaflets, the central largest one up to 8 inches long, are covered on their undersides with fine-silky hairs, many of which fall as the leaves age. Borne in compact racemes along the branches, the flowers are pea-like in structure, about 2 inches long, and 1 inch or more in diameter. They have calyxes velvety brown on their outsides and silvery within, and petals bright orange-red on their insides and, because that color is partly hidden beneath a coating of fine white hairs, salmon-pink on their outsides. There are nine stamens joined and one separate. The fruits, which contain, at one end, a solitary seed, are flat pods, silvery at maturity, and 4 to 6 inches long by 1 inch to 1½ inches broad.

Garden and Landscape Uses and Cultivation. The flame-of-the-forest is a striking and handsome decorative tree for the humid tropics. It does well in brackish, wet, and even water-logged soils, especially those that contain an abundance of organic matter. It is propagated by seed.

BUTIA (Bù-tia)—Yatay Palm. Nine species of tropical and subtropical palms belong in *Butia* of the palm family PALMAE. All are natives of South America. The generic name is a corruption of a native one.

Butias are feather-leaved, bisexual, and have comparatively short, solitary trunks, covered, except sometimes toward their bases, with the remnants of the stalks of fallen leaves. The leaves have stalks with marginal spines and twenty-five to sixty pairs of usually glaucous or gray-green, pointed and bilobed, narrow leaflets. The flower clusters are axillary, each protected by a woody, persistent spathe up to about 3 feet long. They have slender branches with male flowers each with six stamens on their upper parts, and females each with three stigmas and a solitary pistil toward their bases.

The best known species is *B. capitata*, of Brazil, a variable kind represented by

Butia capitata

several botanical and horticultural varieties, and frequently planted in the warmer parts of the United States. Sometimes misidentified as *Cocos australis*, which is a synonym of *Arecastrum romanzoffianum australe*, it is hardy in parts of South Carolina and at San Francisco is recorded as having

withstood temperatures of 12°F. With a stout trunk occasionally up to 15 feet in height *B. capitata* has gracefully arching, durable leaves up to 6 feet long or longer that usually form a dense, but sometimes a rather loose, crown. Its flower spathes are 3 feet long or longer, 2 to 3 inches wide, and glabrous on their outsides. The yellow, pulpy, ovoid to ellipsoid fruits, about 1 inch long, contain one to three seeds. They can be used for making jelly. Varieties of this species are *B. c. odorata*, with broad-conical fruits; *B. c. nehrlingiana*, a larger plant with violet flowers and small red fruits; *B. c. pulposa*, with pulpy fruits 1¼ to 1½ inches across; *B. c. strictior*, with all its leaves erect; and *B. c. virescens*, with brilliant green leaves and succulent, fragrant small fruits, whitish or pinkish at their bases.

Other kinds that may be cultivated include these; *B. bonnetii*, of Brazil, has a trunk up to 4 feet long. Its flower spathes

Butia bonnetii

are hairless on their outsides. The fruits are about ¾ inch long. *B. eriospatha*, of southern Brazil, is up to 20 feet tall and has gracefully recurving leaves and flowering spathes conspicuously covered with brown, woolly hairs on their outsides. *B. yatay*, of Uraguay and Argentina, has a trunk up to 10 feet in height and 1½ feet in diameter that loses its old leafstalks below. Its fruits are up to 2 inches long and about 1 inch wide.

Garden and Landscape Uses. Yatay palms are excellent ornamentals, well adapted for use where space is limited and great height not desired. All are comparatively hardy and may be planted as single specimens or grouped with other plants. They gain height and size slowly and are attractive for cultivating in pots and tubs.

Cultivation. In the open these palms thrive best in fertile, moderately moist soil in full sun. In greenhouses they need shade from strong summer sun, a fairly humid atmosphere, and a minimum night temperature in winter of 50 to 55°F rising by day to 60 or 65°F. At other seasons,

both day and night temperatures may be higher. Water so that the soil is never dry, although in winter it may approach dryness. Well-rooted specimens benefit from dilute liquid fertilizer given biweekly from spring to fall. Propagation is by seeds sown in sandy, peaty soil in a temperature of 75 to 85°F. They take three to four months to germinate. For further cultural details see Palms.

BUTOMACEAE—Butomus or Flowering-Rush Family. This monocotyledonous family, considered by some authorities to include only the genus *Butomus*, and by some it and as many as five others, is accepted here in accordance with the latter concept. Native of the tropics of the Old World and the New World and of temperate regions in Europe and Asia, its members are aquatic or wet-ground herbaceous perennials with foliage all-basal or basal and on the stems. The flowers, solitary or in umbels with involucres (basal collars of bracts), have three each sepals and petals, six, nine, or rarely fewer or more stamens, or stamens and staminodes (nonfunctional stamens), and a whorl of three to many pistils. The fruits are of nearly separate follicles. By some botanists the butomus family is considered to contain the most primitive of all monocotyledons. Cultivated genera are *Butomus*, *Hydrocleys*, and *Limnocharis*.

BUTOMUS (Bù-tomus)—Flowering-Rush. A solitary species of the butomus family BUTOMACEAE, which is closely related to the water-plantain family ALISMACEAE, belongs here. It is native to Europe and Asia and is naturalized in parts of North America, having established itself quite thoroughly in the St. Lawrence River valley and to some extent along the shores of the Great Lakes. An inhabitant of shallow water and muddy pond and lake shores, the flowering-rush (*Butomus umbellatus*) has considerable merit as a garden plant. From the other genera of its family, *Limnocharis* and *Hydrocleys*, the flowering-rush differs in not having milky juice. The name is an ancient Greek one for some wet-soil plant with sharp-edged leaves.

B. umbellatus is a hardy deciduous perennial herbaceous plant with a stout rhizome and, when growing in bogs or shallow water, erect leaves; in deeper water the leaves are floating. They are linear, up to 3 feet in length, and under ½ inch in width. The erect stalks slightly exceed the leaves in length and terminate in loose umbels of up to 1-inch-wide upturned blooms, with individual stalks 2 to 4 inches long. There are numerous flowers in each cluster. They are pale lavender-pink. Each has three spreading sepals and three spreading petals. The former are petal-like in appearance and nearly as big as the true petals. There are nine stamens and six pistils,

Butomus umbellatus

joined at their bases. The fruits consist of six follicles.

Garden and Landscape Uses. The flowering-rush is an effective, easy-to-grow, and thoroughly hardy plant for sunny locations in bogs, wet streamsides and lakesides, and water gardens; it may be grown in containers in ornamental pools. It blooms most freely in muddy soil or shallow water; in deeper water it is more shy. The flowers come in summer.

Cultivation. Division in spring is a simple and effective procedure to obtain increase. Seeds can be used, but they must be fresh and not allowed to dry. Seeds are sown in containers of soil surfaced with about one-half inch sand and submerged so that the sand is an inch or two beneath the water. This plant is not particular as to soil, provided it is wet and passing rich. In the open the flowering-rush may remain undisturbed for years except, possibly, for curbing its spread. When accommodated in tubs or other containers it should be taken out, divided, and replanted every second or third year. The strong outer portions of the clumps are best for replanting.

BUTTER-AND-EGGS is *Linaria vulgaris*.

BUTTERBUR. See Petasites.

BUTTERCUP. See Ranunculus. The Bermuda-buttercup is *Oxalis pes-caprea*. The buttercup tree is *Cochlospermum vitifolium*.

BUTTERFLIES. These are the adults of a group of insects that pass through four distinct life phases. Their eggs hatch into caterpillars that change into pupae from which come butterflies, the females of which lay eggs that give rise to the next generation. Butterflies have much in common with moths. The chief difference is that the antennae of butterflies terminate in knobs, those of moths are either feathery or taper to slender points. Usually butterflies have more slender bodies than moths and generally when at rest their wings are in a vertical position, whereas those of moths commonly are held horizontally or are folded against the body. Also, butterflies do not fly at night except to flutter for short distances if disturbed. The great majority of moths are night fliers, but some fly by day. Butterflies sip nectar and are helpful in transferring pollen from flower to flower. They themselves do no harm to plants, but the caterpillars of many kinds, as for instance those of the common cabbage white butterfly do, and so it behooves gardeners to learn to recognize these harmful kinds and when practicable kill them by swatting. Best control, however, is had by destroying the larvae. See Caterpillars.

BUTTERFLY. As part of their common names the word butterfly is associated with these plants: butterfly bush (*Buddleia*), butterfly-dock (*Petasites hybridus*), butterfly flower (*Schizanthus* and *Bauhinia monandra*), butterfly orchid (*Oncidium kramerianum* and *O. papilio*), golden butterfly orchid (*Oncidium varicosum*), butterfly-pea (*Centrosema virginianum* and *Clitoria*), butterfly-tulip (*Calochortus*), and butterfly weed (*Asclepias tuberosa*).

BUTTERNUT is *Juglans cinerea*.

BUTTERWORT. See Pinguicula.

BUTTON. The word button appears as part of the colloquial names of a number of plants, including button bush (*Cephalanthus*), button cactus (*Epithelantha*), button fern (*Pellaea rotundifolia* and *Tectaria cicutaria*), button mangrove (*Conocarpus erectus*), button pink (*Dianthus latifolius*), button snakeroot (*Eryngium yuccifolium* and *Liatris*), and mescal button (*Lophophora williamsii*).

BUTTONBALL. See Platanus.

BUTTONWOOD. See Platanus and Conocarpus.

BUXACEAE—Boxwood Family. Some plants highly esteemed as ornamentals are included in this family of four genera and approximately 100 species of dicotyledons. The group has a wide natural distribution and includes evergreen trees and shrubs and evergreen and deciduous herbaceous perennials. Its best known examples are boxwoods and the Japanese spurge (*Pachysandra*). The highly regarded lumber of boxwood is used commercially.

The members of this family characteristically have opposite or less commonly alternate, undivided, leathery leaves and small, unisexual, symmetrical flowers without corollas and sometimes lacking calyxes. When present, calyxes are generally of four sepals, sometimes four- to twelvecleft. The males typically have four stamens and sometimes a rudimentary pistil. Female blooms, fewer than the males and occasionally solitary, have two to four styles, separate or united at their bases and wide-spreading. The fruits, capsules or berry-like, contain shining, black seeds. Cultivated genera are *Buxus*, *Pachysandra*, *Sarcococca*, and *Simmondsia*.

BUXUS (Búx-us)—Boxwood, Box. The name *Buxus* is an ancient Latin one. The genus it identifies is one of four that comprise the box family BUXACEAE. It is widely distributed in temperate Europe and Asia, Africa, Malaya, the Philippine Islands, Central America, the West Indies, and South Africa. There are thirty-five species or more.

Boxwoods are evergreen trees and shrubs with opposite, short-stalked, undivided, leathery leaves. The tiny petal-less flowers are of no ornamental merit. They are in axillary or terminal clusters, each usually consisting of one or two females surrounded by several males. The females have six, the males four, sepals. The males have four stamens, the females three pistils. The fruits are approximately spherical, three-horned capsules that explode when ripe to release the glossy black seeds, six from each capsule.

As ornamentals boxwoods rank highly. Esteemed above all other kinds as a landscape feature, English boxwood was brought to the Virginia colonies by the early settlers and planted about their homes. It prospered amazingly, and fine specimens are prominent in many gardens in the upper south. Hard, bony wood of various species is highly prized for engraving blocks, drafting and mathematical tools and musical instruments, turnery, tobacco pipes, inlay work, and furniture. It is durable and fine-grained. The species chiefly used for these purposes are *B. sempervirens*, *B. wallichiana*, *B. microphylla japonica*, and *B. capensis*, the last a native of South Africa not commonly cultivated.

English boxwood (**B. sempervirens**) is a shrub or tree up to about 25 feet or rarely 35 feet high in cultivation. Native specimens in the Caucasus are reported to attain much greater heights. This species is indigenous to Europe, North Africa, and western Asia. One of the best known natural stands is at Boxhill near London, England. There it prospers and reproduces well, in chalky soil. In eastern North America it is reliably hardy without protection about as far north as Philadelphia, Pa.

Characteristics of English boxwood are its crowded branches and branchlets and broad-elliptic, lance-shaped, roundish to

Buxus sempervirens arborescens, as a tall screen

obovate, glossy, smooth leaves under ½ inch wide and from ½ to 1½ inches long. Their undersides are paler than their upper sides. A tree form known as *B. s. arborescens* is in the south called American boxwood, a peculiarly unsuitable designation for a species native only in the Old World. The kinds called English boxwood in the south are more compact varieties that form beautiful billowy mounds of green foliage and add character to many an old garden. Fine specimens are to be seen at Williamsburg, Virginia.

Edging box (*B. s. suffruticosa*) rarely exceeds 3 feet in height, but if left untrimmed it sometimes becomes 4 or 5 feet tall. This is one of the most useful varieties. It sends shoots abundantly from its base. Much esteemed for edging flower beds and paths, by repeated shearing, it can be maintained as a neat hedge up to 1 foot high. Edging box has small, obovate leaves and usually flowers only at the ends of its branches. Its origin is unknown, but it has certainly been cultivated for centuries. It was a favorite in Elizabethan knot gardens.

Other varieties of English boxwood are the following: *B. s. angustifolia* has long, narrow leaves. *B. s. argenteo-variegata* has leaves edged with white. *B. s. aureo-variegata* has leaves that are yellow or variegated with yellow. *B. s. bullata* has broad, wrinkled leaves. *B. s. handsworthiensis* has large, broad-ovate leaves. *B. s. marginata* has yellow-margined leaves. *B. s. myrtifolia*, a low variety, has narrow leaves. *B. s. pyramidata* is an upright, pyramidal bush. *B. s. rosmarinifolia*, a low shrub, has narrow leaves with rolled-back edges. *B. s. rotundifolia* has large, almost round leaves.

Hardiest boxwoods are **B. microphylla** and its varieties, of which *B. m. koreana*, which often does not exceed 1½ feet in height, is one of the most cold resistant. This variety has finely-downy young stems and leafstalks and its midrib above is also hairy. There seems to be at least two forms in cultivation, one low, spreading, and tending to become open in the center as it ages (this sort needs a little shade otherwise its foliage is likely to bronze badly in winter), and another, more erect and sometimes 3 to 4 feet tall. Typical *B. microphylla* differs from *B. m. koreana* in being

Buxus sempervirens

Buxus sempervirens suffruticosa, edging formal beds

The plant commonly grown as **B. harlandii** is not that species but is apparently a variety of *B. microphylla*, probably a low form of *B. m. sinica*. The Chinese species to which the name *B. harlandii* rightly belongs seems not to be in cultivation. The plant known in gardens as *B. harlandii* is 2 to 3 feet tall and has leaves ½ to 1¼ inches long. Not hardy in the north, it succeeds in hot, dry climates better than most boxwoods. A rare native of China, hardy at least as far north as New Jersey, **B. bodinieri** is an attractive shrub about 4 feet tall. It has oblanceolate leaves approximately 1½ inches long, some of which are slightly notched at their apexes.

Buxus bodinieri

quite glabrous. It ordinarily is not more than 3 feet in height. An especially fine and quite hardy boxwood, *B. m. japonica* has splendid dark green foliage and forms a handsome, rounded bush about 6 feet tall. This thrives especially well in California and other warm-climate areas. Good examples are to be seen at the Gray's Summit Arboretum of the Missouri Botanical Garden. The species *B. microphylla* and its varieties are hardy at the Arnold Arboretum, near Boston, Massachusetts.

Other varieties of *B. microphylla* include *B. m. angustifolia* has very narrow leaves. *B. m. aurea* has yellowish foliage. *B. m. latifolia* has broader leaves than the type. *B. m. rotundifolia* has large, bluish-green, rounded leaves. *B. m. sinica* has leaves that are ovate-lanceolate to orbicular. Its twigs, at first downy, are later smooth. In recent years many new clones of *B. microphylla* as well as other kinds have been selected by growers and have been propagated and given horticultural names. One such is *B. m.* 'Kingsville'. Descriptions of these are published in the Bulletin of the American Boxwood Society.

Buxus bodinieri (foliage)

Even less hardy than English boxwood are *B. balearica* of Spain and the Balearic Islands and the Himalayan boxwood (*B. wallichiana*) of the Himalayas. These kinds are suitable for mild climates only. Attaining a maximum height of about 60 feet, but usually considerably lower even in its na-

Buxus microphylla japonica, at Gray's Summit Arboretum, Missouri

Buxus microphylla 'Kingsville'

tive lands, *B. balearica* has roundish-oval leaves ¾ inch to 1½ inches long by about one-half as wide. They are less glossy than those of English boxwood. In southern Europe this is used in gardens as is the English boxwood further north. In its native state growing up to 30 feet in height, but much lower in cultivation, *B. wallichiana* has very downy shoots and narrow leaves 1 inch to 2½ inches long by ¼ to ⅝ inch wide that are not as glossy as those of English boxwood and are hairy at their bases. Its leafstalks are also downy.

Garden and Landscape Uses. Few evergreen shrubs and small trees excel the English boxwood and its varieties for choiceness and dignity. Properly placed they bring to gardens Old World and Colonial American charm. They are redolent of past centuries. As accents in the landscape they are superb either standing free or flanking a doorway or complementing other architectural features, and they can also be used to good effect as hedges. The low-growing edging box is unsurpassed as a bordering shrub in many locations. Other boxwoods can be used as are English boxwoods.

Cultivation. In climates to their liking boxwoods are not difficult to grow. They thrive in almost any well-drained soil including limestone ones. A little shade, at least for part of the day, is helpful, but if the location is not excessively dry they prosper in full sun. They may be transplanted with every expectation of success even when very big.

Boxwoods stand shearing and pruning well and may be kept to a desired size or shape by such regular attentions. Spring, just before new growth begins, is the preferred time for trimming. Specimens that have been neglected and that have become scraggly and unshapely can be renovated by severe cutting back in late winter or early spring followed by the application of

a complete fertilizer and attention to watering during dry weather in the summer following. If suffering from disease or pest, take suitable measures at appropriate times to control these.

Hedges of English boxwood

It is well to keep boxwoods mulched with compost, well-rotted manure, peat moss, or other suitable organic matter. They are surface-rooters and deep cultivation of the soil near them is harmful. Where boxwoods survive in winters severe enough to "burn" their foliage or in other way damage them, protect them from strong winter sun and sweeping winds with screens of burlap or other suitable material.

Propagation is easy by cuttings of mature shoots taken in late summer or early fall and planted in a propagating bed in a cool greenhouse or cold frame or in mild climates in a shady place outdoors. Cuttings of all kinds except Himalayan boxwood root readily. Cuttings of the Himalayan boxwood are less sure to root. Edging box may be increased by digging up plants, dividing them, and replanting the divisions.

Protecting boxwood against winter damage

Winter damage: (a) Foliage "burned" (browned)

(b) Bark killed

An informal border of English boxwood

Pests and Diseases. Boxwoods are subject to a number of pests and diseases and in climates a little too cold for their comfort to injury by winter-kill and sun scald. Among common insect pests are mites, leaf miners, scales, webworms, mealybugs, and the boxwood psyllid, a sucking insect that causes the tip leaves to cup. Nematodes may invade the roots and produce characteristic stunted, witch's-broom-like clusters of roots. The chief diseases are canker, leaf blight, leaf spots, and root rot.

BYBLIDACEAE. The characteristics of this family are those of its only genus, *Byblis*.

BYBLIS (Býb-lis). Australian *Byblis* consists of two species of carnivorous plants comprising the byblis family BYBLIDACEAE. Superficially the genus resembles the sundew family DROSERACEAE, but botanists are uncertain of its affinities. Some are of the opinion that it should be included in the bladderwort family LENTIBULARIACEAE, and strangely, it seems to be remotely related to the pittosporum family PITTOSPORACEAE. The name is of classical origin. It commemorates Byblis, the daughter of Miletus.

So far as is known the only species that has been cultivated in the United States is **B. gigantea,** which was first flowered at Longwood Gardens, Kennett Square, Pennsylvania from seed collected near Perth in 1958–59. This plant closely resembles in growth the Portuguese-sundew (*Drosophyllum lusitanicum*), but unlike it, its long, slender, sticky-glandular leaves do not, after they die, form a skirt of dried foliage around the stems of mature plants. Nor do its young leaves uncoil in the fiddle-head fashion of young fern fronds, as do those of the Portuguese-sundew. Yet another easily observed difference is that the flow-

Rooted cuttings of English boxwood

Byblis gigantea

ers of *B. gigantea* are of various shades of rose-purple, those of *Drosophyllum* are clear sulfur-yellow. As seen in cultivation the plants are under 1 foot tall and have many, mostly erect, very slender leaves furnished along their lengths with hairlike, stalked glands tipped with glistening droplets of a clear viscous fluid that serves to attract and entrap unwary insects. The flowers, which under cultivation have developed within four or five months from seed sowing, are on slender, branching stems. Each has five sepals, five spreading petals, five stamens, a slender style, and measures nearly 1½ inches across. They last for a few days and several may be expanded on a plant at the same time. The fruits are capsules. In its native home *B. gigantea* grows in "sandy swampy places" and in "better drained parts of such swamps" in full sun.

Garden Uses and Cultivation. As a garden plant this is a rare collectors' item. Under cultivation it thrives in acidic, peaty soil and in milled sphagnum moss. It resents root disturbance, and this must be avoided so far as possible when transplanting or repotting. A sunny location in a humid greenhouse where a winter night temperature of 55°F is maintained seems to be satisfactory, but excellent specimens were observed at the Munich Botanic Garden in Germany in full bloom in May in a greenhouse where the winter night temperature was maintained at 65°F. These plants were afforded some shade from strong, direct sun. The use of rainwater or other water that does not have a high content of lime or other solutes is recommended. As with all carnivorous plants the use of insecticides, miticides, and other sprays should be avoided. The other species of the genus, *B. liniflora* is described as having blue flowers.

C

CABBAGE. The name of the familiar vegetable, discussed in the next entry, forms part of the colloquial names of several unrelated plants including these: Australian cabbage palm (*Livistonia australis*), cabbage palm (*Euterpe oleracea* and *Roystonea oleracea*), cabbage palmetto (*Sabal palmetto*), cabbage rose (*Rosa centifolia*), cabbage tree (*Andira inermis* and *Cordyline australis*), deer-cabbage (*Lupinus diffusus*), St. Patrick's-cabbage (*Saxifraga umbrosa*), skunk-cabbage (*Symplocarpus foetidus* and *Veratrum californicum*), and yellow-skunk-cabbage (*Lysichiton americanum*).

CABBAGE. Probably the most popular leaf vegetable, cabbage is esteemed for eating cooked in various ways, fermented as sauerkraut, raw in coleslaw, and red cabbage, for pickling. Its many varieties, horticultural developments of Old World *Brassica oleracea* of the mustard family CRUCIFERAE are grouped botanically as *B. o. capitata*. They are easy to raise. By selecting appropriate varieties and different sowing dates, harvests can be had in many sections from early summer to late fall, and where winters are mild, in winter and spring also. Most varieties do not occupy the land for the entire season. Early crops may be succeeded by late-sown turnips or

Cabbage nearing maturity

other quick-maturing successors, late ones may follow lettuce, peas, or other early-harvested crops. For the entirely different vegetable called Chinese cabbage, see Chinese Cabbage.

Soil for cabbage may be any of various types so long as it is well-drained and fertile. Land capable of producing good corn grows good cabbages. It may be from slightly acid to slightly alkaline, although too much acidity favors the development of club root disease. In preparing soil for planting, spade, rototill, or plow deeply and mix in plenty of humus-forming material such as compost, manure, or a green manure crop, supplemented by a generous dressing of a complete garden fertilizer rich in nitrogen. This is especially necessary to hasten the growth of early crops.

A flat of cabbage plants ready for transplanting

Sow in outdoor seedbeds, or for early harvests, in pots or flats indoors or in a cold frame. Seedlings from outdoor sowings are transplanted to their growing stations, sunny locations outdoors, when a few inches high and easy to handle. Those raised indoors and in frames are transplanted 2 to 3 inches apart in flats or cold frames, and later, when weather permits, are hardened off and transferred to the

open garden. Set the newly-sown pots or flats to germinate in a temperature of about 60°F. Grow the seedlings in full sun where the temperature at night is 50°F, that by day five to fifteen degrees higher depending upon how bright the day. Too high temperatures, shade, and overcrowding result in weak, lanky plants instead of desirable, short, stocky ones.

Plant as early as the ground is workable in spring (light frost will not harm properly-hardened cabbage plants) until as late in summer as will permit the crop to mature before cessation of growth or the onset of hard freezing weather. In mild climates, still later plantings gives crops that continue to grow through the winter, maturing then or later. Spacing depends upon variety. Small-headed kinds may be set at as little distances as 1¼ feet between individuals in rows of 2 feet. Varieties with larger heads need up to 2½ feet between the rows and 2 feet between individuals in the rows. Set the young plants an inch or two deeper than they were in the seedbed, flats, or cold frames, up to their first true leaves. If the ground is dryish, water the plants thoroughly as soon as they are planted.

From now on bend every effort to keep the crop growing without check. This makes for good size and succulence. If after the heads form a severe check occurs, as a result perhaps of the soil becoming dry for a period, and then following irrigation, rain, or fertilizing, growth resumes, the heads are likely to split. Continuous growth is promoted by frequent shallow cultivation, which destroys weeds and aerates the soil, by watering generously at five- to seven-day intervals during dry periods, and by applying when the plants are about half grown, or to spring-set plants earlier and again when they are half developed, a light dressing of nitrate of soda, urea, or other fertilizer that quickly supplies available nitrogen.

Harvesting is delayed until the heads are fully grown and quite firm or hard, but before they burst, except that some or all

Feeling to test if heads are firm enough to harvest

of the earliest crop may be taken somewhat before this stage is reached to satisfy the need for fresh garden greens. Harvesting is done by slicing the heads off the stalks with a heavy knife an inch or two below their bases.

For winter storage select varieties such as Danish ballhead types, especially adapted for the purpose. These have tight, solid heads that keep well, which is not true of all cabbages, for instance, early varieties and flat, drumhead types and the crinkly-leaved types called savoys. Storage may be in root cellars or similar cool, humid places not subject to severe freezing, but kept not more than a few degrees above 32°F, or in outdoor pits covered with straw and a layer of soil. Heads for storing are usually harvested by pulling the plants up intact rather than decapitating. In storage they are stood roots upward to prevent water collecting in the heads.

Varieties of cabbage are numerous. Make selections adapted for specific seasons, uses, and best suited to local conditions. Your Cooperative Extension Agent can advise you. If your land is infected with the disease called yellows, plant only yellows-resistant varieties. These are indicated in seedsmen's catalogs. Among excellent early kinds are 'Early Jersey', 'Early Money', 'Golden Acre', and 'Wakefield'. Good mid-season kinds include 'Copenhagen Market', 'Early Flat Dutch', and 'Glory of Enkhousen'. Late varieties are 'Danish Ballhead', 'Drumhead Savoy', 'Marvin's Savoy', 'Penn State Ballhead', and 'Wisconsin All Season'. Favorite red cabbages are 'Mammoth', 'Red Acre', 'Red Dutch', and 'Red Rock'.

Diseases and pests are fairly numerous and must be promptly and effectively combatted. Information of local application about these is obtainable from Cooperative Extension Agents. The chief diseases against which precautions must be taken are bacterial black rot, which chiefly affects seedlings, club root, yellows (a fungus disease that causes yellowing of the foliage), and a physiological condition called tip burn, the result of excessively acid soil or an imbalance between the amounts of available potash and phosphorus. The chief pests are aphids, caterpillars, harlequin bugs, and that serious pest of all brassica vegetables, root maggots.

CABOMBA (Cab-ómba)—Fanwort, Washington Plant or Fish-Grass. These plants differ greatly in appearance from water-lilies, to which they are related. True, they are aquatics, but except in technical botanical details they give no clear evidence of this kinship. Nevertheless, they are included in the water-lily family NYMPHAEACEAE. The name Cabomba is an aboriginal South American one. There are about seven species of Cabomba, mostly natives of the warmer parts of the Americas, but one extends in the wild as far north as New Jersey and Michigan. They are submersed, slender-stemmed, branching plants with their under-water parts covered with a thin layer of jelly. Their under-water leaves are opposite or whorled (in circles of three or more) and are divided palmately (in hand-fashion) into many slender segments. The floating leaves are undivided and often alternate. The small flowers have three each sepals and petals, which are similar, and three to six stamens.

Commonly grown in aquariums and garden pools, the only species ordinarily cultivated is the Washington plant or fish-grass (C. caroliniana). This familiar native of ponds and slow streams from New Jersey to Ohio, Michigan, Florida, and Texas, has stems 3 to 6 feet long. Its under-water leaves have stalks up to 1 inch long or longer and much dissected blades rounded in outline and 1 inch to 2 inches wide. There are few floating leaves; they are narrowly-elliptic, usually constricted at their middles where the leafstalk is joined to the blade, and often are notched at one end. They are about ¾ inch long. Usually their undersides and stalks are pubescent. The few creamy flowers, about ½ inch in diameter, are produced from the upper leaf axils. They have usually pubescent stalks 1½ to 4 inches long, and six stamens. Its leathery flask-shaped fruits are usually three-seeded. There is a reddish-leaved variety, C. c. rosaefolia.

Garden Uses and Cultivation. The chief uses of this plant are to provide oxygen to and shelter for fish in aquariums and pools. It is commonly sold by purveyors of aquarium supplies in bunches of several shoots with their bases wrapped with a strip of lead or other weighting material. Unless planted in soil such bunches remain attractive and effective for only a month or two; they then must be replaced. In pools with a soil bottom and in containers of soil in pools the shoots root readily if planted in earth a foot or two beneath the surface. Under favorable conditions they grow vigorously. The water must be non-alkaline. A temperature of 55 to 70°F is most satisfactory for growth. This plant will not stand freezing; if not thus exposed, it is hardy about as far north as Philadelphia. These plants are propagated by breaking off pieces of stem and planting them in soil beneath water.

CACAO is Theobroma cacao.

CACCINIA (Cac-cínia). Temperate Asian herbaceous perennials to the number of six species belong in Caccinia of the borage family BORAGINACEAE. The name commemorates Mateo Caccini of Florence, Italy, a seventeenth-century cultivator of rare plants. Caccinias are allied to borage (Borago). They have alternate leaves, and flowers with five-parted calyxes, a slender tubed corolla with five spreading lobes (petals), five unequal fertile stamens, and one style. The fruits are of four seedlike nutlets.

The only kind most likely to be cultivated is C. macranthera crassifolia (syn. C. glauca). This native from Armenia to Afghanistan is leafy and 1 foot to 3 feet tall. It can be expected to be hardy in the north. Its more or less glaucous leaves, up to 10 inches long by nearly 5 inches wide, are linear, lanceolate, or oblong. The lower ones are stalked, those above stalkless. In panicle-like arrangements, terminal or from the leaf axils, the numerous 1-inch-wide flowers are displayed. They are violet-blue, changing to red as they age, and

Caccinia macranthera crassifolia

have corolla tubes not longer than the calyx. From *C. m. crassifolia*, typical *C. macranthera*, which is not known in cultivation, differs in being dwarfer and having its flowers in broader, panicle-like arrangements. Possibly to be found in botanic gardens, *C. strigosa*, native of Iran, is a glaucous herbaceous perennial 1 foot to 2 feet tall. It has oblong to obovate leaves 4 to 6 inches long and bristly-hairy along the midribs and margins. In terminal panicles, the blue flowers have a corolla with a tube longer than the calyx.

Caccinia strigosa

Garden and Landscape Uses and Cultivation. These are as those for perennial kinds of *Cynoglossum*.

CACOUCIA is *Combretum cacoucia*.

CACTACEAE—Cactus Family. All true cactuses are contained in this family of dicotyledons. Many succulent plants the botanically indiscriminating are apt to identify as "cactuses" belong elsewhere, notably in AIZOACEAE, AMARYLLIDACEAE, LILIACEAE, and STAPELIACEAE. Great diversity of opinion exists among botanists as to the number of genera composing the CACTACEAE, liberals opting for more than 200 genera, conservatives for many fewer. The number

of species involved is variously estimated at from about 800 to nearly 2,000.

Except perhaps for a very few species of *Rhipsalis* that occur spontaneously in West Africa and Ceylon, but which may be descendants of sorts introduced there long ago from the New World, the cactus family is native only in the Americas. Many of its members are much esteemed ornamentals, in dry regions for outdoor landscaping, everywhere as indoor plants. There is a very considerable world-wide interest in growing cactuses as a hobby. The edible fruits of some sorts, notably prickly-pears, are marketed commercially.

Cactuses are fleshy perennials with herbaceous or woody stems that generally contain chlorophyll and function in place of leaves, which in most cactuses are reduced to scalelike size or are completely absent. Only in *Pereskia* and *Pereskiopsis* do evident, functional leaves occur.

In size cactuses range from very small to huge tree types, such as the sahuaro. Usually their sap is watery, in a few kinds milky. The branched or branchless stems or plant bodies may be flattened and more or less leaflike, as in many opuntias, cylindrical, ovoid or spherical, ribbed, or with lumpy protrusions called tubercles. They are jointed or jointless. The leaves or scales representing leaves are alternate. A development peculiar to plants of this family are areoles, small specialized areas, generally padlike, from which usually sprout spines, sometimes bristles or glochids, and from which the flowers arise. The latter, solitary or clustered and often colorful and showy, are symmetrical or asymmetrical, and with few exceptions, bisexual. Sepals and petals, commonly numerous, gradually integrate from outside to inside of the bloom. There are many stamens arranged in groups or spirally, and except in *Pereskia* where they are as many as the carpels, one style capped with as many radiating stigmas as there are carpels. The fruits, technically berries, range from small to pear-sized.

Genera of the *Cactaceae* dealt with separately in the Encyclopedia include *Acanthocalycium, Acanthocereus, Acantholobivia, Acanthorhipsalis, Ancistrocactus, Aporocactus, Arequipa, Ariocarpus, Armatocereus, Arrojadoa, Arthrocereus, Astrophytum, Austrocactus, Austrocephalocereus, Austrocylindropuntia, Aylostera, Aztekium, Azureocereus, Backebergia, Bartschella, Blossfeldia, Bolivicereus, Borzicactus, Brasilicactus, Browningia, Carnegiea, Cephalocereus, Cereus, Chamaecereus, Chiapasia, Cleistocactus, Cochemiea, Coleocephalocereus, Coloradoa, Consolea, Copiapoa, Corryocactus, Coryphantha, Craspedia, Cryptocereus, Deamia, Dendrocereus, Denmoza, Discocactus, Disocactus, Dolichothele, Eccremocactus, Echinocactus, Echinocereus, Echinofossulocactus, Echinomastus, Echinopsis, Encephalocarpus, Epiphyllanthus, Epiphyllum, Epithelantha, Erdisia, Eriocactus, Eriocereus, Eriosyce, Erythrorhipsalis, Esco-*

baria, Escontria, Espostoa, Eulychnia, Facheiroa, Ferocactus, Frailea, Glandulicactus, Grusonia, Gymnocactus, Gymnocalycium, Gymnocereus, Haageocereus, Hamatocactus, Harrisia, Haseltonia, Hatiora, Heliabravoa, Helianthocereus, Heliaporus, Heliocereus, Hertrichocereus, Homalocephala, Horridocactus, Hylocereus, Islaya, Isolatocereus, Krainzia, Lemaireocereus, Lepismium, Leptocereus, Leuchtenbergia, Lobivia, Lophocereus, Lophophora, Loxanthocereus, Machaerocereus, Maihuenia, Mamillopsis, Mammillaria, Marginatocereus, Marshallocereus, Matucana, Mediocactus, Mediolobivia, Melocactus, Micranthocereus, Mila, Monvillea, Morangaya, Morawetzia, Myrtillocactus, Neobesseya, Neobuxbaumia, Neochilenia, Neodawsonia, Neogomesia, Neolloydia, Neoporteria, Neoraimondia, Neowerdermannia, Nopalea, Nopalxochia, Notocactus, Nyctocereus, Obregonia, Opuntia, Oreocereus, Oroya, Pachgerocereus, Pachycereus, Parodia, Pediocactus, Pelecyphora, Peniocereus, Pereskia, Pereskiopsis, Pfeiffera, Phellosperma, Pilosocereus, Polaskia, Porfiria, Pseudoespostoa, Pseudorhipsalis, Pterocactus, Pyrrhocactus, Quiabentia, Rathbunia, Rebutia, Rhipsalidopsis, Rhipsalis, Ritterocereus, Rooksbya, Roseocactus, Roseocereus, Schlumbergera, Sclerocactus, Selenicereus, Seticereus, Solisia, Stenocereus, Stephanocereus, Stetsonia, Strombocactus, Strophocactus, Submatucana, Tacinga, Tephrocactus, Thelocactus, Thrixanthocereus, Trichocereus, Turbinicarpus, Weberocereus, Weingartia, Werckleocereus, Wigginsia, Wilcoxia, Wilmattea, Wittia, and *Zehntnerella.*

CACTUSES. Surprising perhaps to readers accustomed to the use of cacti as the plural of cactus, cactuses is the correct English form. There is nothing wrong with using the Latin cacti, but then neither is there with the use of croci as the plural of crocus, yet most people prefer crocuses. Many people have only a vague idea of what constitutes a cactus. They are likely to apply the term to any of a wide variety of fleshy desert plants botanically not even closely related to cactuses. To be a cactus a plant must be a member of the botanical family CACTACEAE, and to be so classified it must have a combination of characteristics including stem features and details of flower and fruit structure not possessed by any other plants. Merely because a plant is fat and succulent and to the untrained eye "looks like a cactus" is no sure indication that it is a cactus, anymore than a whale is a fish because it has much the outward appearance of being one.

To be a cactus a plant must belong to the great major division of botanical classification called dicotyledons. When its seeds germinate they produce two seed leaves (primary leaves). This immediately eliminates from consideration as cactuses such plants as agaves, aloes, and yuccas, all of which have only one seed leaf and belong to the botanical group called monocotyledons. So far as vegetative growth goes, there is only one easily observable feature that sets cactuses apart from all other plants. That is the possession of areoles. Areoles are small, specialized spotlike areas on the stem from which issue all spines and flowers produced. Their surfaces differ from the surrounding tissues in being rough, uneven, hard, and of a different color, and are often covered with woolly hair ranging in color from white to nearly

Cactuses (*Opuntias*) in the Mojave Desert

An exhibit of cactuses at Southport Flower Show, England

Cactuses at The New York Botanical Garden

The spines of cactuses are typically clustered

Cactus flower showing inferior ovary

black. The spines of cactuses, nearly always highly visible, are in clusters, sometimes with one spine much larger and more prominent than the others so that at a hasty glance they may appear to be solitary, but in fact are never so. The cluster arrangement of spines is not found in any other plants that could conceivably be mistaken for cactuses. The spines of most such are solitary, those of the cactus-like euphorbias solitary or in pairs. For other identifying features of cactuses one must look at the flowers. Most cactuses are without obvious leaves, their places being taken by minute, deciduous, scale-like ones, but *Pereskia* and *Pereskiopsis* have sizeable persistent leaves.

Blooms of cactuses have the ovary below the perianth parts, in botanical terminology it is inferior. The many perianth parts are not as they are in most flowers clearly separated into a calyx and corolla, into sepals and petals. Instead, they consist of several series, of which the inner ones, which are clearly petals, gradually and successively give way to more sepal-like ones outward and downward and finally intergrade with more or less leafy scales. Throughout this Encyclopedia the perianth parts for convenience are generally referred to as petals. The stamens are many to very numerous. The single style terminates in several stigmas. The fruits are usually fleshy, sometimes dry, berries.

The vast majority of cactuses inhabit deserts and semideserts but a few, such as eastern North American *Opuntia*, opt for moister habitats. The vast majority grow in the ground, but a sizable group, including *Epiphyllum*, *Rhipsalidopsis*, *Rhipsalis*, and *Schlumbergera*, perch on trees in the manner of many bromeliads and orchids as epiphytes (plants that, unlike parasites, take no nourishment from the trees on which they live). One is apt to think of cactuses as sun-lovers. Most are, but the tree-perchers and even some ground species that inhabit desert regions need shade from strong sun. The latter are kinds that in the wild favor stations where they receive shade from nearby bushes or rocks.

Cactuses are all natives of the Americas except possibly a few species of tree-perching *Rhipsalis* of Africa, the Mascarine Islands, and Ceylon. It has never been satisfactorily established whether these non-Americans are truly natives of the regions they inhabit or are the descendents of plants introduced perhaps inadvertently, at some time in the dim past by man from the Americas. It is certain that other kinds of cactuses, such as the prickly-pears now abundant in Australia, the Mediterranean region, and some other warm, dry regions, are comparatively recent immigrants from

Pereskias are cactuses with normal foliage leaves

Desert cactuses: (a) *Pachycereus*

Epiphytic cactuses: (a) *Epiphyllum*

(b) *Mammillaria*

(b) *Rhipsalis*

(c) *Opuntia*

(c) *Schlumbergera*

the New World. They were unknown to Europeans until after the discovery of America. Book illustrations of biblical scenes and movies portraying activities earlier than the sixteenth century in which cactuses are shown, as they not infrequently are, are clearly in error.

Strange plants wonderously adapted to their environments, cactuses are often amazingly symmetrical, not uncommonly beautiful, occasionally grotesque. Even the oddest are likely to be lovely in bloom. The fruits of some are edible, those of the common prickly-pear being offered in such sophisticated markets as those of New York City and other great urban areas.

The classification of cactuses into genera and species is much confused. Regrettably there is not available any generally accepted authoritative taxonomic interpretation of the family as a whole. In the latest complete monograph (1958), the German Backeberg undoubtedly splits the group into too many genera and far too many species and lesser units, as in all probability did his predecessors the Americans Britton and Rose (1919), although they were more conservative than Backeberg.

The modern tendency as exemplified by Benson, Kimnach, and Weniger in America and Hunt in England is to recognize fewer genera and species, to combine many of those of Backeberg and other recent authors and some of those of Britton and Rose into larger units. If not carried too far this is commendable. But none of the "lumpers," as confirmed splitters of genera somewhat irrelevantly call them, has treated the family as a whole at the species level. They have restricted their studies and interpretations, as Benson has, to limited geographical regions, as Kimnach has to a few genera, or as Hunt has in considering the family as a whole only as to genera. As a result of this, South American, Central American, and Mexican cactuses are especially difficult to interpret conservatively.

In horticulture the general practice has been to accept at least on a tentative basis the finer generic and specific splits and indeed until a more conservative monographer than Backeberg treats the family in its entirety there is little else that anyone concerned with a wide representation of the group can do. In most commercial and amateur cactus collections this is the procedure followed and in the main, without representing firm personal convictions and with full knowledge that it will not please all botanists, this is the one adopted in this Encyclopedia. For the genera of cactuses presented in this Encyclopedia see Cactaceae.

Many colloquial names are used for different sorts of cactuses, among the more common are these: agave cactus (*Leuchtenbergia principis*), ball cactus (*Notocactus*), barrel cactus (*Echinocactus* and *Ferocactus*), beavertail cactus (*Opuntia basilaris*), bishop's cap cactus (*Astrophytum myriostigma*), boxing glove cactus (*Opuntia fulgia mamillata*) bunnyears cactus (*Opuntia microdasys*), button cactus (*Epithelantha*), cardon (*Pachycereus pringlei*), chin cactus (*Gymnocalycium*), cholla (*Opuntia*), Christmas cactus (*Schlumbergera bridgesii*), cinnamon cactus (*Opuntia microdasys rufida*), crab cactus (*Schlumbergera truncacta*), creeping devil (*Machaerocereus eruca*), dahlia cactus (*Wilcoxia poselgeri*), deerhorn cactus or desert night-blooming-cereus (*Peniocereus greggii*), desert Christmas cactus (*Opuntia leptocaulis*), diamond cholla (*Opuntia ramosissima*), dollar cactus (*Opuntia violacea santa-rita*), eagle claws cactus (*Echinocactus horizonthalonius*), early bloomer cactus (*Echinomastus intertextus*), Easter cactus (*Rhipsalidopsis gaertneri*), feather ball cactus (*Mammillaria plumosa*), fishhook cactus (*Ancistrocactus* and *Mammillaria*), flapjack cactus (*Opuntia violacea gosseliniana*), golden barrel cactus (*Echinocactus grusonii*), golden lace cactus (*Mammillaria elongata*), golden stars cactus (*Mammillaria elongata stella-aurata*), grizzly bear cactus (*Opuntia erinacea ursina*), hairbrush cactus (*Pachycereus pecten-aboriginum*), hatchet cactus (*Pelecyphora*), hedgehog cactus (*Hamatocactus setispinus*), hook cactus (*Ancistrocactus*), horse crippler, devil's head, or manco caballo (*Homalocephala texensis*), Indian-fig (*Opuntia ficus-indica*), jumpig cholla (*Opuntia fulgida*), lace cactus (*Echinocereus caespitosus* and *Mammillaria elongata minima*), lady fingers cactus (*Mammillaria elongata*), living rock cactus (*Roseocactus fissuratus*), melon, Turk's cap, or Turk's head cactus (*Melocactus*), mescal button (*Lophophora williamsii*), mission cactus (*Opuntia ficus-indica megalacantha*), mistletoe cactus (*Rhipsalis*), mountain cactus (*Oreocereus*), night-blooming or moon cereus (*Selenicereus*), nipple cactus (*Mammillaria*), old lady or old woman cactus (*Mammillaria hahniana*), old man cactus (*Cephalocereus senilis*), orchid cactus (*Epiphyllum* and *Nopalxochia ackermannii*), organ pipe cactus (*Marginatocereus marginatus* and *Marshallocereus thurberi*), peanut cactus (*Chamaecereus silvestri*), pencil cactus or sacasil (*Wilcoxia poselgeri*), peyote (*Lophora williamsii*), pincushion cactus (*Coryphantha vivipara*), pine cone cactus (*Encephalocarpus strobiliformis*), prickly-pear cactus (*Opuntia*), rainbow cactus (*Echinocereus rigidissimus*), rat tail cactus (*Aporocactus flagelliformis*), sahuaro or giant cactus (*Carnegiea gigantea*), sand dollar (*Astrophytum asterias*), scarlet bugler (*Cleistocactus baumannii*), sea urchin cactus (*Astrophytum asterias* and *Echinopsis*), seven stars cactus (*Ariocarpus retusus*), silver or golden cholla (*Opuntia echinocarpa*), snowball cactus (*Pediocactus* and *Pseudoespostoa melanostele*), star cactus (*Astrophytum ornatum* and *Roseocactus fissuratus*), strawberry cactus (*Echinocereus* and some related sorts), teddy bear cholla (*Opuntia bigelowii*), thimble cactus (*Opuntia longispina corrugata* and *Mammillaria fragilis*), Thanksgiving cactus (*Schlumbergera truncata biflora*), totem pole cactus (*Lophocereus schottii monstrosus*), tuna (*Opuntia*), and white torch cactus (*Trichocereus spachianus*). The plants called red-bird-cactus and cactus-vine are not cactuses. The first is *Pedilanthus carinatus*, the second *Fouquieria splendens*.

Garden and Landscape Uses. As is to be expected, in the United States growing cactuses outdoors is pretty much limited to warm, dry parts of the West and Southwest, but not completely so. A few kinds are hardy and moisture-tolerant enough to survive colder and wetter conditions. Outstanding among these is *Opuntia compressa*. Most cactuses occur natively where summers are hot and annual rainfall does not exceed 1 foot and often is much less.

In the cactus collection at the Huntington Botanical Garden, San Marino, California (*Echinocactus*)

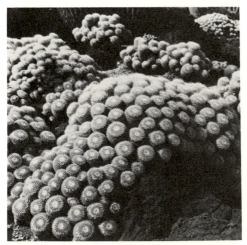

In the cactus collection at the Huntington Botanical Garden, San Marino, California (*Mammillaria*)

Only dedicated cactus specialists are likely to fashion gardens of cactuses alone. It is more usual to combine them with other succulents and dry-region species to achieve desert gardens. These can be quite stunning. Their plants have much character, beauty, and interest and combine well with rocks and boulders. They lend them-

Caladium humboldtii

Cactuses: *Echinocactus grusonii*, opuntias, and other sorts

Calandrinia ciliata menziesii

Calanthe furcata

Calceolaria herbeohybrida varieties

Calceolaria fruticohybrida variety

Calliandra emarginata

Callistephus (China-aster)

Calochortus apiculatus

Callopsis volkensii

selves to informal and semiformal grouping better than precise arrangement. Succulents, including cactuses, come in such a wide range of sizes, forms, and colors that complement and enhance rather than detract from each other, that even tyro landscapers are likely to achieve highly creditable results with arranging them.

Kinds to select from are tall columnar and shorter ones of similar configuration. Some branch in candelabra fashion, others are branchless. There are solitary-stemmed and clustered cactuses and those with stems that sprawl. Certain species make large, nearly-perfect globes or barrels, others tight mounds of smaller spheres, eggs, or cylinders. Nearly all are conspicuously armed with clusters of spines, often formidable, sometimes of less vicious appearance. Some have stems clothed or partly clothed with long hairs. Colors are chiefly in the gray-green to blue-green range, but there are some good greens. The spines may be white, tan, yellow, brown, pink, or red or combinations of these. And then there are the flowers, those of many kinds dramatically handsome and highly colored, those of others less showy.

Cactus-growing indoors is not of course restricted to any one climate. These plants can be raised in greenhouses anywhere. Many of the smaller species are good window and dish garden plants. To accommodate a representative collection, it is better that the greenhouse be devoted to cactuses and other succulents only. Then an environment most favorable to them can be maintained, one drier than that needed by most greenhouse plants. It is true that some more robust cactuses will survive and even prosper in more humid conditions along with other plants, but

Dish gardens with cactuses

most will not and all do better in drier atmospheres. In greenhouses, cactuses may be planted in ground beds or kept in containers. Except in large display conservatories, the latter is usual and better.

In display greenhouses, raised beds of soil of a kind suitable for potting cactuses and very well drained are generally best. Their surfaces can be contoured to achieve variety and rocks or boulders used to give interest. Do not surface the bed with screened gravel or other even-sized stones. That gives a completely unnatural effect. It is not out of character to strew rock chips or stones of varied sizes around, not to completely cover the soil surface except perhaps in small low areas that simulate

desert washes, and not of even density. In some parts let the surface be mostly soil with only the tops of a few stones embedded in it showing. Thicken the stone cover in other places to give the impression of parts of a desert floor from which wind has whipped away the fine soil to leave mostly stones exposed, but still have soil showing between the stones. With a little ingenuity and "feel," very satisfying effects are attainable.

Cultivation. For cactuses outdoors, of first importance is sharp soil drainage. Where this is not natural it can be improved by planting in raised beds and elevated parts of rock gardens. If natural drainage is inadequate underlie the beds with a thick layer of gravel, crushed stone, broken brick, or some similar material. The soil must be porous, not necessarily sandy. Some cactuses grow in alkaline and even saline soils, but the great majority need slightly acid conditions. The most important routine care consists of restricting over-ambitious species from trespassing on their neighbor's territory and of controlling weeds. The last is best done by careful use of the scuffle hoe or cultivator supplemented with a little hand pulling. Do not stir too deeply. Cactus roots are near the surface and are easily injured.

Greenhouses for cactuses must generally be sunny. Only a few cactuses, notably tree-perching (epiphytic) sorts, benefit from some shade from strong sun. The great majority are well satisfied with winter night temperatures of 45 to 50°F and daytime levels not more than five to ten degrees warmer. Too high temperatures in winter are detrimental. Then cactuses are semidormant. At other seasons they benefit from temperatures high as those in nature, always supposing the atmosphere is not heavily humid. A free circulation of air

An amateur's cactus collection

is necessary. Tree-perching cactuses appreciate more atmospheric humidity than desert kinds, but they dislike heavily dank conditions.

Soil mixes for cactuses vary considerably from grower to grower, and excellent results are had by the use of different proportions of common ingredients as well as by varying the components. Successful cultivators are likely to be very sure of the superiority of their favorite mix. Yet there must be and are common denominators to all soils in which cactuses thrive. The first needs are physical. The rooting medium must be sufficiently porous to let water drain readily and to admit air. A second requirement is that it contains the nutrients plants must have. And third it must be within a certain acidity-alkalinity range.

The majority of soil mixes are based on the use of topsoil or loam, sand or perlite, and peat moss, leaf mold, or other acceptable organic matter. Loams vary considerably from predominantly sandy to distinctly clayey. The first are physically acceptable for cactuses, the others can be made so by adding extra grit, sand, or perlite. Except for epiphytic cactuses keep the organic content of the mix low, not more than ⅙ part by bulk of the total, usually less. Desert earths in which most cactuses grow naturally are low in organics. Cactuses are slow growers and most have no foliage. They do not need large amounts of quickly available nutrients, particularly nitrogen, as do plants that produce much leafage and grow rapidly, lettuce and cucumbers, for example. Yet they need nutrients. In the vast majority of instances the trace elements needed, iron, copper, boron, and so on, will be present in the loam in sufficient amounts. Only phosphorus, potash, and nitrogen need perhaps be added. Because cactuses grow slowly add to the soil only those fertilizers that release their nutrients in small amounts over a long time. Bonemeal and hoof and horn meal are excellent and for many kinds it does not come amiss to add a little dried cow manure.

Potting needs attention from time to time, but less frequently than with many faster-growing plants. Large specimens often remain in good health for many years without this attention, but when a specimen becomes so large for its container that it is difficult to water it adequately, or if it becomes top-heavy, it is time to consider a move. More frequent transplanting will be needed with young specimens of some kinds that make a fair amount of annual growth, and repotting is indicated if the soil becomes leached of nutrients to such an extent that occasional fertilizing fails to maintain vigor, or if through poor choice at first or overwatering or other mismanagement the earth becomes pasty, impervious, or otherwise unacceptable to the roots. Late winter or early spring is the best time to repot. Satisfactory growth can be had in porous clay pots and in nonporous plastic ones so long as watering practices are adjusted to compensate for the characteristics of the material. What is important is that the containers have drainage holes and that over these is placed sufficient crocks to ensure that surplus water drains rapidly away. Dish gardens sold by florists are ordinarily without drainage holes and not infrequently are planted with cactuses. In warm, dry rooms these if watered carefully may live for several weeks or even months, but eventually they succumb.

When potting do not give big shifts. Transfer a plant from a 3-inch pot to one 4 inches in diameter, a 4-inch specimen to a 5-inch container, and so on. Only when considerably larger sizes are involved is it desirable to give a 2-inch shift. Spiny cactuses are most easily handled if you wear leather gloves or hold them while they are being tapped out of their pots and positioned in their new ones, by wrapping a handkerchief or larger piece of cloth around them, crossing the ends and giving them a twist, and using them as a handle. If the root balls are stuck so tightly to the sides of the pot that they are difficult to remove, loosen them by poking a stick, for small sizes a pencil will do, through the drainage hole in the bottom of the pot.

Some two or three hours before potting soak the soil of the plants to be moved. See that the potting soil is dampish, but not wet. Do not water newly potted specimens for three days to a week. Then soak the soil thoroughly with a spray fine enough not to wash it. Give no more water until the earth is nearly dry again.

Routine care of cactuses in containers calls for much care in watering. Allow the soil of desert kinds to become nearly dry between applications, then drench it. Do not make frequent light applications. From fall to spring cactuses need very little water, but how often they should be watered depends upon the environment as well as the kind of cactus. In a room where the temperature is 70°F or over, the soil dries more rapidly than in a greenhouse twenty degrees cooler. Globose and other thick-stemmed cactuses need less moisture than slender-stemmed ones. The gardener must exercise judgment based on observation and a little understanding, a mite of common sense. Certainly do not allow the soil to remain dry so long that the stems shrivel.

During the growing season, that is from spring to fall, more especially when new growths are developing, specimens that have filled their containers with roots benefit from fertilizing once every two or three weeks with liquid fertilizer. But dilute this at least twice as much as you would for most other plants. A houseplant fertilizer used at ¼ the concentration recommended by the manufacturer suffices. During the summer months cactuses may be put outdoors, desert kinds in full sun, the tree-perchers in partial shade. The desert kinds can be buried to the rims of their pots in soil, sand, or similar material. Tree-perchers grow better with their containers above ground.

Tree-perching (epiphytic) cactuses such as those of the genera *Epiphyllum*, *Rhipsalidopsis*, *Rhipsalis*, and *Schlumbergera*, natives of wooded regions rather than dry deserts, are treated differently from those that inhabit the latter. They are potted in loose, open, rooting mixtures containing considerable amounts of organic matter, such as coarse compost, leaf mold, or peat moss, and this is kept evenly moist, but not wet, except for a short period of rest following flowering or in some cases in fall in advance of blooming. For these kinds a fairly humid atmosphere is desirable and sufficient shade to keep the stems from being scorched, but not so much that flowering is inhibited. A slight yellowing caused by light is not harmful. Misting the plants with water on bright days is helpful, but not so late that the plants do not dry before nightfall.

Propagation is readily achieved by seeds sown in temperatures of 70 to 90°F. High temperatures promote rapid germination. Spring or early summer are the preferred times to sow. Make sure the soil is porous. A satisfactory mix consists of one part loamy topsoil, two parts peat moss or leaf mold, two parts coarse sand, and one part crushed brick, perlite, or grit, to which may be added a dash each of crushed charcoal and bonemeal and, if the topsoil is too acid, a light sprinkling of ground limestone. But many different mixes are suitable if they meet the needs of porosity and a slightly acid to neutral pH reaction. In place of soil, vermiculite, or milled sphagnum moss may be used. In any case, keep the medium in which the seeds are sown just moist, not wet. Fresh seeds of most cactuses germinate in about a week, some take a little longer, and in a few cases germination may take place sporadically over a period of several months. Temperatures below 70°F are likely to seriously delay or even prevent germination.

Offsets and cuttings are two common means of securing increase. The first consists of taking off and planting easily-detachable, individual shoots (stems), sometimes with some roots attached, that sprout from the base or from above the bases of established plants. No wound or at most only a small one occurs at the point of detachment. Cuttings differ in mostly being pieces not naturally detachable (this is not completely true of those made of pads of opuntias) and that consist of pieces of stem cut cleanly across their bases with a very sharp knife or razor blade. Take care not to crush the tissues when making the

Display of grafted cactuses at Montreal Botanical Garden

cut. When taking cuttings from cactuses with jointed stems, let the base of the cutting be the constricted part of the stem that marks the separation of the joints or segments. Dust the cut surfaces with powdered sulfur, fermate, or charcoal dust and lay the cuttings in a warm, dry place for a week or two before planting to allow the wounds to dry. Cuttings root readily in sand, perlite, vermiculite, or any similar material that admits air and drains freely. Keep it barely moist.

Grafting is a common method of increasing some cactuses and with albino forms devoid of chlorophyll, such as those of *Gymnocalycium*, the only way. The procedure is simple and usually reliable. For information about this see Grafting.

Pests and Diseases. The most commonly encountered animal pests are mealybugs, including species that live on the roots and other above-ground ones, red spider-mites, thrips, and scale insects. Seedlings are apt to be damaged by slugs and sowbugs. Diseases include various rots and virus infections. The former are usually traceable to mechanical injury, ill-drained or poorly-aerated soil, overwatering, or other improper environment. Virus infections are transmitted by insects chewing or sucking on healthy plants after having fed on infected ones and by cutting healthy plants with tools previously used on unhealthy ones without sterilizing them (by dipping in alcohol) between cuts.

CADENDA DE AMOR. See Antigonon.

CADETIA (Cad-étia). Closely related to *Dendrobium* and by some authorities included there, *Cadetia* of the orchid family ORCHIDACEAE numbers about sixty species mostly natives of New Guinea but a few indigenous to Australia, the Molucca Islands, New Caledonia, and the Solomon Islands. The name is in memory of Cadet de Gassicourt, author of a dictionary of chemical terms and formulary in France.

Cadetias are prevailingly epiphytes (tree perchers) but occasionally inhabit cliffs or rocks. Many sorts superficially resemble *Pleurothallis*, but they are readily separated from the plants of that genus by technical details of their minute to small flowers. Their pseudobulbs are slender and stem-like.

Native of New Guinea, **C. ceratostyloides** (syn. *Dendrobium ceratostyloides*) is a tufted species about 6 inches tall with many erect stems. At the apex of each stem there is a lanceolate leaf and one or sometimes two creamy-white flowers with a three-lobed lip.

Garden Uses and Cultivation. Interesting for inclusion in orchid collections, the species described succeeds under conditions appropriate for dendrobiums with intermediate and tropical temperature requirements.

CAESALPINIA (Caesal-pìnia)—Barbados Flower Fence or Dwarf Poinciana or Bird-of-Paradise Flower or Peacock Flower, Divi-Divi. Plants formerly known as *Poinciana*, but not including the royal poinciana (*Delonix regia*), belong here. As now understood, *Caesalpinia* consists of 100 or more species of trees, shrubs, and climbers, widely distributed as natives in the tropics and subtropics. It belongs in the pea family LEGUMINOSAE and bears a name honoring the Italian botanist Andreas Caesalpini, who died in 1603.

Caesalpinias may be prickly or not. They have alternate leaves, twice-pinnately-divided into few or numerous small leaflets. The showy flowers are in panicles or racemes. Not pea-shaped, they are red, orange, yellow, or combinations of these. Each has a short-tubed calyx with five lobes of unequal size, five spreading petals of somewhat irregular size, and ten separate, curved stamens. The fruits are usually flat, linear to ovate or sickle-shaped pods. For yellow-caesalpinia see Peltophorum.

Some species, for instance, the divi-divi, have seed pods that contain much tannin and are used for processing fine leather. From the wood of some, dyes and inks are prepared, and violin bows made. Brazil owes its name to a *Caesalpinia*. In the Middle Ages the wood of *C. sappan* of India was called bresel wood and highly esteemed for dyeing. When, early in the sixteenth century, the Portuguese discovered a similar species, *C. echinata*, in South

Cadetia ceratostyloides

America, that served the same purpose, they transferred the Old World name to it and subsequently to the country from whence it came.

Barbados flower fence, dwarf poinciana, bird-of-paradise flower, or peacock flower (**C. pulcherrima** syn. *Poinciana pulcherrima*) is ubiquitous throughout the tropics. Its original home is not known. A prickly-branched, rather loose shrub 6 to 15 feet tall, it has hairless shoots and foliage, the latter evergreen and of delicate, fernlike aspect. The leaves are up to 1 foot long. Each has twelve to eighteen primary divisions, divided into twenty to twenty-four asymmetrically-oblongish leaflets ½ to ¾ inch long and about one-half as wide. The brilliant blooms, in large, loose, terminal or axillary panicles or racemes, suggest clouds of gaily-colored butterflies hovering over the foliage. They have long, slender stalks, are about 2 inches wide and orange-yellow, with the long-protruding stamens and styles red. The flat seed pods are up to 4 inches long by ½ to ¾ inch wide. Variety *P. p. flava* has beautiful, clear yellow blooms.

A nonprickly, straggly shrub or small tree, **C. gilliesii** (syn. *Poinciana gilliesii*) is a native of South America. Sometimes called bird-of-paradise flower, it is very different from the bird of paradise plant (*Strelitzia*) of South Africa. The shoots of *C. gilliesii* are sticky-hairy. The leaves have many primary divisions, the lowermost opposite, those above more or less alternate. Each has numerous narrow-oblong leaflets ¼ to ½ inch long. Their margins on the undersides are speckled with black. The flowers, in terminal racemes with densely sticky-hairy stems, have pale yellow petals, and brilliant red stamens 4 or 5 inches long. The seed pods are about 4 inches long by ¾ inch wide. Less well known **C. conzattii** (syn. *Poinciana conzattii*), of Mexico, is a small tree with leaves with eight or ten oblong to obovate leaflets, and red or reddish blooms in stalkless racemes. The seed pods are hairy.

Caesalpinia pulcherrima

The divi-divi (*C. coriaria*) as seen in windswept islands of the West Indies and elsewhere in the American tropics, where it is native, is extremely picturesque. In exposed locations it commonly has a more or less leaning trunk and a flat-topped head with branches much prolonged to leeward. In height it varies from 15 feet or less, to twice as tall. Without spines or prickles, it has ferny leaves up to 6 inches long with four to seven chief divisions and a terminal one each with numerous linear-oblong leaflets up to ⅓ inch in length. The fragrant, yellow flowers crowded in terminal and axillary panicles are about one-half as long as the leaves. Their petals are about ⅕ inch long. Shaggy with long hairs, the stamens are longer than the petals. The seed pods are oblong, up to a little over 2 inches long, and curled.

The hardiest species *C. japonica*, as its name implies, is native to Japan. It is a loose, spreading, deciduous shrub, its slender branches well armed with strong, recurved prickles. The leaves have six to sixteen primary divisions each with ten to twenty blunt-oblongish leaflets ½ to ¾ inch long, and pubescent on their undersides. In showy, panicle-like clusters up to 1 foot long are borne the slender-stalked, canary-yellow blooms, the red stamens of which are not much longer than the petals. This is hardy approximately as far north as Washington, D.C.

An evergreen shrub or tree up to about 20 feet tall, *C. vesicaria* is native to the West Indies and Mexico. Densely-branched, it has spiny or spineless, maroon stems. The hairless leaves, 4 to 10 inches long, have two or three primary divisions with a few stalked, obovate leaflets ½ inch to 1½ inches in length, notched at their broad apexes, glossy above and dull on their lower surfaces. In branched or branchless racemes as long or longer than the leaves, the yellow blooms are produced in great profusion. The flat seed pods are about 3 inches long. In southern Florida this sort has proven highly resistant to drought and

storm damage and able to stand neglect better than many shrubs and trees. It thrives in limestone soils.

Garden and Landscape Uses and Cultivation. In climates suited to their well-being, which means except for *C. japonica* tropical and subtropical ones, caesalpinias are excellent landscape and garden furnishings. The taller kinds are useful shade trees, others may be used in beds and as single specimens. The dwarf poinciana makes a charming informal hedge. All need sunny locations, and well-drained, not necessarily rich, soil. The only pruning needed is any thought necessary to shape the plants or restrict them to size. It may be done following the main flush of bloom or early in spring. Propagation is by seeds that germinate more rapidly and evenly if they are soaked in warm water for twenty-four hours prior to sowing.

CAFTA. See Catha.

CAIMITO or CAINITO is *Chrysophyllum cainito*.

CAIOPHORA. See Cajophora.

CAJANUS (Cajàn-us)—Pigeon-Pea. Ancient in cultivation, the pigeon-pea (*Cajanus cajan* syn. *C. indicus*) is important in the tropics and subtropics as a food for humans and domestic animals. The genus, of the pea family LEGUMINOSAE, consists of one or perhaps two species of which there are many varieties. It presumably was originally native of Africa, and is known to have been cultivated in Egypt before 2000 B.C. Its name is aboriginal.

Pigeon-peas are shrubs 3 to 10 feet in height, with alternate leaves each with three elliptic-oblong leaflets, the center one long-stalked, up to 4 inches in length, and silvery beneath with fine hairs. The small, pea-shaped, yellow, yellow and maroon, or orange flowers are in racemes from the leaf axils. The fruits are pointed, hairy pods, narrowed between the seeds, and up to 3 inches in length.

Garden Uses and Cultivation. An especial virtue of the pigeon-pea is its ability to grow and bear in regions too dry for most other food crops. Because of this it is favored in arid regions such as parts of India, the Near East, and some West Indian islands. The seeds are sown in rows. The plants bear the first year and are often grown as annuals, or they may be allowed to crop for three or four, before being plowed under. Besides the edible seeds, commonly called peas, which are employed for stock feed and human food, the pigeon-pea is used for pasturage and hay.

CAJEPUT TREE is *Melaleuca leucadendron*.

CAJOPHORA (Cajóph-ora). Few species of this genus are cultivated. The commonest

is often called *Blumenbachia lateritia*. Its correct name is *Cajophora lateritia*. Sometimes the name is spelled *Caiophora*. The genus consists of sixty-five species of erect and climbing South American annual and perennial herbaceous plants allied to *Blumenbachia* and *Loasa* and belonging in the loasa family LOASACEAE. Most have stinging hairs. Their leaves are opposite, and their yellow, red, or white flowers are solitary in the leaf axils. The fruits are spirally-twisted capsules. The name comes from the Greek *kaio*, burn, and *phor*, bear. It alludes to the stinging hairs.

Although technically a tender perennial, *C. lateritia* is cultivated in the north as an annual. It blooms freely the first year from

Cajophora lateritia

Cajophora lateritia (flowers)

seeds and is attractive because of its curiously-shaped, long-stalked flowers of a muted orange-red. The stems climb to 10 to 20 feet and are furnished with pinnately-divided leaves. The down-facing blooms, about 2 inches in diameter, have five incurved petals densely covered on their outsides with stinging hairs.

Garden and Landscape Uses. As a screening vine where passersby are unlikely to brush against it, and for covering dryish banks, *C. lateritia* has value. It may also be grown over brushwood pea stakes or other such supports as a decorative feature in flower borders. Because of the stinging hairs the flowers are essentially without value for cutting. This plant does well in dryish soil and needs full sun.

Cultivation. Propagation is easy by seeds sown outdoors in spring or earlier indoors and the young plants transplanted to the garden after the weather is warm and settled. For indoor sowing a temperature of 70°F is satisfactory. After they are transplanted individually to small pots the young plants may be grown until almost planting out time in a sunny greenhouse in a temperature of 60 to 65°F. Prior to planting in the garden they should be hardened for a week or ten days by standing them in a cold frame or sunny sheltered location outdoors. A distance of about 1½ feet apart in the garden is appropriate. At the first transplanting the seedlings can be handled with impunity, but later, as a protection from the stinging hairs, it is well to wear gloves when working with them.

CALABASH GOURD. See Lagenaria.

CALABASH TREE is *Crescentia cujete*.

CALABAZILLA is *Cucurbita foetidissima*.

CALADIUM (Cal-àdium). The great arum family ARACEAE contains many notable ornamental foliage plants as well as some prized for their flowers. Among the former none equals in diversity of color patterns and brilliance the fancy-leaved caladiums. These triumphs of the plant breeders' skill are among the most satisfactory and easy-to-grow foliage plants. The genus *Caladium* consists of fifteen species, confined in the wild to tropical America and the West Indies. Only one of the wild species is ordinarily cultivated, and that generally only in choice greenhouse collections. The name *Caladium*, probably of Malayan origin, is not connected with the plants to which it is now applied. The plant often known as *Caladium esculentum*, and commonly elephant's ear, is *Colocasia esculenta*.

Caladiums are stemless herbaceous perennials with underground bulblike parts called tubers. From these arise in season long-stalked, heart-shaped to spear-head-shaped or lanceolate, thin leaves that in very many kinds are peltate, that is the leafstalk is attached some little distance in from the leaf margin. The assemblages commonly called flowers make no appreciable display, but are interesting. They are over-topped by the foliage. Typical of the arum family, these "flowers" look much like jack-in-the-pulpits, and like them, consist of many true flowers with associated parts. Each has a spike or spadix, analogous to the central yellow column in the well-known calla-lily. Arising from the base of the spadix, and partly enveloping it, is a hooded, petal-like bract called a

spathe, the equivalent of the white, petal-like part of the calla-lily. The true flowers are tiny, and crowded along the spadix, females on the lower part, males above. The fruits that follow successful pollination of female flowers are white berries. Caladiums differ from closely-related *Alocasia* and *Colocasia* in technical details of their ovaries, as well as in their leaves usually being much more brightly colored and of thinner texture.

A charming jewel of a plant, *C. humboldtii* (syn. *C. argyrites*), of Brazil, has oblongish-heart-shaped, bright green leaves approximately 2 inches long and clearly spotted with white. Their stalks are two to three times as long as the blades.

Caladium humboldtii

Fancy-leaved caladiums (*C. hortulanum*) are hybrids chiefly of *C. bicolor* and *C. picturatum* of tropical America. Through breeding and selection these have given rise to a tremendous number of beautiful horticultural varieties. Early in this century one Florida grower cultivated more than 2,000 kinds. Far fewer are available today. In their wild forms not much cultivated, *C. bicolor* and *C. picturatum* have leaves with blades up to 1 foot long, variously colored and variegated. Those of *C. bicolor* are broadly-ovate to round-ovate with only a narrow space between their basal lobes, those of *C. picturatum* are narrowly-lanceolate-ovate to narrowly-oblong-ovate, with the basal lobes spreading and widely spaced.

The earliest breeding of garden varieties of fancy-leaved caladiums was done in France during the latter half of the nineteenth century. Some of the early results, including a variety still cultivated named 'Triomphe de l'Exposition', were exhibited in Paris in 1867. Breeding on a substantial scale began in England in 1875, shortly afterwards in Germany and, most importantly, in Brazil. From work done in the last country came such splendid varieties as 'Hortulania' and 'Rio de Janeiro'. By the turn of the century large numbers of fancy-leaved caladiums had been raised in Europe, among them astonishing 'Candi-

dum', still the finest white-leaved kind. Later, breeding was taken up in the United States, first at the Missouri Botanic Garden in St. Louis, later chiefly in Florida, where such fine varieties as 'Edith Mead', 'D. M. Cook', and 'Mrs. W. B. Halderman' were raised. As is to be expected when so many splendid varieties have been developed in places far apart over a period of more than a century, some confusion of identification and naming has resulted.

Fancy-leaved caladiums now in cultivation have foliage ranging from the unbe-

Fancy leaved caladiums: (a) 'Candidum'

(b) 'Mandago'

(c) 'The Thing'

lievably fragile white with narrow green veins of 'Candidum' to the translucent and apparently flimsy, pink-stained-glass window-looking leaves of 'Lord Derby'. Between, are many combinations of green, red, pink, white, and creamy-yellow. Gardeners should make their selections from catalogs of nurseries and specialist dealers in which are described, and often illustrated in color, the varieties offered.

Garden and Landscape Uses. For summer beds and borders, for window and porch boxes and similar uses, and as pot plants for greenhouses and windows, there are no foliage plants more colorful than fancy-leaved caladiums. Given reasonable conditions they are easy to grow, and from spring planting quick displays of color are had. For their best growth deep soil plentifully supplied with organic matter and dampish, but not wet is needed, and a little dappled shade to break the full intensity of summer sun.

Cultivation. In tropical climates caladiums may be left in the ground permanently and may retain some foliage throughout the year. In most parts of the continental United States, it is necessary, and even in Florida advisable, to store the tubers indoors in winter and replant annually. Winter storage must provide protection from frost.

In Florida and similar warm climates, the tubers are planted directly outdoors, but in the north it is more usual to start them inside early and set growing plants out from pots after the weather is warm and settled. To start the rested tubers into growth, set them fairly closely together in flats of peat moss or vermiculite with their tops about 1 inch beneath the surface. Keep them moist and in a temperature of 70 to 85°F. The largest tubers are likely to begin growing first. As soon as leaves sprout and the roots are about 2 inches long, pot the plants either singly in 5-inch pots, or if bigger specimens are needed as container plants, three or more together in larger pans (shallow pots). For the first potting use soil containing much peat moss, humus, or leaf mold, and sand or vermiculite. For subsequent pottings (specimens to be grown in pots will need transplanting to larger containers when their roots begin to crowd) use a higher proportion of good topsoil in the potting mixture. Caladiums prosper at high temperatures and in humid atmospheres. Good light, with shade from strong sun, is needed. The soil must always be moist. After growth is well established regular applications of dilute liquid fertilizer promote continued healthy growth and the production of the finest, most abundant foliage. When, in fall, the plants begin to lose their leaves naturally, gradually reduce the frequency of watering, and finally when the foliage has died, withhold water completely and allow the tubers to rest.

Caladiums as pot plants: (a) Planting the tubers

(b) Potting started tubers

(c) Pressing soil around the roots

(d) Potting completed

(e) Growth well started

(f) Plant in full foliage

Caladiums must be dug from outdoors before frost, brought inside, and gradually dried off. During the dormant period the tubers may remain in the soil in the pots, with the latter laid on their sides under a greenhouse bench or in some other suitable storage place. Alternatively, the tubers may be cleaned of soil, old roots, and tops, and be stored in dry sand, peat moss, or vermiculite in a temperature of 60 to 65°F.

Propagation of caladiums is very easily accomplished by cutting the tubers into pieces, in much the same way as potatoes are cut, in late winter or spring when they are started into growth. Dust the cut surfaces with powdered sulfur, fermate, or powdered charcoal to check any tendency to decay, and plant them as advised above for whole tubers. Seeds from hand-pollinated flowers are used to produce new varieties, but by far the greater proportion of seedlings are poor to mediocre, not more than one out of thousands attaining the high standards of existing varieties.

CALAMAGROSTIS (Calama-gróstis)—Reed Grass. A dozen species of the grass family GRAMINEAE, natives of damp soils chiefly in temperate and colder regions of the northern hemisphere, but one species of East and South Africa, constitute *Calamagrostis*. The name, alluding to the appearance of the plants, is derived from the Greek *kalamos*, a reed, and *agrostis*, a grass. Some sorts are esteemed for hay.

Reed grasses are erect perennials often with creeping rhizomes. Their leaves have long, narrow, flat blades. The flowers are in compact or rarely loose panicles.

Native chiefly to sandy soils in Europe and temperate Asia and naturalized to some extent in eastern North America, *C. epigejos* has creeping rhizomes. It forms dense clumps of stems 3 to 6 feet tall, with hairless leaves up to 2 feet long, and usually up to ⅓ inch wide. The purplish, brownish, or green panicles of blooms are 6 inches to 1 foot long or sometimes longer. At first compact, with age the panicles loosen. They persist through the winter.

Garden and Landscape Uses. The species discussed is attractive for planting at pool sides and in perennial beds, and is used as a source of cut flowers.

Cultivation. No difficulty attends the cultivation of this hardy species, but prospective planters should note that in sandy soils it may become invasive. In clay soils it is much less likely to spread objectionably. It prospers in sunny locations in a variety of moist soils and is easily propagated by division and seeds.

CALAMINT. See Calamintha.

CALAMINTHA (Cala-míntha)—Calamint. This genus of six or seven species is by some authorities included in *Satureja*, but prevailing opinion seems to be that the straight, tubular, thirteen-veined calyxes of its flowers warrant its separation from that genus. It belongs in the mint family LABIATAE and has a name derived from the Greek *kalos*, beautiful, and *minthe*, mint. It is native from western Europe to central Asia.

Calaminthas are aromatic shrubs and subshrubs with opposite, toothed leaves and, in the axils of the upper ones, clusters of asymmetrical blooms. The flowers have more or less two-lipped calyxes and two-lipped corollas, with the upper lip flat and notched at its apex or not. The lower lip is three-lobed, with the middle lobe the largest. There are four nonprotruding stamens and a style with two unequal branches and two stigmas. The fruits are four-seeded nutlets.

Lesser calamint (*C. nepeta* syns. *Satureja nepeta*, *S. calamintha*) is a variable, sparsely- to densely-hairy native of Europe naturalized in North America, 1 foot to 2½ feet tall, with creeping rootstocks. Its blunt,

shallowly- to deeply-round-toothed, ovate leaves are ¾ inch to 1¼ inches long and up to 1 inch wide. The white to lilac flowers, about ½ inch long, are in clusters of ten to twenty. Variety *C. n. glandulosa* has leaves ½ to ¾ inch long with up to five

Calamintha nepeta glandulosa

teeth on each side and flowers in groups of up to eleven. The large-flowered calamint (*C. grandiflora*), of southern Europe, is a sparsely-hairy perennial 9 inches to 2 feet tall. This kind has ovate-oblong leaves up to 3 inches in length with six teeth or more on each side. Its flowers, 1 inch to nearly 1½ inches long, are in clusters of mostly five, sometimes fewer. Wood calamint (*C. sylvatica*) is a hairy species with creeping rootstocks. Native of Europe and 1 foot to 2½ feet tall, it differs from *C. nepeta* in botanical details. The hairs do not protrude from the mouth of the calyx as those of the *C. nepeta* usually do. The pink to lilac flowers, from less than ½ to nearly 1 inch long, have white spots on the lower lip.

Garden Uses and Cultivation. These plants are suited for warm locations in herb gardens, rock gardens, and elsewhere, in poorish, well-drained soil in full sun. Except for shearing the perennials after they are through blooming, no special care is needed. Propagation is easy by seeds, by summer cuttings in a cold frame or greenhouse propagating bed or under mist.

CALAMONDIN. The calamondin (*Citrofortunella mitis*) formerly identified as *Citrus mitis* is now considered a hybrid, the parents of which are *Citrus reticulata* and a species of *Fortunella*, probably *F. margarita*, both members of the rue family RUTACEAE. Hybrids of this parentage are called orangequats.

An attractive ornamental, densely-branched, nearly-thornless evergreen shrub or small tree, *C. mitis* has tangerine-like

fruits of good quality 1 inch to 1½ inches in diameter, acid and excellent for using in the same ways as limes and lemons.

Calamondin

Garden Uses and Cultivation. Calamondins are as hardy or hardier than Satsuma oranges. They are well adapted for landscaping and can be used effectively in foundation plantings. They are also suited for growing in containers to decorate patios, terraces, and similar places and as small greenhouse and window plants. In climates free from freezing and in greenhouses where winter night temperatures are maintained in the 40 to 50°F range, calamondins are easy to grow in any ordinary well-drained soil. Their cultural needs are those of oranges.

CALAMUS (Cál-amus)—Cane Palm, Rattan Palm. This, the largest genus of the palm family PALMAE, is a bewildering group of 375 species of the Old World tropics. Few are cultivated in the Americas, and those usually only in botanical gardens and special collections. The name *Calamus* is from the Greek *kalamos*, a reed. It alludes to the thin reedy stems.

Most species of *Calamus* are climbers, usually with prickly stems. Some have hooked prickles on the midribs on the undersides of the leaves and often the ends of the midribs are furnished with backward-pointing, vicious spines (each representing a modified leaflet) as capable of snagging, holding, and tearing flesh as fishhooks. The spines serve the plants as holdfasts as they climb upward to the light in forests, but they make progress extremely difficult and indeed hazardous for travelers.

The stems of some rattan palms extend for hundreds of feet. The longest measured and recorded, a stem of *C. manan*, in Malaya, was 556 feet long, but a considerably longer one was trampled by elephants before it could be measured. Stripped of their spines and dried, the canes are much used for baskets, cables, chair bottoms, wickerwork furniture, and walking canes. The leaves are alternate, pinnate, and comparatively widely-spaced. Their leaflets are narrow. The flower clusters are axillary, often long and slender and ending in a tail furnished with hooked spines. The long, narrow spathes are hardly or not at all split, a characteristic that distinguishes this genus from *Daemonorops*.

Native to Ceylon, *C. rotang* is attractive as a young plant. Its stems have comparatively few spines and its leaves, 3 to 4 feet long, are dark green and graceful. Another species quite lovely when young is *C. ciliaris*, of Java and Sumatra. It has very slender stems and long, leafless branches with hooked spines. Its hairy leaves are up to 2½ feet long and consist of eighty to one hundred leaflets. The stems have few spines. Brazilian *C. dealbatus* is a thicket-forming species that clambers vigorously over nearby trees and shrubs to heights of 30 feet or more. Its slender stems are plentifully set with brown spines. The gracefully arching, bright green leaves have many arching, linear leaflets. Their stalks and midribs are furnished with hooked spines.

Garden and Landscape Uses and Cultivation. These plants are for collectors of palms who can provide very humid tropical conditions either outdoors in warm frost-free climates or in a greenhouse. Because of the uses to which their stems are put they are suitable for conservatories devoted to tropical plants useful to man. They are not difficult to grow. They require the same cultural conditions as *Phoenicophorium*. For additional information see Palms.

Calamus dealbatus

CALANDRINIA (Calan-drìnia). These relatives of *Portulaca* belong in the same family, the purslane family PORTULACACEAE. They are natives of the Pacific sides of North and South America, and of Australia, and include annuals and herbaceous perennials. The genus comprises 150 species. Its name commemorates a botanist of Geneva, Switzerland, who died in 1758, J. L. Calandrini.

Calandrinias are trailing or erect plants, with all-basal or alternate, usually narrow, fleshy leaves and mostly red or reddish flowers of short duration. From closely related *Talinum* the genus is distinguished by its persistent sepals, and from *Lewisia* by its flowers having only two sepals. The blooms may be solitary and axillary, but more usually are in racemes or clusters at the ends of the branches. They have three to seven, most commonly five, petals, three to fourteen stamens, and a short style with a three-branched stigma. The fruits are many-seeded capsules.

Perennial calandrinias are usually cultivated as annuals. Here belongs the popular *Calandrinia grandiflora*, of Chile, which is 1 foot to 3 feet tall. It has reddish stems and pointed-ovate leaves 4 to 8 inches long and about 3 inches wide that narrow to wide stalks. Its light purple to magenta blooms, each ¾ inch to 1¼ inches across are in racemes. Another showy perennial, also a native of Chile, is *C. spectabilis*. This attains a height of 2 feet and has spatula-shaped leaves. Its flowers, 2 inches wide or wider, are bright purple and in racemes. This kind rarely produces seeds. One of the most attractive calandrinias, an annual or a perennial, is *C. discolor* (syn. *C. elegans*). A Chilean rarely more than 2 feet tall, it has spatula-shaped leaves, gray-green above and purple on their undersides. Its light purple to violet blooms, 2 to almost 3 inches across, are in more or less nodding racemes.

Annual calandrinias include *C. ciliata*, of Peru and Ecuador and its variety *C. c. menziesii*, the red maids of western North America. The latter is the more robust. Very variable, it has sprawling stems 1 foot to 2 feet long. Narrowly-oblanceolate to linear, its leaves are ¾ inch to 3 inches long. The rose-red or rarely white flowers, up to 1 inch in diameter, are in leafy racemes. This variety is native from Arizona to California. The species *C. ciliata* is less showy and smaller in its parts. Its blooms are purple or white and up to ½ inch across. Its stems are up to 1 foot in length. With leafy clusters of small, coppery-pink to brick-red blooms, stems about 1 foot long, and linear-lanceolate, hairless leaves, *C. burridgei* is another attractive South American.

The best garden calandrinia is *C. umbellata*, native to Peru. This beautiful kind is perennial or annual. It forms compact, tufted masses, scarcely more than 3 inches high, of narrow, gray-green, slender leaves 1 inch to 2 inches long, and has a profusion of glowing magenta blooms in many-flowered, umbel-like, terminal clusters. The flowers are upturned, shallowly cup-shaped, and about ¾ inch in diameter.

Garden and Landscape Uses. Calandrinias are nearly always grown as annuals. They are among the most satisfactory and useful annuals for poorish, well-drained

soils in hot, dry, sunny locations. They are admirable for banks, beds, edgings, and for large rock gardens, also for window and porch boxes, urns, and other containers in which plants for summer display are grown. They associate well with succulents. Calandrinias provide brilliant displays of bloom over a long summer season. Their flowers open only in bright weather. Individual blooms are short-lived. They are of no use as cut flowers.

Cultivation. Seeds afford the usual means of propagation, but the perennial kinds can be increased by cuttings. Except in dry, warm climates, when they are treated as perennials, they must be housed in greenhouses over winter. Ordinarily seeds are sown outdoors in spring where the plants are to remain or in a greenhouse in a germinating temperature of 65 to 70°F eight to ten weeks before it is planned to set the young plants in the garden. If sown indoors, the seedlings are transplanted about 2 inches apart to flats, or individually to small pots and are grown in a greenhouse where the night temperature is 55 to 60°F until a week or two before planting out time when they are hardened by being transferred to a sunny cold frame or sheltered location outdoors. Spacing in the garden, both for plants seeded directly and for plants started indoors, may vary from 5 to 6 inches for the less vigorous kinds, such as *C. umbellata* and *C. grandiflora*, up to 9 inches or even 1 foot apart for such robust kinds as *C. ciliata menziesii* and *C. discolor*. Outdoor-sown plants should be thinned to the required distance while young. No special attention is required through the summer.

CALANTHE (Calán-the). Beautiful flower is the literal meaning of *Calanthe*. Derived from the Greek *kalos*, beautiful, and *anthos*, a flower, it is well applied to a genus of 120 species or more of the orchid family ORCHIDACEAE. Cultivated calanthes include some especially lovely man-made hybrids as well as natural species. The genus is distributed in the wild from Japan and China through tropical and subtropical Asia, Indonesia, Tahiti, and Australia to Madagascar and South Africa. One species not known to be cultivated, *C. mexicana*, is a native of South America, Central America, and the West Indies.

Calanthes are mostly ground orchids (terrestrials) that root in the earth, but a few are epiphytes (plants that perch on trees without extracting nourishment from them). Kinds most common in cultivation belong to the first category. There are both deciduous and evergreen calanthes. The former have large, prominent, conical, obscurely-angled pseudobulbs, sometimes constricted to form a waist toward their middles. The pseudobulbs of evergreen kinds are much smaller, globular, and are sheathed by the bases of the leaves. The leaves of calanthes are stalked, broad, and pleated lengthways. The flowers, in erect or nodding, loose or crowded spikes or racemes that come from the bases of the pseudobulbs are white, pink, purple, or yellow. They have spreading sepals and petals, similar or the petals narrower than the sepals. The lip is clawed (narrowed at its base) and has a spreading, three- or four-lobed blade. The column is short and upright.

The most important species horticulturally is deciduous *C. vestita*, a terrestrial kind of Burma and Malaya. This has sil-

Calanthe vestita

very-skinned pseudobulbs up to 8 inches tall, and broadly-lanceolate leaves up to 2 feet long or longer and 4 inches wide. The white to creamy-white flowers, about 2½ inches wide, in arching, downy-stalked racemes up to 3 feet long, have lips usually marked with yellow to orange-yellow at their bases. The lips are four-lobed and have slender spurs. This is a variable species. Among variants that have been given names are *C. v. gigantea*, with flowers, larger than those of the typical species, marked with a bright red blotch at the bottom of the lip; *C. v. regnieri* (syn. *C. regnieri*), which has longer pseudobulbs, blooms later than *C. vestita*, and has more erect flower stalks with smaller white or pink-flushed blooms with rose-pink lips; *C. v. turneri*, the flowers of which are pure white except for a rose-pink eye; *C. v. turneri nivalis*, similar to the last, but without the pink eye, and *C. v. williamsii*, which has blooms with white or pink-suffused sepals, white petals with rose-pink edges, and a rose-crimson lip.

Popular *C. veitchii* is a hybrid between *C. vestita* and deciduous *C. rosea*, the latter a native of Burma. This hybrid has rose-

pink flowers with a white spot at the bottom of the lip. Varieties of this have been named, including *C. v. sandhurstiana*, which has crimson blooms. More complex hybrids include **C. bella** (syn. *C. harrisii*), the parents of which are *C. veitchii* and *C. vestita turneri*. This has large blooms that have white petals and blush-pink sepals and lip, the latter with a white-edged red blotch at its base. A hybrid between *C. veitchii* and *C. sedenii*, named 'Florence', has rosy-purple blooms marked with creamy-white to lemon-yellow on their lips. Variety 'William Murray' is a hybrid of *C. veitchii* and *C. vestita williamsii*. Its flowers have white sepals and petals and carmine-red lips that are darker in their throats.

Evergreen, summer-blooming **C. furcata** (syn. *C. veratrifolia*), a native of Japan, the

Calanthe furcata

Ryukyu Islands, Taiwan, China, Malaysia, and islands of the Pacific, is variable. It has leaves up to 1½ feet long and flower stalks that rise well above the foliage to heights of up to 3 feet. They terminate in crowded racemes up to 4 inches long of white to rose-purple blooms, with sepals and petals about ½ inch long. The lip is three- or four-lobed. Another evergreen, **C. masuca** is native of the Himalayan region. Its leaves are rather narrow, and up to 2 feet long. The flower stalks attain heights up to 2½ feet and terminate in more or less compact racemes. They have long curved spurs, and vary in size, up to 2 inches across. They range in color from rosy-lilac to magenta-red and have a bright orange or golden-yellow warty patch at the base of the lip. This blooms in summer and early fall. Endemic to Taiwan, rare **C. kintaroi** is an evergreen with flowers much like those of *C. furcata* but differing in the shape of the lip which has a broad-heart-shaped center lobe conspicuously indented at its apex and two narrow-oblong side lobes. The blooms, in terminal spikes of several, are about 2 inches long by approximately 1½ inches across their faces. They are purplish-pink to rich purple with a darker patch at the base of the lip. The

leaves are pointed-elliptic and 1¼ feet or more in length.

Calanthe kintori

Garden Uses. The deciduous calanthes discussed above are among the most satisfactory cut-flower orchids, as well as being superb decorative flowering plants for tropical conservatories and greenhouses. On the plants the flower spikes produce their blooms and are decorative for a long period in fall or winter. As cut flowers they last well, even in overheated New York apartments for five or six days or longer. The evergreen kinds treated above are beautiful pot plants for the embellishment of cool and intermediate-temperature greenhouses.

Cultivation. Deciduous calanthes form new pseudobulbs each year, and these, after the foliage dies in late fall, enter a period of dormancy that ordinarily lasts until mid-March or later. To some extent the time of blooming of tropical calanthes is influenced by the time of potting and starting into growth of the pseudobulbs, which normally is done from mid-March into April. Soil consisting of coarse, fibrous

Newly potted pseudobulb starting into growth

loam mixed with dried cow manure and a sprinkling of crushed charcoal and bonemeal suits. Use clean pots. For the largest pseudobulbs those 6 inches in diameter are not too big, for smaller ones 5-inch or even 4-inch containers will be adequate. Make sure they are well drained by filling them one-quarter to one-third their depth with crocks. Some growers start the pseudobulbs into growth in sand and defer potting until new roots an inch or two long have developed, but because the new roots and shoots are very brittle and easily damaged there is little virtue in this practice. It is better to pot directly into the containers in which the plants are to flower.

Tropical calanthes are lovers of warmth and humidity. Following potting they are placed where the temperature ranges from 65°F at night to 85°F on sunny days. Because the young foliage is susceptible to scorching, light shade to break the full intensity of the sun must be given. At first, watering is done sparingly, but as new roots take hold more water is given, and throughout the growing season the soil is kept constantly moist. As the intensity of the sun increases additional shade is likely to be needed, but no more should be given than is necessary to keep the foliage from scorching. After the pots are filled with roots regular applications of dilute liquid fertilizer do much to stimulate vigorous growth, necessary for the production of the good new pseudobulbs and flowers. By the middle of November growth will be completed, and incipient flower spikes will be seen at the bases of the pseudobulbs. Then, lengthen the periods between watering so that the soil is kept much drier. This will encourage the foliage to ripen, turn yellow, and drop, and the flower spikes to develop in all their beauty. Some growers withhold water completely at this stage, but longer and finer flower spikes result if water is given sparingly. While the flowers are in evidence keep the air drier than during the growing season to prevent unsightly spotting of the blooms. The spikes gradually open their blooms over a period of several weeks. When flowering is through, or after the blooms have been cut for floral decorations, remove the plants from their pots, separate the pseudobulbs, and store the new ones in trays in a well-ventilated place where the temperature is about 60°F, until potting time in spring. If increase is desired, the old pseudobulbs, those that have flowered, may be kept also. These, called back bulbs, will not develop new pseudobulbs or flower spikes as big as the younger ones the first year.

Evergreen calanthes have no complete dormant period and, except for keeping them a little drier in winter than at other times, the soil is maintained in a moist condition throughout the year. The kinds discussed above succeed in cool- and inter-mediate-temperature greenhouses. They do not require the high temperatures so favorable to the deciduous calanthes with which we have been concerned. Their needs are essentially those of *Phaius*. For more information see Phaius, and Orchids.

CALATHEA (Cal-athèa)—Peacock Plant, Zebra Plant, Topinambour. Differing from *Maranta* only in technical details, and many of its members often grown under that name, closely-related *Calathea* belongs in the maranta family MARANTACEAE. It comprises 150 species of nonhardy herbaceous perennials, the cultivated ones prized for their beautiful foliage and *C. allouia* grown in the West Indies for its edible tubers, which are used like potatoes. Calatheas are natives of tropical America and tropical Africa. The name derives from the Greek *kalathos*, a basket, and perhaps alludes to the appearance of the heads of flowers of some kinds.

Low to medium-sized or sometimes tall evergreen perennials, calatheas have handsome, often strikingly variegated foliage. Their leaves are stalked, undivided, and without lobes or teeth. From marantas they differ in their flowers commonly being in conelike heads, with spirally-arranged bracts carried low among the foliage instead of in branched panicles usually higher than the leaves, and in their ovaries having three fully-developed cells with one ovule in each. The flowers of *Calathea* have three sepals, three petals, one fertile stamen, and usually five staminodes (nonfunctional stamens), two larger than the others. The fruits are capsules. There is some confusion about the origins of some cultivated kinds and of the application of names to them. Some names used are without botanical standing. For plants often confused with calatheas see Maranta, Ctenanthe, and Phrynium. These following brief descriptions are of kinds more or less commonly cultivated.

Foliage not variegated on its upper surfaces, green or grayish beneath, is typical of the following: *C. allouia*, a tuberous-rooted native of the West Indies, is 4 to 5 feet tall and has leaves with red-striped stalks, lanceolate to oblong blades about 1½ feet long, light green above, silvery-green on their undersides. The white flowers are in ellipsoid heads 4 inches long. *C. crotalifera*, of Mexico, Panama, and Ecuador, 3 to 7 feet tall, has oblong-elliptic to ovate leaves with satiny, green blades up to 2 feet long and with paler midribs. Their undersides are grayish. The yellow flowers are in spikes with greenish-orange bracts. *C. cylindrica*, of Brazil, about 5 feet in height, has thin, long-stalked, light green leaves with short-pointed, lanceolate to elliptic blades 1½ feet long. Its white blooms are in cylindrical spikes approximately 6 inches in length topping 8-inch-long stalks. *C. lutea*, which grows up to 15 feet tall, is a vigorous South American. Its long-stalked, thinnish, broad-elliptic leaves, bright green above, conspicuously corrugated and gray-waxy on their undersides, have blades up to 5 feet long by 2 feet wide. The midribs beneath and the swollen upper portion of the leafstalk like the flowers, are golden-yellow.

Leaves not variegated above, reddish or purplish beneath, are typical of these kinds: *C. acuminata*, of undetermined origin, has slightly-hairy, narrow-lanceolate leaves, with blades up to 1 foot long by 1½ inches wide, dark green above, maroon-red on their undersides. Their pubescent stalks are maroon-red and green. *C. rufibarba*, of Brazil, about 1½ feet tall, has leaves with stalks, midribs, and sometimes entire surfaces clothed with reddish hairs. The asymmetrical, lanceolate to oblanceolate blades up to about 10 inches long have dark purple-maroon undersides. The yellow flowers are in short-stalked, 2-inch-long heads with violet hairy bracts. *C. varians*, of Guiana, has few-leaved tufts of foliage up to about 3 feet in height. Its leaves have hairy stalks spotted with reddish-brown or purple and with their swollen apexes of the same color. Pointed-linear-lanceolate, the blades are about 1½ feet long, green above, purple beneath. The yellow flowers are in short-stalked, 2-inch-long ellipsoid heads with green-warted, chestnut-brown, reddish-hairy bracts. *C. crocata* of Brazil is especially lovely. Up to about 1 foot tall, it has rather short-stalked ovate-lanceolate leaves and, lifted on erect stalks to a little above the foliage, short, erect spikes of orange-yellow flowers with rose-red sepals in the axils of bright orange bracts.

Leaves variegated with white or silvery-gray and with reddish or purple undersides include the following: *C. argyraea*, of Brazil (distinct from the plant usually grown under this name in gardens), is a robust kind with leaves with winged stalks and unequal-sided, oblanceolate blades, glossy and silvery-gray between the grass-green veins. Their undersides are wine-red. *C. eximia* is a tuberous-rooted kind of Central America. Its short-stalked leaves have oblong-ovate, unequal-sided blades up to 1 foot long or a little longer. They have depressed yellowish-green midribs and are grayish-silver with green veins. The brown-hairy undersides are wine-red. The short-stalked, ellipsoid heads of flowers have violet bracts. *C. lancifolia* (*C. insignis* of gardens), of Brazil, has lanceolate leaves with blades 1 foot to 1½ feet long. Their base color, pale yellowish-green, shaded to olive-green toward the margins, is relieved by a very distinct, leaflike pattern of alternate long and short patches, dark olive-green above, rich wine-purple on the undersides. *C. leoniae*, of Ecuador and Brazil, has round-elliptic leaves with stalks nearly equaling their about 8-inch-long

Calathea lancifolia

blades. They have purple undersides. Above, they are rich olive-green with a feathered-edged center stripe of greenish-silvery-gray and a metallic-silvery band midway between it and the leaf margin. The white flowers are in green-bracted, top-shaped heads about 1½ inches long atop 8-inch-long stalks. *C. metallica,* of Colombia and Brazil, is about 1¼ feet tall. Its short-pointed, asymmetrical, elliptic leaves have blades about 6 inches long. Their upper surfaces are dark green relieved with a center band and a jagged narrower one paralleling the margin. The undersides of the leaves are usually purple. The white flowers are in few-bracted cylindrical heads about 4 inches long. *C. picturata* is a Brazilian up to 1¼ feet in height. Its leaves have elliptic blades up to 6 inches long and 3 inches wide, pointed toward both ends. White stripes paralleling the leaf margin and bordering the midrib illuminate the dark green upper surface. The undersides of the leaves are purple. Variety *C. p. argentea* has dark-green-bordered, lustrous, silvery-gray leaves. Those of *C. p. vandenheckei,* thought to be a juvenile form of *C. picturata,* are

Calathea picturata vandenheckei

broad-elliptic and olive-green with a feather-edged band of silvery-white down the center and a narrow jagged silvery stripe paralleling the leaf edge. *C. ornata,* of northeastern South America, in its typical form has leaves in its adult stage without variegation, metallic coppery-green above, light wine-red beneath. The younger foliage is frequently lined with pink or white. Variable and from 1½ to 8 feet tall, this kind has thin, long-stalked leaves, the blades of those of young plants about 8 inches long and lanceolate, those of older ones wider and up to 2 feet long. On stalks up to 1 foot long or slightly longer, the dry-bracted, egg-shaped heads of bloom are about 3 inches long. There are many not always stable garden varieties of this, those best known being *C. o. roseolineata,* which has narrowly-ovate, olive-green leaves prettily marked with pairs of closely-set parallel-penciled leaves, rose-pink in young leaves fading to white later, and *C. o. sanderana,* which has somewhat wider, lustrous olive-green leaves with similar curving pink or white lines in groups of two or three. *C. splendida,* of Brazil, attains a height of up to 1½ feet. Its long-stalked, oblong to oblong-lanceolate, pointed, glossy, wavy leaves have blades approximately 1 foot long. Purple beneath, above they have imposed on a yellowish-green background a distinct pattern of almond-shaped, dark green blotches. The leaf margins are green. *C. undulata,* of Peru, is about 8 inches tall. It has nearly stalkless,

Calathea undulata

asymmetrically-ovate-oblong, downy, wavy-surfaced leaves. They are dark, metallic-green with, when young, a bluish overcast and along the midrib a jagged-edged, silvery-leaden band. The undersides of the leaves are heavily flushed with purple. The white flowers are in short-stalked, top-shaped heads under 1 inch long with white-margined, white-spotted, green bracts. *C. warscewiczii,* native to Costa Rica, robust and about 2½ feet tall, has short-stalked, short-pointed, lanceolate to oblong-elliptic, wavy-edged leaves, dark

Calathea warscewiczii

purple on their undersides, above rich green with an irregular, angled pattern of yellowish-green along the midrib and side veins. The white flowers are in 2-inch-long, short-stalked ellipsoid heads with leathery yellowish bracts. *C. zebrina,* called zebra plant, is a native of Brazil. A vigorous grower, it is 2 to 3 feet tall. Its leaves are oblong-ovate, dark velvety-green with paler-banded veins and margins.

Calathea zebrina

Leaves variegated above with white or silvery-gray, their undersides grayish, are characteristic of these: *C. albicans,* of northeastern South America and Central America, is a low plant with very broad-elliptic leaves, lustrous light green to grayish, obscurely feathered with darker gray. The undersides are grayish-green. *C. bella* (syn. *C. kegeliana*), of Brazil, 1½ feet tall, has asymmetrical ovate leaves heart-shaped at their bases. Their silvery-gray upper surfaces are patterned similarly to the broader ones of *C. carlina,* but the undersides are grayish-green, not as in that kind, red. *C. lucianii,* of tropical South America, has leaves, including their slender stalks, up to 3 feet tall. Their 1-foot-long, broad-oblong-ovate blades have corrugated surfaces. Their upper surfaces are metallic-bronzy-green with a broad, sil-

Calathea bella

Calathea bachemiana

with green and with sharply-defined, almond-shaped blotches of green angling outward from the midrib. **C. carlina,** of Brazil, has asymmetrical, ovate leaves about 7 inches long by 4½ inches wide, lustrous gray netted with yellow veins, bordered narrowly with green and ornamented with a distinct herringbone pattern of dark green slender patches streaking outward from the midrib. **C. leopardina,** of Brazil, is patterned much like *C. concinna,* but is somewhat smaller. Its asymmetrical, lanceolate leaves are clear green emblazoned with triangular, dark green blotches, alternate on either side of the midrib, and not reaching the margin. **C. magnifica,** of Panama, somewhat resembles *C. veitchiana,* but its

Calathea lucianii

silver-gray curving outward and upward from midrib to margin. This is native of Brazil. **C. vittata** is native to Colombia. It has short-stalked, pointed, broadly-lanceolate leaves, with narrow bands alternately bright green and silvery-green, streaking outward and upward from midrib to margin.

Calathea rotundifolia fasciata

Leaves variegated in tones of green or yellow-green, their undersides grayish or greenish are typical of these calatheas: **C. bachemiana,** a Brazilian up to about 1¼ feet tall, has tuberous roots and slender-pointed, unequal-sided, oblong-lanceolate leaves with blades 6 to 10 inches in length. They are greenish-silvery, narrowly edged

Calathea magnifica

feathered pattern of variegation is less deeply-lobed and the undersides of its leaves are gray-green. The base color of the upper surface is green with deeper green variegation bordered with gray. **C. musaica,** a native of Brazil, is low. It has lustrous, broad-arrow-shaped leaves, green beneath and with yellow-green upper surfaces variegated with dark green veins and, diverging from the lateral veins, small dark green bars. **C. wiotii** is a quite small native of Brazil. Its lustrous, light green, elliptic leaves have blades up to 4 inches

very-white band along the midrib. Their undersides are gray-green. The flowers are yellow. **C. mediopicta,** a Brazilian 1 foot to 1½ feet tall, has spreading or recurved, broad, oblong, short-pointed, olive-green leaves boldly striped down their middles with greenish-white. The flowers are blush-white to purplish. **C. micans,** the smallest cultivated kind, native to Brazil and Peru, rarely attains 8 inches in height. Its pointed-elliptic leaves are conspicuously marked above with a broad, longitudinal, central silvery-white band. Beneath, they are silvery-gray. **C. rotundifolia fasciata** has lustrous, almost circular, brown-stalked leaves, their blades up to 9 inches in length and with alternate bands or bars of green and

Calathea wiotii

Calathea lietzei

long with raised, elliptic, dark green blotches angling outward from the midrib. The grayish undersides of the leaves are sometimes tinged with purple. **C. zebrina binotii** resembles *C. zebrina* except for its leaves being rather narrower and gray rather than red on their undersides, and in the bands of dark brownish-green variegation extending from the midrib only about halfway to the leaf margins. **C. z. humilior** differs from *C. zebrina* in its decidedly smaller leaves having olive-green-veined, light grayish-green under surfaces.

Calathea zebrina humilior

Upper sides of the leaves variegated in tones of green or yellow-green and undersides reddish or purple are characteristic of the following: **C. concinna**, of Brazil, has lustrous, yellow-green leaves narrowly edged with darker green and with bands, opposite or alternate on both sides of the midrib, of similar color curving outward and upward and tapering toward the margin. **C. lietzei**, of Brazil, about 1 foot tall, has leaves with oblong-lanceolate blades about 6 inches in length, above alternately banded from midrib to margin with sharply-defined areas of green and silvery-green, purple on their undersides. Young plantlets are borne on erect stolons. **C. lindeniana**, of Brazil, is up to 3 feet tall, has deep

green, broad-oblong-elliptic leaves feathered along the midrib and paralleling the margin with light olive-green. **C. louisae**, of unknown provenance, differs from *C. lindeniana* in having broader leaves, dark

Calathea louisae

green with featherings of pale yellowish-green angling outward from the midrib. The undersides of the leaves are purple. **C. makoyana**, known as peacock plant, a low, tufted native of Brazil has translucent, pale yellow-green, broad-ovate leaves hand-

Calathea makoyana

somely ornamented with fine lines and sharply-defined, elliptic, alternately long and short patches of green reaching outward from the midrib. **C. princeps** is reported to be a juvenile phase of a tall-growing, plain-green-foliaged Brazilian, *C. altissima*. It has large, yellow-green, oblong-lanceolate leaves feathered along both sides of the midrib with blackish-green and with slender dark veins extending to the leaf margins. **C. veitchiana**, of Ecuador and Peru, is much like *C. magnifica*, but the flame-shaped variegation that fills most of the ovate leaf blade is more boldly scalloped along its edges. The upper leaf surfaces are of various tones of green and have brownish-green patches bordered with yellow-green. The pattern carries through to the undersurface where it is duplicated in red against a background of bluish-green.

Leaves variegated on their upper surfaces with brown or red are typical of these: **C. pavonii** is a Peruvian species about 1¼ feet tall. It has somewhat hairy leaves with asymmetrical, pointed-oblong blades 6 to 10 inches long. Greenish beneath, they have upper surfaces with brown patches paired on either side of the midrib. The yellow flowers are in cylindrical spikes. **C. roseo-picta**, of Brazil, is about 8 inches tall. Its very short-stalked leaves have unequal-sided, elliptic blades about 8 inches long and nearly as broad. They are dull green above with the midrib and a slender, jagged streak midway between it and the leaf margin rose-pink.

Calathea roseo-picta

Garden and Landscape Uses and Cultivation. Among the most lovely of tropical foliage plants, calatheas are greatly esteemed as furnishings for shaded, moist locations in tropical gardens and for greenhouses where high temperatures and humidities are maintained. They are splendid for dressing the ground beneath trees and tall shrubs. Given plenty of warmth and moisture they are easy to grow. They revel in rich earth that contains an abundance of organic matter and respond to fertilization.

They do not like sodden soil. Excessive wetness over long periods rots their roots. Most often increase is by division, but seeds can be used. In greenhouses calatheas succeed especially well in ground beds, but good specimens can be had in pots. Syringing the foliage sufficiently early in the day for it to dry before nightfall is highly beneficial. Considerable shade, enough to prevent the leaves from curling in response to too intense light, is needed. Repotting and replanting is done in spring. Mealybugs and red spider mites are the chief pests.

CALCEOLARIA (Calceo-lària)—Slipperwort. Native from Mexico to the Peruvian and Chilean Andes, *Calceolaria* of the figwort family SCROPHULARIACEAE consists of over 300 annuals and nonhardy herbaceous perennials, subshrubs, and shrubs, a few and some hybrids of which are cultivated. Alluding to the shape of the flowers, the name is derived from the Latin *calceolus*, a slipper. Two New Zealand species formerly included in *Calceolaria* belong in closely-related *Jovellana*.

Calceolarias have opposite or whorled (in circles of more than two), undivided or pinnate, lobeless or lobed, usually crinkled leaves. Their mostly yellow, less commonly purple to red, or in cultivated kinds rich bronze-reds, conspicuously spotted, often showy flowers are in irregular-branched clusters. They have a calyx of four sepals, a two-lipped corolla, the lower lip forming a pouch or bag in cultivated kinds large and prominent, the upper one much smaller, usually pouched, and covering the two stamens and short style. The fruits are capsules containing many minute seeds.

Most popular and familiar are two groups of presumably hybrid calceolarias of somewhat obscure, unrecorded ancestry. The first, for convenience grouped as *C. herbeohybrida*, are annuals or are mostly grown as such and are commonly called herbaceous hybrid calceolarias. Their parentage is presumably based on *C. crenatiflora* and *C. corymbosa* probably with infusions from other species. A race in which *C. cana* has played a part as parent includes kinds with hoary leaves and scented blooms. The other group, subshrubby or shrubby perennials, for convenience identified as *C. fruticohybrida*, are in the main derived from *C. integrifolia*.

Herbaceous hybrid calceolarias are splendid decoratives. They have large, soft, hairy leaves and immense trusses of flowers up to 2 inches or more in diameter in a wide range of colors and often splendidly spotted. The hues include creamy-white, bright yellow, orange-yellow, bronze-red, and ruby-red. Hybrid shrubby kinds, for long favorites in Great Britain and northern Europe as summer bedding plants, traditionally planted in combina-

Calceolaria herbeohybrida variety

Calceolaria herbeohybrida variety

Calceolaria herbeohybrida variety

tion with red geraniums and blue lobelias, are not much grown in North America. They include *C. fruticohybrida stewartii*, with showy trusses of bright yellow flowers, *C. f. lymanii*, with showy trusses of bronzy-red blooms, and *C. f.* 'Golden Nugget', with golden-yellow blooms.

Species, as distinct from hybrid, calceolarias grown in gardens include the following: *C. amplexicaulis,* of Peru, shrubby, is 2 to 3 feet tall. It has glandular-hairy stems and stalkless, pointed, oblong-ovate, toothed leaves up to about 3 inches long. Their bases clasp the stems. Nearly ¾ inch in diameter, the yellow flowers are profusely borne in long-stalked, somewhat umbel-like panicles. *C. cana,* of Chile, is an herbaceous perennial, somewhat woody in its lower parts, with mostly basal, spatula-shaped-obovate, densely-white-woolly,

Calceolaria amplexicaulis

blunt, toothless leaves about 1½ inches long, and slender-stalked, branching trusses of about ½-inch-wide, yellow flowers. *C. chelidonioides,* is a native annual of Peru, 1 foot to 2 feet tall, and hairy only in its upper parts. Its pinnate or pinnately-lobed leaves, with the terminal lobe the biggest, are 5 to 8 inches long. In terminal umbel-like clusters with glandular-hairy stalks, the flowers are yellow, about ½ inch long by 1¾ to 2 inches wide. *C. corymbosa,* of Chile, is a herbaceous perennial 1 foot to 2 feet tall. It has double-toothed, heart-shaped basal leaves up to 6 inches long and smaller, toothless, stalkless stem leaves. The ½-inch-wide flowers in branched clusters are yellow with purple spots and stripes. *C. crenatiflora* is a hairy-stemmed, Chilean herbaceous perennial 1 foot to 1½ feet tall. Its deeply-round-toothed, short-stalked basal leaves, up to about 6 inches long, are ovate-oblong to oblong. The few stem leaves, pointed-ovate and toothless, are approximately 2 inches in length. Golden-yellow, spotted or striped with purple, the nearly 1-inch-wide blooms are

Calceolaria integrifolia

in length by up to 1 inch or more in width. The flowers, short-stalked and in rather crowded clusters, are without spots. Ranging in hue from yellow to reddish-brown, they are approximately ½ inch in diameter. *C. mexicana,* of Mexico and Central

Calceolaria polyrrhiza

biosaefolia), a variable hairy annual native from Ecuador to Chile, is from 9 inches to 2 feet tall, and branched. It has usually purplish, slender stems and pinnate or pinnately-lobed, deeply-toothed leaves 5 to 8 inches in length, with two or three pairs of leaflets or lobes. The bases of the stalks of the pairs of leaves are united. In hairy-stalked, open clusters, the pale yellow flowers are about ½ inch long by ⅓ inch wide.

Calceolaria darwinii

Calceolaria mexicana

in loose, branched trusses. *C. darwinii,* native of the Strait of Magellan region, is a choice, almost stemless, low herbaceous perennial. It has hairless, minutely-toothed, wavy-margined leaves up to 3 inches long, and 1-inch-wide, reddish-brown-spotted, yellow flowers on stalks up to 6 inches in length. *C. fothergillii* is a stemless perennial native of Patagonia and the Falkland Islands. It has short creeping rhizomes and crowded, round-apexed, spatula-shaped leaves with scarcely-toothed, densely-hairy margins. They are 1 inch to 1½ inches long. The bases of each pair are united. The solitary, red-spotted, sulfur-yellow flowers, about ¾ inch long, are on usually leafless stalks up to 5 inches in length from the axils of the upper leaves. *C. integrifolia,* of Chile, is a subshrub or shrub 2 to 6 feet tall, its young shoots and leaves more or less sticky-hairy. The crinkled or pebble-surfaced, oblong to oblong-elliptic, round-toothed leaves are 1 inch to 3 inches

America, is a dainty annual 9 inches to 1 foot tall. Its lower leaves are of three leaflets or are three-lobed, those higher on the stems are pinnately-cut or -lobed into toothed, ovate leaflets or segments 1 inch to 2½ inches long. About ¾ inch long by ½ inch wide, the loosely-arranged flowers are soft yellow. *C. polyrrhiza* is a creeping, somewhat hairy native of Patagonia. About 2 inches high, it has lanceolate leaves 2 to 2½ inches long. Its flowers solitary or up to five on glandular-hairy stalks 3 or 4 inches long, usually from the leaf axils, are about 1 inch long by ½ inch wide. They are yellow spotted with purple. *C. tenella,* native to Chile, is a creeper with rooting, reddish, sparsely-hairy stems. Up to about 8 inches tall, it has short-stalked, ½-inch-long, broadly-ovate, blunt, few-toothed leaves. The yellow flowers, about ½ inch long, are carried in twos or threes on stems, each with a pair of small leaves, 3 to 6 inches tall. *C. tripartita* (syn. *C. sca-*

Calceolaria tripartita

Garden and Landscape Uses. Calceolarias are cool weather plants. Most kinds fail to thrive or die in hot and humid climates, an exception being, perhaps, annual *C. mexicana.* Because of this, only hybrid herbaceous kinds that can be conveniently grown from seeds as annuals, and two or three of the *C. fruticohybrida* group and *C. amplexicaulis* that can be raised from cuttings annually, are attempted in most parts of North America. The propagation of these is timed so that their growing season is chiefly fall and winter and their blooming season spring. Even so, except in air-conditioned greenhouses, they are not accounted among the easiest plants to manage.

In California and elsewhere in mild climates, varieties of *C. fruticohybrida* are employed to some extent as bedding plants. In a few places these or other shrubby kinds may be permanent features in gardens. In the Pacific Northwest and similarly climatically favored places, connoisseurs of choice rock plants test their skills with the dwarf species from southern South America. The annual kinds, although easy to manage under a wider range of conditions, are not much grown.

The dwarf perennials, relatively hardy kinds native to southernmost South America, are beautiful rock garden plants impatient also of high summer temperatures and humidities and severe winter cold. They are to be expected to succeed only in parts of the Pacific Northwest and other places favored with fairly uniform, relatively cool, humid climates. This group includes *C. darwinii*, *C. fothergillii*, and *C. polyrrhiza*. Annuals other than the herbaceous hybrids, such as *C. chelidonioides*, *C. mexicana*, and *C. scabiosaefolia*, are pretty but not extravagantly showy plants worthy of considering for use in rock gardens, at the fronts of flower borders, and in greenhouses.

Cultivation. Overriding needs of calceolarias are frostless, cool, humid conditions, sufficient shade to break the intensity of strong sun, and a fairly free circulation of air without exposure to cold drafts or drying winds. Arid atmospheres, brilliant sun, and near scorching heat are not tolerated. The soil must be well drained, at all times uniformly moist, and never for long periods wet.

Herbaceous hybrids are raised from seeds sown in well-drained pots or pans (shallow pots) in soil containing generous proportions of peat moss or leaf mold and sand or perlite. Because the seeds are so small it is important that the surface soil be finely screened and level. Late July to mid-August sowings are usually preferred because the resulting plants then do not have to face a long period of uncontrollable high temperatures. In regions of fairly cool nights and in air-conditioned greenhouses sowings to give larger plants may be made as early as May. Shade the young seedlings fairly heavily and take great care with watering. They are very subject to damping off. When of a size convenient to handle, transplant the young plants, spacing them about 2½ inches apart in flats of porous, fairly-coarse rather than finely-sifted soil containing a scattering of bonemeal and dried cow manure in addition to good topsoil, peat moss or leaf mold, and coarse

sand or perlite. The next move, when the plants in the flats begin to crowd, is to 4-inch pots. Later transfers made as soon as the plants have established a nice network of roots around their balls of soil, are to large containers. Excellent usable specimens can be finished in pots 6 inches in diameter, but larger ones are quite attainable. To help assure the cool, humid conditions in which these plants delight, keep their pots standing on a surface of cinders, gravel, sand or other medium that by periodic damping down is kept constantly moist. Until cold weather arrives the plants can be grown in a shaded, north-facing cold frame. In severe climates they must be accommodated in a greenhouse through the winter. As soon as weather permits, keep the night temperature between 45 to 50°F, before then as cool as practicable. Day temperatures may be five to ten degrees higher. Allow sufficient space between individuals so that their spreading leaves do not crowd. When the final pots become filled with roots start biweekly or weekly applications of dilute liquid fertilizer. No shade is needed during midwinter, but when sunlight strengthens appreciably early in the year light protection is needed. Take particular care in winter not to water excessively. When flowering stalks begin to push up stake them neatly with as few stakes as practicable. Be careful not to wet the flowers. Water causes them to become spotted. Plants can be bloomed earlier than normal by providing them from mid-November on with four hours artificial lighting to extend the natural day length.

Shrubby calceolarias, such as *C. fruticohybrida* varieties and *C. amplexicaulis*, are grown in the same way as the herbaceous hybrids, except that they are propagated from cuttings taken in late summer instead of from seeds, and it is desirable to pinch out their shoots once or twice during their early growing stages to encourage branching. Standards (tree-form specimens) of *C. amplexicaulis* can be had by allowing a rooted cutting to develop without pinching until it is 2 to 2½ feet tall, then pinching out its end, and the ends of branches that develop as a result of this when they are 5 to 6 inches long. The main stem is kept tied to a stake. Any shoots that develop below the head are promptly removed.

Annual calceolarias can be had in bloom in greenhouses and outdoors within a few weeks of seed sowing. Scatter the seeds thinly where the plants are to remain and thin the seedlings to distances that preclude overcrowding or sow in pots and transplant. Choose for these, lightly-shaded places where the soil is damp.

Rock garden calceolarias are most likely in the few regions where they are possible to accommodate to watersides and shaded, moist clefts or crevices, and to experienced

care in alpine greenhouses. Deep-rooted *C. darwinii* is better grown in pots than shallow pans. The soil should contain an abundance of leaf mold. Avoid disturbing established plants unless quite necessary. Increase is by division in spring and by seeds. The most common pests of calceolarias are aphids, whiteflies, sowbugs, slugs, thrips, and leaf nematodes. They are subject to stem rot, root rot, and a bacterial wilt.

CALCIUM CARBONATE. See Lime and Liming.

CALCIUM CHLORIDE. This chemical, used on dirt roads to keep down dust, can have a deleterious effect on vegetation if carried to roots in water that soaks into the soil. Symptoms are scorching of the foliage similar to that caused by lack of sufficient moisture in the ground. Surface grading to carry storm water from the road surface away from the roots of valued plants is the best protection.

CALCIUM METAPHOSPHATE. A high-analysis phosphatic fertilizer with a neutral acid-alkaline reaction, calcium metaphosphate is a good garden fertilizer. It contains about 53 percent available phosphoric acid and may be applied in spring at about ½ ounce to 10 square feet.

CALCIUM NITRATE. Also known as nitrate of lime, this fertilizer contains 15.5 to 16 percent quickly-available nitrogen, about 48 percent calcium carbonate (lime). It reduces soil acidity and so is not generally suitable for acid-soil plants. It may be used in spring and summer at a rate of ½ to 1 ounce to 10 square feet.

CALCIUM SULFATE. See Gypsum.

CALENDULA (Calénd-ula)—Pot Marigold, Field-Marigold. Gaily-colored annuals and herbaceous perennials constitute this genus of twenty to thirty species natives from the Canary Islands to Iran. One, the common pot marigold (*Calendula officinalis*), is an old-fashioned, familiar garden plant, others are occasionally grown in botanical gardens and other special collections. Calendulas belong in the daisy family COMPOSITAE. The name is derived from the Latin *calendae*, the first day of the month and the day when interest must be paid. It alludes to the long period of bloom. Marigold, originally Mary's gold, has reference to the Virgin Mary.

Calendulas have alternate, undivided, lobeless leaves and most commonly large yellow or orange flower heads which, except in double-flowered horticultural varieties, are of the daisy type; that is to say, they consist of a disk or "eye" of short florets surrounded by radiating ray florets that look like petals. In fully double flowers all the florets are rays. Each floret, disk and ray, is really a tiny individual flower. The involucre (collar of bracts at the back of the flower head) consists of one or two rows. The fruits are seedlike achenes.

Common pot marigold (*C. officinalis*) in its wild form is an erect, branched plant 1 foot to 1½ feet tall. It has oblong to oblong-obovate leaves that narrow to their bases and are more or less stem-clasping. The orange-yellow flower heads, 1 inch to 2 inches in diameter, are solitary, terminal, stalked, and have rays that spread by day, but are erect so that the flower head closes at night. The entire plant is covered with fine hairs, is slightly clammy, and when bruised gives off a distinctive odor. Horticultural varieties of pot marigold include various flower forms, mostly fully double, with heads of bloom 3 to 5 inches in diameter and ranging in color from creamy-yellow to brilliant orange. These varieties are listed and described in seed catalogs. American plant breeders have been especially active in developing improved varieties, especially kinds with long flower stalks and fine colored blooms suitable for cutting. Despite the improvements these productions display, the unimproved single-flowered wild type has a distinct charm and is worth a place in the garden. The name pot marigold refers to the use, previously commonly and in Europe still to some extent made, of the flowers of *C. officinalis* for flavoring foods. The chief reasons for growing this popular plant today, however, are as a flower garden ornamental and for the production of cut flowers. It satisfies both purposes well.

Other species of *Calendula* are *C. aegyptiaca,* a 1½-foot-tall, sticky-hairy annual from Egypt and Asia Minor that has linear-lanceolate leaves and short-rayed flower heads about ½ inch in diameter. The field-marigold (*C. arvensis*), of the Mediterranean region, about 1 foot high, is an annual with oblong-lanceolate, sometimes toothed leaves. Its flower heads, 1½ inches across, have yellow ray florets. Another annual, *C. eriocarpa,* is a nearly hairless kind, the precise habitat of which is unknown. It has lanceolate leaves and yellow flower heads about 1 inch across. From Madeira comes *C. maderensis,* a perennial kind that attains a height of 2 feet, with oblong-spoon-shaped, rough leaves and yellow flower heads. The plant known as *C. maritima* is closely related to and is probably only a variation of *C. officinalis.* A sticky-pubescent annual with 1½-inch-wide, yellow flower heads, this kind is endemic to Sicily. Found only in North Africa, *C. maroccana* is an annual closely related to *C. suffruticosa,* but with narrower leaves. The species named *C. sicula* is likely only an extreme form of *C. officinalis,* differing in being almost without hairs and having flower heads about 1 inch in diameter. Its home is southern Italy. Annual

Variety of *Calendula officinalis*

Variety of *Calendula officinalis*

C. stellata, of the Mediterranean region, up to 1 foot in height, has rough, ovate-oblong leaves and yellow flower heads 1 inch to 2 inches in diameter. Also from the Mediterranean region, *C. suffruticosa* is a pubescent annual with a stem that becomes somewhat woody below. Its lanceo-late leaves are more or less toothed. Borne profusely, its yellow flowers are about 1 inch across.

Garden and Landscape Uses. Calendulas are admirable for flower beds and borders and, the wild form of the common pot marigold (*C. officinalis*) for inclusion in

Border of calendulas

herb gardens. As cut flowers they are long-lasting and attractive and can be produced outdoors throughout the summer and at other seasons in greenhouses.

Cultivation. Calendulas, even the rarely cultivated perennial ones, are grown as annuals. Outdoors they need a sunny location and succeed in comparatively poor and even dryish soils. When grown in excessively rich ones they are less successful than in earth of medium fertility. For the production of long-stemmed blooms for cutting, however, the soil must be reasonably moist. Seeds may be sown outdoors in spring or, in regions of mild winters in fall, where the plants are to bloom. If the seeds are broadcast, thin the seedlings to from 8 to 10 inches apart. If they are sown in rows, as is usual for the production of cut flowers, allow 1 foot to 1½ feet between the rows and thin the seedlings to 7 to 9 inches in the rows. For cut flowers harvest the blooms just before they are fully open. Strip their lower stems of leaves, and stand them immediately in deep cool water in shade.

For the production of early flowers outdoors or to have plants to set out early to succeed spring-blooming plants, calendulas can be started indoors from seeds sown about eight weeks before the young plants are to be transferred to the garden, which may be done after all danger of frost is passed. The seedlings are first transplanted, spaced about 2 inches apart, to flats or are set individually in small pots in porous, medium-fertile soil and are grown in a sunny greenhouse, or they may be transplanted to a soil bed in a hotbed or cold frame. Night temperatures of 45 to 50°F, and daytime ones of 55 to 60°F, are ample. Too much warmth results in weak, over-large plants.

Outdoor summer care is not exacting. It consists chiefly of promptly removing faded blooms, keeping weeds under control, and paying early attention to any diseases or pests that may threaten. In dry weather periodic watering is desirable. For the production of cut flowers in greenhouses calendulas are grown in ground beds or benches. They can also be raised in pots

and used for conservatory and greenhouse decoration. For these purposes seeds are sown from late July to January or February and the seedlings transplanted individually to 2½-inch pots (flats to hold more at 2 to 2½ inches apart may be used, but pots are preferable). Before they become crowded in the pots or flats plants grown for cut flowers are planted in the beds or benches, spaced 1¼ by 1¼ feet. A moderately-rich, well-drained soil is most satisfactory. The night temperature should be 45 to 50°F. Day temperatures will normally be five to ten degrees higher. Branching is encouraged by pinching out the tip of the main stem of each plant. Only one flower is permitted to develop on each branch. To make sure of this, all side buds are removed when they are quite small. Eight to twelve fine blooms are to be expected from each plant. About the time the plants touch each other and after they have filled their available soil with roots they may be given weekly applications of dilute liquid fertilizer, but stop these before the blooms show much color. Watering should be moderate at first, more freely done after the plants are well rooted. Plants grown in pots, those about 6 inches in diameter are of suitable size, require the same treatment as bench-grown plants, but are likely to need more frequent fertilizing.

Diseases and Pests. A quite serious leaf spot disease affects calendulas and may destroy the plants. Dusting or spraying with sulfur is the recommended control. Other diseases are stem rots, leaf blights, powdery mildew, smut, and aster yellows. A black mold often grows on the honeydew that spreads over the leaves from aphids. The chief insect pests are aphids, whitefly, caterpillars, thrips, tarnished plant bug, leaf hoppers, blister beetles, and nematodes.

CALIBANUS (Calib-ànus). Much resembling *Nolina*, the only species of *Calibanus* belongs in the lily family LILIACEAE, or according to those who favor the segregation, to the agave family AGAVACEAE. Its name, that of Caliban, the ugly monster of William Shakespeare's *The Tempest*, was presumably suggested by its somewhat ungainly appearance.

Native of Mexico, where its leaves are used for thatching and scouring, *C. hookeri* (syn. *Dasylirion hartwegianum*) has a hemispherical, woody, above-ground, tuberous stem or trunk 1 foot to 3 feet in diameter, much resembling that of the African elephant's foot (*Dioscorea elephantipes*). It has thick, fissured, corky bark and fibrous roots. From it are produced brief branches each terminating in a tuft of slender, wiry, bluish, linear leaves 1 foot to 3 feet long. Each branch blooms once and then dies. The flowers, in broad, rigid-branched panicles from 4 inches to nearly 1 foot long, are unisexual, with the sexes on different plants. They have six purplish

perianth segments or tepals (commonly thought of as petals) and six stamens. The fruits are globular, one-seeded capsules.

Garden and Landscape Uses and Cultivation. This species is of interest to collectors of succulents and other dry-region plants. It requires the same conditions and care as *Nolina*. In their early stages at least, seedlings are reported to make surprisingly rapid growth.

CALICHE. Pronounced cal-ee-che, this is the name given to hardpan deposits of calcium carbonate or mixed carbonates that occur in deserts and semiarid regions. Caliche may be at the surface or inches or feet below ground. It may be granular or compressed and cemented into practically impermeable layers, a few inches to many feet thick. For more information see Desert Gardens.

CALICO BUSH is *Kalmia latifolia*.

CALICO FLOWER is *Aristolochia elegans*. Blue calico flower is *Downingia elegans*.

CALICOTOME (Calicotò-me). Sometimes spelled *Calycotome*, this genus of seven species of the pea family LEGUMINOSAE inhabits the Mediterranean region. Its members are deciduous, spiny shrubs related to brooms (*Cytisus*), from which they differ in their calyxes having no teeth. The name comes from the Greek *kalyx*, calyx, and *tome*, cut, and alludes to the shedding of the tops of the calyxes. Calicotomes have stalked leaves with three stalkless leaflets and yellow, pea-like blooms, clustered or solitary. When the buds open the tops of the calyxes fall away leaving the five-toothed, cup-shaped base. The fruits are several-seeded, linear-oblong pods with winged or thickened margins.

Densely-branched and with many spines ⅓ to ⅔ inch long, *Calicotome villosa* is about 3 feet tall and has shoots thinly clothed with cottony hairs. The stalked flowers, up to ¾ inch long, are generally in clusters of five to fifteen. Softly-hairy on their undersides, the leaves have leaflets from under ¼ to under ½ inch long. Clothed with woolly hairs, the pods are 1 inch long or somewhat longer. From the last *C. spinosa* differs in its flowers usually being solitary and its seed pods without hairs. It is native from Spain to Yugoslavia.

Garden and Landscape Uses and Cultivation. These shrubs are not hardy in the north. They are best suited for Mediterranean-type climates such as that of California. They are attractive general purpose shrubs that can be used effectively for low hedges. They need very well-drained soil and full sun and are propagated by seeds and cuttings. Because they do not transplant well they are grown in containers until they are planted in their permanent locations. They need no systematic pruning.

CALIFORNIA. The word California is used in part of the common names of these plants: California big tree (*Sequoiadendron giganteum*), California bluebell (*Phacelia minor*), California-buckwheat (*Eriogonum fasciculatum*), California-cherry (*Prunus ilicifolia*), California-fuchsia (*Zauschneria californica*), California-geranium (*Senecio petasitis*), California gold fern (*Pityrogramma triangularis*), California-holly (*Heteromeles arbutifolia*), California-laurel (*Umbellularia californica*), California-lilac (*Ceanothus*), California-nutmeg (*Torreya californica*), California pepper tree (*Schinus molle*), California pitcher plant (*Darlingtonia californica*), California-poppy (*Eschscholzia californica*), and California-rose (*Calystegia hederacea florepleno*).

CALLA (Cál-la)—Wild Calla or Water-Arum. This must not be confused with the calla-lily (*Zantedeschia*), a tender native of South Africa quite distinct from our present plant. The wild calla or water-arum (*Calla palustris*) inhabits swamps and shallow water throughout the northern parts of Europe and Asia and in America from Quebec to Alberta, New Jersey and Ohio. The only representative of its genus, it belongs in the arum family ARACEAE, thus although not identical with, it is related to the calla-lily. The name *Calla* is an ancient one used by Pliny. The black-calla is *Arum palaestinum*.

The wild calla (*C. palustris*) has long slender rhizomes that root from the nodes

Calla palustris

and develop clusters of erect, long-stalked, ovate to broadly-heart-shaped leaves with blades 4 to 8 inches across. Each has a well-defined midrib and parallel upswept lateral veins. The spadix (flower spike), up to 1 inch long, is crowded with tiny bisexual flowers. From shortly below it sprouts the

ovate to elliptic white, petal-like spathe (bract). Unlike that of the calla-lily, it does not envelop the spadix, but flares upward and to one side. The stalk carrying the spadix and spathe is 4 inches to 1 foot in length. The blooms appear to early summer and are succeeded by spikes of bright red berries, something like those of the jack-in-the-pulpit, but smaller.

Garden Uses and Cultivation. For swampy places, bog gardens, and wet spots in rock gardens the wild calla is well adapted to a muddy soil, preferably rich with organic matter and acid rather than alkaline. It needs still water; it will not grow where there is a constant flow. The runners travel, so the plant needs a little room to spread. Propagation is very easy by division in spring and by stem cuttings planted in mud in summer. Seeds, freed of their surrounding pulp and sown in sandy, peaty soil kept constantly wet germinate satisfactorily. If sown in pots or pans keep these submerged almost to soil level in water.

CALLA-LILY. See Zantedeschia.

CALLIANDRA (Calli-ándra)—Powder Puff Tree. Fairy Duster. Excellent ornamentals are found in this genus of approximately 100 species of nonhardy trees and shrubs that belongs to the section of the pea family LEGUMINOSAE that includes *Albizzia* and *Acacia*. The name comes from the Greek *kallos*, beauty, and *andros*, stamens, and alludes to the obvious and most showy feature of the pompon flower heads.

Calliandras are mostly spineless. They have alternate, twice-pinnate leaves with few to many leaflets. The flowers, in more or less spherical or hemispherical heads, are brilliant red, purplish, white, or bicolored. Each of the individual blooms of the heads has a toothed or cleft calyx, a small five-parted corolla, and many long, slender, silky stamens with their stalks joined in their lower parts. The fruits are pods with thickened margins, which feature distinguishes *Calliandra* from *Albizzia*. They usually curl markedly after the seeds are discharged. This genus inhabits warm parts of the Americas, Asia, and Madagascar.

The powder puff tree (*C. haematocephala* syn. *C. inaequilatera*) has occasioned much botanical discussion, chiefly because it was first described from plants cultivated in Java and thought to be native there. Not until much later was it discovered by a botanist exploring Bolivia and, on the assumption that it was different from the Javan plant, was given another name. For long it was supposed that the Javan and South American plants were two species, but this is not so. There is no doubt that *C. haematocephala* was introduced to Java from its native Bolivia, quite likely inadvertently with seeds of rubber trees or other desired species, early and without being recorded.

One of the most beautiful and satisfactory tropical ornamentals, *C. haematocephala* is 15 feet or so tall and widespreading. It has leaves with a single pair of major divisions each with four to ten, but most commonly five to eight, leaflets,

Calliandra haematocephala

the basal pair smaller than the others, and the terminal pair largest. The latter are shaped like the outline of a lobster's claw. The leaflets are ¾ inch to 3½ inches long and dark green. In bud the solitary, long-stalked flower heads suggest raspberries. They come from the leaf axils and consist of twenty to forty-five flowers crowded into beautiful, regularly-formed, hemispherical, powder pufflike heads up to 3 inches in diameter. The flowers are displayed in succession over a season of several weeks and commonly are brilliant scarlet. But when plants are raised from seeds considerable color variation occurs, and there are pink-flowered individuals and a rarer variety with pure white blooms.

Beautiful white flowers in hemispherical heads are typical of *C. portoricensis,* of the West Indies. This is a tree up to about 25 feet tall with attractive, ferny foliage. The leaves have two to six pairs of primary divisions 1½ to 3 inches long, and each with ten to thirty pairs of narrow leaflets up to a little over ½ inch long. The long-stalked flower heads are 1¼ to 2 inches across. The seed pods attain lengths of 2 to 4 inches.

Shrubby, or sometimes somewhat climbing, and from 6 to 25 feet tall, *C. surinamensis* has fernlike leaves, 2 to 4 inches long, with two major divisions, each with seven to thirteen pairs of asymmetrically elliptic to ovate, lustrous leaflets up to 1 inch long or a little longer. The flowers, in heads up to 2 inches or more wide, look like white brushes that have been dipped in bright pink ink. The stamens are white in their lower halves, pink above. The fruits are slender, often paired pods about 3 inches long. This kind is native of Surinam.

A large, hairless, slender-branched shrub of Mexico, *C. emarginata* has lustrous leaves with one pair of major divisions each with a terminal pair of leaflets and a solitary, smaller, lower one. The leaflets are somewhat leathery, lopsidedly ovate-oblong, blunt to somewhat pointed, and 1¼ to 2½ inches long. The long-stalked heads of scarlet blooms are 1 inch to 2 inches in diameter. The slender seed pods are up to 4 inches long.

A shrub, 6 feet or somewhat taller, with lacy, very finely-divided foliage and brilliant crimson blooms, *C. tweedii* has long been popular. It is a native of Brazil and has leaves separated into three or four pairs of major divisions that in turn are divided into twenty to thirty pairs of linear leaflets up to ¼ inch long. The flower heads are at the ends of stalks 1 inch to 2 inches long from the leaf axils. They are 3 to 3½ inches across, but less full and regular than those of the powder puff tree. The stamens are more evidently in clusters. A succession of blooms is maintained over a long period.

The fairy duster (*C. eriophylla*) is one of several species that inhabit desert and

Calliandra emarginata

semidesert regions of the southwestern United States and Mexico. A dense, intricately-stiff-branched shrub up to 3 feet or so high but often lower, it has hairy shoots and short-stalked leaves, the latter hairy at least on their undersides, and with usually three pairs of primary divisions up to 1 inch long, each with five to fifteen pairs of narrow leaflets up to ⅕ inch long. The pale to deep pink flowers, in heads 1¼ to 1¾ inches across, are succeeded by slender, velvety seed pods 1½ to 3 inches long.

Calliandra tweedii

Calliandra eriophylla

This species is effective in controlling erosion and provides useful fodder for browsing animals.

Garden and Landscape Uses. For the tropics and subtropics, including Hawaii, southern California, and southern Florida, *C. haematocephala* and *C. portoricensis* are two of the most desirable flowering small trees, adaptable for a variety of purposes, including display as single lawn specimens. For similar regions, *C. tweedii* and *C. surinamensis* are equally dependable and may be used in mixed shrub plantings and beds, and for hedges. These are also excellent for greenhouses, *C. haematocephala* and *C. portoricensis* requiring considerably more space than the last-named kinds, but they respond to repeated pruning well and so it is possible to keep them much smaller than their normal sizes and yet enjoy their blooms. Desert kinds are appropriate only for a warm dry climate, such as that of the Southwest. There they may be used as interesting small shrubs in rock gardens and other plantings. Desert calliandras need full sun. Other kinds prefer full sun, but will stand part-day shade.

Cultivation. Easily raised from seeds and increased by cuttings, preferably set in a propagating bed with mild bottom heat, calliandras are easy plants to grow. Desert types need well-drained, dryish earth, the others any fertile, moderately-moist, but not overwet soil. Prune only as necessary to keep the plants shapely or to limit their size as soon as blooming is through. These plants stand hard cutting back well, and respond with vigorous new growth. In greenhouses a winter night temperature of 55 to 60°F is high enough; by day it may be five to fifteen degrees higher, and at other seasons considerably higher. A humid atmosphere is desirable. Some shade from strong summer sun should be provided. Calliandras are very free from pests and diseases.

CALLICARPA (Calli-cárpa)—Beautyberry, French-Mulberry. Beautyberries are so called because of the unique and lovely colorings of the fruits of many kinds. Their botanical name reflects this. It comes from the Greek *kallos,* beauty, and *karpos,* a fruit. Belonging to the vervain family VERBENA-CEAE, the number of species is reported to be 140, chiefly tropical and subtropical with a few in temperate regions. The group is native to both the Old World and the New. One kind is indigenous to the United States.

Beautyberries are shrubs or trees, the cultivated ones deciduous, with opposite, generally-toothed, leaves. Commonly they are furnished to a greater or lesser extent with a scurf of stellate (star-shaped) hairs. Their insignificant flowers are small and in clusters from the leaf axils. They are whitish, pinkish, or bluish. They have short calyxes that are bell-shaped, four-toothed, or rarely, four-parted. The short-tubed corollas have four lobes (petals). There are four projecting stamens of equal length, and an unbranched style. The approximately spherical, usually shining, berry-like fruits (technically drupes) contain two to four stones (commonly called seeds). In cultivated kinds the fruits are violet to lilac-violet or white.

The American beautyberry or French-mulberry (**Callicarpa americana**) is native from Maryland to Florida, Tennessee,

Callicarpa americana (fruit)

Texas, and in the West Indies. One of the handsomest of the cultivated kinds, it, unfortunately, is not hardy in the north. Up to 6 feet in height and with a scurf of star-shaped hairs, this species has pointed, broad, ovate-oblong leaves up to 6 inches in length and margined with blunt teeth. They are greenish or grayish-green above and whitish or brownish on their undersides. The flowers, in stalkless or nearly stalkless clusters, open from late spring to early summer. They have slightly-toothed calyxes and bluish corollas. The fruits, about ⅙ inch in diameter, are violet to lavender-pink. This kind is native in rich

woodlands and thickets. Variety *C. a. lactea* (syn. *C. a. alba*) has milky-white fruits.

Other kinds not hardy in the north are *C. mollis* and *C. rubella.* Native of Japan and Korea, 8 feet tall or taller, **C. mollis** has its shoots and undersides of its leaves densely covered with soft, starry hairs. Its toothed, ovate-lanceolate leaves are up to 6 inches long. The purplish-pink flowers are followed by dull violet-purple berries. A hybrid between this and *C. japonica* is **C. shirasawana.** Less conspicuously hairy than *C. mollis,* in other respects it is intermedi-

Callicarpa shirasawana (fruit)

ate between its parents. Native of China, Burma, and Assam, *C. rubella* is up to 10 feet tall and handsome in fruit. Of open, branching habit and with downy shoots, it has slender-pointed, lanceolate-oblong to ovate-oblong leaves 4 to 6 inches long, shallowly-toothed and densely-hairy on their undersides. The purplish-pink flowers are in stalked clusters about 1 inch wide. The fruits, ⅒ inch in diameter, are bright rose-purple.

Best of the hardy kinds is **C. japonica,** of Japan and Korea. This beautiful shrub is

Callicarpa rubella (flowers)

Callicarpa japonica

sometimes 15 feet, but often not more than 8 to 10 feet, tall. It has hairless twigs and long-pointed, elliptic to ovate-lanceolate leaves 3 to 6 inches long or sometimes longer, 1½ to 2 inches wide, and toothed from near their bases. Their under surfaces are paler than their upper and are glandular-hairy. The flowers, their calyxes shallowly-toothed, are lilac-pink to nearly white. They are in clusters ¾ inch to 1¼ inches across, with stalks longer than the leafstalks. The shining, rich violet fruits are about ⅙ inch in diameter. Variety *C. j. leucocarpa* has white fruits. Variety *C. j. angustata* is distinguished by its narrower leaves.

Callicarpa japonica leucocarpa (fruit)

Very similar to *C. japonica*, but smaller in all its parts and with its young shoots clothed with a scurf of star-shaped hairs, **C. dichotoma** (syn. *C. purpurea*) is native to Korea and China. It is naturalized in parts of northeastern America. This kind is 3 to

6 feet in height. Its leaves are ordinarily 1¼ to 3½ inches long. They are toothed except toward their bases and apexes, and are light green and glandular on their undersides. The flowers are in clusters ½ to 1 inch across with stalks as long or longer than the leafstalks. They are pink and are succeeded by lilac-violet fruits up to ⅙ inch in diameter.

Callicarpa dichotoma (fruit)

Chinese **C. bodinieri giraldii** (syn. *C. giraldiana*) is an attractive erect shrub that differs from typical *C. bodinieri* in having less hairy and less sharply-toothed leaves. It is also much commoner in cultivation. From 6 to 9 feet in height, it has shoots that are downy at first and narrowly slender-pointed, ovate to lanceolate leaves up to 5 inches long and about 2½ inches wide. They have some hairs on their lower surfaces. The lilac flowers are in hairy, branched clusters, with stalks one-half as long as the leafstalks, and ¾ inch to 1¼ inches across. The lilac-violet fruits are up to ⅙ inch in diameter.

Garden and Landscape Uses. Only in fruit do beautyberries claim particular attention, but then they are so unusual that they invariably surprise those who see them for the first time. Their brilliant displays make an unique contribution to fall landscapes. Their berries remain attractive for a reasonable but not very long, time. They are gone before severe winter weather arrives. For their best accommodation these shrubs need full sun or slight shade and moderately fertile, moistish soil. They are scarcely substantial enough in appearance to be planted as solitary specimens, but they lend themselves to grouping in borders and, in large landscapes, massing in beds.

Cultivation. Increase of beautyberries is very easily had from seeds and by cuttings made of firm shoots in summer planted in a greenhouse or cold frame propagating

bed. When raised from seeds the plants vary somewhat in the size and abundance of their fruits and especially good forms should be selected for planting. No regular pruning is necessary, but if it is desired to limit the plants to size long shoots of the previous year may be shortened very considerably in late winter or early spring. The flowers and fruits are developed along shoots of the current season's growth.

CALLICOMA (Callíc-oma). One species of the cunonia family CUNONIACEAE is the only member of this genus. Its name comes from the Greek *kallos*, beauty, and *kome*, hair. It alludes to the tufted appearance of the heads of bloom. Endemic to Australia, **Callicoma serratifolia** is a tall shrub or a tree up to 40 feet tall. It has woolly-hairy shoots and opposite, undivided, evergreen, coarsely-toothed, broad-elliptic to ovate-lanceolate leaves 2 to 6 inches long and ¾ inch to 2 inches wide. They are glossy above and covered with whitish or reddish-brown hairs on their undersides. Clustered in dense, spherical heads with long-protruded stamens, the yellow flowers are borne from the leaf axils and shoot ends. Up to 1 inch across, the heads are composed of small flowers with four or five tiny sepals, no petals, and ten stamens. The fruits are small, several-seeded capsules grouped in globular clusters.

Garden Uses and Cultivation. Hardy only in mild climates in such areas as southern California, this plant is useful for general planting where an evergreen spring-flowering shrub or small tree is appropriate. It succeeds most surely in well-drained but fairly moist, fertile soil, in sun. It blooms while quite small. It is propagated by seeds, which germinate readily in sandy peaty soil in a temperature of about 60°F, and by cuttings planted in a greenhouse propagating bench.

CALLIOPSIS. See Coreopsis.

CALLIRHOE (Callírho-e)—Poppy-Mallow. Despite their common name, these are neither poppies nor mallows, but they do belong to the mallow family MALVACEAE. The genus, entirely North American, consists of about seven species. Its name is that of the daughter of the river god Achelous of Greek mythology.

Callirhoes are annuals or more often herbaceous perennials with thick, tuberous taproots, and hairy, sometimes roughly so, stems and foliage. The leaves are alternate, and deeply-palmately (in hand-fashion) divided or lobed, with the segments or lobes lobed or toothed. At the bases of the leafstalks are large leafy appendages called stipules. On long stalks from the leaf axils or in terminal racemes, the large, usually colorful flowers make brave displays. In some species there is a whorl (tier) of bracts some distance below the bloom. The flowers have five-lobed calyxes, and five spreading magenta-pink to crimson or more rarely white petals, which differ from those of mallows (*Malva*) in that they are not notched at their apexes, but are irregularly-toothed or frayed there or are cut squarely across. The stalks of the stamens are united, the anthers separate. The doughnut-shaped fruits consist of many seedlike carpels.

A garden favorite, *Callirhoe involucrata* is a variable native from North Dakota to Wyoming, Utah, Missouri, Oklahoma, and Texas. A stout-rooted perennial with sprawling stems sometimes 2 feet long, it has generally deeply five- or seven-parted, and toothed leaves with blades up to 2 inches wide or a little wider. The bright cherry-red to purplish-red or less commonly white blooms are 1½ to 2½ inches across.

Callirhoe involucrata

Other poppy-mallows are cultivated. A perennial native from Georgia to Florida and Texas, *C. papaver* has a long, thin, woody taproot, and upright or sprawling, sparsely-hairy or hairless stems 1 foot to 2 feet long. Its long-stalked, triangular, ovate, or heart-shaped leaves are of three or five long, narrow, sometimes toothed lobes. Bright rose-red to purple-red, the blooms are mostly 2 inches wide or wider. A thick-rooted perennial with erect stems up to about 2 feet tall, *C. alcaeoides* ranges from Illinois to Nebraska, Alabama, and Texas. It has heart-shaped to triangular-heart-shaped leaves with 2- to 4-inch-long blades, the upper ones mostly deeply divided into seven coarsely-toothed segments. The deep purple-pink to white flowers, 1 inch to 2 inches in diameter, are several together in racemes or panicle-like clusters. Native from Missouri to Kansas, Arkansas, and Texas, *C. digitata* is a loose-growing perennial 2 or 3 feet tall, with a carrot-like root and erect or reclining stems. Its five- to seven-parted leaves, with some of the divisions sometimes again deeply lobed,

have blades up to 4½ inches long. The red, purple-red, or white blooms, 1½ to 2 inches wide, are in loose racemes.

Annual *C. leiocarpa* (syn. *C. pedata*), of Texas and Oklahoma, attains heights of 3 feet, or so, and has several slender, upright stems from a thin taproot. The leaf blades, kidney-shaped to ovate, are three- to six-parted or lobed, with the divisions lobed, toothed, or smooth-edged. The 2-inch-wide flowers are from pale pink to red-purple.

Garden and Landscape Uses and Cultivation. Of gay appearance, poppy-mallows are excellent and mostly hardy. They do best in sunny locations where the soil is well-drained and somewhat dryish. Low *C. involucrata* is suitable for rock gardens, border edgings, and similar uses, the taller kinds for flower beds, naturalistic landscapes, and native plant gardens. They are easy to raise from seeds, and the perennials from summer cuttings planted in a greenhouse or cold frame propagating bed. Established specimens need little or no attention. When transplanting is done care should be taken to keep intact as many roots as possible.

CALLISIA (Cal-lísia). About a dozen species of mostly wandering-jew-like plants from the warmer parts of Mexico, Central and South America, and the West Indies, with the greatest concentration of kinds in Mexico and Honduras, constitute this genus of the spiderwort family COMMELINACEAE. The generic name is derived from the Greek *kallos*, beauty, and alludes to the flowers. Callisias are prostrate, evergreen, herbaceous perennials with conspicuously-jointed stems and alternate, ovate to oblong lanceolate leaves with bases that completely envelop the stems. The leaves are successively smaller toward the ends of the stems until the upper ones are mere bracts. The flowers are in paired, stalkless clusters that develop from the axils of the leaves and bracts or in stalked clusters together with a pair of stalkless clusters arising from the same axil. Each bloom has three sepals and three white, pink, or blue petals as long as, or in some species considerably longer than the sepals. There are three or six stamens that have filaments (stalks) without hairs.

The first *Callisia* to be described, as long ago as 1762 by Linnaeus, was *C. repens*, a species that enjoys a wider natural geographical range than any other; it occurs in Mexico, Central America and South America as far south as Brazil and Peru, and throughout most of the West Indies. It is a slender creeper with dark, branching stems up to six feet long and bright green leaves, thin and up to 1 inch long. They are edged with short hairs and their sheathing bases are often striped and pubescent at their apexes. The tiny blooms are white, not showy, and are borne in inconspicuous

clusters in the axils of the upper leaves and bracts. They have three or six stamens.

Quite different *C. elegans*, sometimes misidentified as *Setcreasea striata*, was introduced to cultivation in the United States from Mexico in 1943. This kind has branching stems that may be 2 feet long and, like the leaves, are velvety to the touch because of a fine white pubescence visible only when viewed through a lens. The leaves, ovate to broad-lanceolate, are in two ranks and are mostly 2 to 3 inches long, their margins fringed with hairs. They are dark green with longitudinal paler stripes, and under surfaces green, reddish-purple, or purple. The blooms of *C. elegans* terminate the main stems and short branches and have white petals; they are about ¾ inch across. There are six stamens and a pistil with a brushlike stigma. This species blooms in fall and winter.

Callisia elegans

The plant for long called *Spironema fragrans* and sometimes known as *Tradescantia dracaenoides* is correctly *Callisia fragrans*. It has lax, fleshy stems up to 3 feet long and elliptic-lanceolate leaves that may be 10 inches long by 1½ inches wide. Each stem terminates in a large, branched cluster of fragrant white flowers with six stamens and a brushlike stigma atop a long style. A variety *C. f.* 'Melnickoff' has some or all its leaves longitudinally striped with white, pale yellow, or brown. This species is a native of Mexico.

Garden Uses and Cultivation. Callisias are desirable plants for hanging baskets and pots in warm greenhouses; in frost-free climates they may be planted permanently outdoors. The prostrate ones such as *C. elegans* and *C. repens* are good groundcovers. They root from cuttings with the greatest ease and prosper in any ordinary potting soil kept reasonably moist. They appreciate a minimum temperature of 55°F, a fairly humid atmosphere, and shade from strong sun.

CALLISTACHYS. See Oxylobium.

CALLISTEMON (Calli-stèmon)—Bottle Brush. This aptly-named (from the Greek *kallos*, beauty, and *stemon*, a stamen) genus of Australian evergreen trees and shrubs of the myrtle family MYRTACEAE comprises twenty-five species. Although they withstand a few degrees of frost for short periods, none is hardy in the north. Species and varieties of *Metrosideros* are sometimes misnamed *Callistemon*.

Callistemons have alternate, leathery, cylindrical, linear or lanceolate, toothless leaves, and showy red, purplish-red, or yellowish flowers in cylindrical spikes that, because of the long-protruding stamens, look like bottle brushes. The branches that carry the blooms continue to grow beyond the ends of the flower spikes. The arrangement of the stamens, they are separate instead of united in five bundles opposite the petals, distinguish *Callistemon* from nearly-related *Melaleuca* which is also called bottle brush. The little stalkless flowers have five-lobed calyxes, five petals, many stamens, and a style as long as the stamens. The button-like, woody seed capsules form close cylinders around the stems and remain for two years or more. Partly because of their similarity, and partly because of their tendency to hybridize, cultivated callistemons are often difficult to identify.

Perhaps the most showy bottle brush is *C. speciosus.* A large shrub or bushy tree 20 to 40 feet in height, this sort has nar-

Callistemon speciosus

rowly-lanceolate leaves 2 to 4 inches long, with prominent midribs, and rich red flowers with attractively yellow-tipped stamens in spikes up to 6 inches long. Rather like it, but with proportionately shorter leaves, and less conspicuous golden anthers, lemon bottle brush (*C. citrinus* syn. *C. lanceolatus*), so called because its crushed foliage has a faint odor of lemon, is sometimes 30 feet tall, but more commonly does not exceed 10 feet. Varieties *C. c. splendens* and *C. c.* 'Chico Red' are superior. The

Callistemon citrinus

plant grown as *C. jeffersii,* a broad shrub with reddish-purple flowers that fade to lavender, probably belongs here. Similar, but more rigidly branched, *C. phoeniceus* is a bushy shrub 6 to 8 feet tall with less densely crowded flower spikes than *C. citrinus.* Variety *C. p. prostrata* is a sprawling shrub 5 to 6 feet tall.

Callistemon jeffersii

One of the most popular bottle brushes in California and Florida the weeping bottle brush (*C. viminalis*), closely related to *C. speciosus,* is distinguishable by its strikingly pendulous, willowy branches. At its maximum it may be a tree 60 feet high, but usually is very much lower. When young its leaves, that fully grown are up to 4 inches long, are clothed with bronzy hairs. The long, massive cylinders of bright red blooms are highly decorative. It is best adapted for moist soils and locations protected from sweeping winds. A more vigorous, denser variety with more intensely colored blooms, *C. v. mccaskillii* is by some authorities classed as a variant of *C. citrinus.*

Also red-flowered are *C. rigidus, C. macropunctatus* (syns *C. coccineus, C. rugulosus*), *C. linearis,* and *C. brachyandrus.* As its name indicates, *C. rigidus* is of open, stiff habit.

Callistemon viminalis

It is a slow-growing shrub up to about 20 feet high and 10 feet wide, with crowded, linear to narrow-lanceolate leaves up to 5 inches long, and dense bottle brushes 2½ to 4½ inches long of crimson blooms. In the wild this inhabits dry locations. Quite different in its choice of habitats (it favors wet and even swampy soils), *C. macropunctatus* is 10 to 15 feet tall, but sometimes considerably taller. Its sharp-pointed

Callistemon macropunctatus

leaves are stiff and 1 inch to 2 inches in length. The spikes of scarlet blooms are numerous, 2 to 4 inches long, and very showy. Native of sandy soils, *C. linearis* is a shrub or tree very like *C. rigidus.* It has stiff, narrow leaves 4 to 5 inches long, grooved on their upper surfaces. The dark red flowers are in spikes up to 6 inches long. Sharp-pointed, needle-like leaves ¾ inch to 1½ inches long are characteristic of shrubby *C. brachyandrus.* When young, like the young shoots, they are silky-hairy. The flowers, with red or pink stamens tipped with very conspicuous golden-yellow anthers, are in spikes 2 inches long or slightly longer.

Callistemon brachyandrus

Cream, pale yellow, or pallid pinkish flowers, with stamens up to ½ inch long, in rather loose spikes 2 to 3½ inches long, are borne by fast-growing **C. salignus,** a tree that occasionally is 40 feet tall, but commonly not more than one-third that. Its narrowly-lanceolate leaves are up to 3 inches long. This kind favors moist soils. Variety *C. s. australis* (syn. *C. paludosus*) differs only in the leaf veins being scarcely visible.

Callistemon salignus australis

Remarkable **C. pinifolius** is a variable shrub or tree. Its flowers range from red to bottle green. The green-flowered variant is known as *C. p. viridis.* It has stiff, needle-like leaves 2 to 4 inches long. The bottle brush grown in California as *C. violaceus* is not that species, but probably **C. lilacinus.** It is a dense, rounded shrub 10 to 12 feet tall with spreading branches, rather pale foliage, and dark red bottle brushes about 2 inches long.

Garden and Landscape Uses. Bottle brushes are extremely useful outdoor ornamentals in warm, practically frost-free, sunny climates. They are useful as lawn specimens, for grouping among shrub-bery, and as informal and semiformal hedges. In the main they prefer fairly moist soils. Most do well even where soil drainage is less than good. They bloom when small and are easy to manage in tubs and pots in greenhouses.

Cultivation. To keep bottle brushes as tidy ornamentals it is generally advisable to prune them to shape and to limit the number of new shoots and so prevent crowding, as soon as flowering is through. Specimens accommodated in tubs or other containers should be pruned fairly severely annually. The procedure consists of cutting out surplus shoots, shortening vigorous ones that remain by one-half, and weak ones by two-thirds, of their lengths. In greenhouses, winter temperatures of 45°F by night with increases of five to ten degrees during the day are adequate. Free ventilation must be afforded whenever weather is favorable. Full exposure to sun at all times is necessary. When needed, repotting is done in late winter. A porous, fertile, peaty soil suits best. Water generously from spring to fall, moderately in winter. From spring to fall regular applications of dilute liquid fertilizer are highly beneficial to well-rooted specimens. In summer the plants benefit from being stood outdoors in a sunny place. Propagation is satisfactory by seeds and cuttings. Young plants are encouraged to form shapely specimens by shortening their shoots occasionally to encourage branching.

CALLISTEPHUS (Callís-tephus)—China-Aster. Belonging to the daisy family COMPOSITAE, the China-aster (**Callistephus chinensis**) is the only species of its genus. It is related to *Aster,* but is quite different. Botanical asters are hardy herbaceous perennials, the China-aster is an annual. The two differ greatly in gross appearance, especially in size of bloom and in stem and foliage characteristics. Gardeners commonly call both asters and when they do so without elaboration it is impossible to know whether they refer to the choice annuals that concern us here or to Michaelmas-daisies, the botanists' *Aster.* The prototype of modern China-asters is a native of eastern Asia, one of the very few annuals from that region. Its names is derived from the Greek *kallimos,* beautiful, and *stephanos,* a crown. It alludes to the appendages that accompany the seedlike fruits.

The wild form of the China-aster is little cultivated. It is an erect, branched, rough-hairy plant up to 2½ feet in height with stiffish stems, and alternate, broad, more or less oval, coarsely- and irregularly-toothed leaves. Its flower heads, solitary at the ends of relatively long stalks, are 2 to 3 inches in diameter. They have a large yellow disk or "eye" of bisexual florets and many narrowly-strap-shaped, female ray florets, usually violet or violet-blue, and often called petals. The involucre (collar of bracts at the base of the flower head) is composed of several series, the outer of which are large, green, and leaflike, the inner ones membranous. In this respect *Callistephus* differs from the genus *Aster* in which the involucral bracts are all similar.

In cultivation, the China-aster has proved an extraordinarily variable plant and has produced several distinct races and numerous varieties greatly esteemed by gardeners and rightly considered to be among our choicest annuals. Variation has been in the directions of increasing the size of

Callistephus chinensis, garden varieties (three photos above)

the flower heads, multiplying the number of ray florets to give semidouble and double blooms, altering the form of the florets so that they are incurved, reflexed, quilled (tubular), or partly quilled, developing a wider variety of flower colors, establishing dwarf, intermediate, and tall varieties, and varieties called early, mid-season, and late, that vary in the length of time they take from seed sowing to bloom, and, most importantly, developing disease-resistant strains. The earliest development of this species after its introduction to Europe in 1793 was the result of the work of French horticulturists. Later the British were responsible for much improvement, and more recently American plant breeders have raised fine new strains and varieties. Seedsmen's catalogs list numerous varieties of this handsome annual that come amazingly true from seeds and in all colors except true yellow; the nearest to this so far are creamy-white flowered kinds, with blooms that are yellowish before they fully expand. The blooms of modern varieties are up to 5 inches in diameter, but there are some with very much smaller flowers.

Garden Uses. China-asters are among the foremost cut flowers. For this purpose they rank with the choicest garden blooms, lending themselves well for arrangements, lasting long in water, and affording a great variety of forms and colors. Above all, they have quality, that indefinable something that lifts a flower or plant above the commonplace. They are also first-class annuals for flower beds and borders and for greenhouses as cut blooms and pot plants, although their popularity as greenhouse plants has declined somewhat since methods of growing chrysanthemums have been devised that make it possible to have a succession of those versatile plants in bloom every day of the year.

Cultivation. China-asters are increased only by seeds, which may be sown directly where the plants are to bloom or in containers or seedbeds, and the seedlings transplanted. The latter plan is followed to obtain early blooms outdoors and for greenhouse crops. The plants respond to deep, fertile earth, well drained, yet always moderately moist and neutral or slightly alkaline. A soil that will produce a variety of quality vegetables will grow good China-asters. They need full sunshine and free air circulation, are not satisfactory when crowded in hot, poorly-ventilated places, nor do they prosper where they are subjected to reflected heat from nearby walls. The seeds may be sown broadcast or in drills (rows). The latter method, because it permits easier weed control, is always advisable for cut flower crops. The drills are spaced 1½ to 2½ feet apart. Sowing may be done in spring as early as the ground is workable and additional sowings may be made until mid- or late June to provide successional crops of

bloom. Care should be taken not to sow too thickly, but even so stands of seedlings may be crowded to the extent that it is desirable to thin them. The spacing between the plants should depend on the growth habit of the variety and whether it is growing in rows with considerable space between them or in broadcast patches or groups as, for instance, in a flower border. In the latter case more room is needed between individuals than when they are in rows with plenty of light and air reaching them from two sides.

To have early blooms outdoors, seeds are sown in a greenhouse or hotbed about eight weeks before the resulting plants are to be set out in the garden. A temperature of 55°F is satisfactory for seed germination, and the young plants are grown in full sun in a night temperature of 50°F with a daytime rise of five to ten degrees allowed. The seedlings are transplanted 2½ to 3 inches apart in well-drained flats containing rich soil, are kept growing without any set-back, and are planted outdoors as soon as all danger of frost is passed. At no time must the young plants be permitted to suffer from lack of moisture, but excessive watering, especially in their early stages before their roots have permeated the soil, can be decidedly harmful. Instead of setting the young seedlings in flats, they may be transplanted to a mild hotbed or cold frame (from which frost is excluded) and kept growing there until it is time to transfer them to the outdoor garden. The spacing of plants set in the garden from the flats or frames depends somewhat on the growth habits of the variety, but 9 inches to 1 foot is a fair average.

Good culture is essential to have fine China-asters. Not only must the soil be deep, nourishing, and of agreeable texture, and the location sunny, but regular care must be given throughout the growing season. Clean cultivation is especially important; this means the elimination of all weeds while they are very small and the maintenance of a loose surface layer that admits water and air readily. Clean cultivation is secured by repeatedly stirring the top ½ inch (but not an appreciably deeper layer) of the surface soil with a hoe or cultivator or, after the weather has become fairly warm, keeping the soil mulched with a loose organic mulch. During dry periods the plants should be watered very thoroughly at intervals of a few days. Tall varieties may need staking or some other form of support, and faded blooms must be removed promptly if the flowering season is to be as long as possible. Prompt preventative and remedial measures are necessary if the plants are threatened by diseases or pests.

In greenhouses, China-asters can be had in bloom from fall to late spring. To achieve this, it is desirable to supply supplemental illumination because, although the plants

may bloom during periods of short day length, their stems do not elongate sufficiently for their flowers to be useful for cutting. By lengthening the day through the use of lights so that the hours of darkness are not more than nine and one-half, good results are obtained. Lighting that is satisfactory for chrysanthemums is appropriate for China-asters, although it need not necessarily be as intense. Asters need full sun and a winter night temperature of 50°F with an increase of five to ten degrees during the day. Higher temperatures result in fewer-rayed flowers and weaker stems. The atmosphere should be dryish rather than highly humid. From seed sowing to bloom takes from four to five and one-half months depending upon the time of sowing and the variety. The seeds are sown in well-drained pots, pans, or flats of light soil, and as soon as they are big enough to handle comfortably, are transplanted about 2 inches apart to flats or individually to small pots. From these they are planted into benches or ground beds, with about 8 by 8 inches between plants. The soil must be a fertile, reasonably porous one; if it is at all acid it is advisable to mix in some lime. The plants do not need pinching, but to ensure fine blooms for cutting they should be disbudded, which involves removing all side buds and shoots that develop from the branches from the main central stem while they are quite small. Because of the grave danger of infection with fusarium wilt disease, in greenhouses the same soil should not be used twice for China-asters unless it is steam-sterilized between crops.

Diseases and Pests. China-asters are subject to several infections and infestations. The two most serious diseases are a virus called aster yellows and a fungus wilt. The former is transmitted from infected plants of China-asters and various other species, including common plantains (*Plantago*) and the ox-eye daisy (*Chrysanthemum leucanthemum*), by leaf hoppers. Control of these is necessary to avoid infection. This is accomplished by spraying or dusting or by growing the plants under screens of aster cloth, which prevent entry of the leaf hoppers. Controls for wilt disease consist of relying upon wilt-resistant varieties and of sterilizing the soil, preferably with steam. This is a soil-borne disease and great care must be exercised not to spread the disease by infected soil carried on tools or shoes or by adding infected plants to compost piles. Other diseases include root rot, stem rot, and rust. The chief insect pests are leaf hoppers, aphids including root aphids, beetles, tarnished plant bug, red spider mites, and nematodes.

CALLITRICHACEAE—Callitriche Family. The characteristics of this family of dicotyledons are those of its only genus, *Callitriche*.

CALLITRICHE (Callít-riche)—Water-Star-wort. The name of this genus is pronounced in four syllables. Originally used for some other plant, it is derived from the Greek *kallos*, beauty, and *thrix*, hair, but is without evident application to the present genus. Water-starworts (*Callitriche*) number about forty species of mostly small, aquatic herbaceous plants. The group is cosmopolitan in its natural distribution with several species in North America. It is the only genus of the water-starwort family CALLITRICHACEAE. Its members are stemmed plants with undivided, opposite leaves and minute unisexual flowers without sepals or petals. The males are reduced to a single stamen, the females to a solitary pistil, which are as simple structures as flowers can be. They are solitary, in twos or threes, in the leaf axils, and sometimes are accompanied by a pair of bracts. A strong lens is necessary to examine the blooms satisfactorily.

An underwater or a floating perennial, native throughout temperate parts of the northern hemisphere and in southern South America, **C. palustris verna** (syn. *C. palustris*) of North America, Europe, and Asia has submersed linear leaves usually under ½ inch long. Those that surface are oblanceolate to obovate and are in rosettes at the ends of the stems, thus forming floating green stars that are the reason for the common name water-starwort. Differing chiefly in recondite characteristics of the minute fruits, **C. stagnalis** is wild from Pennsylvania to Mississippi and, reportedly, in Michigan and Wisconsin, as well as Europe, Asia, and North Africa. Another kind with both submersed and floating leaves, **C. hermaphroditica**, ranges from Quebec to Alberta, Oregon, New England, and California, and is common in Europe and Asia. This differs from the previous two in having all its leaves similar, linear and nearly threadlike; they are up to ½ inch long or slightly longer.

Garden Uses and Cultivation. Water-starworts are primarily for aquariums. They may be grown in pools by keen collectors of aquatic vegetation. Some ornamental fish feed on them and thus damage or destroy them. They need, or thrive best in, cold water; most will not live in heated tanks. Best for that purpose is *C. stagnalis*. Water-starworts need strong light and may be planted in mud or in sand and gravel with some mud content. They are very easily propagated by cuttings planted in the rooting medium; it is usually necessary to weight the cuttings with stones or by other means to prevent them from floating to the surface.

CALLITRIS (Callì-tris)—Cypress-Pine. The Australian, Tasmanian, and New Caledonian genus *Callistris* of the cypress family CUPRESSACEAE is closely related to Australian *Actinostrobus* and African and Mada-

gascan *Widdringtonia*, both previously included in it. As now interpreted, *Callitris* differs from *Actinostrobus* in its cones not being surrounded at their bases by closely-pressed scales and from *Widdringtonia* in its scalelike adult-type leaves being in threes instead of twos, in its leaves being usually bigger, and in its cones having usually six or eight instead of four scales. The sixteen species of *Callitris* are among the very few conifers native to Australia, Tasmania, and New Caledonia. The name comes from the Greek *kalli*, beautiful, and *treis*, three. It alludes to the leaves, cone scales, and other parts being in threes.

Cypress-pines are evergreen trees and shrubs with firm bark and short, upright branches with numerous slender branchlets. Adult-type leaves of plants that have outgrown the juvenile stage are pressed, except for their triangular tips, closely against the shoots. Juvenile-type leaves of young plants are narrow and pointed and in whorls of four. The fruiting cones remain on the plants for several years after they have shed their seeds. In Australia the wood of several cypress-pines is used for construction, interior trim, furniture, fences, and other purposes, and is reportedly termite-proof. It is fragrant and often handsomely figured. From cypress-pines also are derived oil used in perfumery, and resin.

The Murray-River-pine (*C. columellaris* syn. *C. glauca*), a shrub or tree up to 80 feet tall, is widespread in Australia and has usually glaucous foliage. Its leaves are about ⅒ inch long and its spherical cones, in clusters or solitary, are in a little over ½ inch in diameter. The durable wood of this species is much esteemed. The tree grows well in hot, dry climates. The black cypress-pine (*C. endlicheri* syn. *C. calcarata*) is sometimes 80 feet in height, and erect and pyramidal. Its leaves are tiny and scalelike and its cones, solitary or in clusters, are about ½ inch long and not quite as wide. This species provides good tanbark and useful resin, as well as handsome lumber. The Tasmanian cypress-pine (*C. oblonga*) is indigenous to the islands from which it derives its common name and there is fairly abundant along river banks. A shrub or tree up to 25 feet tall, its leaves are under ¼ inch long and its solitary or clustered cones ½ to 1 inch long. The common cypress-pine (*C. preissii* syn. *C. robusta*) is an important timber tree of southern Australia that at its finest attains a height of 100 feet, but under much less favorable conditions is a shrub. Its leaves are not much over ⅛ inch in length and its cones, often broader than high, are about 1 inch in diameter. The Oyster Bay cypress-pine (*C. rhomboidea* syn. *C. cupressiformis*) inhabits coastal areas both on the mainland and in Tasmania, but reaches its best development in Tasmania. It attains a height of about 50 feet and has green or

glaucous leaves approximately ⅛ inch long. Its spherical cones are up to ½ inch wide.

Less well known than the sorts described above, *C. morrisonii* of New South Wales is a tree 20 to 30 feet tall with erect glaucous branchlets furnished with tiny leaves set more closely together than those of other species. The cones, solitary or in clusters, are spherical and about ¾ inch in diameter.

Callitris morrisonii

Garden and Landscape Uses. These plants are suitable for cultivation in warm regions where little or no freezing occurs. They may be used for much the same purposes as true cypresses (*Cupressus*) and false-cypresses (*Chamaecyparis*), as solitary specimens, in groups, or for screens and hedges.

Cultivation. Cypress-pines grow in any moderately-fertile, well-drained soil in full sun. They withstand dry conditions well and are adaptable to seaside locations. Any pruning needed to shape them may be done just before the new season's growth begins. They are increased by seeds sown in sandy, peaty soil and by cuttings of firm shoots inserted under mist or in a propagating frame in a humid greenhouse or cold frame. As young plants they are attractive for growing in pots and tubs. They succeed in any ordinary potting soil in a sunny greenhouse where the night temperature in winter is about 50°F. For further suggestions on culture see Conifers.

CALLOPSIS (Callóp-sis). The only species of *Callopsis* of the arum family ARACEAE is endemic to East Africa. Its name is derived from that of another genus of the family, *Calla*, and the Greek *opsis*, of similar appearance.

Callopsis volkensii

An evergreen, stemless, herbaceous plant, *C. volkensii* has a short, branching, underground rootstock and bright green, short-stalked, long-heart-shaped, round-toothed leaves with blades 3 to 5 inches long by 2 to 3 inches wide. As is usual in the arum family, what appear to be flowers are inflorescences, arrangements of many flowers and associated parts. The true flowers are minute and without sepals or petals. They are crowded on a yellow spike called a spadix that is the equivalent of the similar organ in the center of a calla-lily. A pure white, broad-ovate bract or spathe about 1 inch long and much longer than the spadix sprouts from just below the spadix; unlike that of the calla-lily (often thought of as a petal) it does not envelop the spadix, but spreads in much the manner of those of anthuriums. The fruits are berries.

Garden Uses and Cultivation. A delightful subject for humid, tropical greenhouses, terrariums, and in the tropics for shaded rock gardens and similar accommodations, this kind gives little trouble to gardeners. It revels in rich soil with an abundance of decayed organic matter, such as compost, leaf mold, or peat moss, kept damp, but not constantly wet. Temperatures of 60 to 70°F or higher are appreciated. Propagation is easy by division.

CALLUNA (Cal-lùna)—Heather. The name heather is often used indiscriminatingly in North America to include plants that are more properly heaths, as well as true heathers. This is unfortunate, since heaths are members of the genus *Erica*, whereas the heather is *Calluna*. Both belong in the heath family ERICACEAE, but there are significant and easy ways to detect botanical differences. Chief of these is that in *Erica*

the urn-shaped to tubular corolla, tipped with four tiny lobes, is the colored, showy part of the flower and is longer than the calyx, whereas in *Calluna* the deeply-four-parted colored calyx is the showy portion of the bloom and is longer than and hides the corolla. Thus, if the colored part of the flower is in one piece, the plant is *Erica*, if it is divided to its base into four parts, it is *Calluna*. The name, derived from the Greek *kallunein*, to sweep, alludes to the use of heather for making brooms. In lands where it is plentiful it is also used for thatching.

Heather consists of only one highly variable species, *C. vulgaris*, but there are numerous varieties. It is widely known as Scotch heather, but this gives no indication of the extent of the plant's natural range. True, it is a floral emblem and pride of the Scots, whose land it clothes and, in fall, colors with a rosy-lavender glow over many thousands of acres of moorland and mountainside, but it is equally as plentiful

Calluna vulgaris

in many other parts of northern Europe and adjacent Asia and has even established a foothold as a naturalized immigrant of long standing in parts of North America.

Heather (*C. vulgaris*) is a small-foliaged evergreen shrub from 6 inches to 3 feet tall, hairy or hairless, with opposite, narrow leaves ordinarily about ½ inch long, that overlap each other in four rows. The flowers, many together in one-sided racemes, are about ⅛ inch long and typically purplish-pink, but varying somewhat in the wild and to a greater extent in cultivation. White heather (*C. v. alba*) is considered by the Scots to be a symbol of good luck. It occurs sporadically among wild plants and is grown in gardens.

Since there are numerous varieties of heather, it would serve no useful purpose to attempt to describe all or even most here. Certainly well over fifty are grown in North America and are to be found in the nursery catalogs of specialists. Of those most meritorious the following is a selection: *C. v. alba*, is white flowered. *C. v. alba-plena*, a dwarf, has double white blooms. *C. v. aurea* is low and has yellow-tinted foliage. *C. v.* 'County Wicklow' is a dwarf spreader with double lilac flowers. *C. v. cuprea* has yellow young shoots that become reddish-bronze in winter. *C. v. foxii* is extremely dwarf and bright green, with rosy-purple flowers. *C. v. hammondii* is tall and white flowered. *C. v.* 'H. E. Beale', one of the best, is late blooming and has long spikes of bright pink double blooms. *C. v.* 'J. H. Hamilton' has large pink blooms and is dwarf. *C. v.* 'Mair's Variety' is tall and has white blooms. *C. v.* 'Mrs. Pat' has light rosy-purple flowers and foliage that in spring is light pink. *C. v.* 'Mrs. Ronald Gray' is dwarf and prostrate and has reddish flowers. *C. v. nana* is a dwarf with purple blooms. *C. v. serlei argentea* has silvery-white young shoots. *C. v. s. aurea* has young shoots of bright yellow. *C. v. s. rubra* bears dark reddish-purple flowers late in the season. *C. v.* 'Sister Anne' has pink blooms and is low.

Calluna vulgaris (flowers)

A heather garden

Calluna vulgaris, garden varieties (three photos above)

Garden and Landscape Uses. In Great Britain and some other parts of Europe, heathers are much more extensively employed in than in North America. Often entire heather gardens are planted. These usually include, in addition to heathers, hardy heaths and other companionable shrubs such as brooms (*Cytisus*). Heathers are also used as groundcovers, at the fronts of shrub plantings, and in rock gardens. They have much to recommend them and should be more freely planted in parts of North America where they prosper.

They are hardy well north into New England and flourish especially well in the Pacific Northwest. They are not plants for regions of searing summer heat or long periods of dryness. They do well by the sea.

Other conditions must be met if heathers are to be happy. The soil must be acid, not necessarily strongly so, but at least on the acid side of neutral. And it should be lean and "hungry," too poor in available nitrogen and other nutrients for the well-being of most garden shrubs. An over-rich diet results in lush growth that is likely to die in winter. Heathers will stand part-day shade, but best results are had in exposed locations where there is free air circulation. They are not plants for stuffy, dark corners. In cold climates north- and west-facing slopes are often to their liking. Their flowers are useful for cutting and may be dried as everlastings.

Cultivation. In preparing the soil for heathers it is well to mix in very thoroughly, liberal amounts of acid peat moss and, if the earth is clayey, plenty of coarse sand. Spring is generally the best time to plant, but where winters are not excessively severe they may be set out in early fall. Spacing of 9 inches to 1 foot between individuals, depending upon the vigor of the variety, is satisfactory for most kinds. Very strong growers may be given a little more space. Following planting, a mulch of peat moss or other congenial organic material should be installed, and it is well to maintain such a covering at all times. A very important routine chore is that of shearing the plants fairly severely each year in early spring. If this is not done they tend to develop old woody stems much subject to splitting. If pruning is done at

times other than spring the plants may be killed or at least subjected to a severe setback. Where winters are very cold and there is little or only sporadic snow cover, a light layer of branches of pine or other evergreen placed over the plants in late fall ensures against damage from strong winter sun.

Propagation of the wild species is by seeds sown in sandy peaty soil kept uniformly moist in a cold frame or cool greenhouse in late winter or spring, or by cuttings. Varieties root readily from short cuttings made from the shoot tips in summer and planted in a mixture of sand and peat moss in a cold frame or under mist.

CALLUS. The mass of new cell growth that first develops from and around wounded plant tissue is called callus. Cuttings placed in environments favorable for rooting commonly develop outgrowths of callus tissue from their cut bases. Such developments consist of irregular masses originating from the cambium and nearby tissues. Contrary to common belief, callus formation is independent of and without direct bearing on root development. To the extent that the callus inhibits invasion of the tissues of the cuttings by funguses and other decay-producing organisms it is beneficial, but in some instances, notably with slow-rooting woody cuttings such as those of certain conifers, it may develop to such an extent that it interferes with absorption of water. This may be relieved by paring the callus with a sharp knife, then replanting the cutting. Callus tissue also plays an important part in grafting. The mingling and interlocking of such callus tissues developed by both scion and understock is an important first step to successful union.

CALOCARPUM. See Pouteria.

CALOCEDRUS (Calocéd-rus). Previously included in *Libocedrus*, this genus of three species of evergreen conifers is related to arbor-vitae (*Thuja*). Most commonly cultivated is the incense-cedar (*Calocedrus decurrens* syn. *Libocedrus decurrens*), a native of Pacific North America. The other kinds inhabit eastern Asia. The name is derived from the Greek *kalos*, beautiful, and *Cedrus* the name of the true cedars, and implies a similarity in appearance. The genus belongs to the cypress family CUPRESSACEAE. It differs from *Thuja* in its cones having four or six scales (if six the upper two are joined), only two of which are fertile.

The incense-cedar (*C. decurrens*) inhabits mountain regions from Oregon to Baja

Calocedrus decurrens in California

California and is sometimes more than 180 feet in height with a tapering trunk up to 8 feet or more in diameter. It has cinnamon-red, deeply-furrowed bark, more or less upright branches, and dark green foliage. Through youth and middle age the trees are columnar; in advanced age they are broader and less regular in outline. The branchlets form flat, fernlike sprays. The scalelike adult leaves, in pairs that alternate on opposite sides of the twigs so that they are in four rows, are pressed closely to the shoots for most of their length, only their short, pointed tips spread outward. On the main shoots they are about ½ inch long, but toward the tips of the branchlets much shorter. The juvenile leaves of young trees are longer and a greater proportion of their length consists of the spreading tips. Both male and female cones are solitary at the ends of the shoots. Most frequently they are on separate branches of the same tree. The fruiting cones ripen at the end of their first season; they are slender, up to 1 inch in length, and usually have six scales, with only the middle two

fertile. Varieties are *C. d. aureovariegata*, with yellowish patches of foliage and not especially ornamental, *C. d. columnaris*, of narrow columnar, compact habit, *C. d. compacta*, a low-growing, compact kind, and *C. d. glauca*, with glaucous blue-green foliage.

Calocedrus decurrens columnaris

One of the most distinct and beautiful conifers, the incense-cedar, unlike many western American trees, thrives in eastern North America and is reasonably hardy. Very handsome plantings of it are to be seen at Longwood Gardens, Kennett Square, Pennsylvania, and there are good specimens as far north as Long Island, New York. At Boston, Massachusetts, it lives outdoors in sheltered locations only. The name incense-cedar alludes to the pleasant fragrance of its wood, which is excellent for building and for the manufacture of lead pencils. A fungus dry rot often affects large specimens in the wild and reduces their value for lumber. The foliage of the incense-cedar is less pungent when crushed than that of arbor-vitae.

Other kinds include *C. formosana* (syn. *Libocedrus formosana*), an endemic of Taiwan and much less hardy than *C. decurrens*. It is 75 feet in height and often has a crooked trunk. Its cones are from slightly less to slightly more than ½ inch long and have four scales, two fertile. From western China comes *C. macrolepis*. It is up to 100 feet in height, has a whitish trunk and larger, flatter, and thinner leaves than *C. decurrens*. Its branchlets are stouter than those of *C. formosana* and the fertile ones longer. The cones are ¼ to ½ inch long and have six scales. This species is decidedly more tender than *C. decurrens*. In China its wood is esteemed for making coffins.

Garden and Landscape Uses. One of the stateliest and most formal of evergreens

(*C. d. columnaris*, the kind most commonly planted, is particularly strict in outline), the incense-cedar ranks high among ornamental conifers. It is especially appropriate where strong vertical lines are needed in the landscape and can be used effectively to line avenues and to provide accents. It has much the same exclamation point effect as the Lombardy poplar, with the advantage that it is never without foliage. A very attractive way of using this tree is to plant several in a group that has depth as well as length so that the specimens toward the rear of the group are seen between those that front it. Space must be allowed for the full development of each tree without crowding, which means that they should be about 15 feet apart.

Cultivation. A somewhat acid to neutral, well-drained, deep, and reasonably fertile loamy soil that is never excessively dry provides ideal conditions for these trees; they are not adapted for limestone soils. They need full sun and shelter from cold, sweeping winds. Little is required in the way of annual maintenance, no pruning, for example, but they benefit from the ground around them being kept mulched with compost or other suitable organic material. Propagation is best effected by seeds sown in sandy peaty soil in a cold frame or cool greenhouse, but increase can also be had by cuttings. These should be taken in late summer and consist of side shoots 2 to 3 inches long, with a sliver-like heel of old wood attached; they should be planted under mist or in a humid cold frame or greenhouse propagating bench. Incense-cedars under cultivation are notably free of pests and diseases. For more information see Conifers.

CALOCEPHALUS (Calocéph-alus). This genus of the daisy family COMPOSITAE is entirely Australian and includes annuals, herbaceous perennials, and small shrubs. The only one cultivated is *Calocephalus brownii* (syn. *Leucophyta brownii*), a stiff, wiry-branched, white-woolly shrublet,

Calocephalus brownii

about 1 foot in height, that inhabits coastal areas, often growing among rocks where it receives salt spray. Its slender stems are clothed with alternate, blunt, linear leaves up to ⅙ inch long. The flower heads are in silvery, globular clusters about ½ inch wide. The name *Calocephalus* is from the Greek *kalos*, beautiful, and *kephale*, head, and refers to the flower clusters. The genus comprises fifteen species.

Garden Uses. The chief value of *C. brownii* is as a foliage plant to use with other foliage and flowering plants in summer beds. For this purpose it is especially esteemed in Europe. In a warm, dry, nearly frost-free climate, such as that of southern California, it may be grown permanently outdoors. It is a good plant for seaside gardens.

Calocephalus brownii edging a bed of coleuses

Cultivation. New plants are obtained from cuttings taken in late summer and fall. They are wintered in sunny greenhouses where the night temperature is about 50°F and the day temperatures a few degrees higher. The young plants need a porous sandy soil; excessively wet conditions must be avoided. They are pinched once or twice to encourage branching and are planted outdoors after all danger of frost has passed and the weather is warm and settled. Seeds can also be employed as a means of propagation.

CALOCHORTUS (Calo-chórtus)—Mariposa-Lily, Butterfly-Tulip, Globe-Tulip, Star-Tulip, Fairy Lantern, Cat's Ear, Sego-Lily. In pronouncing *Calochortus* the "ch" takes the sound of "k." It is the name of a charming genus of bulb plants of the lily family LILIACEAE, confined in the wild to western North America and Central America, from the Dakotas and Nebraska to British Columbia and Guatemala. The name, from the Greek *kalos*, beautiful, and *chortus*, grass, alludes to the aspect of the plants. There are about sixty species. The first to be discovered, *C. elegans* was collected by Lewis and Clark in 1814 in what

is now Idaho. The edible bulbs of these plants were used as food by the Indians.

Calochortuses are herbaceous, perennial, deciduous plants with bulbs that have smooth, membranous coats or, in a group previously segregated as the genus *Cyclobothra*, netted, fibrous coats. The leaves are mostly broadly- to narrowly-linear, generally hairless, often glaucous. The stems may be leafy or leafless, branched or not. There is one basal leaf, which may or may not persist until the flowers open, and sometimes leaves so low on the stem that they appear almost basal. There may be other, alternate leaves higher on the stems that are successively smaller from the base upward. Solitary small bulblets are frequently present in the axils of the lowermost leaves. In species of the *Cyclobothra* section these, if present, are in the axils of the upper leaves and bracts and are not solitary. The flowers are up-facing, horizontal, or nodding. In form they range from nearly globose to lantern-shaped or broadly-bell-shaped. They come in a wide range of colors and combinations. There are three usually lanceolate sepals and three considerably bigger and broader obovate petals, often conspicuously bearded, and in nearly all species with a gland or glandlike development at the base that may be clothed with hairs or projections called processes. There are six stamens and a three-parted stigma that usually sits directly on the ovary without an intervening style. The fruits are capsules. Botanists recognize three sections within the genus. For convenience the kinds considered here are similarly arranged. The dimensions given for the flowers of up-facing kinds are those of wide open specimens.

Mariposa-lilies and butterfly-tulips are the common names of calochortuses that belong to the botanical section of the genus identified as *Mariposa*. These have smooth-coated bulbs and most commonly branchless stems. Their up-facing, broadly-bell-shaped blooms have lanceolate petals sparingly hairy only near the gland. The seed capsules are erect, three-angled, or narrowly-three-winged. Almost always the basal leaf has completely withered before the bloom opens. Species of mariposa-lilies are often difficult to delimit. They include the following: *C. catalinae*, of grassy slopes chiefly near the coasts of southern California and Catalina Island, has usually branched stems 9 inches to 2½ feet tall, and 3½- to 4-inch-wide, white to lilac blooms usually with a purple spot at the bottom of each sepal and petal and with the glands clothed with long, slender processes. The petals are longer than the sepals. The anthers are lilac. *C. clavatus*, endemic to California, is one of the handsomest species. It frequently has branched stems, zigzag and 1½ to 3 feet tall. Its leaves are broadly-linear, its flow-

ers, in clusters of up to six, cup-shaped and 3 to 6 inches wide. They are yellow with a zigzag brown line on each obovate petal above the circular, deeply-depressed gland, which is clothed with short, much-branched processes. The petals are commonly much longer than the sepals. The anthers are red-brown to purplish. *C. excavatus*, endemic to California, closely resembles *C. nuttallii*, but is more slender and the petals of its blooms are without a brown or purplish spot above the gland. Up to 1½ feet tall, this kind has white flowers suffused and streaked with purple. *C. flexuosus*, native of arid hills and mesas from Colorado to Arizona, Nevada, and California, has in well-developed specimens, semitrailing or semitwining, branched, one- to four-flowered stems 9 inches to 1¼ feet long. Its leaves are linear. The 2- to 3-inch-wide, white to lilac-pink blooms have on each petal a cross-band of yellow above the gland and usually a purple spot on the narrow shaft or claw below. The gland, thickly covered with short, branched processes, is surrounded by a few hairs. The sepals, shorter than the petals, are similarly marked. *C. gunnisonii* ranges in the wild in mountains from South Dakota to Montana, Utah, Arizona, and New Mexico. It has linear leaves, and stems 9 inches to 1½ feet tall bearing up to three white to purplish or pale yellow blooms 3 to 4 inches wide, greenish toward their centers, often with a narrow cross-band of purple on each fan-shaped petal above the gland and with a purple spot on the claw of the petal. The gland, thickly covered with short processes, is surrounded by hairs. The sepals are marked similarly to the petals. *C. invenustus*, of California, is 6 inches to 1½ feet tall. Closely related to *C. nuttallii*, it has a basal leaf much shorter than the stem and white to dull lavender or greenish-gray blooms 1½ to 3 inches wide, sometimes spotted on the claws of the petals, but usually without a purple spot or blotch above the gland. This kind grows natively in dry soils, usually in pine woodlands. *C. kennedyi* inhabits desert and semidesert parts of Arizona, southern California, and adjacent Mexico. From 4 to 8 inches tall or occasionally considerably taller and closely related to *C. nuttallii*, it has glaucous, linear leaves and bears umbel-like groups of up to six 3-inch-wide blooms. Their yellow to orange or brilliant scarlet hue distinguishes this from *C. nuttallii* as do the smaller glands of the petals. The glands are thickly covered with slender processes. The petals and sepals generally have at their bases black or purple marks. *C. leichtlinii* also approaches *C. nuttallii* in appearance, but is readily distinguished by its flowers having petals without a membrane surrounding the gland and its anthers having arrow-shaped bases. This native of gravelly soils in open forests from South

Dakota to Oregon and California is 8 inches to 2 feet tall, has a very narrow basal leaf shorter than the stem, sometimes one or two slender stem leaves, and white to smoke-colored blooms commonly tinged with pink or lavender and on each petal a red to almost black spot above the gland. In clusters of two to five, or rarely solitary, they are 1½ to 3 inches wide. *C. luteus* is a slender-leaved Californian native of grasslands and forest throughout

Calochortus luteus

almost the length of the state and on Santa Cruz Island. It usually favors clayey soils. It varies considerably in size and in the markings of its petals, but is relatively constant in their basic deep yellow hue. Its stem, rather slender, sometimes branched, 9 inches to nearly 2 feet tall, carries up to four 2½- to 3½-inch-wide blooms sometimes blotched and usually penciled in their lower parts with reddish-brown. The glands on the petals, crescent-shaped, are densely-clothed with short, hairlike processes. The name *C. l. citrinus* is often used for the kind with blotched petals. *C. macrocarpus* is distinct and very handsome. Endemic in dry sagebrush country from Montana to Nevada, British Columbia, and California, it has nearly leafless stems up to about 2 feet tall and linear leaves that tend to curl at their tips. The stems carry one to three 3- to 4-inch-wide, satiny, lavendar, creamy-white and purple, or purple blooms with a central, longitudinal green vein or band down each petal. The petals are usually shorter than the long-pointed sepals and are moderately bearded above the gland. The anthers are long and slender. *C. nuttallii,* the sego-lily, the state flower of Utah, is the most widely distributed species in the wild. Somewhat variable, it occurs in dry soil from the Dakotas to Montana, Nebraska, Idaho, Arizona, and New Mexico. Its sparsely-foliaged stem, usually branchless, is up to about 1½ feet high. It has one to four 2- to 3½-inch-wide, rather fragile-looking blooms. They are

white, tinged or lined with lilac or magenta, the fluted petals, yellow at their bases, and marked above the circular, depressed gland with a purple spot or band. The sepals, usually shorter than the petals, are similarly decorated. Variety *C. n. bruneaunis*, from Montana to Oregon and California, has notably pointed, narrow petals. *C. splendens* is endemic to dry soils in California and Baja California and offshore islands. From 9 inches to 2 feet tall and

Calochortus splendens

usually branched, its stems carry up to four blooms 3 to 4 inches wide. They are pinkish-lilac to lavender, with a purple spot near the bottom of each sepal, and sometimes similarly spotted near the gland of each silky petal. The glands, frequently clothed with matted, branched processes, are sometimes naked. The petals are longer than the sepals. The anthers are blue or purple. *C. superbus,* endemic to California, is a close ally of *C. luteus* and *C. vestae* and resembles some forms of *C. venustus*. From 1¼ to 2 feet tall, it is usually readily distinguishable from these by the narrow glands on its petals being A-shaped, and from the first two by the color of its flowers. They are white to yellowish or lavender with sepals and petals generally penciled with purple below and with a reddish-brown to purplish blotch encircled by bright yellow. The glands are densely clothed with short, branched processes. The anthers are purplish to yellowish. *C. superbus* has pointed-linear leaves and bears up to three 2½- to 4-inch-wide blooms with petals usually longer than the sepals. *C. venustus* is tremendously variable. A Californian, specimens of different hues and mixtures usually occur together in the wild, some with much the aspect of *C. superbus*. Several color forms have at various times been named as varieties of *C. venustus* or as separate species. The most reliable distinguishing feature of this kind is the rectangular glands on the petals. They are covered with short, hairlike processes. Also, the

tips of the narrow, pointed sepals, which are about as long as the petals, curl backward. From 1 foot to 2½ feet or more in height, the usually branched stems have flowers singly, in twos, or in threes, from 2½ to 4 inches wide. White to lavender, purple, dark red, or yellow, the petals have at their middles a dark red blotch, often a paler one higher, and sometimes another above that. *C. vestae,* the largest-flowered kind, is native to California. A distinguishing characteristic is that the petals of its blooms have a more or less double-crescent-shaped gland thickly covered with short hairs. Its stem bears one to three blooms 3 to 4 inches wide or wider with petals usually longer than the sepals. Their white to purplish petals have a conspicuous reddish-brown blotch surrounded by a zone of pale yellow and on their undersides are penciled with red or purple.

Calochortuses of the botanical section *Eucalochortus* are for the most part of more northern origin than other kinds and so in general are more hardy. With the exception of one species that reaches southern California, all are natives of more northern parts of that state and of higher latitudes in the Pacific Northwest. They have a large basal leaf, leafy or leafless stems, and erect or nodding, spherical to broadly-bell-shaped or saucer-shaped flowers in umbel-like clusters. Their petals are hairy above the more or less depressed gland. A characteristic feature of members of this group is the orbicular to short-oblong, three-winged, erect or nodding fruits. These sorts belong: *C. nitidus* (syn. *C. eurycarpus*) has erect white, lavender, or purple flowers with a purple central blotch. The plants, about 1½ feet tall, have blooms 2½ to 3 inches in diameter. This is native from Montana to Washington and Nevada. *C. greenei,* native of California and adjacent Oregon, is up to 1 foot tall. It has up-facing, long-stalked, bowl-shaped, lilac to purplish blooms 2 to 3 inches wide, with a zone of darker purple on each petal above the crescent-shaped, deeply-depressed gland. There are up to five blooms on each stem. *C. howellii,* an endemic of Oregon, occurs in dry, rocky soil. From 1 foot to 1½ feet in height, its stems bear one to four up-facing, yellowish-white cupped flowers approximately 2 inches wide, their petals, longer than the sepals, have purplish hairs toward their bases. They are succeeded by erect seed capsules. *C. lyallii* inhabits dry slopes from Washington to British Columbia. Up to 1½ feet in height, but often shorter, this kind has stems with occasionally as many as nine up-facing or inclined blooms. They are 1 inch to 1½ inches wide, white sometimes tinged with purple, and usually have a crescent of purple on each petal above the gland and on each sepal. The seed pods are erect. *C. monophyllus* is a Californian distinct from its closest rel-

Calochortus gunnisonii

Calochortus macrocarpus

Calochortus kennedyi

Calopogon pallidus

Calothamnus species

Camellia japonica variety

Camellia japonica variety

Camellia japonica variety

Campanula medium, hose-in-hose variety

Canna generalis variety

atives by reason of its generally freely-branched stems and deep yellow flowers. This attractive kind rarely exceeds 9 inches in height and in the wild favors partially shaded locations. Its stems usually have one to three leaves. The erect or inclined blooms, with a dark reddish-brown blotch at the base of each densely-bearded and fringed petal, are 1 inch to 1¼ inches wide. *C. tolmiei* (syns. *C. maweanus, C. purdyi*) is exceedingly variable. It favors dry, rocky, or sometimes moist soils from Washington to California. Its stem usually branched, up to 1 foot tall, bears one to five or occasionally more erect, white, rose-pink- or purple-tinged blooms with hairy petals longer than the sepals and an upward-arched gland. *C. uniflorus* is a close ally of *C. monophyllus* from which it may readily be distinguished by its much shorter, usually branchless stems and fewer larger blooms and by the abundance of bulblets it develops in the axils of its leaves. The blooms, lilac generally with a purple spot on each petal, are 1½ to 2 inches across, and are greatly overtopped by the leaves. This is native to California.

Other sorts with up-facing blooms, as opposed to nodding ones, are characteristic of these species of the *Eucalochortus* section: *C. apiculatus* grows in dry, open woodlands from Alberta to British Columbia, Montana, and Washington. The possession of a nearly circular, small gland on each petal readily distinguishes it from related kinds. From 9 inches to 1½ feet tall, its stem, usually leafless above, carries up to six or sometimes more white to straw-yellow, erect or spreading, 2- to 2½-inch-wide blooms sometimes with purple pencilings. The solitary basal leaf is up to 1 foot long by ½ inch wide. *C. coeruleus*, called cat's ear, resembles *C. elegans* from which it may be distinguished by its flowers having more conspicuously fringed and heavily bearded petals, not minutely-warty on their upper sides, and by its large oblong instead of lanceolate anthers. Native in gravelly and organic soils in open, evergreen woodlands in California, this kind rarely exceeds 6 inches in height. Its fuzzy-petaled flowers, from one to ten on each stalk and bluish, are about 1 inch wide. Variety *C. c. nanus* is smaller and has smaller anthers. *C. elegans*, endemic to Idaho, Washington, and Oregon, is about 6 inches in height. Differences between it and closely-related *C. coeruleus* are given above. The blooms of *C. elegans* are greenish-white often with a crescent of purple above the gland on each petal and a blotch of the same color on each sepal.

Nodding, globose, or lantern-shaped blooms are characteristic of these four species of the *Eucalochortus* section: *C. albus*, the white fairy lantern or globe-tulip, ranges practically throughout the length of California and offshore islands. Variable, it has branched, leaf-bearing stems 1 foot to 2 feet tall with several slender-stalked, nodding, globose-bell-shaped blooms 1 inch to 1½ inches long, white to rosy-pink and sometimes suffused with brown. Their strongly concave petals, one-third again as long as the sepals, are clothed with long, yellow hairs. The glands on the petals are crescent-shaped. *C. amabilis*, of California, much like *C. pulchellus*, has somewhat smaller, deeper yellow blooms, their petals with glands margined with a fringe of short hairs, but otherwise hairless. The stems, 9 inches to 1½ feet tall, are usually branched. The slender-stalked, spherical to spherical-bell-shaped, nodding flowers are ¾ to 1 inch long. Their petals are not longer than the sepals. *C. amoenus*, the purple fairy lantern, is a Californian akin

Colochortus amoenus

to *C. albus*. It differs from that species in its nodding to more or less erect flowers being deep lavender-pink to rose-pink and in the glands on their petals having a lower membrane extending across their bases instead of only part way. The blooms, ¾ inch to 1¼ inches long, are sparsely furnished with long hairs. *C. pulchellus*, endemic to Mount Diablo in California and a close relative of *C. amabilis*, has branched stems 1 foot to 1½ feet tall or sometimes taller with up to twelve globose, lemon-yellow, nodding, long-stalked blooms 1 inch to 1¼ inches long and wide. Their petals are conspicuously fringed and on their insides are sparsely-hairy to their tips.

The *Cyclobothra* section of *Calochortus* includes a few species that are not infrequently cultivated under the name *Cyclobothra*. Their give-away characteristics are the netted coats that cover the bulbs and the seed capsules being much longer than wide and having three wings. The flowers nod or face upward according to species. Kinds belonging here include these: *C. barbatus* (syns. *C. luteus, Cyclobothra lutea*), native of Mexico. This has usually branched stems 1 foot to 2 feet tall and generally two nodding, more or less bell-shaped, yellow or purplish blooms, their petals a little longer than the sepals, fringed and densely clothed on their insides with slender hairs. The flowers are 1½ to 2 inches wide. *C. obispoensis*, of southern California, is quite

Calochortus uniflorus

different in appearance from all other kinds. It has slender, branched stems 1 foot to 2 feet tall and usually in twos, and blooms about 1 inch wide. Flat when open and facing upward, they have reflexed, slender yellow sepals markedly longer than the petals. The latter are yellow to orange-yellow with purplish-brownish apexes. They are clothed with a shag of long, slender hairs especially toward their bases. *C. plummerae,* of southern California, differs from allied *C. weedii* in having pinkish to rose-pink blooms with rarely fringed petals not bearded to their apexes. The stems are 1 foot to 2 feet tall. The up-facing, bowl-shaped flowers are usually paired, about 3 inches in diameter. *C. weedii,* a very variable native of California and Baja California, has several botanically named varieties. Generally similar to *C. plummerae,* it differs from that species in having yellow to orange flowers with usually fringed petals often tipped, edged, or flecked with brown. They are covered with yellow hairs.

Garden and Landscape Uses and Cultivation. Like their distant cousins, tulips, calochortuses do not settle down well as permanent residents in regions with climates markedly different from those they know in the wild, nor are they likely to multiply under such conditions. Although in the main they are less cold-tolerant than tulips, experience in the East indicates that low temperature is not the chief factor barring their successful acclimatization. The chief villains of the piece are excessive wetness and alternate freezing and thawing. Every effort must be made to mitigate these. In the vicinity of New York City a fair number of kinds located favorably have been grown successfully and have survived 0°F without apparent harm. Among the hardiest calochortuses are *C. albus, C. amabilis, C. howellii, C. macrocarpus, C. nuttallii, C. tolmiei,* and *C. uniflorus.* For their best display, calochortuses need mild winters and warm, dry summers. Yet they are so lovely that it is worth considerable effort and some expense to have them. Therefore ambitious northern gardeners set them at the bottoms of south-facing "cliffs" in rock gardens and at the bases of walls similarly oriented. They take care that soil drainage is perfect and after the ground has frozen to a depth of an inch or so insulate the site with a blanket of branches of evergreens, salt hay, or dry leaves over which a sheet of plastic mulch is spread and weighted down. By such contrivances calochortuses will bloom in northern gardens, but they do not increase, a true test of a plant's satisfaction with its environment, but gradually and sadly become fewer with each passing year. So, northern gardeners, do as you do with tulips, obtain a few new bulbs each fall and set them in the most favorable spots you have and enjoy them while they

deign to stay with you. Because calochortuses benefit from a period of summer dryness, in regions of summer rains many gardeners prefer to dig the bulbs immediately after their foliage has died naturally and store them indoors in a cool, airy place through their season of rest. Do not plant too early—otherwise growth may begin too soon and be harmed by freezing. As with tulips, late fall, but before the ground freezes, is the best time to plant.

In western gardens where climates are the same or similar to those under which these delightful bulb plants grow as natives much less difficulty accompanies their taming. There they are admirable in rock gardens, native plant gardens, and some sorts in flower beds.

CALODENDRUM (Calo-déndrum)—Cape-Chestnut. Two species of South Africa and tropical Africa belong to this genus of the rue family RUTACEAE. The only one known in cultivation is a handsome ornamental flowering tree. The generic name is derived from the Greek *kalos,* beautiful, and *dendron,* a tree. It is the Cape-chestnut *Calodendrum capense.*

The Cape-chestnut, or as it is called in South Africa, wild-chestnut, is one of the most conspicuous native trees there. In coastal areas and in cultivation in America, *C. capense* is evergreen; it is reported to be deciduous in inland Africa, where its leaves

Calodendrum capense

turn bright yellow before they drop. Round-headed and with wide-spreading branches, it is 60 or 70 feet high, but is often lower in the open. Its handsome, lustrous, dark green leaves are mostly in twos, but sometimes in threes. They are 4 to 6 inches long, short-stalked, pointed-ovate or obovate, unlobed, each with a prominent mid-vein and parallel laterals branching from it at nearly right angles. They are marked with tiny translucent spots. The flowers, in terminal clusters 6 or 7 inches long and about as broad, make a magnificent show in

spring or early summer. They are faintly fragrant and pale pink to rich mauve marked with purple, glandular dots. Each has five slender, spreading petals, five sterile, petal-like stamens, and five normal stamens, and is 1½ inches long. The fruits are dry, woody, globular capsules covered with sharp knobs or tubercles. They are 1½ to 2½ inches in diameter and each has several seeds. After the seeds are dispersed the husks often hang on the trees for a considerable time.

When the famous Swedish botanist Carl Peter Thunberg saw this tree in Africa in 1772 he was so entranced by it that he went to unusual effort to collect botanical specimens; this he accomplished by cutting off flowering branchlets he could not reach by shooting them down with a gun. The lumber of the Cape-chestnut is fairly hard, but bends easily, and in its homeland is one of the most useful of woods. It is esteemed for furniture, yokes, tool handles, tent bows, planking, and other purposes. An oil obtained from the fruits can be used for making soap.

Garden and Landscape Uses and Cultivation. Only in a warm climate, such as that of southern Florida and southern California, is this tree hardy. It is a fine ornamental and grows quite rapidly. It responds best to deep, reasonably fertile, fairly moist soil and a sunny location. No pruning or other special care is needed. As a foliage plant this species is attractive for growing in pots and tubs in large greenhouses and conservatories, but indoors it is unlikely to bloom unless there is space for it to attain quite a large size. It succeeds in any ordinary fertile soil in well-drained pots or tubs in a minimum winter temperature of 50 to 55°F. A moderately humid atmosphere and good light with a little shade from strong sun suits. Water freely from spring through fall, more moderately in winter. Well-rooted specimens benefit from weekly or biweekly applications of dilute liquid fertilizer from spring through fall. Container-grown specimens may, with advantage, be stood outdoors during summer. Any pruning necessary to shape the plants or restrict their size may be done in late winter or early spring, but may involve loss of the season's blooms. Propagation is by fresh seeds sown in sandy peaty soil in a temperature of about 70°F, and by cuttings of firm shoots inserted in a propagating bed in a greenhouse or under mist, in summer.

CALONYCTION. See Ipomoea.

CALOPHACA (Calóph-aca). Low deciduous shrubs and herbaceous plants comprise this genus of ten species of the pea family LEGUMINOSAE. They are natives from southern Russia to Burma and China. One is cultivated. The name comes from the Greek *kalos,* beautiful, and *phake,* lentil.

The lentil (*Lens*) is a related plant. Calophacas have alternate, pinnate leaves, with an uneven number of leaflets, and pea-shaped, yellow or violet flowers in axillary racemes, or rarely solitary. Their calyxes have five slightly unequal teeth. Nine of their stamens are united, one is free. The seed pods are cylindrical, pubescent and glandular.

Native from southeast Russia to the Ukraine, and hardy throughout New England, *Calophaca wolgarica* is up to 3 feet tall and has leaves of five to eight pairs of ovate-elliptic to nearly-round leaflets up to ½ inch long. The racemes are four- to six-flowered and glandular-hairy. The bright yellow corollas are ¾ to 1 inch long. The slender pods, each with usually one or two seeds, are up to 1¼ inches long.

Garden Uses and Cultivation. This shrub has attractive foliage and in early summer is pretty in bloom. It needs full sun and a sharply-drained, dryish soil. The only pruning necessary is a shortening of any long straggling shoots in late winter. Propagation is by seeds sown as soon as they are ripe and by grafting onto *Laburnum* or *Caragana*.

CALOPHYLLUM (Calo-phýllum)—Kamani or Alexandrian-Laurel, Maria or Santa Maria. The garcinia family GUTTIFERAE includes *Calophyllum*, which consists of more than 100 species of trees of tropical Asia and tropical America. The name derives from the Greek *kalos*, beautiful, and *phyllon*, a leaf, and refers to the handsome foliage.

Calophyllums have opposite, leathery leaves, with very many fine parallel veins that run at wide angles from midrib to the leaf margins. In axillary or terminal racemes or panicles, unisexual and bisexual flowers are on the same plant. Each bloom has four to twelve sepals and petals, and numerous stamens. The fruits are single-seeded, the seed being inside a shell, covered with a fleshy layer or skin. Another plant, *Danae racemosa*, is also and perhaps more aptly, called Alexandrian-laurel.

Valuable commercial products are obtained from this genus. Several species, including *C. inophyllum*, are sources of high-grade lumber, that of this kind is called Borneo mahogany. The lumber of *C. brasiliense* is used for ship and furniture building, and construction. From the seeds of *C. inophyllum*, dilo or domba oil, employed medicinally and for burning for illumination is obtained. Seeds of *C. brasiliense* yield an illuminating oil, and the bark of that sort a yellow gum used medicinally.

The kamani or Alexandrian-laurel (*C. inophyllum*) in its native tropical Asia is up to 120 feet in height, but in cultivation in southern Florida it is of much more modest dimensions. It has a stout, often leaning trunk and open head. The leaves, similar to those of the broad-leaved rubber plant

(*Ficus elastica decora*), have short, flattish stalks and broad oblong-elliptic to obovate blades up to 8 inches long, glossy dark green above, and with slightly thickened margins. The exquisitely-fragrant, cup-shaped, white flowers, in loose clusters of four to fifteen, are ½ to 1 inch across, have four sepals and four to eight petals, and rather resemble orange blossoms. Often, this species blooms twice each year. The stones of the globular, green, yellow, or reddish fruits are surrounded by a thin skin.

A New World species, the Maria or Santa Maria (*C. brasiliense* syns. *C. antillanum*, *C. calaba*), native of shorelines in the West Indies is reported to at times attain a height of 150 feet, but as known in cultivation it usually is not more than one-half that height and is even smaller as grown in Florida. Its leaves, not more than 6 inches long, are like those of the previous species, but thinner and rather narrower. The fragrant, cup-shaped, white flowers, about ⅓ inch across, are in clusters shorter than the leaves. The males have forty to fifty stamens, bisexual flowers eight to twelve. The fruits are ½ to 1 inch in diameter.

Garden and Landscape Uses and Cultivation. Both species discussed are handsome ornamentals very useful for shade and as avenue and street trees. In Florida the Maria succeeds better than the Asian species. It is commonly planted in Puerto Rico and other parts of the American tropics for ornament, and in forest areas. For the latter purpose it is chosen because of its ability to grow on eroded and degraded soils.

CALOPOGON (Calo-pogon)—Grass-Pink Orchid. This wholly North American and West Indian genus of terrestrial orchids comprises four species, most endemic to the southeastern United States. Members of the orchid family ORCHIDACEAE and inhabitants of acid bogs, wet pinelands, and similar habitats, they are discouragingly averse to being tamed as garden plants. The name, given in allusion to the flowers having a bearded lip, comes from the Greek *kalos*, beautiful, and *pogon*, a beard.

Calopogons are deciduous. They have underground tuber-like organs from which develop one, or rarely, two grasslike leaves and a loose, slender raceme of two to several flowers with wide-spreading, similar sepals and petals and a conspicuously bearded lip, uppermost of the six flower segments, which is unusual among the native orchids of North America.

The hardiest species *Calopogon tuberosus* (syn. *C. pulchellus*) blooms in summer and is native from Newfoundland to Minnesota, Florida, and Texas. Its slender leaf is up to 1¼ feet in length. The flower stem, 1 foot to 2 feet high or a little higher, carries three to fifteen rose-pink to purplish-

pink blooms about 1¼ inches wide. Their lips, broadly fan-shaped toward their apexes, have a crest of white hairs tipped with magenta-pink and yellow.

Native of the southeastern United States, *C. barbatus* is 6 inches to 1½ feet in height. It has leaves less than ¼ inch wide and up to 7 inches long. The racemes are of usually five or fewer, but up to eight, rose-pink or less commonly white flowers, each about 1¼ inches in diameter. They open in rapid succession. Somewhat similar *C. multiflorus* of the southeastern United States has racemes of up to ten purplish or crimson blooms and is 6 inches to 1½ feet tall.

Garden Uses and Cultivation. Attempts to grow these orchids should be made only under conditions that very closely approximate those under which they grow in the wild. This means extremely-acid, wet soil, and a sunny location. A bog garden or favored spot in a rock garden may make possible success with these choice natives. Increase is by natural multiplication. Additional information is given under Orchids.

CALOSTEMMA (Calo-stèmma). Four species of nonhardy bulb plants of the amaryllis family AMARYLLIDACEAE comprise *Calostemma*. Natives of Australia, they have a name derived from the Greek *kalos*, beautiful, and *stemma*, a crown. It alludes to the corona of the flowers.

Calostemmas have all-basal, grasslike leaves that soon wither and leafless flowering stalks that terminate in an umbel of blooms with at its base two or three membranous, linear bracts. The flowers have perianths with a short tube and six lobes (petals) forming the funnel-shaped part of the bloom. The six stamens have stalks with wings united into a tubular, toothed crown or corona. The style is slender, about as long as the perianth. The fruits are capsules.

Its flowers reddish-purple to pink, *C. purpureum* is about 1 foot tall and has brown-coated bulbs ¾ inch to 1½ inches in diameter and leaves about 2 inches wide. The flowers are ½ to ¾ inch long with individual stalks as long or longer. Except that its blooms are yellow and ¾ to 1 inch long, *C. luteum* scarcely differs from the last.

Garden Uses and Cultivation. These are for collectors of the rare and unusual. They are suitable for outdoor cultivation in warm, dryish climates and for cool greenhouses. They respond to conditions and care that suit crinums.

CALOTHAMNUS (Calo-thámnus)—Net Bush, One-Sided Bottle Brush. The beautiful evergreen Australian shrubs of the myrtle family MYRTACEAE that constitute *Calothamnus* total twenty-five species. They resemble callistemons, but are more graceful than most kinds of that better-known group, and their flowers do not form such evident bottle brushes. The well-chosen botanical name is derived from the Greek *kallos*, beautiful, and *thamnos*, a bush.

Calothamnuses have slender, alternate leaves, and commonly, showy flowers in usually one-sided spikes or clusters. The blooms are produced along shoots of the previous year's growth. The alternate, stiff leaves are flat or cylindrical. The blooms are close to and sometimes partly embedded in the stems. They have tubular calyxes with four or five lobes, four or five petals, and many stamens much longer than the petals and united at their bases into groups. The fruits are capsules enclosed in the hardened calyx tubes.

One of the best-known kinds is *C. quadrifidus.* This, a shrub 5 to 8 feet tall, is decorated in season with few-flowered, one-sided, stalkless clusters of 1-inch-long, brilliant red blooms each with four groups of flat-stalked stamens. Its slender, flat, heathlike leaves are ½ to 1 inch long or sometimes a little longer.

Two of the most attractive calothamnuses are *C. villosus* and *C. homalophyllus.* As its name implies *C. villosus* has woolly-hairy foliage. The needle-like, incurved,

Calothamnus villosus

Calothamnus villosus (flowers)

crowded leaves are grayish and about 1 inch long. The red flowers of the one-sided clusters have calyxes with five, instead of the more usual four, teeth. This handsome species is 5 to 7 feet tall. Beautiful *C. homalophyllus* is 4 to 8 feet tall and has round-apexed, narrowly-oblong to linear, flat, thick leaves that taper to their bases, and are 1 inch to 1½ inches long. The 1-inch-long crimson blooms are in spikes. A white-flowered variety is cultivated in Australia.

Its foliage rough to the feel, *C. asper* has short, dense, one-sided clusters of brilliant red blooms. From ½ to 1 inch long, its crowded leaves are narrowly-linear. When young they are clothed with abundant silky hairs. This species is about 6 feet in height. From 6 to 8 feet tall, *C. sanguineus* has crowded, slender needle-like leaves ½ to 1½ inches long that when young often are silky-hairy. Its flowers, in one-sided clusters or short spikes, have finely-silky-hairy calyxes and are about 1 inch long. Compact and up to about 5 feet tall, *C. rupestris* has crowded, needle-like, mostly curved leaves up to 1½ inches long. The crimson flowers, in clusters of few, have conspicuously woolly-hairy green calyxes. Very distinct *C. longissimus* is a shrub 1½ to 4 feet tall with curving, pinelike leaves 6 inches to 1 foot long. The dark red flowers, partially embedded in the corky tissue of the stems, have hairy calyxes. They are in clusters.

Garden and Landscape Uses and Cultivation. As garden and landscape decoratives, calothamnuses serve the same purposes as similar-sized callistemons, and need the same conditions and care. They are beautiful shrubs for California-type climates, distinguished by warm, dry summers and mild almost or quite frost-free winters. Most calothamnuses succeed in exposed, hot, dry places, and near the sea. Well-drained, porous soil, improved by the addition of peat moss or other decayed organic matter, is to their liking. Too much watering is to be avoided. Australian experience suggests that fertilizing and excessive pruning tend to inhibit blooming. The only cutting necessary, and this should be done as soon as flowering is through, is any absolutely necessary to shape the specimens or limit their size. Propagation is easy by seeds. Cuttings can also be used as a means of increase.

CALOTROPIS (Caló-tropis)—Crown Flower, Giant-Milkweed. Milkweeds, of the genus *Asclepias,* so familiar in the Americas and especially in the natural flora of the United States, do not occur as natives of the Old World. But to tropical Africa and Asia, the closely-related genus *Calotropis* is endemic. It consists of six species, one of which, *C. gigantea,* has become naturalized in the West Indies, and belongs in the milkweed family ASCLEPIADACEAE.

From *Asclepias* the Old World group differs in technical details of the scales that form the corona of the flower. Its name comes from the Greek *kalos*, beautiful, and *tropis*, a keel, and alludes to the blooms. In Hawaii these are made into leis.

The genus *Calotropis* comprises milky-juiced shrubs or small trees, commonly freely-branched, with large, undivided, almost stalkless, opposite, hairy or hairless leaves. The flowers are in broad clusters. They have a five-parted calyx, glandular on its inside, a bell-shaped to somewhat wheel-shaped corolla with five broad lobes (petals), and a corona (crown) of five fleshy scales joined to the stamen tube. The fruits, usually in pairs, are pods, containing seeds with silky hairs or floss. The juice of these plants is likely to irritate the skin. A strong fiber called madar is prepared from the bark of *A. gigantea* and the floss of the seeds is used in the same ways as kapok.

In India the blooms are sacred to Shiva, the destroyer, and the god of love Kama is depicted as having the flower buds on one of his arrows.

The giant-milkweed (*C. gigantea*), 6 to 15 feet tall, has woolly shoots and broad, obovate leaves 4 to 10 inches long and woolly-hairy on their undersides. The sweetish, fragrant, rose-pink to purplish or white flowers, in solitary or branched umbels, have petals that bend downward and with age become twisted. The fruits are 3 to 4 inches long. Differing in having more oblong, pointed leaves, white and purple blooms with erect petals, in cottony hairy umbels, and fruits 4 to 5 inches long, *C. procera* attains a height of up to 15 feet. It is a native of India, Syria, and North Africa.

Calotropis procera

Garden and Landscape Uses and Cultivation. These are handsome plants of bold, architectural aspect and prevailingly gray coloring. They are evergreen and withstand drought without distress. On the plains of India, in other parts of their natural range, and on the drier islands of the West Indies, they stand out among other vegetation that is seared as a result of long periods without rain. They are excellent for gardens in warm, dry regions. Deep-rooted, they are probably difficult to transplant when large. They may be raised in containers, and transferred to their final quarters from these. Full sun and well-drained soil are essential. Propagation is easy by seeds and by cuttings in a greenhouse propagating bench. It is important not to keep the cuttings too wet.

CALPURNIA (Cal-púrnia). Six species of African shrubs or small trees compose this genus of the pea family LEGUMINOSAE, the name of which commemorates Calpurnius, an imitator of Virgil, and was applied because of the close relationship of *Calpurnia* and *Virgilia*. From *Virgilia* calpurnias differ in having yellow blooms, and very flat, sharp-edged seed pods. They have pinnate leaves, with an uneven number of leaflets, and axillary or terminal racemes, sometimes branched, of pea-like blooms. The calyxes of the flowers are five-toothed, the reflexed standard or banner petal is two-lobed at its apex. There are ten stamens, separate or joined only at their bases, and a curved style. The fruits are stalked, usually broadly-linear, sometimes slightly-winged pods containing compressed seeds.

South African *C. aurea* is a shrub up to about 10 feet tall. Its somewhat leathery

Calpurnia aurea

leaves have from four to six, rarely more, pairs of blunt, broad-elliptic to oblong leaflets and a terminal one, sparsely-hairy on their undersides, and 1 inch to 1¾ inches long. The abundant yellow blooms are ½ inch long. The linear seed pods, up to 3 inches long by ½ inch wide, are thinly-hairy. Among other species of this genus surely worth introducing to cultivation is *C. floribunda,* of South Africa, a beautiful shrub about 6 feet tall that is covered with drooping panicles of golden pea-like blooms.

Garden and Landscape Uses and Cultivation. These handsome shrubs form excellent general purpose embellishments in warm, sunny, frost-free, or essentially frost-free climates. They are very showy in bloom and have attractive foliage. They need full sun and succeed in ordinary soils that are well drained. No special care is needed. Any pruning required to shape or control them is done immediately after flowering. Propagation is easy by seeds. Cuttings may also succeed.

CALTHA (Cál-tha)—Marsh-Marigold. Twenty temperate-region and arctic species constitute *Caltha*. Several, the most familiar of which is the marsh-marigold, or cowslip of New England, are attractive enough to warrant the attention of gardeners. All are hardy herbaceous perennials belonging in the buttercup family RANUNCULACEAE and favoring wet and marshy habitats. The generic name is an ancient Latin one, probably for the marigold (*Calendula officinalis*).

Calthas have vigorous root systems, succulent stems, and glabrous, rounded to kidney-shaped, undivided, lobeless, usually toothed leaves, heart-shaped at their bases. The showy parts of the yellow, white, or pink, usually cup-shaped flowers, commonly accepted as petals, are sepals. There are five or more. There are no petals. The stamens are numerous and conspicuous. There are five to fifteen small, podlike follicles. The spring foliage of the marsh-marigold is collected, cooked, and eaten in New England as "cowslip greens."

Marsh-marigold (*C. palustris*), a variable native of northern Europe, Asia, and North America, occurs in swamps, bogs, watersides, and wet woods. It grows from 8 inches to 2 feet high and has hollow stems. The basal leaves are long-stalked, those above becoming progressively shorter-stalked until the uppermost are nearly stalkless. The bright yellow blooms, ¾ inch to 1½ inches across, are produced in considerable abundance. They resemble huge buttercups. A variety of special interest to gardeners is *C. p. monstruosa,*

Caltha palustris

which has large, attractive, double, yellow flowers. Another, *C. p. tyermanii*, is a yellow-flowered kind that does not usually exceed 6 inches in height. Distinguished by its single flowers being white, *C. p. alba* is native to the Himalayas. Pale yellow, double blooms are borne by *C. p. pallida-plena*. Native from Alaska to Washington and Colorado, *C. leptosepala* has attractive, solitary, white flowers. It attains a height of about 1 foot and, except for sometimes one on the stem, all its leaves are basal. Variety *C. l. grandiflora* has larger flowers. Another white-flowered, or bluish-flowered kind is *C. biflora,* which ranges as a wildling from Alaska to California. This has no true stem, and as its name indicates, its flowers are usually in pairs.

A very handsome species, *C. polypetala* (curiously ill-named in view of the fact that calthas have no petals), of Asia Minor and the Caucasus, spreads vigorously by stolons and is sometimes 2 to 3 feet tall. Its leaves are up to 1 foot in diameter, its bright yellow flowers, 3 inches. Closely resembling *C. palustris*, but smaller in all its parts, *C. radicans* is a native of northern England and Scotland. Its flowers are up to 1½ inches in diameter. Another low-

Caltha radicans

Caltha palustris (flowers)

growing close relative of *C. palustris* is *C. laeta,* which has butter-yellow flowers, solitary or several on each stalk. This kind occurs natively from southern and central Europe to the Himalayas. Quite different from any of the above is *C. natans,* which grows in ponds and slow-moving streams from Alaska to Wisconsin and Minnesota and also in northern Asia. When rooted in submerged soil its stems float on the surface, otherwise they trail over the soil surface. Its flowers, under ½ inch in diameter, are white or pink.

Southern hemisphere calthas are little known in North America. Several are attractive. They require decidedly cool, moist summers for their successful cultivation. Hailing from New Zealand, *C. novae-zelandiae* is a low, fleshy plant that inhabits alpine regions and has leaves with the basal lobes bent upward or completely turned over onto the blade. A curious botanical feature is that, reversing the usual order, the stomata (leaf pores) are on the upper rather than the lower leaf surfaces. A similar folding upward of the leaf lobes occurs in several South American species. It has been suggested that this provides air-still areas in which the stomata can function more efficiently than if they were exposed to wind. The New Zealand caltha has solitary, pale yellow, scented flowers. An abundant native of Tierra del Fuego is *C. dioneaefolia.* Its specific epithet refers to the fact that its glossy leaves closely resemble those of venus fly tray (*Dionaea*) in miniature. They are oval and tiny and are densely clustered on a short, thick stem. The flowers are pale yellow. Andean species include *C. sagittata,* which has scalloped, kidney-shaped leaves that have upward-folded basal lobes and proportionately large solitary flowers, and *C. appendiculata,* which has wedge-shaped leaves and solitary flowers with narrower sepals.

Garden and Landscape Uses. Calthas are displayed to best advantage when planted along the margins of lakes, ponds, or streams and in bog or water gardens. The smaller kinds are well suited for growing in wet soil in rock gardens. The flowers are attractive and last well in water when cut. It is worth noting that as an ornamental the European form of the marsh-marigold (*C. palustris*) is superior to the native American phase of the species. It has been observed by growers in New York that this does not, as the native form often does, become something of a nuisance because of self-sown seedlings springing up in abundance in moist soils.

Cultivation. No special difficulties attend the cultivation of calthas. They are easily increased by division in early fall or early spring and may be had from seeds sown as soon as they are ripe in moist or wet soil under cool conditions. Plant in fall or early spring. Fertile soil containing an abundance of organic matter is best. It should be always moist, but it is not necessary for it to be completely saturated and boglike, although such a condition is quite conducive to satisfactory growth.

CALVARY-CLOVER is *Medicago echinus.*

CALYCANTHACEAE—Calycanthus Family. This dicotyledonous family of two genera of usually aromatic, deciduous and evergreen shrubs occurs natively in North America, eastern Asia, and northern Australia. Its sorts have opposite, undivided leaves, and solitary flowers with a variable number of spirally-arranged perianth parts that change gradually from sepal-like to petal-like from outside to inside of the blooms. There are five to thirty stamens, the inner ones nonfunctional and properly identified as staminodes, and several to many pistils in a hollowed receptacle. The fruits consist of a number of one-seeded achenes enclosed in the fleshy receptacle. The genera are *Calycanthus* and *Chimonanthus.*

CALYCANTHUS (Caly-cánthus)—Sweet Shrub, Sweet-Scented Shrub, Carolina-Allspice. Old-fashioned favorites, common in gardens of last century, these native American shrubs are not planted as often as they were formerly. Perhaps the great influx of Asian shrubs and their popularization during the twentieth century is responsible for this. Possibly modern taste calls for more dramatic displays of color than sweet shrubs provide. Whatever the cause, their popularity has waned. Yet few of the kinds that have displaced them can compete with sweet shrubs in fragrance. That delicious and most precious quality of theirs is reason enough for tucking at least one specimen in some corner of the garden to which one may repair in summer to enjoy the scented blooms and, perchance, nostalgic memories.

The name *Calycanthus* comes from the Greek *kalyx,* a calyx, and *anther,* a flower, and refers to the structure of the blooms. The genus belongs to the calycanthus family CALYCANTHACEAE, the only other representative of which is *Chimonanthus.* There are four species of sweet shrubs. All except one are hardy in the north. They are deciduous and have rather large, opposite, toothless leaves roughened by tiny warts on their upper surfaces, and rich brown or yellowish-brown flowers, which are usually very fragrant. The blooms, borne at the ends of short lateral branchlets, have many petal-like parts that represent both sepals and petals. There are numerous stamens and many pistils. The fig-shaped fruits are capsules containing many achenes (commonly called seeds).

The hardiest and most freely planted is the Carolina-allspice (*C. floridus*). Although in the wild not found north of Virginia (it extends south to Florida), it is

Calycanthus floridus

Calycanthus floridus (flowers)

hardy through most of New England and was once much esteemed there as a dooryard shrub. It is up to 10 feet in height and width. Its leaves are narrow-elliptic to ovate and 2 to 5 inches long. Their undersides are densely grayish pubescent. The rich dark reddish-brown blooms, borne in June and July, are 2 inches across and sweetly fragrant. When bruised, all parts of the plant have a camphor-like fragrance as does the dry wood. A closely-related species, *C. mohrii,* differs chiefly in the fruits being scarcely rather than conspicuously contracted at the mouth. A native from Tennessee to Georgia and Alabama, it is slightly more tender than *C. floridus.*

From the above kinds *C. fertilis,* native from Pennsylvania to Georgia and Alabama, differs mainly in that the glaucous undersides of its leaves are hairless or only slightly pubescent. It is rather less hardy than the Carolina-allspice, and its blooms are less fragrant. They are greenish-purple to warm red-brown. The fruits are strongly contracted at the mouth. Variety *C. f. ferax* has the undersides of its leaves green rather than glaucous. A dwarf variant with leaves up to 3½ inches long and green beneath is *C. f. nanus.*

Native of moist soils in California, *C. occidentalis* is not ordinarily hardy in the

Calycanthus fertilis

East north of Philadelphia. It is less compact than the others and has bigger leaves and blooms. From its eastern relatives it is easily distinguished when in leaf by its axillary buds, which are visible. In the other species they are hidden by the bases of the leafstalks. The Californian sweet shrub attains a height of 10 to 12 feet and has ovate to ovate-lanceolate leaves 3 to 8 inches long, bristly-hairy above and green and hairless or slightly pubescent beneath. The blooms, 2 to 3 inches in diameter, are less pleasantly fragrant than those of the other species. They are brownish-purple with tawny ends to the sepals. The bell-shaped fruits are not contracted at the mouth.

Garden and Landscape Uses and Cultivation. Sweet shrubs provide good foliage and are suitable for borders, solitary lawn specimens, informal areas, and native plant gardens. The fragrance is esteemed. They are of easy culture, prospering in any reasonably fertile soil that is well-drained and not excessively dry and tolerating shade or sun. Increase is easily had by dividing sizable plants, by removing rooted suckers, by layering, and by sowing seeds in spring in sandy peaty soil. These shrubs require no regular systematic pruning.

CALYCOPHYLLUM (Calyco-phýllum)—Lemonwood. Six species belong in this genus of evergreen and partially evergreen trees and shrubs of the madder family RUBIACEAE. Named from the Greek *kalyx*, calyx, and *phyllon*, a leaf, in allusion to the curious petal-like development of the calyxes of some species, the group is indigenous to the West Indies and tropical America. Some kinds are of importance for their lumber, notably the lemonwood, the wood of which, in the United States, is much esteemed for the manufacture of bows.

Lemonwood (**Calycophyllum candidissimum**) is a slender, semideciduous tree 40 to 65 feet in height, with opposite, broad-ovate, bluntly-pointed, 2- to 3-inch-long leaves. In spring, in terminal clusters, the white, bell-shaped flowers are borne.

Within each cluster the blooms are in threes. The two outer flowers of each three have calyxes with four equal ¼-inch-long lobes. The center bloom has three such calyx lobes, and one broad, rounded, creamy-white, petal-like, and 1 inch to 1½ inches long. The petal-like calyx lobes are the extremely showy parts of the flowers; they remain attractive for long periods.

Another white-flowered species of considerable display value and charm, but without the expanded calyx lobes so prominent in the last, is *C. spruceanum,* of Brazil. This slender tree attains heights of up to 90 feet. It has grayish-green bark that changes to reddish-brown, and sheds annually. The leaves are opposite, thin, 3 to 4 inches long, broadly-pointed-ovate, and dark green. The numerous small, hairy blooms are in terminal, branching clusters 3 to 8 inches across.

Garden and Landscape Uses and Cultivation. Very attractive in bloom, the calycophyllums described are useful for general landscaping in southern Florida, Hawaii, and other humid tropical and near-tropical places. They succeed in ordinary soils and locations and are propagated by seeds and cuttings.

CALYCOTOME. See Calicotome.

CALYPSO (Calýp-so). Its name commemorating the Greek nymph Calypso, this genus of the orchid family ORCHIDACEAE has only one species. A lovely native of high latitudes and some mountains throughout the northern hemisphere, it is occasionally cultivated. In North America it is found in moist evergreen forests from northern New England and New York to Michigan, Minnesota, and Alaska and, in the western mountains, as far south as California and Arizona.

From 4 to 8 inches tall, *Calypso bulbosa* is a herbaceous perennial with a small bulb from which comes in fall a solitary basal leaf. The leafstalk and pointed-broad-ovate blade are each 1½ to 2 inches long. The flower, solitary on a stem sheathed at its base by two or three scales, comes in May or June. The blooms have three linear-lanceolate sepals and two similar lateral petals, each from almost ½ to ¾ inch long, and pale purple. The prominent, pouched, slipper-like lip is about ¾ inch long, whitish with a yellowish tip, and with red-brown markings and a crest of three lines of golden-yellow hairs.

Garden Uses and Cultivation. This choice orchid is a treasure for those dedicated to growing native plants and for skilled rock gardeners. Often difficult to satisfy, best results are had by duplicating as nearly as possible the conditions it favors in the wild. Constantly-moist, sandy soil containing an abundance of leaf mold or peat is appropriate, as is a cool, partially-shaded location. A light covering of leaves or

branches of evergreens over winter is helpful where snowfall is sparse or intermittent. Propagation is by careful removal of offsets. For further information see Orchids.

CALYPTRIDIUM (Calyp-trídium). The name of this genus of about six species, alluding to the manner in which the petals of some kinds fold over the seed capsule as they age, is from the Greek *kalyptra,* a cap or covering. Endemic to western North America, *Calyptridium* belongs to the purslane family PORTULACACEAE. As treated here it includes the one or two species that some botanists isolate as *Spraguea*.

Calyptridiums are annual or herbaceous perennials with basal or alternate, spatula-shaped leaves and small flowers in curved or coiled spikes or headlike clusters of spikes. The blooms have two papery or papery-margined sepals, two or four petals, one to three stamens, and a style with two stigmas. The fruits are capsules.

Pussy paws (*C. umbellatum* syn. *Spraguea umbellata*) is a variable annual or more or less perennial native from the Rocky Mountains to British Columbia, California, and Baja California. Its has a dense rosette of mostly basal leaves from just over ½ inch to 3 inches long, and several prostrate to semierect stems 2 to 10 inches long that carry either a few smaller leaves or none. The flowers, on heads of curving spikes, have persistent, whitish sepals and, scarcely longer than them, four rosy-pink petals ⅛ to ¼ inch long. More persistently perennial *C. u. caudiciferum* (syns. *Spraguea umbellata caudicifera, S. multiceps*) has rounder leaves under ½ inch long.

Garden Uses and Cultivation. Very attractive plants for sunny rock gardens, *C. umbellatum* and its variety need gritty, well-drained soil and full sun. They are hardy to considerable cold, but are intolerant of wet winters and long periods of hot, humid weather. This means that they are in the main better suited to western than eastern gardens. Once established, the plants should remain undisturbed. They do not transplant readily. Propagation is by seed.

CALYSTEGIA (Caly-stègia)—California-Rose. By many botanists this genus of twenty-five species of the morning glory family CONVOLVULACEAE is retained in *Convolvulus*. Those who regard it as a separate entity segregate it on the basis of technical differences in the pollen grains and construction of the ovary. A more easily observable characteristic that helps, but does not assure correct assignment of cultivated kinds is that in *Calystegia* the bracts just below the flowers are large, leafy, and almost or completely enclose the calyx, whereas in *Convolvulus* they are small or minute. Also, the blooms of *Calystegia* are usually solitary, those of *Convolvulus* often occur in clusters. The name, from the Greek *kalyx*, calyx, and *stege*, a covering, alludes to the pair of bracts beneath the flowers.

Calystegias, natives of tropical and temperate regions, are vining or creeping, hairless or nearly hairless herbaceous perennials, with undivided, lobeless or palmately-lobed leaves. The blooms come from the leaf axils. White, pink, or purplish, the flowers are fairly large. The species of *Calystegia* have five sepals, a pleated, funnel-shaped, sometimes slightly five-angled corolla, five nonprotruding stamens, and a slender style with two stigmas. The fruits are spherical capsules.

The California-rose is a double-flowered variety of **C. hederacea,** often misidentified as *C. japonica*. It is hardy in southern New England and naturalized in some parts of North America. A vigorous vine with twining, nonwoody stems up to 20 feet long, this kind has arrow-shaped to lanceolate leaves 2 to 4 inches long, usually with basal lobes and densely clothed with minute hairs. The bright pink, solitary blooms, cleft into narrow petal-like lobes and 1 inch to 2 inches wide, are freely produced throughout the summer. They remain open for several days. The single-flowered species of *C. hederacea,* which seems not to be cultivated, is native to Japan, Korea, and China.

Quite pretty in bloom but generally too invasive to be admitted to gardens, Rutland beauty or bindweed (**C. sepium**) of North America, northern Europe, and northern Asia has twining stems a few feet long, long-stalked, triangular-ovate leaves, and solitary white or pinkish flowers up to 2¾ inches in diameter.

Calystegia sepium

Garden and Landscape Uses and Cultivation. Caution must be exercised in placing the California-rose otherwise its proclivity for invasive takeover of areas adjacent to where it is planted can spell trouble. So long as this is clearly borne in mind this vine can be used to good effect to ornament walls, fences, tree stumps, other supports, and rocky banks. It thrives in any ordinary soil in sunny locations. It does not set seeds. Propagation is by division in spring.

CALYTHRIX (Calý-thrix)—Fringe-Myrtle. The name of this genus is often spelled *Calytrix*. It consists of forty species of evergreen, heathlike, Australian shrubs of the myrtle family MYRTACEAE. The name is derived from the Greek *kalyx*, calyx, and *thrix*, hair, in allusion to the long hairlike ends of the calyx lobes.

Fringe-myrtles have small, scattered, undivided, heathlike leaves, and pink, lilac, violet, yellow, or white, small, starry, many-stamened flowers in considerable numbers.

An attractive shrub, compact, almost or quite hairless, and up to about 4 feet in height, **Calythrix sullivanii** has fresh green, short-linear, three-angled leaves about ¼ inch long. Its white or pinkish blooms are borne freely in small clusters at the ends of branches and branchlets. Other species that would certainly be worth introducing and testing include *C. alpestris, C. glutinosa,* and *C. tetragona*.

Garden and Landscape Uses and Cultivation. These are plants for sandy peaty, somewhat acid soils of rather low fertility, and full sun. They can be grown outdoors only where there is little or no frost and are suitable for climates similar to that of California. Although they stand considerable dryness during their season of growth, they appreciate reasonable supplies of moisture. Light pruning, to shape the bushes, should be done as soon as blooming is through. Propagation is by seeds and cuttings.

CALYTRIX. See Calythrix.

CALYX. The calyx is the part of a flower formed of the outer set of floral parts, the sepals. Commonly green or greenish and of leafy texture, in the bud stage it surrounds and encloses the other floral parts, protecting them from injury by inclement weather and other causes. Some few flowers, those of willows, for example, have no calyxes. Collectively the calyx and corolla form the perianth. If their parts (sepals and petals) are similar they are correctly identified as tepals, but more often if not as accurately when they are petal-like as they are in lilies and tulips, for example, they are all called petals. The sepals may be separate or joined below into a calyx tube with the tips of the individual sepals clearly recognizable as calyx lobes or calyx teeth. Less often, the sepals are completely united into a truncate, lobeless and toothless calyx tube.

CAMAROTIS. See Sarcochilus.

CAMAS or CAMASS. This is the common name of *Camassia*. Species of *Zigadenus* are named death-camas, poison-camas, and white-camas.

CAMASSIA (Camás-sia)—Camas or Camass or Quamash. These are beautiful hardy bulb plants, natives only of North America and there, except for one of the about six species, confined as wildlings to the West. In appearance they suggest giant squills (*Scilla*) or smaller, more delicate editions of *Eremurus*. They belong to the lily family LILIACEAE. The name *Camassia* is adapted from camass or quamash, Indian designations for these plants that have been adopted as their English common names.

To the Indians of the West camassias were of great importance. Their bulbs were boiled and eaten as a staple food. Rights to exploit vast natural stands were of prime importance and the fields where they grew in great abundance were regarded as tribal property to be defended against intruders. Bloody wars were fought to establish possession and settle disputes about these. The last such, the Nez Perce war of 1877, was brilliantly and desperately, but unsuccessfully waged by Chief Joseph and his braves to prevent appropriation of their camass grounds by trespassing white men. But camass was of importance not only to the original Americans. Many early explorers and settlers employed them to stave off hunger and at times starvation. Members of the Lewis and Clark expedition used them extensively for these purposes and at times were entirely dependent upon them for food. Later, where they were abundant, they were exploited as hog feed. The camass, which held an honored place in Indian legend, played an important role in the white man's settlement and development of the West.

Camassias have solitary or clustered, black- or brown-coated, ovoid bulbs and all-basal foliage. Their leaves, sheathing at their bases, are long, narrowly-lanceolate, toothless and hairless, prostrate or weakly-erect at maturity. The slender, erect, branchless flowering stalks, those of some kinds up to 4 feet tall, terminate in racemes of well-displayed starry flowers that open in succession from below upward. Each has six spreading perianth parts commonly called petals, but more properly tepals. These are usually blue or violet-blue, more rarely cream or white. There are six stamens slightly shorter than the petals and a slender style ending in a three-lobed or three-parted stigma. The fruits are few- to many-seeded subspherical to egg-shaped or oblong capsules. Individuals within the species differ considerably in the sizes of their parts, flower colors, and other details. Technical differences must be considered to establish positive identification.

Common camass (**C. quamash** syn. *C. esculenta*) is distinguished by its usually slightly asymmetrical flowers having one petal curved downward, the others upward, many of its blooms being open at one time, and their petals, after withering, remaining for a long period without dropping. Also, its seed pods are held tightly against the main flower stem. From 1 foot to 3 feet in height, this kind has leaves usually under ⅔ inch wide, and flowers, ranging from white through pale and deep blue to violet, five to forty in each raceme. They are 1¼ to nearly 3 inches across. The anthers are yellow to purple. The common camass is native in moist meadows from Montana to British Columbia, Utah, and California. Several varieties of this attractive species have been recognized and named.

Ranging as a native of moist soils from British Columbia to California, *C. leicht-linii* differs from the last in having symmetrical flowers with petals that soon drop.

Camassia leichtlinii

Not more than three blooms are usually open at one time, and the seed pods do not press against the central stalk. The flowers, white to cream, blue, or purple, are in racemes up to 4 feet in height of up to sixty blooms, but often considerably fewer. They are 2¼ to 3¼ inches across.

The other western North American species are *C. cusickii* and *C. howellii*. A rare native of hillsides in northeastern Oregon, *C. cusickii* differs from *C. quamash*, to which it is closely allied, in having longer, clustered bulbs, somewhat potato-like in aspect, and more numerous, broader leaves, the latter ¾ inch to 1½ inches wide. Also, the bulbs are unpleasantly pungent and inedible. Limited in the wild to southwestern Oregon, rare *C. howellii* inhabits grassy meadows in company with *C. leicht-linii*. From that species it differs in blooming slightly later and in having subspherical, glossy seed capsules up to ⅔ inch long containing five or fewer seeds instead of dull, egg-shaped ones ⅔ to 1 inch in length with six to twelve seeds.

Camassia cusickii

Sometimes called wild-hyacinth, the most eastern camass is *C. scilloides* (syn. *C. fras-eri*). Native of prairies and open woodlands from Pennsylvania to Minnesota, Georgia, Alabama, and Texas, this sort is distinguishable from *C. quamash*, *C. leicht-linii*, and *C. cusickii* by its nearly spherical seed capsules and from *C. howellii* by its withered petals seldom closing over the seed capsules and usually remaining separate to their bases. The leaves of this are commonly 1 foot long by usually under ½ inch wide. The racemes of 1-inch-wide, pale blue, blue-violet, or sometimes white flowers are carried to heights of 1 foot to 2 feet. Mostly they are of fifteen to forty blooms, sometimes many fewer or many more.

Garden and Landscape Uses. Just why such beautiful natives as these are not more freely planted is difficult to understand. Certainly lack of decorative merit or adaptability to cultivation are not reasons. Lovelier by far than many more familiar plants esteemed by gardeners, they are as easy to grow as squills and daffodils. Unlike tulips and hyacinths, if provided with conditions at all to their liking, they take up permanent residence and do not need to be renewed every two, three, or four years. True, most kinds do not multiply by offsets as do daffodils and many other bulbs. Because of this, except where conditions favor the development of self-sown seedlings, these camassias do not increase. Besides their suitability for decorating landscapes the flowers of camassias are excellent for cutting for use in arrangements.

In the wild most members of this genus inhabit rich damp meadows, which are often inundated with water for considerable periods in the spring, but dry in summer. As garden plants they are tolerant of a wider range of habitats and make themselves at home in any fertile soil that does not lack for moisture early in the year, yet is not waterlogged. Camassias stand wetter soils than most bulbs, but in the East at least, poor soil drainage that results in

excessive wetness in winter is detrimental. After the foliage dies in early summer dryness does no harm. These bulb plants are best in full sun, but adapt well to part-day shade. Naturally gregarious, they show to best advantage when massed. Colonies of not less than one dozen are about the smallest for satisfactory effect (and very charming pictures can be had with such), but for really stunning results they should be planted in hundreds by watersides, in meadows, open woodlands, and other places where they can be naturalized and left pretty much to themselves. They are naturals for gardens of native plants. Camassias bloom at the same time as May-flowering tulips and, in flower beds and borders, associate with them so far as display values are concerned, to the benefit of both. The softer hues of camassia blooms intensify and complement the more strident ones of many tulips and the contrasting shapes and forms of the blooms are flattering to each other.

Cultivation. Care needed by camassias is minimal. Plant them in fall 6 to 8 inches apart with the tops of the bulbs about 4 inches beneath the ground surface. Then, so long as they flower satisfactorily, leave them undisturbed. Should they show signs of deterioration dig them up immediately after the foliage has died, sort the bulbs to size and either replant immediately or store them in a dry place until early fall and then replant in deeply-spaded, fertilized, and conditioned ground. Winter covering is not necessary. If the ground is poorish, an early spring application of a complete garden fertilizer is beneficial. Propagation is usually by seeds. Bulb cuttings can be used.

CAMBIUM LAYER. A thin layer of cambium, or more precisely vascular cambium cells, between the bark and underlying tissues of the stems, including trunks, branches, and twigs of dicotyledonous trees and shrubs, and of the roots is called the cambium layer. Consisting of meristem, cells capable of dividing, it is responsible for the production of new wood on the inside of the layer and new bark on its outside. From the cambium new tissue develops to heal and cover wounds and pruning cuts and cuts made at the bases of cuttings. Successful grafting and budding are based on bringing the cambium layers of understocks and scions into close contact and tying them to maintain their positions.

CAMELLIA (Cam-éllia). Camellias are among the most beloved and useful garden ornamentals. In mild parts of North America, especially in the south and on the Pacific Coast, they serve much the same landscape purposes that evergreen rhododendrons do in cooler regions adapted to them. Probably these two are the most widely appreciated of all groups of flowering evergreen shrubs or sometimes trees. Camellias are grown in greenhouses as well as outdoors. They cannot be generally regarded as reliably hardy north of Washington, D.C. True, in favored localities and sheltered sites they may survive for a longer or shorter number of years as far north as Long Island, New York, but they can scarcely be relied upon to do this, and exceptional winters, which rather than average ones are the true tests of hardiness, will surely spell disaster there.

The genus *Camellia,* comprising about eighty species and very many garden varieties, is native to Japan, China, and Indomalaysia. It belongs in the tea family THEACEAE and as now interpreted includes the group previously separated as *Thea* to which the common tea plant of Boston tea party fame belongs. The name commemorates the Moravian Jesuit priest and traveler Georg Josef Kamel whose name was latinized as Camellus. He resided in the Philippine Islands and died in 1706.

Camellias have alternate, short-stalked, leathery, undivided, toothed leaves. Their stalked or apparently stalkless blooms, solitary or in clusters of few and white, pink, red, variegated, or yellow are terminal at the ends of one-year-old shoots and branches or come from the leaf axils. They have five deciduous or persistent sepals sometimes more or less united at their bases and in some species associated with a few sepal-like bractlets. There are five to twelve, or in horticultural varieties sometimes more, petals. The outer of the numerous stamens, sometimes separate, are often joined to the bases of the petals. The slender styles, as many as the carpels, are united in their lower parts. The fruits are subspherical or angular woody capsules.

Camellia history is fascinating. For hundreds, possibly thousands of years before Europeans or Americans were aware of their existence these lovely shrubs were cultivated and treasured in the Orient. First knowledge about them came to the West from pressed dried herbarium specimens sent from China to England in the first year or two of the eighteenth century by a Scottish physician named James Cunningham. The kind he sent was later named *C. japonica.* We are without accurate record of when the first live camellia plant was brought to Europe, but it is believed that it arrived in England before 1739. It was almost the close of the century before much interest developed in these plants, an interest that increased during the early years of the nineteenth century. New varieties were introduced from China, others were raised in Europe and soon in America from seeds. The first camellia in America was a single, red-flowered one imported from England by John Stevens of Hoboken, New Jersey. Others soon followed. The new introductions were grown in greenhouses in the north. Just when they were first taken to the south is not known precisely, but it was probably within the first decade or two of the nineteenth century. David Landreth, the first seedsman of the United States, opened a store in Charleston, South Carolina, in 1818. Since he was one of the earliest growers of camellias in the country, there is little doubt that this business venture played a substantial part in the dissemination of camellias in the south. In 1852, James Warren of Boston, Massachusetts imported into California what are believed to be the first camellia plants to reach the West. From about 1860 until the second decade of the twentieth century, interest in camellias waned both in the United States and Europe. About 1920 a renascence that has continued unabated to the present began. This interest is handsomely sustained and promoted by the American Camellia Society, founded in 1945.

The common camellia (*C. japonica*) is cultivated in a multitude of horticultural varieties. A much-branched, full-foliaged shrub or tree up to about 40 feet tall, native of forests in Japan, the Ryukyu Islands, and Korea, this kind has lustrous, short-pointed, ovate to elliptic, shallowly-toothed quite hairless leaves 2 to 4 inches long. The wild species has seemingly stalkless flowers solitary at the ends of short branchlets, red, 2½ to 4 inches wide, and with five to seven roundish petals. The stamens are joined at their bases for up to two-thirds of their length into a fleshy cylinder. The ovaries are hairless. The more or less an-

(a) *Camellia japonica,* garden variety

(b) *Camellia japonica,* garden variety

(c) *Camellia japonica,* garden variety

(d) *Camellia japonica*, garden variety

(e) *Camellia japonica*, garden variety

'Guilio Nuccio' has semidouble coral-pink blooms 5 inches or more in diameter. The inner petals are fluted. One of the very best camellias, this is of vigorous, erect growth. 'Herme' and its several sports are tall. They have slightly-fragrant, semidouble blooms, variously patterned in deep pink and white or on some branches sometimes solid pink. The freely-produced flowers are 3 to 3½ inches wide. 'Lady Clare', of rather willowy, pendulous growth, has semidouble blooms about 4¾ inches in diameter. They are carmine-rose with darker veins and splashes of darker color, and sometimes white spots. 'Tomorrow' has fully double to peony-type pink blooms 5 inches or more in diameter. The bush is robust, of somewhat open, pendulous habit. 'Ville de Nantes', bushy and slow growing, has semidouble deep red flowers blotched with white. Their petals are fringed and fluted. 'White Empress' is a vigorous, semidouble-flowered variety, its color white, yellowish-tinted at the bases of the petals. The blooms are 4½ inches wide.

Sasanqua camellias, varieties of *C. sasanqua*, a forest shrub or tree of Japan and the Ryukyu Islands, bloom in fall and winter mostly ahead of *C. japonica* varieties. The wild type is distinct from its many improved horticultural varieties in having white single blooms 1½ to 2 inches wide. A usually loose, rather straggling shrub or small tree, **C. sasanqua** has obovate to narrow-elliptic leaves 1½ to 3½ inches long. Hairless except along the midribs on their upper sides, they have round-toothed margins. The flowers in the wild are white and 1½ to 2 inches wide. Their ovaries are hairy.

Garden varieties of sasanquas have white to deep rose flowers, smaller and rather flimsier than those of *C. japonica* varieties, and the individual blooms are comparatively short-lived. Contrary to opinion, sasanquas are not more cold-resistant than

gular fruits are ¾ to 1 inch long by one-half as wide. A subspecies or natural variety of the common camellia by some authorities accepted as a separate species, the snow camellia (*C. j. rusticana* syn. *C. rusticana*) is native of Japan and the Ryukyu Islands. This kind is cultivated in a number of garden varieties, among them white-, pink-, red-flowered ones and some with double blooms. In the wild *C. j. rusticana* occurs at higher altitudes than *C. japonica*. It may be hardier.

Varieties of *C. japonica* are so plentiful (750 are grown in the Norfolk Botanical Garden in Virginia) that it would be futile here to attempt to describe or even enumerate even one-tenth of them. Available kinds are listed by nurserymen. In books devoted to camellias, varieties are described and often pictured. A poll taken of members of the American Camellia Society who grow camellias from Washington, D.C. to Texas showed the following to be among the most popular in that region. Most of them are also highly regarded in

other regions where camellias are grown. 'Adolphe Audusson', of compact habit, has semidouble red blooms over 5 inches in diameter. 'Betty Sheffield', of compact habit, has 4- to 5-inch-wide flowers varying from semidouble to peony-type to fully double. They are white with the petals bordered with pink or red. 'Debutante', of vigorous, upright growth, bears an abundance of light pink, peony-type blooms 3½ to 4 inches wide. 'Donckelari', a comparatively hardy slow grower of bushy habit, has 4- to 5-inch-wide, semidouble red flowers splashed to varying degrees with white. 'Drama Girl', of robust, pendulous habit, has rich salmon-rose-pink blooms well over 5 inches wide. 'Dr. Tinsley' is a compact bush. Its semidouble rose-type blooms, pale pink becoming deeper at the edges of the petals, are 3 to 3½ inches across. 'Flame' has red flowers with darker veins. They are about 5 inches in diameter.

A variety of *Camellia sasanqua*

japonicas. They do have greater tolerance for adverse soils and atmospheres and adapt better to sunny locations. In habit sasanquas range from bushy and upright to spreading and almost vinelike. A selection of the best kinds includes 'Cleopatra', semidouble, rose-pink; 'Hugh Evans', erect with pendulous branches, flowers pink; 'Jean May', double, shell pink; 'Setsugekka', large, white, semidouble blooms; and 'Sparkling Burgundy', ruby-pink. Spreading or partially vining varieties include 'Mine-No-Yuki' large, white, double; 'Tanya', single rose-pink; 'White Frills', white, semidouble. Certain varieties of C. sasanqua are identified horticulturally because they bloom, respectively, earlier or later than the run of sasanqua varieties as C. hiemalis and C. vernalis. To the first belong 'Shishi-Gashira', rose-red, semidouble to double; 'Showa-No-Sakae', pale pink, sometimes marked with white; and 'Showa Supreme', peony-type pale pink blooms sometimes marked with white. In the C. vernalis group are 'Dawn', semidouble white suffused with pink, and 'Hiryu', rich red, double.

Reticulata camellias, varieties of Chinese C. reticulata, were cultivated in European and American gardens for more than 100 years before the wild species from which they were derived became known. A shrub or tree up to about 35 feet in height, C. reticulata has leathery, broad-elliptic to slightly-obovate, fine-toothed, pointed, usually dull, hairless leaves 2 to 4½ inches long by approximately 1 inch to 2¼ inches wide. The rosy-red blooms are solitary near the shoot ends. About 3 inches wide, they have sepals silky-hairy on their outsides and five to eight petals. The lower halves of the outer stamens are united into a tube. The first C. reticulata introduced to European gardens was a semidouble-flowered garden variety brought to England from China in 1820 by a Captain Rawes of the East India Company. This variety is still cultivated as 'Captain Rawes'. At least two other varieties were brought shortly afterward from gardens in coastal Chinese cities to Europe. One of these, double flowered, and given the name 'Robert Fortune', is still grown. Not until 1938 did the Western world learn that there existed in gardens in the interior province of Yunnan many other splendid varieties of C. reticulata, and another decade passed before the first of these were sent out of China to the United States and New Zealand. The Kunming reticulatas as these varieties are called (they were imported from the city of K'un Ming) have been cultivated in that part of China for over 1,000 years. In the eleventh century a Chinese writer described seventy-two varieties.

Garden varieties of reticulatas tend to be of loose, lank, rather graceless habit, and tall. Out of bloom they have little to recommend them as ornamentals. Their flowers are magnificent, generally semidouble, of immense size and with the inner petals deeply fluted and wavy. Kinds to be recommended for greenhouse cultivation and outdoors where they succeed, which is not in all areas where other camellias prosper, include these: 'Buddha', reported to be a hybrid of C. reticulata and C. pitardii is a fast grower with immense rose-pink blooms. 'Butterfly Wings' has flowers, reportedly up to 9 inches in diameter, with wavy rose-pink petals. 'Cornelian', sometimes misidentified as 'Chang's Temple', has pink and white blooms and is a variegated-flowered variant of the next. 'Crimson Robe' has semidouble, wavy-petaled, bright red flowers. 'Lion Head' has solid red blooms. It is often misidentified as 'Cornelian', the blooms of which are variegated. 'Purple Gown' is of compact growth. Its large, peony-type to fully double flowers are purplish-red. 'Shot Silk' grows fast, is of open habit, and has loose, brilliant pink, semidouble flowers. 'Tali Queen' is the correct name for the variety usually misidentified as 'Noble Pearl'. The latter has smaller, deep red flowers with smooth edges to the petals. The blooms of 'Tali Queen' have heavily crinkled or notched, bright red petals.

The hybrid swarm to which the name C. williamsii is applied has as parents C. japonica and C. saluenensis. Its single or semidouble flowers more closely resemble those of the former than those of the latter, but in growth and foliage characteristics C. williamsii varieties favor C. japonica. The shoots are hairless, the leaves up to almost 4 inches long by over 2 inches wide. The pink-flushed white, pale pink to deep rose-pink blooms 2 to 5 inches across, have the densely-hairy ovaries of C. japonica. Varieties that belong here include these: 'Bonnie Marie', erect and compact, has large, semidouble to anemone-type, pink flowers. 'Brigadoon', of compact, upright habit, has semidouble, fuchsia-pink flowers. 'Donation' has large and beautiful, semidouble, purple-pink flowers borne freely along the slightly drooping stems. 'E. G. Waterhouse' has fully-double, pale pink flowers of medium size. 'Flirtation', of vigorous growth, produces single, silvery-pink blooms. 'J. C. Williams' has somewhat pendulous branches and cupped, single, pink flowers of medium size. 'Robbie' is an erect, compact bush with very large, purplish-pink, semidouble blooms.

A spectacular species, **C. granthamiana** was not known until 1955. Then a single specimen, the only one that has ever been found, was discovered growing natively in Hong Kong. About 15 feet tall, this has short-stalked, oblong-elliptic leaves approximately 4 inches long by up to 2 inches wide. The solitary, white blooms, 4½ to nearly 6 inches in diameter, have the stamens separate except where they are joined to the petals. This species differs from all others except the next in having the sepals and bractlets persistent and present with the fruits. Also native of Hong Kong, **C. hongkongensis** is a tree up to 30 feet tall. It differs from C. japonica in the three styles of its flowers being separate, the ovaries hairy, and in having narrower, sharper-

Camellia reticulata

Camellia granthamiana

Camellia granthamiana (flowers)

pointed leaves. The solitary, terminal flowers are bell-shaped, approximately 1½ inches long, and have six or seven crimson petals.

One of the hardiest species, Chinese *C. cuspidata* is an erect, rather slender shrub 6 to 15 feet in height. It has hairless shoots. Its narrow- to broad-elliptic, hairless leaves, bronzy when young, are 1 inch to about 3 inches in length by up to 1 inch wide. Pure white, the 1½ inch-wide flowers have dense central clusters of yellow-anthered stamens, united only at their bases. A hybrid between this and *C. saluenensis*, named 'Cornish Snow', has larger blooms pink-tinged on their outsides. Closely allied to *C. cuspidata* and also Chinese, *C. fraterna* differs in its shoots, flower stalks, and calyxes being densely-hairy. Up to 15 feet tall, this kind has elliptic to elliptic-oblong leaves 1½ to 3 inches long and fragrant white or whitish-lilac flowers about 1½ inches across. Also akin to *C. cuspidata*, Chinese *C. tsaii* is a shrub up to 15 feet or a tree up to 30 feet in height. This differs from *C. cuspidata* in having decidedly hairy shoots and white flowers with stamens united into a distinct fleshy tube at their bases. A dense shrub up to about 8 feet tall by almost as wide, it is notable for its very thin, minutely-toothed leaves. The double flowers, about 1½ inches wide, are blush-rose-pink. Introduced from China about 1917, *C. saluenensis* has proven of value to hybridizers, especially in the development of comparatively hardy varieties. A shrub 10 to 15 feet in height, it has finely-toothed, pointed-lanceolate to elliptic-lanceolate leaves 1½ to 2½ inches long,

without hairs except on the midribs of the undersides. Singly or in pairs at the ends of short shoots, the usually darker-lined, blush-pink flowers have five petals 1 inch to 1½ inches long. In cultivation since its original introduction from China to England in 1819, and not found since, *C. maliflora* undoubtedly came from a garden. Possibly it is of hybrid origin. Of neat habit, it may attain a height of 20 feet or so. Its rose-pink flowers paling to white toward their centers are not quite fully double. They are 1½ to 2 inches across.

Chinese *C. oleifera* is cultivated in the Orient for the excellent oil its fruits yield. This, called tea oil, is used for cooking and in soaps, shampoos, and other products. Similar oils are obtained from *C. sasanqua* and *C. sinensis*. A shrub or tree of rigid habit, *C. oleifera* in the wild attains 25 feet in height, but is considerably smaller in

Camellia oleifera

cultivation. Closely related to *C. sasanqua*, it differs in its blunter, thicker leaves, densely-hairy bud scales, and large fruits. Its stiff, usually slightly obovate, leathery leaves 1½ to 3 inches long, are regularly toothed. Except sometimes for their short stalks, they are hairless. From 2 to 2½ inches wide, mostly from the axils near the shoot ends, the flowers are white. The fruits are about 1 inch long.

The tea plant (*C. sinensis* syn. *Thea sinensis*), native of China and of which leaves are infused to make the popular beverage, has short-stalked, hairless, dull, shallowly-toothed, lanceolate leaves up to 4½ inches long by 1½ inches wide. The fragrant blooms, 1 inch to 1½ inches across, solitary or in clusters of up to three, are white and have numerous stamens with yellow anthers. Variety *C. s. assamica*, the source of much of the commercial tea crop of Ceylon and other warm regions, is a tree that, unpruned, may attain a height of 50 feet. It has proportionately longer, thinner leaves than the typical species. It is native to Indochina, Thailand, Assam, and southern China. A near relative of the tea plant, *C. taliensis* of China, up to 10 feet tall or taller, has broadly-elliptic to obovate, pointed, toothed leaves 3 to 6 inches long by about one-half as wide. Solitary or in twos or threes, the white flowers, their stamens many and with yellow anthers, are up to 2½ inches in diameter. There are eight to ten petals. Before the blooms open they swell in balloon-like fashion to buds about 1 inch across.

Garden and Landscape Uses. Camellias are treasured as single specimens in lawns

A *Camellia japonica* variety, in light woodland

and other places, for grouping behind lower plants, for foundation plantings, for setting along the fringes of woodlands and in the interiors of open ones, and for employing as screens and informal hedges. Trailing varieties of *C. sasanqua* can be used effectively as groundcovers. Camellias are splendid in large greenhouses, conservatories, and lath houses. They can be cultivated in ground beds or in tubs or other containers. Some kinds lend themselves to espaliering on walls and, the sasanqua varieties particularly, for training as bonsai. Generally some shade from strong sun is

necessary or desirable, but many sasanqua varieties succeed in sunny locations so long as water supplies are adequate. As cut flowers camellias must usually be taken without appreciable stem. They are delightful when displayed in shallow saucer-like containers. Their blooms are much in favor as corsages.

Cultivation. Well-drained, slightly-acid, fertile soil, containing an abundance of humus and never excessively wet nor dry is ideal for camellias. Over-deep planting is anathema. Do not set them deeper than they were previously and take precautions against them settling too deeply because of the loosened ground in which they are planted sinking later. Be sure to tramp the under soil firm before putting the plant balls in place and set them with their tops 2 to 3 inches above the level of the surrounding soil. As with most evergreens, it pays handsomely to do a good job in readiness for planting. The holes should be at least twice the diameter of the root balls, more is all to the good. If the ground water (water table) is high, and it is not practicable to drain it away, good results can be had by planting on mounds or beds 1 foot to 2 feet above the general soil level. Before planting spade in very generous amounts of organic matter, compost, leaf mold, peat moss, or forest litter. In addition, add well-rotted cow manure or if this is not available

some dried cow or sheep manure. Do not use chemical or other concentrated fertilizers. Ideally, the root run should consist of approximately 50 percent organic material.

Planting may be done at almost any time, but by far the best is when the plants are not in active growth. In mild regions fall planting, in colder areas spring planting, is preferred. Camellias can even be moved in bloom. This makes the arranging of colors to advantage easy. Container-grown specimens adapt more quickly to new locations than those dug from the open ground. Small nursery-grown plants are often transplanted with bare roots, but with others it is practically essential to take a good ball of soil properly protected by wrapping in burlap or in the case of very large specimens by being boxed. If the location is exposed to sun or wind protect the transplants until they are thoroughly reestablished by covering them with a burlap or lath screen or canopy. Protection will be needed throughout the first season and perhaps longer. Unless this is done the foliage will almost certainly be scorched. Such scorching is particularly likely to occur if in positioning the plant the side previously pointed north is pointed south.

Routine care of established plants consists of supplying sufficient water to prevent them suffering during dry periods. Do this with fairly well-spaced deep soakings rather than more frequent applications that wet only the upper few inches. The maintenance of a permanent mulch is of tremendous help in conserving ground water, moderating soil temperatures, and, with some types of mulches, providing nourishment. Humidity is of great importance to camellias. In regions such as California where this is low at times, overhead spraying or misting, either with portable sprayers or syringes or by a fixed installation of overhead misters is highly beneficial. Fertilize cautiously. Camellias are easily harmed if too much fertilizer is given. The best fertilizers to use are formulated especially for camellias, rhododendrons, and similar acid-soil plants. Never exceed the amounts recommended by the manufacturer. Often it is wise to use less. Apply only when the ground is thoroughly moist.

Pruning normally needs little attention. Most camellias make shapely specimens without the aid of knife of shears. Nevertheless, some pinching back of young shoots may be needed to encourage branching, especially with young specimens. Attend to this before the shoots become hard. Other pruning may involve the removal from the interiors of the bushes of thin, unpromising branches and, of course, cutting out any dead wood.

Disbudding is done to obtain larger blooms and with varieties that produce more flower buds that the roots can supply with moisture to make sure the best buds

A camellia trained as a bonsai

are retained. If not done these may be shed or at least not develop properly. It is often advantageous to limit by disbudding the number of flowers carried by young plants. This permits their energies to be more definitely concentrated on the production of strong new growth. Disbudding to increase flower size consists of removing from each shoot all except one flower bud. Do it as soon as late summer or early fall as the flower buds, which become fat as they develop, can be distinguished from the more slender, pointed growth buds.

Propagation can be achieved in various ways. Seeds germinate readily when freshly gathered, less surely if they have been stored. Stored seeds are helped by pouring boiling water over them and allowing them to soak for twenty-four hours before sowing. Sow in a sandy peaty soil, covering the seeds to the equivalent of their own diameters. Protect from rodents and birds. After two to three weeks inspect the seeds, pinch back the roots of those that have sprouted and developed roots over 1 inch long, and replant them immediately. This encourages desirable branching. When the seedlings are 2 to 3 inches high transfer them to individual small pots. Seeds other than those of wild species do not reproduce the parent plant true to type. Usually the flowers of seedlings of horticultural varieties are inferior. In any case the plants bloom only after six or seven years. The chief purpose of raising seedlings is to have understocks for grafting.

Grafting is a popular and reliable way of increasing camellias. Usually the cleft graft is employed using understocks from pencil thickness up to about 2 inches thick. Winter or spring is the preferred time. Bark grafting in spring and splice (whip) grafting in greenhouses in winter, using slender, potted understocks are techniques sometimes employed. Less rarely used is the method called inarching. For further details see Grafting and Inarching.

Cuttings afford an easy way of multiplying camellias. They result in own-root plants and so eliminate any chance of change in the characteristics of the variety being propagated due to the influence of the understock. Also avoided is the chance of branches of understock developing in competition with those of the desired kind. Leafy stem cuttings made from firm shoots of the current season's growth give good results. From mid-June to the end of July is a favorable time for taking those of most kinds. They root readily under mist or in a greenhouse or cold frame propagating bed in any standard rooting medium. A mixture of peat moss and coarse sand or perlite is very satisfactory.

Greenhouse cultivation of camellias is based on the same principles as that outdoors. During fall to spring when temperatures can be controlled that at night is best kept as close to 35 to 45°F as possible.

During the day whenever outdoor weather permits keep the greenhouse temperature at 50°F. On all favorable occasions ventilate freely. Indoors as out, camellias need a constantly moist, but not stagnant, poorly-drained soil and a humid, but not dank atmosphere. Careful attention to watering, damping down, and syringing assure a desirable atmosphere. Too high temperatures during the fall to spring bud-forming and flowering periods are likely to result in dropping buds and blooms. Immediately after flowering is over, however, the night temperatures should be increased to 55 to 60°F, day temperatures five to ten degrees higher. Also, maintain a more humid atmosphere then and make sure that there is sufficient shade to prevent scorching of the foliage, but not so much that the young growth stimulated by the increased warmth and moisture is weak. During this growing period take particular care that adequate amounts of water are supplied. Judicious applications of dilute liquid fertilizer are also in order. Container specimens in need of potting or retubbing should be given that attention just as new spring growth starts. Make sure the containers are well drained and use a nourishing, porous soil rich in leaf mold, peat moss, or rich compost. The plants may, and if in ground beds must, stay in the greenhouse throughout the summer, but container plants are better put in a shaded place outdoors or in a lath house then, with their pots or tubs buried to their rims in sand, cinders, sawdust, wood chips, or similar material.

Pests and Diseases. The numbers of these that may affect camellias are many. Some of the pests such as aphids, mealybugs, scale insects, red spider mites, and thrips will be recognized by most experienced amateur gardeners. With others it will often be necessary to seek the diagnostic skills of County Extension Agents or other specialist authorities as well as their council as to controls. Much the same is true of diseases, some of the best known of which are leaf spots, flower blights, and root rots.

CAMOENSIA (Camo-énsia). Of the two West African species of woody vines of the pea family LEGUMINOSAE that compose this genus, one is cultivated in tropical and warm subtropical places where it can be grown outdoors and is sometimes accommodated in large greenhouses and conservatories. It is *Camoensia maxima.* The name of this genus commemorates the Portuguese poet Luis Camoens.

Camoensias are evergreens with leaves of three leaflets and flowers structured like pea blooms, but very much larger and of quite different aspect. The petals narrow at their bases to claws. The stamens are not joined. The fruits are broad, flattened pods. In *C. maxima,* the leaflets are 5 to 6

Camoensia maxima

Camoensia maxima (flowers)

inches long. The white blooms, six to eight together in racemes from the leaf axils, have frilled petals marked with yellow. The largest petal, the standard, is about 4 inches long by nearly as wide. The others are about 1 inch wide and are shorter than the standard. The seed pods are 6 to 8 inches long.

Garden and Landscape Uses and Cultivation. This plant is useful only where a vigorous tropical vine can be accommodated with plenty of room to spread. Planted in a ground bed in a sunny tropical greenhouse at The New York Botanical Garden, this magnificent vine blooms freely each December and sometimes in the summer as well. For its comfort it needs a porous, fertile soil through which water drains readily, exposure to full sun, and a minimum winter night temperature of about 60°F. The day temperatures at that season may exceed that at night by five to fifteen degrees according to the brightness of the day. A humid atmosphere is needed, and the support of a pillar or wires to which it is trained is essential. Pruning, done in winter after blooming is finished, consists of removing all unwanted branches and shortening those that have bloomed to within 2 or 3 inches of their bases. Propagation is by seeds sown in sandy peaty soil in a temperature of 75 to 80°F and by cuttings, the latter set in a propagating bed of sand, vermiculite, or perlite, if possible with some bottom heat so that the rooting medium is maintained five to ten degrees higher than the air temperature of 70 to 75°F.

CAMOMILE OR CHAMOMILE. This is *Chamaemelum nobile* (syn. *Anthemis nobile*). Once much used for its supposed tonic and fever-allaying properties, it is now of minor medicinal importance. It is a favorite for inclusion in herb gardens, and in Europe, and perhaps very infrequently in North America, is occasionally employed as a grass substitute in lawns. As such it stands mowing, but upkeep in the matter of controlling weeds and other details is likely to be considerably more onerous than with grass, and the turf does not wear as well as grass. In days past it was a fancy in England to form garden seats of beds of camomile, and this is still rarely done in period gardens.

The cultivation of camomile presents no special difficulties. It is most rapidly established by planting small divisions in early fall or spring, but can also be raised from spring-sown seeds. Recommended spacing between plants is 3 to 6 inches. It resents too much wetness, thriving best in fertile, well-drained, dryish soil, and demands full sun. The dried flower heads are used as a herb. These should be picked, or better cut with scissors, since picking results in too much stem and leaf being taken, as soon as they are fully expanded, and laid out thinly in a dry, airy, shady place and turned occasionally until they are quite dry. Then, they are stored in tightly-stoppered jars or other containers. A recommended way of making camomile tea is to pour a pint of boiling water over one-half ounce of dried flower heads and allow them to soak for ten minutes. Then strain the liquid, and if desired add milk or cream and honey or sugar. The resulting infusion is said to be helpful as a tonic, to reduce feverish colds, and to alleviate indigestion. Sweet-false-camomile is *Matricaria recutita*. Scentless-false-camomile is *Tripleurospermum maritimum inodorum*.

CAMPANULA (Cam-pánula)—Bellflower, Canterbury Bells. Little bell is the literal translation of *Campanula*. It derives from the Latin *campana*, a bell. It is apt in reference to the flowers of many kinds, but there are others with much flatter blooms more reminiscent of a star than a bell. This genus of 300 species belongs in the bellflower family CAMPANULACEAE. Mostly hardy herbaceous perennials, but including some annuals and biennials and a sprinkling of nonhardy perennials, some of which are subshrubby, campanulas or bellflowers as natives are widely distributed chiefly in the northern hemisphere. They are most abundant in Europe. The names of some kinds are confused in cultivation. In addition to natural species a goodly number of hybrids are grown.

Campanulas range from dwarf, tufted plants to kinds with sprawling, or tall, erect stems. Commonly the basal leaves are very different from those of the stems, which are alternate and few to numerous according to kind. The flowers are solitary, in headlike clusters, racemes, spikes, or panicles. Prevailingly they come in tones and shades of blue, lavender, or purple, or are white. Rarely they are pale yellow. Bell-shaped to funnel-shaped, wheel-shaped, or starlike, the blooms have a five-lobed calyx, a five-lobed or five-petaled corolla, five stamens, their stalks usually dilated at their bases, and a single style, unlike that of closely related *Adenophora*, not surrounded by a deep cuplike disk or gland and terminating in most cultivated kinds in a three-branched stigma. The fruits are capsules opening by terminal or basal pores.

Two of the most satisfactory flower garden hardy perennial bellflowers are *C. lactiflora*, of the Caucasus, and *C. glomerata*, of Europe and Asia, the latter somewhat naturalized in North America. From 3 to 6 feet in height, **C. lactiflora** has branched stems and sharply-toothed, ovate-lanceo-

Campanula lactiflora

late, stalkless leaves 2 to 3 inches long. The 1¼- to 1½-inch-wide flowers are in ample panicles usually composed of groups of threes. They are broadly-bell-shaped, typically pale blue, but varying to deeper hues as in *C. l. caerulea* and to white-flowered *C. l. alba*. Popular **C. glomerata** at a glance might deceive one into thinking it is not a bellflower. Instead of being displayed separately, its bright violet-blue, funnel-shaped, up to 1-inch-long flowers with petals flaring are densely bunched in crowded, globular heads at the tops of the stems and from the upper leaf axils. From 1 foot to 2 feet tall, hairy or hairless, this bellflower has rough leaves, its basal ones long-stalked and with blunt, round-toothed, narrow-ovate to narrow-heart-shaped

Camomile

Campanula glomerata

Campanula glomerata (flowers)

blades 4 to 5 inches long. The ovate to ovate-oblong stem leaves, mostly stalkless and somewhat stem-clasping, are 3 to 4 inches in length. Native to Europe and Asia, this beautiful bellflower is somewhat naturalized in North America. There are horticultural varieties with white and with double flowers and *C. g. dahurica*, with intensely rosy-purple to violet-purple blooms in heads larger than those of the typical species, 3 inches wide or wider. Dwarf *C. g. acaulis*, smaller in all its parts, is 3 to 6 inches tall.

The peach-leaved bellflower (*C. persicifolia* syns. *C. grandis*, *C. latiloba*) is a hardy perennial well suited for flower borders. An old favorite, it is a native of Europe and Asia. Hairless, this kind has erect stems 2 to 3 feet tall, sometimes branched near their tops and the branches upright. The basal leaves are numerous, narrowly-oblanceolate, tapered to their bases, blunt at their apexes, and 4 to 8 inches long. They have round-toothed margins. The comparatively few, finely-toothed, 4- to 6-inch-long stem leaves are linear-lanceolate to linear or the lower ones narrow-spatula-shaped. Upturned, about 1½ inches in length and generally wider than long, the broadly-bell-shaped flowers are lavender-blue to blue-violet. Those of *C. p. alba* are white, those of *C. p. moerheimii* white and double. There are also double blue-flowered variants. In all kinds the blooms are spaced rather distantly and irregularly in long, terminal racemes. Other varieties are *C. p. dasycarpa*, with hairy seed capsules; *C. p. minor*, the flowers of which are not more than 1 inch wide; and finest of all, *C. p.* 'Telham Beauty', a tetraploid with very large and handsome blue blooms.

The Scottish bluebell or harebell (*C. rotundifolia*) is native to North America, Europe, and northern Asia. Its botanical name may seem to be inappropriate because far from being round the leaves mostly in evidence at flowering time are long and slender. But basal leaves present earlier in the season and sometimes findable even at blooming time are long-stalked, nearly round, and ½ to 1 inch in diameter with scalloped margins. The slender stems, erect or sometimes more or less procumbent at the base, are 6 inches to about 1½ feet tall. They are well-clothed throughout most of their lengths with grassy leaves 1½ to 3 inches long, mostly linear, the lower ones narrowly-lanceolate. The bell-shaped flowers are occasionally solitary, more commonly in racemes of few to sev-

Campanula persicifolia

Campanula rotundifolia

eral. About 1 inch long, they hang from long, slender stalks. The calyxes are without appendages between their lobes. Variety *C. r. alba* has white flowers. The blooms of *C. r. flore-pleno* are double. In *C. r. soldanellaeflora* the corollas of the semi-double blooms are shredded to their bases into many narrow, sharp-pointed lobes.

More hardy herbaceous perennials, these moderately tall to tall and with nodding or deflexed, bell-shaped flowers, include the following: **C. alliariaefolia,** of Asia Minor and the Caucasus, has woolly stems up to 3 feet tall, usually branched in their upper parts, and leaves gray-hairy above, white-woolly on their undersides. The lower leaves, large, stalked, and ovate-heart-shaped to kidney-shaped, have round-toothed margins. The stem leaves gradually decrease in size and have successively shorter stalks upward and finally become stalkless. The short-stalked, creamy-white, 2-inch-long flowers are solitary from the upper leaf axils. Conspicuous appendages alternate with each of the calyx lobes. *C. divaricata* inhabits rocky mountain woodlands from Maryland to Kentucky, Alabama, and Georgia. It has slender, much-branched stems and is 1 foot to 2 feet or a little more in height. Its short-stalked, linear-lanceolate to ovate-lanceolate leaves are 1¼ to 3¼ inches long. The slender-stalked, light blue flowers, about ⅓ inch long, are produced profusely in broad, airy panicles. *C. grossekii,* of central Europe, has much the aspect of *C. trachelium* but its flowers droop and have calyxes with conspicuous appendages between their lobes. From 2 to 3 feet tall, this sort has angled, usually hairy, leafy stems, and rough-hairy foliage. The leaves are all stalked, those below broadly-heart-shaped and irregularly double-toothed, the upper ones ovate-lanceolate. Bell-shaped and in racemes, the 1-inch-long, violet-colored flowers have corollas lobed to about one-third their lengths. The calyxes are bristly-hairy. *C. longistyla,* 1½ to 2½ feet tall, is native to the Caucasus. More or less hairy, it has branched stems. Its basal leaves have long, winged stalks and lanceolate-ovate blades. The stem leaves are stalkless and narrower. The pendulous, amethyst-violet blooms are urn-shaped to bell-shaped. When the flowers are fully open the styles protrude. Their calyxes have appendages between their lobes. *C. punctata* (syn. *C. nobilis*), native from Siberia to Japan, has

Campanula punctata

angled, branched stems 1 foot to 2 feet tall that, like the foliage, are hairy. The long-stalked basal leaves have broad, heart-shaped-ovate, blunt-toothed blades 3 to 5 inches long. The stem leaves are ovate to lanceolate, the lower ones stalked, those above stalkless. The 2-inch-long, semi-

drooping or drooping, bell-shaped blooms are generally conspicuously spotted on their insides, but some variants have blooms without spots. The lobes of the white to clear lilac corollas extend about one-third of the way to their bases. There may or may not be appendages between the calyx lobes. *C. rapunculoides,* of Europe and eastern Asia, spreads vigorously by un-

Campanula rapunculoides

derground stolons (runners) to form large clumps of slender, erect, leafy stems 2 to 4 feet tall. Hairy or hairless, it has long-stalked ovate to heart-shaped, round-toothed basal leaves, their blades 1 inch to 3 inches long. The short-stalked to stalkless, sharp-toothed stem leaves, up to 4 inches long, are lanceolate-ovate. In usually one-sided racemes, the about 1-inch-long, bluish-violet flowers are bell-shaped. Their corollas are cleft to nearly one-half their lengths into pointed, flaring petals. Inside they are slightly bearded. *C. rhomboidalis,* an inhabitant of European mountains, is 1½ to 2 feet tall. It has slender, hairless or nearly hairless, angled stems, branched in their upper parts and leafy. The leaves are stalkless or nearly so, pointed-ovate, toothed, and 1 inch to 2 inches long. The purplish-blue to violet-blue or occasionally white, bell-shaped flowers, ¾ inch long, are few together in loose, not one-sided racemes. *C. sarmatica,* softly-hairy, is 1 foot to 2 feet tall. Its stems are usually without branches. Its basal leaves are long-stalked, their pointed blades arrow-shaped to heart-shaped. They are roundish-toothed, 3 to 5 inches long. The stem leaves are smaller and comparatively narrower. Rather widely spaced in one-sided terminal racemes, the narrowly-bell-shaped, lilac flowers are lobed to one-third of their lengths into pointed petals. They are 1½ inches long, velvety on their outsides. The styles do not protrude. Leafy appendages alternate with the corolla lobes and are early deciduous. This is a native of the Caucasus.

Additional hardy herbaceous perennials medium-tall to tall, with flowers predominantly facing upward or inclined upward, include these: *C. latifolia,* of Europe and Asia, 3 to 5 feet high, is erect. It has

Campanula latifolia

spreading roots and almost hairless, branchless or nearly branchless stems. The leaves are rough-hairy, the basal ones long-stalked and with pointed-oblong-ovate blades with heart-shaped bases and toothed margins are up to 6 inches long. Those above are smaller and proportionately narrower. In fairly-short, terminal leafy racemes, the purple-blue flowers, somewhat under 1½ inches long and narrowly-bell-shaped, have corollas with lobes (petals) about one-third the length of the bell. Variety *C. l. macrantha* has larger, more richly colored flowers. The flowers of *C. l. alba* are white. The Brantwood bellflower (*C. l. eriocarpa*) is lower than the species and has bristly-hairy seed capsules. *C. trachelium,* a variable kind 2 to 3 feet tall, is a vigorous spreader. Native to Europe, North Africa, and Asia, it is naturalized in North America. Rough-hairy to a greater or lesser degree, the coarsely-double-toothed, ovate-lanceolate leaves are 2 to 3 inches long, the lower ones long-stalked, those above shorter-stalked. The broadly-bell-shaped flowers, about ¾ inch long, have erect rather than spreading petals, bearded on their insides. They are rich blue-purple to purple and usually tend to droop when fully open. Variety *C. t. alba* has white blooms. The flowers of *C. t. alba-plena* are white and double. Double blue flowers are borne by *C. t. caerulea-plena.* Native of mountains in Greece and Italy, *C. versicolor* is 2 to 3 feet tall, has long-stalked, deeply-toothed, oblong to ovate basal leaves, heart-shaped at their bases, and

Campanula latifolia macrantha

Campanula versicolor

1 inch to almost 2 inches wide, face upward. In color they are typically bright blue ranging in variants to tones of lavender-blue and mauve and to white. Among the several forms to which names have been given one of the most distinct is *C. c. turbinata*. This is somewhat procumbent and has longer bell-shaped flowers than

Campanula carpatica turbinata

Campanula latifolia macrantha (flowers)

Most popular of dwarf, hardy, perennial bellflowers, **C. carpatica** is called tussock bellflower, but the name is not widely used. This native of eastern Europe is a rewarding species, easy to grow and extremely free-flowering. There are many varietal forms, some named, some not. Typically hairless and clump-forming, this kind has many slender, branching, leafy stems more or less spreading at their bases, from 6 inches to 1½ feet long. Except that the basal ones are longer-stalked, the leaves are all similar. They have short-pointed, ovate, more or less round-toothed blades with squared to heart-shaped bases, 1 inch to 1½ inches long. The solitary, long-stalked, broadly-bell-shaped blooms,

the typical species. The flowers of *C. c. alba* are white. Those of *C. c.* 'White Star' are white and exceptionally large. Several excellent hybrids have *C. carpatica* or *C. c. turbinata* as one parent. One of the most

smaller sometimes nearly toothless stem leaves, the uppermost almost stalkless. The flowers, 1 inch or more in diameter in spikelike racemes, are shallow and have a dark violet-colored throat and wide-spreading light blue lobes (petals).

Campanula trachelium

Campanula carpatica

distinct, an attractive free-bloomer, *C. haylodgensis* probably has *C. cochlearifolia* as its other parent. It is 3 to 5 inches tall and bears a profusion of delightful double or semidouble, more or less up-facing, blue blooms. In appearance this kind does not resemble closely either parent. Probably the result of a mating between *C. carpatica* and *C. tommasiniana*, the hybrid *C. stansfieldii* is an excellent small bellflower. It has downy foliage and starry, violet, bell-shaped blooms on stems 4 to 5 inches high.

Campanula haylodgensis

Hardy perennial bellflowers for rock gardens and similar places where free-blooming plants of low stature can be displayed to advantage include many fine species, varieties, and hybrids. In addition to *C. carpatica* and *C. glomerata acaulis*, discussed previously, there are these now to be described. Others are likely to be listed in catalogs of specialist dealers in rock garden plants. To aid in identification these low campanulas are presented here as two groups, those in which the flowers are usually solitary on the stems and those that normally carry two to several blooms on each stem.

These are solitary-flowered, hardy, dwarf bellflowers: *C. allionii,* of screes and stony soils in the mountains of Italy and southern France, develops a deep taproot from the top of which stem underground fleshy stolons ending in rosettes of small, spatula-shaped to narrow-oblong or linear, gray-green, slightly-hairy leaves 1 inch to 2 inches long. The up-facing or inclined, purple, lavender-blue, rosy-lilac, or white blooms are on stems 2 to 4 inches tall. Much resembling individual blooms of Canterbury bells, they are bell-shaped, about 1¾ inches long by 1 inch to 1½ inches wide. Variety *C. a. alba* has white blooms. Those of *C. a. grandiflora* are rich purple and exceptionally large. *C. cenisia,* similar to *C. allionii* in habit of growth, is native in sunny alpine screes along the Swiss-Italian border and eastward. It has basal rosettes of usually downy, obovate

leaves under ½ inch long. The 1- to 3-inch-tall stems bear toothless, hair-fringed, ovate-oblong leaves and from hairy flower buds develop up-facing, clear steely-blue, ¾-inch-wide, starry-bell-shaped blooms. *C. excisa,* a tufted or mat-forming native of Switzerland, grows among rocks in light shade. It has many threadlike, branchless stems 3 to 6 inches tall, leafless above, with toothless or almost toothless, slender-pointed, linear leaves on their lower parts. The nodding, light violet, shallowly-bell-shaped blooms, about ¾ inch long and lobed to about one-half their lengths, are borne in rich profusion. The bases of the clefts between the lobes (petals) are rounded like punched-out holes. *C. pulla* is a beautiful, tufted native of the eastern European Alps. It has slender, underground stolons and stems 3 to 4 inches high sometimes hairy toward their bases. The leaves are hairless, those higher on the stems stalk-less, narrow-ovate to linear, the lower ones short-stalked, broad-ovate, and obscurely-toothed. The slender-stalked, long-ish-bell-shaped blooms are glossy violet-blue, ¾ to 1 inch long, and shallowly-lobed. *C. pulloides,* an intermediate hybrid between *C. pulla* and probably *C. carpatica,* is about 6 inches tall, hairier than *C. pulla,* and with larger, shallower, beautiful violet blooms. *C. raineri* is at home on limestone cliffs in northern Italy. More or less hairy,

Campanula raineri

this kind is tufted and 2 to 4 inches tall. It has slender, underground stolons and erect, branched stems. Its ashy-gray leaves, the larger, lower ones about 1 inch long by ½ inch wide, have short stalks, with oblong-spatula-shaped, bluntly-toothed blades. The china-blue, broadly-bell-shaped flowers are solitary at the branch ends. They face upward. *C. tridentata,* of the Caucasus, is tufted and 3 to 4 inches tall. Similar to if not identical with plants grown as *C. bellidifolia* and *C. saxifraga,* also from the Caucasus, it has a deep taproot and numerous rosettes of erect, leafy, branchless stems and linear to linear-lanceolate or spatula-shaped leaves, toothless or the lower ones

with margins round-toothed above their middles, tapered at their bases. From ¾ to 1 inch long, the up-facing flowers are blue to blue-purple or violet-purple.

These hardy low bellflowers have usually few to several flowers on each stem. They are suitable for rock gardens and similar places: *C. barbata* attains 1 foot to 1½ feet in height or may be considerably lower. It is native to southern Europe. It has basal rosettes of very short-stalked, blunt, rough, linear to oblong-lanceolate or oblanceolate, often wavy-edged leaves 2 to 5 inches long. The erect stems carry one to three narrow-oblong leaves. From their tops and near their tops are displayed up to six 1-inch-long, short-stalked or stalk-less, pendulous, lavender-blue, bell-shaped blooms bearded on their insides. The corolla lobes (petals) extend for about one-third of the length of the blooms. *C. caespitosa,* of the southern European mountains, is densely tufted. It has a deep taproot, but is without stolons. From 3 to 6 inches tall, the slender stems have, mostly toward their bases, small, glossy, ovate, toothed leaves. The blue horizontal flowers, few on each stem, are about ¾ inch long. *C. cochlearifolia* (syn. *C. pusilla*) is a nearly or quite hairless native of mountains in Europe. A rock garden delight, it spreads satisfyingly and blooms profusely. Its shiny foliage has much the aspect of that of *C. caespitosa,* but is more loosely arranged. The leaves of the basal rosettes are ovate and somewhat toothed, those higher on the 4- to 6-inch tall stems are narrow-lanceolate. Few together or occasionally solitary, the blooms nod or are held more or less horizontally. They vary in color from medium purple through blue and pale blue to white. Some color forms have been named, such as *C. c. alba,* with white flowers, and *C. c.* 'Miranda', with light china-blue blooms. *C. collina* is a 1-foot-tall, somewhat hairy native of the Caucasus that in favorable environments spreads with considerable zeal. Its erect, branchless stems have a few leaves much smaller and narrower than the basal ones. The latter have long stalks and slender-pointed, ovate-oblong, round-toothed blades 1 inch to 2 inches long. Deep purple and about 1 inch in length, the blooms nod or are held horizontally from the stem ends. They are bell-shaped, with big recurved corolla lobes (petals). *C. elatines,* a low bellflower of Italy and the Balkan Peninsula, is represented in cultivation by a number of natural varieties some botanists and many horticulturists treat as separate species. It is probable, too, that at least some garden plants of this relationship are hybrids between different elements of *C. elatines.* Such hybrids are conveniently grouped as *C. adria.* Typical *C. elatines,* tufted, has a thick rootstock. It has many ground-hugging, hairy or hairless stems up to about 8 inches in length, and gray-

Campanula collina

Campanula elatines elatinoides

Campanula elatines fenestrellata

Campanula elatines garganica

downy to hairless, glossy foliage. The long-stalked, sharply-toothed leaves are roundish-heart-shaped below, on the upper parts of the branches, pointed-ovate. Their blades are up to 1 inch long. Very freely produced, the shallow-bell-shaped, up-facing blooms, up to ¾ inch wide and solitary or in twos or threes, are arranged in raceme- or panicle-like fashion. They have intensely violet-blue corollas with long-pointed petals and a distinctly protruding style. The major varieties of *C. elatines* include compact *C. e. elatinoides* (syn.

C. elatinoides), which has prostrate, densely-hairy stems, gray-hairy leaves, and flowers smaller than those of the typical species. Its foliage glossy and hairless, *C. e. fenestrellata* (syn. *C. fenestrellata*) is compact and has rather small leaves and well-displayed, violet-blue flowers deeply lobed into comparatively long, recurved petals. Gray-hairy foliage and up-facing, starry, purple-blue, or in one variant white, flowers borne raceme fashion on semitrailing branches, are characteristic of *C. e. garganica* (syn. *C. garganica*). This robust variety is without stolons, but develops a central clump of short stems. Its blooms have long petals and a style that protrudes only slightly. From the last, *C. e. istriaca* (syn. *C. istriaca*) differs chiefly in having slimmer, longer branches and flowers with long-protruding styles.

C. piperi, an inhabitant of rock crevices in the Olympic Mountains, Washington, is tufted, hairless, and 2 to 4 inches tall. It has branchless, leafy stems. The sharply-toothed leaves are spatula-shaped to wedge-shaped, ½ inch to 1¼ inches long. Usually one to three on a stem, less often solitary, the bright blue or less commonly white, ¾-inch-long, up-facing flowers are broadly-bell-shaped, with sepals about as long as the corolla. *C. portenschlagiana* (syn. *C. muralis*) is closely related to *C. elatines*.

Campanula cochlearifolia

Campanula elatines istriaca

Campanula portenschlagiana

Campanula medium

and at the end of each branch a solitary, saucer-shaped, five-lobed, up-facing bloom, violet-blue with a white center or in *C. r. alba* white.

Canterbury bells (*C. medium*) is a popular, fairly hardy biennial. Typically 3 to 4

Hairless and 6 to 9 inches tall, this native of southern Europe has long-stalked, irregularly-toothed, kidney-shaped to nearly circular basal leaves and ovate stem leaves. The up-facing, funnel-shaped flowers are so plentiful they nearly hide the foliage. *C. poscharskyana,* of Dalmatia, is another ally of *C. elatines.* This rampant bellflower has

Campanula poscharskyana

more or less decumbent, spreading, slender, hairless stems up to 1 foot long or longer and hairless to downy foliage. The leaves are coarsely-toothed. The lower ones are 1 inch to 1½ inches wide and heart-shaped. The upper leaves are narrower. The broadly-funnel-shaped, lavender-blue flowers are in panicle-like arrangements. *C. tommasiniana,* of Italy, is compact, tufted, hairless, and without stolons. Its slender stems 6 inches to 1 foot long or sometimes longer, at first erect, droop later under the weight of the blooms. The leaves, linear-lanceolate, toothed, and up to 2 inches long, are all on the stems. The generally nodding flowers are several to many near the stem ends. Pale blue, they have nearly cylindrical, tubular, short-petaled corollas up to ¾ inch in length. *C. waldsteiniana,* of Dalmatia and Croatica, resembles the last in growth habit. A high-altitude alpine, this kind is 3 to 9 inches in height. It has chiefly pointed-lanceolate leaves and a few broader, blunt lower ones. The three to five lavender-blue to violet-blue flowers on each stem are deeply-lobed, somewhat star-shaped, and face upward. *C. zoysii,* an alpine, mat-forming native of central Europe, is tufted and 2 to 3 inches tall. It has sparingly-branched stems and toothless leaves, the basal ones ovate to obovate, the stem ones more or less oblanceolate. Lavender-blue and held horizontally, the flowers have narrowly-urn-shaped, tubular corollas about ½ inch long, puckered at their mouths.

Annual bellflowers, for the most part inferior to cultivated biennial and perennial kinds, are rarely grown. The best is quite charming *C. ramosissima,* of Asia Minor. Similar to and probably not specifically distinct from *C. loreyi* of Italy, this is bushy, hairless, and 6 inches to 1 foot tall. It has stalkless, toothless, elliptic to obovate leaves

Campanula medium (flowers)

feet tall, but in some horticultural varieties not more than 2 feet high and compact, it is erect and rough-hairy. It has bold basal rosettes of oblanceolate to nearly-obovate, round-toothed leaves 6 inches to nearly 1 foot long, and shorter, stalkless, more or less clasping stem leaves, somewhat wavy and round-toothed. The stalked, solitary or paired blooms are in long, erect racemes. In its wild form this species has bell-shaped to urn-shaped, violet-blue flowers smaller than those of garden varieties, which come in white and a range of hues from pale to deep pink, rose-red, lav-

Campanula medium calycanthema

of the Azores that prospers in California. Branched from the base, it has stems 1 foot to 2 feet tall. The coarsely-toothed, thick, clammy to sticky leaves, oblong to spatula-shaped, are 3 to 4 inches long. Normally white with a yellow ring at their bases, the 2-inch-long, narrowly-urn-shaped to bell-shaped blooms are in short racemes. A pale pink-flowered variety is also cultivated.

Campanula vidalii

ender, blue, and purple, with the corolla tube a full inch in diameter and with five short, spreading or rolled-back lobes (petals). Unique among cultivated campanulas, the stigma is five-lobed. In addition to the kind with a simple corolla with a leafy green calyx, other forms of Canterbury bells are commonly grown. In one, known as hose-in-hose, the calyx is represented by a second colored, petal-like bell enclosing the corolla proper. In another, called cup and saucer Canterbury bells and identified as *C. m. calycanthema*, the colored and petal-like calyx spreads to form a flattish saucer upon which the cuplike corolla stands. Double-flowered varieties with as many as three additional bells inside the outer one are also grown. This species is native to southern Europe.

Rampion (*C. rapunculus*) is a hairy biennial, native to Europe, North Africa, and western Asia as far as Siberia. It was formerly cultivated as a salad vegetable for its swollen, fleshy roots and young leaves. The stems are erect, 2 to 3 feet tall, and sometimes branched near their tops. The lower leaves are short-stalked, obovate, and slightly-toothed. The upper ones are stalkless, toothless or almost so, and linear-lanceolate. Up-facing or ascending, the open-bell-shaped to funnel-shaped, lilac-blue or white blooms are in erect, loose, long, slender racemes. They are about ½ inch long and have calyx lobes almost as long as the corolla.

Chimney bellflower (*C. pyramidalis*), well grown, is one of the glories of its race. Native to southeast Europe, it regretably

Campanula pyramidalis

is not hardy in the north. A perennial that often "blooms itself to death," and so is likely to die after flowering, it is ordinarily grown as a biennial. Stately in bloom and 4 to 6 feet tall, this kind has a dominant, stout main stem that branches freely from the base and has numerous short flowering branchlets creating an effect justifying the botanical name. The basal and lower stem leaves of the chimney bellflower are long-stalked. They have glandular-toothed, heart-shaped-ovate blades 2 inches long. The leaves higher on the stems are narrower, pointed-ovate. The many up-facing, saucer-shaped to flattish, light blue to white flowers have very slender, wide-spreading calyx lobes mostly shorter than the corolla tube. A nonhardy perennial, charming *C. vidalii* is a subshrubby native

Star of Bethlehem is the name used in New England and some other parts of North America for delightful, evergreen, perennial *C. isophylla.* This common name is also used for very different *Allium umbellatum*, so one must be a little wary in

Campanula isophylla

interpreting it. Not hardy in the north, this campanula is much esteemed as a greenhouse and window plant. Native of Italy, it is more or less downy to nearly hairless. It has trailing or drooping stems and heart-shaped-ovate, toothed leaves, the lower ones long-stalked, those nearer the flowers with shorter stalks and narrower blades. The blades of the lower leaves are 1 inch to 1½ inches long. Borne in great profusion singly on branchlets with bracts, the blooms spread their petals to form saucer-shaped to flat, five-pointed stars 1 inch or more in diameter. They have wide-spreading, narrowly-linear calyx lobes as long as or longer than the corolla tube. The corollas are lilac-blue to clear light blue. The style is conspicuously protruded. Variety *C. i. alba*, practically hairless, has pure white flowers. The blooms of *C. i. caerulea*

Campanula isophylla alba

are blue. The foliage of *C. i. mayi* is clothed with soft gray down. Handsomely white-

Campanula isophylla mayi

variegated foliage is characteristic of *C. i. variegata*. Except for its smaller, more pointed, glossy, hairless leaves and its

Campanula isophylla variegata

flowers having calyx lobes usually shorter than the corolla tube, **C. fragilis,** a non-hardy species native of southern Italy,

Campanula fragilis

scarcely differs from *C. isophylla*. Another sort not reliably hardy in the north, *C. arvatica* of Spain is delightful for growing in pans (shallow pots) in an alpine greenhouse or cold frame. A tufted, hairless perennial 2 to 3 inches tall with stems up to 8 inches long, it has stalked, round-heart-shaped, basal leaves less than ½ inch long and stalkless or nearly stalkless, lozenge-shaped, sharply-toothed stem leaves. Its widely-bell-shaped, blue or white flowers are 1 inch to 1¼ inches wide.

Garden and Landscape Uses. Bellflowers are among the most important and useful flower garden ornamentals. From among them can be chosen kinds to decorate flower beds and borders and naturalistic landscapes and some to use as edgings. Others provide a wealth of bloom in rock

Campelia arvatica

gardens after the main flush of spring floral display has passed. Many are admirable cut flowers. As a container plant for ornamenting patios and similar places and greenhouses, impressively tall *C. pyramidalis* is outstanding. Much lower *C. isophylla* and *C. fragilis* are delightful in pots, pans, and hanging baskets in greenhouses, window gardens, and on porches and, where winter-hardy, in rock gardens.

Few, very few, cultivated bellflowers are not hardy in the north. Here belong *C. isophylla*, *C. pyramidalis*, and *C. vidalii*. These are satisfactory outdoor perennials only in mild, nearly frostless climates. Elsewhere they must be grown indoors at least in winter. Of hardy kinds, the uses of Canterbury bells are discussed under Canterbury Bells. The others fall into two chief groups, taller bellflowers adaptable for flower beds and borders and lower ones for rock gardens and similar locations. Among the latter are such adaptable and easy-to-grow kinds as *C. carpatica*, *C. elatines* and its varieties and its hybrid brood grouped under the name *C. adria*, as well as such kinds as *C. poscharskyana*, *C. portenschlagiana*, and *C. rotundifolia*. Certain low bellflowers are more exacting in their requirements and are likely to succeed only under rather specialized rock garden conditions such as many choice alpine plants need.

Cultivation. The cultivation of Canterbury bells is detailed under Canterbury Bells. Other hardy biennial bellflowers, of which only *C. longistyla* and *C. rapunculus* are here discussed, need similar care. Tall hardy perennials, those employed to decorate flower beds and borders and supply cut flowers, are easy to satisfy. They will grow in full sun, but most are not adverse to a little light shade during the hottest part of the day. They respond to ordinary garden soil of reasonable fertility, well drained but not deficient in moisture. Plant in spring or early fall. For the most satisfactory effects set the plants in groups of three or more. Within the groups space them according to the height and vigor of their kind, from 9 inches to 1½ feet apart. Subsequent care is that usual for most hardy herbaceous perennials and includes such routine procedures as weed control, watering in dry weather, and the annual application in early spring of a dressing of fertilizer. Staking is needed for many kinds and is especially important for several that have stems that tend to be brittle, and hence subject to storm damage. Attend to this early in the season and do it as neatly and unobtrusively as possible. Low hardy perennial bellflowers of the easy-to-grow group, such as *C. carpatica*, thrive under the same conditions as taller kinds but need less space between individuals and no staking.

Rock garden bellflowers are most likely to give satisfaction planted in crevices between rocks or in dry walls or on rock ledges where their roots can reach back for considerable distances into cool, damp but not wet, very gritty earth. They are also suitable for moraines and screes and for alpine greenhouses and cold frames. In regions of hot summers, locations where there is some shade during the intense heat of the day are most favorable. For some dwarf bellflowers the rooting medium, with advantage, may contain a liberal admixture of crushed limestone, others are much better with soil neutral or slightly acid. There is room for experiment here. Among those that benefit from limestone are *C. caespitosa*, *C. fragilis*, *C. raineri*, and *C. zoysii*. Those that dislike limestone include lovely, but difficult *C. cenisia*, *C. excisa*, and *C. piperi*. The propagation of dwarf bellflowers is done by division, cuttings, or seeds according to kind.

Container cultivation of *C. isophylla*, *C. fragilis*, and *C. pyramidalis* indoors presents no special problems. These appreciate nourishing, reasonably porous soil kept moderately moist at all times and, when their containers are well filled with healthy roots, benefit from regular applications of dilute liquid fertilizer. Cool growing conditions are essential, and light shade from the strongest sun. From fall to spring temperatures at night of 45 to 50°F are sufficient. Increases of five to ten or, on sunny days, fifteen degrees are allowable. On all favorable occasions ventilate the greenhouse, cold frame, or other place where they are kept freely. In summer a lightly-shaded location outdoors is to the liking of these bellflowers. Refurbish and repot *C. isophylla* and *C. fragilis* each late winter or early spring. The most satisfactory means of securing increase of these kinds is by cuttings made in spring of moderately firm shoots inserted in sand, vermiculite, or perlite in a greenhouse propagating bench or approximately similar environment. When the cuttings are rooted, pot them individually in small pots. Later, when well established in these, plant them few

to several together in pans (shallow pots) or hanging baskets.

Procedures to secure good specimens of the chimney bellflower (*C. pyramidalis*) differ slightly from those appropriate for *C. isophylla* and *C. fragilis*. Seed affords the best method of securing plants. Sow in February or March in a temperature of 50 to 55°F. Transplant the young seedlings as soon as they are large enough to handle, first to small pots then successively to larger ones until they occupy containers 6 to 7 inches in diameter. In summer keep the plants lightly shaded, outdoors or in a cold frame, with their pots partially buried in a bed of sand, peat moss, or similar material. Before severe frost transfer them to a well-protected greenhouse with a night temperature of 45 to 50°F and in daytime five to ten degrees higher. Water fairly generously. In February pot the plants into the containers in which they are to bloom. These may be 8- to 10-inch pots or tubs. When the flowering spikes begin to push up, fertilize regularly. Although the chimney bellflower is actually a perennial it gives much the best results when treated as a biennial.

Annual bellflowers may be raised from seeds sown in spring directly where the plants are to bloom or from seeds sown earlier indoors and the seedlings grown along in flats or small pots until the weather is suitable for them to be planted in the garden. If raised from outdoor sowings, thin the seedlings to stand 4 to 6 inches apart. Plants raised indoors may be allowed the same spacing when transplanted outside.

CAMPANULACEAE — Bellflower Family. Many desirable ornamentals belong in this assemblage of sixty to seventy genera and possibly 2,000 species of dicotyledons. Widely dispersed as natives of temperate and subtropical regions, and to a lesser extent of tropical mountains, the kinds of the bellflower family are mostly annuals, biennials, herbaceous perennials, and subshrubs. A few are shrubs or trees. As interpreted by most modern botanists and as accepted here, the CAMPANULACEAE includes the group sometimes segregated as the lobelia family LOBELIACEAE.

Most members of this family have milky sap. Their leaves are undivided, generally alternate, less commonly opposite, rarely whorled (in circles of more than two). The symmetrical to markedly asymmetrical flowers are bell-shaped, funnel-shaped, or star-shaped or are tubular and often strongly two-lipped. They are solitary, in racemes or panicle-like inflorescences, or sometimes are in compact heads with involucres (collars of bracts) at their bases.

The blooms have calyxes with from three to ten, but usually five lobes. The corollas, if asymmetrical, usually slit along one side, mostly have five lobes or less

often five separate petals, but a few members of the family have three or four, and some six corolla segments. Rarely the corolla is lacking. Typically there are as many stamens as corolla lobes or petals. There is one sometimes-branched style and two to five stigmas or one stigma with two to five lobes. The fruits are usually capsules, less often berries. Cultivated genera include *Adenophora*, *Asyneuma*, *Campanula*, *Canarina*, *Centropogon*, *Codonopsis*, *Cyananthus*, *Downingia*, *Edraianthus*, *Githopsis*, *Heterotoma*, *Hippobroma*, *Hypsela*, *Jasione*, *Laurentia*, *Legousia*, *Lobelia*, *Mindium*, *Monopsis*, *Ostrowskia*, *Phyteuma*, *Platycodon*, *Pratia*, *Symphyandra*, *Trachelium*, and *Wahlenbergia*.

CAMPELIA (Campèl-ia). Native from Mexico to northern South America, this genus of the spiderwort family COMMELINACEAE consists of about three species of nonhardy, herbaceous perennials with much the aspect of *Dichorisandra*, but with flower clusters quite distinct. The meaning of the name appears to be unexplained.

Campelias have one or more erect or decumbent, often branchless, fleshy stems with alternate, short-stalked, lanceolate to oblanceolate leaves the bases of which sheath the stems. As they emerge, the stalks that carry the blooms of the flowers pierce these sheaths. The paired flower stalks nestle between two leafy bracts that terminate each flower stalk and branch. Each bloom has three each sepals and petals, the former succulent, white or white and purple, the latter white and short-lived. The filaments (stalks) of the six stamens are hairy on their lower parts. There is one style. The fruits are capsules.

Only one species is known to be cultivated, *Campelia zanonia*. This is represented by the normal, green-leaved form

Campanula zanonia 'Mexican Flag'

and by a variety, *C. z.* 'Mexican Flag', which is sometimes identified as *C. z. albolineata*. The green-leaved kind, similar to the variety except that it grows more robustly and has plain foliage, has minor merit as an ornamental, but *C. z.* 'Mexican

Flag' has highly decorative foliage. It attains a height of about 2½ feet and has thick, erect stems striped white or pink. The leaves, mostly toward the tops of the stems, are elliptic to oblanceolate and up to 1 foot long by 3 inches wide. They are variegated with longitudinal bands of creamy-white of various widths and have red-purple margins. The degree of variation varies from leaf to leaf, and some individuals are almost all white.

Garden Uses and Cultivation. The only usefulness of *C. z.* 'Mexican Flag' is as an ornamental foliage plant for tropical greenhouses and outdoors in the humid tropics. It needs fertile soil containing an abundance of organic matter that is always uniformly moist and shade from strong sun. In greenhouses a minimum temperature of 65 to 70°F and a constantly moist atmosphere are necessary; day temperatures may be allowed to rise to 75 or 80°F and in summer even higher. Specimens that have filled the receptacles they are in with roots benefit from weekly applications of dilute liquid fertilizer from spring to fall. Repotting should be given attention in late winter or spring. Increase is secured by division and by cuttings set in a greenhouse propagating bench; slight bottom heat encourages rooting.

CAMPERNELLE. This is *Narcissus odorus*.

CAMPHIRE. See Lawsonia.

CAMPHOR TREE is *Cinnamomum camphora*.

CAMPHORA OFFICINARUM is *Cinnamomum camphora*.

CAMPHOROSMA (Camphor-ósma). One species of *Camphorosma* is cultivated. The genus, named because of its prevailing aromatic qualities, from camphor and the Greek *osme*, an odor, comprises about eleven species of subshrubs, herbaceous perennials, and annuals. It ranges from the Mediterranean region to central Asia, and belongs in the goosefoot family CHENOPODIACEAE.

Camphorosmas have alternate leaves, more or less round in section, and small, bisexual or female flowers with bell-shaped, four- or five-toothed perianths, four or five stamens, and a style with two, or occasionally three, stigmas. The flowers are solitary or are crowded in cylindrical to ovoid spikes. The small fruits (technically achenes) are enclosed in the persistent calyxes.

Heathlike or lavender-like in aspect, *C. monspeliaca* is subshrubby, compact, not more than 1½ feet tall, and redolent of camphor. Its shoots, ascending or prostrate, are woolly-hairy. In the axils of awl-shaped, rigid leaves, up to ⅓ inch long, are tufts of smaller ones. The minute blooms, which come in summer, are crowded in cylindrical to ovoid spikes. Their styles are red. The seeds are black. This species is native from the Mediterranean region to far north in Russia.

Garden and Landscape Uses and Cultivation. This camphorosma is attractive and is especially well adapted for seaside locations and saline soils. It thrives in dryish, sandy soils in full sun. Propagation is by summer cuttings, and by seeds. Any pruning needed to shape the plants is done in early spring. Although American experience, probably with stock secured from Europe, indicates that this shrub is not hardy in the north, its native range suggests that plants raised from seeds collected at the northern limits of its natural distribution would survive much colder climes.

CAMPION. See Lychnis and Silene.

CAMPSIDIUM (Camp-sídium). This genus of one species of evergreen vine of Chile and Argentina belongs in the bignonia family BIGNONIACEAE. Its name alludes to its resemblance to *Campsis*. Attaining a height of 40 to 50 feet, **Campsidium valdivianum** has angular shoots and finely-pinnate, hairless leaves of nine to fifteen stalkless leaflets ¾ inch to 1½ inches long and usually toothed in their upper parts. It has neither tendrils nor aerial roots. The tubular, bright orange flowers, in pendulous racemes of six to ten, have five short corolla lobes and four stamens, the ends of the two longer of which extend slightly from the mouth of the bloom. The seeds are in slender podlike capsules 3 to 4 inches long.

Garden Uses and Cultivation. No great success appears to have attended efforts to have this species flower in the deep south. It probably is adapted to conditions in southern California. It is sometimes grown in cool conservatories in loamy, well-drained soil. Pruning consists of removing weak and crowded shoots and shortening flowering shoots to close to their bases as soon as blooming is through. A greenhouse with a minimum winter night temperature of about 50°F is satisfactory. Watering should be done freely spring through fall, more sparingly in winter. Propagation is by cuttings and seeds.

CAMPSIS (Cámp-sis)—Trumpet Vine. Two deciduous woody vines that climb by aerial, more or less plentiful rootlets are the only species of this American and Asian genus of the bignonia family BIGNONIACEAE. The name is from the Greek *kampsis*, a curve or bend, in allusion to the curved stamens. From *Bignonia, Pyrostegia, Tecomaria*, and certain other closely-related genera trumpet vines are distinguished by having aerial roots and orange to red flowers with the stamens included in instead of protruding from the corolla. These plants are also called trumpet creepers.

Campsis radicans at Princeton University

The genus *Campsis* has opposite leaves with an odd number of toothed leaflets. The large, very short-stalked, trumpet-shaped flowers have unequally-five-toothed calyxes, and corollas with five spreading lobes (petals), three of which are larger than the others. They are borne in showy terminal clusters in summer and early fall. There are two long and two short stamens. The fruits are slender, spindle-shaped capsules containing many winged seeds.

Common trumpet vine (*C. radicans* syns. *Bignonia radicans*, *Tecoma radicans*), native of moist woods, roadsides, and fence-rows from New Jersey to Ohio, Florida, and Texas, is hardy at least as far north as Massachusetts. It often occurs as an escape from cultivation. Up to 30 feet tall or taller, this kind has leaves of five to thirteen, but commonly nine to eleven leaflets, pubescent, at least along the midribs on the undersides. The flowers, about 3 inches long and 2 inches wide, are usually orange with scarlet corolla lobes. Their calyxes are one-third or less the length of the corolla tube and have short teeth. Yellow-flowered *C. r. flava* is quite lovely.

Chinese trumpet vine (*C. grandiflora* syn. *Bignonia chinensis*) is not as tall as the American species and develops aerial roots sparsely or sometimes not at all. Its leaflets, usually seven to nine, are quite glabrous and its orange-scarlet flowers have calyxes lobed to their middles. The flower clusters of this native of China and Japan

Campsis radicans (flowers)

Campsis radicans flava

are larger and looser than those of the American kind, and the corolla tube is up to twice as long as the calyx. The blooms are about 3 inches in diameter. Chinese trumpet vine is not hardy in the north. A hybrid between it and the American trumpet vine is named **C. tagliabuana.** Intermediate in flower size, hardiness, and other characteristics between its parents, it generally has leaves with seven to eleven leaflets, usually pubescent on the veins beneath. The flowers have calyxes much shorter than their corolla tubes and divided for about one-third of their lengths. The popular variety 'Mme. Galen' belongs here.

Garden and Landscape Uses. Trumpet vines are excellent for covering masonry walls, tree stumps, trunks of palms and other bare-stemmed trees, and large rock outcrops, but they are unsuitable for growing against wooden buildings because of the difficulty they pose when painting becomes necessary. They may be maintained as bushy specimens by suitable pruning and, given this treatment, make attractive hedges. Although they stand some shade, they are at their finest only in full sun. A fertile, moderately-moist soil suits them best.

Cultivation. It is well to cut trumpet vines back to within a few inches of the ground at planting time. This encourages branching and the production of young shoots that are the only ones that attach themselves to supports. Once they have achieved the size desired, annual pruning in late winter or early spring is in order. This consists of cutting back all shoots of the previous year's growth to within two or three inches of their bases and the removal of any thin, straggly, and crowded ones. In poor soils these vines benefit from a spring application of fertilizer to encourage the production of strong flowering shoots. Propagation is easy by seeds, leafy cuttings in summer, hardwood cuttings in fall, and by layers and root cuttings.

Diseases and Pests. Leaf spots, powdery mildews, and a leaf blight, none likely to

be very serious, infect trumpet vines. They are also attacked, rarely with serious results, by scale insects, whitefly, and mealybugs.

CAMPTOSEMA (Campto-sèma). This genus of approximately one dozen species of rather rare nonhardy evergreen shrubs and vines of the pea family LEGUMINOSAE is endemic to South America. The name *Camptosema* derives from the Greek *kamptos*, curved, and *sema*, a standard. It alludes to the curved appendages on each side of the bases of the standard or banner petals of the flowers.

Camptosemas have alternate leaves of usually three, rarely more, pinnately-arranged leaflets, or sometimes only one leaflet. Their pea-like flowers, in racemes from the leaf axils, have tubular calyxes.

Long misidentified in cultivation as *Dioclea glycinoides*, Argentinian and Uruguayan *C. rubicundum* is an excellent twining vine of refined appearance. It has hairless leaves of three oblong to narrow-elliptic leaflets 1 inch to 2 inches long, up to ¾ inch wide, and rounded and often notched at their apexes. The ruby-red blooms, with standard petals ¾ to 1 inch long and smaller wing petals and keel, are scattered rather than massed. They are attractive to hummingbirds.

Garden Uses and Cultivation. Rather rare in cultivation, the species described here succeeds with little trouble in southern California. It withstands light frosts, and even if killed to the ground by somewhat greater cold, is likely to recover and renew itself by shoots from the base. It is well adapted as a neat vine for small and larger gardens and for greenhouses. Remarkably free of pests and diseases, this kind succeeds in ordinary, well-drained soil where it receives sun for at least half of each day. It responds well to occasional pruning to prevent it becoming tangled and overgrown, and appreciates watering regularly in dry weather and occasional fertilizing. Propagation is by seed, layering, and cuttings.

CAMPTOSORUS (Campto-sòrus)—Walking Fern. Two species of evergreen ferns, one native in North America the other in eastern Asia, constitute this genus. Only the former is likely to be cultivated. They belong in the asplenium family ASPLENIACEAE and develop clusters of undivided, toothless fronds (leaves) from short, erect rhizomes. The fronds narrow gradually from comparatively broad bases to long drawn-out, slender apexes. The linear or oblong, straight or flat, clusters of spore capsules on the undersides of the leaves chiefly follow the veins. The name walking fern is applied because the tips of the fronds root into the ground and give rise to new plants. In this way the plants spread. The name *Camptosorus* is from the

Greek *kamptos*, bent, and *soros*, a heap. It alludes to the irregularly-arranged clusters of spore-producing bodies.

The American walking fern (*C. rhizophyllus*) is a charming plant. It has lanceolate-linear fronds, heart-shaped at their bases, 2 inches to 1 foot long, and up to 1¼ inches across at the base. It inhabits rocks, most commonly those of a limestone nature, less frequently it is found on tree trunks or growing in leaf mold. Its native range extends from Quebec to Ontario, Minnesota, Georgia, Arkansas, and Oklahoma.

Camptosorus rhizophyllus

Garden Uses. The attractive appearance of this fern and its interesting habit of growth commend it to the consideration of keen plantsmen and gardeners. It is always fun to display it to visitors, especially to children who are intrigued by its name and the manner of its "walking."

Cultivation. Rarely a robust grower, the walking fern should be given a choice spot in a well-shaded part of the garden where the air is humid and not disturbed by sweeping winds and where its roots are not called upon to compete with those of more vigorous, hungry neighbors. An almost pure organic soil, such as leaf mold, loose humus or non-acid peat moss, with some coarse sand mixed in and interspersed with chunks of limestone or tufa rock, provide an agreeable rooting medium. The soil should be moderately moist at all times. A winter cover of a light layer of branches of pine or other evergreen that holds its leaves when cut is beneficial. Increase is usually by separating rooted plantlets that develop at the ends of the fronds. Spores may also be used for propagation.

CAMPTOTHECA (Campto-thèca). A deciduous tree, rare in cultivation, *Camptotheca acuminata*, of China, is the only representative of this genus of the nyssa family NYSSACEAE. From the sour gum (*Nyssa*) it differs in having dry, 1-inch-long, three-winged, elliptic fruits, many together in globular heads. Not hardy in the north, it is suitable for southern California and other areas where severe frosts are not a threat. Its name is derived from the Greek *kamptos*, curved, and *theke*, a cell. The alkaloid camptothecin, obtained from this species, has been investigated as a possible anticancer drug.

Reported to attain, in its native range, a height of 80 feet, but in cultivation lower, *C. acuminata* is a fast-growing species of pyramidal outline. It has alternate, ovate, toothed leaves with strongly-marked pinnate veins angling sharply upward from the mid-vein. The leaves are up to 6 inches long and when young are bronzy. The flowers, attractive to bees and butterflies, are in globular heads that are solitary or in racemes. The blooms are small and have ten, long-protruding, white stamens. The cup-shaped calyxes are slightly-five-toothed. There are five slender-stalked stamens of unequal length and a two-branched style. Each head of flowers ends in a female bloom, with male flowers clustered near it. There are also bisexual flowers. The fruits are brown and glossy.

Garden and Landscape Uses and Cultivation. This is a tree for those interested in the rare and unusual. Attractive in bloom and useful for shade, it grows in any ordinary soil and is easily raised from seeds and from cuttings taken in May or June and planted under mist in a temperature of about 70°F.

CAMPYLANTHUS (Campy-lánthus). One of the seven species of *Campylanthus* is cultivated. Belonging to the figwort family SCROPHULARIACEAE, the genus consists of shrubs not hardy in the north. They are natives of the Canary and Cape Verde islands, Arabia, Socotra, and West Pakistan. The name, from the Greek *kampylos*, a curve, and *anthos*, a flower, alludes to the curved corolla tubes.

Native to the Canary Islands, *C. salsoloides* attains heights of 3 to 6 feet. It has slender shoots, and erect, alternate, rather crowded, stalkless, linear to oblanceolate leaves ½ inch to 1½ inches long and not more than 1/12 inch wide. The small, bright pink flowers are in racemes 2 to 4 inches in length near the branch ends. They have calyxes with five hairy lobes. The corolla has a short, slender, curved tube and five spreading, pointed lobes (petals) that form a face ⅜ inch wide. There are two stamens. The fruits are capsules.

Garden and Landscape Uses and Cultivation. The species considered here is suitable for outdoor cultivation as an ornamental in warm, dryish climates. It succeeds in well-drained soils in sunny locations. It may also be accommodated in large conservatories where winter night temperatures are about 50°F and those by day a few degrees higher. Increase is by seeds and cuttings.

CAMPYLOBOTRYS. See Hoffmannia.

CAMPYLOCENTRUM (Campylo-cèntrum). Belonging in the orchid family ORCHIDACEAE, and native from Florida to Argentina, *Campylocentrum* consists of thirty-five species. Its name, from the Greek *kampylos*, a curve, and *kentron*, a spur, alludes to the spurs of the flowers.

Campylocentrums as wildlings grow perched on trees or sometimes cliffs or rocks. They are without pseudobulbs and include completely leafless kinds with brief stems and chlorophyll-containing roots that photosynthesize food, and others with rooting, branching stems and two-ranked, usually fleshy, alternate leaves. The tiny flowers are in spikes or racemes of few to many, those of leafless kinds coming from the centers of the root clusters or sides of the stems, those of the others from the leaf axils. The blooms are tubular, mainly greenish or yellowish, and have similar sepals and petals and a three-lobed lip with a usually curved, conspicuously-swollen spur.

Native from Mexico to Cuba and South America, *C. micranthum* has erect or sometimes pendulous stems, with elliptic-oblong leaves 2 to 4 inches long by ¾ inch wide. Its one-sided flower spikes 1 inch to 1½ inches long are of many flowers, white or yellowish-white with olive-green corolla tubes, less than ½ inch long, in two up-pointing rows. For the plant sometimes called *C. porrectum* see Harrisiella.

Campylocentrum micranthum

Garden Uses and Cultivation. Campylocentrums are suited only for keen collectors of unusual orchids who are also experienced growers. The leafless species are difficult to domesticate and rarely persist for long under cultivation. Leafy kinds are more amenable. Afforded conditions agreeable to angraecums, they may succeed attached to slabs of tree fern trunks or bark. It is important that they never become dry. For more information see Orchids.

CAMPYLONEURUM (Campylo-nèurum)—Strap Fern. Twenty-five species of ferns of the polypody family POLYPODIACEAE comprise *Campyloneurum*, the name of which derives from the Greek *kampylos*, curved, and *neuron*, a nerve. It alludes to the leaf veins. By some authorities these western hemisphere ferns are included in *Polypodium*.

Campyloneurums are epiphytes, that is, they perch on the trunks and branches of trees without extracting nourishment from their hosts, or are terrestrial. Medium to large, they have creeping, scale-clothed rhizomes and usually clustered, more or less leathery, hairless fronds (leaves) that are rarely pinnate, more commonly strap-shaped, undivided, and without marginal teeth. The spore-case clusters, near the ends of veinlets, are round and well distributed over the lower sides of the fronds.

Native from the Everglades of Florida to Brazil, *C. phyllitidis* (syn. *Polypodium phyllitidis*) is reminiscent of a large hart's

Campyloneurum phyllitidis

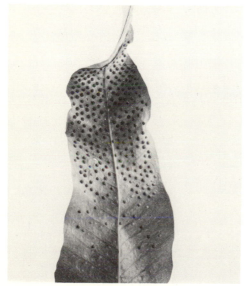

Campyloneurum phyllitidis (spore-case clusters)

tongue fern (*Phyllitis scolopendrium*). It has bright, glossy green, pointed, stalkless, strap-shaped leaves 1 foot to 3 feet long by 1 inch to 4 inches wide that narrow gradually to their bases. Less robust *C. angustifolium* (syn. *Polypodium angustifolium*) is wild from Mexico to South America, and in the West Indies. Its leathery, narrow-linear leaves are up to 1½ feet long and ¼ to nearly 1 inch wide. They narrow gradually to their bases and often have rolled-under margins.

Campyloneurum angustifolium

Other sorts cultivated include **C. costatum,** of Costa Rica and the West Indies, which has thickish rhizomes and linear-oblong to paddle-shaped, lobeless and toothless leaves 9 inches to 1½ feet long, with the clusters of spore capsules in rows between the veinlets that angle outward from the midrib, and West Indian **C. vexatum,** the slender elliptic to pointed-oblan-ceolate fronds of which are 4 inches to 1 foot long and tapered to both ends.

Garden and Landscape Uses and Cultivation. These are as for tropical species of *Polypodium*. In greenhouses the species described above are well suited for growing in ground beds, pots, and tubs. For additional information see Ferns.

CAMPYLOTROPIS (Campyló-tropis). Sixty-five species of Asian deciduous shrubs and subshrubs of the pea family LEGUMINOSAE compose *Campylotropis*. Similar to *Lespedeza*, they are little known in cultivation. The name, alluding to the curved keels of the blooms, comes from the Greek *kampylos*, curved, and *tropis*, a keel.

These have slender-stalked leaves, with three leaflets, and generally purple, pea-like flowers in racemes, or more rarely panicles, from the leaf axils or terminal. The slender-stalked blooms, their stalks jointed below the five-parted calyx, the two upper lobes of which are somewhat united, are most commonly solitary in the axils of persistent or deciduous bracts. The flowers have five petals, and ten stamens of which nine are joined and the other

free. There is one style. The fruits are one-seeded pods.

Native to China, *C. macrocarpa* in aspect resembles *Lespedeza thunbergii*. Hardy in southern New England, it is about 3 feet tall, and has leaves with elliptic to oblong leaflets up to 2 inches long. They are silky-hairy on their undersides, hairless above. The flowers, a little less than ½ inch long, are in somewhat crowded racemes up to 3½ inches long.

Garden and Landscape Uses and Cultivation. The species described is appropriate for the fronts of sunny shrub borders and similar locations. It thrives in ordinary well-drained soil and is raised from seeds.

CANADA SNAKEROOT is *Asarum canadense*.

CANADA THISTLE is *Cirsium arvense*.

CANAIGRE is *Rumex hymenosepalus*.

CANANGA (Can-ánga)—Ylang-Ylang. The common name ylang-ylang is also that of the exotic Oriental and Pacific island perfume obtained from *Cananga odorata*. An oil obtained from the flowers of this species, called cananga oil, is a valuable and extremely important ingredient in modern perfumery and is present in almost all perfumes. The name *Cananga* is derived from a native one. The genus consists of two or three trees of the annona family ANNONACEAE, natives of tropical Asia. They have alternate, lobeless and toothless leaves. Borne in the leaf axils, their fairly large flowers have three sepals and six petals in two rows of three; the petals are long, narrow, and of nearly equal size.

The ylang-ylang (**Cananga odorata** syn. *Canangium odoratum*), native to India, Java,

Cananga odorata

and the Philippines, a rather open-headed tree up to 80 feet high, but usually smaller, has rather brittle, somewhat drooping branches that tilt upward toward their ends and have down-curved tips. Its sharp-pointed, ovate-oblong leaves may be 8 inches long. They are glossy above and sparsely-hairy on their undersides. The flowers are profuse and deliciously fragrant, greenish at first, maturing to rich ivory-white. They have pendulous petals 1½ to 2 inches long, and many crowded stamens. One or two blooms are on each short flower stalk. The oblong-cylindrical fruits are greenish and almost 1 inch in length.

Garden and Landscape Uses. In the tropics and warm subtropics, this species may be used as a specimen planted in the vicinity of the house or other location where its fragrance can be enjoyed to its fullest. Because it does not cast dense shade it is a good lawn tree and is also quite often used in avenues. In some countries it blooms twice each year. It is grown in Florida and Hawaii.

Cultivation. In suitable climates cultivation of the ylang-ylang is simple. It thrives in ordinary soil and is easily raised from seed.

CANARINA (Can-arìna). For more than a century following its discovery, this group of the bellflower family CAMPANULACEAE was thought to consist of one species, a native of the Canary Islands. At the end of the nineteenth and beginning of the twentieth centuries other kinds were found in East Africa, thus confirming for this genus of three species an unusual pattern of natural distribution. The genus *Canarina*, the name of which refers to the islands where it was first discovered, differs from *Campanula* in having fleshy edible berries instead of dry capsules. Also its flower parts are commonly more numerous. It consists of slender-stemmed, herbaceous perennials with leaves opposite or in circles of three, and large, bell-shaped blooms with usually six calyx lobes, six corolla lobes (petals), as many stamens as corolla lobes, and a slender style.

In its home islands *C. canariensis* (syn. *C. campanula*) occupies shaded ravines and woodlands, where it attains heights of 3 to 6 feet or sometimes more. It is a rather glaucous, semiclimbing or trailing plant, with stalked, rather triangular, leaves the blades of which are up to 3 inches long. They are jagged-toothed and more or less lobed toward their bases and are in twos or sometimes threes. The flowers, solitary at the ends of the slender stems and axillary branches, are up to 2 inches long and approximately as wide across the mouth. They are yellow, heavily flushed with brick-red to purplish-brown.

From the last *C. eminii*, of tropical East Africa, differs in having tuberous roots. Its slender, pendulous stems have pairs of ovate leaves 1½ to 3 inches long, toothed or lobed at their bases, and not as long-pointed as those of *C. canariensis*. The flowers are terminal, 2½ inches long, and slen-

derer than those of *C. canariensis*. They are dull yellow with green stripes and have red-striped calyxes. From East Africa also comes *C. abyssinica,* a tuberous-rooted kind similar to *C. eminii,* but with less elongated leaves, and smaller, pinkish-orange to streaked-with-red blooms on stalks with a marked spiral twist. The stamens are conspicuously broadened at their bases. The nearly spherical fruits are yellow to tomato-red.

Garden Uses. Canarinas are not hardy in the north, but can be grown in cool greenhouses, and outdoors in regions of little or no frost where the climate is neither oppressively torrid nor humid. They may be expected to prosper under conditions that suit the marguerite or Paris-daisy (*Chrysanthemum frutescens*), and to be well adapted for California and regions with similar climates. They provide interesting variety in flower gardens and require well-drained, fertile soil fairly rich with leaf mold, compost, or other organic material. They may be planted where they receive part-day shade.

Cultivation. Propagation is by seeds, division, and cuttings started in spring in a greenhouse propagating bench that has gentle bottom heat. Generous supplies of water are needed when the plants are growing actively, with much less given in winter. The tuberous-rooted kinds may be kept quite dry then. Light shade from strong summer sun is needed. Repotting or replanting in greenhouses is done annually in January or February at the very beginning of the new season of growth. A greenhouse winter night temperature of 45°F is satisfactory, with a rise of five or ten degrees by day.

CANARY. This word forms part of the common names of these plants: canary-balm (*Cedronella canariensis*), canary bird bush (*Crotalaria agatiflora*), canary bird flower or canary bird vine (*Tropaeolum peregrinum*), and canary grass (*Phalaris*).

CANAVALIA (Canav-àlia)—Jack-Bean or Horse-Bean or Chickasaw-Lima-Bean. More or less twining or trailing prostrate herbaceous plants of the pea family LEGUMINOSAE compose this genus of fifty species of the Old and New World tropics. They have leaves of three leaflets, and purple, rose-pink, or whitish pea-like blooms in long-stalked racemes. The calyxes are two-lipped, the standard or banner petal large and rounded, the wing petals narrow, and the keel incurved. The fruits are pods. The name is derived from an aboriginal one.

The jack-bean, horse-bean, or Chicka-saw-lima-bean (*Canavalia ensiformis*), probably native to the West Indies, in warm climates is grown as food for livestock, and its seeds, reported to be poisonous when eaten fresh and immature, when young are cooked and eaten like string beans.

They can be roasted and used as a coffee substitute. The fruits of related *C. obtusifolia* are eaten raw, salted, and cooked.

Almost or quite hairless, *C. ensiformis* is bushy, with little tendency to climb. Its strongly-veined leaves are of ovate-oblong to ovate leaflets each 5 to 8 inches long and one-half or more as wide. The blooms are small and pale purple. At maturity the pods are up to 1 foot long or a little longer.

Garden Uses and Cultivation. Except as an interesting species to include in educational collections of plants of use of man, the jack-bean has no garden importance. It thrives in a variety of soils and tropical conditions. An annual, its seeds are sown about 6 inches apart in rows 3 feet apart.

CANCERWORT. See Kickxia.

CANCHALAGUA is *Centaurium venustum*.

CANDELILLA is *Euphorbia antisyphilitica*.

CANDLE. This word appears in the common names candle-berry (*Aleurites moluccana*), candle bush (*Cassia alata*), candle plant (*Senecio articulatus*), and candle tree (*Parmentiera cereifera*).

CANDLENUT is *Aleurites moluccana*.

CANDLEWOOD is *Fouquieria splendens*.

CANDOLLEA. See Hibbertia.

CANDYTUFT. See Iberis.

CANE and CANES. The essentially straight stems of such plants as blackberries, raspberries, and certain roses that attain considerable lengths, are much the same thickness throughout; usually not retained for longer than one to three years, they are commonly called canes. The stems of bamboos are also canes. Those of certain types furnish most of the canes used for staking plants.

CANE-REED is *Arundinaria gigantea*.

CANELLA (Can-élla)—Wild-Cinnamon. This, the type genus of the canella family CANELLACEAE, consists of two species of evergreen trees, one native of Florida and the West Indies, the other of northern South America. From *Cinnamodendron*, the only other genus of the family, *Canella* differs in its clusters of flowers being at the shoot ends instead of in the leaf axils. The name, a diminutive of the Greek *kanna*, a reed, alludes to the bark being rolled in a manner suggestive of reeds.

Canellas have aromatic bark, and berries sweet when ripe but earlier pungent, that can be dried and used like hot pepper. The flesh of pigeons that feed on the berries acquires a pleasing, distinctive flavor. Canella bark has been used as a tonic, a stimulant, and an aromatic. The leaves are alternate, undivided, and bespeckled with little translucent dots. The flowers have three overlapping, persistent sepals, five thick petals that soon fall, and a short, thick style ending in a faintly two-lobed stigma. The fruits are subspherical and contain three or four large seeds.

Native of Florida and the West Indies, wild-cinnamon (*C. winterana* syn. *C. alba*), white-barked, is up to 50 feet tall, but commonly smaller. Its short-stalked, round-ended, obovate-elliptic leaves are 2 to 3 inches long. The red to purple flowers are ⅓ inch wide or a little wider. The berries, about ⅓ inch in diameter, when ripe are crimson or purplish-black.

Garden and Landscape Uses and Cultivation. The species described here is a fine, straight-trunked, round-headed tree that in Florida and other warm regions with little or no frost can be put to good use as an ornamental. It stands partial shade, succeeds in ordinary, reasonably fertile soil, and is propagated by seeds.

CANELLACEAE—Canella Family. This family of dicotyledons consists of sixteen species of aromatic trees and shrubs distributed among five genera and natives of the West Indies, warm parts of South America, Africa, and Madagascar. They have alternate, undivided, leathery leaves and flowers solitary, in clusters, or racemes. The blooms have four or five sepals, four to twelve separate or united petals or none, twenty to forty stamens joined as a tube, and one style with two to five stigmas. The fruits are berries. Only *Canella* is likely to be cultivated.

CANISTEL is *Pouteria campechiana.*

CANISTRUM (Canís-trum). Alluding to the cupped collar of bracts that contains the flower clusters, the name *Canistrum* comes from the Latin *canistra*, a flat basket. It is that of a genus of about seven species of the pineapple family BROMELIACEAE, natives of Brazil and one of Trinidad.

Canistrums grow mostly as tree-perchers (epiphytes) that take no nourishment from their hosts, but use them only as places to lodge, or on rocks, or more rarely in the ground. Their evergreen leaves, with sheathing, broadened, water-holding bases, are in dense, rather large rosettes. They are linear to sword-shaped, toothed, and more or less furnished with scurfy scales. Arising from the center of the rosette, the short to tall flower stalk is topped by a compact spike or dense head of green, yellow, or blue blooms sitting in a whorl (collar) of broad, colored bracts. The individual flowers have three each sepals and petals, the latter separate to their bases, the sepals similarly separate or nearly so. The petals each have a pair of small, frilled, scalelike appendages or calluses.

There are six stamens and a style about as long, ending in a three-branched stigma. The fruits are many-seeded berries.

Kinds cultivated include *C. aurantiacum,* a robust Brazilian with finely-toothed leaves 1 foot to 2 feet long and about 2 inches wide. They are green, often spotted or mottled with a deeper shade of green. Up to 1 foot tall, the erect flowering stalk terminates in a basket of orange and bright red bracts filled with a spherical head of from fifty to one hundred 2-inch-long, orange-yellow flowers. Smaller, Brazilian *C. cyathiforme* has broad rosettes of 1-foot-long, wide, soft-toothed leaves mottled with darker green. The reddish-pink flowering stalk elevates the clusters of yellow flowers and their attendant collar of rigid, reddish bracts well above the foliage. Another Brazilian, *C. fosteranum* has tubular rosettes of finely-toothed, gray-green leaves 2 feet long by 2 inches wide obscurely and irregularly marked with brown. The white flowers, in clusters with rose-pink bracts, are atop rosy-red stalks. More variable than others described here, *C. lindenii* has rosettes up to 3 feet wide of light green leaves with darker mottlings. Its crowded heads of green and white blooms are 2 to 3 inches in diameter. They may, in the varieties as well as in the typical species, be low in the center of the rosette or lifted to a height of up to 8 inches or so above it. Variety *C. l. roseum* has darker foliage with the undersides of the leaves stained with rose-pink. Variety *C. l. viride* is often somewhat bigger than the typical species. Its floral bracts are green.

Canistrum lindenii

Hybrid *C. leopardinum,* the parents of which are believed to be *C. ingratum* and *C. l. roseum,* has broad rosettes up to more than 3 feet wide of mottled green leaves that, when the plant is grown in good light, assume purplish-red tones with fleckings of deep purple. From the center of the rosette is lifted a compact, brilliant maroon flower head.

Canistrum leopardinum

Garden and Landscape Uses and Cultivation. These are beautiful plants for outdoors in the humid tropics and subtropics and for greenhouses and other indoor locations where a more or less greenhouse-like environment can be maintained. They require conditions and care that suit aregelias, guzmanias, and most other epiphytic bromeliads. For more information see Bromeliads or Bromels.

CANKER. Cankers are diseases of usually, but not exclusively, woody plants that manifest themselves as local lesions, called cankers, on trunks, stems, or other parts. The affected areas shrink, die, and often crack and become open wounds with the under tissues exposed. In some cases, sap oozes from the affected parts. Cankers, small at first, soon increase in size and not infrequently completely girdle stems and branches. They seriously interfere with the upward movement of water with the result, sometimes aggravated by toxins secreted by the canker-causing fungus, that the foliage wilts and die-back of the shoots occur. Many canker diseases are caused by fungi; others are caused by bacteria. Common examples are those of apples, roses, maples, delphiniums, and spruces. For some cankers, for example bleeding canker and basal canker of maples, there are no known cures. Others are more or less effectively treated by pruning out affected parts or by spraying with fungicides. Preventive measures include avoidance of injury to stems, branches, and trunks, removal of dead wood, fertilizing and watering to promote vigorous growth, and in the case of cankers caused by organisms that persist in soil, such as crown canker of roses, by using only steam-sterilized soil.

CANKERWORMS or INCHWORMS. These, the larvae of caterpillars of small moths, defoliate trees of many kinds and are especially obnoxious near sitting areas. They have the distressing habit of lowering themselves on silken threads, becoming entangled with and crawling over the hair and other parts of the body or clothing. Populations of cankerworms, or inchworms or measuring-worms as they are sometimes called, vary tremendously from year to year from comparatively few to infestations of such magnitude that it is actually possible to hear them crunching the foliage. Two kinds are widely distributed in the United States, the fall cankerworm and the spring cankerworm. The moths of the first emerge from the pupae in the ground in late fall. After mating, the wingless females crawl up trees and deposit eggs in compact masses. These hatch in spring about the time new foliage develops and the caterpillars feed on the leaves until late spring when they retire to the soil to pupate. Females, also wingless, of the spring cankerworm crawl up tree trunks in late winter or early spring to lay their eggs, which hatch in a month or so. The behavior of the resulting larvae is the same and as distressing as that of the fall cankerworm.

CANNA (Cán-na)—Indian Shot. The genus *Canna* is the only one in the canna family CANNACEAE. It consists of fifty-five species, natives of tropical and subtropical America. The name is from the Greek *kanna*, a reed. It alludes to the stems.

These well-known tropical and subtropical foliage and flowering plants have stout, clustered rootstocks and erect, unbranched stems bearing large, alternate, more or less paddle-shaped, prominently-veined, lobeless leaves with the lower parts of their stalks sheathing the stems. Their flowers, which in garden kinds are large and showy, come in red, yellow, cream, and various intermediate shades such as apricot and flame, and are sometimes spotted with colors other than the ground hue. They are in terminal clusters. Botanically the blooms are of peculiar structure, having three small green sepals, three greenish, sepal-like petals, and two to five petal-like staminodes (stamens modified to look like petals), one reflexed and forming a lip to the flower. The fruits are three-angled dry capsules containing very hard, round, shot-like seeds, which account for the common name of Indian shot sometimes applied to *Canna indica*.

The edible canna (*C. edulis*) is a native of South America and the West Indies. It bears tubers, called tous-les-mois, which are eaten. From them is also obtained an easily digestable starch called Queensland arrowroot. The edible canna has purple stems and attains a height of 10 feet. Its leaves, about 2 feet long, have purplish undersides. The flowers are bright red with the three upper staminodes, 2½ inches in length, verging to orange. The roots of certain other species are also used as food locally in Africa and South America. In Africa the seeds of *C. bidentata* are used for necklaces and rosaries.

Canna edulis (flowers and fruits)

Endemic from South Carolina to Florida, *C. flaccida*, about 5 feet tall, has green stems and leaves up to 2 feet long by 5 inches wide. Its yellow flowers have strongly-reflexed petals and three staminodes up to 3 inches long. This species has played an important part as a parent of the orchid-flowered garden hybrid cannas. Indian shot (*C. indica*) is naturalized in the southern United States as an introduction

Canna indica

from tropical America. It is 4 to 7 feet tall and has green stems and leaves and bright red flowers with an orange lip spotted with red. The three upper staminodes are 2 inches long. Native of the West Indies and tropical South America, *C. glauca* is 4 to 6 feet tall. It has hairless stems and slender-pointed, thinly white-edged, grayish, lan-

ceolate leaves up to 1½ feet long. In usually branchless racemes the pale yellow, sometimes orange-tinged flowers have three, obovate staminodes about 3 inches long and sometimes two-lobed, and a narrower lip notched at its apex.

Canna glauca

Hybrid cannas of complex and not fully understood parentage are the kinds commonly grown for ornament. They have handsome bold foliage and gorgeous, often brilliantly-colored, large flowers. Few if any plants so easy to grow for summer display in North American temperate region gardens provide such rich tropical displays. Hybrid cannas have been grouped under two botanical names, the common garden canna (*C. generalis*), which includes the original French Crozy hybrids, and the orchid-flowered cannas (*C. orchiodes*), which are later developments more popular for garden planting. With a wide variety of flower colors, *C. generalis* has blooms up to 4 inches in diameter that are not tubular, petals not reflexed, and usually four erect staminodes. The foliage may be green, bronzy, or purplish. The orchid cannas (*C. orchiodes*) differ in having flowers with five staminodes and tubular bases, up to 6 inches wide or sometimes wider, and have petals that on the second day after the bloom opens become reflexed. There are many varieties. A recent development among orchid cannas is a dwarf large-flowered strain raised by Wilhelm Pfitzer of Stuttgart, Germany and called Pfitzer's dwarf cannas. These are 2½ to 3 feet tall and come in a range of beautiful colors. Named varieties of hybrid cannas including the new dwarfs are described and sometimes illustrated in seedsmen's and bulb dealers' catalogs.

Garden and Landscape Uses. Cannas at one time fell into poor repute among people of good taste because of their too frequent and often inappropriate use. Stiff, formal, often circular, and frequently mounded beds, planted with tall cannas ringed with salvias, coleus, acalyphas, dusty miller, and other exotic-looking species dotted lawns in parks, erupted in front of courthouses and other public places,

Capsicum annum variety

Carnation, a Malmaison variety

Carlinia acanthifolia

Cattleya aurantiaca

Cattleya intermedia alba

Cattleya percivaliana

Cattleya hybrid

Celosia cristata plumosa variety

Cedrus atlantica glauca

Caulifower

Centaurea dealbata variety

Canna generalis variety

Canna orchiodes variety

and marred the tranquility of private estates. They were used vulgarly to bring the worst of Victorian taste to the outdoors, and the practice was common well into the present century. Cannas need not be used incongruously, but can be employed tastefully to create elegant and quite stunning effects without ostentation. In part this is possible because of the refined colors and color combinations of modern hybrids and in part because of the dwarfer stature of many of the newer varieties. Change of taste, of course, accounts for the desire to use these plants less extravagantly.

Hybrid cannas can in good conscience be highly recommended for use, as modern taste suggests, massed in beds and borders to produce large scale effects or planted in groups of three to a dozen in mixed flower borders. The dwarf varieties are splendid for porch boxes and other on-the-ground containers (they are too big for most window boxes). Because of the strict lines of their stems and the boldness and simple shapes of their handsome leaves they associate well with architectural features and can often be planted near buildings with satisfying results. Scale is an important factor in locating cannas. They are massive and must be planted either where they contrast or harmonize, without discordance or any sense of overpowering surrounding vegetation and other features.

Cultivation. In the warmer parts of the southern United States and Hawaii, cannas can be left in the ground all winter. In colder areas it is necessary to dig and store the roots. They sometimes fail in storage because of wrong treatment. The procedure is to cut the stems to within 6 inches of the ground as soon as the foliage has been lightly damaged by frost, dig the roots with as much soil clinging to them as possible, and store them in a dry place away from furnaces or other sources of heat, in a temperature of 40 to 50°F. The soil attached to the roots may need sprinkling occasionally to prevent it from becoming so dry that the roots shrivel, but under no circumstances should it be kept wet.

Propagate in late winter and spring. It is possible to raise cannas from seeds, but this is rarely done except by breeders of new varieties or when seeds are the only available sources of botanical species. Seeds sown without treatment germinate very irregularly, in any sowing the seedlings are likely to appear sporadically over a period of several months. Quicker and much more regular germination is secured by filing a nick through the hard outer coat of each seed before sowing. An alternative, but less sure, method is to soak the seeds for twenty-four hours in warm water before they are sown. Seeds sown in sandy peaty soil kept evenly moist in a temperature of 75 to 90°F germinate without difficulty. By far the commonest method of increase is by division of the rootstocks. In tropical and subtropical regions this is done by lifting plants or parts of plants from the ground at the beginning of the growing season, cutting them into suitably-sized pieces, and replanting or, if they have been stored over winter, dividing the rootstocks and planting the divisions directly outdoors. Elsewhere division is done when the rootstocks are removed from storage for starting into growth. The rootstocks are cut into pieces 2 to 3 inches long with one, or certainly not more than two of the conspicuous large "eyes" or buds to each, and are laid closely together, eyes upward, on a couple of inches of peat moss, leaf mold, or soil covered with a thin layer of sand spread over the bottom of a flat or shallow box, and are just covered with the same material and watered thoroughly. The flats are then put where a temperature of 70°F is maintained. If it is possible to provide bottom heat five to ten degrees higher by standing the flats over hot water pipes or a bed warmed by electric heating cables, so much the better, especially if divisions are made early. Without bottom heat there may be some loss from rotting. Division is done from the end of February on. When the eyes have produced shoots about 3 inches long the young plants are potted individually into 3½- or 4-inch pots in fertile porous soil and are grown in a sunny greenhouse with temperatures of 60°F at night rising to 70°F or more by day. Because the divisions do not all start into growth at once it is usually necessary to remove some from the flats in which they are started before the others. The plants are gradually hardened before they are planted outdoors.

Soil and location affect success with cannas. They need full sun and are at their best in deep, fertile earth that does not lack for moisture, but has adequate subsurface drainage. Deep spading and the incorporation of compost, peat moss, leaf mold, or other decayed organic matter as well as a generous application of a complete fertilizer containing nitrogen in a slow-acting form (organic or ureaform nitrogen) prepare poor soils for cannas.

Planting outdoors should not be done until the soil is fairly warm and the weather is settled. When it is safe to set out such tender plants as peppers and eggplants and coleus and scarlet salvias, cannas may be planted. The plants may be spaced about 1½ to 2 feet apart. Summer care is

Planting cannas: (a) Set young pot-grown plant in a hole of ample size

(b) Fill around plant with soil and press firmly

not exacting. Weeds must be kept down, which early in the season is done preferably by shallow cultivation, but after hot weather arrives can be in part accomplished by mulching. In dry weather regular soakings with water prevent the soil from becoming excessively dry. By the prompt removal of faded blooms, the exhausting effort of seed production is forestalled, and as a result more blooms are produced over a longer season. Also the plants look tidier.

CANNABIS (Cán-nabis) — Hemp, Marijuana. Best known in America as marijuana, and in the Orient as bhang, hashish, ganja, and charas among other names, preparations of the drug derived from the only species of this genus are habit-forming narcotics. The plant belongs in the mulberry family MORACEAE, or according to some interpretations to a family of its own, the CANNABIDACEAE.

In many parts of the world, especially Asia, this drug is used extensively, and often illegally, for smoking and drinking. In small amounts it results in euphoria, but larger amounts induce hallucinations, delirium, catalepsy, and may even cause the user to become fanatical and run amok.

The meanings of the names bhang, cementer of friendship, ganja, increaser of pleasure, and charas, leaf of delusion, reflect its effects. But the drug, like so many harmful ones, has also medicinal uses; it is employed in the treatment of nervous disorders and to relieve pain. The name of the genus is a modern rendition of *kannabis*, the ancient Greek name of the plant. Apart from its virtues and disrepute as a drug plant, *Cannabis sativa,* a native of Asia naturalized in North America, serves mankind in other important ways. The tough fibers of the inner bark of its hollow stems, fibers 3 to 9 feet long, are the hemp from which are made ropes, cordage, sails, mats, and sacks, and also oakum used for caulking. Hempseed oil, expressed from the seeds, is used in manufacturing paints, varnishes, and soaps, in illumination, and as a food.

The marijuana plant is a coarse, strong-smelling, bushy annual, 3 to 15 feet in height, with alternate, thin leaves of three to nine slender, toothed leaflets arranged palmately (their bases arising from a common point at the apex of the long stalks). The lower leaves are usually opposite, the upper, alternate. The small, green, unisexual flowers, in leafy panicles or clusters, are without petals and are not showy. The sexes are usually on separate plants. The females are in short dense clusters and have two slender stigmas, the males are in longer, looser clusters and have five sepals and stamens. The fruits, usually called seeds, are technically achenes. The strongest fibers come from male plants. In the United States cultivation of this plant is forbidden except by Federal permit.

CANNACEAE—Canna Family. The genus *Canna* is the only one of this family of monocotyledons. It is described under Canna.

CANNON BALL TREE is *Couroupita guianensis.*

CANS. In warm regions, especially in dry climates, nurseries have long grown plants for sale in metal cans. Originally containers that had been used for oil or other products were employed, but ones manufactured especially for the purpose are now commonly available. Plants raised in this fashion in mild parts are often shipped and sold in other regions.

Planting from cans, as from other containers, makes possible setting trees, shrubs, and other plants when it would be impracticable to transplant from open ground. Unless cans are tapered so that root balls can be easily knocked out as from pots it is necessary to cut the cans to remove them. The simplest way is with a special tool, and it is often possible to have the nursery do this for you. If you undertake to cut cans with tin shears or other improvised tools wear heavy gloves and take care not to be cut by the sharp edges of the metal. Do not break the root ball when removing it from the can.

CANTALOUPE. See Muskmelon or Melon.

CANTERBURY BELL, WILD. This name is applied to *Phacelia minor.*

CANTERBURY BELLS. Favorite, easily-grown, old-fashioned flowers, Canterbury bells are botanically *Campanula medium.* A

Cannabis sativa (male)

Cannabis sativa (female)

botanical description is given under that name in this Encyclopedia. Here we are concerned only with their garden uses and how to grow them. Their chief employments are for grouping in flower beds and borders, for use as cut flowers, and to a lesser extent for growing in pots to decorate greenhouses, patios, terraces, and such-like places. For all such uses they are admirable. Seeds are obtainable that give flowers of specific colors, such as dark blue, light blue, purple, rose-pink, and white, and as single-flowered, double-flowered, and cup-and-saucer types.

To have fine Canterbury bells sow seeds in May or June in a cold frame or lightly-shaded bed outdoors where there is no danger of disturbance by animals, rain washes, or other cause. The seed is very small, so make the surface of the seedbed fine and level either by careful raking or by spreading a layer of sifted soil over it. Be sure the soil is porous and of agreeable texture. Mixing in leaf mold, well-rotted compost, or peat moss, and if the earth is clayey, coarse sand or grit, is desirable. Sow in drills (furrows) ¼ to ½ inch deep, 6 inches apart. Keep the bed moist, but not constantly saturated. When the seedlings sprout keep the soil between the rows stirred shallowly and promptly pull out any weeds.

Transplant the seedlings before they begin to crowd, to their detriment, and before they become too big, to a nursery bed. Do this when their second pair of leaves are half grown and the plants are of a size that you can pick them up conveniently. Make sure the soil in the nursery bed is in good heart, that is, in a condition of fertility that would encourage the growth of the general run of vegetables and flowers. Set the plants in their new quarters in rows 1 foot apart. Allow 6 inches between indi-

(b) Single-flowered variety

Canterbury bells: (a) A garden bed

(c) Cup-and-saucer variety

viduals in the rows. Summer care consists chiefly of suppressing weeds by cultivating shallowly and frequently or by mulching, and of watering thoroughly at about weekly intervals in long dry spells.

When fall comes, in mild climates you may transfer the plants to their flowering stations, spacing them 1 foot to 1½ feet apart, or you may leave this until early spring. Where winters are at all severe, it is better to delay the move until spring; in regions where temperatures are likely to drop below 10°F it is well to grow the plants in cold frames or at least to give them the protection of a layer of salt hay, branches of evergreens (discarded Christmas trees come in handy for this), or other suitable cover that will moderate heaving of the ground due to alternate freezing and thawing. Do not put the cover in place until the ground is frozen to a depth of a couple of inches. Remove it gradually early in spring.

Excellent pot specimens of Canterbury bells can be had by carefully digging plants from a nursery bed in September or October, keeping as large a ball of soil around the roots as conveniently possible, and potting them in containers large enough to hold them without undue crowding. Pots 8 inches in diameter usually will be about right. Water the newly-potted plants thoroughly and put them in a cold frame. Shade them lightly for a week or two and until really cold weather comes ventilate the frame freely. Leave them in the frame until January or February, then move them to a sunny greenhouse where the night temperature is 45 to 50°F, that by day five to fifteen degrees higher depending upon the brightness of the weather. Water freely and when the flowering stalks begin to push up initiate a program of weekly applications of dilute liquid fertilizer. Plants handled in this way will bloom in March or April. If you want pot plants for later bloom follow the same procedure but either do not bring them indoors until later than January or February or leave them in the cold frame to develop at their natural rate in spring. Even then they will come into bloom a little ahead of plants in the open ground.

CANTUA (Cán-tua). Less than twelve species of nonhardy, evergreen, South American shrubs or sometimes small trees constitute *Cantua*. The name is a modification of the native name of one kind. The group belongs in the phlox family POLEMONIACEAE.

Cantuas have stalkless or short-stalked, alternate or clustered, undivided, smooth-edged or toothed leaves. The white, yellow, red, or violet flowers, generally in terminal clusters, more rarely solitary, are long-tubular. They have short, five- or occasionally three-lobed, bell-shaped calyxes, and five short corolla lobes (petals).

There are five stamens that may or may not protrude. The fruits are many-seeded capsules.

Best known is *C. buxifolia* (syn. *C. dependens*), of Bolivia, Peru, and northern

Cantua buxifolia

Cantua buxifolia (flowers)

Chile. From 4 to 10 feet tall, this freely-branching shrub has downy young shoots and elliptic or lanceolate, downy or hairless leaves, rarely exceeding 1 inch in length, that are toothless, or those on flowerless shoots sometimes with a few teeth. The blooms, at first upright, but later pendulous, are in crowded clusters at the shoot ends. They are funnel-shaped, 2½ to 3 inches long, and pinkish-red with the corolla tubes usually striped with yellow. The stamens about equal the corolla tubes in length. The flowers of *C. candelilla* have more slender corolla tubes and do not expand markedly at the mouth. They vary in color from yellow to tangerine-red and are 2 to 3 inches long. The stamens protrude.

Garden and Landscape Uses. Cantuas prosper outdoors in warm-temperate and subtropical regions where little or no frost is experienced. They are adaptable to climates such as that of California and are beautiful general-purpose flowering shrubs for sunny locations and ordinary soil. They can also be grown in large containers or ground beds in sunny greenhouses.

Cantua candelilla

Cultivation. Cantuas may be raised from seeds, or from cuttings made of firm shoots, planted in a greenhouse propagating bench or under mist. Outdoors the only particular care needed is a little pruning to shape them and to thin out ill-placed or crowded branches. This is done as soon as blooming is through. Indoor specimens are pruned the same way. They grow well in fertile, well-drained soil watered to keep it evenly moist from spring to fall and kept slightly drier in winter. Well-rooted specimens benefit from judicious applications of dilute liquid fertilizer. On all favorable occasions the greenhouse should be ventilated freely. Winter night temperatures of about 50°F are appropriate with a five to ten degree increase by day allowed. In summer container-accommodated specimens may, with advantage, be stood in a sunny location outdoors. Cantuas are prone to infestation by red spider mites. Prompt spraying with a miticide may be necessary.

CAPE. Usually but not invariably alluding to the plant being native to the Cape of Good Hope region or adjacent parts of South Africa, this word forms part of the names of various plants including Cape-chestnut (*Calodendrum*), Cape-cowslip (*Lachenalia*), Cape-dandelion (*Arctotheca*), Cape-fuchsia (*Phygelius capensis*), Cape-gooseberry (*Physalis peruviana*), Cape-honeysuckle (*Tecomaria capensis*), Cape-ivy (*Senecio macroglossus*), Cape-jasmine (*Gardenia jasminoides*), Cape-marigold (*Dimorphotheca*), Cape-pondweed (*Aponogeton distachyus*), Cape-primrose (*Streptocarpus*), Cape-tulip (*Homeria*), and Capeweed (*Arctotheca*).

CAPE BULBS. Rarely used now, the term Cape bulbs was once much employed by gardeners and is frequent in old literature. It alludes to plants native to South Africa, many of the Cape of Good Hope region, that have bulbs or corms. Among the most familiar Cape bulbs are albucas, antholyzas, babianas, brunsvigias, crocosmias, freesias, homerias, ixias, lachenalias, and sparaxises.

CAPER BUSH. See Capparis.

CAPER SPURGE is *Euphorbia lathyrus*.

CAPEWEED. See Arctotheca.

CAPILLARY BENCHES. These are benches (tables), usually in greenhouses, designed so the soil of pot plants stood upon them is kept uniformly moist by capillary attraction, thus eliminating the need for hand watering. The benches must be absolutely level and waterproof. This last can be assured by covering them with polyethylene plastic film turned up at the bench edges to form a shallow tray.

The benches are filled to a depth of an inch or two with sand, or a mat of an absorbent feltlike or wicklike fabric is spread over them. By wicks leading from reservoirs of water or any of several other devices, the sand or mat is kept constantly wet.

No crocks are used in pots of plants grown on capillary benches. This, because it is essential that the soil in the pots and the wet sand or mat form a continuous system through which water will rise from the bench to the soil surface by capillary action. To make sure that good contact is established when placing a pot on a capillary bench, press it down firmly and at the same time give it a slight twist.

Soil texture is important to success with this technique. If too fine, the soil is likely to be kept over-wet, if too coarse, too dry. A little experimenting is likely to be needed to determine the best mixtures for particular plants.

Plants can be grown successfully without hand watering for years by this method, but in the main it is better suited for batches of one sort of plant, similar in size and potted in the same soil mixture, which at potting time has been packed to the same degree of firmness than it is for collections of different kinds in different soils and of various sizes and stages of growth. The growth of algae on the sand or mat can be troublesome in that it interferes with the free flow of water. Such growth can be controlled by the use of algicides.

CAPILLARY MATS. These are feltlike fabrics of synthetic fibers manufactured for use in capillary watering systems employed in growing pot plants. Chiefly used in greenhouses, the capillary method of watering can be adapted to the cultivation of houseplants in pots up to the 6-inch size. Position pieces of capillary mat cut to the appropriate sizes in the bottoms of shallow trays and keep them constantly wet either by drenching them periodically or by having a portion of the mat droop into a container of water from which water can be drawn by capillary action. The level of the water should not be more than 2 to 3 inches below the mat. When setting the pots in place, be sure to press their bottoms firmly into the fabric of the mat. If a growth of algae appears on the mat (its rapid development is likely to indicate excessive fertilization), soak the mat for thirty minutes in water to which some laundry detergent and laundry bleach, at the rate of one-half a cup to one pail of water, have been added, then rinse it two or three times with clear water before replacing it in the tray. For more information see the Encyclopedia entries Capillary Benches, and Greenhouses and Conservatories.

CAPOLLIN is *Prunus capuli*.

CAPPARIDACEAE—Caper Family. About six hundred and sixty species of dicotyledons disposed in more than forty genera constitute the caper family. Natives of most tropical, subtropical, and some temperate regions, they are commonly trees, shrubs, or occasionally woody vines, often spiny, rarely herbaceous. The dried or pickled flower buds of *Capparis spinosa* are the capers used for seasoning foods.

Hairy or scaly, plants of the caper family have alternate, usually toothless leaves, undivided or of separate leaflets that spread in finger-like fashion from the tops of the leafstalks. Their generally asymmetrical flowers, usually in racemes, less commonly solitary, are bisexual, or unisexual with both sexes on the same plant. They have four to eight each sepals and petals or the latter sometimes lacking. There are six to many stamens and one short or long, slender style ending in a usually two-lobed or headlike stigma. The fruits are capsules or elongate berries. Cultivated genera are *Capparis, Cleome, Euadenia,* and *Steriphoma*.

CAPPARIS (Cáp-paris)—Caper Bush. The genus *Capparis* of the caper family CAPPARIDACEAE consists of 250 species of warm-climate shrubs and trees that differ from most members of the caper family in having berries as fruits. The name is derived from *kapparis*, the ancient Greek name for the caper bush, or possibly is a modification of the Arabic *kaper*. Pickled flower buds of *C. spinosa*, are the capers of commerce. They are used for flavoring. Those of some other kinds are eaten locally.

Members of this genus have alternate, undivided leaves and, generally, spines that represent stipules (appendages at the bases of leafstalks). The solitary flowers have usually four, rarely five, each of sepals and petals, and numerous stamens. The fruits are long-stalked berries.

The caper bush (*C. spinosa*) is a straggling, deciduous shrub, native from the Mediterranean region to India. It is 3 to 4½ feet in height and has short, recurved spines. The leaves, blunt or notched at their apexes, are ovate to nearly round and often rather fleshy. They are about 2 inches long. The white or pale lilac blooms, 2 to 3 inches in diameter, have four sepals, four petals, and forty to fifty conspicuous, projecting stamens with lavender stalks. When mature the fruits burst to reveal pale red flesh in which are embedded purple seeds. Variety *C. s. inermis* is either without spines or has quickly deciduous spines. Its leaves are decidedly fleshy.

Garden and Landscape Uses and Cultivation. In California, Florida, and other warm-climate areas, capers may be grown outdoors. In colder regions, they are sometimes cultivated in greenhouses, but not commonly. They grow without difficulty in any well-drained soil in sun. Propagation is by seeds or by cuttings made of firm, short shoots. In greenhouses a minimum temperature of 55°F is satisfactory.

CAPRIFIG and CAPRIFICATION. See Fig.

CAPRIFOLIACEAE — Honeysuckle Family. Many handsome ornamentals belong in this family of fourteen genera of dicotyledons. The group consists of deciduous and evergreen shrubs, small trees, more or less woody vines, and a few herbaceous plants. It is native principally in the north temperate zone, a few sorts in warmer regions. There are nearly 500 species.

Opposite, undivided or rarely pinnate leaves occur in this family. The symmetrical to markedly asymmetrical and often two-lipped flowers are usually in sometimes raceme-like clusters. They have a five- or four-toothed calyx, a five- or four-lobed, tubular to wheel-shaped corolla, five or four stamens, one style or none, and one to five stigmas. The fruits are firm-fleshed or juicy berries or drupes or achenes or capsules. Cultivated genera include *Abelia, Alseuosmia, Diervilla, Dipelta, Kolkwitzia, Leycesteria, Linnaea, Lonicera, Sambucus, Symphoricarpos, Triosteum, Viburnum,* and *Weigela*.

CAPSICUM (Cápsi-cum) — Pepper, Red Pepper. The fifty species of *Capsicum* of the nightshade family SOLANACEAE are all natives of warm parts of the Americas. Most familiar of the genus are the sweet peppers of the vegetable garden and kitchen, widely used raw in salads, and cooked stuffed with meat and in other ways. Products of other kinds of capsicums are paprika, cayenne pepper, and chili powder. Small-fruited varieties called Christmas peppers are popular as florists' and home greenhouse pot plants. Although commonly known as peppers and red peppers, capsicums are not related to *Piper nigrum*, the source of the familar white and black peppers used as table condiments. The name *Capsicum* comes from the Greek *kapto*, to bite, in allusion to the hot, biting taste of the fruits. Columbus introduced capsicums to Europe. As early as 1493 Peter Martyr recorded that the discoverer of America had found that the natives there esteemed certain plants more pungent than the pepper of the Caucasus. In those days of tremendous interest in and need for spices, this was a noteworthy discovery. But the history of capsicums goes back much further. For hundreds or probably thousands of years they had been cultivated in South America.

Capsicums, although commonly grown as annuals, are woody subshrubs and shrubs related to *Solanum*. Typically they branch freely. Their alternate, undivided, toothless, hairless or pubescent leaves range from narrow-lanceolate to elliptic, and broad-ovate. The white, greenish, or purple-tinged flowers, upturned or down-facing, are solitary or in twos or threes. They have very brief, usually five-pointed, calyxes, wheel-shaped, generally five-lobed corollas, commonly five, often bluish stamens, and a style tipped with a headlike stigma. The fruits, technically berries, are podlike and many-seeded. They vary greatly in size, shape, and color according to species and variety. Mostly they are very pungent.

The botany of the many varieties of cultivated capsicums has been variously interpreted. Some authorities have grouped all together as manifestations of the single species *C. frutescens*, but a more discerning point of view that recognizes among them derivatives of five species, of which *C. frutescens* is one, seems to find more acceptance. A hard-wooded shrub 6 to 8 feet tall, *C. frutescens* has usually pointed leaves variable shapes and sizes. The flowers, sometimes solitary, but more frequently in pairs or several from each node, are from ⅜ to ½ inch wide or wider, and greenish-white or yellowish-white. The fruits are very varied. Some of the tiny-fruited bird peppers, naturalized in the southern United States and many warm regions, belong in *C. frutescens*. The only variety cultivated extensively in the United States is 'Tabasco', a small-fruited kind employed in the preparation of Tabasco sauce. Differing from *C. frutescens* in its shorter, thicker flower stalks, its blooms three to five at a node, and in other details, *C. sinense* is provisionally recognized as distinct, although further study may reveal it to be only a variant of *C. frutescens*. The most important species horticulturally and agriculturally is *C. annuum.* To it belong, with the exception of 'Tabasco' referred to above, virtually all the better-known varieties of peppers grown in temperate regions. Its importance is largely based on its ability to crop when grown as an annual in regions of short growing seasons, and upon its including both pungent (hot)- and sweet (mild)-fruited varieties. The distinguishing characteristics that separate *C. annuum* from *C. frutescens* are that the flowers of the former are clear white to dingy-white, and are usually solitary, occasionally in twos. Very variable in growth and

Capsicum annuum

Capsicum annuum small-fruited variety

foliage, varieties of *C. annuum* differ in their fruits more than those of any other species of *Capsicum*. According to variety, the fruits are from less than ½ inch to 1 foot long. They may be globular, ovoid, conical, oblongish, or slender and tapered and red, yellow, or brown when ripe.

White flowers, with greenish-yellow or tan markings dissected by a network of veins in their throats, distinguish the cultivated varieties of *C. baccatum*, identified as *C. b. pendulum*, from *C. frutescens* and *C. annuum*, which they otherwise much resemble. The varieties of this species fruit early and are popular in South America. They are little known in North America, but at least one is grown in Hawaii. The fruits, depending upon variety, are of diverse shapes and sizes. When ripe they are orange-yellow to red.

Most distinctive of the species of cultivated peppers, *C. pubescens* differs from the others in having flowers with purple corolla lobes (petals) and fruits with nearly black instead of light-colored seeds. Also, its leaves are wrinkled and hairy. From mild to strongly pungent, the fruits at maturity, orange, brown, or red, are of various shapes and sizes. This species, which needs a long growing season, is little known in North America.

Garden Uses and Cultivation. For these consult Peppers.

CAPSULE. A capsule is a dry fruit containing more than one cell or compartment that usually opens when ripe to permit the escape of the seeds. In effect it is a compound pod.

CAPULIN. See Muntingia.

CARAGANA (Cara-gàna)—Pea-Tree, Pea-Shrub. To the pea family LEGUMINOSAE belongs this temperate Asian genus of some eighty species of deciduous shrubs, or more rarely small trees. The cultivated kinds are valued especially for their extreme hardiness and displays of yellow flowers. The name is derived from a Mongolian one.

Caraganas are spiny or spineless, with the spines in cultivated plants often represented by bristles. The leaves are alternate and pinnate. They have an even number of small leaflets and usually a spinelike end to the midrib. In some species the leafstalk remains after the leaflets fall, hardens, and becomes a spine that persists for years. Pea-like and commonly yellow, the flowers are clustered or solitary. They come in spring or early summer. The erect standard or banner petal curls back at the sides to form claws. There are nine stamens joined and one separate. The fruits are straight, short, cylindrical, slender pods.

The Siberian pea-tree (*Caragana arborescens*) is erect, usually narrowly so, and up to 20 feet tall. Native to Siberia and Manchuria, and hardy well north in Canada, it has leaves 1½ to 3 inches long with four to six pairs of bright green, obovate to elliptic leaflets ½ to ¾ inch in length. Like the shoots they are hairy when young. Almost or quite ¾ inch long, the yellow flowers, on stalks up to 1½ inches long, are in groups of up to four or sometimes solitary. Especially graceful, *C. a. lorbergii* has ferny leaves with very narrow leaflets ½ to 1 inch long and narrower, less showy flowers than those of the typical species.

Caragana arborescens lorbergii

In *C. a. pendula* the stiff, but not graceless branches grow downward. Contorted branches are characteristic of the dwarf *C. a. nana*.

Somewhat similar to *C. arborescens* and nearly, but not quite as hardy, **C. microphylla,** of Siberia and northern China, is 6 to 10 feet tall and has spreading branches. Its leaves, each ending in a small spine, are 1½ to 3 inches long and have six to nine pairs of elliptic to obovate leaflets much smaller than those of *C. arborescens*. The flowers are solitary or sometimes paired, yellow, and about ¾ inch in length. A hybrid between *C. arborescens* and *C. microphylla* named **C. sophoraefolia,** and intermediate between its parents, has leaves with usually six pairs of leaflets.

Caragana sophoraefolia

Not hardy in climates more severe than that of southern New England, **C. decorticans** is a shrub or small tree of Afghanistan that has leaves with three to six pairs of elliptic to obovate leaflets ¼ to ½ inch long. The blooms are yellow.

One of the better pea-shrubs, **C. maximowicziana** is hardy well north in Canada. Densely-branched, wide-spreading, and 3 to 4½ feet tall, it has short-stalked yellow flowers ¾ to 1 inch long. Its leaves have two or three pairs of oblong-lanceolate, bright green leaflets under ½ inch long. As hardy as the last, **C. spinosa** differs in having both pinnate leaves of two or four pairs of oblong-obovate to linear-lanceolate leaflets and leaves on the same branch, with leaflets spreading almost in hand-fashion, and in the spiny ends of their midribs being much longer, from ¾ inch to more than 2 inches. This species may be low or up to 6 feet in height. Its usually solitary, short-stalked flowers are yellow and ¾ to 1 inch long. In *C. s. foliosa* the leaflets are longer and more crowded.

Leaves with one or two pairs of leaflets only are characteristic of several species of pea-shrubs, including *C. sinica* (syn. *C. chamlagu*), *C. frutex*, *C. pygmaea*, and *C. aurantiaca*. The first two are hardy well north in Canada, the next is slightly less hardy, and the last persists as far north as southern New England. From the other three, northern Chinese *C. sinica* differs in its unequal-sized pairs of leaflets being widely spaced. The leaflets are obovate to more or less wedge-shaped, and ½ inch to 1½ inches long. Much-branched and 4 or 5 feet in height, it has slender, angled shoots, and dark green, lustrous foliage. The solitary, reddish-yellow flowers are 1 inch long or a little longer. When bruised the bark of this kind has a licorice-like odor. About 9 feet in height and upright, **C. frutex** (syn. *C. frutescens*), which in the wild ranges from southern Russia to Siberia, has slender branches and leaves with obovate to oblong-obovate, dull green leaflets ¾ to 1 inch long. Solitary, in twos or threes, on stalks about equaling their own lengths, the yellow flowers are ¾ to 1 inch long.

Caragana frutex

Very like each other and the prettiest of the pea-shrubs, *C. pygmaea* and *C. aurantiaca*, both of northern Asia, are up to 3 feet tall. These are erect, with gracefully-arching, slender, few-branched branches, or sometimes are prostrate. The leaves are nearly stalkless and have linear-oblanceolate leaflets from ⅓ to slightly over ½ inch long. Solitary and abundant, the short-stalked flowers are ¾ to 1 inch long, those of *C. pygmaea* yellow, those of *C. aurantiaca* orange-yellow. They hang for long distances along the undersides of the branches.

Garden and Landscape Uses. In the main caraganas make no special appeal where more ornamental shrubs can be grown, but the hardier kinds are very useful and acceptable in regions of cold winters, and where summers are hot and dry. The Siberian pea-tree, especially, is valuable as a windbreak and screen, and other kinds serve these purposes too. Because of its finely-cut foliage *C. arborescens lorbergii* is one of the most decorative, and *C. a. pendula*, with its weeping habit, one of the most distinctive. The latter is usually grafted high on understocks of *C. arborescens* so that its rigid, downsweeping branches are displayed effectively. The most attractive kinds in bloom are *C. aurantiaca*, *C. pygmaea*, and *C. maximowicziana*. All do best in poorish, well-drained soil in full sun.

Cultivation. Caraganas do not transplant readily when old and well established, therefore they should be planted in permanent locations as young, comparatively small specimens. Any pruning needed to improve their shapes or contain them to size is done as soon as flowering is through. No other care is ordinarily needed. New plants of the species can be raised from seeds (it is advisable to steep them in water at about 190°F for a few hours before sowing), or, like the horticultural varieties must be, by propagating them vegetatively by cuttings taken in summer and planted under mist, or in a greenhouse or cold frame propagating bed, preferably with a little bottom heat, or by grafting in spring in a greenhouse onto seedling understocks of *C. arborescens*.

CARALLUMA (Caral-lùma). More than 100 species of *Stapelia* relatives, natives of dry areas from Africa to the Mediterranean region and Burma, constitute *Caralluma* of the milkweed family ASCLEPIADACEAE. The name is based on an unsupported belief that a people of India called one species car-allum.

Carallumas are low, seemingly leafless, perennial succulent herbaceous plants, to the nonbotanical viewer cactus-like in appearance. Their green or gray-green, sometimes mottled stems are erect or are prostrate below and upright at their ends. Essentially of the same thickness throughout, they are not round or nearly round, but in cross section are markedly four-, five-, or six-angled. The angles, more or less toothed, on young stems have minute, three-angled, scalelike leaves. These soon fall. The flowers, those of some species foul-smelling, are variously colored. Frequently they are beautiful, often quite astonishing in aspect. They develop from the bases, from along the grooves toward middles, or from the apexes of younger shoots. They are usually clustered, sometimes forming tight spheres. Rarely they are solitary. Bell- to wheel-shaped, they have a calyx of five sepals, a corolla with five lobes (petals) not joined at their tips, and a bell-shaped, tubular or less commonly flat basal portion. The corona or crown in the center of the bloom is of two parts, usually distinct, but in some kinds the outer and inner corona are combined and appear to be one. The coronas are lobed. The stalks of the stamens are joined to form a tube around the style. The fruits are paired, podlike follicles.

The only carallumas native to Europe are the typical form of *C. europaea*, endemic to the islands of Lampedusa and Linosa in the Mediterranean Sea, *C. e. confusa*, which occurs in Spain, and *C. munbyana hispanica*, a Spanish variety of a North African species. Varieties of *C. europaea* occur in coastal North Africa. The finger-thick, small-toothed, four-angled stems of *C. europaea* are gray-green. The almost odorless, nearly ¾-inch-wide, wheel-shaped, fleshy flowers are in stalkless clusters of about twelve near the tips of the stems. They are pale greenish-yellow mottled and banded with dull purple. The corona bears ten small yellow knobs. Spanish *C. e. confusa* has a less deeply-lobed corolla and is without yellow knobs on the outer corona. North African varieties *C. e. affinis*, *C. e. simonis*, *C. e. maroccana*, and others differ in minor details.

North African *C. munbyana* has soft, fresh green, four-angled, wavy-toothed stems ½ inch or so thick and 2 to 6 inches tall. Produced from near the stem apexes in groups of up to ten, the unpleasantly-scented, short-tubed deeply-lobed, hairless flowers have velvety, brown petals less than ⅓ inch long that do not spread widely and have strongly recurved margins. Spanish *C. m. hispanica* has more slender stems and flowers, with proportionately longer petals. Native of Morocco, where it inhabits limestone mountains, *C. hesperidum* has grayish to greenish-white, often purplish-mottled stems 3 to 4½ inches long with sharp-pointed, conical teeth about ¾ inch long. Practically stalkless, the star-shaped, ½-inch-wide flowers, in clusters of two to ten from more or less the upper parts of the stem, are very dark chocolate-brown with a tiny, cream center.

Caralluma hesperidum

The Canary Islands has one native species, *C. burchardii*. Similar to *C. europaea*, and its irregular stems resembling exaggerated ones of that species, the islander differs in the ten-toothed outer coronas of its flowers being bowl-like instead of divided into little pouches and in the face of the bloom being so densely clothed with white hairs that its surface is not visible.

Caralluma burchardii

Variety *C. b. maura*, which differs from the typical species in its flowers being smaller, more bell-shaped, and stalked instead of stalkless, is endemic to Morocco. Another native of Morocco, 4-inch-tall *C. joannis* has trailing, branched stems sometimes 3 feet in length. The shoots, green and about ½ inch thick, have four rounded, small-toothed angles. In stalkless clusters of two to ten, the blooms have red-spotted, yellow centers and velvety, purple petals ¼ inch long or slightly longer with a few margin hairs near their apexes.

Several southern African species are cultivated. Its stems erect, up to about 4 inches tall, and with four rounded, toothed angles, *C. caudata* is variable. Several varieties are recognized. One, *C. c. fusca* has uniformly purple blooms. The stalked flowers come in clusters of several from the bases of the shoots. Shaped like starfish, they are nearly 4 inches in diameter, have five long, spreading, tapering, lanceolate petals, canary-yellow with pink or purple spots, and margined sparingly with red hairs. Canary-yellow-flowered *C. lutea* extends from South Africa into adjacent parts of Africa. This kind has subterranean and above-ground stems, the latter crowded, 1½ to 4 inches long, ½ to ¾ inch thick, sharply four-angled and long-toothed. The beautiful starfish-shaped blooms, which unfortunately stink like stale fish, are 1½ to 2½ inches across. They are in clusters of three to about twenty-four from the middles or lower parts of the young shoots. The pointed, narrowly-lanceolate, spreading, long petals are fringed with delicate purple hairs. The plant previously identified as *C. vansonii*, which has blooms up to 4½ inches in diameter and less sturdy stems than typical *C. lutea*, is by some botanists included in that species.

Erect and bushy *C. mammillaris*, of South Africa, has stout, slightly glaucous-green, branched stems 6 inches to 1½ feet tall and ¾ inch to 1½ inches in diameter, with five or six conspicuous angles often irregularly spiraled around them. The angles are furnished with sharp-pointed, conical, brown-tipped spines ¼ to ½ inch long. The flowers, in clusters of three to twenty from the ends of the branches or lateral, are rich velvety-purplish-black inside, pale green outside. The long, pointed, more or less erect rather than spreading petals have rolled-back margins, which account for their slender appearance. In contrast to the last, the 2-inch-wide, nearly flat flowers of South African *C. melanantha* have broad, comparatively short, pointed petals fringed with fine hairs. Typically deep purple-black, but varying somewhat in color, with concentric wrinkles toward their centers, and usually covered with short hairs, they are in clusters of three to five from the middles of the shoots. Forming clumps 3 to 4 inches high, the stems, ¾ to 1 inch thick, have four angles with spreading, pointed teeth. Variety *C. m. sousae* of Portuguese East Africa differs in having more slender petals and in details of the corona. Handsome-flowered *C. nebrownii*, of tropical Southwest Africa, forms tufts of gray or gray-green marbled with dull red, wavy-toothed, four-angled stems up to 7 inches long by about ¾ inch thick. Very evil-scented, the nearly flat, starry flowers, in clusters of fifteen to thirty, are 3½ to 4 inches across. Uniformly blackish-brown, they have spreading, triangular to ovate-lanceolate petals with slightly recurved margins, sparingly fringed with slender, purple hairs. Variety *C. n. pseudonebrownii*, with small clusters of flowers irregularly marked with yellow, comes from less tropical areas to the south of the range of *C. nebrownii*. Much-branched and bushy, South African *C. ramosa*, up to 1 foot tall, has erect, slightly round-toothed, four-angled, slightly glaucous, gray-green stems shaded with dull purple, ½ to 1 inch or a little more in diameter. The blackish-purple flowers, in small clusters from the grooves between the stem angles near the stem ends, are about ½ inch wide.

Garden Uses and Cultivation. These interesting, easy-to-grow succulents make the same appeals and require the same conditions and care as stapelias. They lend themselves to growing in pans (shallow pots) better than in normally deep pots. They are interesting window plants. For further information see Succulents.

CARAMBOLA is *Averrhoa carambola*.

CARAWAY is *Carum carvi*.

CARBON DISULFIDE. Sometimes used by qualified operators as a soil fumigant, carbon disulfide or carbon bisulfide, as it is sometimes called, is too dangerous for use by amateurs. A heavy liquid, on exposure to the atmosphere it quickly evaporates into a poisonous, highly explosive gas, heavier than air and injurious to living plants.

CARDAMINE (Cardámin-e)—Bitter-Cress, Lady's Smock or Cuckoo Flower. The name *Cardamine*, pronounced in four syllables, belongs to a group of about 160 species of the mustard family CRUCIFERAE, widespread in temperate regions. Most kinds are too weedy in appearance to be considered for gardens. The name comes from the ancient Greek *kardamon*, applied to some plants of the family and probably derived from *kardia*, the heart, and *damao*, I overpower, in allusion to the plants' once supposed ability to deaden pain.

Bitter-cresses are annual, biennial, and hardy, hairy or hairless perennial herbaceous plants, sometimes with rhizomes, and with undivided leaves, lobed or not, or dissected pinnately into separate leaflets. The small to medium-sized flowers have four sepals. Rarely they are without petals, more commonly there are four that spread to form a cross. Mostly they have six slender-stalked stamens, two, shorter than the others, associated with semicircular glands. Unusual for the mustard family, some species have fewer than six stamens. The fruits are slender, cylindrical or four-angled pods with many flattened, wingless seeds that when ripe are discharged explosively.

The lady's smock or cuckoo flower (**C. pratensis**) is widely distributed as a native in northern parts of North America, Europe, and Asia. It is an erect, hairless perennial, without rhizomes, and 9 inches to 1½ feet tall. Its long-stalked basal leaves and sometimes the lowest stem ones, have up to eight broad-ovate to rounded leaflets, with the terminal one, up to ¾ inch long, bigger than the others and angularly-toothed. Most of the stem leaves are shorter-stalked and have much narrower, usually linear, leaflets. The slender-stalked flowers, pale lilac or light pink, and from a little over ½ to 1 inch across, are in crowded racemes that lengthen as the seed pods develop. They have obovate petals, six stamens with yellow anthers, and a pistil with a two-lobed stigma. They are succeeded by almost erect seed pods 1 inch to 1¾ inches long. The lady's smock develops buds in the axils of its basal leaves that are capable of growing into new plants. Variety *C. p. palustris*, which occurs in bogs and swamps from New Jersey, to Ohio, Minnesota, and throughout Canada, has white flowers. The terminal leaflets of the basal leaves are not lobed, and the leaflets of the stem leaves are often much contracted. Most beautiful, *C. p. flore-pleno* is profuse with racemes of bloom that suggest those of slender, graceful, small stocks.

Long-stalked basal leaves with three rounded, shallowly-toothed leaflets, purplish on their undersides and ½ to 1 inch wide, distinguish **C. trifolia**, a 6-inch-tall native of central and southern Europe. It has no stem leaves, or quite small ones of three or only one leaflet. The pink or white flowers, with yellow anthers, are about ¾ inch across. This species has creeping, knobby rhizomes.

Garden Uses. The single-flowered lady's smock has mild merit as a garden plant. It is suitable for herb gardens, wild gardens, rock gardens, and other informal areas where the soil is moist and it receives full or part-day sun. The double-flowered variety, which comes true from seed, is choicer and quite lovely. It has the same uses. Dwarfer *C. trifolia* is best accommodated in dampish soil in rock gardens.

Cultivation. Cardamines are very easily raised from seeds and by division. The lady's smock can also be grown from leaf cuttings. The buds that form naturally at the bases of the leaves of the lady's smock also afford means of increase. These plants are hardy and need no special attention.

CARDAMON is *Elettaria cardamomum*.

CARDIANDRA (Cardián-dra). Eastern Asia is home to the five species of *Cardiandra*, a genus of herbaceous, sometimes subshrubby perennials of the saxifrage family SAXIFRAGACEAE, named from the Greek *kardia*, a heart, and *andros*, male, in allusion to the shape of the stamens. From *Deinanthe* the genus differs in its leaves being alternate, or rarely nearly opposite and its flowers having more than one style. It is related to *Hydrangea*, but the latter consists of shrubs and woody vines with opposite leaves.

Cardiandras are sparsely-hairy and have undivided, toothed, lanceolate to oblong leaves, and terminal clusters of two types of blooms. The more numerous are small and bisexual, but there are a few larger, marginal, sterile flowers with three, often colored, decidedly showy, petal-like calyx lobes (sepals). The calyxes of the fertile flowers are four- or five-toothed. There are five small petals, many stamens, and three styles. The fruits are many-seeded capsules.

Native of mountain woods in Japan, and the only species that occurs there, **C. alternifolia** has usually branchless stems, 8 inches to 2½ feet tall, and coarsely-toothed, elliptic leaves, 4 to 8 inches long and 1 inch to 2½ inches wide. The flowers, in loose clusters, are white, pink, or blue and borne in summer.

Garden Uses and Cultivation. Not hardy in the north, in milder climates this species is adapted for flower borders, rock gardens, and similar places. It needs light shade and shelter from strong winds. A peaty, moist soil that drains well is most

to its liking. Propagation is by summer cuttings and seeds.

CARDINAL. As part of their common names this word appears in cardinal climber (*Ipomoea sloteri*), cardinal flower (*Lobelia cardinalis*), cardinal sage (*Salvia fulgens*), and cardinal's guard (*Pachystachys coccinea*).

CARDIOCRINUM (Cardio-crìnum). Formerly included with the true lilies in *Lilium*, this genus of three Asian species is now segregated as a separate entity of the lily family LILIACEAE. The name, alluding to the shape of the leaves, is from the Greek *kardia*, a heart, and *krinon*, a kind of lily.

Cardiocrinums have large bulbs, with scales that overlap like shingles on a roof. Their long-stalked leaves, unlike those of lilies, are broadly-heart-shaped and net-veined. When the bulbs have attained sufficient size and strength, usually when they are three or four years old from offsets, each produces a stout, erect, rigid flowering stem. After blooming is finished the bulb that flowered dies, but offsets generally develop. The fruits are capsules.

Most magnificent is Himalayan **Cardiocrinum giganteum** (syn. *Lilium giganteum*). From 6 to 10 feet in height, this has leaves that, except for those uppermost on the flowering stems, have channeled stalks about 1 foot long. Their blades are broadly-heart-shaped, and up to 1 foot to 1½ feet in length. Those of the flowering stems gradually diminish in size upward. White slightly tinged with green, and purple at the bottoms of their throats, the trumpet-shaped blooms, which may be 6 inches long or longer, are in terminal racemes of up to twenty. They come in summer. Variety *C. g. yunnanense* is lower and has foliage that at first is reddish-brown.

The other two species are *C. cathayanum* (syn. *Lilium cathayanum*) of central China and *C. cordatum* (syn. *Lilium cordatum*) of Japan. Generally similar to *C. giganteum*, but much less impressive, **C. cathayanum** is 1 foot to 4½ feet tall, and normally has one to three narrowly-funnel-shaped flowers, greenish-white on their outsides and creamy within. The Japanese species **C. cordatum**, like *C. giganteum*, has white blooms with purple on their insides. There are up to twenty on a stem. Its stem leaves are mostly in a single crowded whorl (circle) midway up the stems, which are 4 to 6 feet tall. This is less handsome and less hardy than *C. giganteum*.

Garden and Landscape Uses. Impressive *C. giganteum* has been grown and has flowered in eastern North America including New England. It is, however, capricious and is to be recommended only to skilled gardeners willing to pamper it and to experiment. In the Pacific Northwest, where summers are relatively cool and humid, and winters not excessively cold, cardiocrinums can be planted with greater expectation of success. They need light, nutritious soil that contains an abundance of leaf mold or similar decayed organic material and affords a deep root-run. Well-rotted manure mixed into the soil a few inches beneath the bulbs is helpful. A location in the dappled shade of deep-rooted trees, and where nearby shrubs such as rhododendrons provide shelter from winds, is likely to prove most favorable.

Cultivation. Planting is done in early spring. The bulbs are set with their tips at ground level. The maintenance of a mulch of leaf mold, rich compost, or peat moss about the plants helps by keeping the soil in the uniformly moist, but not wet, and cool condition most favorable to these plants. A spring application of a fertilizer of a kind prepared for bulbs is beneficial. Propagation is by seeds, handled in the same way as those of lilies, and by offsets.

CARDIOSPERMUM (Cardiospérm-um) — Heart Seed, Balloon Vine. Only two of the fourteen members of tropical and subtropical *Cardiospermum* are in general cultivation. The genus is a member of the soapberry family SAPINDACEAE. Its name is from the Greek *kardia*, heart, and *sperma*, a seed. It refers to the heart-shaped white spot that marks each black seed.

Heart seeds are vigorous, extensively-branching, tendril-climbing vines with grooved stems and alternate, biternate (twice three-lobed), coarsely-toothed leaves. The flowers are white and in axillary clusters, each of which has two opposite tendrils. Individual plants may have blooms all of one sex or both unisexual and bisexual flowers. The flowers have four sepals and four petals of unequal size, eight stamens, and a three-branched style. The fruits are membranous, inflated capsules.

Balloon vine (*C. halicacabum*) attains a height of 10 or 12 feet. It is commonly cultivated as an annual, although it may be biennial and sometimes perhaps a short-lived perennial. Native of tropical and subtropical regions around the world, it is naturalized in the southern United States. The balloon vine has hairless stems and leaves, the latter pointed-ovate or pointed-oblong and up to 4 inches long. Its flowers are 1¼ inches across. The fruits are three-angled capsules only slightly longer than broad. They are pubescent and about 1 inch across. A perennial, the evergreen heart seed (*C. grandiflorum hirsutum*) differs in having densely-hairy stems, usually downy undersides to its less sharply-pointed and longer-stalked leaves, and pointed capsules much longer than broad. They are 1½ to 2 inches long and hairy. The evergreen heart seed climbs to a height of 30 feet or more.

Garden and Landscape Uses. As an annual the balloon vine can be grown outdoors in summer in most regions where gardens are cultivated, but the evergreen heart seed is adaptable only for regions of mild winters such as southern California. They succeed in any ordinary garden soil in full sun and are suitable for covering fences, pergolas, arbors, trellises, porch screens, and other supports where a rapid-growing mantle of light, ferny foliage is advantageous.

Cultivation. These vines are easily raised from seeds, which take about three weeks to germinate in a temperature of 65 to 70°F. In the north they are usually sown indoors about two months before the young plants are to be planted outside and are grown until planting time in small pots in fertile porous soil, but they may be sown directly outdoors and this is the usual practice in mild climates where the growing season is long. The evergreen heart seed is also raised from cuttings usually taken in spring. For rapid coverage the plants may be spaced 1 foot to 2 feet apart. In dry weather copious watering at weekly intervals is highly beneficial.

CARDON is *Pachycereus pringlei*.

CARDOON. One of the lesser known vegetables, the cardoon requires a long season of growth and, as it is not winter-hardy in the north, it is best adapted for cultivation in the south and west. Botanically *Cynara cardunculus* and a close relative of the artichoke, this is native of North Africa and western Asia.

Cardoon

Cardoons are esteemed for their edible, blanched, thickened leafstalks rather than, as are artichokes, for their unopened flower buds. The leafstalks are spiny in the French variety, which is considered superior to the nonspiny Spanish kind. They are prepared by boiling or occasionally are eaten raw.

In mild climates sow seeds outdoors in early spring in hills (not raised above ground level) 2 to 3 feet apart in rows of 3 feet. Set three or four seeds in each hill and thin the seedlings until only the strongest one remains. Alternatively, sow in 4-inch pots in March in a greenhouse or hotbed where the temperature is 50 to 55°F and thin the seedlings to one in each pot.

Before planting indoor-raised plants in the garden, which may be done at tomato-planting time, harden them by standing them in a cold frame or sheltered place outdoors for about a week. Soil for cardoons must be deep, fertile, and well prepared.

Care through the summer consists of doing everything possible to promote healthy growth. To this end, keep down weeds, water deeply in dry weather, and fertilize regularly. In exposed locations secure staking of each plant may be necessary.

Blanching begins in fall and requires six to eight weeks. It is best achieved by drawing the leaves together, tying their tops to form a celery-like bunch, and wrapping this in heavy, lightproof paper, securely tied, or by slipping a cardboard cylinder over the plant so that all except the tops of the leaves are protected from light. The older method of hilling soil to exclude light involves a great deal of work and is likely to encourage rotting. In the north cardoons may be dug in fall with considerable root balls and replanted in a dark, cool cellar or other frostproof place to complete the blanching.

CARDUNCELLUS (Cardún-cellus). Comprising twenty species of the daisy family COMPOSITAE, the mostly Mediterranean region genus *Carduncellus* has a name that is diminutive of *Carduus*, a genus of thistles. It alludes to the appearance of the plants.

Herbaceous perennials, *Carduncellus* species have alternate, lobed or spine-toothed, more or less thistle-like leaves and heads of usually blue, tubular florets. The involucres (collars of bracts at the backs of the heads of bloom) are of several rows of overlapping bracts. The fruits are seedlike achenes.

Native of North Africa and Sicily, *C. pinnatus* is hardy at New York City. It is stem-

Carduncellus pinnatus

less or has an extremely short stem so that it looks much like the stemless form of *Carlina acaulis*. Its rosettes are of wide-spreading, narrow-ovate-elliptic, pinnately-lobed or pinnately-divided, spine-toothed leaves 3 to 5 inches long. The flower heads may be as big as a hen's egg and 1½ to 2½ inches wide. Their petals are light blue. Curious and quite beautiful *C. rhaponticoides* of the Atlas Mountains in Algeria forms a flat rosette 6 to 7 inches across of coarsely-toothed, spatula-shaped leaves with dull reddish-purple stalks and midribs. At the center a stalkless, tight rounded head of lavender flowers develops.

Carduncellus rhaponticoides

Garden Uses and Cultivation. The first sort described is an unusual, attractive plant for sunny locations in rock gardens. It thrives in poorish, well-drained, gritty or stony soil and is propagated by seeds or division. A specimen persisted in the Thompson Memorial Rock Garden at The New York Botanical Garden for more than thirty-five years. The second sort described may be expected to respond to similar conditions.

CARDUUS (Cárdu-us)—Plumeless Thistle. Although sometimes suggested for use as garden plants, few if any of this group of more than 100 species of the daisy family COMPOSITAE are worthy of cultivation. At most the more showy kinds might be naturalized or grouped in informal landscapes. They are hardy, annual, biennial, and perennial, spiny herbaceous plants, natives of Europe, Asia, North Africa, and the Canary Islands, and naturalized in North America and many other parts of the world. The name is the ancient Latin one for thistles.

Plumeless-thistles (*Carduus*) differ from plumed thistles (*Cirsium*) in that the hairs (the pappus) that accompany the ovaries and seed-like fruits are not plumose (feathery). Among the kinds that have been suggested of possible interest to gardeners are

C. kerneri, of Europe, a much-branched biennial or perennial 2 to 3 feet tall, with solitary or paired, rose-purple flower heads 2½ inches wide, and *C. pycnocephalus,* of the Mediterranean region, a hoary annual up to 4 feet in height, with deeply-lobed leaves, and rose-purple flower heads.

Plumeless thistles thrive in ordinary soils in full sun, and are easily raised from seeds.

CAREX (Càr-ex)—Sedge. Possibly two thousand species of chiefly grasslike herbaceous perennials of the sedge family CYPERACEAE constitute the genus *Carex*. Called sedges, they are widely distributed throughout the world and are especially abundant in temperate and arctic regions. A few kinds inhabit tropical mountains. Most are natives of wet soils. The botany of the group is complicated, and species are often difficult to identify except by specialists. The name *Carex* comes from the Greek *keiro*, to cut. The allusion is to the minutely saw-toothed leaf edges, which in some kinds are sharp enough to cut a hand they are drawn swiftly across.

Sedges differ from grasses in having solid triangular stems (those of grasses are round and hollow), leaves in three ranks instead of two, with their lower parts forming sheaths that completely surround the stems instead of being slit down one side as are the leaf sheaths of grasses. The flowers of sedges are very different from those of grasses. Small, green, and unisexual, they occur commonly in dense heads or spikes that arise from the axils of leaves or bracts. They are without sepals or petals. The males have three stamens, the females a solitary pistil, with two or three styles. Generally the same plant bears both sexes either in separate spikes or with male and female flowers segregated in different parts of the same spike. From related *Cyperus* and *Scirpus* sedges differ in having the pistil enclosed in a sac. From *Carex* closely-related *Cymophyllus fraseri* (syn. *Carex fraseri*) differs in having leaves without a definite midrib and in technical details.

A few sedges are cultivated for ornament; the vast majority are of no horticultural importance. Native to New Zealand, *C. comans* (syn. *C. vilmorinii*) forms dense tufts of very slender, pale green or reddish leaves 1 foot to 1½ feet long. Its male flowers are in narrow, solitary or paired, short-stalked or stalkless, terminal spikelets, its females in lateral spikelets in clusters of three to seven. The spikelets are about 1 inch long. First collected by Dr. James Morrow, who accompanied Commodore Perry's expedition to Japan and China, and named in his honor, *C. morrowii,* often called in gardens *C. japonica,* is an attractive evergreen. It forms tufts of stiff, bright green, long-pointed, flat leaves about 1 foot long, and has flower spikes ½ inch to 1½ inches long, the males terminal, the

females in clusters of two to four. Variety *C. m. variegata*, in which the leaves have a white line paralleling each margin, is the kind usually grown. From 2 to 5 feet tall, quite handsome *C. pendula,* a native of damp soils in shaded locations in Europe, North Africa, and western Asia, has upper leaves with yellowish-green blades shorter than the stems, ½ to ¾ inch wide, more or less keeled, and glaucous on their undersides. The upper spikes, 2½ to 4 inches long, are of male flowers, the female flowers are in widely-spaced pendulous spikes 2¾ to 6 inches long. Vigorous *C. riparia,* of Europe, is a waterside species 3 to 4 feet tall, with glaucous, sharply-keeled leaves ¼ to ¾ inch wide. Attractive, much less robust *C. r. aurea* has golden-yellow leaves with only small stripes of green. The

Carex riparia aurea

leaves of 2- to 3-foot-tall *C. r. variegata* are green striped with white.

Carex riparia variegata

Native American sedges are occasionally planted to ornament watersides and other moist-soil places. They are so numerous, and many are so similar, that it is quite impracticable and would be other than helpful to describe them in detail here. Interested persons should refer to books dedicated to describing local floras. Among kinds likely to attract the attention of gardeners are **C. crinita,** which occurs in wet woods throughout eastern North America, has leaves up to ½ inch wide and several feet long and drooping flower spikes and attains a height of 2 to 5 feet, and **C. plantaginea,** another hardly woodland species, 1 foot to 2 feet in height, that inhabits eastern North America to as far south as North Carolina, Georgia, and Kentucky. The last named has leaves up to 1 inch wide and 1 foot long or longer, and erect flower spikes.

Garden and Landscape Uses and Cultivation. The evergreen *C. morrowii* and *C. comans* are sometimes grown as pot plants in greenhouses and as border or edging plants in conservatories. In climates with moderate winters they may be used for the latter purposes outdoors. They stand some shade and grow well in any fertile, decidedly moist soil. They are very readily increased by division, which is best done in early spring when new growth is just beginning. Hardy native American sedges grow without difficulty in wet soils in sun or light shade. They are propagated by seed or by division. The only care generally needed is any necessary to restrain their spread.

CARICA (Càr-ica)—Papaya or Pawpaw. Only one species of this genus of forty-five is much known horticulturally. It is the tropical papaya or pawpaw, which must not be confused with completely different *Asimina triloba,* a native tree of the United States, also known as pawpaw. The genus *Carica* belongs to the pawpaw family CARICACEAE. It members are all natives of the American tropics. The name comes from the Greek *karike,* a kind of fig with leaves that suggest those of the papaya.

Caricas are small, normally short-lived trees, with more or less succulent and herbaceous, usually branchless trunks. They contain milky, caustic sap and have alternate, long-stalked, undivided leaves deeply-lobed in palmate (handlike) fashion. Their flowers have small, tubular calyxes, five united or separate petals, ten or five stamens, and a stalkless stigma. Within the species various rather complicated arrangements of the floral parts may occur. The fruits, often very large, are melon-like or cucumber-like in shape. Technically they are berries.

The digestive enzyme papain is contained in the milky juice of the leaves and unripe fruits of the papaya. In the tropics meat is often wrapped in papaya leaves and left overnight to tenderize it. Papain prepared from papayas is used in commercial meat tenderizers and for clarifying beer, and medicinally.

The papaya or pawpaw (*C. papaya*) is exceptionally 35 feet, more usually not more than 25 feet, tall. Its trunk is light green, hollow, and generally without branches. Forming a terminal crown, the

Carica papaya

Carica papaya (flowers)

leaves have hollow stalks 2 feet long or longer, and nearly round blades up to 2 feet in diameter. They are deeply seven-lobed, with the lobes pinnately-lobed, and glaucous on their undersides. Individual trees are usually unisexual, but predominantly male specimens sometimes have a few female flowers. The blooms are fragrant and yellow, the stalkless, approximately 1-inch-long, funnel-shaped males, in slender panicles up to 3 feet long, have corollas with tubes twice as long as the lobes (petals). The females, solitary or in clusters of two or three, have shorter corolla tubes and five long, twisted petals up to 1 inch long. The hollow, pointed, melon-like fruits contain numerous shiny, black seeds the size of small peas and with a gelatinous coating. They weigh from one to twenty pounds or more, and have thick skins, yellow to orange when ripe, and sweet, bland, firm, yellow to orange flesh.

Less commonly cultivated are the following. A tree up to 20 feet high with three-lobed or lobeless leaves that in shape suggest those of an oak, *C. quercifolia* has small, hardly edible, golden-yellow fruits. The mountain papaya (*C. pubescens*) is a stout-trunked tree with round-bladed leaves over 1 foot in diameter, deeply cut into five

pinnately-cleft lobes. This has hardly edible, yellow, furrowed, white-fleshed fruits. The leaves of *C. goudotiana* are deeply lobed in palmate (handlike) fashion. This has pale yellow fruits tinged with magenta-red. These species respond to the same conditions and care as the papaya.

Garden and Landscape Uses and Cultivation. For these see Papaya.

CARICACEAE—Pawpaw Family. Fifty-five species of American and African, small, rarely-branched, soft-wooded trees distributed among four genera constitute this family of dicotyledons. Only one is well known, the papaya (*Carica papaya*).

The components of the family have milky sap and alternate, usually palmately-lobed, much less frequently lobeless, large, generally long-stalked leaves clustered as a crown at the apex of the trunk. The small, unisexual or bisexual flowers, one or both sexes on the same plant, are without decorative value. They are solitary or in racemes or clusters, have five-lobed calyxes and corollas, or the latter may be of five separate petals, five or ten stamens, and five fan-shaped to wedge-shaped styles set directly on the ovary or atop a short style. The fruits, including the large, melon-like ones of papaya, are technically berries. The only genus cultivated is *Carica*.

CARICATURE PLANT. See Graptophyllum.

CARISSA (Carís-sa)—Natal Plum, Hedge-Thorn, Karanda. As here presented this genus of the dogbane family APOCYNACEAE comprises about thirty-five species of the native floras of Africa, the warmer parts of Asia, and Australia. Other plants that some authorities include here are treated separately as *Acokanthera*. The name *Carissa* is aboriginal.

Carissas are warm-climate, much-branched, evergreen shrubs and small trees, with milky juice, opposite, leathery leaves, and white, pink, or purple flowers in terminal or apparently lateral clusters. The flowers have slender, cylindrical corolla tubes, five spreading petals that are twisted in bud and overlap each other to the left or right, and stamens joined to the upper part of the inside of the corolla tube. The fruits, technically berries, are ellipsoid or spherical. Those of the Natal-plum are made into a sauce similar in flavor to cranberry sauce. The fruits of *C. edulis* and *C. ovata* are used for jams and jellies and are eaten out of hand. Those of *C. carandas* are used similarly, and before they ripen are made into green pickles.

The Natal-plum (*C. grandiflora*), of South Africa, is a spreading shrub up to 18 feet in height armed with stout, two-pronged spines up to 1½ inches long. Its ovate leaves have tiny spurlike points at their apexes and are 1 inch to 3 inches long. The fragrant blooms about 2 inches in diameter

Carissa grandiflora (flowers)

Carissa grandiflora (fruits)

Carissa grandiflora nana (flowers)

Carissa grandiflora nana (fruits)

Carissa bisponosa

and with petals overlapping to the left and at least twice as long as the corolla tubes, are clustered at the ends of the shoots. Ovoid to elliptic, the scarlet fruits are 1 inch to 2 inches long, contain reddish pulp and eight to sometimes more than twice that number of seeds. Variety *C. g. horizontalis* is prostrate or semiprostrate and compact, *C. g. nana*, possibly identical with *C. g. minima* and *C. g. prostrata*, is low-growing, spineless, and has smaller leaves. Another spiny South African species, the hedge-thorn (*C. bispinosa* syn. *C. arduina*),

is about 10 feet tall. It differs from the Natal-plum in having its flowers about ½ inch wide with corolla tubes approximately twice as long as the petals. In bud petals twist to the right. The bright red fruits are from slightly less to slightly more than ½ inch long and contain one or two seeds.

The karanda (*C. carandas*), of India, is a large shrub or small tree up to 20 feet in height, with spines, often forked and 1 inch to 2 inches long, and blunt, broad-ovate to oblong or obovate leaves 1 inch to 3 inches long. The fragrant white or pale pink flowers, ¾ to 1 inch wide, have corolla tubes about ¾ inch long, about twice

the length of the petals. The blooms are in twos or threes. At first red, but black when ripe, the ellipsoid fruits, ½ to 1 inch long, contain four to six seeds. Closely related to the karanda and perhaps not specifically distinct is **C. spinarum.** It differs chiefly in its leaves, ½ to 1½ inches long, being acute or having a short, spurlike point rather than being blunt, and in its flowers being about ¼ inch wide and having corolla tubes about ½ inch long. It is a native of India and Ceylon.

Other sorts cultivated include *C. edulis* and *C. ovata*. A branched, straggling, usually spiny shrub of Egypt, **C. edulis** has ovate leaves up to 2 inches long, white to purple flowers ¾ inch long in terminal clusters, and purple to black fruits about ¼ inch in diameter. A native of Australia, *C. ovata* is about 4 feet tall, has ovate leaves about ¾ inch long and fruits about as long.

Garden and Landscape Uses. Hardy only in the warmest parts of the United States and elsewhere in the subtropics and tropics, carissas include sorts of great value as ornamentals as well as some more or less esteemed for their edible fruits. Among the former are the Natal-plum or matungula and its varieties. They can be employed to good effect as lawn specimens and in shrubberies and foundation plantings. A prime use for notably thorny kinds, such as *C. grandiflora, C. bispinosa,* and *C. carandas,* is as hedge plants. The Natal-plum and its varieties are also grown as pot plants in greenhouses and to some extent as houseplants.

Cultivation. These are sun-loving plants, but stand part-day shade. They thrive in any ordinary garden soil and may be pruned to any extent necessary to keep them shapely and to prevent them outgrowing allotted reasonable space. Pruning, however, is not needed on any regular basis unless they are being grown as formal sheared hedges. In greenhouses most prosper if afforded a minimum winter night temperature of 50 to 55°F rising a few degrees by day and warmer at other seasons, and a little shade from strong summer sun. They may be kept indoors or be stood outdoors in summer. Any fertile, porous potting soil suits them, and they may be accommodated in well-drained pots, tubs, or ground beds. When needed, repotting is done in spring and at that season any necessary pruning receives attention. The soil must always be reasonably moist and from spring to fall regular applications of dilute liquid fertilizer promote good growth. Propagation is usually by cuttings of firm shoots inserted in a greenhouse propagating bench, but seeds, sown in sandy peaty soil in a temperature of 60 to 70°F, also provide a ready means of increase.

Pests. Mealybugs and scale insects are the most common pests.

CARLINA (Car-lìna). Twenty species of thistle-like annuals, biennials, and herbaceous perennials comprise this European and temperate Asian genus of the daisy family COMPOSITAE. The name alludes to a belief that the army of Charlemagne (Carolinus) was cured of the plague by one of these. Their roots contain a purgative principle and were formerly employed medicinally.

Carlinas have spiny foliage, and flower heads of all disk florets similar to those that form the "eyes" of daisies. Ray florets, in daisies the petal-like ones, are absent, but the inner bracts of the involucre, papery, shining, and colored at their tips, spread outward from the disk and give the impression of being petals. The involucre is the collar of bracts that in plants of the daisy family is behind the florets and forms the base of the flower head. In *Carlina* the outer involucral bracts are green and leathery. The fruits are achenes.

Native of mountain pastures and stony places in southeastern Europe and adjacent Asia, *C. acanthifolia* is a hardy perennial 1 foot to 2 feet tall with spreading leaves, oblong in outline and, the upper ones particularly, deeply-pinnately-cut into spiny-toothed lobes. The leaves are velvety-white beneath and often also on their upper sides. The flat, stalkless, usually solitary flower heads, nestle at the centers of rosettes of foliage. They are 4½ to 5 inches across. Their inner bracts are lustrous pale yellow or whitish, the ones immediately behind are blackish and have spiny, comb-like teeth, the outermost are lanceolate and leafy. Another hardy perennial, *C. acaulis* is stemless or may have stems up to 1 foot in height. Its deeply-pinnately-lobed, spiny leaves have few or no hairs and are in large rosettes. The whitish to reddish flower heads, generally similar to those of *C. acanthifolia,* are 2 to 5 inches in diameter and have pale yellow or white inner involucral bracts that are sometimes pinkish or brownish at their bases. This species inhabits rocky places and poor pastures in the mountains of Europe. Its cut flower heads are used by country people as weather indicators. When the air is dry the bracts spread widely, when humid, they close.

Garden and Landscape Uses and Cultivation. The most appropriate locations for these plants are sunny rock gardens, dryish slopes, and similar places where their curious, pale, miniature, sunflower-like flower heads can be advantageously displayed. They grow with minimum trouble. The kinds described are reliably perennial. Any ordinary, well-drained soil is appropriate, those containing lime especially favorable. Seeds sown indoors or out in spring afford a ready means of propagation.

CARLUDOVICA (Carlu-dovìca)—Panama Hat Plant. This group of three species of Central and tropical western South America belongs to the cyclanthus family CYCLANTHACEAE. It consists of stemless or very short-stemmed plants, with foliage resembling that of palms, and small, unisexual flowers arranged similarly to those of aroids (members of the arum family ARACEAE). The name honors King Carlos IV of Spain and his wife Ludovia. Other plants previously included in *Carludovica* are now placed in *Asplundia, Dicranopygium, Sphaeradenia,* and other genera.

Carludovicas have leaves with stalks three to five times as long as their Maltese-cross-shaped blades. The latter are as broad

Carlina acaulis

or broader than long and are divided into four, or more rarely three or five, lobed or toothed, wedge-shaped segments. The flower stalks, from the leaf axils, are about one-third as long as the leafstalks. They terminate in a cylindrical to club-shaped spadix (fleshy, spikelike axis crowded with small blooms) at the bottom of which are three or four soon deciduous spathes (bracts). The female blooms are sunken in the tissue of the axis of the spadix. Each is encircled by four male blooms that form a square, and the squares are arranged spirally around the axis. The fruits are four-sided berries joined to each other in crowded heads. When they peel from the axis on which they are borne they reveal their inner sides, which, like the axis, are bright red. The material of which Panama hats are made is prepared from young leaves of *C. palmata* by bleaching and slicing them into slender strips.

The Panama hat plant (*C. palmata*) is widely distributed as a native chiefly of wet forests in Central and South America. Beyond its range of natural distribution it is often naturalized. This sort is a rather variable species with leaves with slender, channeled stalks 3 to 10 feet long or sometimes longer, and blades 1 foot to 3 feet wide. The ends of the leaf lobes droop.

Carludovica palmata

Carludovica palmata (fruits)

The fruiting spadix, about 6 inches long, has somewhat the appearance of a long-stalked corncob.

Garden and Landscape Uses and Cultivation. Handsome foliage ornamentals, carludovicas are easily grown outdoors in humid, tropical environments, and in greenhouses. They may be accommodated in ground beds or large containers. Their needs and care are those of tropical palms. Well-drained, fertile soil, kept uniformly moist, and shade from strong sun are to their liking. Well-rooted specimens are greatly benefited by regular applications of dilute liquid fertilizer. Propagation is by division, and by seed from which the surrounding pulp has been removed sown in a temperature of 70 to 80°F.

CARMICHAELIA (Carmich-aèlia). The "ch" in *Carmichaelia* is pronounced as "k." The plants identified by this name comprise about forty species of the pea family LEGUMINOSAE. With the exception of one endemic to Lord Howe Island, all are natives exclusively of New Zealand. Their name commemorates Captain Dugald Carmichael, who introduced many plants to Great Britain. He died in 1827.

Carmichaelias are nonhardy shrubs and small trees of diverse habits. As adults most kinds are leafless or essentially so. In their juvenile stages they have small, undivided or pinnate leaves. A few kinds, even at maturity, are leafy during the early part of the growing season. The much flattened or nearly cylindrical branchlets contain chlorophyll and function in the manner of leaves to photosynthesize foods. Pea-like and often fragrant, the flowers are in branched or branchless racemes, or sometimes are solitary. They have bell-shaped, five-toothed calyxes, a more or less round standard or banner petal, somewhat sickle-shaped and eared wing petals, and an incurved keel. There are ten stamens of which nine are united and the other free, and one slender style tipped with a minute, headlike stigma. The fruits are leathery pods, with the dried style forming a beak at the apex. At maturity the center part of the pod drops out leaving a ringlike frame.

Foliaged early in the season with hairy leaves of three or five leaflets, *C. grandiflora* is a much-branched, spreading shrub up to 6 feet tall. Its drooping, flattened branchlets are finely-ribbed. The fragrant, pale purple blooms, veined and blotched with violet, and often with white keels, are about 1/3 inch long. They are in stalked, five- to twelve-flowered racemes. The long-beaked, straw-colored to brown seed pods are nearly 1/2 inch long. Variety *C. g. alba* has white flowers. Also leafy in spring, *C. odorata* attains heights of 6 feet or more. From the last, it is distinguishable by the ground color of its seeds being yellowish or greenish instead of brown. Of bushy

habit, it has pendulous, much-flattened, grooved branchlets, and leaves with five or seven leaflets. The fragrant, lilac-rose-pink, or purple-veined, white flowers, 1/6 inch in length, are in stalked, branchless racemes of rarely more than ten. The straw-colored, one- or two-seeded pods are 1/4 inch long.

Lovely *C. williamsii* grows wild in coastal regions. In bloom the showiest of the genus, this is a shrub or tree with a maximum height of perhaps 18 feet. It has much-flattened, hairless, grooved and jointed branchlets up to 1/2 inch broad. Juvenile specimens have leaves with one to three narrow leaflets. Adult plants are without leaves or have at most extremely few. The flowers, from the notches along the edges of the stems, are yellowish, veined and blotched with purple. Occasionally solitary, they are more often in single or paired racemes of two to five. They are 3/4 to 1 inch long or sometimes a little longer. The red seeds, sometimes mottled with black, are in pods 3/4 inch long.

From 2 to 6 feet tall, *C. petriei* has loosely-branched, round, not flattened branchlets, with sometimes a few little leaves. The flowers are fragrant, whitish flushed with purple and with a greenish-white keel purplish toward its apex. The dark brown pods, up to nearly 1/2 inch long, contain black-mottled, greenish seeds.

Carmichaelia petriei

Completely different *C. flagelliformis* is 3 to 6 feet tall or occasionally taller. It has extremely-slender, pendulous branches, and in its juvenile state leaves with one to three minute, reverse-heart-shaped leaflets hairy on their undersides. The very tiny blooms, up to four from each notch, are flushed and veined with purple. About 1/5 inch long and dark brown, the pods contain one or two more or less black-mottled seeds.

From 3 inches to 1 foot tall, *C. enysii* and *C. uniflora* form mats or cushions of leafless stems and short branchlets. The branchlets of *C. enysii* are about 1 inch long, much

Carmichaelia enysii

flattened, and ¹⁄₁₆ inch wide. Tiny suborbicular leaves are borne in the juvenile stage only. The flowers, ⅕ inch long, are violet or purplish, with darker veins. They are up to three together in racemes, or sometimes solitary. The one-seeded pods, on drooping stalks, are suborbicular and about ¼ inch long. Less compact **C. uniflora** has slender, compressed branchlets about 1 inch long, with blunt apexes. The flowers, usually solitary, but occasionally paired, are about ⅓ inch long, and whitish, with purple at the base of the standard or banner petal and with purple veining.

The name *C. australis*, applied to plants in cultivation is without botanical precision. Plants so identified are probably mostly *C. arborea* or perhaps some closely-related species such as *C. aligera, C. cunninghamii, C. egmontiana,* or *C. solandri*. A shrub up to 15 feet tall, with narrow, flat branches, **C. aligera** is leafless when mature. The tiny leaves have mostly three leaflets. The flowers, in racemes of three to six, are white with purple veins toward the base of the standard petal. The seeds are yellowish-green mottled with black.

Garden and Landscape Uses and Cultivation. Not hardy in the north, carmichaelias are interesting and useful for garden planting in milder climates such as those that prevail on the Pacific Coast and throughout much of the Southwest. The dwarf kinds are excellent for rock gardens, the others for shrub plantings of various kinds. They are easy to grow, succeeding under much the same conditions that suit brooms (*Cytisus*). Part-day shade, or if adequate water is available, full sun, and thoroughly well-drained, dryish soil are appreciated. They may be expected to prosper near the sea. As large specimens, transplanting may be resented. The best procedure is to set out young plants from pods. Once established little attention is needed. No pruning is ordinarily necessary. Propagation is by seed.

CARNATIONS. Among the choicest of flowers, carnations include kinds best suited for greenhouse cultivation and others that prosper outdoors. They are horticultural developments of *Dianthus caryophyllus*, of the pink family CARYOPHYLLACEAE. The name alludes to the prevailingly pink blooms of the wild species. It is a modification of the Latin *carnatio*, fleshiness.

The wild progenitor of carnations is a subshrubby perennial, native from southern Europe to India. Its conspicuously-jointed stems, branched above, are 1 foot to 3 feet tall. They have opposite, fleshy, linear, keeled leaves 3 to 6 inches in length. The deliciously fragrant flowers of *D. caryophyllus*, 1 inch or sometimes more across, are pink, purple, or white. They are without beards in their throats. Each has a five-toothed, tubular calyx, five toothed petals, ten stamens, and two styles. The fruits are capsules.

Carnations have been cultivated for at least 2,000 years. They are discussed in the writings of Theophrastus. An old English name for them was gilliflowers. By the latter part of the sixteenth century many varieties were being cultivated in Europe, all quite different from modern carnations. They flowered only in summer. By the middle of the eighteenth century, however, there had been developed in France varieties that in mild climates bloomed more or less repeatedly without need for a period of winter rest. It was from these that modern perpetual flowering carnations were eventually derived as also were the now rarely grown class of large-flowered, summer-blooming varieties called malmaisons, the first of which was raised in France in 1857.

Modern perpetual flowering or tree carnations, the kinds grown in greenhouses, have ancestries that trace back to varieties that originated in France about 1840. These were subsequently improved by further breeding in France. Brought to the United States some fifteen years later, they gained popularity, and American breeders developed new varieties. The first of these was distributed in 1858, but it was not until nearly the end of the century that the modern perpetual flowering type was introduced. This was the remarkable 'Mrs. T. W. Lawson', raised in Massachusetts in 1895. The free-flowering newcomer had long, strong stems, long-lasting, rose-pink flowers, and bloomed almost continuously. It is an ancestor of numerous varieties cultivated today. Mr. Peter Risher who raised 'Mrs. T. W. Lawson' sold the entire stock of it to Mr. T. W. Lawson for a great sum. The price was variously reported to be from $10,000 to $30,000. Since

Modern greenhouse carnations

the introduction of 'Mrs. T. W. Lawson', plant breeders have effected tremendous improvements in greenhouse carnations.

Modern varieties bloom over a long period and provide large numbers of splendid, stiff-stemmed, fragrant blooms in a wide variety of solid colors and combinations. New varieties are produced regularly and undoubtedly breeders will continue to introduce them to meet the demand for novelty and improvement as well as to replace older ones that "run out" because of virus infection or other causes. New varieties are mostly raised as seedlings, but sometimes they occur as mutants or "sports." These carnations are grown in tremendous numbers in greenhouses as commercial cut flowers and to a lesser extent by amateurs. Their blooms last well in water.

In greenhouses carnations are grown in benches or sometimes ground beds and are propagated from cuttings (seed is used

Carnations in a greenhouse bench

only for the production of new varieties) taken in winter or very early spring. The cuttings must be from healthy plants. They consist of the terminal portions of shoots with stout stems and closely-spaced leaves. Cuttings made from long, straggly shoots or thin ones do not produce good plants. A recommended procedure is to break off the upper six inches of the stem to be used as a cutting and without trimming it with a knife (which may transmit virus diseases) insert it in the propagating bench. Many gardeners, however, follow the practice of cutting off the lower leaves and slicing the stem across just beneath a node.

Plant the cuttings in sterile sand or perlite and at first keep them under intermittent mist or lightly shaded. It is advantageous if sufficient bottom heat is supplied to keep the rooting medium 60 to 65°F. The air temperature should be about ten degrees lower. Carnation cuttings under favorable conditions root in three to four weeks. They are then ready for potting individually into 2½- or 3-inch pots.

After potting they can remain in 2½-inch containers about a month or in 3-inch containers about two months before it is necessary to plant them out or repot them. As soon as the newly-potted cuttings become established and begin to grow pinch out their tips to encourage branching. The time of planting must be considered in determining when to take the cuttings. Grow the young plants in full sun in an airy greenhouse where the night temperature is 50°F and that by day five to ten degrees higher. From the small pots the carnations may be planted outdoors in spring and there continue their growth until July when they are lifted and planted in the greenhouse, or they may be planted directly in the greenhouse benches or beds. The second method is preferable. A third possi-

Carnation ready for planting in greenhouse bench

bility is to repot the small plants into 3¼- or 4-inch pots and grow them in these in the greenhouse for benching later. This procedure is useful when the benches or beds are not available for planting early.

Whether grown outdoors or in, the plants are pinched during the early part of the season several times, no shoot being permitted to exceed 6 inches in length without having its end nipped out. The last pinch is given in early August.

Beds or benches in which carnations are to be planted are filled with porous, but not excessively rich, loamy soil that has a good organic content, is approximately neutral (pH 6 to 7 or slightly higher), and permits the free passage of water. Space plants 8 to 9 inches apart and set them "high," that is with the tops of the root balls standing slightly above the surrounding soil. This minimizes danger of loss from rot diseases. For a week or two after planting, shade the greenhouse lightly and take great care not to overwater. The best practice is to soak the soil near the plants, but to keep it dry between them. For support, rows of horizontal wires are stretched over the beds or benches between the

plants and as the stems lengthen strings are stretched crossways between these to form a pattern of squares that hold up the stems, or alternatively special grids of wire mesh with large openings are used.

Cool, airy, but not drafty, conditions are necessary. A night temperature from fall to spring of 48 to 52°F rising to 55 on dull days and to 60°F on sunny ones is satisfactory. Humidity should be comparatively low. Excessive moisture in the atmosphere encourages disease. Watering must always be done with care so that although the plants never suffer from lack of moisture, the soil is not constantly saturated. Fertilizing must be done circumspectly to avoid the development of soft, lush, disease-prone growth. Applications are ordinarily not needed in late fall and early winter.

Disbudding is done to secure longstemmed, large, solitary blooms. To effect this, remove side or lateral shoots that develop from the upper parts of the stems, including those immediately below the terminal bud, as soon as they are large enough to handle. After cropping is over discard the plants. If they are diseased burn or bury them. Then the greenhouse should be thoroughly cleaned and sterilized before a new crop is planted. If steam sterilized, the soil can be planted with carnations again, otherwise install new soil for each new planting. Strict hygiene at all stages is necessary for the successful cultivation of carnations.

Disbudding a carnation

Garden carnations include grenadin, marguerite, and border kinds. They are easily grown in sunny locations where the soil is well-drained. In the north it is often best to grow most kinds as annuals. The grenadins are not greatly changed from the wild species. Their very fragrant flowers are single or partly double, and they are delightful plants of unassuming appearance for brightening summer flower beds and for cutting. They may be grown as annuals or biennials and, under favorable conditions, will sometimes persist for more than two years. They are the hardiest carnations. Marguerite carnations, although really perennials, may be grown as annuals or biennials and usually it is better to do this than to keep them more than two years because with age they tend to become unkempt. Marguerite carnations begin blooming in early summer and continue to fall. They are 9 inches to 2 feet tall and their flowers come in a wide range of colors. They are not quite as hardy as the grenadins, but nevertheless they withstand considerable cold and may be expected to overwinter in southern New England with a little cover. Border carnations are less winter hardy than the other kinds mentioned and not widely grown in America, although a few varieties are offered by dealers. They resemble greenhouse carnations, but are lower and have smaller flowers. Border carnations are usually grown as perennials and propagated from cuttings. A strain called Chabaud carnations flower the first year from seeds if started early indoors, and may be cultivated as annuals.

Diseases and Pests. Carnations are subject to a number of diseases, especially rots, wilt, and rust. Grown under good conditions and not in wet, unkindly soils, outdoor carnations are usually not unduly troubled. Should disease attack, it is usually simplest to destroy affected plants promptly, although at the first sign of infection with rots it may be helpful to spray several times at weekly or ten-day intervals with a sulfur fungicide and this practice is recommended as a preventative of rust as well. Greenhouse carnations are subject to these same diseases and a number of others including several serious viruses. Growers should become familiar with the latest recommendations of specialists. These may be had from State Agricultural Experiment Stations. The chief pests outdoors and in are slugs, cutworms, aphids, caterpillars, thrips, and red spider mites.

CARNEGIEA (Carn-ègiea)—Sahuaro or Giant Cactus. Few cactuses are as well known, at least by reputation, as the sahuaro or giant cactus of Arizona, southeastern California, and adjacent Mexico. This solitary-stemmed or candelabra-branched species, 20 to 40 feet high or sometimes higher, and with a trunk diameter of up to 2 feet, has been pictured repeatedly by cartoonists, comic strip illustrators, and others depicting desert scenes. It not uncommonly appears as atmosphere in western films. Its name commemorates the Scottish industrialist and philanthropist, Andrew Carnegie, who died in 1919. Some botanists include *Carnegiea* in *Cereus*.

The sahuaro (*C. gigantea* syn. *Cereus giganteus*), sole representative of its genus of the cactus family CACTACEAE, is protected

Young *Carnegiea gigantea* specimen in the botanic garden, Mexico City

Older *Carnegiea gigantea* specimens in the wild

in Saguaro National Monument and Organ Pipe Cactus National Monument, both in Arizona. It is the official state flower of Arizona. A massive, but by no means the most massive or tallest cactus (several Mexican and South American species are larger), the sahuaro may weigh eight to ten tons. Its columnar stems have twelve to twenty-four blunt ribs with brown-woolly areoles (locations on cactuses from where spines arise) about 1 inch apart along them. The main stem is solitary or may develop one to several stout branches that curve outward and then upward parallel with the trunk. These main branches may branch similarly. From each areole develops several spines, the central ones up to 3 inches, the surrounding ones up to ¾ inch, long. The white or cream, fragrant flowers, borne near the tops of the stems, are about 4½ inches long and wide. They open by day and close after a few hours. The red fruits are 2½ to 4 inches long, spiny at their bases, and contain red pulp and many small black seeds.

Sahuaro fruits are edible. They formed and still form an important staple in the diet of Indians. From the seeds they prepare a nutritious flour. They eat the pulp both raw and preserved. The woody skeletons of this cactus are used as major supporting members in constructing Indian hogans.

Woodpeckers dig holes for nesting into the stems of sahuaros, and the plants are visited by hummingbirds and other birds, moths, bees, and other pollinating creatures seeking nectar, and by fruit-eating bats.

The sahuaro's adaptation to its environment is remarkable. From its base a vast network of shallow roots spreads beneath the desert floor for 50 feet or more in all directions. These rapidly absorb water from infrequent rains and transport it to storage tissues within the trunk and branches. Following such an addition, which in the case of a large sahuaro may amount to more than a ton of water, the stems swell markedly. If a long dry period has preceded the rain they are shrunken, somewhat shriveled, and the vertical ribs have been drawn closer together as the grooves between them deepened. But now the tissues plumpen, the skin expands like the bellows of a concertina, and the pleats become less pronounced. Then the whole cycle begins again, a slow but inevitable loss of moisture under the influence of desert sun and wind and a gradual shrinkage of the tissues until the next, usually far distant, refreshing downfall.

Despite the preservation of presently standing sahuaros in National Monuments, there is serious doubt about the ultimate survival of the species there and some other places. Government action protects them from direct harm by man, and their formidable spines ward off most sizable animals. But slow climatic changes since the end of last century coupled with overgrazing, an increase in populations of rodents and weevils that feed on cactus seeds, the spread of a bacterial rot disease, and other factors are responsible for the failure of sufficient young plants to start and maintain themselves to replace those that die from age and other causes.

Garden Uses and Cultivation. This species does not take kindly to cultivation. At best, transplanted specimens, and these are to be found occasionally in botanical collections, linger for a few years and die. Recently, there has been considerable scientific investigation into raising young plants from seeds. It is believed that fairly exact conditions of light, moisture, and temperature are needed for success. Under laboratory conditions seeds germinated after being placed on moist filter paper in a temperature of 77°F for about twenty-four hours, and then being exposed to light of up to 230 foot-candles in a temperature of 77 to 86°F. To gardeners wishing to experiment, this clearly indicates that, after sowing, the seeds should not be covered with soil, but should be exposed to moderate light, and that the medium on which they are sown should be evenly moist. But the prospective propagator of sahuaros must not expect too much. It is estimated that under natural conditions at age ten young plants are about 4 inches tall, that they are twenty years old before their spines develop, and that before a specimen attains a height of 8 to 10 feet and blooms for the first time forty or fifty years have elapsed. For further information see Cactuses.

CARNIVOROUS OR INSECTIVOROUS PLANTS. Although both adjectives are used for plants that trap small creatures and digest their bodies as sources of nutrients, the former is the more accurate. The diet of these plants is by no means restricted to insects, but includes other small animals unwary or unfortunate enough to be caught. Certainly mites, sowbugs, and little frogs are frequent victims, and according to report it is not unknown for giant-pitchered *Nepenthes* occasionally, but undoubtedly rarely, to capture small mice and creatures of like size. These plants are therefore carnivores (flesh eaters) rather than strict insectivores (insect eaters).

Carnivorous plants are a fascinating group. They belong to several botanical families and inhabit most parts of the world. They occur in various habitats, but invariably where available nitrogen is lamentably scarce. Because of this, the nitrogen obtained from the bodies of their prey is of special significance. Yet probably none of these plants is dependent upon its catch. They can prosper, at least in cultivation, without meat in their diet.

The trapping mechanisms of carnivorous plants are various. In the Venus's fly trap (*Dionaea muscipula*) rapid movement is involved. This remarkable species snaps shut the halves of its leaf blades around its victims with all the effectiveness and almost the speed of the rat traps they resemble. The aquatic *Aldrovanda* behaves in much the same way.

The leaves of sundews (*Drosera*) also move. Their bristle-like tentacles curl over the victim, but very slowly. Sundews entrap their prey by the flypaper method. The captured are held fast by dewy drops of nondrying sticky liquid that tip every

Dionaea muscipula

Drosera binata

Pinguicula caudata with trapped insects

bristle-like tentacle of the leaves and contain digestive enzymes. Related *Drosophyllum* and unrelated *Byblis* and *Pinguicula* operate similarly.

Drowning is the fate of creatures trapped by pitcher plants of the genera *Cephalotus*, *Darlingtonia*, *Heliamphora*, *Nepenthes*, and *Sarracenia*. In all of these the traps are leaves modified into pitchers, cunningly designed to prevent the escape of the captured, and partly filled with liquid containing digestive enzymes.

Bladderworts (*Utricularia*) employ a somewhat different mechanism. They have finely-dissected leaves, some segments of which are little bladders fitted with complex trap-door arrangements that close rapidly on and deny escape to small creatures that enter.

Darlingtonia californica

Nepenthes species

grew upward, and from its upperside, branches several feet in length spread horizontally.

Dr. Liche described attending a religious ceremony involving the sacrifice of a young girl. The victim, he said, was forced by a group of dancers intoxicated from drinking a ''native ferment'' to climb into the tree and drink a ''holy'' intoxicating liquid contained on top of the plate. Then the tree ''seemingly so dead and motionless a moment before'' coiled its palpi about the girl. Its branches ''began to writhe'' and the leaves to ''rise slowly'' until the thorns ''were closing on her with the force of a hydraulic press.'' A pinkish mixture trickled down the trunk. This ''the maddened natives fought and trod each other down to get one mouthful of the intoxicating fluid from the tree and the blood of the human sacrifice.''

Five years later a similar account of a ''man-eating tree'' said to have been observed in the Philippine Islands by W. C. Bryant, an American planter, was published. Bryant's tree differed in structure

Utricularia alpina

Stories of an entirely fictitious ''man-eating tree'' crop up from time to time in newspapers and magazines oriented more to sensation than fact. Mostly they are traceable to reports of such a plant, which allegedly had been discovered long before, that appeared in magazines, newspapers, and even scientific journals from 1878 to 1892. Dr. Carle Liche, who claimed to have seen the tree in Malagasy (Madagascar) in 1878, described it in a letter to Dr. Omelius Fredlowski. He said that in the southern part of the island there existed a very rare 10-foot-tall tree, with a barrel-shaped trunk resembling a huge pineapple. Its top, 8 to 9 feet in circumference was, reported Dr. Liche, capped with a plate-like growth from which hung eight leaves 10 to 12 feet long and 1 foot wide and ''strewn with huge venomous looking thorns.'' From underneath the plate six stamen-like ''palpi''

Sarracenia species

from the one said to exist in Malagasy, but the horrifying details of its action were not less dramatic. In 1925 the author of this story maintained "the tree is there and in the main the account is true."

CAROB is *Ceratonia siliqua.*

CAROLINA. As parts of the common names of plants, Carolina is used for these: Carolina-allspice (*Calycanthus floridus*), Carolina moonseed (*Cocculus carolinus*), Carolina-vanilla (*Trilisa odoratissima*), and Carolina yellow-jessamine (*Gelsemium sempervirens*).

CAROSELLA is *Foeniculum vulgare piperitum.*

CARPANTHEA (Carpán-thea). The origin of the name *Carpanthea* is obscure. The genus it identifies belongs in the carpetweed family AIZOACEAE and is endemic to South Africa. It consists of two species.

Carpantheas are succulents, with opposite leaves and flowers that suggest daisies in gross appearance, although they are constructed on a very different botanical plan (a daisy head consists of numerous florets, each technically a flower; in the carpetweed family each bloom is a single flower). The blooms are produced profusely. They have five sepals, numerous narrow petals, and many stamens. The fruits are capsules. The only species cultivated is an annual grown for its showy yellow blooms. Formerly known as *Mesembryanthemum pomeridianum*, its correct name is *C. pomeridiana*. It is erect, branched, up to 1 foot tall, and has spoon-shaped to lanceolate, stalked, somewhat hairy leaves 1½ to 4 inches long by up to 1 inch wide. The long-stemmed, bright yellow blooms, 1¾ to 2½ inches across, are solitary or in twos or threes at the stem ends. They open only during the afternoon.

Garden Uses and Cultivation. This is especially useful for dry soils and sunny situations. It is appropriate for edgings, the fronts of flower beds and borders, slopes, and rock gardens. Seeds may be sown outdoors in spring, lightly raked into the soil surface, and the young plants thinned to 5 or 6 inches apart, or they may be started indoors in a temperature of 60 to 65°F about two months earlier, and the young plants grown, spaced about 2 inches apart, in flats, to be planted outdoors after the weather is warm and settled. In flats they need porous, well-drained soil of moderate fertility. They are watered rather sparingly so that the soil is kept dryish rather than too wet. Full sun and dryish atmospheric conditions are needed.

CARPEL. Each structural unit of the pistil of a flower is called a carpel. When more than one, the carpels of an individual bloom may be united, partly united, or separate. Morphologically carpels are generally believed to represent leaves.

CARPENTERIA (Carpentèr-ia) — Tree-Anemone. One species endemic to California is the only representative of *Carpenteria* of the saxifrage family SAXIFRAGACEAE. A rarity in the wild, it occurs in only a few locations in the foothills of the southern Sierra Nevada. The name honors Professor William Carpenter of Louisiana, who died in 1848.

The tree-anemone (*C. californica*) is an erect, evergreen shrub 3 to 15 feet in height, with pithy, quadrangular branches and opposite, lobeless, toothless, lanceolate to oblong leaves, hairless and bright green above, their undersides covered with fine white pubescence. The leaves, 2 to 4½ inches long and up to 1 inch wide, are opposite and close together on the branches so that the shrub is well furnished with attractive foliage. Appearing in early summer, the beautiful, pure white flowers have five to seven each persistent sepals and broad petals, a central bunch of many stamens with conspicuous yellow anthers, and a short, persistent style with a five- to seven-lobed stigma. The blooms are 2 to 3 inches in diameter, have the scent of mock-orange, and are solitary or in clusters of three to seven. The fruits are conical capsules. The tree-anemone is closely related to mock-orange (*Philadelphus*) from which it differs chiefly in having evergreen foliage and flowers with more than four petals and one rather than four styles.

Garden and Landscape Uses. This highly ornamental shrub, not hardy in regions of cold winters, is at its best in a warm-temperate climate such as that of California

where little frost is experienced and excessive wetness, especially in winter, is not a problem. Under such conditions, *C. californica* is admirable as a solitary accent specimen or intermixed with other shrubs. It can be used effectively in foundation plantings and lends itself to espaliering.

Cultivation. Well-drained, sandy soil and a sunny, sheltered location are most appropriate for this plant. No systematic pruning is needed, but each year as soon as flowering is through cut out any weak or dead shoots. Propagation is by suckers, summer cuttings under mist or in a humid propagating greenhouse or cold frame, layering, and seeds sown in spring in sandy peaty soil or milled sphagnum moss. Great care must be exercised in watering the seedlings. Excessive wetness causes them to die from damping-off disease.

CARPET BEDDING. See Bedding and Bedding Plants.

CARPHEPHORUS (Car-phéphorus). There appears to be no accepted common name for this genus of the daisy family COMPOSITAE. Closely related to *Liatris*, but with long-stalked flower heads ½ to ¾ inch wide in loose clusters rather than spikelike arrangements, all four species of *Carphephorus* are natives of the southeastern United States. The name may come from the Greek *karphos*, a dry stalk or particle and *phoreus*, to bear.

Herbaceous perennials, these plants have unbranched stems, and alternate, narrow, toothless leaves, those toward their bases larger than those above. The rosy-purple flower heads are of all disk florets (the kind that form the central portions of the flower

Carpenteria californica

heads of daisies). There are no ray (petal-like) florets. At the back of each flower head is an involucre (collar) of several rows of bracts. The fruits are seedlike achenes.

The stems of *C. bellidifolius,* essentially hairless, are 1 foot to 1½ feet tall. Narrowly-spatula-shaped, the leaves are up to 3 inches long. The flower heads are in loose, slender-branched clusters. Finely-hairy stems 1 foot to 3 feet tall characterize *C. corymbosus.* Its lower leaves are spatula-shaped, those toward the top of the stem wedge-shaped, elliptic, or ovate.

Garden and Landscape Uses and Cultivation. In their wild ranges carphephoruses are sometimes transplanted to ornament grounds and gardens and for inclusion in collections of native plants. They are rarely grown elsewhere and just how far north they are hardy is not recorded. They succeed in ordinary soils in sunny locations and are propagated by seed.

CARPINUS (Car-pìnus) — Hornbeam or Blue-Beech or Water-Beech or Ironwood. The hornbeams (*Carpinus*), traditionally associated with hop-hornbeams, hazels, and birches in the birch family BETULACEAE, are by some authorities considered to compose, with *Ostrya* and *Ostryopsis,* the hornbeam family CARPINACEAE. There are some thirty-five species, all of the northern hemisphere, most from eastern Asia. The name is the ancient Latin one of the common European species.

Hornbeams are deciduous, hard-wooded, smooth- or scaly-barked trees or rarely shrubs, with zigzag twigs and alternate, toothed leaves, more or less in two ranks, and with unbranched, parallel veins running outward from the midribs. Their flowers are unisexual, with the sexes in separate catkins on the same plant. Male catkins are pendulous and slender and composed of ovate, scalelike bracts with several short stamens, forked at their apexes, in their axils. Female catkins, shorter than males, are terminal on the branchlets. Their flowers are in pairs in the axils of bracts, which with the minute bractlets at the bases of the flowers enlarge to conspicuous size and leafy appearance as the small, ribbed nutlets that are the fruits develop. Hornbeam wood is extremely hard and rather difficult to work. It was much used for wheel spokes and axils and was employed for making charcoal for gunpowder. It is excellent fuel.

American hornbeam, blue-beech, water-beech, or ironwood (*C. caroliniana*) inhabits moist woodlands from Nova Scotia to Minnesota, Florida, and Texas. A tall shrub or tree up to 40 feet in height, but usually lower, it has a picturesque, fluted, bluish-gray to ash-colored trunk, often divided fairly low down into a few major branches. The oblongish, ovate to obovate, sharply-toothed leaves, 3 to 4 inches long, are bluish-green, and have seven to fifteen

pairs of veins angling from the mid-vein. From ¾ inch to 2 inches long, the fruiting catkins, egg-shaped to short-cylindrical, have wide-spreading, loosely-arranged, narrow, three-lobed bracts. Variety *C. c. pyramidalis* is distinctly conical.

Common European hornbeam (*C. betulus*) under favorable circumstances is up to 80 feet in height. Much like the American

Carpinus betulus

species, it differs in its winter buds being hairless, slenderly-spindle-shaped, and ¼ inch long or longer. Those of *C. caroliniana* are hairy at first, and about ⅛ inch long. Also, its leaves are hairier on their undersides and rather thicker, and have their seven to fifteen pairs of side-veins more definitely impressed than those of American hornbeam. The fruiting catkins are similar to those of American hornbeam. Native from Europe to Iraq, this thrives inland better than near the sea. It is hardy in southern New England. Several distinct varieties exist. Two with branches more upright than is typical of the species are *C. b. columnaris* and *C. b. fastigiata* (syn. *C. b. pyramidalis*). The first, very compact and

Carpinus betulus fastigiata

slow-growing, becomes egg-shaped as it ages. The other, more or less conical at first, grows more rapidly, and with age becomes looser in habit and rounded. Compact *C. b. globosa* differs from *C. b. columnaris* in being more rounded and without a definite central trunk. Weeping (drooping) branches distinguish *C. b. pendula* and even more elegant *C. b. pendula dervaesii.* A variety with deeply-lobed leaves, the lobes toothed, is *C. b. asplenifolia.* Similar *C. b. incisa* differs in having shorter, smaller, irregularly- and coarsely-toothed leaves, with only about six pairs of side-veins. This kind has sometimes been wrongly named *C. b. quercifolia,* which designation is correctly applied to a variant in which some, but not all the branchlets have smaller, more or less oaklike leaves, with broad, rounded, toothed lobes.

Japanese *C. japonica* (syn. *Distegocarpus carpinus*) is hardy farther north than European hornbeam. Up to 50 feet in height, but usually lower, it is a graceful tree with wide-spreading branches, scaly bark, and downy young shoots. Its oblong-lanceolate leaves are pointed, and 2 to 4½ inches long by up to 1¾ inches wide. They have twenty to twenty-four pairs of veins, and toothed margins usually with large and smaller teeth alternating, but sometimes with the teeth again toothed. This species has conelike fruiting catkins with tightly-packed, overlapping, toothed bracts that enfold and surround the nutlets, but that do not form bladder-like pouches around them as in the hop-hornbeam (*Ostrya*). This same characteristic is typical also of *C. cordata,* a very fine native of Japan, Korea, and China, which is readily distinguish-

Carpinus cordata

able from *C. japonica* by its larger, wider leaves, up to 5½ inches long and 2¾ inches wide and more deeply-heart-shaped at their bases, and by its bigger winter buds. It is a shapely tree 40 to 50 feet high.

Japanese *C. laxiflora,* up to 50 feet tall, has shoots silky-hairy when young, and ovate to elliptic, slender-pointed leaves 1½ to 3 inches long by approximately one-half as wide, heart-shaped at the base and hairless except for tufts in the vein axils on the undersides. The fruiting catkins are pendulous, loose, and up to 2¾ inches long. Graceful *C. turczaninovii,* of northern China and Korea, is a tree about 20 feet tall with hairy young shoots and ovate leaves 1¼ to 2½ inches long. The fruiting catkins are about 2 inches long.

Not common in America, *C. orientalis* is well worth planting. Hardy in southern New England and native of southeastern Europe and Asia Minor, this slow-growing species is sometimes 50 feet tall, but is usually much lower, and sometimes is not much more than a tall shrub. It is easily distinguished from the other kinds discussed here by its smaller foliage. The sharp-pointed, double-toothed, ovate leaves are 1 inch to 2 inches long by ½ to 1 inch wide. They have twelve to fifteen pairs of side-veins, and silky hairs along the midribs. The fruit clusters have ovate bracts that are toothed, but unlike those of American hornbeam and *C. betulus,* not lobed. Another lesser known species, Japanese *C. tschonoskii* (syn. *C. yedoensis*), is a graceful tree up to 50 feet in height. It has ovate to ovate-oblong, pointed leaves up to 3½ inches long with twelve to fifteen pairs of side-veins. From *C. betulus* and *C. caroliniana* this differs in the floral bracts being densely-hairy and those of the fruit clusters being lobed on one side only. It is hardy in southern New England.

Carpinus tschonoskii

Garden and Landscape Uses. Hornbeams are beautiful for displaying as individual specimens, and the common European kind especially, for use in sheared hedges, which, like those of beech, retain their old, browned leaves throughout the winter. Hornbeams are admired for their shapely and sometimes picturesque outlines, and particularly for their handsome, beechlike foliage that in fall often assumes

Carpinus betulus: (a) As a hedge, in summer

(b) As a tall screen, in winter

beautiful shades of yellow or red. Fall color is much less impressive in the European hornbeams than in other kinds. Hornbeams are notoriously difficult to transplant, and failure is very likely to follow attempts to move the native kind from the wild. Young, well-grown nursery specimens are much more likely to survive transplanting. They should always be moved with a ball of soil about their roots. These are good trees for using as single specimens, and the European kind for hedges.

Cultivation. Hornbeams are not particular as to soil. They grow even in dryish, rocky ones. Following transplanting it is important to keep the earth moist by mulching and by irrigation during dry spells during the first summer. When sheared as hedges or in other formal ways two clippings a year are advisable, one about midsummer and one after growth has ceased in fall. Propagation of the species is best accomplished by seeds. These may be sown in cold frames as soon as they are ripe, or be stratified in a temperature of 40°F for four months and then be sown in a greenhouse, or in spring in a cold frame or outdoor bed. They germinate irregularly. Varieties, and species when

seed is not available, may be increased by grafting or budding onto understocks of European hornbeam, and by layering. They are susceptible to infestations of scale insects.

CARPOBROTUS (Carpo-bròtus) — Hottentot-Fig, Sea-Fig. Because of the extensive use of the Hottentot-fig in California and in other areas with warm, dry climates for planting on banks along freeways and other places where erosion threatens, the genus *Carpobrotus* is familiar. It comprises about twenty-four species of subshrubs, natives of South Africa, the Pacific coasts of North and South America, Australia, and New Zealand. Formerly included in *Mesembryanthemum* and belonging in the carpetweed family AIZOACEAE, it is distinguished by its flowers having mostly ten to sixteen stigmas and its fleshy fruits. The latter are edible. The name comes from the Greek *karpos*, fruit, and *brotus*, edible, and refers to the fruits.

These plants have prostrate, usually trailing, angled stems and very fleshy, sharply-three-angled, opposite leaves with the bases of each pair joined. Their flowers, superficially daisy-like, but botanically of very different structure, are cream to yellow, reddish, or purple. They are solitary, comparatively large, and open fully only in sun.

The Hottentot-fig (*C. edulis*), a native of South Africa, has long trailing stems and

Carpobrotus edulis

leaves up to 3 inches long or longer with finely-toothed keels. Its flowers are 2½ to 3½ inches across and are most commonly pale straw-yellow, but they vary to rose-purple. Another South African species, *C. acinaciformis* has long stems and sickle-shaped leaves up to 3 inches long. Its flowers are large and rosy-purple. Similar to the Hottentot-fig, but with leaves not more than 2½ inches long and not toothed along their keels and purple flowers about 2 to 3½ inches in diameter, the sea-fig (*C. chilensis*) inhabits Pacific coasts from Or-

Carpobrotus chilensis, a natural stand

egon to Washington, and in Chile. The Australian *C. glaucescens* has rose-purple flowers with purplish-brown anthers. Its leaves do not exceed 2 inches in length and are more or less glaucous. Less well known *C. sauerae* of South Africa has thick, spreading stems and bluish- to grayish-green leaves, triangular in section and up to 3½ inches long. From 3½ to 4 inches in diameter, its flowers have many bright rosy-purple petals. The fruits are edible.

Garden and Landscape Uses. Carpobrotuses are favorites for cultivating in collections of succulents, outdoors in appropriate climates, and in greenhouses. They stand slight frost only. They are excellent groundcovers for dry places and thrive near the sea. They prosper best in full sun and need well-drained soil. When used to clothe very steep slopes the increasing weight of the branches of the Hottentot-fig (and of other kinds) may, as they grow older and bigger, cause great patches of the plants to tear away and leave unsightly scars. Because of this, it is better to limit their use to slopes of not more than about forty-five degrees.

Cultivation. Since every piece of leafy stem roots with the greatest enthusiasm if stuck into porous soil or sand maintained on the dryish side and since seeds sprout readily, there are no problems of propagation. Nor, under anything like reasonable growing conditions, is there any difficulty in growing these plants. In greenhouses a winter night temperature of 40 to 50°F is appropriate and on all favorable occasions the structure should be freely ventilated. Watering should be moderate from spring through fall, always allowing the soil to become nearly dry before an application is made. Less water is needed in winter.

CARPODETUS (Car-pódetus)—Puta-Puta-Weta. Because in its native New Zealand the wood of this tree is usually perforated by insect galleries wrongly supposed to be the work of a repulsive insect called the weta, the tree is known by the native names of puta-puta-weta, puna-weta, and kai-weta. As a matter of fact, although the holes are often inhabited by wetas, they are made by the larvae of an entirely different insect, a moth. The puta-puta-weta (*Carpodetus serratus*) is the only representative of its genus, a member of the saxifrage family SAXIFRAGACEAE. Its botanical name is derived from the Greek *karpos*, a fruit, and *detos*, bound, and alludes to the nature of the fruits.

A flat-topped evergreen tree or shrub 15 to 30 feet tall with branches that spread in fan-fashion, *C. serratus* has alternate, short-stalked leaves, ovate-oblong to elliptic, sharply-toothed, 1 inch to 2 inches long, and beautifully veined and marbled with yellow-green. The white, fragrant blooms are in broad axillary and terminal clusters shorter than the leaves. They are about ⅛ inch in diameter, and have five or six sepals, petals, and stamens. They are succeeded by black, pea-sized fruits that take several months to ripen.

Garden and Landscape Uses and Cultivation. The chief use of this species is as an outdoor ornamental in mild climates such as those of parts of California. Occasionally it is grown in greenhouses and conservatories and can be employed, container-grown, to decorate terraces and similar places. The puta-puta-weta grows satisfactorily in sun in well-drained, slightly-acid soil that contains an abundance of peat moss or other decayed organic matter and is always moderately moist. It is propagated by seeds and summer cuttings.

CARRIEREA (Carrièr-ea). The French botanist and horticulturist Elie Abel Carrière, who died in 1896, is honored in the name of *Carrierea* of the flacourtia family FLACOURTIACEAE. This genus inhabits eastern Asia and comprises three species of deciduous trees of which only one seems to be cultivated. They have alternate leaves and terminal racemes or panicles of flowers with five sepals, no petals, numerous stamens shorter than the sepals, and three or four three-lobed styles. The fruits are capsules containing winged seeds.

Much like *Idesia*, to which it is related, and native of central China, *C. calycina* develops a broad crown up to 45 feet tall. Its long-stalked, elliptic, ovate, or oblong-ovate, short-pointed, round-toothed leaves are 3 to 6 inches in length, about one-half as wide as long, hairless, and lustrous on both sides. The cup-shaped flowers, with broad, yellowish-white, downy sepals ¾ inch long, are in erect downy clusters or short racemes of about ten at the branch ends. They come in early summer. The fruits are spindle-shaped, downy, and 2 to 4 inches long.

Garden and Landscape Uses and Cultivation. Adapted for outdoor planting in the milder parts of the United States, the rather rare species described is effective as

Carpobrotus sauerae

an ornamental. It makes no special demands, succeeding in any fairly good, well-drained soil in sunny locations. It needs no regular pruning and is increased by seeds, summer cuttings under mist or in a greenhouse propagating bench, and root cuttings.

CARRION FLOWER. This name is applied to *Stapelia* and *Smilax herbacea*.

CARROT. One of the most popular root vegetables, carrots are cultivated varieties grouped as *Daucus carota sativa* of the pretty wild flower called Queen Anne's lace (*D. carota*). This member of the carrot family UMBELLIFERAE is widely naturalized in North America. Carrots are esteemed as human food, cooked and raw, and as livestock feed. They are of easy cultivation and are raised for summer and fall use and, except for animal feed, to a lesser extent for winter storage. In mild climates fall sowing gives crops harvested in winter and spring.

Soil for carrots should be fertile, mellow, free of stones and clods, and fairly deep. One of a fairly loose, somewhat sandy, rather than compact, clayey character is preferred; it should be slightly acid to neutral, but if properly managed crops can be had from a wide variety of earths. Newly turned sod land is not suitable. Do not use fresh manure in preparing the ground because it encourages the development of branched, unshapely roots and excess foliage at the expense of root growth, but residues in the soil from manure used for a previous crop such as cabbage, peas, or onions are favorable. It is advantageous to spade, rototill, or plow under liberal amounts of well-decayed compost, a green manure crop, or similar organic material that does not contain as much readily available nitrogen as manure. Mix in before sowing a dressing of a complete garden fertilizer, one rather high in phosphoric acid and potash, or use a regular garden fertilizer, and if the ground is poor in those nutrients supplement it with light dressings of superphosphate and muriate or sulfate of potash.

Carrot seeds are small and germinate slowly. A first sowing is made as early in spring as the ground is workable to be followed by later ones about every three weeks until nine or ten weeks before the expected date of the first killing frost. For winter storage, sow about three months before harvesting. Sow three or four seeds to the inch about ½ inch deep in rows 1 foot to 1¼ feet apart. To mark the rows and to help break the surface soil crust scatter radish seeds along with those of the carrots at the rate of three or four to the foot. When of table size the radishes may be pulled and eaten.

Carrot varieties fall into two groups, earlies that develop relatively quickly tender roots used shortly after harvesting and lates that take longer to grow and are adapted for winter storage. Only the former are much grown in gardens. In addition, varieties are classified according to the forms of their roots as short or stump-rooted, half-long, and long. The shorter types are best adapted for all except deep soils. Recommended short and half-long varieties are 'Chantenay', 'Danver's Half-Long', 'Red-Cored Chantenay', and 'Scarlet Nantes'. Among long-rooted varieties are 'Gold Pak', 'Gold Spike', 'Imperator', and 'Nantes'.

Growing season care begins with thinning the seedlings, a rather tedious job if the seeds were sown too thickly. Do not thin to the final spacing in one operation. Go over the rows twice at an interval of about two weeks. The end objective is to have the plants 1 inch to 1½ inches apart for crops to be harvested when about half grown, 2 to 3 inches apart for winter storage carrots. Weed control is very important. It involves hand pulling in the rows and frequent shallow cultivation or mulching between them. Do not allow weeds to become sizable; destroy them early. In dry weather water deeply periodically, but do not overdo this in the later stages of growth or the roots may crack. Availability of moisture is much more important during the first few weeks after sowing. Harvest young carrots, they are most tender and flavorful when not more than half grown, by pulling selectively from the rows, taking the largest and more crowded first, leaving the others a week or more longer. Pull only as needed for use. Freshly harvested carrots have much better flavor than if they have been out of the ground a week or more. Late carrots for storage are harvested at one time, just before hard freezing weather arrives. The task is made easier if the ground is loosened with a spading fork before pulling, or if the roots are dug, taking care not to injure them, with that tool.

Storage may be in a root cellar or other dark, cool, fairly humid place or in outdoor pits. The temperature should be not much above freezing. If the atmosphere is too dry, pack the roots in slightly damp soil, sand, or peat moss. Young carrots can be preserved by processing and freezing.

Diseases and pests are not numerous. Failure of seedlings to appear may result from sowing too early. A virus disease spread by leaf hoppers, carrot yellows, is checked by controlling the hoppers. A leaf blight may occur. Caterpillars and in some regions the carrot rust fly, the larvae of which tunnel through the outer layers of the roots, are sometimes troublesome. Consult your Cooperative Extension Agent about control measures.

CARROT WOOD, AUSTRALIAN is *Cupaniopsis anacardioides*.

CARRUANTHUS (Carru-ánthus). Technical details of the fruits (capsules) distinguish the only species of this genus of the carpetweed family AIZOACEAE from closely related *Bergeranthus*. The name is derived from *carru*, the equivalent of Karroo, the name of desert regions in South Africa, and the Greek *anthos*, a flower. Native to South Africa, **Carruanthus ringens** (syn. *C. caninus*) is a short-stemmed, fleshy-rooted,

Carruanthus ringens

clump-forming plant, with very thick, succulent, glossy, gray-green, three-angled, toothed, densely-crowded, erect or inclined leaves, flat on their upper surfaces. They are up to 2 inches long or slightly longer by approximately 1 inch wide. The leaves narrow to their bases, have deep chinlike apexes, and somewhat resemble those of *Faucaria*. The mostly solitary flowers, on erect stalks up to 4 inches long, are freely produced. Yellow, they are tinged red on the undersides of their petals, and like those of other plants of the *Mesembryanthemum* complex have a deceivingly daisy-like aspect. From daisies they differ in that each bloom is a solitary flower, not a head compounded of numerous florets. They are not hardy.

Garden Uses and Cultivation. These are identical with those of *Bergeranthus*. For further information see Succulents.

CARTERARA. This is the name of hybrid orchids the parents of which include *Aerides*, *Renanthera*, and *Vandopsis*.

CARTHAMUS (Cár-thamus)—Safflower or False-Saffron. This genus of thirteen species belongs in the daisy family COMPOSITAE and at one time was called *Kentrophyllum*. It is native from the Canary Islands through the Mediterranean region to Central Asia. Its name is derived from the Arabic *qurtom*, or the Hebrew *qarthami*, to paint, and refers to the value of some species as dyes. These are rigid, spiny-leaved, thistle-like annuals with flower heads lacking ray florets, but furnished with spiny, leaflike involucres (collars of bracts) that have a somewhat similar appearance. The flowers are whitish, yellow, or purple. The fruits are seedlike achenes.

The safflower or false-saffron (*Carthamus tinctorius*) has blooms much es-

Carthamus tinctorius

teemed as the source of red and yellow dyes. Mixed with talc, they were used as rouge. In addition, it serves other purposes. The seeds can be eaten by humans and are good poultry and cattle feed, and from them is obtained an edible oil that is also used in paints, varnishes, and linoleum. The plant is up to 3 feet in height and has broadly-ovate, finely-spiny-toothed leaves. The orange heads of bloom are 1 inch to 1½ inches across. It is a native of Europe and Asia.

From the Mediterranean region hails *C. lanatus,* about 3 feet tall, with fiddle-shaped basal leaves and deeply-lobed stem leaves. Its 1-inch-long flowers are dull yellow. A native of Greece, *C. leucocaulos* has pale pink flowers, white stems, and deeply-cleft leaves.

Garden Uses and Cultivation. Although of no very great decorative merit the plants described above are suitable for informal areas and, the safflower, for including in collections of useful plants that interest herb gardeners. They grow best in a fairly heavy loamy soil, from seeds sown in early spring where the plants are to bloom. The seedlings are thinned to about 6 inches apart. The blooms are not suitable for use as cut flowers.

CARUM (Càr-um)—Caraway. This group of about twenty species belongs to the carrot family UMBELLIFERAE. Its members inhabit temperate parts of Europe and Asia. American plants previously included in *Carum* are segregated as *Perideridia.* The name is derived from the Greek *karos,* applied to some plant of the carrot family.

Carums are tap-rooted annuals, biennials, and perennials, with hairless stems and foliage. Their leaves are once- or twice-pinnately-divided. The tiny, white

or occasionally pink flowers are in umbels composed of smaller umbels. The blooms are without sepals and have five petals, notched at their tips. The flattened fruits are ovoid to oblongish and have longitudinal ridges.

Caraway (*C. carvi*), native to Europe and Asia, freely naturalizes in many parts of North America. It is a biennial 1 foot to 3 feet tall with hollow, grooved stems, and carrot-like leaves 6 to 10 inches long and twice divided into slender segments. The stalks of its umbels are of unequal lengths. The petals are deeply notched. The fruits are oblong, strongly-ribbed, and about ⅛ inch long.

Carum carvi

Garden Uses. The only species of any horticultural significance is caraway. This is likely to be grown only in herb gardens and among collections of plants useful to man. Its seeds, popular for flavoring, are used in rye bread, cakes, soft cheeses, and other foods, and in the manufacture of the liqueur kümmel.

Cultivation. Caraway gives best results in deep fertile soil that never dries unduly, but is well drained. A sunny location is needed. Seeds are sown in June, either where the plants are to remain or in beds from which the young seedlings are transplanted to their permanent places. A distance of 1 foot to 1½ feet should be allowed between individuals. There is some evidence that transplanting, and nipping the ends off the taproots at that time, is advantageous in developing strong-branching root systems.

CARYA (Càry-a)—Hickory. Hickories are a group of twenty-five deciduous trees nearly all natives of eastern North America, a few of eastern Asia. They constitute the genus *Carya* of the walnut family JUGLANDACEAE. The name is derived from *karya,* the Greek name for the walnut. From walnuts (*Juglans*) and wingnut (*Pterocarya*) hickories are easily distinguished by their branchlets having solid rather than lamellated (horizontally-layered) or chambered pith.

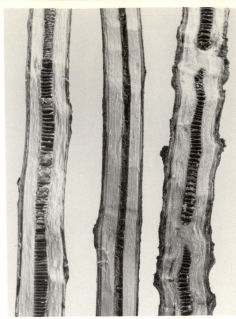

Solid pith of *Carya* branchlet contrasted with laddered piths of *Pterocarya* (left) and *Juglans* (right)

Caryas have alternate, pinnate leaves with an odd number of leaflets, all except the terminal one in opposite pairs. When young the leaves are hairy and glandular. The flowers are without petals, the males in pendulous catkins from the leaf axils, the females in terminal spikes. Individual trees bear both sexes. Neither is decorative. The fruits are nuts enclosed in thick green husks that at maturity split completely or partway into four segments. Characteristically the trees have ovoid or oblong crowns. Their lumber, tough, elastic, and straight-grained, is especially esteemed for uses where resistance to impact is important, as with handles of hammers, axes, and golf clubs, and as shafts and wheel spokes for horse-drawn vehicles. It is one of the finest fuel woods and is commonly employed for smoking bacon, hams, and other meats. Chief commercial nuts are the pecan and the shagbark hickory.

Hickories are among the noblest of American forest trees and include many worth planting as ornamentals and nut trees. The affection in which they are held by the American people is indicated by the sobriquet Old Hickory applied to President Andrew Jackson. Undoubtedly most of the rails split by Abraham Lincoln were hickory. That wood was valued above all others for rail fences, and hickory trees were plentiful in the region where Lincoln spent his youth.

The pecan *C. illinoinensis* (syn. *C. pecan*) is the biggest species. Under forest conditions that attains a maximum height of about 175 feet. It has a rounded head of sturdy branches and leaves of eleven to seventeen leaflets. The pecan is the fastest growing kind. It chiefly inhabits rich, moist bottomlands from Iowa and Indiana to Al-

Carya illinoinensis

Carya ovata, tree in foliage

Carya ovata (bark)

abama, Texas, and Mexico, but may be grown as far north as southern New York and Massachusetts, although in such northern climes it does not crop satisfactorily. Chiefly this is a tree for regions of long, warm summers and fairly mild winters. It is believed that the Indians planted it through the Mississippi valley and elsewhere and so extended its original natural range. In the southern states it is much planted for its delicious nuts, and many choice horticultural varieties, selected as bearers of superior nuts, have been given varietal names and are propagated vegetatively. The bark of the pecan is deeply furrowed. Its buds are yellow and, like the young shoots, hairy. The fruits are oblong and in spikes of three to twelve. The smooth, light brown nuts are thin-shelled, noticeably longer than broad, and have sweet meats. In superior types they may be 2½ inches long by more than one-third as wide.

Shagbark hickory (*C. ovata*) also has delicious nuts, and varieties of superior quality have been segregated, named, and are propagated vegetatively. Shagbark hickory is so called because of the ragged appearance of its trunk, which results from the shedding of its bark in long, jagged, hard plates that remain attached by their upper ends with their lower ends lifted away from and reflexed outward from the trunk. The tree has a columnar trunk and may attain or exceed 100 feet in height. In the open it has an ovoid head with erect upper branches and the lower ones somewhat pendent. Its twigs are scurfy-pubescent at first, but soon are glabrous. The leaves are of five or sometimes seven finely-toothed, pointed-elliptic leaflets that often have red

stalks and when young are scurfy-pubescent. The fruits are subglobose and up to 2½ inches long. They have thick husks that split to the base and contain a slightly flattened, broad-obovoid or ellipsoid, rather thin-shelled, white nut. Shagbark hickory has a natural distribution from southern Quebec to Minnesota, the Carolinas, Mississippi, Arkansas, Louisiana, and Texas.

Kingnut or big shellbark hickory (*C. laciniosa*) up to 120 feet in height, is handsome. It has a shaggy-barked trunk sometimes 4 feet in diameter that resembles that of the shagbark hickory, but the bases of its bark plates do not ordinarily lift so far from the trunk. When growing in the open it has an oblongish head, with somewhat drooping lower branches. Its twigs, pubescent when young, are later orange and almost hairless. The leaves have five to nine, but mostly seven, oblong-lanceolate, toothed leaflets, pubescent beneath. The fruits, the largest of any hickory, are solitary or in twos and threes. They have thick, woody rinds and contain thick-shelled, compressed, yellowish-white nuts almost as flavorful as those of shagbark hickory. The big shellbark hickory is indigenous from New York to Iowa, Tennessee, and Oklahoma.

Mockernut (*C. tomentosa*) is so named because its nuts "mock" those who eat

them by presenting a small amount of meat inside extraordinary thick shells. This is native from Massachusetts and Nebraska, Florida, and Texas. Despite its colloquial name, the kernels of its nuts are sweet and delicious, but it takes quite some effort to extract them. Handsome, and up to 100 feet in height, *C. tomentosa* has a symmetrical, rounded head and a trunk up to 3 feet in diameter. The lower limbs tend to be pendulous. Its twigs are hairy. The leaves are of seven to nine pointed, toothed, oblong-lanceolate leaflets, densely-pubescent and glandular on their undersides and decidedly fragrant when crushed. Their stalks and midribs are hairy. The fruits of the mockernut, subspherical or pear-shaped, are up to 2 inches long. They have thick husks that split almost to their bases. The slightly-angled, somewhat flattened, nearly globose or ellipsoid nuts are brown.

Bitternut (*C. cordiformis*) is a handsome, broad-headed native from Quebec to Min-

Carya cordiformis

nesota, Florida, and Louisiana. It attains a height of up to 100 feet and has light brown bark and twigs that are rusty-pubescent when young, and lustrous reddish-brown later. Its pointed-lanceolate, toothed leaflets number five to nine. At first they are pubescent beneath, especially along the veins. The more or less globose or ovoid fruits have thin rinds, are four-winged above their middles, and split to somewhat below that. The nearly smooth, slightly compressed, approximately globose or ovoid nuts have thin shells. Their kernels are bitter and astringent.

The pignut (*C. glabra*) also has bitter nuts. This kind occurs from Maine to Ontario, Florida and Mississippi. A handsome tree, up to 125 feet tall, it has dark, fissured bark, glabrous or nearly glabrous twigs, and leaves of three to seven, but commonly five, sharply-toothed, pointed, oblong to oblong-lanceolate, nearly glabrous leaflets. Its obovoid fruits, slightly winged toward their apexes are about 1 inch long. Ordinarily they split only to their middles. Variety *C. g. megacarpa* has larger fruits and bigger, thicker-shelled nuts. The sweet pignut (*C. ovalis*) is very similar. The differences are that its fruits are ovoid, with husks that eventually split to their bases, and the kernels of the thin-shelled nuts are sweet. On old trees the bark is often shaggy. Because of this the tree is sometimes called false shagbark hickory. The leaves have five to seven leaflets and often red stalks. The fruits are very variable in shape, but mostly are subglobose or ellipsoid.

Other kinds include these: *C. aquatica*, the bitter pecan, is a 90-foot-tall native of the southeastern United States. It has leaves of seven to thirteen leaflets, and irregularly-angled, bitter nuts, mostly as wide as long. *C. cathayensis*, the Chinese hickory, attains a height of 60 feet. Native of eastern China, it has orange-red twigs and leaves with five or seven short-stalked leaflets that are scurfy-yellow beneath and hairy along their midribs. The obscurely four-winged, obovoid fruits contain sweet nuts from which an oil used in pastries is expressed. They are sold in Chinese markets. The wood is used for tool handles. *C. myristicaeformis*, the nutmeg hickory, native from South Carolina to Arkansas and Mexico, and hardy as far north as Long Island, New York is up to 90 feet in height. It has leaves of five to seven leaflets that are yellow-hairy when young, but later lose their hairs. The usually solitary, ellipsoid or ovoid fruits have nuts with sweet meats.

Garden and Landscape Uses. Hickories are beautiful ornamental trees of great value for shade and for landscape decoration. They are good park trees. Characteristically they are tall, sturdy, straight-trunked, and have good-looking foliage that changes to rusty-greens, yellowish-greens, orange-browns, and sometimes clear yellow before leaf fall. Most thrive best in deep, rich, moist earth, but the pignut, mockernut, and shagbark hickory prosper in drier soils. With the exceptions of the pecan and the bitter pecan the cultivated sorts are hardy in the north. They are rather slow growers.

Cultivation. Hickories develop long taproots and because of this do not recover well from transplanting. This is especially true of specimens moved from the wild. By far the best plan is to set out only nursery-grown trees of comparatively small size that have been transplanted every year or two. Many gardeners recommend raising these trees from seeds planted directly where the trees are to grow. Hickories require no special attention in the matter of pruning. Propagation is usually by seeds, which may be sown outdoors in fall or stratified and sown in spring. Protect the seedbed from squirrels and other rodents. Suckers from the roots are some-

times used for propagating purposes, and superior varieties are grafted onto seedling understocks (usually *C. cordiformis*) in the greenhouse in spring. Splice grafting or veneer grafting are the methods usually employed.

Diseases and Pests. Hickories are subject to leaf spot diseases, a witches' broom fungus, powdery mildews, and crown gall. The principal insects that attack them are gall aphids, bark beetle, cigar casebearer, twig-girdler, borers, June beetle, caterpillars, and scale insects. They may also be infested with mites.

CARYOPHYLLACEAE—Pink Family. Comprising approximately 1,600 species of annuals, biennials, herbaceous perennials, and a few subshrubs distributed among more than fifty genera, this family of dicotyledons, of nearly worldwide natural distribution, is especially abundant as to sorts in temperate and cold regions. Its members include carnations, gypsophilas, pinks, sweet williams, and a number of other much esteemed flower garden ornamentals.

The stems of members of the pink family usually have distinctly swollen joints. The opposite leaves, with the bases of pairs united or connected by a line across the stem, without lobes or teeth, have parallel veins. The flowers are sometimes solitary, more often in sprays or clusters variously branched. They are bisexual or unisexual, with the sexes on different plants. The calyxes are of four or five sepals or have four or five lobes. There are four, five, or less commonly no petals, eight, ten, or occasionally fewer stamens, and two to five separate or united styles. The fruits are capsules or less often berries. Genera cultivated include *Agrostemma*, *Arenaria*, *Cerastium*, *Dianthus*, *Gypsophila*, *Herniaria*, *Lychnis*, *Paronychia*, *Petrocoptis*, *Petrorhagia*, *Sagina*, *Saponaria*, *Scleranthus*, *Silene*, *Stellaria*, *Telephium*, and *Vaccaria*.

CARYOPTERIS (Cary-ópteris)—Bluebeard, Blue-Spirea. Summer- and fall-blooming shrubs are too scarce for gardeners to neglect any that hold promise, and when their flowers are pleasing blue or violet-blue that is an added attraction. Such are found in *Caryopteris*. Belonging to the vervain family VERBENACEAE, this is an eastern Asian genus of fifteen species of deciduous, small shrubs, subshrubs, and herbaceous plants. Its name, alluding to its fruits, is from the Greek *karyon*, a nut, and *pteron*, a wing.

Bluebeards have opposite, short-stalked, toothed or toothless leaves and an abundance of little flowers in axillary clusters. The blooms have bell-shaped, deeply-five-lobed calyxes that are persistent and enlarge as the fruits develop, a short-tubed corolla with five lobes, one of which is fringed and bigger than the others, two

pairs of protruding stamens, and a slender style cleft at its apex. The dry fruits split into four slightly-winged nutlets.

Most handsome are a group of hybrids identified as *C. clandonensis*, the parents of which are *C. incana* and *C. mongholica*. Several have been given varietal names such as 'Blue Mist' and 'Heavenly Blue'. The original hybrid, 'Arthur Simmonds', was raised in England. From 2 to 4 feet tall, the members of this complex are soft-wooded shrubs or subshrubs intermediate between and better garden plants than their parents. They are hardy in sheltered locations in southern New England, although their tops may be winter-killed there.

Less hardy than the hybrids, *C. incana* (syn. *C. mastacanthus*) exceptionally is 6 feet tall, commonly much lower. Ovate to ovate-oblong, its coarsely-toothed leaves, ¾ inch to 2 inches long or sometimes longer, have dull green, somewhat downy upper surfaces. Their undersides, like the stems and flower clusters, are gray-hairy. The flowers are violet-blue. This is a native of Japan and China.

Extremely hardy *C. mongholica* is from northern China and Mongolia. About 3 feet tall, it has grayish-green leaves, toothless except in variety *C. m. serrata*, in which they are sparsely-toothed and more hairy on their undersides than above. The clusters of blue flowers are of nine or fewer blooms, and from the upper leaf axils form panicle-like spires.

Garden and Landscape Uses and Cultivation. Sun-loving plants, bluebeards may be used advantageously at the fronts of shrub plantings and in perennial flower beds, where their grayish foliage and displays of blue or violet blooms blend pleasingly with other late summer and fall flowers. If their tops are killed in winter or are pruned quite hard in spring, the plants renew themselves with a profusion of new shoots that flower the first season. When treated in this way bluebeards have more the aspect of herbaceous perennials than shrubs. A spring application of a complete fertilizer, and a mulch maintained around them, encourages vigorous growth.

As pot plants bluebeards are sometimes grown for greenhouse decoration. Summer-rooted cuttings are grown in pots to bloom during their second summer and succeeding ones. From fall to spring they are kept in a greenhouse where the temperature is 40 to 50°F. In spring they are repotted and grown under conditions that suit chrysanthemums. In summer they are best outdoors in a sunny place with their pots buried nearly to their rims in sand, peat moss, or other such material. Before frost they are moved to a cool greenhouse. Throughout the growing season watering and application of dilute liquid fertilizer requires regular attention. Plants can also be raised from seed.

Caryopteris incana

rable ropes and brushes. From the trunk a nourishing sago is extracted. The Indian wine palm has a stout solitary trunk 80 to 100 feet in height. Its leaves are up to 20 feet long and 12 feet wide and have drooping lateral branches. The individual leaflets are dark green, rigid, and strongly-veined. Their terminal leaflets are jagged at their tips, and the lateral ones have long oblique ends coarsely-toothed for usually more than one-half the length of the outer margin of the leaflet. The pendulous flower clusters are 10 to 12 feet long. Male flowers have forty stamens or more. The fruits are ¾ inch in diameter and reddish.

Quite different **C. mitis** is 25 to 40 feet in height; from around the base of its trunk suckers develop freely as it ages. Its leaves, lighter green than those of *C. urens*, attain a maximum length of about 9 feet and have much thinner leaflets that are not strongly-veined and have toothed edges that commonly do not extend for more than one-half the length of the outer margin of the leaflet. The flower clusters are much shorter than those of *C. urens*. The male flowers have fifteen to twenty-five stamens. This palm is native from India to Java and the Philippine Islands. Chinese **C. ochlandra** is a single-trunked tree up to 80 feet tall with leaves with fish-tail-shaped

CARYOTA (Caryò-ta)—Fish-Tail Palm. Not well understood botanically, *Caryota* of the palm family PALMAE consists of about a dozen handsome species, natives from tropical Asia to Australia. It is suspected that some plants in cultivation are hybrids. The generic name is from the Greek *karyon*, a nut.

Fish-tail palms vary greatly in size and have a solitary trunk or one main trunk with secondary trunks arising as suckers from around its base. Often the trunks are partly covered with persistent fibrous remains of leafstalk sheaths. Caryotas are remarkable because their leaves are normally twice-pinnate, an unusual arrangement with palms. Young specimens may have once-pinnate leaves, and very occasionally an older plant has thrice-pinnate ones. The leaflets are triangular or fish-tail-shaped, with the irregularly-toothed end forming the base of the triangle and the apex of the triangle attached to the stem. The veins of the leaflet splay outward from the base to the broad tip. The flower clusters are solitary, one at a node, with the green or purple flowers mostly in groups of one female flanked by two males. The males usually have numerous stamens. The small, one- or two-seeded, red to blackish fruits contain an irritating principle. Caryotas belong to that small group of palms that bloom only once. When after many years the tree attains maturity the first flower clusters appear high among the leaves, then in succession downward others de-

velop. Finally, when the last, the lowermost, has bloomed and fruited the leaves and trunk wither and die. The full life cycle of the individual is completed.

The Indian wine palm or toddy palm (**C. urens**), of India, is the source of a refreshing beverage called toddy, which is boiled

Caroyta urens

down to obtain a crude sugar called jaggery and is fermented and distilled to produce the alcoholic drink arrack. The fibers of the leaf sheaths of this species, called kittul fiber, are used as a substitute for horsehair and for making strong and du-

Caryota ochlandra

leaflets. The flowers, the sexes on separate trees and the males with many stamens, are in drooping clusters 5 to 7 feet in length. The persistent fruits are spherical, about ¾ inch in diameter and deep red. Native from Australia to India and the Philippine Islands, **C. rumphiana** has a solitary trunk 60 feet or more in height. Its leaves, up to 20 feet long, have stiff, blunt-toothed leaflets 1 foot or more in length shaped like one-half a fan. The flower clusters are 2 feet long or longer. The stamens of the male flowers number thirty or more.

Garden and Landscape Uses. Fish-tail palms are beautiful decoratives for out-

Caryota rumphiana

doors in tropical and subtropical climates free or nearly free of frost. They are effective in groups and as solitary specimens and associate charmingly with other palms and tropical vegetation by providing a pleasing change of foliage pattern. They are splendid for tub cultivation and may be used with excellent effect in conservatories and as florists' decorative plants.

Cultivation. Fish-tail palms thrive in any ordinary, reasonably moist garden soil, in sun or light shade. They are best propagated by fresh seeds sown in sandy, peaty soil in a temperature of 80 to 90°F. Those that sucker can be increased by very careful division. After removal with as many roots as practicable, pot the suckers in porous, sandy, peaty soil and keep them in an extremely humid atmosphere where the temperature is 75 to 90°F. Shade them from direct sun for a few weeks.

Pot or tub specimens thrive in greenhouses where a minimum winter night temperature of 60 to 65°F is maintained and a day temperature five to ten degrees higher, and where night and day temperatures at other seasons are ten degrees or more above those maintained in winter. The containers must be well drained. Any coarse, porous, fertile potting soil yields satisfactory results. When the pots or tubs are filled with healthy roots apply dilute liquid fertilizer every other week from spring through fall. For additional information see Palms.

CASCARA SAGRADA is a product of *Rhamnus purshiana*.

CASEBEARERS. Moths and their larvae called casebearers are distinguished by the larvae, which feed on leaves, flowers, fruits, or seeds, having portable pouches or cases or tubelike structures in which they live or hibernate. See Caterpillars.

CASHEW OR CASHEW NUT is *Anacardium occidentale*.

CASIMIROA (Casi-míroa)—White Sapote. Only one of the half-dozen species of this genus of tropical and subtropical American evergreen trees and shrubs is ordinarily cultivated. It is the white sapote (*Casimiroa edulis*), esteemed especially in Mexico for its edible fruit. Named to honor the eighteenth-century Spanish botanist Casimiro Gomez de Ortega, *Casimiroa* belongs in the rue family RUTACEAE.

Casimiroas have alternate, leathery leaves occasionally undivided, but more often of three or more leaflets arranged in hand-fashion. Usually they are beset with translucent dots. The small, bisexual blooms are in clusters or panicles in the leaf axils or at the branch ends. Generally their tiny calyxes are five-lobed. Commonly there are five petals and the same number of stamens. Often the stalkless stigmas are three- to five-lobed. The pulpy fruits are large, approximately globular, and contain two to five seeds.

A broad-crowned tree up to 50 feet or sometimes more in height, *C. edulis* is warty-trunked and has long-stalked leaves with three to seven leaflets 3 to 5 inches long, glossy on their upper sides, slightly-hairy beneath, obovate or lanceolate, and with obscurely-toothed or toothless edges. When they first unfold they are bronze. The greenish flowers, not more than ½ inch across, are succeeded by thin-skinned, greenish-yellow, slightly-flattened-spherical fruits 3 to 4 inches in diameter that con-

tain somewhat peach-flavored, sweetish to slightly bitter, pale yellow, soft flesh. This species is native from Mexico to Central America.

Garden and Landscape Uses and Cultivation. In California, Florida, and other warm parts of the United States, the white sapote is sometimes planted for ornament and fruit. It succeeds, without special care, in open locations in ordinary, well-drained soil and is remarkably drought resistant. It may be propagated by seeds, but if edible fruits are desired superior varieties should be chosen and increased vegetatively. This is usually done by shield budding onto strong seedlings when they are about 3 feet tall. Seedlings should have their tops pinched out to encourage branching, and it is recommended that young plants be accommodated in cans or other containers until they are about 3 feet tall. Then they are suitable for setting in their permanent locations.

CASSABANANA is *Sicana odorifera*. The name is sometimes misapplied to *Benincasa hispida*.

CASSAVA. See Manihot.

CASSIA (Cás-sia)—Senna. Widely distributed in tropical, subtropical, and temperate regions, *Cassia*, of the pea family LEGUMINOSAE, considered in a broad sense comprises some 500 to 600 species that

Casimiroa edulis

some authorities favor splitting into several genera. Its name is an ancient Greek one of some unidentified aromatic plant.

Cassias include trees, shrubs, herbaceous perennials, and annuals, the latter not cultivated. The bark and foliage of many kinds emit an unpleasant odor when crushed. Some are more or less spiny. Their leaves are alternate, two-ranked or spiraled around the stems. Sometimes very small, they are pinnate without a terminal leaflet and with or without one or more glands on the leafstalk or midrib. The more or less asymmetrical flowers are solitary or in racemes or panicles. They have calyxes with five quite asymmetrical sepals and a corolla of five nearly equal-sized petals narrowing to slender shafts (claws) at their bases. There are five or ten stamens frequently of unequal lengths and often not all fertile. The fruits are stalked or stalkless, few- to many-seeded, cylindrical, flattened, four-angled or four-winged pods. Several species, notably *C. fistula*, are cultivated for their leaves, which are dried and used medicinally and for the pods, used similarly. The seeds are used in leis and necklaces.

The pink shower, coral shower, or horse cassia (*C. grandis*), of tropical America, is a deciduous tree 20 to 50 feet tall or, under favorable conditions in its native regions, sometimes twice that height. It has a spreading crown. Its shoots, leafstalks, and stalks of the flowering parts are clothed with short, rusty hairs. The leaves, 6 inches to 1 foot long, are of eight to twenty pairs of blunt, oblong leaflets 1 inch to 2½ inches long by ½ to ¾ inch wide, hairy on their undersides. The flowers, ½ inch wide or a little wider, in drooping lateral racemes up to 10 inches long, are from nearly white to deep rose-pink, often with some yellow. From 1 foot to 2 feet long or longer by about 1½ inches wide, the nearly cylindrical, blackish, woody seed pods contain a bitter, laxative pulp.

The apple-blossom shower (*C. javanica*), a deciduous tree on occasion 80 feet tall in its homelands, but in cultivation ordinarily much lower, when young has spiny trunks and branches. Native to Java, Sumatra, and the Philippine Islands, this has leaves with from five to fifteen or occasionally up to twenty pairs of broad-elliptic to oblong leaflets 1 inch to 2 inches long by approximately one-half as wide. The appendages (stipules) at the bottom of the leafstalks are big. The flowers, in spreading or more or less drooping racemes up to 6 inches long, have dark red or reddish-brown stalks and calyxes, and petals 1 inch to 1¼ inches long that change from pale red to dark red with paler blotches and finally become pale. The black pods, 8 inches to 2 feet long by 1¾ inches wide, contain 75 to 100 seeds.

Jointwood or pink-and-white shower (*C. nodosa*) differs from *C. javanica* in not hav-

ing a spiny trunk and branches and in the calyxes of its red-stalked flowers being green and in its more lustrous, up to 1-foot-long leaves having up to a dozen pointed, oblong or ovate-oblong leaflets 1¼ to 2¼ inches long by almost one-half as wide. At first downy, they are later hairless. The appendages (stipules) at the bottom of the leafstalks are tiny. The fragrant flowers in short, broad clusters up to about 4 inches long, from the older parts of the shoots, are first pale, but become pink or pink blotched with white and finally yellowish-pink. Their petals are 1 inch to nearly 1½ inches long. The dangling, pencil-like, cylindrical, black seed pods are 1 foot to 2 feet long. There are three long stamens with stalks swollen at their middles. This, in its native Malaya, attains heights of up to 90 feet and has a large, buttressed trunk. The rainbow shower (*C. hybrida*) is an intermediate hybrid between *C. javanica* and *C. fistula*. Seedlings exhibit considerable variation. The flowers are of various hues from creamy-yellow to apricot, orange, and red.

The golden shower, pudding pipe tree, or Indian-laburnum (*C. fistula*) is a graceful, deciduous native of India and Ceylon frequently planted elsewhere in the tropics and subtropics. One of the most beautiful of flowering trees, this is about 30 feet tall or sometimes taller, with leaves, sometimes coppery when young, 1 foot to 1½ feet long, their stalks and midribs without glands. Each has four to eight pairs of leaflets 4 to 7 inches long. In loose, pendulous racemes 8 inches to 1½ feet in length, from the older shoots, the light to deeper bright yellow, 1½- to 2-inch-wide, fragrant blooms on stalks as long as the flowers are broad are most often displayed while the trees are leafless. They have ten fertile stamens, three much longer than the others, and are succeeded by glossy, nearly black, cylindrical, straight pods 1 foot to 2 feet long by up to 1 inch wide. The seeds, walled off in individual compartments, are embedded in sweet, sticky pulp.

The kassod tree (*C. siamea*), native to southeast Asia and the East Indies, is naturalized in the West Indies. An evergreen tree up to 40 feet in height, this kind has leaves of seven to twelve pairs of thickish, elliptic-oblong to slightly ovate leaflets, usually tipped with a little point, hairless above, finely-hairy on their undersides, 1¼ to 3 inches long by ½ to 1 inch wide. There are glands on the midribs. The flowers, in crowded racemes from the leaf axils and forming terminal panicles 6 inches to 1 foot long or longer, are bright yellow. They have petals ½ to ¾ inch long and seven fertile stamens. Nearly straight, the flat seed pods, 6 to 9 inches long by ½ inch wide or a little wider, are much thickened along their edges. Crown-of-gold tree (*C. spectabilis*) is a handsome native of Argentina. From 15 to 30 feet in height, but

in the wild sometimes attaining twice that, and evergreen or partially evergreen, this has leaves, mostly toward the outer parts of the branches, with ten to twenty pairs of elliptic-oblong to lanceolate-oblong leaflets 1 inch to 3 inches long by about one-third as wide as long. Its bright yellow flowers, with petals up to 1 inch long or longer, are in panicles 1 foot to 3 feet long. The seed pods are black, cylindrical, and 6 inches to 1 foot in length.

Other tree cassias in cultivation include these: *C. leptophylla* is an open-crowned, evergreen or nearly evergreen graceful, Brazilian tree about 25 feet tall. It has spreading, somewhat pendulous branches. The deep yellow blooms, 2 to 3 inches wide, are in spikelike racemes 6 to 8 inches long. *C. moschata,* the bronze shower, is a deciduous, broad-headed tree of Central and South America up to 75 feet tall. It has leaves of ten to eighteen pairs of oblong leaflets approximately 2 inches long, velvety-hairy on both sides. Its flowers are in slender, loose racemes. They are orange-yellow to yellow, ¾ to 1 inch wide. The pods are cylindrical, 1 foot or more in length, ½ to ¾ inch in diameter. They contain musk-scented pulp. In Hawaii this species blooms freely, but does not produce seeds. *C. multijuga* is deciduous or in some climates evergreen. It is a round-headed tree up to 20 to 25 feet tall, a native of tropical America and the West Indies. Its feathery leaves are 5 to 9 inches long. They have fifteen to forty pairs of leaflets ½ to 1 inch long, paler on their undersides than above, each ending in a tiny point. The rich yellow flowers, 1 inch to 2 inches wide, are in broad, terminal panicles up to 1 foot long. Each bloom has two long and eight short stamens. The flat, brownish seed pods may be 6 inches long or sometimes longer by ½ to ¾ inch wide.

Shrubby cassias, a few sometimes attaining the dimensions of small trees, will now be described in alphabetical sequence. Ringworm cassia (*C. alata*), so called because it is used by natives to treat ringworm and other skin afflictions, is also called, because of its racemes of bloom, candle bush and candlestick cassia. Native of tropical America, it is naturalized in other warm parts of the world. A straggling shrub up to about 8 feet tall, it has leaves 1 foot to 2 feet in length with eight to twenty pairs of blunt-oblong leaflets each ending in a tiny point 2 to 4½ inches long by 1 inch to 3 inches wide, but occasionally bigger. The bright yellow blooms, 1 inch to 1½ inches wide, are in erect, crowded, spikelike racemes, 1 foot to 2 feet long, accompanied by orange bracts. The seed pods are winged, black, and 6 to 8 inches long by nearly ¾ inch wide. Native to Puerto Rico, St. Thomas, and Tortola, *C. antillana* is a somewhat vinelike shrub, its stems up to 25 feet long. From 3 to 8 inches in length, the leaves have two pairs of leaflets with a gland on the midrib between each pair. The leaflets, obliquely-ovate to elliptic, are up to 4 inches long. From 1 inch to nearly 2 inches wide, the yellow flowers are in short racemes forming showy clusters at the branch ends. The pendulous seed pods are 3 to 8 inches long by about ½ inch wide. Very distinctive, the wormwood cassia (*C. artemisioides*) is native to Australia. A bushy shrub, this has beautiful silvery-gray shoots and feathery foliage. The delicately-divided leaves have three or four pairs of narrow-linear leaflets. The abundant flowers are sulfur-yellow, ½ inch to a little more in diameter, in short clusters from the leaf axils. The seed pods, flat, and 2½ to 3 inches long by about ¼ inch wide, are clustered toward the tops of the branches. A scrambling, evergreen shrub of the American tropics 5 to 10 feet tall, Christmas bush (*C. bicapsularis* syn. *C. candolleana*) is naturalized in other warm parts of the world including Florida and Hawaii. It has leaves with hairy stalks and midribs, three to five pairs of blunt, elliptic-oblong-obovate leaflets ½ inch to 1½ inches long by up to ¾ inch wide, with a short-stalked gland on the midrib between the lowest pair of leaflets, and a tiny point at the tip of each leaflet. The yellow flowers, ¾ inch to 1¼ inches wide, are in spikelike racemes forming panicle-like arrangements at the branch ends. The cylindrical seed pods are 4 to 6 inches long and somewhat over ½ inch thick. A deciduous shrub or small tree 4 to 15 feet tall, with a crown often broader

Cassia corymbosa

than high, *C. corymbosa,* of Argentina, has ascending, forked branches. Its leaves are of three, or less often four pairs of somewhat sickle-shaped, lanceolate leaflets 1¼ to 1½ inches long, with an obscure gland between the lowermost pair. Its rich golden-yellow, cupped blooms are in small but numerous, stalked, terminal and axillary clusters. The individual flowers are ¾ inch to 1¼ inches wide. The seed pods are up to about 4½ inches long by about ⅜ inch wide. East African *C. didymobotrya* (syn. *C. nairobensis*) is naturalized in parts of North America. A wide-spreading, densely-foliaged evergreen shrub of rangy habit, this attains a height of 7 to 15 feet. Its

Cassia didymobotrya

leaves, chiefly near the branch ends and 6 inches to 1 foot long, have eight to sixteen pairs of 1¼- to 2-inch-long, oblong to ovate-elliptic leaflets, each with a tiny point at its tip. The 1½-inch-wide, golden-yellow flowers are crowded in long-stalked, upright, spikelike racemes up to 1 foot long. They are ill-scented. The flat seed pods are up to 4 inches long by ¾ inch wide. An erect shrub up to 10 feet tall or sometimes a small tree, *C. laevigata,* of tropical America and West Africa, resembles *C. surattensis,* but has leaves with only three to five pairs of leaflets that are ovate-lanceolate usually narrowing gradually to pointed apexes to oblong-elliptic or narrowly-ovate. They tend to droop. They are up to 3 inches long by about 1 inch wide. The yellow flowers, in racemes from the upper leaf axils that form loose, panicle-like groupings, are 1 inch to 1¼ inches wide. The seed pods are cylindrical, lustrous dark brown, and 2¼ to 4 inches long. This is naturalized in Hawaii. Ranging in the wild from New Mexico and Arizona to South America, *C. leptocarpa* is an evergreen, hairless to hairy shrub 3 to 6 feet tall and as broad as tall. Its leaves have four to eight pairs of ovate to ovate-lanceolate leaflets 1¼ to 4 inches long by up to 1½ inches wide. There is a gland close to the base of the leafstalk. Its bright yellow to light orange blooms, ½ to ¾ inch wide, are in axillary and terminal racemes grouped to form large panicle-like displays. The seed pods, hairy or hairless and often curved, are up to 1 foot long by not more than ¼ inch wide. Brazilian *C. splendida* well deserves its name. It is a hairless shrub up to about 10 feet tall with leaves of two pairs of blunt or pointed, elliptic to oblong leaflets 1 inch to 4 inches long by up to 1¾ inches wide. There is a gland on

Cassia artemisioides

the leafstalk between the lower pair of leaflets. About 3 inches wide, the rich orange-yellow blooms, each with seven fertile stamens and three sterile ones (staminodes), are in showy, panicled racemes. An evergreen broad shrub or small tree with widely-arching branches, *C. surattensis* (syn. *C. glauca*), of tropical Asia and Australia, is naturalized in Florida. The leaves, approximately 6 inches long, have eight to twenty pairs of oblong-elliptic leaflets 1¼ to 2 inches long. They are glaucous on their undersides. In long-stalked, umbel-like racemes that form panicle-like clusters at the branch ends, the orange-yellow or sometimes light yellow flowers are 1 inch to nearly 1½ inches across. The flat seed pods, 3 to 6 inches long, terminate in a distinct point. Native from Mexico to South America, the woolly senna (*C. tomentosa*) is a robust evergreen shrub 8 to 15 feet tall. Its leaves are of six to eight pairs of 2½-inch-long, oblong to oblong-elliptic leaflets, green above, white-hairy on their undersides. The deep yellow flowers, in short, erect racemes that form leafy, more or less panicled clusters at the branch ends, are 1 inch to 1¼ inches wide. The flattened seed pods are up to about 5 inches long by ¼ to ⅜ inch wide.

Hardiest of cultivated cassias are two North American herbaceous perennial species called wild senna. Native in moist, open woodlands and at streamsides from Pennsylvania to Iowa, Florida, and Texas, *C. marilandica* survives as a garden plant considerably north of its native range.

Cassia marilandica

From 3 to 6 feet tall, hairless except sometimes hairy in the flowering parts, this has leaves usually of four to eight pairs of oblong to elliptic leaflets ¾ inch to 2 inches long, with a tiny point at the tip of each. There is a gland on the leafstalk. The approximately 1-inch-wide flowers are in

clustered racemes from the leaf axils. Up to 4 inches long by ⅓ to nearly ½ inch wide, the seed pods are of joints (sections, each containing one seed) markedly wider than long. More copiously flowered than the last, *C. hebecarpa* inhabits similar places from Massachusetts to Michigan, North Carolina, and Tennessee. From 3 to 6 feet in height, it has leaves of usually six to ten pairs of oblong to elliptic leaflets ¾ inch to 2 inches long, each tipped with a tiny point. The many-flowered racemes from the leaf axils form showy, terminal panicles. The blooms are bright yellow, ¾ to 1 inch across. The seed pods, up to 4½ inches long by approximately ⅓ inch wide, are of joints noticeably longer than wide.

Garden and Landscape Uses. Cassias are among the most useful ornamental flowering trees and shrubs for the tropics and subtropics. They come in considerable varieties of sizes, types of foliage, and flower colors, as evergreens and as leaf-losers. Kinds suitable for moist, and kinds adaptable to dry, climates are available. They lend themselves according to kind to many general landscape uses, as street trees, lawn specimens, in foundation plantings, for inclusion in beds and borders of trees and shrubs, and as border and screen plantings. In addition, *C. didymobotrya* behaves splendidly as a pot plant for growing in a cool greenhouse. From seeds sown in summer excellent 1-foot-tall specimens can be had in full bloom the following May. Cassias are sun-lovers, adapted to a variety of soils so long as they are well drained.

Cultivation. The chief attention to give cassias is an annual pruning. Not all need this, but to maintain their shape and to contain them to size many do. Prune after flowering, hard or lightly depending upon the type of growth. Compact, neat growers such as the wormwood cassia do not require cutting back severely, but strong, vigorous growers such as the candle bush and crown-of-gold tree respond well to that treatment. Propagation is usually by seed. Cuttings of some kinds can be rooted in greenhouse propagating benches or under mist.

CASSIA BARK TREE is *Cinnamomum cassia*.

CASSIA FLOWER TREE is *Cinnamomum loureiri*.

CASSIE is *Acacia farnesiana*.

CASSINE. This is a common name of *Ilex cassine*.

CASSINE (Cas-sìn-e). This genus of usually evergreen tropical trees and shrubs belongs to the staff tree family CELASTRACEAE. Represented in the native floras of the Old and New Worlds, *Cassine* comprises possibly eighty species. Its name is

an American Indian one for a kind of holly (*Ilex*).

These plants have opposite or alternate, undivided, laurel-like, toothed or toothless leaves. Their inconspicuous, greenish or whitish flowers are in axillary or lateral clusters. The calyxes are generally of four or five sepals. There are four or five petals, longer than the sepals, and four or five stamens. The style, solitary and very short, ends with a two- to five-lobed stigma. The fruits are largish drupes (fruits structured like plums).

The false-olive (*C. orientalis* syn. *Elaeodendron orientale*) is a shrub or small tree with thick, opposite or alternate leaves, the adult ones quite different from the juvenile, which are much slenderer and have a red mid-vein. Adult leaves are 2 to 3 inches long, bluntly-obovate with wedge-shaped bases, and have round-toothed or scalloped margins. Less than ¼ inch wide, the yellowish-green flowers are in crowded clusters shorter than the leaves. The fruits are the size of olives. South African *C. capensis* (syn. *Elaeodendron capense*) is a shrub or tree up to about 30 feet tall. It has spreading, pendulous branches. The short-stalked, opposite leaves are somewhat leathery, elliptic-ovate to broad-elliptic, with slightly-toothed, rolled-under margins. They are mostly 1½ to 3 inches long, but sometimes larger, and from narrow to quite broad. The tiny, yellowish flowers are freely produced in branched clusters. The 1-inch-long fruits are red. Australian *C. australis* (syn. *Elaeodendron australe*) is a tree 30 to 40 feet tall. It has mostly opposite, blunt or bluntish, ovate to oblong-lanceolate, toothed or toothless leaves. The flowers have four each sepals, petals, and stamens. The fruits ripen red, are egg-shaped to spherical, and about ½ inch long. Much narrower leaves distinguish *E. a. angustifolium*.

Bermuda olive-wood bark (*C. laneana* syn. *Elaeodendron laneanum*) is a tree up to 45 feet high, endemic to Bermuda. In the open it is branched to the ground. The branches are upright, the shoots densely leafy. Somewhat lustrous on their upper sides, the leaves are short-stalked, oblanceolate, and distantly-toothed. They are 2½ to 4 inches long and nearly one-half as wide as long. The flowers are in axillary clusters about 3 inches wide. Ovoid to spherical, the glossy, yellowish-white fruits, ½ to 1 inch long, contain a sweet, white flesh. Closely related *E. attenuata*, of Cuba and the Bahamas, differs in having pale green foliage and yellow-green fruits.

Garden and Landscape Uses and Cultivation. The sorts discussed above are good-looking foliage evergreens for general landscape uses in tropical and semitropical climates. Their flowers and fruits make little display. These species succeed in open locations in ordinary soil and grow readily from seeds. They may also be increased by terminal and single-eye cuttings in a propagating bench in a tropical greenhouse, or under similar conditions.

CASSINIA (Cas-sínia). Evergreen shrubs or rarely herbaceous plants, often of heathlike aspect, constitute *Cassinia* of the daisy family COMPOSITAE. Of the fewer than thirty species, native of New Zealand, Australia, and South Africa, none is hardy in the north. The name commemorates the French botanist Viscomte Alexandre Henri Gabriel Cassini, who died in 1832.

Cassinias are densely-foliaged. They have alternate, undivided, lobeless, and toothless leaves. Their small, tubular flower heads, in the axils of chaffy bracts, are composed of little tubular florets. They are very numerous and form flattish panicles or clusters at the ends of the branches. Except sometimes for a few threadlike outer ones that are female, the florets are bisexual and five-toothed. There are no petal-like ray florets. The small, seedlike fruits are achenes.

The hardiest species *C. fulvida* is a New Zealander, a bushy, slender-stemmed shrub

Cassinia fulvida

up to 6 feet tall, with distinctly-sticky young shoots. Its linear leaves, up to ⅓ inch long and about one-half as wide, are at first yellowish or rusty-hairy on both surfaces. As they age they lose the hairs from their upper sides, but retain them on their under surfaces. The clusters of white flower heads are 1 inch to 3 inches wide. Very similar *C. leptophylla,* of New Zealand, differs from *C. fulvida* in having numerous scales among the florets of its flower heads instead of not more than one or two. Also, its shoots are not sticky, and the hairs on its foliage are whitish or grayish.

Differing from the kinds described above chiefly in its leaves being widest above their middles, *C. vauvilliersii* is sometimes 9 feet tall. Native to New Zealand, it has thickish stems, and leaves ¼ to nearly ½ inch long clothed with rusty hairs on their undersides, and when young, above. The

younger shoots are sticky, the white flower heads in dense clusters. In variety *C. v. albida* the hairs on the leaves are white, those on the upper surfaces soon falling. From it *C. v. canescens,* also white-hairy, differs in having leaves up to ¾ inch long that retain the hairs on both their upper and lower sides through maturity.

Cassinia vauvilliersii

Native to Australia, **C. aurea** is a shrub 6 to 10 feet tall. It has slender, linear to linear-lanceolate, glandular leaves up to 2 inches long. Its little flower heads are in crowded clusters 2 to 3 inches wide. Their scales are bright yellow at their tips.

Garden and Landscape Uses and Cultivation. In regions of mild winters and moderate summers cassinias are more likely to succeed than under greater extremes. They do well near the sea and in other open, sunny sites. Although not outstanding ornamentals, they are worth planting in a small way to give added interest and variety to shrub beds and informal groups. They succeed in ordinary soils, preferably ones that contain fairly generous amounts of peat or other organic material. The only pruning needed is a little judicious thinning out of crowded or excessively lanky branches from time to time. If the bushes become too tall and overgrown, they can be restored by cutting them back in late winter or early spring to within 1 foot of the ground, and following this by applying a dressing of fertilizer and a mulch of peat moss, compost, or some similar material and making sure that they are watered periodically during dry spells in summer. Propagation is very easy by seeds and by summer cuttings in a greenhouse or cold frame propagating bed or under mist.

CASSIOPE (Cassì-o-pe) — White-Heather. Twelve species of choice, dwarf, creeping or prostrate evergreen shrubs constitute *Cassiope* of the heath family ERICACEAE.

They inhabit arctic, subarctic, and alpine regions in North America, Europe, and Asia, often carpeting large expanses with heathlike vegetation. Two sorts with opposite leaves and terminal flowers by some authorities are segregated as the genus *Harrimanella*. The name is that of the mother of *Andromeda*, in Greek mythology.

Cassiopes have opposite, scalelike, overlapping leaves or linear, spreading ones in four ranks. Their solitary, axillary, or terminal white to pinkish, nodding blooms have four or five overlapping calyx lobes, bell-shaped corollas with four or five lobes (petals), eight or ten stamens, one style, and one stigma. The fruits are capsules containing minute seeds.

Sorts with flowers terminal on the stems are *C. hypnoides* (syn. *Harrimanella hypnoides*) and *C. stellerana* (syn. *Harrimanella stellerana*). Native of arctic regions and tops of high mountains in North America, Europe, and Asia, **C. hypnoides** is 2 to 3 inches high and has leaves up to ⅙ inch long pressed against the stems and white or pink-tinged flowers about ⅓ inch long, with pointed calyx lobes and corolla lobes about as long as the corolla tubes. Endemic to northwestern America and northeastern Asia, **C. stellerana** forms loose mats. Its spreading leaves are about ⅛ inch long. The flowers are white and about ⅕ inch in length. They have blunt calyx lobes, and corollas much longer than the corolla tubes.

Sorts with flowers from the axils of the leaves include those now to be considered. Circumpolar in its natural distribution, *C. tetragona* has spreading to ascending stems 4 inches to 1 foot long furnished with four rows of closely-overlapping, oblong-lanceolate leaves ⅙ inch long set in such a way that the shoots are four-sided. The back side of each leaf has a deep longitudinal groove. Arising from the leaf axils, the creamy-white sometimes pink-tinged blooms, rarely more than ¼ inch in length and slightly constricted at their mouths, have stalks four to six times as long as the leaves. In this characteristic they differ from those of *C. t. saximontana*, of Alberta and the Yukon, which has flower stalks not more than three times as long as the leaves. Distinguishable from *C. tetragona* by the backs of its leaves being ridged longitudinally instead of furrowed, white-heather (**C. mertensiana**) is native from mountains in California to Alaska. Up to 1 foot tall, this kind has four rows of somber green, tightly-overlapping, ovate-lanceolate, stalked leaves ¼ to ³⁄₁₆ inch long, which give a four-angled effect to the shoots. The creamy-white, cup-shaped, short-stamened blooms on threadlike stalks have ⅓-inch-long corollas with four or five reflexed, shallow petals. Like *C. mertensiana* in that its minute, ¹⁄₁₂-inch-long, ovate leaves are not grooved down their backs, **C. lycopodioides** has prostrate, wide-spreading stems. Native to Alaska and Ja-

Cassiope mertensiana

pan, it has thread-stalked, bell-shaped, five-petaled, white blooms ¼ inch long. European gardeners report that plants from Japanese sources are much easier to grow than those from Alaska. Variety *C. l. rigida* (syn. *C. l. major*) of Japan has larger leaves and flowers, the latter more cylindrical and with longer, proportionately narrower petals.

Like those of *C. tetragona* deeply longitudinally grooved down their backs and in four overlapping rows that give a four-sided form to the shoots, the leaves of shrubby *C. fastigiata* differ from those of that species in having membranous edges fringed with fine hairs. Also, they are less closely pressed to the stem. The more widely bell-shaped flowers of this sometimes 1-foot-tall native of the Himalayas are white and ⅜ inch wide. Distinguished from *C. fastigiata*, which it otherwise much resembles, by the absence of thin, membranous margins to its ¼-inch-long leaves, *C. wardii* is another Himalayan. Its hairy-stalked, broadly-bell-shaped, white flowers are tinged with red at their bases inside. They have recurved, broadly-triangular petals approximately ⅜ inch long.

Interesting hybrids between species of *Cassiope* have been developed and named in Great Britain. Here belong 'Badenoch' and 'Randle Cook', their parents *C. lycopodioides* and *C. fastigiata*, 'Edinburgh', a chance hybrid between *C. tetragona* and *C. fastigiata*, 'Muirhead', its parents *C. lycopodioides* and *C. wardii*, and 'George Taylor', its parents *C. fastigiata* and *C. wardii*.

Garden Uses and Cultivation. Except where summers are truly cool and humid cassiopes are likely to spell heartbreak for would-be cultivators. They are plants that enthusiastic, even experienced growers of alpines must approach with respect. Successful growers emphasize the necessity of a soil that never becomes dry and a location where the plants are never exposed to drying winds, fierce sun, or high temperatures. A little shade, but certainly not too much, may be advantageous. Cassiopes require good light. An annual top dressing

with a mixture of peat moss and sand is likely to be beneficial. Propagation is by cuttings and, for mat-forming kinds, by division. Cuttings root slowly under mist in a mixture of peat moss and sand.

CAST IRON PLANT. See Aspidistra.

CASTALIS (Cast-àlis). Three species of South African herbaceous perennials, previously included in and generally resembling *Dimorphotheca*, are segregated as *Castalis* on the basis of the ray florets of their flower heads not producing fertile fruits. They belong in the daisy family COMPOSITAE. The name is taken from that of the nymph Castalia.

These are erect plants with alternate, toothed, lobeless to pinnately-lobed leaves and, at the ends of the branchlets, solitary flower heads with white, purple, yellow, or orange ray florets. The disk florets are bisexual, the rays neuter. The seedlike fruits are achenes. Because prussic acid is developed in the foliage and other parts of these plants, they can poison livestock.

Cultivated since 1774, when it was brought to England from the Cape of Good Hope, *C. tragus* (syn. *Dimorphotheca aurantiaca*) is not the plant commonly grown in gardens as *D. aurantiaca*. That is *D. sinuata*. Growing from a woody rootstock, the branchless or sparingly-branched stems of *C. tragus* attain a height of about 1 foot, are woody toward their bases, and bear on the same plant toothless and wavy-toothed, linear-oblong leaves up to 3 inches long by ½ inch wide. The bright orange-yellow flower heads are 2 to 2½ inches wide. Variety *C. t. pinnatifida* has most of its leaves more deeply-toothed than those of the species.

One of the most beautiful plants of the *Dimorphotheca* relationship is *C. spectabilis* (syn. *Dimorphotheca spectabilis*). Up to 1¼ feet in height, its few to several erect stems come from a woody rootstock. The younger shoots and leaves are clothed with short, glandular hairs. The leaves are 1½ to 2½ inches long, up to ½ inch wide, and lanceolate to narrowly-elliptic. Those on the stems are usually toothless. The flower heads, up to 3 inches in diameter, have violet centers and ray florets of a lovely mauve-purple. Because of similarities in their appearance this species, perhaps not in cultivation, has been confused with *Osteospermum ecklonis* (syn. *Dimorphotheca ecklonis*).

Garden and Landscape Uses and Cultivation. The recommendations made under these headings under Dimorphotheca apply here also. Castalises are not frost-hardy.

CASTANEA (Cas-tànea)—Chestnut, Chinquapin. The genus *Castanea* of the beech family FAGACEAE consists of twelve species of deciduous trees or less often shrubs,

natives of temperate parts of North America, Europe, and Asia. The name is the ancient Latin one of the Spanish chestnut. Chinquapin is used as a common name for some species of *Castanopsis* as well as for some of *Castanea*.

The sorts of this genus have two-ranked, toothed leaves with many conspicuous parallel veins angling outward from their midribs. The small flowers are unisexual, both sexes on the same tree or bush. Male blooms are in more or less erect, slender catkins from the leaf axils. Female blooms are at the bases of predominantly male catkins, or sometimes from separate leaf axils. Usually they are in threes, nested in a prickly involucre (collar of bracts). Both sexes have a six-parted calyx and are without corollas. Males have ten to twenty stamens, females seven to nine styles. The fruits, large brown nuts with a big, pale basal scar, are one to three, but occasionally more, inside a spherical to ovoid prickly husk, a development of the involucre.

Because of a devastating blight that has infected chestnuts in North America since the beginning of the twentieth century, and has practically wiped out all sizable examples of the native species, it is unrealistic to recommend for planting any than the resistant Chinese chestnut and the almost as resistant Japanese chestnut. The American chestnut (*C. dentata*), once one of the noblest inhabitants of the forests of eastern North America and an immensely important lumber tree attained heights up to 100 feet. It still exists in the wild as sprouts from old stumps and perhaps sometimes as seedlings. These occasionally reach an age and size when they bear some nuts, but invariably within a few years they succumb to the blight and die. Despite careful searches by large numbers of qualified people no resistant example of the American chestnut has been found. The chinquapin (*C. pumila*), native of the middle Atlantic and southeastern United States, is a suckering shrub or tree 25 to 45 feet tall of little ornamental merit. Chestnuts commonly sold for eating are the imported produce of the Spanish chestnut (*C. sativa*), a native of Europe, North Africa, and western Asia. Unfortunately this splendid species is subject to chestnut blight in North America.

The Chinese chestnut (*C. mollissima*), native of China and Korea, is a tree up to about 60 feet tall, with densely-hairy young shoots and twigs. It has pointed, oblong-lanceolate leaves 3 to 7 inches long, coarsely-toothed, but the teeth flat rather than needle-like for most of their lengths. The under surfaces of the leaves are softly-hairy. On their upper sides the leaves are hairy only along the veins. The nuts, about 1 inch in diameter, are mostly two or three in each hairy-spined husk. Selected varieties, chosen for the superior qualities of

Castanea sativa

Castanea savita (bark)

Castanea sativa (fruit)

Castanea mollissima (fruits and foliage)

their nuts for eating, have been made. The best of these are 'Abundance', 'Kuling', 'Meiling', and 'Nanking'. In addition some hybrids of promise have been developed between the Chinese chestnut and other species. Here belong 'Essate-Jap', 'Kelsey', and 'Sleeping Giant'.

The Japanese chestnut (*C. crenata*) is native to Japan. From the Chinese chestnut it can be distinguished by its young shoots soon becoming hairless, and the closely-spaced teeth of its leaves being needle-like

for a considerable distance from their apexes, sometimes to their bases. This is a shrub or tree up to about 30 feet tall. Its oblong-lanceolate leaves are 3 to 6 inches in length. When young their undersides are hairy. The nuts, 1 inch or more in diameter, are in burs with wide-branching spines, usually two or three nuts in each husk.

Garden and Landscape Uses and Cultivation. Chinese and Japanese chestnuts are decidedly ornamental as well as being sources of food for humans and animals.

Castanea crenata (flowers)

They are attractive in foliage. The leaves color yellow, bronze, and warm browns before they fall. Chestnuts thrive best in deep, well-drained soil, which is slightly acid rather than alkaline. They stand dryish conditions better than many trees and prefer sunny locations. Individual trees of Chinese chestnut are more or less sterile to their own pollen. To assure fruiting, two or more varieties or seedlings must be planted in proximity. Propagation is by seeds and by grafting and budding onto seedlings of Chinese chestnut. The seeds must be sown as soon as they are ripe in an outdoor bed protected from food-seeking animals. Or they may be mixed with slightly damp peat moss or vermiculite and stored in polyethylene bags for three months in a temperature of 40°F, and then sown in a cool greenhouse. The Chinese chestnut is hardy through much of New England, but if frosts occur in mid-June when the trees are in flower, or in fall before the fruits mature, they will not fruit satisfactorily. The Japanese chestnut is hardy approximately as far north as New York City.

CASTANOPSIS (Castan-ópsis) — Chinquapin. The common name chinquapin also belongs to *Castanea pumila*. Except for the giant chinquapin, a species by some authorities considered as belonging to the separate genus *Chrysolepis*, the genus *Cas-*

tanopsis is little represented in cultivation. It comprises about 120 species, mostly Asian, with two natives of western North America. Related to chestnuts (*Castanea*), *Castanopsis* belongs in the beech family FAGACEAE. Its name derives from the Greek *kastana*, chestnut, and *opsis*, resembling.

Castanopsises are nonhardy evergreen trees or rarely shrubs with alternate, undivided, toothed or toothless, two-ranked or five-ranked, leathery leaves. The petalless flowers are unisexual and have five or six sepals. The males, each with ten or twelve stamens, are in erect, branched or branchless spikes. The females, mostly in separate, short spikes or sometimes at the bottoms of spikes of which most of the flowers are males, have three styles. The fruits, which ripen in their second year, are nuts, one to three usually completely enclosed in an asymmetrical, approximately egg-shaped to spherical husk (involucre), spiny, or covered with tubercles or interrupted cross ridges, that opens by splitting irregularly.

Giant chinquapin (*C. chrysophylla* syn. *Chrysolepis chrysophylla*), native from Nevada to Oregon and California, is a handsome tree up to more than 120 feet tall, but frequently lower. It has deeply-furrowed bark and pointed, ovate-oblong to oblonglanceolate, toothless leaves 2 to 6 inches long. Above, they are lustrous dark green. Their undersides are clothed with a persistent scurf of golden-yellow scales. The fluffy spikes of creamy-white flowers are slender and 1 inch to 1½ inches long.

Males occupy most of their lengths with, at the bottom, usually two groups of three to seven female blooms. Sometimes the females are lacking. The subspherical, densely-stiff-spined, mostly solitary fruits are, including the spines, 1 inch to 1½ inches in diameter. Golden chinquapin (*C. c. minor*) is a shrub or tree 3 to 15 or rarely 30 feet tall. Its leaves, usually folded upward along their midribs, have richly golden-yellow undersides. They do not exceed 3½ inches in length. This variety intergrades with the typical species.

Bush chinquapin or Sierra chinquapin (*C. sempervirens* syn. *Chrysolepis sempervirens*), a native of dry rocky areas and slopes from Oregon to California, is a broad, round-topped shrub about 8 feet tall. It naturally forms thickets and has mostly blunt, oblong-lanceolate, flat leaves 2½ to 3½ inches long, grayish-green to yellowish-green above, rusty-hairy on their undersides. The fruits, resembling those of giant chinquapin, are ¾ inch to 1¼ inches in diameter.

Garden and Landscape Uses. Castanopsises are not hardy in the north. In milder climates, the giant chinquapin is a stately ornamental appropriate for featuring as a specimen. The golden chinquapin can be used similarly. It makes an effective hedge and is also satisfactory for growing in large containers to decorate terraces, patios, and similar places. It may be pruned to shape periodically, the beginning of a new growing season being an appropriate time to attend to this. The bush chinquapin is useful as a shrubby groundcover that by pruning or shearing can be kept moderately low.

Cultivation. These chinquapins usually grow slowly in their early stages, but somewhat more vigorously later. Once established they require minimal care. They succeed in poor, dry soils in sunny locations. Propagation is by seed.

CASTANOSPERMUM (Castan-ospérmum) — Moreton-Bay-Chestnut, Black-Bean. The only species of this genus, a native of Queensland and New South Wales, is planted as an ornamental in many parts of the tropics and warm subtropics. Belonging to the pea family LEGUMINOSAE, its name refers to the similarity in appearance its seeds have to those of chestnuts and is derived from the generic name of the chestnut, *Castanea*, and the Greek *sperma*, seed.

The Moreton-bay-chestnut (*Castanospermum australe*) is a handsome, compactheaded, evergreen tree up to about 60 feet but sometimes considerably more in height, with dark, glossy green, leathery foliage that, like other parts of the plant, is hairless. The leaves are usually alternate, up to 1½ feet in length, and consist of an odd number, eleven to fifteen, of broadly-oblong leaflets 3 to 5 inches long. The 6-inchlong, short-stalked or stalkless racemes of long-stemmed, pea-shaped flowers, with recurving upper petals, are tucked close to the trunk and main branches as well as on limbs high in the crown; were it not for their bright colors they often would likely pass unseen. But they are brilliant as well as variable. Upon opening, the petals and ten protruding stamens are clear yellow, as they age they change to orange and finally red. At all stages the calyxes are orange and the pistil is tipped with red. Because of the successional opening of the flowers in individual racemes each cluster displays a rich assortment of warm xanthic and rubicund tones. The blooms are succeeded by cylindrical, leathery or woody pods 6 to 9 inches long and about 2 inches wide, each containing about six chestnutlike seeds, which are poisonous raw but are safe cooked. They are eaten by the Australian aborigines. The bark of young shoots crushed has a strong odor of cucumber. The Moreton-bay-chestnut produces high-class lumber that resembles walnut and is decidedly handsome. In its native land it is esteemed for furniture and cabinetwork.

Garden and Landscape Uses and Cultivation. This deep-rooted species is excellent as a specimen tree in home grounds, parks, and other public places, and for avenues. It thrives in deep moist soil of ordinary fertility and does especially well on the banks of streams or lakes where its roots have access to constant supplies of moisture. It is propagated by seed.

Castanopsis chrysophylla (fruit)

CASTILLA (Cast-ílla)—Mexican Rubber or Panama Rubber. Once a source of commercial rubber, although never as important as *Hevea brasiliensis*, the Mexican rubber or Panama rubber (*Castilla elastica* syn. *Castilloa elastica*) is one of ten species of a tropical American genus of the mulberry family MORACEAE. The name commemorates Juan Diego del Castillo, an eighteenth-century pharmacist and a botanical explorer of Mexico.

The Mexican rubber tree (*C. elastica*) ranges in height from 50 to 150 feet and has horizontal or drooping branches. Its young shoots are woolly-hairy and its leaves are thickly covered with hairs especially on their undersides. They are elliptic-obovate to oblong, 1 foot to 1½ feet long, 3 to 6 inches broad, and short-stalked. The blooms are inconspicuous. The compound fruits, about 1½ inches in diameter and conspicuously knobbly, consist of many individuals about ¾ inch long. They are sweetish and edible.

Garden and Landscape Uses and Cultivation. Attractive for general planting in Florida and other warm climates, the Mexican rubber tree is propagated by seeds and by cuttings. It grows rapidly and adapts to ordinary soils, preferring those that are deep and fertile. As a young plant it appreciates some shade.

CASTILLEJA (Castil-lèja) — Painted Cup, Paint Brush. Because they are semiparasites on the roots of other plants and because these relationships are neither well understood nor easily provided for, castillejas are generally not easy to cultivate. They have never been grown widely in gardens. This is unfortunate, since many of the about 250 species are highly ornamental. The genus, which belongs in the figwort family SCROPHULARIACEAE, is entirely American except for one species that occurs also in Asia. The name commemorates the eighteenth-century Spanish botanist Castillejo.

Castillejas are annuals, biennials, and herbaceous perennials, with alternate, narrow leaves that in some species are lobed (especially the upper ones). The flowers, interspersed with often bright red or yellow bracts, are in dense, terminal spikes. They have tubular calyxes with two or four lobes and compressed, tubular, two-lipped corollas, the upper lip of which is much longer than the often tiny, three-toothed lower one. The stamens and style are enclosed by the upper lip. There are two pairs of stamens. The fruits are many-seeded capsules.

Because of their limited susceptibility to cultivation there is little purpose in discussing many kinds. They are described in books dealing with wild flowers and in floras of the regions of North America in which they occur. Among the more brightly colored and attractive kinds is the Indian paint brush (*C. californica* syn. *C. affinis*), a perennial species of California and Baja California with bright red blooms, and the scarlet paint brush (*C. coccinea*), native from Ontario to Manitoba, Louisiana, and Oklahoma, that has yellow flowers and scarlet bracts. This is an annual.

Garden Uses and Cultivation. Attempts to grow castillejas are mostly made by gardeners who specialize in native plants. About the only sensible advice is to duplicate as closely as possible conditions under which the species grow naturally, paying particular attention to their companion plants and attempting to include these in the garden planting. Propagation is by seed.

CASTOR-BEAN or CASTOR OIL PLANT is *Ricinus communis*.

CASTOR POMACE. The residue of castor beans from which the oil has been expressed, castor pomace, is employed as a fertilizer. See Fertilizers.

CASUARINA (Casu-arìna)—Australian-Pine, She-Oak or Beefwood. To the botanically uninitiated, members of this most important genus, of the casuarina family CASUARINACEAE are likely to suggest evergreen conifers rather than hardwood trees and shrubs. This because they have no evident leaves and the slender green branchlets that do the work of photosynthesis from a little distance away have much the aspect of the foliage of conifers. Closer examination reveals them to be distinctly jointed and so more like the stems of horsetails (*Equisetum*) than like conifer needles. Casuarinas are also sometimes confused with desert species of *Tamarix*, but these do not have jointed stems or bear fruiting cones. The forty-five species of this genus are restricted as natives chiefly to Australia and New Caledonia, with a few species in other Pacific islands and Malaysia, and possibly East Africa. The name is derived from that of the cassowary. Its drooping branches fancifully resemble the feathers of that bird. Casuarina timber is extremely dense, hard, and so heavy that it sinks in water or barely floats. At least one species, *Casuarina equisetifolia*, is naturalized in Florida.

Casuarinas have in place of leaves tiny scales, joined to form toothed sleeves around the joints (nodes) of the longitudinally-grooved young shoots. Male flowers, borne in long spikes, consist of a single stamen between a pair of scales representing the perianth. More evident, female blooms are in globular heads. These terminate short branches and as they pass into fruit become compact, woody cones. They have spiraled scales or bracts with a pistil between each pair. The fruits are compressed, seedlike nuts.

The horsetail tree (*C. equisetifolia*), of Australia, is 40 to 60 feet high and up to 20 feet wide. Its grayish-green branches

Casuarina equisetifolia

and branchlets droop gracefully. Their nodes or joints are less than ½ inch apart. The spikes of male flowers are about ¾ inch long. The fruiting cones are ½ inch in diameter. The tree often grown as *C. equisetifolia* is quite similar to *C. cunninghamiana* or a hybrid between that species and *C. glauca*. Native of Queensland and New South Wales, *C. cunninghamiana*, 30 to 50 feet tall, is most easily distinguished from *C. equisetifolia* by its globular, fruiting cones being not more than ⅓ inch in diameter. From *C. equisetifolia*, the mountain she-oak or coast beefwood, of Australia and Tasmania, *C. stricta* differs in the joints of its dark green branchlets being more than ½ inch apart. This has fruiting cones 1 inch in diameter.

Casuarina stricta (branchlets and flowers)

Garden and Landscape Uses and Cultivation. In warm climates casuarinas are extremely useful ornamentals. They are adapted for a variety of locations, being especially suitable for use near the sea and in semidesert regions. The tree types are good street trees. Some even thrive on beaches, just above high water mark. They tolerate salt spray, high winds, much heat, and wet or dry soils. They need no special care and are easily increased by seed. They can also be grown from cuttings.

CASUARINACEAE—Casuarina Family. Two genera constitute this family of sixty-five species of dicotyledons. Natives of southeast Asia, the Mascarene Islands, Polynesia, and Australia, they are evergreen trees and shrubs with green or gray-green, jointed, usually deciduous shoots and branchlets that are often mistaken for leaves. The true leaves are tiny scales in whorls (circles of more than two) around the nodes (joints) of the generally deeply-grooved, cylindrical shoots. In this, the casuarina family resembles horsetails (*Equisetum*). The flowers are tiny and unisexual, the males with perianths of one or two scales and one stamen, the females in dense heads or spikes that become cone-like and dry are of a single pistil and without perianths. The fruits are thin, winged nutlets. The only genus cultivated is *Casuarina*.

CAT or CAT'S. These words are used as part of the common name of the following plants: cat-tail (*Typha*), cat-thyme (*Teucrium marum*), cat's claw (*Macfadyena unguis-cati*, *Pithecellobium unguis-cati*, and *Schrankia nuttallii*), cat's ear (*Calochortus* and *Hypochoeris*), cat's valerian (*Valeriana officinalis*), and red-hot-cat-tail (*Acalypha hispida*).

CATABROSA (Cata-bròsa)—Brook Grass. The genus *Catabrosa* consists of four North American, European, and Asian species of the grass family GRAMINEAE. Its name, derived from the Greek *katabrosis*, eating away, alludes to the eroded appearance of the lower scales of the flower spikelets. Catabrosas are aquatic and wet-soil herbaceous perennials with creeping rhizomes and loose panicles of mostly two-flowered spikelets.

Brook grass (*C. aquatica*) inhabits shallow water and wet soils in northern North America, Europe, and Asia. From 1 foot to 3 feet tall, it has stems with lower parts prostrate and rooting. The soft, flat, hairless blades of its leaves are up to 4 inches long by ¼ inch wide. Its loose, erect, pyramidal, yellowish-brown panicles of flowers are 4 to 8 inches long. The foliage of *C. a. folio-variegata* is handsomely marked with lengthways stripes of green and yellow.

Garden and Landscape Uses and Cultivation. The species described and its variety are occasionally cultivated in watery soils and at the margins of ponds and streams. They are easily propagated from divisions and, the typical species, by seeds.

CATALPA (Catál-pa)—Indian Bean. Eleven species of *Catalpa*, natives of North America, the West Indies, and eastern Asia, are deciduous and evergreen trees, the evergreens confined in the wild to the West Indies. The name is derived from the Cherokee Indian one of some species. This genus, which belongs in the bignonia family BIGNONIACEAE, is closely related to the empress tree (*Paulownia*) of the figwort family SCROPHULARIACEAE, to the extent that the two genera represent a bridge between the families. Catalpas are handsome and decorative in foliage and flower. They bloom in summer. The soft, coarsely-grained wood of the deciduous species is of no commercial importance, but is durable in the ground and is used for fence posts and fuel. That of the evergreen yokewood (*C. longissima*) is hard and is used locally for construction material and carts.

Catalpas have branchlets with thick pith and without terminal buds, large, opposite or whorled, long-stalked, entire or coarsely-lobed, undivided leaves, with usually purple, glandular spots in the axils of the veins beneath, and showy blooms in terminal panicles or racemes. The flowers are bell-shaped. They have two-lipped or irregularly-split calyxes. The corollas have five spreading lobes (petals), the three lower larger than the two upper. Of the five stamens, two are fertile. The two-lobed style slightly exceeds them in length. The fruits are long, slender, cylindrical capsules that hang in bunches. These suggested the common name Indian-bean. They contain many flattened, oblong seeds with a tuft of white hair at each end.

Common catalpa or Indian-bean (*C. bignonioides*), native from Georgia to Florida and Mississippi and sometimes naturalized in other states, was the first kind known. It was cultivated in Europe in 1726. Hardy through most of New England, this is a broad, round-headed tree usually not more than 45 feet tall but occasionally 55 or 60 feet tall. Its leaves, often in whorls of three, emit an unpleasant odor when crushed. They are ovate, slightly heart-shaped or wedge-shaped at their bases, abruptly pointed at their apexes, and up to 10 inches long. Sometimes they have two lateral lobes. They are light green, pubescent on their undersides, especially on the veins, and nearly hairless above. The broadly-pyramidal panicles are of many fragrant flowers almost 2 inches in diameter, with frilled petals. They are white with two yellow stripes inside, thickly spotted with purplish-brown. The slender pods, 6 to 20 inches long, remain on the trees, a little untidily, until well into the winter. Variety *C. b. nana*, is a dwarf that rarely blooms. This is frequently grafted onto 6- or 7-foot-tall stems of *C. bignonioides* to produce a round-headed specimen often misnamed *C. bungei* (true *C. bungei* is quite different). See additional kinds below. Variety *C. b. aurea* has yellow foliage;

Catabrosa aquatica folio-variegata

Catalpa bignonioides

Catalpa bignonioides (flowers)

Catalpa speciosa, in fruit

C. b. koehnei is distinguishable by its yellow leaves with green veins and a green blotch below the center of the leaf.

Western catalpa (**C. speciosa**) is also sometimes called Indian-bean. Native from Illinois to Indiana, Tennessee, and Arkansas, and sometimes naturalized elsewhere in the United States, it grows to a height of 90 feet. From *C. bignonioides* it differs in having fewer-flowered panicles and in the flowers being 2 to 2½ inches wide and only sparsely spotted with purplish-brown. Its leaves taper to longer points and are not malodorous when bruised. They are rounded or heart-shaped at their bases, downy on their undersides, and up to 1 foot long. Western catalpa is somewhat hardier than the common catalpa.

A hybrid between Asian *C. ovata*, and American *C. bignonioides* is **C. hybrida.** This fine ornamental, intermediate between its parents and about 40 feet tall, was raised in Indiana by John C. Teas about 1874. Its leaves, which more closely resemble those of its Chinese than its American parent, are purplish as they unfold and become green later. Slightly-hairy beneath, they are larger than those of *C. ovata*, sometimes 2 feet in diameter. The flowers are much like those of *C. bignonioides*, but smaller and mostly in longer panicles. Variety *C. h. purpurea* has black-purple shoots

Catalpa speciosa (flowers)

and young leaves. In *C. h. japonica* the leaves are wider, more abruptly pointed, and nearly hairless beneath.

The French-oak, Spanish-oak, or yoke-wood (**C. longissima**) is an evergreen West Indian species up to 60 feet in height. It is grown in Hawaii, southern Florida, and other tropical and near-tropical climates for ornament and shade. In Hawaii it is used for reforestation. This kind has opposite or whorled (in circles of more than two), pointed, narrow-oblong to elliptic, thin leaves 3 to 4 inches long, and panicles of white and pink-tinted blooms. Its slender fruits are 1 foot to 2 feet long. Another evergreen, **C. punctata,** also of the West Indies, has blunt, leathery leaves and very fragrant, light yellow flowers. Attaining heights of 25 to 30 feet, it inhabits swamps and wet soils. Both evergreen kinds are sometimes placed in a separate genus, *Macrocatalpa.*

Catalpa bignonioides aurea

Catalpa hybrida

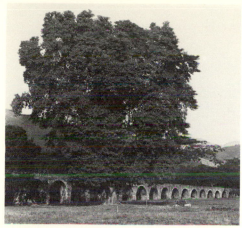

Catalpa longissima

Additional kinds include these: *C. bungei* (not to be confused with *C. bignonioides nana* often known by that name) is a pyramidal Chinese tree up to 40 feet in height with narrowly-triangular-ovate, glabrous leaves, dark green above, paler beneath, and up to 7½ inches long. The flowers, less freely borne than those of most kinds, are white with purple spots. The pods are 1 foot to 1¼ feet long. This is hardy at Boston, Massachusetts. *C. b. heterophylla* has several pointed teeth near the bases of its leaves. *C. fargesii* is a handsome native of China that attains a height of 60 feet. Its broadly-ovate, taper-pointed leaves are up to 6 inches long and are densely clothed beneath with branched hairs. Its flowers, rosy-pink to purplish spotted with brown, are in racemes. *C. f. duclouxii* has hairless leaves and pink blooms with orange spots. Both *C. fargesii* and its variety are hardy in southern New England. *C. ovata*, of China, has yellowish flowers, striped orange and purple-spotted inside, in panicles. It attains a height of 30 to 45 feet and has broad-ovate, often shallowly- sometimes irregularly-lobed leaves, abruptly-pointed and up to 8 inches long. *C. o. flavescens* has yellow flowers. These two are hardy through most of New England.

Garden and Landscape Uses. Despite catalpas being among the handsomest of flowering trees and blooming when few other kinds are making any floral display, they are a little difficult to use to good advantage. Unless carefully placed somewhat incongruous effects can result. Their large, usually light green leaves produce a distinctly exotic look. Catalpas do not blend with other trees and shrubs as successfully as many trees. They are apt to be a little too insistent in the landscape picture. Well located, they can be extremely effective and are among the most beautiful of trees when in bloom. They are usually seen to better advantage in sophisticated garden landscapes than in natural or naturalistic ones. They can be used successfully as lawn specimens and in association with buildings and other architectural features. They are also useful as specimen

trees in parks and for planting in groups, with ample space between individuals, along parkways and in similar developments. The dreadful examples of dwarf *C. bignonioides nana* grafted atop bean-pole-like understocks of other kinds to produce mop-head monstrosities usually sold as *C. bungei* (a calumnious usage of a perfectly good name of another species) should be banished forever from American gardens. Completely without aesthetic merit, they are easily replaceable with better plants.

Cultivation. Catalpas find any ordinary, reasonably moist soil agreeable, but grow best in distinctly fertile ones. They need sunny locations and abhor exposed windy sites. These trees transplant without difficulty and grow without special care. Once of planting-out size, they need no regular pruning, but as young specimens in nurseries some is needed to make sure that they develop branchless trunks 9 or 10 feet in height. Because their branch ends have no terminal buds, they produce each spring two or three new leaders from each. All except one should be removed from the shoot that is to form the trunk. Propagation is usually by seeds, but increase can be had by leafy cuttings under mist in summer, by root cuttings, and by grafting onto seedling understocks in a greenhouse in late winter.

Diseases and Pests. The chief diseases are leaf spots, powdery mildews, and wood decays. Insect enemies are caterpillars of the sphinx moth, mealybugs, and maggots of a midge that chew the interior tissues of the leaves.

CATAMODES. This is the name of orchid hybrids the parents of which are *Catasetum* and *Mormodes*.

CATANANCHE (Catanán-che) — Cupid's Dart. Cupid's dart (*Catananche caerulea*) is an old-fashioned, summer-blooming, hardy herbaceous perennial, one of five species of a genus of the daisy family COMPOSITAE. The name comes from the Greek *katanangke*, a powerful incentive, and takes cognizance of the use, by Greek women, of cupid's dart in love philters.

Catananches are annuals and herbaceous perennials with linear or lanceolate leaves clustered near their bases, and blue, occasionally white or yellow, flower heads atop long stalks. The flower heads have involucres (collars of bracts below the blooms) of several rows of bracts, with the upper ones membranous or chaffy and without green coloration. The florets are all strap-shaped (of the type that composes dandelion flowers and look like petals). These are Mediterranean region natives.

Cupid's dart (*C. caerulea*) is 2 to 2½ feet tall and has much the aspect of chicory (*Cichorium intybus*), from which it differs in its flower heads being long-stalked instead of stalkless. Its lanceolate to oblanceolate

leaves have hairs and are up to 1 foot in length. Sometimes they have a few marginal teeth. About 2 inches across, the slender-stalked flower heads typically are blue. In variety *C. c. alba* they are white, and in *C. c. bicolor* white with blue bases to the florets. The outer florets spread widely and have square, toothed apexes.

Garden Uses and Cultivation. Cupid's dart is suitable for beds and borders in full sun and succeeds in dryish soils. Its flowers are attractive for cutting and may be dried as everlastings. This is done by harvesting them before they are fully open, tying them in small bundles, and hanging them upside down in a dry, shaded, airy place for a few weeks. The cultural needs of this plant are of the simplest. It needs no special care. Propagation is by seeds, which, sown early, give plants that flower the same year, and by division in early fall or early spring.

CATANOCHES. This is the name of orchid hybrids the parents of which are *Catasetum* and *Cycnoches*.

CATAPODIUM (Cata-pòdium). Closely related to *Festuca*, *Poa*, and *Scleropoa*, this genus of four Mediterranean region and western European grasses, of the grass family GRAMINEAE, includes one sometimes cultivated for ornament and naturalized in warmer parts of the United States. The name is from the Greek *kata*, down to, and *podium*, a foot, and has reference to the stalkless or nearly stalkless spikelets.

Catapodiums are low annuals with slender, wiry stems and leaves with flat, linear blades. The flower panicles or racemes are stiff and flat and are composed of somewhat flattened spikelets, of three to twelve flowers, without awns (bristles).

In Europe called fern grass, *Catapodium rigidum* (syn. *Scleropoa rigida*) is common in the western part of that continent and is naturalized in many other parts of the world including the United States. Up to 8 inches in height, its stems are in tufts or sometimes solitary. The slender leaves have blades rarely over 4 inches long. The flower panicles, dense or rather loose, are 1 inch to 3 inches long with bases two-thirds as wide as they are long. The spikelets, up to ⅓ inch in length, are three- to ten-flowered, green or purplish. Bright green *C. r. major*, with stems up to 1 foot tall, and larger, looser, panicles, is the kind usually cultivated.

Garden Uses and Cultivation. This little grass makes a modest display when grown in flower beds or among collections of grasses, and its panicles may be cut and used fresh or dried in flower arrangements. Its cultivation is simple. Seeds are sown in spring in ordinary garden soil in sunny locations, and the seedlings are thinned sufficiently for the plants not to crowd unduly.

CATASETUM (Cata-sètum). Among the most remarkable of orchids, catasetums have often large, frequently beautiful, curiously structured blooms. The genus to which they belong occurs in the wild from Mexico to Peru and Brazil. It belongs to the orchid family ORCHIDACEAE. There are seventy species. The name, from the Greek *kata*, downward, and *seta*, a bristle, refers to the antennae usual in the male flowers.

Species of *Catasetum* are generally epiphytes, growing on trees without taking nourishment from them. Related to *Cycnoches* and *Mormodes*, they have fleshy, ovoid to spindle-shaped pseudobulbs covered with large sheaths and large, deciduous longitudinally-pleated leaves narrowing to their bases. Commonly they produce many aerial roots. Some species have bisexual flowers. In others the blooms are unisexual, the sexes very dissimilar, often borne at different seasons, and frequently borne on separate plants. Because of this, there has been and is considerable confusion in applying names to catasetums. Not infrequently male and female plants of the same species have been given different names. The branchless flower stalks come from the bases of the pseudobulbs. Erect or arching, they have few to many blooms. Usually more or less equal and rather fleshy, the sepals and petals are spreading or reflexed. The rigid, fleshy lip is deeply-concave, helmet-shaped or pouched with the margins of the opening often toothed or fringed. In male blooms the column is usually long and fleshy and generally has a pair of long, down-pointing antennae. The shorter, stouter column of the female flower is without antennae. These, or part of the column itself if antennae are absent, when touched cause the explosive ejection of the masses of pollen. Each pollen mass has a sticky disk at its base. This enables it to adhere to a visiting insect and thus obtain transportation to another bloom the creature visits, and if it be female or bisexual to fertilize it. Male blooms are more numerous than females.

The national flower of Venezuela **C. pileatum** (syn. *C. bungerothii*) is probably the most lovely of catasetums. It has pseudobulbs 5 to 9 inches long by one-third as wide. The pointed-lanceolate leaves are up to 9 inches long by 2 inches wide. Arching flower stalks carry up to nearly twelve flattish, ivory-white to delicate yellow blooms sometimes exceeding 4 inches in diameter, and richly fragrant. Their sepals and petals are lanceolate. The almost round to broader, basin-like to nearly flat lip, about 2½ inches in diameter, has below its middle a sometimes orange depression. Widespread as a native of South America, **C. macrocarpum** is variable and vigorous. It has pseudobulbs up to 1½ feet long by 5 inches thick. Its oblong-lanceolate leaves may be 3 feet long by 4 inches wide. The

Catasetum pileatum

Catasetum macrocarpum

3- to 4-inch-wide blooms are in arching racemes of up to twelve, and up to 1½ feet long. Their pointed, more or less brown-spotted sepals and petals are light green to yellow. The deeply-pouched lip terminates in three sharp teeth. Similar **C. integerrimum** (syn. *C. oerstedii*) has wider sepals and petals and the orifice of the lip fringed with hairs. Similar **C. viridiflavum,** of Panama, has nodding green flowers with the interior of the lip marked with yellow. An excellent intermediate natural hybrid, variable and handsome **C. splendens** has as parents *C. pileatum* and *C. macrocarpum.* Its flowers, rather smaller than those of *C. pileatum,* have shallow to deep lips.

Catasetum callosum

Catasetum callosum (flowers)

Catasetum viridiflavum

Other species cultivated include the following: *C. barbatum,* of Guiana and Brazil, is a ground orchid with more or less pendulous flower stalks, and 2-inch-wide, fragrant, black-flecked, greenish blooms, with bearded lips. **C. bicolor,** of Panama, has

short pseudobulbs and smaller leaves than most catasetums. Its arching to drooping racemes are of fragrant blooms about 3½ inches wide, the sepals and petals of various combinations of chocolate-brown, brownish-green, green, purplish-green, and pink, the lips white or yellow marked with red-brown or purple. **C. callosum,** of Venezuela and Colombia, has blooms with brownish sepals and petals about 2 inches long and red-dotted, green lips. **C. fimbriatum,** of Brazil, has arching, loose racemes up to 1½ feet tall of seven to fifteen fragrant blooms about 1½ inches wide. Yellowish, they are spotted and flecked

with red. The yellow, fan-shaped lip is sometimes tinged with green. **C. saccatum christyanum** (syn. *C. christyanum*), of Brazil, has drooping, loose racemes up to 1½ feet long of up to eight or nine fragrant flowers 4 inches across. They have red-dotted, greenish sepals and petals and greenish to brownish-pink lips. The petals and lip are fringed with rose-pink hairs. **C. warczewitzii** (syn. *C. scurra*), of Central America and northeastern South America, has pseudobulbs up to 4 inches long. Its leaves, deciduous and usually absent at flowering time, are 1 foot to 1½ feet long and up to 3 inches wide. The pendulous

Catasetum barbatum

Catasetum barbatum (flower)

racemes are of several 1- to 1½-inch-wide, often fragrant, white to greenish-white blooms striped lengthwise with light green. Similarly colored and with chocolate-colored veining deep in the throat, the lip has a strongly-fringed center lobe and a pair of erect side ones frilled at their margins.

Garden Uses and Cultivation. These fascinating orchids of easy cultivation are suitable for beginners as well as more experienced orchid collectors. They thrive in well-drained, not-too-large pots or hanging baskets in tightly packed tree fern or

Catasetum warczewitzii

Catasetum warczewitzii (flowers)

osmunda fiber or fir bark. Repotting must be done before the rooting medium becomes stale or sour. Catasetums enjoy warmth and a humid atmosphere. Minimum winter night temperatures should be 60 to 65°F with increases by day of five to fifteen degrees. When in active growth generous, but not excessive supplies of water are needed. Care must be taken not to allow water to lodge in the bases of the leaves of the young shoots. If it does rot is likely to result. Regular mild fertilization during the growing season does much to encourage strong growth and flowering. When the new pseudobulbs have attained full size and maturity a rest period of three or four weeks, during which time water is withheld, is needed. For more information see Orchids.

CATBRIER. See Smilax.

CATCH CROP. This is a quickly maturing crop, usually a salad or vegetable, but sometimes a flowering annual, produced by sowing between rows of another crop that will occupy the ground for a much longer time or by sowing on a patch of ground that will be vacant for a short time only. See Intercropping or Companion Cropping.

CATCHFLY. See Silene. German catchfly is *Lychnis viscaria*. For catchfly-gentian see Eustoma.

CATERPILLAR PLANT. See Scorpiurus.

CATERPILLARS. These are the larvae of butterflies and moths, the only one of the four life stages through which these insects pass in succession in which they feed destructively. And feed caterpillars do, many of them greedily and not uncommonly on the choicest garden plants. Some kinds confine their attentions to one kind of plant, others adapt to a more varied diet. Caterpillars have soft, usually cylindrical, wormlike bodies with a head furnished with chewing mouth parts and thirteen other segments. The first three behind the head have each a pair of jointed legs. Further to the rear are usually five, sometimes fewer, pairs of jointless false legs, one pair each on the sixth to ninth body segments behind the head and one pair on the rearmost segment.

Caterpillars may be spiny, hairy, or smooth. Often they are beautifully colored. In size they vary from very small to up to 6 inches long or longer and 1 inch in diameter. Some, called hornworms, have a large, hornlike projection from the rear end of the body. Others, called cankerworms, inchworms, loopers, or measuring-worms, are without false legs in the middles of their bodies and travel by arching their bodies in a series of looping movements. Tent caterpillars live gregariously in large tents they build of a silky material they spin; others, leaf tiers, leaf rollers, and webworms, spin other kinds of webs. Female bagworms spend their entire lives inside little bags or tents. Some leaf miners are caterpillars. Slug caterpillars are practically without feet. And so it goes. The manners of life of the larvae of butterflies and moths are very various. As they grow, caterpillars shed their skins several times and generally assume new forms and coloring after each molt. Because of this, fully grown ones may be completely different in appearance from the young of the same species.

Before changing into the butterfly or moth, which is the adult stage of the insect of which the caterpillar is the larval stage, the creature pupates. It goes into a dormant condition for a period. The pupae of moths are enclosed in cocoons (bags made of silken threads), those of butterflies often have hard shells and are called chrysalids. The pupae may be attached to trunks, branches, twigs, or other plant parts or hidden in bark crevices and other out-of-the-way places or in the ground.

Controls for caterpillars include hand picking and spraying or dusting with stomach poisons or less commonly contact insecticides. In special cases other measures are employed, for example burning the nests of tent caterpillars with torches and banding tree trunks with a sticky substance to trap the wingless female moths as they ascend to lay eggs. For specific, up-to-date recommendations applicable to special cases and particular geographical regions consult Cooperative Extension Agents, the State Agricultural Experimental Station, or other reliable authorities. The spines and hairs of a few caterpillars loosen easily and become embedded in parts of the body brought into contact with them. They can cause serious irritation. Beware of handling spiny and hairy caterpillars. Because of their similar appearance the larvae of some sawflies, relative of bees and wasps rather than butterflies and moths, are sometimes called caterpillars. They differ from the caterpillars of butterflies and moths in having more than five pairs of false legs in addition to three pairs of jointed legs.

CATESBAEA (Cates-baèa)—Lily-Thorn. Despite not being a lily relative, but belonging to the madder family RUBIACEAE, the most commonly cultivated member of this genus of ten species has a colloquial name that is descriptive. The plant is exceedingly thorny and has blooms of lily-like aspect. The name *Catesbaea* honors Mark Catesby, an American naturalist, who died in 1749.

Catesbaeas are spiny shrubs, natives of the West Indies, with tiny-flowered *C. parviflora* extending into Florida. They have opposite or clustered, small leaves, prevailingly broad-ovate or oblong, and solitary white or yellow blooms from the leaf axils. The flowers have four sepals, a tubular, funnel-shaped corolla with four short lobes (petals), four stamens, and a solitary style. The fruits are spherical berries.

The lily-thorn (*C. spinosa*) is an evergreen, vase-shaped shrub up to 8 or sometimes 15 feet tall, and formidably armed with sharp spines 1 inch to 1½ inches long. Native of the Bahamas and Cuba, it has ovate to oblong leaves shorter than the spines. The arching stems are festooned in season with handsome, creamy-yellow, hanging, trumpet-like blooms about 6 inches long. The yellow, globular to egg-shaped fruits, about 2 inches long, are edible.
Garden and Landscape Uses and Cultivation. The beautiful lily-thorn described here grows naturally in dry, rocky ground, and under cultivation succeeds under similar circumstances. It is suitable for subtropical climates, and thrives in full sun. It is useful for background planting, and for use as a single specimen where its thorniness is not disadvantageous. It is also effective as a hedge. Propagation is by seeds and by cuttings.

CATHA (Cà-tha)—Khat or Cafta. Arab peoples use the leaves of the only species of this genus to make a tea-like beverage. It belongs to the staff tree family CELASTRACEAE and is indigenous to Africa, Arabia, and Madagascar. Its name is derived from its Arabic one.

Khat or cafta (**Catha edulis**) is an evergreen, hairless shrub up to 10 feet in height, with thickish, narrowly-elliptic to oblanceolate, stalked, toothed leaves up to 4 inches long. Mostly they are opposite, but on vigorous shoots may be alternate. In short clusters from the leaf axils, the small white blooms have five-toothed calyxes, and five each petals and stamens. The fruits are club-shaped to cylindrical, three-angled, ⅓-inch-long capsules that remain throughout the winter and split to reveal their up to three bright red seeds.
Garden and Landscape Uses and Cultivation. Planted in the south, California, and other mild-climate regions, khat is of interest because of the economic use made of it by Arabs and because of its ornamental appearance. It serves as a general purpose shrub in sun or part-shade and succeeds in ordinary garden soil. It is easily multiplied by seeds and by cuttings.

CATHARANTHUS (Cathar-ánthus) — Madagascar-Periwinkle. To this genus the Madagascar-periwinkle, long known to gardeners and botanists as *Vinca rosea*, belongs. Critical study has shown it to be sufficiently distinct from *Vinca* to warrant the reclassification and consequent name change. The chief differences between *Vinca* and *Catharanthus* are that the latter consists of non-woody, annual or perennial herbaceous plants with soft, deciduous leaves and flowers usually in twos or in threes in the leaf axils. The blooms have slender cylindrical, instead of narrowly-funnel-shaped corolla tubes. As in *Vinca,* the five corolla lobes spread horizontally, but the mouth of the corolla tube is closed with bristle-like hairs, not as with *Vinca* either open or closed by scalelike appendages. In *Catharanthus* the seed pods contain fifteen seeds or more, in *Vinca* six to eight. With the exception of *C. pusillus* of India, the genus *Catharanthus*, consisting of five species, is confined to Madagascar. It belongs in the dogbane family APOCYNACEAE.

The Madagascar-periwinkle (*C. roseus* syn. *Vinca rosea*) is the only species known to be cultivated in America. Not only is it a popular garden annual, it has escaped from cultivation and naturalized in parts of the south, as it has in many subtropical and tropical regions. This erect, pubescent plant, 1 foot to 2 feet tall, has more or less oblong leaves, narrowed to their bases to short stalks and rounded and with a tiny spinelike protrusion at their apex. In the typical species the blooms are magenta-rose, often with a reddish eye. Variety *C. r. albus* has white blooms, those of *C. r. ocellatus* are white, with a red or carmine eye. The flowers face upward and are about 1½ inches in diameter.
Garden Uses. The Madagascar-periwinkle is one of the most satisfactory plants to grow as a flower garden annual in areas where hot summers occur. It revels in high

Catharanthus roseus

temperatures and high humidity and blooms without letup for weeks or months, usually until killed by frost. Well suited for beds, borders, and window and porch boxes, it is also attractive in pots in window gardens and greenhouses.

Cultivation. Because it needs a long growing season an early start must be made when raising plants for summer display. Seeds are sown, or cuttings are taken from stock plants wintered in a greenhouse, in February. They are started in a temperature of 65 to 70°F. The young plants are potted individually in 2½- or 3-inch pots and kept in a sunny, fairly humid greenhouse with a night temperature of 55 to 60°F and day temperatures five to fifteen degrees higher. When 3 or 4 inches tall their tips are pinched to promote branching. The plants are not transferred to the garden until the weather is warm and settled; prior to planting out they should be hardened for a week or two in a cold frame or in a sheltered, sunny place outdoors. A planting distance of 10 inches to 1 foot between individuals is appropriate. The Madagascar-periwinkle is satisfactory in any ordinary garden soil not lacking moisture. Although good drainage is necessary, it needs moist earth. In dry weather water regularly.

CATJANG is *Vigna unguiculata cylindrica*.

CATKIN. This is a particular type of inflorescence or natural arrangement of the flowers of some kinds of plants. It is a special type of spike that has scaly bracts and is often flexuous. The "pussies" of pussy willows are catkins, so are the inflorescences of other willows and of birches, hazels, and oaks. Plants with catkins are usually wind-pollinated.

Catkins: (a) Birch

(b) Willow

CATMINT, CATNIP, or CATNEP is *Nepeta cataria*.

CATOPSIS (Cat-ópsis). Although its twenty-six or more species are not among the most showy members of the pineapple family BROMELIACEAE, to which it belongs, *Catopsis* is represented in cultivation by a few kinds. It ranges in the wild from Florida through Mexico and Central America to northern South America and the West Indies. Its name, from the Greek *kato*, beneath, and *opsis*, appearance, may allude to the plants being viewed from below.

These, generally epiphytes (tree-perchers that take no nourishment from their hosts), sometimes elect to grow on rocks. They have rather elegant rosettes of smooth-edged, soft leaves, dusted on their under surfaces with almost chalky-white scales. In some kinds the foliage is speckled or barred. The usually branched, flowering stalks, erect, arching, or drooping, carry many small white or yellow blooms that have three sepals, three petals separate to their bases, six stamens that do not protrude, and a short style. The fruits are capsules.

Species native in southern Florida as well as in Central and South America and, the second also in the West Indies, are C.

berteroniana, C. floribunda, and C. nutans. In the wild favoring full sun, **C. berteroniana** has erect, vase-shaped rosettes 1½ to 3 feet tall. The channeled, strap-shaped, arching, yellow-green leaves broaden at their bases, where they are chalky-white. Stout and stiffly-erect, the yellow to bronzy flowering stalks have overlapping basal bracts and broad, green floral ones. Fragrant and white, the blooms have sepals ½ inch long or longer and shorter petals. The stamens are of unequal lengths. Many-leaved rosettes of pea-green foliage are typical of shade-loving **C. floribunda.** Its arching leaves, 8 inches to 1¼ feet long, narrow abruptly from a broad base and then taper gradually to a long-pointed apex. The semipendulous to drooping flowering stalk, much-branched toward its end and 1 foot to 2 feet long, has functionally unisexual, white or yellowish blooms with sepals decidedly under ½ inch long. Rosettes of broad, pointed, strongly recurved, bright green leaves up to 1 foot long are characteristic of **C. nutans.** The branchless or few-branched, usually arching, slender flowering stalks of this, up to 1 foot in length, bear blooms with bright yellow petals that flare outward near their apexes. The three outer stamens are longer than the inner ones.

Kinds not native in the United States include these: **C. compacta,** of southern Mexico, has compact rosettes of many brownish leaves 8 inches to 1 foot long by about 2 inches wide. They have, especially toward their bases, a chalky-white coating. The white blooms are on erect, branched flowering stalks. **C. morreniana,** of southern Mexico and Central America, has open

Catopsis morreniana

rosettes of spreading and ascending, glossy, strap-shaped leaves 4 to 8 inches long, and tall, openly-branched, erect flowering stalks with yellow bracts and tiny pale yellow blooms. **C. nitida,** of Central and northern South America and the Greater Antilles, has erect, tubular rosettes 9 inches to 1½ feet tall of a few broad, channeled, glossy leaves that above spread outward. Slender and erect or somewhat arching, the branchless or few-branched flowering stalk bears tiny white-petaled blooms. **C. sessiliflora** is native from southern Mexico to southern Brazil and in the West Indies. It has funnel-shaped rosettes 6 inches to 1 foot tall of arching leaves. The branchless or few-branched, slender flowering stalk, well above the foliage, is topped by a spike of little white-petaled blooms largely hidden among the wide green floral bracts.

Garden Uses and Cultivation. The chief appeal of these plants is to fanciers of bromeliads. They need conditions and care appropriate for tillandsias. For more information see Bromeliads or Bromels.

CATS. Probably the chief objection to cats in gardens is that they scare away and, as opportunity affords and not without certain enthusiasm, more effectively reduce the bird population. Were these activities directed only to English sparrows, crows, pigeons, and other such nuisances few would object, but unfortunately, *Felis domestica* is not selective. One helpful device is to have pussy wear a bell around the neck. Feeding stations, nesting boxes, baths, and other encouragements for birds should be protected against cats by placing them 5 feet or more above the ground and well away from bushes or other concealment for lurking felines. Sheet metal cones extending for 1 foot or more around single posts supporting nesting boxes and about 6 feet above the ground will prevent cats from reaching the boxes.

Cats also cause trouble scratching in seedbeds and other choice places. Strategically placed chicken wire fences or guards foil this activity. To attract cats in gardens, if for any reason you wish to do this, plant catmint (catnip), common valerian, or *Actinidia polygama*. Unexplainably, these are all highly pleasing to cats.

CATTLEYA (Cátt-leya). To those without horticultural or botanical leanings the word orchid almost invariably brings to mind cattleyas for they are the most popular and most showy orchids commonly available from florists. It is cattleyas that so often are made into corsages for young ladies attending such important events as proms. It is they that are responsible for the name orchid-pink applied to a color. Cattleyas are the only orchids known to a large segment of the population, yet they number only sixty out of an estimated world population of orchids of 20,000 species. In addition to the species, kinds that occur in the wild, there are innumerable natural and man-made hybrids. It is these that are most commonly cultivated. This genus belongs in the orchid family ORCHIDACEAE.

The genus *Cattleya* is confined to the warmer parts of the Americas from Mexico to South America and the West Indies. Its name commemorates William Cattley, an English collector and grower of rare plants, who died in 1832. Cattleyas are epiphytes, in their native haunts they perch on trees without taking sustenance from their hosts. They are evergreen and have slender to much-swollen stems or pseudobulbs. Each stem or pseudobulb has one to three thick, leathery leaves. Solitary or several on a stem, usually from the tops of the pseudobulbs, but in some kinds on leafy stems arising from their bases, the blooms of most cattleyas are large and brightly colored. They have three petal-like sepals, two petals similar to them or the petals considerably broader, and a three-lobed lip, which represents a third petal, that curves around or encloses the column, but is not joined to it. The middle lobe of the lip is large and showy. There are four pollen masses (pollinia) as contrasted with the six characteristic of the allied genus *Laelia*. There are many hybrids, designated *Laeliocattleya*, between *Laelia* and *Cattleya*.

The autumn cattleya (**C. labiata**), of Brazil and Trinidad, is typical of a group of species, by some authorities reduced to varieties of *C. labiata*, that have pseudobulbs with one leaf. The pseudobulbs of typical *C. labiata*, which blooms in late summer and fall, are club-shaped and somewhat flattened. The blooms, seven or fewer together, are 6 to 7 inches wide. Their sepals and much broader, wavy petals are bright rose-pink or paler. The lip, narrower than the petals and with a deeply-notched, frilled center lobe, is velvety crimson to magenta-purple with a yellow throat streaked with reddish-purple. The spring cattleya or Easter orchid (**C. mossiae** syn. *C. labiata mossiae*), differs from the last in having usually longer, narrower pseudobulbs and in its spring- to early-summer-borne, fragrant blooms having a crinkled lip as wide or wider than the petals. From 5 to 7 inches or more across, and two to five or more together, the blooms have rose-pink to whitish sepals and much broader, wavy-edged petals. The exceptionally large, deeply-cleft lip, frilled at its

Cattleya dowiana

margins, rich velvety purple to crimson mottled and veined with lavender-rose, has a purple-veined, golden-yellow throat. This kind is native of Venezuela.

Others of the *C. labiata* relationship include these: *C. l. chocoensis* (syn. *C. l. quadricolor*) has smaller flowers than *C. labiata*, which never open fully, but are more or less bell-shaped. Very fragrant, they have white or lilac-tinted sepals and petals, the latter much wider than the sepals, and a yellow lip with a purple blotch. **C. dowiana** (*C. l. dowiana*), of Costa Rica, resembles *C. labiata* in growth, has 6-inch-wide flowers up to six on a spike, with buff-colored sepals, very large, crisped-margined yellow petals, and a rich crimson-purple lip wider than that of *C. labiata* and patched or streaked with yellow. **C. eldorado** (syn. *C. l. eldorado*) is smaller than *C. labiata*. Native of the Amazon region, this has a very short spike of three or fewer fragrant blooms 4 to 6 inches across. They have comparatively narrow, pale rosy-lilac sepals and petals and a pronouncedly-tubular lip blotched with purple and yellow in the throat. The blooms of *C. e. virginalis* are pure white with yellow throats. **C. gas-**

Cattleya mossiae

Cattleya gaskelliana

kelliana (syn. *C. l. gaskelliana*) is a variable native of Venezuela that not infrequently has fragrant blooms much like those of *C. mossiae*. Mostly not over 5 inches wide, the delicate lavender to amethyst-purple blooms, commonly more or less suffused or marked with white, have a large, frilled, rosy-mauve lip blotched or veined with rich amethyst-purple, with a yellow to orange-yellow throat streaked with magenta and with a pair of white blotches at the sides. *C. lueddemanniana* (syn. *C. l. lueddemanniana*, of Brazil and Venezuela, has smoother more nearly cylindrical pseudobulbs and usually longer leaves than *C. labiata*. Its flowers, not infrequently exceeding 8 inches in diameter, are very fragrant. Up to five in each spike, they are pale purplish-rose suffused with white. The more or less wavy petals are very much broader than the sepals. The narrowly-tubular lip has a notched, nearly round, frilled, amethyst-purple center lobe with a pair of yellow or white blotches at the throat. *C. mendelii* (syn. *C. l. mendelii*) is a variable native of Colombia, similar in habit to, but usually less vigorous than *C. trianaei*. Its fragrant blooms, up to five on a spike, and up to 7 inches wide, have white or blush-pink sepals and wavy petals and a wide lip with a rich crimson-purple in its outer portion sharply demarcated from the lower, often reddish-streaked, yellow part. *C. percivaliana* (syn. *C. l. percivalliana*), of Venezuela, grows chiefly on rocks. This has flowers 4 to 5 inches across, similar to those of *C. mossiae*, but commonly smaller and more richly colored. It chiefly blooms in winter. *C. rex* (syn. *C. l.*

rex), native to Brazil and Peru, blooms in summer. Its striking, fragrant blooms, 5 to 7 inches wide, have sepals and very broad, wavy-margined petals creamy-white to yellowish or sometimes deeper in color. The markedly-frilled, large lip is magenta-crimson with a yellow throat. *C. trianaei* (syn. *C. l. trianaei*) is robust and very var-

iable. Blooming from midwinter to spring, it is called the Christmas orchid. The flowers, two or three on each spike, sometimes exceed 7 inches in diameter. They have sepals and broader, usually crisped petals ranging from white to amethyst-pink or purple. The frilled, yellow-throated lip, which usually does not spread widely, is rich magenta-crimson or sometimes considerably paler. Similar *C. t. schroederae* (syn. *C. schroederae*), usually more fragrant, has larger blooms with broader petals and more conspicuously frilled lips, purple and yellow in their throats. The sepals and petals are usually pale lilac-pink. This is native to Colombia. It blooms from spring to summer. *C. warneri* (syn. *C. l. warneri*) is exceptionally fine. Brazilian, it is much like *C. labiata*, except for its blooming season. The flowers, which exhibit considerable variation in color, are typically 6 to 7 inches or even more in diameter. Usually their sepals and petals are pale rose-pink with deeper shadings and the fringed lip is usually rich crimson-purple sometimes more darkly veined, with a yellow throat streaked with light lilac or white. *C. warscewiczii* (syn. *C. l. warscewiczii*), of Colombia, has immense and handsome blooms, exceptionally 11 inches in diameter, commonly 7 to 9 inches. The sepals and petals, the latter broader, are soft rose-pink. The deeply-cleft lip is rich crimson-purple, sometimes bordered and mottled with a lighter hue. The throat is golden-yellow, often lined with purple, and with a pair of large pale yellow or white blotches. Variety *C. w. alba* has blooms that except for a

Cattleya percivaliana

pair of yellow patches in the throat are pure white. It was sold in 1910 for $10,000.

These also have one-leaved pseudobulbs: *C. lawrenceana*, of Guiana and Brazil, has pseudobulbs 1 foot to 1¼ feet long terminating in a narrow leaf. The short-stalked spikes, borne in early summer, are of up to eight fragrant, 4- to 5-inch-wide blooms with rosy-purple to white sepals and petals and a slender-tubed, deeply-cleft, rarely wavy-edged, white-throated, brilliant purple lip with a maroon stripe. *C. luteola* is a chiefly, but not exclusively winter-blooming native of Brazil, Peru, and other parts of northern South America. It has laterally-compressed, elliptic pseudobulbs 2 to 4 inches long. The 1½- to 2-inch-wide blooms, up to six on a spike and with petals as broad or only a little broader than the sepals, are sometimes fragrant. They are lemon-yellow with a whitish or white lip sometimes streaked or blotched inside with red. *C. maxima* is a splendid native of Colombia, Peru, and Ecuador. Its usually cylindrical pseudobulbs are up to 1¼ feet in length. The fragrant flowers, sometimes 6 inches wide, but often rather smaller, are in spikes of from three to fifteen up to 1 foot long. They have light pink sepals and petals and a frilled pale rose-pink lip with a yellow band with rosy-purple lines branching from it running the length of the tube. The blooms come in winter. *C. walkeriana*, of Brazil, is small. Its up to 5-inch-long, egg-shaped, stalked pseudobulbs often rather distantly spaced along zigzag rhizomes occasionally have two leaves, elliptic-oblong and up to 5 inches long. The flowers come from the rhizomes near the bottoms of the pseudobulbs. One or two on each leafless, 3-inch-tall stalk, they are up to 4½ inches wide. The sepals and petals, the latter twice as wide as the former, are bright

rose-purple to pinkish-lilac. The lip is darker and crimson-veined.

Pseudobulbs with two leaves and flowers that come in spring or spring and summer are characteristic of these: *C. elongata*, of Brazil, has pseudobulbs up to more than 2 feet long, and flower stalks as long, carrying up to ten blooms. About 3 inches wide and varying somewhat in color, the flowers are fragrant. They have narrow, coppery-brown, purplish-brown, or green, sometimes purple-spotted sepals and petals and a usually magenta-red to magenta or dark-lined, rose-pink lip. *C. intermedia* (syn. *C. amethystina*), of Brazil and Uru-

guay, has slender pseudobulbs up to 2 feet tall or taller. The flowers have narrow, light lavender-pink to rosy-purple sepals and petals and a similarly colored lip with a deep rose-magenta to violet-purple blotch. Usually in spikes of up to five, the fragrant blooms are 4 to 5 inches across. Taller *C. i. alba* has pure white flowers. *C. skinneri* has mostly club-shaped pseudobulbs, rarely attaining lengths of 1 foot to 1½ feet. Usually not all of the up to ten blooms of each spike opening simultaneously, the flowers are 2 to 3 inches wide or a little wider, rose-purple to purple with the lip generally deeper colored than the sepals and petals

Cattleya intermedia

Cattleya luteola

Cattleya intermedia alba

and the throat whitish. The petals are considerably broader than the sepals. This species is native of Central America. *C. s. autumnalis*, which flowers in summer, has smaller flowers with deep purple throats.

Cattleya skinneri

Cattleya aclandiae

Two-leaved pseudobulbs and flowers displayed in summer and early fall are typical of these: *C. aclandiae* has nearly cylindrical pseudobulbs up to 4 inches in height each with two or three leaves. A native of Brazil, its solitary or paired, fragrant flowers are 3 to 4 inches wide. From green to yellowish-brown the sepals and petals have many large purple-brown spots and blotches. The three-lobed lip does not surround the column. It and the column are magenta-red, the side lobes of the lip paler than the center one. The latter is golden-yellow at its base. *C. aurantiaca* (syn. *Epidendrum aurantiacum*), of Mexico, Guatemala, and Honduras, is vigorous. It has slender, spindle-shaped pseudobulbs up to 1¼ feet tall. Its crowded spikes of up to twenty bright orange to orange-red flowers has similar lanceolate sepals and petals. They usually do not open fully. When expanded they are 1½ inches across. *C. forbesii* is a Brazilian with clusters of 1-

Cattleya skinneri autumnalis

Cattleya aurantiaca

Cattleya forbesii

gether and 2½ to 3 inches across, are much like those of *C. skinneri.* The blooms of *C. b. grandiflora* and *C. b. splendens* are larger. They are rose-pink to purple with a deeper-colored lip. **C. citrina,** called the tulip cattleya because of the form of its long-lasting blooms, is distinct. A native of Mexico, it has rounded pseudobulbs about 2 inches long, drooping, strap-shaped leaves, and pendulous, long-stalked, rarely paired, usually solitary, bell-shaped, delightfully fragrant flowers that never fully open. They have bright lemon-yellow sepals, broader petals, and a large, frilled, golden-yellow lip often with a white border. **C. deckeri** (syn. *C. guatemalensis*), a natural hybrid between *C. aurantiaca* and *C. skin-*

Cattleya deckeri

foot-tall, rather slender, cylindrical pseudobulbs. The flowers, 3 to 4 inches wide or a little wider, vary considerably in hue, but commonly have yellowish-green to olive-green sepals and petals of nearly equal width and a three-lobed lip whitish outside, inside red with a whitish margin and a red-veined, yellow throat. **C. schilleriana,** a Brazilian, has 1-inch-tall, slender pseudobulbs. Its fleshy, waxy, fragrant blooms, solitary or in twos, and about 4 inches wide, have narrow, usually darker-spotted, deep brownish-green to green sepals and wavy-edged petals, a reddish-purple to rose-red lip with darker lines, and a yellow throat.

Fall, winter, or sometimes early spring flowers with two-leaved pseudobulbs include the following: **C. bicolor,** of Brazil, has canelike pseudobulbs 1½ to 3 feet long. The strongly-fragrant, 3- to 4½-inch-wide blooms have sepals and broader petals generally tawny to brownish-green. The lobeless lip, much narrowed below its flared, crisped-margined outer part, is rosy-purple somtimes bordered with white. **C. bowringiana** is a Central American species with 1- to 1½-foot tall, slender pseudobulbs. The flowers, from few to many to-

neri, occurs in Central America. It has club-shaped pseudobulbs up to 6 inches long and short racemes of few to many flowers with 2-inch-long, spreading, yellowish to rose-pink sepals and petals and a yellow-throated, magenta-red to carmine lip. **C. granulosa,** of Brazil and Guatemala, has slender, stemlike pseudobulbs 1¼ to 2 feet

Cattleya aurantiaca (flowers)

Cattleya citrina

in length. The blooms of the up to seven-flowered spikes are approximately 4 inches wide and sometimes wider. They are fragrant and somewhat variable in hue. Commonly the sepals and petals are olive-green with rich brown spots, and the strongly three-lobed lip is white with a rough-surfaced patch of reddish-purple. The sepals and petals of *C. g. buyssoniana* are without spots. The blooms of *C. g. russelliana* and *C. g. schofieldiana* are bigger than those of the typical species. *C. guttata* has canelike pseudobulbs up to 3 feet tall or taller. This native of Brazil has long-stalked spikes of sometimes more than twenty waxy blooms each 2 to 4 inches across. Their sepals and petals are yellowish-green, dotted brownish-red to nearly crimson. The lip has a usually bright, rose-purple middle lobe and whitish side ones, but this species exhibits considerable variation in flower color. *C. harrisoniana*, of Brazil, has slender pseudobulbs up to 1½ feet long. Its 4-inch-wide flowers in racemes of two to five have pale orchid-lavender sepals and petals and a cream to pinkish lip with a yellow spot. Variety *C. h. alba* has flowers that are white except for a lemon-yellow spot in the throat. Those of *C. h. gigantea* are bigger than is typical of the species. The sepals and petals of *C. h. maculata* are dotted with purple. Rose-pink sepals and petals dotted with purple are characteristic of *C. h. maculata*. Large flowers with rose-pink sepals and petals and a creamy-white lip are borne by *C. h. superbissima*. The blooms of *C. h. violacea*

have deep violet sepals and petals and an orange spot on the lip. *C. loddigesii*, of Brazil and Paraguay, is a very good species, more robust than, but otherwise somewhat resembling *C. forbesii*. Its pseudobulbs are canelike, 1 foot to 2 feet tall. The spikes are of two to seven blooms up to 4 inches wide or sometimes a little wider. Their sepals and broader petals are blush-white to lilac-tinged, light rose-pink. The slightly-lobed lip is pale to deeper lilac-rose to rose-pink. *C. nobilior* (syn. *C. walkerana nobilior*), of Brazil, has pseudo-

bulbs 4 to 5 inches long. From one to three on stalks, unusual for cattleyas that come from the bases of the pseudobulbs, the 3- to 4-inch-wide or slightly wider flowers are rosy-lilac with a cream-colored blotch veined with lilac on the lip.

Garden Uses and Cultivation. Among the most popular orchids, cattleyas are easy to manage and for the most part give fine returns for the effort expended in growing them. They are primarily adapted for greenhouses and for lath houses or outdoors in the tropics, but it is by no means

Cattleya nobilior

Cattleya harrisoniana

impossible to achieve a degree of success with them in sunrooms and windows where the humidity is not disappointingly low. The many magnificent hybrids, the newer ones sometimes extraordinarily high priced, represent the acme of hybridizers achievements, but many untampered-with species are well worth growing and are likely to give satisfaction and pleasure.

Cattleyas succeed in any of the several rooting mediums commonly used for epiphytic orchids. Those of bark are easily available and commonly used. It is usual to accommodate most kinds in pots, but they can also be placed on rafts and slabs of tree fern and on cork-covered artificial trees. A humid, but not oppressively dank atmosphere is needed and for the great majority what greenhouse gardeners call intermediate temperatures. This means winter night levels of 58 to 60°F rising five to fifteen degrees by day depending upon the brightness of the weather. At other seasons higher temperatures are in order, but then the greenhouse should always be ventilated moderately. Cattleyas develop wonderfully rich green and seemingly healthy foliage when afforded considerable shade. This is apt to mislead the uninitiated into thinking that they are surely going to flower well. Not so; to bloom prolifically these orchids need all the light they will stand without the leaves being scorched. This means that they will assume a yellower appearance than they would under more shade, but the growth will be firm and flower production will be encouraged. If the rooting medium is well drained, as it must be for success, quite generous supplies of water are needed while active growth is taking place, but after the new pseudobulbs have matured water should be reduced for two or three weeks to encourage them to ripen. Cattleyas benefit from regular fertilization. They should be repotted and divided whenever they begin to outgrow their containers and when there is suspicion that the rooting medium is becoming stale or sour. This is likely to involve repotting every second or third year. For more information see Orchids.

CATTLEYOPSISGOA. This is the name of orchid hybrids the parents of which are *Cattleyopsis* and *Domingoa*.

CATTLEYOPSISTONIA. This is the name of orchid hybrids the parents of which are *Broughtonia* and *Cattleyopsis*.

CATTLEYTONIA. This is the name of bigeneric orchid hybrids the parents of which are *Broughtonia* and *Cattleya*.

CAULANTHUS (Caul-ánthus)—Wild-Cabbage or Squaw-Cabbage or Desert Candle. Native of dry and desert parts of western North America, *Caulanthus* is a genus of possibly twenty species of the mustard family CRUCIFERAE. It is closely allied to *Thelypodium*, the chief difference being that the flask-shaped calyxes of its flowers are narrower at their tops than just beneath. The name, from the Greek *kaulos*, a stem, and *anthos*, a flower, alludes to the manner in which the flowers are borne.

Caulanthuses are annuals and herbaceous perennials, hairless or nearly so. Their stems are more or less inflated, their alternate, undivided leaves short-stalked or stalkless. The flowers have four each sepals and purple, purplish, or white, spreading petals, six stamens, one style, and a deeply-lobed stigma. The fruits are erect, slender, cylindrical pods.

Wild-cabbage, squaw-cabbage, or desert candle (*C. inflatus* syn. *Streptanthus inflatus*) is a tap-rooted annual 1 foot to 2½ feet tall. Usually branchless, it has erect, curiously and conspicuously inflated, hollow, spindle-shaped stems, the upper parts naked of foliage and fancifully suggestive of yellow candles. The lower portions are foliaged with stem-clasping, undivided, toothless leaves. The lowest leaves are fiddle-shaped, those above ovate to oblong. They are up to 4 inches long. The short-stalked flowers, purple changing to white,

¾ inch or more in diameter, and crisped at the tips of their petals, decorate the naked portions of the candles, which terminate in a short tip formed of unexpanded purple buds. The slender seed pods are 2 to 4 inches long.

Garden and Landscape Uses and Cultivation. The unusual-looking species described is of interest for including in native plant gardens in regions where it is indigenous and for growing as something of a curiosity elsewhere. It needs full sun and sharply-drained, dryish soil. Seeds afford the only practicable means of propagation. Because this species does not transplant well the seeds should be sown where the plants are to remain, or the young plants should be grown in pots until they are set in their flowering locations.

CAULARTHRON (Caul-àrthron) — Virgin Orchid. The very similar members of *Caularthron* of the orchid family ORCHIDACEAE are regarded by some authorities as constituting two species, by others as many as six. The genus, native of tropical Central and South America and Trinidad, was formerly called *Diacrium*. Its name from the Greek *kaulos*, a stem, and *arthron*, a joint, alludes to the pseudobulbs.

Caularthrons generally perch on trees (they are epiphytes) or sometimes on rocks. Their pseudobulbs, fleshy, longitudinally furrowed, and mostly hollow, have at their tops a few leathery, evergreen leaves, and in season often long stalks bearing few to several loosely arranged blooms. From those of *Epidendrum* the flowers differ in the position of the lip, which spreads from the bottom of the column, is nearly as long as the sepals, and has two spreading or reflexed side lobes, a broad-triangular center one, and a pair of erect horns from the base. They have rather similar, spreading sepals and petals.

The virgin orchid (*C. bicornutum* syn. *Diacrium bicornutum*), which blooms in

Caularthron bicornutum

spring and summer, is very handsome. Its spindle-shaped, conspicuously jointed, hollow pseudobulbs, are in clusters. The three to five blunt, oblong-lanceolate leaves are up to 8 inches in length. The fragrant, waxy, long-lasting blooms, 2 to 3 inches across, are five to twenty on each slender, up-to-1-foot long or longer, flower stem. They are ivory-white, with the backs of the short-pointed, elliptic sepals and petals sometimes suffused with pink or lavender. The small lip, its lower half sprinkled with crimson spots, has a lanceolate center lobe, and two short, erect side lobes.

Less robust than the virgin orchid, and with white or pink- or lavender-tinged blooms up to 1½ inches in diameter, *C. bilamellatum* (syn. *Diacrium bilamellatum*) has blooms, few to many together, on stalks, sometimes branched, up to 3 feet in length. The side lobes of the lip are very small or absent. On the center lobe are a pair of triangular, fleshy calluses. This kind blooms in winter and spring.

Garden Uses and Cultivation. These orchids are relatively easy to grow and are worthy of being included in collections. They respond to the conditions that suit cattleyas, and appreciate maximum light, short of intensities that scorch the foliage. Suspended baskets or pans (shallow pots) are the most satisfactory containers. For more information see Orchids.

CAULIFLOWER. This, one of the brassica vegetables, is *Brassica oleracea botrytis* of the mustard family CRUCIFERAE. Except in climates and soils especially suited to its needs, cauliflower is difficult or impossible to grow. Even where these factors are

Cauliflower

agreeable it is more exacting than any other of the cabbage tribe. It is extremely intolerant of heat and drought. Basic to success are a sufficiently long, cool, humid, frost-free growing season and deep, fertile, well-drained, fairly moist soil that contains abundant organic matter and available nitrogen. Commercial production in the United States is largely confined to western New York and Long Island, mountain regions in Colorado and Texas, and coastal California and Washington, but, like most vegetables, cauliflowers can be raised in home gardens in regions unsuited to their commercial production, but not where the environment differs too radically from the ideal.

If you wish to grow cauliflower at home make sure that the soil is deeply spaded, plowed, or turned with a rototiller and that generous amounts of rotted manure, compost, or other available decomposed organic material are mixed in. In addition, prior to planting, incorporate a liberal dressing of a complete garden fertilizer fairly high in nitrogen.

You may prefer as many home gardeners do to start with purchased young plants. This is fine if you get sturdy specimens, not overgrown and not harmed by neglect, crowding, drying of the roots or other cause. Otherwise, raise plants from seeds. This is easy. The time to sow depends upon where you garden, when you expect to harvest, and how long the variety you select takes to maturity. In northeastern North America cauliflowers are planted to mature in summer and fall, on the Pacific Coast over a much longer period. You may sow the seeds in outdoor beds in mild climates, and for late crops in more severe ones. Where spring comes late it is usually better to sow in a greenhouse or hotbed early enough to have strong young plants ready to set out as soon as danger of frost is past. Sow the seeds and handle the young plants as advised for cabbage.

Choose a cloudy day for planting out. If you can afford space, set the rows 3 feet apart with 2 feet between the plants in the rows. If you must be less generous diminish these distances by 6 inches each way. Be sure to set the plants 2 or 3 inches deeper than they were previously (they will root from the stems). Immediately after planting water them individually and thoroughly. There is no need at this stage to soak the entire ground between the plants.

Care during the growing season is simple. Weeds must be kept down. Do this by frequently stirring the surface soil with a scuffle hoe or other effective cultivator or by mulching. If you elect to cultivate, be careful not to go deeper than about 1 inch, otherwise you will injure feeding roots. In dry weather water regularly. Deep soakings at weekly intervals usually suffice, but however often water is needed to keep the crop growing it must be given. It is very detrimental to cauliflowers to have their growth checked and a spell of dry weather without water being given will result in this. Soon after the curds (the white heads that form the chief edible part) begin to form, when they are about 3 inches in diameter, shade them to preserve their whiteness and protect them from inclement weather. Do this either by drawing the larger outside leaves together to form a tent over the heads and tying their tops together or securing them with a rubber band or by snapping the midrib of one leaf and positioning the blade over the curd. Harvest the heads while they are yet tight and compact, before they assume a ricey

appearance. Cauliflowers are subject to the same pests and diseases as cabbage. Favorite varieties are 'Dwarf Erfurt', 'Snowball', and 'Super Danamerica'.

CAULOCATTLEYA. This is the correct name for orchid hybrids the parents of which are *Cattleya* and *Caularthron*. Formerly such plants were named *Diacattleya*.

CAULOPHYLLUM (Caulophýll-um)—Blue Cohosh or Papoose-Root or Squaw-Root. One American species and an eastern Asian native that some authorities regard as a variety and others as a distinct species are the only members of *Caulophyllum*, a genus closely related to the barberries (*Berberis*) and by some authorities included with them in the barberry family BERBERIDACEAE, but by others segregated, along with *Leontice* and *Bongardia*, as the leontice family LEONTICACEAE. The name derives from the Greek *kaulos*, a stem, and *phyllon*, a leaf, and applies because the stem appears to be the stalk of a large, divided leaf.

Caulophyllums are deciduous herbaceous perennials with thick, underground, knotted rhizomes from which arise solitary stems each bearing near its apex an almost stalkless, large, two or three times divided leaf, with the leaflets sometimes three-lobed. The small flowers, each with six sepals, petals, and stamens, and a solitary pistil, are in terminal clusters; they are prevailingly greenish-yellow or yellow and are succeeded by fruits that burst soon after flowering to expose two naked seeds that are berry-like at maturity. The petals are scarcely recognizable as such, being reduced to glandlike bodies very much smaller than the sepals.

American Indians used the blue cohosh to facilitate childbirth, a fact reported to the medical profession early in the nineteenth century, which resulted in it being employed later in the treatment of various uterine disorders as well as for bronchitis, rheumatism, hysteria, and many other troubles, but it is no longer an official drug in the United States.

The American species **C. thalictroides** called blue cohosh, squaw-root, and papoose-root, is indigenous from New Brunswick to Manitoba, South Carolina and Mississippi. It attains a height of 1 foot to 2½ feet and has the three leaflets of its leaves deeply-cut into three slender-pointed segments. Its flowers are yellowish-green, or sometimes purplish, and ⅓ inch wide. This kind is attractive in foliage, and its deep rich blue seeds, ¼ to ⅓ inch long, are ornamental in fall. Japanese **C. robustum** (syn. *C. thalictroides robustum*), not known to be in cultivation in North America, differs scarcely at all from its American counterpart.

Garden Uses and Cultivation. Although by no means the showiest of American

Cauliflower, with leaf broken over curd to preserve whiteness

woodland plants, the blue cohosh is of agreeable appearance and is well worth planting in woodlands and wild gardens. Its Asian relative, scarcely known in cultivation, has no attractions beyond those of the American species except, perhaps, as an item for collectors of the unusual. When unfolding, the young foliage of the blue cohosh is a pleasing reddish-purple and throughout the summer is attractive and well displayed. The chief ornaments, however, are the fruits, which remain decorative for a long season. The blue cohosh needs deep, rich, dampish woods soil and thrives best in fairly dense shade. For the best effects it should be planted in substantial clumps. Propagation is easy by division in early fall or spring and by cuttings made from the rhizomes. Seeds sown in a cold frame or a protected bed outdoors as soon as they are ripe also provide reliable means of increase. If sown in fall, some seeds will germinate the next spring, others not until a year later.

CAUTLEYA (Càut-leya). The difference between this Himalayan genus of five or six species and closely related *Roscoea* is that its three petals are of approximately the same size, instead of the upper one being much the bigger. Named in honor of the British naturalist Sir P. Cautley, who died in 1871, *Cautleya* belongs in the ginger family ZINGIBERACEAE and consists of nonhardy, herbaceous perennials, some of which, including those described below, sometimes grow as epiphytes perched on trees, in the manner of many orchids and bromeliads.

Suitable for outdoor cultivation in climates with little or no frost, *C. gracilis* (syn. *C. lutea*) is a pleasing, graceful kind that looks something like a diminutive, refined canna. It is up to 1½ feet tall and has erect tufts of stems, bracted at their bases, with four to six stalkless, ovate to ovate-oblong leaves, purple or striped brownish-purple on their undersides, and 5 to 10 inches long. The upper leaves are narrower than those below. The flowers are constructed like those of *Roscoea*. There are six to eight in each loose spike. They are 1½ to 2 inches long, and have two-lobed, red-purple calyxes, and yellow corollas with two-lobed lips rather less than ¾ inch in length. Up to 2½ feet tall, *C. spicata* (syn. *C. petiolata*) has flower spikes with very dark maroon bracts and bright yellow, strongly contrasting flowers. Its leaves resemble those of the last species.

Garden Uses and Cultivation. For warm, nearly frostless climates and for cultivation in ground beds or containers in greenhouses, cautleyas are attractive. They need deep, fertile, reasonably moist soil and some shade and are easily propagated by division at the beginning of their season of active growth and by seed. In greenhouses, temperatures during their season

of winter dormancy of 50 to 55°F are satisfactory. When in growth, night temperatures of 55 to 60°F and day temperatures five to fifteen degrees higher, or more in summer, produce good results. A humid atmosphere is desirable. When dormant they are kept dry, at other times they are watered freely. Applications of dilute liquid fertilizer sustain well-rooted clumps in summer.

Cautleya spicata

CAVANILLESIA (Cavan-illèsia)—Quipo. Up to five species of tropical American tall trees of the bombax family BOMBACACEAE belong in *Cavanillesia*. The name commemorates Antonio José Cavanilles, a director of the botanical garden at Madrid, Spain. He died in 1804.

The leaves of cavanillesias are undivided. They are palmately (in hand-fashion) five- to seven-lobed. The smallish pink flowers have a five-lobed calyx, five petals, and a column of stamens separated above into five bundles. There is one style. The fruits are five-winged, usually one-seeded capsules.

Native from Panama to Colombia, the quipo (*C. platanifolia*) is a deciduous tree up to 90 feet tall. It has soft, light wood similar to balsa, and smooth, light-colored

Cavanillesia platanifolia

bark. Nearly hairless, its leaves are large and shallowly five- to seven-lobed. The flowers are red. The one-seeded fruits are about 3 inches wide.

Garden and Landscape Uses and Cultivation. The species described is grown in Hawaii, southern Florida, and other essentially tropical areas. It adapts to a variety of soils and conditions and is propagated by seed.

CEANOTHUS (Cean-òthus) — California-Lilac, Blue Brush or Blue Blossom, Buck Brush, Jim Brush, Deer Brush, New Jersey-Tea. The exclusively American genus *Ceanothus* of the buckthorn family RHAMNACEAE, in the wild is chiefly confined to the Pacific Coast region, but also repre-

Ceanothus species in the wild

sented in the east, contains many handsome ornamentals. Its members are shrubs and small trees notable for their pretty and abundant blooms. In addition to the fifty-five species, there are many natural and man-made hybrids. The name is from *keanothos*, the ancient Greek for some other kind of plant of the buckthorn family.

There are evergreen and deciduous ceanothuses. Usually their undivided leaves are alternate, more rarely opposite. They are smooth-edged or toothed. The little flowers are in dense, axillary or terminal panicles or racemes of small umbels. They have five each somewhat petal-like sepals, petals, and stamens, and a three-parted style. The dry fruits, those of some kinds with usually three prominent horns, separate into three small nutlets.

The tallest species *C. arboreus* is an evergreen shrub or tree 10 to 25 feet in height. It has softly-hairy shoots and alternate, three-veined, broad-ovate to elliptic, toothed leaves 1 inch to 3 inches long, white-hairy on their under surfaces. The fragrant, light blue flowers are in short-stalked clusters 2 to 6 inches long. This endemic of islands off the coast of California is likely to hybridize with the blue brush or blue blossom and some other species when they are grown in proximity. A hy-

Ceanothus arboreus

Ceanothus thyrsiflorus repens

Ceanothus griseus

Ceanothus griseus (flowers)

brid between *C. arboreus* and *C. griseus*, named 'Ray Hartman', attains heights of 10 to 15 feet and is as broad as high. Its bright blue flowers are in loose clusters.

Blue brush or blue blossom (*C. thyrsiflorus*) is an erect evergreen shrub, commonly 4 to 8 feet in height, but sometimes attaining twice or more that maximum and becoming treelike. Native from Oregon to California, it has angled, green shoots and alternate, prominently three-veined, oblong-ovate to broadly-elliptic, glandular-toothed leaves 1 inch to 3 inches long, sparsely-hairy on the conspicuously raised veins beneath. The flowers are dark to light blue, rarely almost white. In the wild this hybridizes freely with other species. Unfortunately blue brush in some localities is excessively subject to insect pests. Variety *C. t. repens* is prostrate. The chief dif-

ference between *C. cyaneus* of California and the blue brush is that the branchlets of the former have small, glandular tubercles, and the veins on the undersides of the leaves are not conspicuous and raised. Its bright blue flowers are in panicles sometimes more than 9 inches long. One of the most beautiful ceanothuses, *C. cyaneus* is often short-lived in cultivation. Excellent hybrids derived from it are 'Mountain Haze', 'Sierra Blue', and 'La Primavera'. Similar to the blue brush, but with leaves with rolled-under margins, **C. griseus** (syn. *C. thyrsiflorus griseus*) is endemic to California. Prostrate or low-spreading *C. g. horizontalis* is much like *C. thyrsiflorus repens*. Excellent garden vari-

eties of this are *C. g. horizontalis* 'Hurricane Point', a sparsely-flowered, fast-grower

Ceanothus griseus horizontalis

about 2 feet tall and with a spread of more than 30 feet and light blue blooms, and *C. g.* 'Yankee Point', as tall as the last and with a spread of 8 feet. This has bright blue flowers. Other garden varieties are *C. g.* 'Louis Edmunds', 4 to 5 feet tall and 12

Ceanothus thyrsiflorus

feet wide, and *C. g.* 'Santa Ana', 4 to 8 feet high and with a spread of up to 20 feet.

Evergreen shrubs sometimes exceeding 10 feet in height, the first sometimes a small tree, *C. spinosus*, *C. leucodermis*, and *C. megacarpus* are natives of California, with the first two extending into Baja California. The ultimate branches of *C. spinosus* and *C. leucodermis* are stiff and more or less spiny. They spread at nearly right angles to main stems. The leaves are alternate, toothless or toothed, those of *C. spinosus* elliptic to oblong with one chief vein from the base and ½ inch to 1¼ inches long, those of *C. leucodermis* elliptic-oblong to ovate, up to 1 inch long, with three prominent veins from the base. The flowers of both are pale blue to white. Those of *C. spinosus* are in much-branched panicles 2 to 6 inches in length, those of *C. leucodermis* in usually branchless panicles mostly up to 3 inches long. From these *C. megacarpus* differs in not having rigid, wide-spreading ultimate branches and in its fruits having large, hornlike appendages. Compact and 3 to 12 feet tall, it has mostly alternate, spatula-shaped to obovate leaves up to ¾ inch long, with more or less rolled-under margins. Hairless and dull green above, they are hairy on their undersides. The white flowers are on short side shoots each bearing several ½-inch-wide clusters. Variety *C. m. pendulus* has whiplike, more or less drooping branches. The plant previously named *C. m. insularis*, a native of islands off the coast of California and distinguished by its leaves being nearly all opposite and its fruits being not or scarcely horned, is *C. insularis*.

Evergreen shrubs up to 10 feet tall, but often lower, are *C. crassifolius*, *C. cuneatus*, *C. ramulosus*, and *C. sorediatus*. Except the last, these have opposite leaves and horned seed capsules. Rather stiffly branched, white-flowered *C. crassifolius* has broad-elliptic to obovate, ¾- to 1¼-inch-long, usually sharp-toothed leaves, densely-white-hairy on their undersides and with rolled-under margins. Its flowers are in nearly stalkless, rounded clusters. This is very drought resistant. Variety *C. c. planus* has leaves less densely-hairy beneath, with less markedly revolute margins. Buck brush (*C. cuneatus*) differs from *C. crassifolius* in its spatula-shaped to obovate, toothless leaves not being densely-white-pubescent beneath and in their margins not being rolled under. This blue- to white-flowered native of California varies considerably and hybridizes freely with other species. From the two previous species *C. ramulosus* is distinct by reason of its spreading or arching, comparatively slender branches and branchlets. Its elliptic to roundish or obovate, toothed or toothless, nearly stalkless leaves are up to ¾ inch long and hairy beneath. The lavender, light blue, or whitish flowers are in small, stalked umbels. Al-

ternate-leaved *C. sorediatus*, or Jim brush, is dense, rigidly-branched, and has somewhat spiny branchlets. Its elliptic to ovate, distinctly three-veined, lustrous green leaves have glandular-toothed margins and paler undersides. Mostly without branches, the crowded clusters of light to dark blue flowers up to 1¾ inches long are on somewhat shorter stalks.

Evergreen shrubs approximately 3 to 6 feet tall include *C. dentatus*, *C. impressus*, *C. purpureus*, and *C. greggii*. All are natives of California, the last extending into Mexico. The first two are closely related. Densely-branched, they have alternate, hairy leaves with a single prominent vein from the base and more or less rolled-under, toothed margins. The leaves of *C. dentatus* are narrowly-oblong to elliptic, those of *C. impressus* elliptic to nearly round with the veins on the upper surfaces deeply impressed. Typical *C. impressus* is low, variety *C. i. nipomensis* attains heights up to 9 feet. The flowers are deep blue. A variety especially adapted to garden conditions is *C. i.* 'Mountain Haze'. Erect or spreading, *C. purpureus* has wavy-edged, spine-toothed, holly-like, opposite leaves, broadly-elliptic, glossy green above, paler and minutely-hairy on their lower sides. They are ½ to 1 inch long. In several-flowered umbels, the flowers are dark blue to purple. The fruits are horned. Related to *C. crassifolius*, but with leaves not densely-white-hairy beneath, and differing from *C. cuneatus* in its leaves having mostly concave upper sides and its fruits with usually small lateral horns, *C. greggii* has opposite, elliptic-ovate to oblanceolate leaves up to a little more than ½ inch long. The short-stalked umbels of creamy-white flowers are lateral.

Low-growing evergreen ceanothuses include some very useful garden plants. Here belongs the squaw carpet or Mahala mat (*C. prostratus*), native from Washington to California. This forms carpets up to about 1 foot tall, as much as 10 feet wide, of prostrate, rooting stems and shoots, the latter downy. The thickish, opposite, holly-like, coarsely-spine-toothed leaves are ¼ to 1 inch long and about one-half as wide. Their undersides are downy to hairless. The blue to lavender-blue or whitish flowers are in 1-inch-wide clusters of twelve to twenty at the ends of short leafy shoots. Closely similar *C. pumilus* (syn. *C. prostratus profugus*) is a high altitude native of the Siskiyou Mountains with leaves not more than ⅕ inch long. Typically with ground-hugging branches that spread to a length of 5 to 6 feet, *C. gloriosus* is a mat-forming Californian 4 inches to 2 feet tall. Its opposite, elliptic to oblong, roundish, pinnate-veined leaves are ½ inch to 1½ inches long, up to 1 inch wide, dark green above and paler on their undersides. Their margins, at least in their upper parts, are finely-toothed. Its clusters of deep blue to

lavender-blue flowers have stout stalks. This kind adapts well to gardens. Variety *C. g. exaltatus*, an inland form of this chiefly coastal species, is erect, up to 6 feet tall, with deep lavender-blue flowers. Rarely exceeding 3 feet in height, but often considerably lower, *C. foliosus* (syn. *C. austromontanus*), of California, is an evergreen with flexuous, glandular-pubescent shoots. Its alternate, lustrous, oblong-elliptic to broadly-elliptic, wavy-edged, glandular-toothed leaves are ¼ to ¾ inch in length. Paler beneath than on their upper sides, they are somewhat hairy along the veins. The flowers are blue, in branchless or branched clusters.

Two evergreen hybrids of uncertain ancestry found wild in California the middle of the nineteenth century and introduced then to European gardens are *C. veitchianus* and *C. lobbianus*. Perhaps the result of a chance mating of *C. thyrsiflorus* or *C. griseus* and *C. rigidus*, *C. veitchianus* is a handsome shrub 10 to 12 feet tall. It has

Ceanothus veitchianus

lustrous, obovate, pinnate-veined, glandular-toothed leaves, grayish on their undersides. In gardens this is sometimes wrongly identified as *C. dentatus*. The parents of *C. lobbianus*, which has since its original discovery been found wild near Monterey, are believed to be *C. griseus* and *C. dentatus*. From *C. veitchianus* this hybrid differs in its leaves being distinctly three-veined from their bases. Its flowers are bright blue.

Hybrids of especial interest because their parents are a spring-blooming and a summer- or fall-blooming kind are *C. burkwoodii* and *C.* 'Autumnal Blue'. The parents of the first are *C.* 'Indigo' and *C. floribundus*, those of the latter one of the *C. delilianus* complex and *C. thyrsiflorus*. Raised in England, *C. burkwoodii* is an evergreen up to about 6 feet tall, with somewhat lustrous, toothed, broad-elliptic leaves ½ inch to 1¼ inches long by one-half as wide, grayish-hairy beneath and with hairless upper surfaces. Borne in late summer and fall, the bright blue flowers are in panicles 1 inch to 2 inches long. From this, *C.* 'Autumnal Blue' differs in having bigger, glossier, more distinctly three-veined leaves and larger panicles of paler flowers.

Deciduous, the deer brush (*C. integerrimus*), 3 to 12 feet tall, has alternate, broadly-elliptic to oblong leaves sometimes slightly toothed at their apexes, but otherwise smooth-edged. They are paler, generally hairy on their lower surfaces, 1 inch to 2½ inches long. The clusters of white to more rarely dark blue or pink flowers are 2 to 6 inches long. This variable Californian is given to hybridizing with other species. It does not usually adapt well to garden conditions. Closely related to deer brush, but generally flat-topped, only 2 to 4 feet tall and with oblong, toothless, hairless or nearly hairless, deciduous leaves ½ to 1 inch long, *C. parvifolius* inhabits the Californian Sierra Nevada. The blue flowers are in scarcely branched panicles ½ inch to 1½ inches long.

New Jersey-tea (*C. americanus*) owes its colloquial name to the belief that its leaves were used in the American war of Independence as a substitute for tea. Native of coastal North America from Maine to Florida and Texas, and adaptable to poorish soils, this deciduous, summer-blooming shrub is 2 to 3½ feet tall. Alternate and ovate to ovate-oblong, its dull, finely-toothed leaves, three-veined from their bases, are 1½ to 4 inches long, pubescent to nearly hairless on their undersides. The little white flowers are in large terminal panicles of long-stalked clusters 1 inch to 2 inches in length on shoots of the current season's growth.

Ceanothus americanus

A better ornamental than the last, *C. ovatus* has alternate, deciduous leaves. Its native range is more inland than that of New Jersey-tea. It extends from Vermont to Colorado and Texas. Rarely much exceeding 2 feet in height, this erect, more compact species differs from New Jersey-tea in having blunter, more lustrous, elliptic to elliptic-lanceolate leaves with nearly

hairless undersides. Its red fruits are quite decorative.

Other deciduous, alternate-leaved kinds include *C. fendleri, C. sanguineus,* and *C. caeruleus.* Native from South Dakota to New Mexico and Arizona, *C. fendleri* is rarely more than 2 feet tall, and sometimes procumbent. It has somewhat spiny branches and elliptic to elliptic-lanceolate, finely-toothed or toothless leaves up to 1 inch long, short-hairy and grayish-green beneath. In terminal clusters up to a little more than 1 inch long, the bluish-white flowers are on leafy side branchlets. This is hardy in southern New England. Up to about 12 feet tall and not hardy in the north, *C. sanguineus* has round to ovate or obovate, toothed leaves 1 inch to 3½ inches long, slightly-hairy on their undersides. Borne on short branches of the previous year's growth, the small white flowers are in slender, leafless panicles up to about 5 inches long. This is native from Montana to British Columbia and California. Mexican and Guatemalan *C. caeruleus* (syn. *C. azureus*) attains a maximum height of about 8 feet. This has its shoots, undersides of its foliage, and flower stalks clothed with grayish hairs. Toothed, and 1 inch to 2 inches long, its thickish leaves are ovate. In panicles up to 6 inches long of dense clusters that develop from near the ends of shoots of the current season's growth, the flowers are rich blue. This species has played an important part in the parentage of many hybrid ceanothuses, some of them hardy.

Ceanothus pallidus roseus

Hybrids of considerable merit raised in France, the offspring of *C. americanus* and *C. caeruleus,* are classified as *C. delilianus,* the typical form of which has sky-blue flowers. One or more of these hybrids, which are usually deciduous, but may in warm climates retain their foliage, crossed with *C. ovatus* gave rise to deciduous kinds to which the name *C. pallidus* is applied. Chief among the hybrids are 'Ceres', with large panicles of pale pink blooms, 'Gloire de Plantieres', a low kind with dark blue flowers, 'Gloire de Versailles', with handsome panicles of powder-blue blooms, 'Henri Desfosse', resembling the last, but its flowers darker, 'Indigo', with the darkest blue flowers of all, 'Leon Simon', its flowers light blue, 'Marie Simon', the blooms of which are rose-pink, 'Perle Rose', with carmine-pink to rose-pink blooms, and 'Topaz', its flowers indigo-blue. The *C. delilianus* hybrids are generally not hardy in the north, but at least some of the *C. pallidus* ones are, including pale pink-flowered *C. p. roseus.* These hybrids flower at the ends of their current season's shoots.

Garden and Landscape Uses. Among western North America's finest contributions to the list of ornamental flowering shrubs, the species native to that region and their hybrid progeny are, most sadly, not hardy in the north. They are cultivated to a considerable extent in California and other favorable West Coast regions, and many garden varieties additional to those listed above are grown. In Great Britain they thrive in the milder parts and are commonly espaliered on walls. Displayed in this fashion, and as free-standing shrubs, they are superb. The prostrate kinds are admirable for covering banks and are splendid furnishings for rock gardens. Because many Western ceanothuses are naturally rather short-lived and because they are prone to succumb to root rot diseases in watered garden areas it is well to provide for their replacement from time to time. This can be done by raising a few new ones from cuttings every two or three years. Ceanothuses native east of the Rocky Mountains and at least some of their hybrids classed as *C. pallidus* are less magnificent than their Pacific Coast relatives, but they are hardy and are worth planting for variety, and the species of course for display in native plant gardens.

Cultivation. Ceanothuses are not difficult to manage. They adapt well to most well-drained soils of average quality and to full sun or at most to shade for a small part of each day. To prune them intelligently some understanding of their flowering habits is necessary. They fall into two groups, evergreen kinds that bloom in spring on shoots developed the previous year and deciduous sorts that bloom late at the termination of shoots of the current season's development. Prune these last in late winter or early spring by cutting back severely, close to their bases, all shoots of the previous year's growth. Unless you wish to limit their size, improve their shape, or espalier them, no pruning is necessary with spring bloomers. If you do prune, attend to it immediately flowering is through. Then, shorten all outward-pointing branches of espaliers back close to their bases. Propagation of most ceanothuses is easily achieved by summer cuttings under mist or in a greenhouse or cold frame propagating bed. The species may also be raised from seed.

CEARA RUBBER. See Manihot.

CECROPIA (Ce-cròpia) — Trumpet Tree, Snakewood. The name *Cecropia* is believed to commemorate Cecrops, the builder and first king of Athens, originally named Cecropia. That cecropia trees and certain fierce biting ants commonly live under an arrangement beneficial to both is undoubtedly true. Whether this symbiotic relationship is fortuitous or the result of intelligence is arguable. It is certain that the trees can get along perfectly well without the ants, but whether or not the ants can live without cecropias is less certain. The arrangement works thus. Between their joints the stems of most cecropias are hollow, but without any opening to the outside. Near the top of each section of stem there is, however, a thin place in the stem wall. Through this a gravid ant bites its way, takes up residence inside, and there raises its family. But the tree supplies more than

housing for its tenants. The swollen bases of its leafstalks, close to the entrances to the ants' apartments, develop on their undersides nourishing bodies upon which the insects feed. As these are eaten new ones grow. So much for the contribution made by the trees to the ants. Of what benefit are the insects to the trees? Chiefly the protective one of fighting off creatures that would otherwise destroy their foliage and flowers, especially certain leaf-cutting ants. This, with one notable exception, they certainly do. Sloths, apparently immune to, or disdainful of, the attacking ants, feed almost exclusively on the foliage and buds of cecropias. Shaking the branches of an ant-colonized cecropia causes the fierce creatures to rush out and attack any intruder, a fact that many an unwary traveler has discovered to his intense discomfort. Despite this, certain Indian tribes harvest the hollow stems and make from them the trumpets they use for communicating over fairly long distances, and the light wood is used for floats and other purposes. It is most interesting that one species of *Cecropia*, with stems so covered with wax that they are unclimbable by leaf-cutting ants, has neither thin places in its stems through which the gravid insects can tunnel nor does it develop food bodies to nourish them.

Cecropias are fast-growing trees that often are the first to occupy clearings, and by foresters are generally looked upon as weed trees. From a considerable distance their crowns of large, glistening umbrella-shaped leaves stand out prominently from other forest foliage, especially when they are disturbed by wind and their silvery undersides are displayed. There are about 100 species, but only one is at all commonly cultivated. Fortunately for gardeners they prosper without association with the ants that in many parts of their native territories inhabit them. Belonging in the mulberry family MORACEAE, or according to some botanists to the nettle family URTICACEAE, the genus *Cecropia* is entirely tropical American and West Indian. It consists of milky-juiced, unisexual trees with large, alternate, palmately-lobed or -divided leaves clustered near the ends of the few branches, and conspicuously white-felted on their under surfaces. Their leafstalks are attached to the blades well in from their margins and, unless the leaf consists of separate leaflets, without any opening or gap from leaf margin to leafstalk. The tiny flowers, without petals, form umbels of dense spikes, but are without appreciable decorative value. The fruits are small nuts arranged in spikes.

The trumpet tree (*C. peltata*) is cultivated in Florida and elsewhere. It should be noted that the name trumpet tree is also applied to *Tabebuia*. This species may attain a height of 70 feet. At the ends of its few, rather awkwardly placed branches it car-

ries leaves with stalks 1 foot to 1½ feet long and blades 1 foot to 2½ feet in diameter. They have seven to eleven lobes extending less than halfway to the centers of the leaves. The upper surface is practically hairless, but beneath, the leaves are densely felted. In Puerto Rico the wood is made into excelsior and is used for manufacturing insulation board. This species is abundant in Puerto Rico and other parts of the West Indies and is indigenous also from Mexico to northern South America.

Another species of trumpet tree, the snakewood (*C. palmata*), native of Central and South America and the West Indies, is cultivated. It differs chiefly from *C. peltata* in having leaves usually lobed to beyond their middles. Also, the fruit clusters of *C. palmata* are almost twice to much more than twice as long as the 3-inch ones of *C. peltata*.

Garden and Landscape Uses and Cultivation. For imparting a modernistic note to tropical landscaping cecropias serve a good purpose. They grow quickly, are rather short-lived, cast little shade, and scarcely interfere with the growth of plants beneath or near to them. They prosper in ordinary garden soils and are easily raised from seed.

CEDAR. As a common name without qualification cedar applies to species of the genus *Cedrus*, which includes the Atlas, Cyprian, and deodar cedars and the cedar of Lebanon. Other plants having the word cedar as part of their colloquial names are Australian red-cedar (*Cedrela australis*), Bermuda-cedar (*Juniperus bermudiana*), cedar-of-Goa (*Cupressus lusitanica*), Chilean-cedar (*Austrocedrus*), cigar-box-, Spanish-, or West-Indian-cedar (*Cedrela odorata*), Clanwilliam-cedar (*Widdringtonia juniperoides*), Colorado red-cedar (*Juniperus scopulorum*), ground-cedar (*Lycopodium complanatum*), Himalayan pencil-cedar (*Juniperus macropoda*), incense-cedar (*Calocedrus decurrens*), Japanese-cedar (*Cryptomeria japonica*), Mlanji-cedar (*Widdringtonia whytei*), pencil- or red-cedar (*Juniperus virginiana*), Southern red-cedar (*Juniperus silicicola*), stinking-cedar (*Torreya taxifolia*), Tasmanian-cedar (*Athrotaxus*), Western red-cedar (*Juniperus occidentalis* and *Thuja plicata*), West-Indian-cedar (*Cedrela odorata* and *Juniperus barbadensis*), white-cedar (*Chamaecyparis thyoides*), and Willowmore-cedar (*Widdringtonia schwarzii*).

CEDRELA (Céd-rela) — West-Indian-Cedar or Spanish-Cedar or Cigar-Box-Cedar. The pleasing fragrance of old-time cigar boxes was attributable to the wood of which they were constructed, commonly that of *Cedrela odorata*. Modern cigar boxes are more rarely made from it. This aromatic, beautifully colored lumber, however, as well as similar ones from other species of the genus, are highly esteemed for interior trim, clothes closets, wardrobes, chests, fine furniture, and boats. They are insect resistant. Several species of *Cedrela* are cultivated as ornamentals. The genus, which belongs in the mahogany family MELIACEAE, consists of seventeen species and is represented in the natural floras of the tropics and subtropics of both eastern and western hemispheres. At one time the Old World species were considered to form the separate genus *Toona*. One *Cedrela* is hardy as far north as southern New England.

These are tall trees with much the aspect of the tree-of-heaven (*Ailanthus*), although they belong in a quite different botanical family. They have pinnate leaves. The leaflets are slightly toothed or smooth-edged. The flowers are in large axillary or terminal panicles. They are small, whitish or greenish, and have a four- or five-lobed calyx and the same number of petals, the lower parts of which, although quite separate, form a tube. There are four to six fertile stamens and sometimes the same number of staminodes (non-functional stamens). The style is tipped with a disk-shaped stigma. The fruits are woody capsules containing winged seeds. The name is from that of the genus *Cedrus* and alludes to the similarity of the woods.

The West-Indian-, Spanish-, or cigarbox-cedar (*Cedrela odorata*), a native of the West Indies and tropical America,

Cedrela odorata

sometimes attains an imposing 100 feet in height. It has a tall or rounded head. When crushed or cut, its foliage, stems, twigs, and bark have a garlic-like odor and flavor. The deciduous leaves, up to 2 feet long or sometimes longer, have five to eleven pairs of lanceolate to ovate, long-pointed, short-stalked leaflets 2 to 6 inches long. They are somewhat lustrous above and have dull undersides. Shorter than the leaves, the flower clusters consist of numerous yellowish-green blooms. The fruits, ¾ inch long, remain on the tree throughout the fall and winter. Their seeds are winged at their lower ends. This species is planted in southern Florida.

A native of the warmer parts of India and Burma, **C. toona** is planted in southern Florida, southern California, and other warm frost-free or almost frost-free regions. It is somewhat hardier than the West-Indian-cedar. Almost evergreen, it is up to 70 feet in height and has leaves of five to ten pairs of pointed, ovate-lanceolate leaflets that are not toothed, but may have wavy margins. They are 3 to 6 inches long. Its clusters of honey-scented white flowers are shorter than the leaves. The fruits, ¾ to 1 inch long, contain seeds winged at both ends.

The Australian red-cedar (**C. australis**) is very similar to *C. toona* and by some botanists is considered to be a variety of it. Deciduous, and reported to attain heights of 100 to 180 and sometimes even 200 feet, it produces one of the most highly prized of Australian lumbers. It has fragrant white or pink flowers. This native of New South Wales and Queensland is cultivated in Hawaii.

The hardiest kind is **C. sinensis**, of China. Deciduous, and in its native land up to 70 feet tall, it is usually somewhat lower in cultivation. A handsome ornamental, this species is readily distinguished from the somewhat similar appearing tree-of-heaven (*Ailanthus*) by its leaves, the five to ten pairs of leaflets that, unlike those of the tree-of-heaven, are without lobes or conspicuous teeth and without glands near their bases. The leaves of *C. sinensis* are 10 to 20 inches long, the leaflets oblong to oblong-lanceolate, pointed and distinctly short-toothed, are 4 to 8 inches long. Their undersides are paler than their upper. The whitish flowers are in clusters much longer than the leaves. The fruits are also very different. Those of *C. sinensis* are capsules 1 inch long that contain seeds winged at their upper ends.

Garden and Landscape Uses. Cedrelas are admirable shade trees. They are effective on lawns, in parks, and as street and avenue trees.

Cultivation. Fertile loam not lacking for moisture suits cedrelas best. No special attention or care is needed. Propagation is by seeds, and by cuttings and root cuttings set in a greenhouse propagating bed kept a few degrees warmer than the air temperature.

CEDRONELLA (Cedron-élla)—Canary-Balm or Balm-of-Gilead. The only species of *Cedronella* of the mint family LABIATAE is by some authorities included in nearly related *Dracocephalum*, from which its flowers differ in having a symmetrical instead of a two-lipped calyx. The name, alluding to the cedar-like fragrance, is a diminutive of the Latin *cedrus*, a cedar.

Canary-balm or balm-of-Gilead (**C. canariensis** syns. *C. triphylla*, *Dracocephalum canariense*) is an aromatic shrub 3 to 5 feet tall, a native of the Canary Islands and Madeira. It has opposite, stalked leaves of three oblong-lanceolate, coarsely-toothed leaflets, conspicuously-hairy on their undersides, less so above, and 1½ to 4 inches long. The flowers, pale purple-violet, lilac, or white and ¾ to 1 inch long, are crowded in whorls that are parts of terminal, cylindrical, dense, sometimes interrupted spikes or heads 2 to 4 inches long.

Garden Uses and Cultivation. Canary-balm is pleasant for growing in pots and tubs, and in regions of essentially frostless winters it is a welcome permanent addition to herb gardens. In harsher climates it can be wintered in cool, sunny greenhouses or approximately similar environments and be planted outdoors each spring. It does best in well-drained, porous, moderately fertile soil in full sun. Increase is easy by cuttings and seeds.

CEDRUS (Céd-rus)—Cedar. The name cedar is loosely applied to many quite different evergreen plants and, with appropriate adjectival modifications, is correctly used for several others. Thus we have whitecedar (*Chamaecyparis thyoides*), incense-cedar (*Calocedrus decurrens*), cigar-box-cedar (*Cedrela odorata*), and red-cedar (*Juniperus virginiana*). For none of these is the name cedar alone appropriate. When used without a prefix it should be reserved for true cedars, members of the genus *Cedrus*.

The genus name is a form of *kedros*, used by the ancient Greeks to designate a resinous tree. The genus it identifies includes four, or according to some authorities three, species that occur naturally in five separated localities from the western end of the Mediterranean in North Africa to the western Himalayas. Each isolate consists of a single species with the cedar of Lebanon present in two regions. The Atlas cedar (*C. atlantica*) abounds in the mountains of Algeria and Morocco. The Cyprian cedar (*C. libani* syn. *C. libani brevifolia*) is endemic to Cyprus. In the Taurus and Anti-Taurus mountains of Asia Minor and in the mountains of Lebanon the cedar of Lebanon (*C. libani*) occurs, and far to the east the deodar cedar (*C. deodara*) forms forests extending from the eastern Himalayas to Nepal.

Differences between species of *Cedrus* are slight, and none is very closely related to any other tree. The nearest relatives are the larches, which are all deciduous. No doubt the wild colonies of cedars that now exist are remnants of a common ancestral type that in ancient geological times formed a more or less continuous forest.

Cedars are generally handsome evergreen coniferous trees of the pine family PINACEAE that, with the exception of the Cyprian cedar and the deodar, are hardy in fairly sheltered locations about as far north as New York City, or the hardy form of the cedar of Lebanon, to southern New England. They have two kinds of branchlets, leading shoots that lengthen several inches each year and are furnished with solitary leaves arranged spirally. Along these, develop stubby branchlets called spurs, which normally lengthen only a fraction of an inch each year and which have leaves clustered at their tips. Occasionally the spurs develop into leading shoots. The needle-like leaves are quadrangular or sometimes triangular in section. Their flowers, petal-less and sepal-less, are unisexual, with both sexes on the same tree. The males are in upright, cylindrical catkins about 2 inches long that shed clouds of yellow pollen at maturity. The females are in ovoid cones at first purplish, later green, and about ½ inch long, but maturing to 3 to 5 inches long. The cones are erect and take two to three years to mature. The seeds are winged.

Most famous of cedars is the cedar of Lebanon (*C. libani*), which attains a height of about 125 feet and at its finest has a

Cedrus libani

huge trunk with a maximum girth of nearly 50 feet, great wide-spreading branches, and ample rich, dark green foliage. This is the species to which frequent mention is made in the Bible. It was the most massive tree known to the ancient Israelites. From its fragrant lumber the Temple and Palace of King Solomon were constructed and also his great Porch of Judgment and a domicile for his wife, a Pharoah's daughter. Other ancient potentates exploited Lebanon's cedars. So much destruction was wrought that the original stands largely disappeared and all now left are pitiful remnants of Lebanon's once majestic and glorious cedar forests. That this should happen is not surprising when we recall that King Solomon once conscripted 30,000 Israelites and 150,000 slaves and under the direction of 3,300 supervisors sent them to aid an army of slaves of King Hiram of

Tyre in lumbering operations in Lebanon. Even without modern power tools such populations wrecked massive and irreparable destruction. Of the cedars that remain in Lebanon the best known are small groves at an elevation of more than 6,000 feet in the Kedisha valley. In the Taurus and Anti-Taurus mountains of Asia Minor the species is more plentiful. The cedar of Lebanon is pyramidal when young, with age it develops massive, spreading branches and becomes flat-topped. Its leading shoot arches or droops, and its twigs are usually minutely-downy. The leaves of this cedar are needle-like and ¾ inch to 1¼ inches long. Its cones are barrel-shaped, from 3 to 5 inches long by about one-half as wide. Horticultural varieties of *Cedrus libani* are *C. l. argentea*, which has silvery-blue foliage, *C. l. aurea*, with yellowish leaves, *C. l. nana* (syn. 'Comte de Dijon'), a dwarf compact form, and *C. l. pendula,* with drooping branches.

At the instance of Professor Sargent, then Director of the Arnold Arboretum, early in the present century a collector was sent to obtain seeds of the Lebanon cedar from the coldest area in which it was known to grow, the Cilician Taurus. There, at elevations to 7,000 feet, snow lies on the ground for five months of each year and the climate is severe. From seeds received at the Arnold Arboretum in 1902 trees were raised that have proved decidedly hardier than stocks of the cedar of Lebanon originating in softer climates. This hardy race lives through southern New England winters with nothing worse than scorching of the foliage in exceptionally severe years.

Closely resembling the cedar of Lebanon and hardiest of the genus except for the especially cold-resistant race of the cedar of Lebanon just mentioned, the Atlas cedar (*C. atlantica*) attains a height of about 120 feet. Its young shoots are downy, and it has leaves ½ inch to 1 inch long, curved

Cedrus atlantica

toward their tips and noticeably stouter than those of the cedar of Lebanon. Its leading shoot grows stiffly upright. The cylindrical cones are 3 inches long by up to 2 inches wide. When raised from seeds the Atlas cedar varies considerably in the color of its foliage from a good green to a pronounced silvery-blue. Named horticultural varieties are *C. a. aurea*, a yellowish-leaved kind of no special merit, *C. a. glauca*, with silvery-bluish foliage and seemingly hardier than the type, and *C. a.*

Cedrus atlantica glauca

pendula, a very beautiful form with long, slender, pendulous, whiplike branches. The Cyprian cedar (*C. libani*) is decidedly less attractive than other species. It resembles the cedar of Lebanon, but has shorter cones and leaves ¼ to ½ inch long. The tree is about 40 feet tall. Its appearance is that of a rather starved cedar of Lebanon. Tenderest of cedars is the deodar (*C. deodara*). This prospers only in moderately mild climates. It succeeds well in California and in Great Britain, but in eastern

Cedrus atlantica (male catkins)

Cedrus atlantica pendula

Cedrus deodara

belts, pillows, and mattresses; it has the virtue of not matting even when packed tightly. Its remarkable qualities are largely due to the fact that the fibers, which surround the seeds, are hollow. The kapok tree is cultivated and naturalized in many tropical parts of the world. The name *Ceiba* is derived from a Caribbean Indian one for a canoe; the trunks were used for dugouts.

The kapok or silk-cotton tree (**C. pentandra**) exceptionally attains a height of 120 feet or more, and not unusually from 75 to 100 feet. Its crown may have a spread of 150 feet. Like the red-silk-cotton tree its stout, horizontal branches are in tiers, usually of three, and as is the trunk, are sparsely or densely covered with cone-shaped prickles. The trunk is conspicuously buttressed, the buttresses flangelike and larger than those of the red-silk-cotton; they may extend to a height of 10 feet. Other differences are the usually smaller leaves with shorter leafstalks of the kapok, and its blooms being off-white to pinkish rather than the commonly bright red of the blooms of *Bombax malabaricum*.

Ceiba pentandra

Garden and Landscape Uses. The cedars are among the most magnificent and stately of conifers, well suited for planting in avenues and as lawn specimens. Because they spread so widely at maturity it is important to allow ample space for their full development. If crowded they are likely to prove disappointing as ornamentals. Located where they have ample light and space they retain their lower branches throughout most of their life and form grand masses of perpetual verdure.

Cultivation. Cedars grow best in deep, fertile, reasonably moist, loamy soils that are well drained. They will not tolerate waterlogged ground. Seeds afford the most satisfactory means of propagation, but horticultural varieties cannot be increased in that way and are grafted onto seedlings in greenhouses in winter.

Diseases. A tip blight or die-back disease and various root rots sometimes attack cedars.

CEIBA (Cèi-ba)—Kapok or Silk-Cotton Tree. It is important to distinguish the kapok or silk-cotton tree of this genus from the red-silk-cotton tree (*Bombax malabaricum*). Both belong in the bombax family BOMBACACEAE. Both are tropical trees. The genus *Ceiba* consists of ten species and is represented in the spontaneous floras of both the Old and New worlds. The kapok or silk-cotton tree (*C. pentandra* syn. *Eriodendron anfractuosum*), possibly originally American, is now common in many parts of the tropics. It is of commercial importance as the source of kapok, a lightweight, water-resistant fiber used in life

The leaves of the kapok have five to nine elliptic to oblanceolate, drooping or recurved leaflets that spread from the apex of the 3- to 8-inch-long leafstalks like the fingers of a hand. The leaflet blades are up to 6 inches in length and sometimes have a few teeth at their margins. In clusters of two to seven, about 1½ inches across, the short-lived flowers have five-lobed calyxes, five pubescent petals, and five bundles of stamens united at their bases and longer than the petals. They have a milky odor. The fruits are woody capsules, oblong to spindle-shaped, 3 to 6 inches long by 2 inches in diameter, that open by splitting along five longitudinal lines. They contain, embedded in a thick mass of white, grayish, or brownish floss, numerous round, dark, pea-sized seeds.

The wood of the kapok tree is very light in weight, soft, and without lasting quality. It is used to a limited extent for packing boxes and matches. The flowers are attrac-

North America it is not generally reliable north of Washington, D.C. In a wild state it may be 250 feet tall. The deodar has the longest leaves of any. They are 1 inch to 2 inches long. Its leading shoot arches gracefully and its branches, always downy, are pendulous at their ends. The cones are about 4 inches long by 3 inches wide. Horticultural varieties of *C. deodara* are *C. d. argentea*, with silvery-blue leaves, *C. d. aurea*, with yellowish foliage, *C. d. pendula*, with a pendulous leading shoot and drooping branches, and *C. d. prostrata*, a low, spreading form.

tive to bees, and the species is rated a good honey plant. An oil useful as an illuminant and for making margarine and soap is obtained from the seeds.

Garden and Landscape Uses and Cultivation. Easily raised from seeds and cuttings, the silk-cotton tree, especially during its early years, is a rapid grower. It is a good shade tree, but the floss from its seed pods can be a minor nuisance. Only in warm climates where frost is rarely or never experienced does kapok thrive. Planted as a shade tree in Florida and Hawaii, it succeeds in ordinary soils. Propagation is by seed.

CELANDINE. This is the name of *Ranunculus ficaria,* sometimes called the lesser celandine. The greater celandine is *Chelidonium majus.* The celandine-poppy is *Stylophorum diphyllum.* The tree-celandine is *Macleaya.*

CELASTRACEAE—Staff Tree Family. Deciduous and evergreen trees, shrubs, and woody vines numbering fifty-five genera and 850 species are accounted for in this family of dicotyledons. They are widely distributed through temperate, subtropical, and tropical regions and include many prized as ornamentals.

Members of the staff tree family have alternate or opposite, undivided leaves and small, greenish or yellowish, symmetrical, bisexual or unisexual flowers. If the blooms are individually male and female, those of any one plant are predominantly of one sex with commonly a few of the other sex or bisexual blooms present. They have four or five sepals united at their bases, four, five, or rarely no petals, four, five or less commonly ten stamens, one short style and a headlike or indistinctly two- to five-lobed stigma. The fruits are capsules, drupes, samaras, or berries, their seeds often with a brightly colored covering called an aril. Cultivated genera include *Cassine, Catha, Celastrus, Euonymus, Maytenus, Paxistima,* and *Tripterygium.*

CELASTRUS (Celást-rus) — Bittersweet or False-Bittersweet. Mostly deciduous, climbing, clambering, or twining shrubs and vines make up this genus of the staff tree family CELASTRACEAE. Rarely they are evergreen. Some, not cultivated, attain heights of 150 feet. There are thirty species, natives of the Americas, eastern Asia, islands of the Pacific, and Madagascar. The name is from the Greek *kelastros,* an evergreen tree, and was applied by Theophrastus to a *Phillyrea.*

Celastruses show considerable diversity in their foliage between species, and often on the same plant. The leaves are undivided, chiefly from elliptic to nearly orbicular. The inconspicuous flowers, in axillary or terminal panicles or racemes, are typically greenish-white. They have

five-lobed, persistent calyxes, and five small, usually reflexed petals. In cultivated kinds, and indeed in all except a few Central and South American species that have bisexual blooms, the flowers are unisexual with the sexes nearly always on separate plants. Male flowers have five fertile stamens, and females five infertile ones (staminodes). Female blooms have a columnar style tipped with a more or less lobed functional stigma, in males there is a vestigial pistil. The fruits are usually showy. They are approximately rounded capsules that split to reveal their colored inner surfaces and brightly colored seeds. Some plants previously included in *Celastrus* belong in *Gymnosporia.* The plant once named *C. orixa* is *Orixa japonica.*

The bittersweet of North America (*C. scandens*) in the literature, but rarely in conversation, is called false-bittersweet to distinguish it from the Eurasian bittersweet (*Solanum dulcamara*). It is also known as waxwork. This kind is native from Quebec to North Carolina and New Mexico, at times climbing to a height of 60 feet. Its hairless leaves are elliptic to obovate, toothed, and 1¾ to 4½ inches long by up to 2¼ inches wide. The flowers and fruits are in terminal panicles or racemes 2 to 4 inches long. About ⅓ inch wide, the orange-yellow fruits contain crimson seeds and are well displayed above the foliage. From the last the Japanese, Chinese, and Korean *C. orbiculatus* differs in its flowers

Celastrus scandens: (a) Fruits unopened

(b) Fruits open, showing seeds

Celastrus scandens (fruits unopened)

and fruits being in clusters from the leaf axils of its current year's shoots. A vigorous climber up to 40 feet tall, it has chiefly obovate to orbicular, toothed leaves that vary considerably in shape and are ¾ inch to 4½ inches long and ¾ inch to 3½ inches wide. The flowers are in clusters of three to seven, on male plants they are very occasionally terminal as well as axillary. The subspherical, orange-yellow fruits, containing red seeds, are mostly hidden until the foliage falls. This species is hardy throughout New England. Resembling *C. orbiculatus*, but easily distinguished because the pith of its shoots is in laddered, horizontal layers instead of a solid cylinder, **C. rosthornianus** (syn. *C. loeseneri*) is sometimes considered superior, but there seems little to choose between the two. It is hardy in southern New England. Another hardy kind, **C. flagellaris**, survives in southern New England. It comes from northern China, Korea, and Japan and is easily identified by the two persistent spines at each node (joint) of the stem and by the marginal teeth of its leaves being bristle-tipped. Sometimes aerial roots develop from the stems. This is a climbing shrub with broadly-elliptic to nearly round leaves up to 2 inches long or slightly longer. The flowers are in axillary, few-flowered clusters. The fruits are spherical, about ¼ inch across, and orange-yellow.

Suitable only for mild climates and not hardy in the north, **C. paniculatus** is a variable native of southeastern Asia, Ceylon, and the Philippines. Its most characteristic phase has broadly-obovate to almost round leaves, sometimes 5 inches in length. The plant attains heights up to 30 feet. The flowers are in terminal panicles mostly 2 to 4, but sometimes up to 8 inches long. The subspherical fruits are yellowish-brown.

The largest-leaved celastrus, well worth cultivating for its foliage alone, is **C. angulatus,** a native of China. This is hardy at New York City and probably further north. Up to 30 feet in height, it has broadly-elliptic to nearly circular, toothed leaves 4 to 6 inches long or a little longer. The flowers and fruits are in terminal panicles 4 to 8 inches long. The nearly spherical fruits are almost ½ inch across and are yellow with orange seeds. Angled instead of round young shoots, much larger leaves, and larger, more crowded panicles of flowers, and shorter-stalked fruits distinguish this from the American bittersweet.

Garden and Landscape Uses. Bittersweets have many uses. They can be employed to clothe posts and other supports and hide walls, rocks, tree stumps, and the like. For covering banks *C. flagellaris* is especially well adapted; other kinds can be put to the same use. In some locations the thorny character of *C. flagellaris* is an advantage. Bittersweets make no appreciable floral display, and except for *C. angulatus,* their foliage is rather ordinary. Their displays of fruits, however, can be extremely beautiful and remain attractive through most of the winter. Cut and brought indoors they are excellent long-lasting decorations. Because of the segregation of sexes it is important when planting to set mostly female plants with one male to every six or eight females to serve as a pollinator.

Cultivation. Among the most amiable of plants so far as cultivation is concerned, bittersweets thrive in any ordinary soil in sun or part-day shade. The only attention generally needed is any little pruning required to keep the plants tidy or to limit their size. This may be done in late winter or spring. New plants are easily raised from seeds sown as soon as they are ripe in fall, or stratified and sown in spring, but the seedlings will average, of course, about 50 percent each males and females. Vegetative propagation of plants of known sex is usually the best procedure. This can be done by summer cuttings under mist or in a greenhouse or cold frame propagating bed, by root cuttings, by suckers, and by layers. The chief pest of these plants is euonymus scale.

CELERIAC, KNOB CELERY, or TURNIP-ROOTED CELERY. A cultivated form of the species from which celery is derived, celeriac (botanically *Apium graveolens rapaceum*), belongs to the carrot family UMBELLIFERAE. It differs from celery in having as its edible part a tuberous, knobby stem commonly called the root. The leaves, similar to those of celery, but considerably smaller and shorter-stalked, are not used as food. Celeriac is eaten as a cooked vegetable, in soups, and raw in salads. It has a pleasant, celery-like flavor. A favorite variety is 'Giant Prague'.

Except that it does not require blanching, the cultural needs of this crop are essentially those of celery. It thrives best in cool, fairly moist, fertile soils well supplied with organic material, in full sun. Seeds may be sown outdoors where the crop is to remain, but at least for summer harvesting, it is usually preferred to sow in a greenhouse or hotbed where the temperature is about 60°F about eight weeks before the plants are to be set in the garden and, as is done with celery, to transplant the seedlings to flats or cold frames to make some growth before they are set in the garden.

Planting outdoors, in rows 1 foot to 1½ feet apart, with 6 to 8 inches between plants in the rows, may be done as soon as there is no longer danger of frost. For a succession crop, sow in drills ¼ inch deep in the open ground from the middle to the end of May and thin the seedlings to the required spacing. Care of celeriac in the garden consists of keeping down weeds by frequent shallow cultivation and watering generously during dry spells. One, or on poorish soils two, spaced about a month apart, light applications of fertilizer may be stirred into the surface soil during the growing season.

Harvesting is done in summer and fall before severe frost and when the roots are 3 inches or more in diameter. Pull up the plants, twist off their tops, and trim off all side roots. They may be stored for winter used in a cool cellar or similar place packed in slightly damp soil, sand, or peat moss. Diseases, to which celeriac seems more resistant than celery, and pests are those of celery.

CELERY. Celery is less easy to grow in home gardens than many vegetables, yet it is such a universal favorite that some enthusiastic amateurs are not discouraged. Modern strains of this vegetable have been bred over a long period from *Apium graveolens*, a European species of the carrot family UMBELLIFERAE.

The first requirement for producing good celery is deep, rich, mellow soil that at no time lacks moisture, but is well drained. It should contain abundant humus and so, unless the ground is a muck or peat type, both of which are admirable, it is important to mix to a depth of 9 inches or 1 foot or more with spade, rototiller, or plow generous amounts of partly decomposed manure, compost, or other decayed organic material.

Another point to bear in mind is that this crop needs a long growing season. In the north, sow seeds indoors early in spring to have plants to set in the garden in June to be harvested in late summer and fall. In the south, sow in late summer or fall to have plants to harvest in winter and spring. Home gardeners without a greenhouse are likely to do better buying young plants from a nearby nursery or garden center than trying to raise them in a window or other makeshift place. In any case be sure to secure strong plants that have not been unduly crowded before they are planted out.

To raise celery from seeds fill pots, pans, or flats with a porous, sandy soil mix containing abundant leaf mold, peat moss, or humus. Sift the upper ½ inch through a screen with a ¼-inch mesh and make it perfectly level. Because the seeds are small cover them with the barest sprinkling, not more than ⅛ inch, of the same soil or fine sand. After sowing, cover the containers with glass or polyethylene plastic film, shade them with paper and put them where the temperature is maintained at 65 to 70°F. Celery seed germinates slowly and the baby seedlings are frail. It takes about ten weeks from seed sowing for the plants to become big enough to plant outdoors. During this time take care that the soil is not allowed to dry. Celery seedlings that suffer from dryness are likely to become plants that "run to seed" early instead of

Young celery growing vigorously

developing into fine edible table plants. Transplant the seedlings to flats 5 inches deep or to a hotbed in rich soil as soon as their second pair of leaves are well developed. Allow 3 to 4 inches between individuals. Maintain a night temperature of 60°F, five to fifteen degrees more by day. Exposure to temperatures of 50°F or lower causes premature bolting or running to seed.

For planting outdoors choose a cloudy, humid day. Formerly it was the practice to set the young plants in trenches 10 inches to 1 foot deep and later as growth developed to fill these gradually with soil, taking care that none fell into the hearts of the plants. After the heat of summer had passed, additional soil was banked against the plants to effect blanching. This involved a great deal of work and was practical only where the fertile soil was 1¼ to 2 feet deep. It is now more usual to plant in shallow trenches or on the level and to blanch by other means.

Set the plants, not deeper than they were previously, in single rows spaced 1½ to 2 feet apart or in double rows 9 inches apart with 2½ to 3 feet between the pairs of rows. Allow 6 to 8 inches between plants in the rows. Water the plants thoroughly as soon as they are set. Should the weather be bright during the first few days after planting afford shade by sticking small leafy branches into the ground near them, by covering the rows with lath or burlap shades, or in some other convenient way.

Care during the growing season consists of doing everything possible to promote healthy growth. Cultivate shallowly at frequent intervals to eliminate weeds before they attain appreciable size. Soak the ground with water whenever it shows any indication of dryness. Every three weeks or so apply a light dressing of readily available high nitrogen fertilizer. Sprinkle this along both sides of the rows of plants and a few inches from them. Nitrate of soda at 1½ ounces to each 10 feet of row or its

equivalent in other fertilizer is satisfactory. Alternatively, water the plants with dilute liquid fertilizer at weekly intervals.

Blanching to bleach the stalks of most of their green color and tenderize them is needed with most celeries. It even improves the eating qualities of kinds designated as self-blanching. But, nutritionists tell us, blanched celery is less rich in vitamin A than green celery. Blanching can be done by standing boards 10 inches to 1 foot wide on edge along each side of the plants, and staking them into position. Soil is then gradually filled between the boards and around the plants taking care not to get any into their hearts and leaving their leafy tops free. A simpler method with early celery is to wrap each plant with a 1-foot strip of stout building paper tied into place or to slip over each a 4-inch cardboard cylinder or drain tile.

Celery wrapped for blanching

Celery wrapped for blanching

Blanching by banking soil around the plants without board supports was believed by old-time gardeners to produce celery of superior eating quality. For this, celery plants set in trenches have soil gradually filled around their bases as the season advances. After the hottest weather of

summer is over, hilling up or banking begins. First all suckers from the bottoms of the plants are taken off, and the top of each is pulled together and tied with string to prevent the possibility of soil entering the heart. Then, when the plants are dry, soil dug from along each side of the row is heaped against the plants as a long ridge, but except for the sides being patted to shape, is not compacted. The leafy tops of the plants are left uncovered. Celery continues growing well into fall and as the plants stretch additional soil is added.

Before the ground freezes hard, dig the celery and replant it closely together in a root cellar, protected cold frame, or deep trench covered with boards and hay or straw, where the temperature is 35 to 40°F. Alternatively, cover the soil ridges outdoors with straw or leaves and dig the plants as needed and as weather permits through the winter.

Digging celery for storage

Varieties of celery that need blanching are 'Cornell 619', 'Florida Golden', 'Golden Plume', 'Golden Self Blanching', and 'Michigan Golden'. Green varieties include 'Emerson Pascal', 'Giant Pascal', 'Summer Pascal', and 'Utah'.

Pests and Diseases. These include tarnished plant bug, carrot rust fly, early and late blights, and leaf spot. In certain areas a condition called black heart, believed to be caused by insufficient calcium occurs, in others brownish cracks on the stalks may be caused by boron deficiency. For knob or turnip-rooted celery see Celeriac, Knob Celery, or Turnip-Rooted Celery.

CELERY-TOP-PINE is *Phyllocladus asplenifolius*.

CELMISIA (Cel-mísia). With the exception of one native of Australia and Tasmania, this genus of sixty species or more is endemic to New Zealand and nearby islands. Difficult to grow and little known in America, a few species are occasionally attempted by enthusiastic rock gardeners. In British gardens it is more common, but there, and indeed even in New Zealand, many kinds defy the skills of cultivators.

Named after Celmisius, son of the nymph Alciope, *Celmisia* belongs in the daisy family COMPOSITAE. Its members are stemless or short-stemmed herbaceous perennials with rosettes of all basal leaves or leaves with sheathing bases arising from short stems and overlapping. In most kinds the foliage is abundantly clothed with silvery or buff-colored silky hairs. The solitary, daisy-like flower heads are comparatively large and usually stalked. Their ray florets, white and narrowly-strap-shaped, are female, the five-lobed tubular disk ones, usually yellow or more rarely purple, are bisexual. The fruits are seedlike achenes.

Kinds that have proven most amenable to cultivation include *C. coriacea*, which has short stems and silvery lanceolate leaves 8 inches to 2 feet long and flower heads 1½ to 3½ inches wide, on stalks 1 foot to 3 feet tall; *C. hieracifolia*, a mat-forming kind with short stems, obovate to linear-oblong leaves covered below with buff-colored hairs and up to 5 inches long and flower heads ¾ to 2 inches across, on stalks up to 10 inches long; *C. hookeri*, with rosettes of erect, lanceolate leaves, gray-green above, silvery beneath, and 3-inch-wide flower heads with narrow rays; *C. lindsayi*, a mat-forming kind with procumbent woody stems, linear to lanceolate leaves up to 8 inches long, smooth on their upper surfaces and white-hairy beneath, and flower heads 1 inch to 2 inches wide

Celmisia hookeri

Celmisia lindsayi

Celmisia hieracifolia

atop thin stalks; and *C. spectabilis*, a thick-stemmed, mat-former with narrowly-linear leaves up to 6 inches long, nearly smooth above and heavily covered beneath with white or buff hairs, and flower heads about 1½ inches wide.

Celmisia spectabilis

Other prized sorts are *C. discolor* and *C. monroi* which, like those described above, are natives of New Zealand. Subshrubby *C. discolor* forms broad, flat cushions of prostrate stems. In rosettes at the ends of the branches the 1- to 1½-inch-long, oblong- to obovate-spatula-shaped, toothed leaves are somewhat hairy on their upper surfaces and densely white-hairy beneath. Slender, glandular-hairy stalks 4 to 6 inches long support flower heads up to 1¼ inches wide. A tufted perennial 6 to 8 inches tall in bloom, *C. monroi* has rigid, all basal, toothless lanceolate-elliptic to elliptic leaves up to 6 inches long and with recurved margins. They are silvery on their upper sides and densely white-hairy beneath. Topping stoutish, densely white-wooly stalks, the flower heads are up to 1½ inches in diameter.

Celmisia discolor

Celmisia monroi

Garden Uses and Cultivation. In humid regions of mild winters and not excessively torrid summers, celmisias are worth trying in rock gardens. Sandy, gravelly, scree soil that contains some peat, with, if practicable, underground watering, the conditions provided in what rock gardeners call a moraine, and a place in full sun is most likely to favor these plants. Propagation is by seed and careful division.

CELOSIA (Celòs-ia)—Cockscomb. With few exceptions the sixty species of *Celosia*, of the amaranth family AMARANTHACEAE, are unknown to gardeners. All are natives of the tropics or subtropics. Those most commonly cultivated are annuals. The genus is a close relative of *Amaranthus*, but differ in the stalks of its stamens being joined in their lower parts to form a tube around the style and in the fruits having more than one seed. The name *Celosia* is from the Greek *kelos*, burned, and refers to the color and appearance of the flower clusters. Celosias have alternate, usually lobeless leaves and small flowers in dense chaffy spikes at the ends of the main stems and branches.

The cultivated celosias are nearly all derivatives of *C. argentea*, a hairless native of the tropics that attains a height of 2 to 3

Celosia argentea

feet and has linear-lanceolate to lanceolate-ovate leaves. The upright or lax flower spikes of this erect plant are 2 to 4 inches long and silvery-white. The wild form of *C. argentea* is not particularly showy, but is worth growing to a limited extent as a matter of interest. A horticultural tetraploid derivative of *C. argentea*, named *C. cristata,* includes some of the showiest annuals. They are divided into two groups, those with plumelike heads of red or yellow flowers that constitute the plumosa

Celosia cristata: (a) Yellow-flowered plumosa variety

(b) Red-flowered plumosa variety

(c) Cockscomb variety

group and to which are referred sorts listed as *C. childsii* and *C. thompsonii* and the sorts called cockscombs. The latter, which also come in red and yellow, have fantastically crested, flattened, broad, fanlike flower clusters, the result of the fusing of the branches and branchlets in a phenomenon known as fasciation. This occurs rarely and sporadically in lilies and many other flowers, but in cockscomb it is characteristic and hereditary.

A species more rarely cultivated is *C. huttonii,* a 2-foot-tall, bushy annual from Java that has red foliage and cylindrical spikes about 2 inches long of red flowers. Quite different is *C. floribunda,* native to Baja California and sometimes grown in gardens in southern California and other areas with mild climates. This is a much-branched, hairless shrub up to 12 feet in height with triangular-ovate to ovate, green or glaucous leaves up to 8 inches long and numerous tiny flowers in tight panicles. Seedsmen sometimes apply the designation *floribunda* to varieties of *C. argentea*.

Garden Uses. Except *C. floribunda,* which is a shrub of interest for planting in beds and borders in mild climates, the cultivated celosias are annuals well adapted for summer display in gardens and for growing as pot plants in greenhouses. They revel in hot, sunny weather, create displays over a long season, and produce flowers useful for cutting.

Cultivation. Annual celosias are raised from seeds that may be sown directly outdoors in early spring or be sown indoors and the seedlings transplanted to flats or individually to small pots and later transferred to the garden or potted into larger containers if the plants are to be grown to blooming size in a greenhouse. Sowing outdoors where the plants are to remain is as satisfactory a method as any for the production of flowers for cutting. The seeds are sprinkled very thinly along very shallow drills spaced 2 to 3 feet apart and the young plants are thinned to about 1 foot apart. For flower beds and borders it is often more convenient to sow the seeds outdoors in a nursery seedbed, and when the seedlings are large enough to handle easily to transplant them to their flowering locations spacing them 1 foot to 1½ feet apart according to the space needs and vigor of the variety. Sow seeds indoors to give plants for outdoors about eight weeks before the young plants are set in the garden, which should not be done until the weather is warm and settled, about the time it is safe to plant peppers and eggplants. They are spaced as suggested above for plants transplanted from outdoor nursery seed beds.

The soil for best results must be deep, fertile, and at all times reasonably moist. To have good annual celosias they must be grown throughout without check. This is especially true of the cockscomb varieties.

Exposure to cold, unnecessary damage to the roots when transplanting, or excessively dry soil are likely to result in stunted, inferior plants and smaller heads of bloom. Summer care consists of weeding and watering as needed, and staking tall-growing kinds.

Pot specimens are raised from seeds sown in greenhouses as detailed above, but instead of transferring the plants outdoors from flats or the first small pots they occupy they are repotted into successively larger containers until those in which they are to bloom are attained. For the cockscomb varieties these may be 5 or 6 inches in diameter, for the plumose-flowered kinds 5 to 8 inches in diameter. The potting soil should be coarse, fertile, porous, and pressed moderately firmly about the roots. Unless it is open enough to admit air and drain freely root, growth is not satisfactory and rotting is apt to occur. Celosias should be grown throughout in a minimum night temperature of 60 to 65°F and by day 70 to 75°F before the greenhouse needs to be ventilated. Full sun and high humidity are desirable while the plants are making their main vegetative growth, but later as they approach full bloom, they can with advantage to the lasting of the display be kept in a more airy, less humid, and somewhat cooler environment and be lightly shaded. In their later stages of growth, after their final pots are filled with healthy roots, they benefit from weekly or semiweekly applications of dilute liquid fertilizer, but these should be discontinued a little before the blooms reach their maximum development.

Shrubby *C. floribunda* thrives in sunny locations in any ordinary garden soil. It is propagated by cuttings and by seeds.

Diseases and Pests. Celosias are subject to fungus leaf spot infections and virus curly top disease and to infestations of red spider mites and nematodes.

CELSIA (Cél-sia)—Cretan Bear's Tail, Cretan-Mullein. Closely related to mulleins (*Verbascum*) are the sixty species of *Celsia*, a genus of the figwort family SCROPHULARIACEAE, native from the Mediterranean region to India and South Africa. Celsias include annuals and biennials and herbaceous and subshrubby perennials. From mulleins they differ in their flowers having four instead of five stamens. Their name commemorates the distinguished Swedish botanist Olaus Celsius, who died in 1756.

Celsias are not hardy in the north. They have alternate, usually toothed, sometimes pinnately-lobed leaves, and racemes or spikes of yellow flowers with five-parted calyxes, short-tubed corollas with five deep lobes (petals), and four stamens. The fruits are capsules containing many small seeds.

A subshrubby, evergreen, woolly-hairy perennial 1½ to 4 feet tall, the Cretan bear's tail (**Celsia arcturus**) is a native of Crete and Asia Minor. Its lower leaves are fiddle-shaped, its upper oblong. The flowers, in slender, lax racemes, are long-stalked, about ¾ inch wide, and are yellow marked with purple. They have beautiful, violet-bearded stamens.

Celsia arcturus

Very handsome, the Cretan-mullein (**C. cretica**) is a stiffly erect biennial of the Mediterranean region, and 4 to 6 feet tall.

Celsia cretica

Its stem, sometimes branched, but commonly not, is furnished to the bottom of the flower spike with leaves that gradually diminish in size from the base upward. The lower ones are fiddle-shaped to oblong, those above oblong. The clear yellow flowers, about 2 inches in diameter, have their two-lobed upper lips somewhat deeper colored than the three-lobed lower ones. There are two chocolate-brown marks near the base of the upper lip, and the two upper stamens are fuzzy with hairs of the same hue. The blooms face outward. Individuals remain in good condition for several days and a succession is maintained over a long period. This is a somewhat variable species. Seeds of only the largest flowered, most attractive specimens should be selected for sowing.

Low and almost stemless, **C. acaulis**, of Greece, has congested basal rosettes of round- to jagged-toothed, oblongish leaves, about 1 inch long. Its ½-inch-wide flowers, yellow with orange stamens, are borne through a long summer period. This species is reported to hybridize with *Verbascum phoeniceum*. Hybrids between these two genera are named *Celsioverbascum*.

Garden Uses. Celsias are usually cultivated in greenhouses, but they can be grown outdoors in climates not too dissimilar from those of Mediterranean lands. Where winters are mild and summers warm they are good flower garden plants. Dwarf *C. acaulis* is attractive in rock gardens in mild climates. It is also grown in alpine greenhouses.

Cultivation. As biennials celsias are raised from seeds sown in June. In mild climates they can remain throughout the winter in garden beds of moderately rich, well-drained soil, but in greenhouses the seedlings are transferred to flats or small pots, later to 4-inch pots, and then to larger ones as growth makes necessary. For *C. cretica* the final containers may be 6 or 7 inches in diameter, for *C. arcturus* smaller pots are satisfactory. Coarse, porous, fertile soil is needed. It is important that cool, airy growing conditions be provided. A little shade during their early stages and again after the buds show is advantageous. The winter night temperature should not exceed 50°F, with a daytime rise of five to ten degrees permitted. Even in climates as cold as that of New York City *C. cretica* winters satisfactorily in a well-protected cold frame. Watering should be moderate through the winter, generous later. After the final pots are filled with roots regular applications of dilute liquid fertilizer are highly beneficial.

CELTIS (Cél-tis) — Sugarberry or Hackberry. Deciduous or rarely evergreen trees or less commonly shrubs numbering eighty species constitute *Celtis* of the elm family ULMACEAE. They inhabit the northern hemisphere and tropics in the southern hemisphere. The name is an ancient Greek one for some tree bearing a sweet fruit, not certainly a hackberry.

Hackberries have alternate, usually fairly long-stalked, undivided, toothed or toothless leaves with three veins radiating from the unequal-sided base of the blade. The small blooms, bisexual and unisexual ones on the same plant, appear with the leaves. Male blooms are clustered near the bottoms of the new shoots. Bisexual flowers are solitary or sometimes in twos from the leaf axils above. The blooms have a four- or five-lobed calyx, four or five stamens, and the bisexual ones, a very short style bearing a pair of spreading, recurved stigmas. The fruits are small, dark-colored, egg-shaped to spherical drupes (fruits structured like plums) containing a single seedlike stone. Those of a few kinds are edible. It is not always easy to distinguish between different species of hackberry.

Extremely hardy **C. occidentalis,** native from Quebec to Manitoba, North Carolina, Alabama, and Kansas, attains a maximum height of about 120 feet. Straight-trunked and with spreading or somewhat drooping branches, it has lustrous, ovate to oblong-ovate leaves, rounded or somewhat heart-shaped at their bases, their blades 2 to 4½ inches long. Hairless except sometimes on the veins of their undersides, in fall they become yellow. The orange-red to black-purple fruits, up to a little more than ⅓ inch long, have slender stalks longer than the leafstalks. The surfaces of the stones they contain are conspicuously pitted. From the last, **C. sinensis,** a native of China, may be distinguished by its shorter-stalked leaves and the stones of its fruits being smooth-surfaced rather than pitted. Attaining heights of up to 60 feet, this kind has pointed, ovate to oblong-ovate, round-toothed leaves with wedge-shaped bases and somewhat hairy undersides. Its dark orange fruits have stalks about as long as the leafstalks. Variety **C. s. japonica,** is a phase of this species indigenous to Japan, Korea, and China.

Sugarberry or Mississippi hackberry (**C. laevigata**), not hardy in climates harsher than that of southern New England, is native in wet soils from Illinois to Florida and Texas. Broad-headed and up to about 100 feet tall, it has more or less pendulous branches. Its long-pointed, slightly sickle-shaped, oblong-lanceolate leaves, 2 to 4 inches long, are hairless except for a short time when young. They have wedge-shaped to rounded bases. From ¼ inch to a little more in diameter, the slender-stalked fruits are orange-red to purplish-black.

Not hardy in climates harsher than approximately that of Washington, D.C., **C. australis** is native to southern Europe, North Africa, and western Asia. It has a roundish, egg-shaped head and is 40 to 75 feet tall. Its long-pointed, sharply-toothed, elliptic-ovate to oblong-lanceolate leaves

Celtis laevigata, in winter

Celtis laevigata, in summer

are grayish-pubescent on their undersides, dark green and rough to the touch above, at their bases oblique and more or less wedge-shaped or rounded. They are 2 to 6 inches in length and have stalks up to a little over ½ inch long. The fruits are dark purple.

Other nonhardy kinds, planted in Hawaii and other tropical and subtropical regions, are **C. kraussiana,** the only South African species, and **C. trinervia,** of Java.

A deciduous tall shrub or tree up to 80 feet tall, **C. kraussiana** has pointed-ovate leaves sometimes slightly over 2 inches long, often smaller. The nearly spherical fruits are ⅙ inch long. A tall tree, **C. trinervia** has elliptic, oblong-elliptic, or obovate-oblong, toothless leaves ¾ inch to 4 inches long. The ellipsoid fruits are ½ inch long.

Garden and Landscape Uses. These somewhat elmlike relatives of elms are of less distinguished appearance than elms. They may be used as single specimens and in other ways. In the south they are planted as street trees.

Cultivation. Hackberries grow readily in a variety of soils and locations and require no special care. They are raised from seeds sown as soon as they are ripe or after being mixed with slightly damp sand or vermiculite and stored in a temperature of 40°F for three months. Propagation may also be by grafting onto understocks of **C. occidentalis.**

CELTUCE. The name of this vegetable, sometimes called asparagus lettuce, is a made one combining portions of the names of celery and lettuce. The plant has no botanical affinity to celery, but is a form of lettuce. Botanically it is *Lactuca sativa asparagina.* Said to have been brought to the United States from an area near the Chinese-Tibetan border, celtuce has much the aspect of a loose romaine lettuce, but unlike that familiar salad is not eaten raw but cooked like broccoli. The edible parts are the stems.

To raise good crops of celtuce sow seeds in spring, where the plants are to stay, in fertile soil in a sunny location. Space the rows 1½ feet apart and as soon as the seedlings are big enough to handle comfortably thin them to about 1 foot apart. Keep weeds down, and water liberally in dry weather. The stems are ready for harvesting as soon as their bases are about 1 inch in diameter and until flower buds appear. Cut them close to the ground, strip off the foliage, and peel before cooking. A recommended method of preparation is to cut the peeled cores into 1-inch lengths, boil them in a small amount of water for a few minutes, drain, and then bake them in a casserole with cheese sauce and bread crumbs.

CENIZO is *Leucophyllum frutescens.*

CENTAUREA (Cen-taurèa)—Basket Flower, Cornflower, Dusty Miller, Mountain-Bluet, Sweet Sultan, Mountain-Bluet. Mostly natives of the Old World, but represented also in the native floras of North and South America and one in Australia, the 600 species of *Centaurea* of the daisy family COMPOSITAE include several well-known and some lesser appreciated worthy ornamentals. Some are annuals, others herbaceous or more rarely subshrubby perennials, hardy and nonhardy. Their name is derived from the Greek *kentauros*, a centaur, in reference perhaps to these plants being used medicinally. The centaur Chiron was believed to have taught mankind the healing qualities of plants.

Centaureas have alternate leaves, undivided, lobeless, and toothless, or pinnately-divided, pinnately-lobed, or toothed. Some kinds, popularly called dusty millers, a vernacular name they share with certain kinds of *Artemisia, Lychnis,* and *Senecio,* are admired for their densely-felted, white-hairy stems and foliage. The small to large flower heads, as usual in the daisy family, are of many florets, each technically a flower, and are backed by a collar of bracts called an involucre. The bracts in *Centaurea* are in several overlapping rows and are often fringed or appendaged. Sometimes they are prickly. The flower heads are without true ray florets (petal-like ones characteristic of daisies), but the marginal florets are sometimes much enlarged and petal-like and are often frilled. The fruits are seedlike achenes.

Popular annual centaureas (the first, perennial in the wild, is cultivated as an annual) are the basket flower, the cornflower, the bachelor's button, or blue bottle, and the sweet sultan. Basket flower (**C. americana**) is one of the very few New World species of the genus. Native from

Centaurea americana

Missouri to Louisiana and Mexico, this rather coarse, branchless or sparsely-branched species has ovate-lanceolate leaves mostly without lobes, 2 to 5 inches long, the lower ones often stalked, those above stalkless. From 2 to 6 feet tall, it bears solitary, pink to rosy-purple flower heads 4 to 5 inches wide, with showy, enlarged, dissected petal-like marginal florets. The bracts of the involucre are fringed. The blooms of *C. a. alba* are white. Cornflower, bachelor's button, or bluebottle (**C. cyanus**), native to southeastern Europe and

Centaurea cyanus

naturalized in parts of North America, is an old-time garden favorite. From 1 foot to 3 feet tall and branched, it has young stems and foliage furnished with white, cottony hairs. Its linear leaves are 3 to 6 inches long. The lower ones are sometimes toothed or pinnately-lobed. On erect, slender stalks the blue, purple, pink, or white flower heads, 1 inch to 1½ inches in diameter, have showy, enlarged, petal-like, incised marginal florets. The bracts of the involucre are fringed. Variety *C. c. florepleno* has double blooms. A race of compact plants up to 1 foot tall known as *C. c. nana-compacta* includes 'Jubilee Gem' with rich blue double flower heads. Sweet sultan (**C. moschata**), native of the Orient, is erect and hairless. Branched from the base and about 2 feet tall, it has leaves toothed or pinnately-lobed, with the lobes toothed. The fragrant, white, yellow, or pinkish-purple, solitary flower heads, about 2 inches in diameter, terminate long stalks. They have showy, petal-like marginal florets and smooth-edged involucral bracts. Annual **C. imperialis** is a variant or perhaps a hybrid of *C. moschata.* It is similar to but has flower heads twice as big as those of *C. moschata.*

Hardy herbaceous perennial centaureas include the favorite mountain-bluet (**C. montana**), sometimes called perennial

Centaurea montana

cornflower. This easy-to-grow kind has erect, mostly branchless stems 1 foot to 1½ feet tall. Its cornflower-like flower heads, 1½ to 3 inches wide, are typically bright blue, in variety *C. m. alba,* white, in *C. m. rubra,* rosy-red, in *C. m.* 'Parkham', lavender-purple. They have enlarged, petal-like marginal florets. The toothed leaves, broadly-lanceolate to obovate-lanceolate, have stalks extended as wings down the stems. The involucral bracts have black-fringed edges. Leaves somewhat silvery-hairy on their undersides, but green and hairless above are characteristic of **C. dealbata,** a hardy herbaceous perennial native

Centaurea dealbata

of Asia Minor and Iran. From 1 foot to 2 feet tall, this has pinnately-divided or cleft into coarsely-toothed, oblong-lanceolate to obovate leaflets or lobes, and lower leaves that are 1 foot to 1½ feet long and stalked. The upper ones, considerably smaller, are usually stalkless. The short-stalked, somewhat thistle-like flower heads, solitary at the ends of the branches of the flowering stems, 2 to nearly 3 inches wide, have red inner florets and rosy-pink to white or in horticultural varieties red, outer ones. The involucral bracts are deeply fringed. Compact *C. d. steenbergii* has rosy-crimson flower heads. Yellow-flowered **C. macrocephala** is a hardy herbaceous perennial native of Armenia. This attains heights of 2½ to 3 feet. Its stems are scarcely branched or branchless. Its toothed, ovate-lanceolate leaves gradually diminish in size upward. From 3 to 4 inches in diameter, the thistle-like flower heads, the stems thickened just below them, are globose and of all similar florets. The rusty-colored bracts of the involucre are fringed.

Dusty miller-type centaureas (not to be confused with other plants known by this name) have stems and both sides of the leaves intensely whitened with thick, felty coverings of hairs. Subshrubby perennials, they are not hardy in the north. Belonging here are *C. ragusina, C. cineraria,* and *C.*

Centaurea macrocephala

gymnocarpa. Native to Crete and Dalmatia, bushy, and 2 to 3 feet tall, **C. ragusina** has branchless stems, leafless or nearly so in

Centaurea ragusina

Centaurea cineraria

their lower parts. Its leaves, pinnately-lobed into lobed or lobeless, ovate to obovate segments have the upper lobes the biggest. The flower heads, individually long-stalked and without spreading marginal florets, are yellow. Solitary or sometimes in twos or threes, they are 1 inch to 1½ inches wide. Variety *C. r. compacta* is of denser habit. Native to the Balkans, **C. cineraria** (syns. *C. rutifolia*, *C. candidissima*) has leaves deeply-pinnately-cleft into linear-lanceolate segments. The rather small, individually short-stalked, clustered, pale purple flower heads have slightly enlarged marginal florets and hair-fringed, somewhat spiny involucral bracts. In gardens *Senecio leucostachys* is often misidentified as *C. candidissima*, which name properly is a synonym of *C. cineraria*, and *C. cineraria* is frequently grown as *C. gymnocarpa*. True **C. gymnocarpa** differs technically from *C. cineraria* in its flower heads being without a pappus. An erect, branching subshrub up to 3 feet tall, this kind has leaves mostly twice or sometimes once pinnately-cleft into blunt, oblong, or linear, toothless segments. The rosy-purple flower heads are

Centaurea gymnocarpa

solitary or few together at the branch ends. Their involucral bracts have short hairs at their apexes. This is native to Capri.

Occasionally cultivated **C. pulcherrima** is a beautiful hardy herbaceous perennial up to 2½ feet tall. Native of the Caucasus, it has foliage hairless above, gray-hairy beneath. From *C. dealbata* it differs in its flowering stems not branching. Up to about 7 inches in length and toothed or pinnately-cleft, its leaves are stalked. The solitary, purple flower heads, 2 to 2½ inches across, have enlarged, fringed marginal florets. The conspicuously-fringed involucral bracts are light brown. Also Caucasian, **C. bella** forms a wide, low mound of cobwebby-hairy stems and foliage. Its fiddle-shaped leaves are pinnately-cleft into elliptic to

obovate lobes, white-hairy on their undersides. About 1¾ inches across, the pinkish-lavender to light purple flower heads have much-enlarged, deeply-frilled outer flowers. The flower heads terminate stalks 9 inches to 1¼ feet long.

Centaurea bella

Native to Asia Minor, **C. hypoleuca** is a perennial 1½ to 2½ feet tall. Its coarsely-pinnate leaves, with dull green upper surfaces, are white-hairy beneath. They are up to 1 foot long, the lower ones obovate to fiddle-shaped, those above oblong. The solitary flower heads 3 to 3½ inches across, and lavender-pink to rosy-purple, have much-enlarged and frilled outer florets.

Centaurea hypoleuca

European **C. triumfettii,** 1 foot to 2 feet tall, has short rhizomes. Its linear-lanceolate to ovate-lanceolate leaves, the lower ones stalked and sometimes toothed or lobed, are white-hairy on both surfaces. The blue to red-purple flower heads, 2 to 2½ inches across, have enlarged, raylike outer florets. Attractive *C. t. cana* (syn. *C. cana*), native of rocky limestone regions in southern Europe, has sparsely-lobed, oblong-lanceolate basal leaves and long-pointed, linear-lanceolate stem leaves, all very white-hairy. Its flower heads are on stalks 4 inches to 1½ feet tall.

Centaurea triumfettii cana

Garden and Landscape Uses. Various kinds of centaureas serve different garden purposes. The basket flower, cornflower, and sweet sultan are esteemed as annuals for flower beds, borders, and cut flowers. Sometimes they are grown in greenhouses for late winter and spring display. The hardy perennials are good flower garden ornamentals that supply useful cut blooms. They make but slight demands on the skill of the cultivator and adapt to all ordinary garden soils, generally responding best to those reasonably fertile and moist. All grow best in full sun, but the mountain-bluet tolerates light or part-day shade. The gray to nearly white attractive foliage of the dusty miller centaureas is their chief charm. Grown as perennials in warm, dry climates, they are also commonly raised on an annual basis there and in harsher climates for mixing with other plants in summer flower beds. They provide beautiful foils for colorful flowers of all kinds and themselves add an appearance of coolness and a much appreciated tone of quality. Plants raised in pots especially for the purpose, or carefully lifted in early fall from the outdoors and potted, make useful winter cool greenhouse foliage plants.

Cultivation. Sow the annuals outdoors in early spring or in fairly mild climates in fall. If in rows, as is most convenient for cut flowers, space those for cornflowers and sweet sultans 1 foot to 1½ feet apart, for basket flowers 1½ to 2 feet. Thin the seedlings sufficiently to prevent excessive crowding, but not too severely because centaureas, unlike many annuals, seem to bloom most profusely when just a little tight for room. Subsequent care involves cultivating to keep down weeds, watering in moderation in dry weather, prompt removal of faded blooms and, particularly with taller kinds, staking or the provision of other neat supports. When watering sweet sultans avoid, if possible, overhead sprinkling.

Hardy herbaceous kinds benefit from being divided and replanted every third or fourth year. Because it spreads by underground stems it may be necessary to reduce the size of clumps of mountain-bluet more frequently. Do this in fall or spring by digging out unwanted portions. An annual application of a complete garden fertilizer in spring is usually all that is needed to keep these plants vigorous. As a group they stand dryish conditions fairly well, but benefit from periodic watering during long dry spells. Little or no staking is needed.

Dusty miller-type centaureas favor porous, dryish soils and revel in full sun. They may be managed as perennials in dryish climates with little frost. The only attention they then are likely to need is the trimming of faded flower heads and any pruning needed to shape them. Most often they are grown as annuals either from seeds sown in a greenhouse in spring or from cuttings managed in much the same manner as those of geraniums. The cuttings are made in late summer or early fall, rooted in sand, perlite, vermiculite, or other medium in a greenhouse or cold frame propagating bed. After rooting they are potted individually and grown in a frostproof frame or greenhouse where the temperature by night is 40 to 50°F and by day not more than ten degrees higher. Take care throughout the winter to keep the soil dryish, but not dry. To raise dusty miller centaureas from seed sow at 60 to 65°F about twelve weeks before it is safe to set the plants in the garden, about the time that tomatoes and geraniums may be planted outdoors. Transplant the seedlings to flats or individual small pots and grow them in full sun where the temperature is 50 to 55°F at night, five to fifteen degrees higher by day.

CENTAURIDIUM. See Xanthisma.

CENTAURIUM (Cent-aùrium)—Centaury, Canchalagua, Mountain-Pink. Widely distributed as natives in many warm and temperate regions except tropical and South Africa, *Centaurium* contains fifty species of the gentian family GENTIANACEAE. It has also been named *Erythraea.* The name is an adaptation of *kentaurion,* used by Dioscorides for *C. minus,* possibly the plant according to Greek mythology used to cure an arrow wound made by Hercules in the foot of the centaur Chiron.

Centauriums are small annuals, biennials, and herbaceous perennials with much the aspect of *Sabatia.* They have opposite, undivided, lobeless, toothless, stalkless leaves in alternate pairs set at right angles to those next above and below. The lower ones may form rosettes. The pink, yellow, or rarely white flowers are in loosely-branched clusters or spikes. They have tubular, four- or five-parted calyxes, slim-tubed corollas with four or five wide-spreading lobes (petals), as many stamens as petals, and a slender style terminated by a two-lobed stigma. The fruits are capsules. The kinds discussed here are annuals or biennials.

Two somewhat similar European species, *C. erythraea* (syn. *C. umbellatum*) and *C. pulchellum,* are naturalized mostly in dampish soils in North America. From 4 inches to more than 1 foot tall, **C. erythraea** has slender stems, branched above. Its

Centaurium erythraea

leaves are pointed and oblong to elliptic, the lowermost in rosettes. Bright rose-pink to whitish, the nearly stalkless flowers, about ½ inch across, are in flat-topped clusters. From this, **C. pulchellum** differs in its stems branching from their bases, in the bottom leaves not forming rosettes, and in its smaller flowers being stalked and much more loosely disposed.

The canchalagua (*C. venustum*) inhabits dry soils in California. From 6 inches to 1½ feet tall, it has stems branched above. Its leaves, up to 1 inch long, are ovate to oblong. The stalked blooms, rose- to purple-pink with red-dotted white throats, or rarely white, are ¾ to 1 inch across. Similar *C. calycosum* attains heights up to 2 feet. More loosely branched than *C. venustum*, its lower leaves tend to be oblanceolate. The blooms are rose-pink with white centers. This sort grows in damp places from Utah to California, Texas, and Mexico.

Mountain-pink (*C. beyrichii*), native of usually gravelly, often limestone soils in Texas and perhaps New Mexico, is one of the most beautiful of its race. It forms mounds 6 inches to 1 foot or so tall covered with bright pink flowers about 1 inch in diameter, with corolla tubes twice as long as the calyx. Its leaves are slender-linear, mostly ¾ to 1 inch long. Native chiefly of dry and limestone soils from Missouri to Texas, *C. texense* has smaller flowers with corolla tubes scarcely longer than the calyx. About 1 foot tall, it has slender stems loosely fork-branched above. The linear to linear-lanceolate leaves are up to ¾ inch long. The fairly long-stalked, pink flowers are nearly or quite ½ inch wide.

Garden Uses and Cultivation. Although not very well known to gardeners, these are plants of considerable charm for growing as annuals in rock gardens and at the fronts of borders, as well as in collections of plants that have been used medicinally, and appropriate species in native plant gardens. They succeed from seeds sown in early spring where the plants are to remain, the seedlings being thinned just enough to prevent undue crowding. Sandy soil and locations with just a little shade from the strongest sun are suitable for most kinds, but conditions may be modified to meet known preferences of individual species.

CENTAURY. See Centaurium.

CENTIPEDE, GARDEN. The creature that goes by this name is not a true centipede, but a symphylan. Symphylans differ from centipedes (which do not harm plants) in having fewer legs, twenty-four in twelve pairs as against thirty or more, no eyes, and no poison claws. The garden centipede is about ¼ inch long, it avoids light, works below the ground surface, and so is rarely seen. It injures plants by chewing the roots of a wide variety of kinds. It inhabits damp places where there is abundant organic material, such as manure and leaf mold. The eggs of this pest are laid in clusters deep in the ground. They hatch within a week or ten days into minute young with only six pairs of legs. At each

successive molt they gain additional legs until the full complement of twelve pairs is attained. Soil sterilization affords the best control.

CENTIPEDE PLANT is *Homalocladium platycladum*. Centipede grass is *Eremochloa ophiuroides*.

CENTRADENIA (Centra-dènia). Six Mexican and Central American species of herbaceous perennials and low subshrubs compose *Centradenia* of the melastoma family MELASTOMATACEAE. Two are cultivated in greenhouses. The generic name, from the Greek *kentron*, a spur, and *aden*, a gland, refers to the anthers.

Centradenias have quadrangular stems, with the angles often winged, and opposite leaves with those of each pair markedly dissimilar in size or one may be lacking. The blooms are produced very abundantly in clusters. They are pink or more rarely white, with slightly four-angled calyx tubes and four petals. There are eight stamens, unequal in size. The fruits are many-seeded capsules.

In cultivation up to about 2 feet tall, but reported to attain heights of 4 feet in the wild, and bushy, *C. grandifolia* has stems distinctly four-winged, and stalked, ovate-lanceolate to ovate leaves, the longest of each pair always from the lower sides of the stems, 3 to 7 inches in length, 1 inch to 2 inches wide, curved, and ending in long points. The under surfaces of the leaves are red, their upper sides dark green. They have four or five very evident veins. The clear rose-pink flowers, about 1 inch in diameter, have very unequal-sized stamens.

Differing in its stems not being winged, although they are obscurely angled, its

narrowly-lanceolate leaves being three-veined and usually not more than 2 or 3 inches long, and its stamens being of nearly equal lengths, *C. floribunda*, of Mexico and Central America, is a lower

Centradenia floribunda

Centradenia floribunda (flowers)

Centradenia grandifolia

plant than *C. grandifolia*. Its short-stalked leaves are green above and softly-hairy and red on the veins beneath. Its flowers are pink and nearly 1 inch across.

Garden Uses. Cultivated centradenias are pretty for providing winter color in greenhouses and conservatories. They are suitable for blooming in 4- or 5-inch or larger pots, and, although individual blooms do not last long, the plants make a fine display for several weeks.

Cultivation. A humid greenhouse in which the minimum winter temperature is 55°F suits centradenias best. Good light is important. A little shade from strong summer sun is needed, but not too much; especially at other seasons shade is likely to be detrimental. Too much results in weak stems and loose, unattractive plants. In summer these plants respond to conditions that suit most begonias. Excessively oppressive, hot and humid environments are not to their liking. The greenhouse in which they are grown should be ventilated sufficiently to avoid such environments. When well grown centradenias are sufficiently sturdy to support themselves with little or no staking. The soil best adapted for their needs is a porous fertile one of a sandy peaty character. It should be watered sufficiently often to keep it evenly moist, but never for long periods wet. When the plants are well rooted in the pots in which they are to bloom weekly applications of dilute liquid fertilizer are of benefit. Centradenias are best raised from cuttings each year; old plants are less satisfactory than young ones. Cuttings root with great ease and rapidity in a greenhouse propagating bench. They are inserted from late winter to early summer depending upon the size of plants needed. To promote bushiness and the production of shapely, compact specimens the tips of the growing shoots are pinched out two to four times, the last pinch in July.

CENTRALS. Spines of cactuses that originate from the center of an areole are called centrals as opposed to radials, which sprout from near the periphery of an areole.

CENTRANTHUS (Centrán-thus)—Red-Valerian or Jupiter's Beard. The name of this genus of a dozen species of the valerian family VALERIANACEAE has also been spelled *Kentranthus*. The group consists of annual and perennial, sometimes somewhat subshrubby, herbaceous plants that in the wild inhabit Europe and the Mediterranean region. The name, from the Greek *kentron*, a spur, and *anthos*, a flower, was applied because the corollas are spurred at their bases.

The small flowers of centranthuses are crowded in terminal clusters. Their calyxes are of five to fifteen slender divisions that increase in size after the blooms fade. The slender-tubular, red, pink, or white corol-

las are spurred, or have a small conical projection at their bases, and have five lobes (petals). There is one stamen. The membranous fruits contain a solitary seed.

Red-valerian or Jupiter's beard (**Centranthus ruber** syns. *Valeriana rubra; V. coccinea*) is a worthy, popular, hardy perennial. Bushy, erect, hairless, and somewhat glaucous, it attains heights of 1½ to 3 feet and has toothless or nearly toothless, ovate to lanceolate leaves up to 4 inches long. The upper leaves are stalkless. The brilliant red, fragrant blooms, about ½ inch long, come from late spring to early fall and have spurs one-half as long as the tubes of the corollas. Variety *C. r. atrococcineus* has flowers of deeper red than the typical kind. In *C. r. roseus* the blooms are pink. Those of *C. r. albus* are white.

Another perennial, **C. angustifolius**, differs from the last in having linear-lanceolate or linear, toothless leaves up to 3 inches long. From 1 foot to 2 feet in height, it has fragrant, coral-red blooms borne in spring and early summer, with spurs one-half as long as the corolla tubes. A white-flowered variant is *C. a. albus*. Perennial **C. longiflorus**, 1½ to 3 feet tall, has many upright stems, branched above, and linear to ovate, toothless leaves 1¼ to 4 inches long. The abundant, pinkish to lilac flowers in erect showy panicles, have a corolla tube ½ to ¾ inch long, a spur nearly as long.

Centranthus longiflorus

Two annual kinds, *C. calcitrapa* and *C. macrosiphon*, are grown. The former hails from southern Europe, the latter from Spain. From slightly less than to more than 1 foot tall, **C. calcitrapa** has ovate or fiddle-shaped lower leaves and pinnately-cut upper ones up to 3 inches long. Its flowers are white tinged with red. Up to 2 feet in height, compact and glaucous, **C. macrosiphon** has ovate, lobed or toothed leaves up to 3 inches long and rose-pink blooms larger than those of *C. ruber*. In variety *C. m. albus* the flowers are white. Variety *C. m. nanus* is dwarfer.

Garden and Landscape Uses. Centranthuses are delightful, easily grown flower

garden plants well suited for beds and borders, and if grown in poor soil so that they remain low, for rock gardens. The perennial kinds supply satisfactory cut flowers, but for this purpose the annuals are less adapted. All grow freely in ordinary, well-drained soils, including those of limestone derivation, and prefer sunny locations. The perennials are often rather short-lived, commonly not persisting longer than three to five years. Because of this, and because when large they do not transplant readily, it is desirable to raise new plants fairly frequently.

Cultivation. All centranthuses are easily raised from seed, and the perennials also by division in spring or early fall. Once established they need little attention beyond watering during dry weather, keeping down weeds, and removing faded heads of bloom if seeds are not required. The perennials benefit from a spring application of a complete garden fertilizer. After they have been frosted in fall their tops are cut off close to the ground. Seeds of annual kinds may be sown outdoors in early spring where the plants are to stay, or indoors in a temperature of 55 to 60°F about eight weeks before the last frost is expected, and the young plants set in the garden later after having been transplanted 2 inches apart into flats or small pots and grown in a sunny greenhouse where at night the temperature is 50°F and by day five to ten degrees higher. Spacing in the garden may be 6 inches to 1 foot between individual plants.

CENTRATHERUM (Centrá-therum). Of the daisy family COMPOSITAE, the genus *Centratherum* consists of about twenty species of herbaceous or subshrubby natives of warm parts of the Americas. The name, presumably from the Greek *kentron*, a spur, and *antheros*, a barb or spine, is not of obvious application.

Centratherums branch freely, have alternate, stalked, toothed leaves and, usually terminating the branches, rather thistle-like hemispherical to bell-shaped flower heads of numerous tubular florets with a collar (involucre) of large leafy bracts. The fruits are achenes.

A kind sometimes cultivated as *C. intermedium* is probably **C. muticum**, native from Mexico to South America, or possibly is highly variable **C. punctatum**, of Central America. The differences between these are technical. From 1 foot to 2 feet tall, the plant cultivated has hairy stems and foliage. Its thinnish leaves, about 2 inches long, nearly 1 inch wide, and coarsely-toothed, have depressed veins. The flower heads, approximately 1½ inches wide, are bright lavender to blue-purple.

Garden Uses and Cultivation. The sort described may be grown outdoors in warm, frost-free climates and is useful also as a greenhouse ornamental and houseplant. It

logs and in cactus collections the generic splits are usually maintained and so without any strong conviction that it is the best botanical one that procedure is followed in this Encyclopedia. For some genera botanical "lumpers" include in *Cephalocereus* see *Austrocephalocereus, Backebergia, Coleocephalocereus, Haseltonia, Micranthocereus, Neobuxbaumia, Neodawsonia, Pilocereus, Pilosocereus,* and *Stephanocereus.* The name *Cephalocereus* comes from the Greek *kephale,* a head, and *Cereus,* the name of another cactus genus. It alludes to the topknot of hairs called a pseudocephalium developed by flowering-size specimens.

In its broad sense *Cephalocereus* consists of treelike and shrubby cactuses. They

Cephalocereus species

have thick, columnar, erect, spreading, or less frequently procumbent stems, conspicuously ribbed and spiny. The areoles (positions on the stems of cactuses from which spines and flowers are borne) are usually of two kinds, the ones that bear flowers being usually closer together than those that develop only spines and having long woolly hairs and bristles that form the dense beard or collar (pseudocephalium). The funnel- to bell-shaped, rather small blooms open at night. They have short perianth tubes naked in their lower parts, scaly above. There are numerous stamens. The flattened-spherical to top-shaped fruits may be spiny or scaly. They contain many black seeds. This genus is native to tropical and subtropical America.

The old man cactus (*C. senilis*) is a great favorite with fanciers. When well grown and unblemished it is one of the most beautiful of all cactuses. Young specimens are the most perfect and lovely. In its native Mexico this favors limestone soils, may attain heights up to 45 feet, and is believed to sometimes live for 200 years. It has erect, columnar, branched or branchless stems up to 1 foot or more in diameter. They have twenty to thirty conspicuous, spiny ribs, in young specimens fewer. From each areole sprout three to five yellow or gray spines and twenty to

thirty coarse hairs up to 5 inches long. At first the hairs are silvery-white, later they become grayish or yellowish. These, of course, form the beard of the "old man." Very old specimens are likely to shed the beard from all except the upper 3 feet or so of the stems. Flowers are not borne until the plants are approximately 20 feet tall. Then at one side of the stem near its apex the pseudocephalium develops. It consists of a great mass of hairs similar to those lower on the stems, but shorter and mixed with brown wool. The funnel-shaped, pink flowers 2 to 3 inches long or perhaps sometimes longer and wide, open at night. Their lower parts are hidden among the hairs and wool of the pseudocephalium. The purple-red fruits contain black seeds. Variety *C. s. longisetus* has hairs up to about 10 inches in length.

Garden and Landscape Uses and Cultivation. The old man cactus is certainly as near a "must" as any species can be for any fairly representative collection of cactuses, outdoors in dry, warm desert areas, and in greenhouses. It is not difficult to grow, but nevertheless requires a certain amount of understanding and intelligent care. It revels in maximum sunshine and indoors should be where the temperature in winter does not fall below 50°F. Water with circumspection. In summer allow the soil to become nearly dry, then saturate it. In winter allow it to dry even further before watering. Some growers recommend "shampooing" the beard if it has become matted or dirty, but this helps only if it is surface grime not if, as happens with age, the hairs have become discolored. To shampoo wash carefully with a brush dipped in mild soap suds taking care not to damage the somewhat brittle hairs. Rinse with clear water to remove all traces of soap and when the hairs have dried comb them in an upward direction to fluff out the beard.

Propagation may be by cuttings or by grafting onto strong-growing species of *Trichocereus.* Seeds germinate readily and within about four years give plants about 4 inches tall. The general needs and care of the old man is that of other kinds of desert cactuses. For more information see Cactuses.

CEPHALOPHRYS. This is the name of orchid hybrids the parents of which are *Cephalanthera* and *Ophrys.*

CEPHALOPHYLLUM (Cephalo-phýllum). Among the most beautiful of the vast array of succulent plants of South Africa once lumped as *Mesembryanthemum,* but now divided into many genera, is *Cephalophyllum.* Its name, from the Greek *kephale,* a head, and *phyllon,* a leaf, has reference to some species producing crowded, distantly spaced, headlike rosettes of foliage on prostrate, elongated stems. This genus belongs to the carpetweed family AIZO-

ACEAE. There are seventy species. None is hardy.

Cephalophyllums may be cushion-like subshrubs with much-branched, but not elongating stems or may have long, runner-like stems that, like the runners of strawberries, radiate from the parent plant and bear dense tufts of foliage that root into the ground. The smooth, fleshy, slender, curving leaves are subcylindrical or three-angled and are usually besprinkled with dark, translucent dots. Generally in threes, less commonly in twos or solitary, the very large and showy white, yellow, pink, coppery-red, or red blooms have numerous separate feathery stigmas, and are on branched stalks. In form they are daisy-like, but they are single blooms, not like daisies, heads of many florets. The fruits are capsules.

Shrubby and from 1 foot to 2 feet tall, *C. spongiosum* is a native of sandy coastal regions. Its ½-inch-thick, runner-like stems,

Cephalophyllum spongiosum

spongy inside, bear tufts of one to three pairs of upright leaves, one of each pair longer than the other. They have flat, white-scaly upper sides, are up to 4 inches long and about ⅓ inch wide, and from somewhat less to more than ½ inch deep. The vermilion blooms, on stalks approximately 2 inches long, are 2 to 2½ inches in diameter. Cushiony, *C. subulatoides* forms compact clusters of crowded, spreading, gray-green leaves, each pair more or less at right angles to the pairs below and above. The leaves, 2 to 3 inches long, subcylindrical, and sprinkled with tiny dots, are ⅓ inch wide or a little wider. Purple-red, and up to 1¾ inches in diameter, the flowers are on stalks up to 3 inches in length.

Sorts with procumbent stems include these: *C. alstonii* has stems up to about 1½ feet long and upright tufts of somewhat incurved, subcylindrical, gray-green leaves freely sprinkled with tiny dark-green dots and slightly flattened on their top sides. They are up to 3 inches long and approximately ⅓ inch wide. From 2 to more than 3 inches in diameter, the dark ruby-red flowers have violet anthers. *C. anemoniflorum* has running stems and erect branches with one to three pairs of erect to spreading, somewhat incurved, slightly three-angled, bluish or reddish leaves ¾ inch to 1¼ inches long. Shrimp-pink with white centers, the flowers are about 2 inches in diameter. *C. aureorubrum* has prostrate stems up to 7 inches

Cephalophyllum aureorubrum

long. Its blunt, gray-green leaves with flattish upper surfaces and rounded undersides are from 2 to 3½ inches long by up to ⅓ inch wide. Nearly 1½ inches in diameter, the flowers are magenta-red with golden-yellow centers. *C. ceresianum* has slender, angled, trailing stems up to 1 foot

Cephalophyllum ceresianum

long. Its leaves, cylindrical to three-angled and soft and 3 to 4 inches long, taper to their apexes. About 1¼ inches across and with stalks 1 inch to 1½ inches long, the light golden-yellow flowers are obscurely streaked with red on the backs of the petals. *C. dissimile* has curved stems up to 2 feet long, and crowded, subcylindrical

Cephalophyllum gracile

leaves 2 to 3½ inches long by up to ⅓ inch wide at the base and tapered toward their three-angled apex. The yellow flowers have stalks 2 to 3 inches long. *C. gracile* has angled, trailing stems and erect flowering branches. At first upright, later curved to spreading, its leaves are slender and ¾ inch to 1½ inches long. Their upper sides are channeled, their undersides rounded. The flowers are lemon-yellow to golden and 1¼ inches in diameter. *C. tricolorum* has procumbent stems and twisted branches. Its cylindrical-tapering, light green to gray-green, sometimes reddish leaves 2 to 3¼ inches long by up to ¼ inch thick are sprinkled with tiny dots. The flowers, solitary or in groups of up to six, are up to 2 inches, or a little under, wide. They are pale yellow with the bases of the petals dark red to purple and their undersides red toward their apexes.

Garden and Landscape Uses and Cultivation. In warm, dry climates that approximate those in which the plants grow as natives, such as the desert and semidesert regions of the southwestern United States, cephalophyllums are suitable for outdoor collections of succulent plants for rock gardens and for similar selected uses. They need full sun and grow most freely in porous, sandy soil. They are also of interest to the fancier of succulents who keeps his treasures in a greenhouse or on a sunny window sill. Indoor winter temperatures should be about 50°F at night and five to fifteen degrees more by day. At other seasons higher temperatures are in order, but always as much ventilation as practicable must be given to keep the air from becoming too humid or stagnant. These plants

must never be overwatered. In winter they are best kept dry, at other seasons they should be well watered at intervals, but not until the earth is nearly dry. Propagation is very easy by cuttings and by seeds.

CEPHALOSTACHYUM (Cephalostàchyum). This genus of a dozen species of bamboos of the grass family GRAMINEAE is native to Indo-Malaysia and Madagascar. The name is from the Greek, *kephale*, head, and *stachys*, a spike. It alludes to the form of the flower clusters.

The species of *Cephalostachyum* form tall clumps. They are adapted for cultivation outdoors in warm, frost-free, or nearly frost-free climates only. Their spikelets of flowers are in dense, spherical heads at the ends of the branches or are scattered in large clusters; they bristle with leaflike bracts.

Native to Burma, *C. pergracile* has canes about 40 feet tall, with branches that bear leaves up to 1 foot long or sometimes longer and 1½ inches wide. The leaves are hairy along their margins. This is an attractive ornamental suitable for planting in Hawaii and the warmer parts of Florida and California and for growing in large tropical greenhouses and conservatories. It needs moist soil. For additional information see Bamboos.

CEPHALOTACEAE. The characteristics of this dicotyledonous family are those of its only genus, *Cephalotus*.

CEPHALOTAXACEAE — Plum-Yew-Family. The only genus of this family of gymnosperms is *Cephalotaxus*.

CEPHALOTAXUS (Cephalotáx-us) — Plum-Yew. The name *Cephalotaxus* is derived from the Greek *kephale,* head, and the botanical name of the true yews *Taxus.* In aspect its members resemble yews and by some authorities are placed in the yew family TAXACEAE. Others regard *Cephalotaxus* as the sole representative of the family *Cephalotaxaceae,* a view accepted here.

This genus, native from the eastern Himalayas to Japan, includes seven species. From true yews, plum-yews differ in having their branches opposite or in whorls (circles of more than two), in their leaves being usually marked on their undersides with a pair of broad white stripes, and in their seeds being completely enclosed in fleshy pulp. From *Torreya* which plum-yews also resemble, they are distinguished in their leaves not being furrowed lengthwise on their undersides, in not being sharp-pointed, and in their buds being covered with more numerous scales. Plum-yews are attractive, usually unisexual, evergreen trees and shrubs. Their pointed-linear, scarcely-stalked leaves spread all around vertical leading shoots. On laterals they form two distinct rows. Along their upper sides is a conspicuous midrib. Somewhat resembling plums or olives, the fruits ripen in their second year.

The best known plum-yews are *C. harringtonia* and its varieties. This name, originally applied to a male form with longer leaves and longer-stalked cones than normal, long cultivated in Japan and with no exact replicas found in the wild, is now used by Japanese botanists for a natural population that inhabits Japan, Korea, and northern China. This is the population to which the name *C. h. drupacea* is often applied as a means of distinguishing the natural species from the cultivated form on which the name *C. harringtonia* was originally bestowed. It has spreading branches and abruptly-pointed leaves ¾ inch long by up to a little more than ⅛ inch wide. Those on lateral shoots angle upward and outward in two rows that form a V. The ovoid, obovoid, or rarely spherical fruits, greenish at first but becoming purplish when ripe, are about 1 inch long. Variety *C. h. nana,* a mountain plant of Japan, is a spreading shrub with erect branches. Horticultural varieties include *G. h. fastigiata.* With much the appearance of the Irish yew (*Taxus baccata fastigiata*), this has erect branches and leaves not in two rows but spread around the shoots in all directions. A low grower, *C. h. koreana* of Korea is a tufted shrub 3 to 5 feet tall, probably hardier to cold than other kinds. Japanese *C. h. nana,* up to 6 feet in height, spreads by suckers and has upright branches. A low grower with spreading branches has been named *C. h. prostrata.* Up to 12 feet tall, *C. h. sinensis* has linear-lanceolate leaves that spread and taper to a fine point and are 1 inch to 1½ inches long by up to ⅛ inch wide. Its slightly pear-shaped fruits, broadest at their apexes, are about 1 inch long. Golden-

Cephalotaxus harringtonia fastigiata

C. harringtonia fastigiata as a hedge

yellow fruits, smaller and rounder than those of other kinds, are characteristic of *C. h. sphaeralis.*

The Chinese plum-yew (*C. fortunei*) attains a maximum height of 40 feet, but in cultivation is usually lower and often shrublike. Its linear, tapering, glossy, slightly-arched leaves, 2 to 3 inches long, spread in two nearly horizontal ranks. They are longer and narrower, more slender-pointed and spaced farther apart on the shoots than those of *C. harringtonia.* The egg-shaped, olive-green fruits are about 1¼ inches long by one-half as wide. Varieties of this species are *C. f. alpina* with shorter leaves and stalkless male cones, *C. f. brevifolia,* with short leaves, *C. f. concolor,* not more than 3 feet in height and indistinctly banded on the undersides of its leaves, and *C. f. longifolia* with leaves longer than those of the typical kind. Another Chinese species, rare *C. oliveri,* is a low, sturdy shrub. It has very closely-set leaves ¾ to 1 inch long by up to ⅛ inch wide. Their undersides have a pair of longitudinal glaucous stripes, and they are in two ranks that spread horizontally in one plane.

Garden and Landscape Uses. Plum-yews are primarily mild-climate trees and shrubs, although in sheltered locations most kinds

Cephalotaxus harringtonia (fruits)

listed above will live outdoors in southern New York, but there never grow as large as they do in more salubrious climates. They are especially useful for shaded places where they succeed better than in full sun and may be used effectively as single specimens or in groups. They are useful for foundation plantings and as backgrounds to flower borders.

Cultivation. Plum-yews have a fairly wide range of tolerance as to soils in which they will grow, but are best satisfied with those that are well-drained, but reasonably moist and on the sandy side. Before planting, it is well to improve the site by spading into the soil liberal quantities of compost, rotted manure, leaf mold, or peat moss to a depth greater than that of the root ball. Plum-yews transplant without difficulty. A good ball of soil should be maintained undisturbed around the roots, and following planting it should be watered thoroughly and mulched.

Propagation is best effected by seeds, but horticultural varieties and species of which seeds are unavailable must be multiplied in other ways. Cuttings, taken in summer or fall and inserted under mist or in a humid cold frame or greenhouse propagating bed, give satisfactory results, as does veneer grafting in a greenhouse or cold frame in summer. Make cuttings of only terminal shoots if it is desired to have offspring duplicate the parent in habit. Cuttings made from side branches are likely to develop into misshapen, spreading plants without any definite leading growths. Sow seeds as soon as ripe or obtainable in well-drained containers of sandy, peaty soil in cold frames or outdoors, or stratify them and sow in spring. Seeds not newly gathered may not germinate until the second spring after sowing.

CEPHALOTUS (Cephal-òtus) — Australian Pitcher Plant. Sufficiently distinct from other plants to merit a botanical family of its own, the Australian pitcher plant belongs in the cephalotus family CEPHALOTACEAE. It is the only species. Although it has pitchers similar to those of American pitcher plants (*Sarracenia*) and Asian pitcher plants (*Nepenthes*), it is related to neither. It has merely adopted the same way of life. It supplements the meager nourishment it obtains from the bogs in which it lives by trapping and digesting insects and other small prey, using the nitrogen from their bodies to aid its growth. Botanists suppose that *Cephalotus* may be distantly related to saxifrags. The name, from the Greek *kephalotes*, headed, alludes to the stamens.

The Australian pitcher plant (**C. follicularis**) is a herbaceous perennial with short, woody rhizomes that produce 2- to 3-inch tall rosettes of two types of leaves, the upper ovate, flat, green, and of normal appearance, the lower formed into pitchers 1 inch to 3 inches long, with down-pointing teeth on the insides of their rims. The

pitchers are light green shaded with maroon and have red-veined lids. The white, petal-less, bisexual flowers are in crowded, panicle-like clusters atop stalks up to 2 feet tall. They have six sepals, and twice as many stamens. The fruits are technically one-seeded pods (follicles).

Garden Uses and Cultivation. This is a choice plant for the collector of rarities. It is most successfully grown in a cool greenhouse (winter minimum temperature 45 to 50°F) in good light. Because a very humid atmosphere is needed it is often wise to place it under a bell jar or in a terrarium, but care must be taken to ventilate sufficiently so that exposure to sun does not overheat the enclosed air. Good drainage is important. The rooting medium may be a mixture of coarse peat moss, live sphagnum moss, and sand, together with a little partly rotted leaf mold. Pans (shallow pots) are suitable containers. They should be kept standing in an inch or two of water, preferably rain water, so that moisture may constantly rise by capillary action. Propagation is by careful division in spring just before new growth begins and by seeds sown on the surface of finely-chopped live sphagnum moss at a temperature of about 55°F.

CERARIA (Ceràr-ia). The five species of *Ceraria*, of the purslane family PORTULACACEAE, inhabit tropical and South Africa. They are related to *Portulacaria* from which they differ in their flowers in clusters or axillary racemes being prevailingly unisexual. Very occasionally single blooms are bisexual. The name honors the wife of the botanist who first described the genus.

Cerarias are sparsely-foliaged small trees, shrubs, or shrublets. Their little fleshy leaves, in pairs or clusters, are flat or cylindrical. Their flowers have two short, persistent sepals and five larger petals. Male blooms have five stamens, females five staminodes (aborted stamens) and a two- or three-branched stigma on a very short style or directly on the ovary. The fruits are capsules.

A compact, hairless shrub 9 inches or so tall and up to 1 foot across, **C. pygmaea**

Ceraria pygmaea

(syn. *Portulacaria pygmaea*) is a native of South Africa. It has a stout, woody-based, erect stem or trunk and forked, cylindrical branches, the lower spreading, the upper spreading or deflexed. From ⅓ to ½ inch long and approximately ⅓ inch wide, the rough-surfaced, bluish-green to yellowish-green leaves are ovate-wedge-shaped. The whitish flowers, with pale pink outer petals, are in stalkless, terminal clusters of two to six.

Garden Uses and Cultivation. An interesting addition to collections of succulents, this requires the same conditions and care as *Portulacaria*. For more information see Portulacaria and Succulents.

CERASTIUM (Cerás-tium)—Snow-in-Summer. A nearly cosmopolitan group of about sixty, mostly cool-temperate-region species constitutes *Cerastium* of the pink family CARYOPHYLLACEAE. Best known to gardeners by the pleasant and popular snow-in-summer, and the sometimes troublesome invader of lawns, the mouse-ear-chickweed (*C. vulgatum*), the genus contains a few species that are cultivated. Its name is derived from the Greek *keras*, a horn, in allusion to the usually curved seed pods.

Cerastiums are annuals and herbaceous perennials, sometimes slightly woody toward their bases and usually hairy. They have opposite leaves and generally clustered, but sometimes solitary blooms. The flowers are white and have five, or rarely four, sepals, as many petals, generally cleft or notched into two lobes or rarely wanting, five to ten stamens, and usually five, rarely fewer, styles. The fruits are cylindrical, many-seeded capsules.

Snow-in-summer (*C. tomentosum*) is a vigorous, creeping, freely-branched, de-

Cerastium tomentosum

ciduous perennial that forms billowing mats up to about 1½ feet tall. It has grayish to whitish stems, and foliage with twisted hairs, and in late spring or early summer, masses of white flowers. The blooms, ½ to ¾ inch in diameter, are in clusters of seven to fifteen. The leaves are linear-lanceolate to lanceolate, and ½ to 1 inch long by not more than ⅕ inch wide. This is a hardy native of Europe. Similar but superior, **C. biebersteinii** is a native of the Crimea. It is 4 inches to 1 foot tall and generally is more compact and has whiter stems and foliage than *C. tomentosum;* like it it has twisted hairs. The leaves and flowers average somewhat larger than those of *C. tomentosum.* Also better than common snow-in-summer is **C. boissieri,** of Spain, Corsica, and Sardinia. Forming loose mats 4 inches to 1 foot tall, this grayish or greenish plant is less hairy than the last two. The upper parts of its stems, and the flower stalks, bracts, and sepals are densely-glandular. Its stiff, spreading to recurved leaves, pointed to nearly bristle-tipped, are narrowly-lanceolate and ⅓ to ⅔ inch long. They have prominent midribs. The flowers are in groups of up to seven or occasionally are solitary. They are more intensely white and larger than those of *C. tomentosum.* The seed capsules are not curved. Closely related to *C. boissieri,* and an inhabitant of Gibraltar and North Africa, **C. gibraltaricum** is up to 1 foot tall, and glandular-pubescent. Its linear-lanceolate, nearly bristle-tipped leaves attain maximums of 1½ inches long by ⅓ inch wide and are fringed with hairs. The midribs are conspicuous on their undersides. The long-stalked flowers are in groups of five or fewer, or are sometimes solitary. From *C. boissieri* this species differs in its seed pods being twice as long as the sepals instead of as long as or only slightly longer.

Others of the snow-in-summer group are *C. grandiflorum* and *C. candidissimum,* the first indigenous to the Balkan peninsula, the other to Greece. Both are densely-white- to yellowish-hairy, 6 inches to 1 foot in height, and have lanceolate to linear leaves, those of the former very narrow and 1 inch to 2½ inches long, those of the latter not ordinarily exceeding ¾ inch. The flowers of **C. grandiflorum** justify its specific name; they have snowy-white petals ¾ inch long. The petals of **C. candidissimum** are less than ½ inch long.

Less rampant than snow-in-summer and similar irresponsible kinds is **C. alpinum.** A variable native of arctic, subarctic, and alpine parts of Europe, it is 2 to 8 inches tall and often compact. Obovate to elliptic-oblanceolate, its leaves are hairy or not. The flowers, in groups of five or fewer or sometimes solitary, have petals ½ to ¾ inch long. The seed capsules are narrowed and curved in their upper parts. Variety *C. a. lanatum* is extremely hairy. Not exceeding 4 inches in height and often smaller, **C. uniflorum** has slender leaves up to ½ inch long, and flowers in ones to threes with petals not more than ½ inch long, cleft halfway to their bases. This kind inhabits the mountains of Europe.

Plants previously named *C. lerchenfeldianum* and *C. thomasii* are provisionally included as subspecies of variable *C. ar-*

A rock garden planting of *Cerastium tomentosum*

vense, a complex that inhabits most of Europe, temperate Asia, and North America. Its members are perennials that may be pubescent and glandular, but never have long, soft hairs. They are 2 inches to 1 foot tall or sometimes taller, loosely matted to cushion-like, and have flowers in groups of few to many with petals up to ½ inch long or longer.

Garden and Landscape Uses and Cultivation. Cerastiums are chiefly useful for rock gardens, and the more vigorous ones, such as the ubiquitous snow-in-summer, for edgings, banks, dry walls, and similar uses. For the most part they are hardy and grow without trouble in sunny locations in well-drained, even stony soils. Many prosper in soils of limestone origin as well as those of neutral and even acidic character. They are easily raised from seed and may be increased by division in spring or fall.

CERATONIA (Cerat-ònia) — Carob, St.-John's-Bread. According to legend the fruits of the only species of this genus of the pea family LEGUMINOSAE were the locusts eaten in the wilderness by John the Baptist and the husks that the prodigal son ate. For centuries in Europe carob fruits have been called locusts, and the name was transferred by early colonists to two American trees that reminded them of the carob. These are the kinds we now call locust (*Robinia*) and honey-locust (*Gleditsia*). Actually the similarities between the American trees and the carob are slight. The name is derived from the Greek *keration,* a horn. It alludes to the fruits.

The carob (**Ceratonia siliqua**) is an evergreen attaining a maximum height of about 50 feet, but often is lower. Native to the Mediterranean region, it has a broad, round head and leathery, pinnate leaves with two to five pairs of broad-elliptic to nearly round or obovate, dark green leaf-

lets 1 inch to 4 inches long. From the trunk and branches develop dense racemes, up to 6 inches in length, of reddish or greenish, unisexual or bisexual flowers. They are not pea-like. They have a five-lobed calyx, no petals, and five stamens. The fruits are flat, broad, beanlike pods up to 1 foot long. They contain several small, hard seeds

Ceratonia siliqua

Ceratonia siliqua (flowers)

embedded in a mealy, nutritious pulp. The pods are sweet and are much liked by animals and are palatable to humans, children especially being fond of them. The seeds, remarkably uniform in size and weight, are believed to be the original carat weights of jewelers. They have also been used as weights by apothecaries.

Garden and Landscape Uses. The carob flourishes in Mediterranean-type climates, regions of hot, dry summers and cooler, but frostless or essentially frostless, winters. It stands drought well, and brilliant sun, and grows in ordinary well-drained soil. As a rule it can be cultivated wherever oranges thrive. It is an attractive ornamental, useful as a street tree, lawn specimen, and for other landscape purposes, and in some parts of the world is much cultivated for stock feed.

Cultivation. The carob is propagated by seeds, which germinate more quickly if they are soaked for two or three days in water before they are sown, by budding (a form of grafting) selected forms onto seedlings, and by cuttings in a greenhouse propagating bench with a little bottom heat. Because it does not transplant well young specimens should be grown in containers until they are planted permanently. In greenhouses and conservatories this tree is sometimes grown for ornament and as an example of plants useful to man. It does well where the winter temperature by night is 45 to 50°F and by day is five to ten degrees higher. It needs good light. Porous, fertile soil, watered to keep it moderately moist, but allowing it to dry somewhat between waterings, suits its needs. Well-rooted specimens benefit from occasional soakings with dilute liquid fertilizer. Repotting, needed by large specimens at intervals of several years only, is done in late winter or early spring. That is an appropriate time also to do any pruning required to restrain growth and promote shapeliness.

CERATOPETALUM (Cerato-pétalum)—New South Wales Christmas Bush, Coachwood. Five species of the cunonia family CUNONIACEAE comprise *Ceratopetalum*, a genus of Australian and New Guinean trees and shrubs. The name, derived from the Greek *keras*, a horn, and *petalon*, a petal, alludes to the staghorn lobing of the petals of *Ceratopetalum gummiferum*. The lumber of the coachwood (*C. apetalum*) is esteemed for cabinets, boats, tool handles, masts, and other purposes, and is regarded as scarcely inferior to hickory.

Ceratopetalums have opposite leaves, undivided or of two or three leaflets. The flowers, in terminal clusters or panicles, are remarkable for their persistent calyxes, which enlarge and becomes brightly colored as the small, hard, achene-like fruits they surround mature. Depending upon the species, they may or may not have pet-

als. There are ten stamens. The fruits are capsules.

New South Wales Christmas bush (*C. gummiferum*), a tree 30 to 40 feet tall, or in the wild sometimes considerably taller, re-

Ceratopetalum gummiferum

ceived its specific designation because of the large amount of clear red gum that exudes when its bark is wounded. In its homeland much favored as a garden ornamental and for supplying cut branches for indoor decoration, the New South Wales Christmas bush has stalked, lustrous, lanceolate leaves each of three, shallowly-toothed leaflets 1½ to 3 inches long and ¼ to a little over ½ inch wide. Its plentiful, but not very showy whitish flowers, in loose panicles 3 or 4 inches long, have deeply three- to five-lobed petals. As they age the calyxes, also deeply five-lobed, enlarge to nearly 1 inch across, and change from white through pink to glorious red. They give a gorgeous, long-lasting display.

A silvery-white-barked, handsome tree 50 to 60 feet tall, coachwood (*C. apetalum*) has glossy, conspicuously-veined, stalked leaves, usually undivided, but sometimes of two or three leaflets. The elliptic leaves and leaflets 4 to 6 inches or occasionally up to 1 foot long, are one-third to one-half as broad as their length, and are toothed. The inconspicuous whitish flowers, in long-stalked terminal and axillary clusters 3 to 4 inches across, are without petals. As the fruits develop the calyx enlarges to a diameter of ¾ inch and becomes rich crimson or purplish-red. All parts of this tree when crushed are pleasantly aromatic.

Garden and Landscape Uses and Cultivation. In California and other warm-temperate, essentially frost-free regions the species described are adapted for general landscaping. The New South Wales Christmas bush is well displayed as a single specimen and is suitable for hedges. Ordinary nonalkaline garden soils and sunny locations are satisfactory. Propagation is by seeds, and by cuttings of firm, but not hard shoots, planted under mist or in a greenhouse propagating bench.

CERATOPHYLLACEAE — Hornwort Family. The characteristics of this family of dicotyledons are those of its only genus. See Ceratophyllum.

CERATOPHYLLUM (Cerato-phýllum) — Hornwort or Coon Tail. Three or four geographically widely distributed species of *Ceratophyllum* are the only members of the hornwort family CERATOPHYLLACEAE. They are usually rootless, underwater plants with long, branching stems. Their finely-dissected leaves, thrice divided into slender segments, are in whorls (circles) along the stems, but are usually most densely aggregated toward their ends. The unisexual flowers are minute and insignificant. The name, derived from the Greek *keras*, a horn, and *phyllon*, a leaf, refers to the manner in which the leaves are branched. The fruits of hornworts are an important food of water birds.

The best known hornwort or coon tail is *C. demersum,* a species common and abundant in quiet water throughout temperate North America, from Quebec to British Columbia southward, as well as in the Old World. It mostly grows in large dense masses and has the divisions of its leaves markedly toothed along one side and fruits (achenes) with two spines at their bases. The closely related *C. echinatum,* indigenous to the eastern United States and Mexico, has achenes with several spines from the sides as well as a basal pair, and its leaf divisions are nearly or quite toothless. These plants sink at the approach of winter and rise in spring.

Garden Uses and Cultivation. Hornworts are effective oxygenators. They assist in making the water habitable by fish. For this, as well as to provide fish with cover and shelter, they are grown in aquariums and garden pools. They are planted by simply dropping pieces into the water or inserting them in below-surface soil in a pond or aquarium. No care is needed.

CERATOPTERIS (Cerat-ópteris) — Water Fern, Floating Fern. This, the only genus of the water fern family PARKERIACEAE (syn. *Ceratopteridaceae*), consists of two or possibly more species of tropical and subtropical aquatic ferns. They are cultivated to ornament pools and aquariums, and in parts of the tropics are eaten as salads. Although described as annuals, they are often perennial in cultivation. The name is from the Greek *keras*, a horn, and *pteris*, a fern, and refers to the hornlike lobing of the sterile fronds.

These quite fleshly-leaved water ferns float free or root in mud. They consist of rosettes of two distinct kinds of fronds (leaves), spreading sterile ones once to three times pinnately-lobed, and more erect fertile ones twice to four times pinnately-lobed with the ultimate divisions much narrower than those of the sterile fronds. The margins of fertile fronds are rolled under and protect and practically hide the lines of sporangia (sporebearing organs). In appearance the plants vary considerably depending upon whether they are under water, floating, or rooted in mud. When not immersed they commonly produce young plantlets freely along the margins of the sterile fronds.

The western hemisphere *Ceratopteris pteridoides,* native from Florida to Brazil, has sterile fronds up to 10 inches long, with blades broadly triangular in outline and a little longer than wide. They are divided one to three times into triangular lobes and have short leafstalks decidedly swollen at their middles. The fertile fronds are up to 1¼ feet in length and deeply divided once to three times into slender segments.

Ceratopteris pteridoides

From the above, the eastern hemisphere *C. thalictroides* differs in the blades of its once or twice divided sterile fronds being oblong in outline and considerably longer than broad and the leafstalks being slender throughout. Its sterile fronds are twice to four times divided into slender segments.

Ceratopteris thalictroides

Garden Uses and Cultivation. The garden uses of these water ferns have been

given. They need hot, humid conditions and thrive in tropical greenhouses and in aquariums where water temperatures of 68 to 78°F can be maintained, and the atmosphere humid. They prefer slightly acid soils and water and under favorable conditions make very rapid growth. Because of their vigor, when grown submersed in aquariums it is usually best to plant them in a relatively infertile medium such as unwashed river sand mixed with a little unfertilized soil. In greenhouses, and outdoors in warm climates, they may be planted in mud at watersides or floated without attachment to soil. Bright light with a little shade from strong sun produces the best results, but these plants can be grown with artificial illumination only. Where light is not intense the older plants die in winter, but small plantlets that develop on their leaves can usually be brought through satisfactorily.

CERATOSTIGMA (Cerato-stígma). Closely related to, and in gardens often called *Plumbago,* ceratostigmas differ from that genus in having flowers with non-glandular calyxes and stamens attached to the middles of the corolla tubes. There are eight species, natives from China to India and in tropical Africa. They belong in the plumbago family PLUMBAGINACEAE. The name *Ceratostigma* is derived from the Greek *keras,* a horn, and stigma, the part of the female element of a flower that receives the pollen. It alludes to hornlike projections on the stigmas.

The group contains hardy and tender herbaceous perennials and tender shrubs that have alternate, usually somewhat bristly leaves fringed with hairs and terminal and axillary clusters of mostly blue or blue-purple phloxlike blooms. The flowers have five-lobed calyxes and slender-tubed corollas with five wide-spreading lobes (petals). The fruits are capsules.

The hardiest species is *C. plumbaginoides* (syn. *Plumbago larpentiae*). This native of China is herbaceous and 9 inches to 1 foot tall. It spreads freely by slender, un-

Ceratostigma plumbaginoides

derground rhizomes and has numerous, much-branched, angled, slightly-hairy, reddish stems. The nearly stalkless leaves are obovate, ¾ inch to 2 inches long, and hairless except for their eyelashed margins. The bright purple-blue flowers, with obcordate petals, are borne over a long period in late summer and fall. They are ¾ inch across. This fine species is hardy at least as far north as New York City.

A deciduous shrub 3 to 5 feet tall, slender-branched and with bright blue flowers whitened toward their bases and with rosy-red corolla tubes, *C. willmottianum* is not reliably hardy in climates harsher than that of Washington, D.C. It has angled, bristly, often purplish stems, and lanceolate to obovate, pointed leaves up to 2 inches long and up to ¾ inch wide. They are bristly-hairy on both surfaces. The many flower clusters, about 2½ inches across, are composed of blooms ½ to ¾ inch wide, with obovate petals. They open over a long period in summer and fall.

Garden and Landscape Uses. The species last discussed is an admirable shrub for mild climates. Toward the northern limits of its tolerance of winter cold its roots may live even though its stems are killed. Then, it renews itself in spring and blooms freely in summer. It is splendid for late bloom and associates quite stunningly with yellow-flowered plants. Its foliage colors quite prettily in fall. This species is useful for borders, inclusion in foundation plantings, and many other purposes. It needs full sun and well-drained, reasonably fertile soil.

The lower-growing *C. plumbaginoides* thrives best in full sun, but tolerates part-day shade. It is a first-class groundcover and edging plant and is excellent for fronts of flower borders and rock gardens. Not only are its flowers attractive, in fall its foliage assumes pleasing bronzy and reddish tones. In addition to its value as a permanently placed plant, it can be easily handled in pots as a bedding plant to succeed earlier summer displays. For this purpose it can be extremely effective used with chrysanthemums, the latter planted as accent or dot plants in a carpet of the ceratostigmas.

Cultivation. Ceratostigmas thrive in soils of moderate fertility that are well-drained, but never excessively dry. A fairly high organic content is appreciated, especially by *C. plumbaginoides.* A liberal admixture of compost, humus, or peat moss with the soil is generally advantageous. Planting may be done in spring or early fall with the former usually preferable. Propagation is easy by cuttings and, in the case of *C. plumbaginoides,* by division.

As a bedding plant the procedure for handling *C. plumbaginoides* is to lift stock plants in fall and set them closely together in flats of sandy soil. They are watered thoroughly and placed in a cold frame where they are protected from very severe freezing by the frames being covered with mats in very cold weather, or they may be kept in a greenhouse or other place where the temperature is 40 to 50°F. In February or March the clumps are divided and the pieces potted into 4-inch pots. They are then kept a little warmer, in a sunny greenhouse or frame, and are watered regularly. After danger of frost is over they are plunged (buried to the rims of the pots) outdoors in sand, coal ashes, peat moss, or other suitable material, in full sun, and there they remain until needed for planting in the display beds. An occasional fertilization with dilute liquid fertilizer is helpful after the pots are filled with roots.

CERATOSTYLIS (Ceráto-stylis). Not frequent in cultivation, although some of its about sixty species are decidedly attractive, *Ceratostylis*, of the orchid family ORCHIDACEAE, is endemic to Indo-Malaysia and Polynesia. Its name derives from the Greek *keras*, a horn, and *stylis*, a small pillar.

Many species when not in bloom have much the appearance of tufts of grasses or of rushes, but this is not true of the one described here. The blooms are small, but frequently brightly colored.

Its native territory the Philippine Islands, where it grows as an epiphyte (perched on trees), *C. rubra* forms loose clusters of pencil-thick stems furnished

Ceratostylis rubra

with fleshy, evergreen, pointed-linear, recurved leaves, channeled lengthwise, and 4 to 5 inches long by ½ inch wide. Solitary or in twos, the wide-opening, short-stalked, freely-produced blooms are 1 inch to 1½ inches across. They have similar salmon-pink to brick-red sepals and petals and a very small, usually whitish or yellowish lip.

Garden Uses and Cultivation. These are orchids for enthusiastic collectors. They respond to the care and culture that suit

tropical bulbophyllums. The species described does well when attached to a slab of tree fern trunk. For more information see Orchids.

CERATOTHECA (Ceratothèc-a). One of the nine species of this African genus of the pendalium family PEDALIACEAE is cultivated. The generic name comes from the Greek *keras*, a horn, and *theke*, a case, in allusion to the two-horned seed capsules. Ceratothecas have mostly opposite, ovate leaves, and short-stemmed, asymmetrical flowers with two lips, the lower much longer than the upper, singly in the leaf axils.

A native of South Africa, *Ceratotheca triloba* is 4 to 6 feet tall and has hairy, quadrangular stems and heart-shaped to triangular, three-lobed, round-toothed or sometimes smooth-edged leaves up to 8 inches across. The flowers, hairy and resembling those of foxgloves (*Digitalis*), are lilac, often with purple stripes on their insides, and are about 3 inches long. The individual blooms do not last long; the flowers are not useful for cutting.

Ceratotheca triloba

Garden Uses and Cultivation. A handsome flower garden ornamental, *C. triloba* is best adapted for regions that assure a long growing season. In the north it may be grown by sowing its seeds indoors in a temperature of 70 to 75°F about ten weeks before the plants are to be set in the garden, which may be done when it is safe to plant out tomatoes, and growing the young plants, individually in 3-inch pots. This species needs rich, fairly moist soil and a sunny location not unduly exposed to wind; a spacing of 9 inches to 1 foot between plants is satisfactory. Blooming begins in late summer and lasts through fall. Summer care consists of weeding, watering adequately in dry weather, and staking and tying to prevent breakage.

This is also an attractive plant for pot culture in greenhouses. For this purpose the seeds are sown in August and the plants kept growing throughout the winter in a greenhouse where the night temperature is about 50°F and the day temperature a few degrees higher. This plant needs a fertile, porous soil and during its period of active growth abundant supplies of water. When well established in pots regular applications of dilute liquid fertilizer are helpful.

CERATOZAMIA (Cerato-zàmia). This is one of three genera of the cycad family CYCADACEAE that are natives of Mexico, the present genus exclusively so. The name, from the Greek *keras*, a horn, and *Zamia*, the name of another genus of the family, alludes to the scales of the cones having each two rigid horns or spines. The presence of these separates *Ceratozamia* from *Zamia*.

Ceratozamias are handsome, short-trunked, palmlike evergreens with a crown of stiff pinnate leaves, the leaflets of which are lanceolate or oblong-lanceolate. The reproductive bodies are in cones, those of *Ceratozamia* with their scales in vertical series.

Of the four species one or two are cultivated. A good ornamental that attains a height of 4 to 6 feet, somewhat variable, thick-trunked *C. mexicana* has leathery leaves 3 to 9 feet in length, with fifteen to

Ceratozamia mexicana

twenty or more pairs of prickly-stalked, narrow- to broadly-lanceolate, toothless leaflets up to 1 foot long or sometimes longer. This species in the wild grows in deep shade. Male and female cones are on separate plants, the former, on hairy stalks, are longer and more slender than the females which are 9 inches to 1 foot long and about one-half as wide. Variety *C. m. latifolia* has leaves with broader leaflets of nearly equal size. The leaves of *C. m. longifolia*, narrower than those of the typical species, are of unequal size.

Garden and Landscape Uses and Cultivation. These are admirable ornamentals, well suited for outdoor cultivation in the tropics and subtropics, and are excellent as tub and large pot specimens. For further information see Cycads.

CERBERA (Cèr-bera). Six species compose *Cerbera*, of the dogbane family APOCYNACEAE. They are natives of tropical Asia and islands of the Pacific and Indian oceans. The native American species previously included belong in *Thevetia*. The name, derived from that of the three-headed dog Cerberus, which according to mythology guarded the entrance to the infernal regions, alludes to the poisonous attributes of the genus.

Cerberas are evergreen, milky-juiced trees or shrubs with alternate, undivided, lobeless leaves and clusters of flowers with deeply-five-cleft calyxes and tubular, cylindrical to funnel-shaped corollas, hairy in their throats and with five spreading petals. There are five stamens and one style. The solitary or paired fruits are drupes containing one seed.

Widely dispersed as a native of many islands and Asian coasts of the Pacific, *C. manghas* is a shrub or tree up to 40 feet tall. Its leaves, crowded toward the branch ends, are oblanceolate with short-pointed apexes. From 6 inches to 1 foot long and up to about 2½ inches wide, they have glossy upper surfaces. The abundant, fragrant, red-centered, white flowers in large, terminal clusters are about 1 inch long by 1 inch to 3 inches across. The pink to black, spherical to egg-shaped fruits are 2 to 4 inches long. The seeds are said to be the only poisonous part of this species.

Garden and Landscape Uses and Cultivation. The sort described, a useful ornamental for tropical and subtropical regions, is cultivated to some extent in Hawaii and southern Florida. It succeeds in sunny locations in ordinary soils, doing especially well near the sea. Propagation, easy by seeds, can also be accomplished by cuttings.

CERCIDIPHYLLACEAE—Cercidiphyllum or Katsura Tree Family. The characteristics of this family of dicotyledons are those of its only species, the katsura tree (*Cercidiphyllum japonicum*).

CERCIDIPHYLLUM (Cercidi-phýllum) — Katsura Tree. One species of deciduous tree of eastern Asia is the only representative of the katsura tree family CERCIDIPHYLLACEAE, which is closely related to the trochodendron family TROCHODENDRACEAE. It is handsome and distinctive. Because of the similarity of its foliage to that of redbud, the name, from *Cercis*, the redbud, and the Greek *phyllon*, a leaf, was given.

Cercidiphyllums have two kinds of branches, long ones and short, spurlike ones. Their opposite, stalked, undivided leaves are broadly-ovate to round, with heart-shaped bases. The main veins spread from the leaf base like the fingers of a spread hand. The trees are unisexual. The flowers appear in spring before the foliage, but make no appreciable display. They are small and without calyxes or corollas. The many red-anthered stamens of the males are short-stalked. Female blooms have three to five podlike carpels and very slender, rose-purple styles. The fruits, follicles containing many small, winged seeds, remain on the trees throughout most of the winter.

The katsura tree (*Cercidiphyllum japonicum*), of Japan and China, is wide-spreading and 60 to 100 feet in height. Its trunk often branches near the ground into several large secondary trunks. Even on young specimens the bark is longitudinally spirally furrowed. The bluntly-toothed leaves, glaucous on their undersides, have blades 1½ to 3 inches long and about as wide, and reddish stalks ¾ to 1 inch long. The seeds are winged at one end only. The variety named *C. japonicum sinense*, of China, tends to be taller and less disposed to make several trunks than *C. japonicum*; otherwise it is similar. Variety *C. j. pendulum* has drooping branches. Variety *C. j.*

magnificum syn. *C. magnificum*), native of Japan at higher altitudes than the species, has bark that does not become furrowed until the trees are of advanced age. Its leaves are 3 to 4 inches across, its seeds winged at both ends.

Garden and Landscape Uses. A noble specimen for lawns and other places where there is ample room for it to spread its limbs widely, or for less spacious accommodations if restricted to a single trunk, the katsura tree and its varieties have the virtue of being never, or at best very rarely harmed by pests or diseases. They have distinctive foliage, yet not different enough to look out of place or bizarre in American landscapes, that becomes yellow to scarlet in fall before it drops. These trees are hardy throughout most of New England. For their best development they need deep, dampish, fertile soil; they prosper in those of a limestone nature. In their early years they grow quite rapidly and are then proportionately much narrower than later.

Cultivation. Seeds afford the most satisfactory means of increasing stocks of cercidiphyllums. They are sown in sandy peaty soil in late winter or spring in a cool greenhouse or cold frame. Cuttings may be made in summer and rooted under mist. Alternatively, they can be taken in early spring from plants brought into a greenhouse and forced into early growth, and can be planted in a greenhouse propagating bench. Layering is also practicable.

CERCIDIUM (Cercíd-ium) — Palo Verde. This genus of ten species of the warmer parts of America consists of deciduous shrubs and trees of the pea family LEGUMINOSAE. They are remarkable for their green branches and branchlets, which give reason for their common name, one also applied to related *Parkinsonia*. Because the branches and shoots, which are spiny at the nodes or at the ends of short branchlets contain chlorophyll they are able to synthesize food and thus assist in the work of the foliage. The name from the Greek *kerkidion*, a weaver's shuttle, refers to the shape of the pods.

Cercidiums have twice-pinnate leaves with one to three pairs of primary segments divided into numerous leaflets and midribs rounded instead of flattened as they are in *Parkinsonia*. The nearly symmetrical, not pea-shaped, yellow flowers are in short racemes or clusters from the leaf axils. They have five each sepals and petals and ten separate stamens that are hairy at the bottoms of their stalks. The fruits, flattened or cylindrical pods, are somewhat constricted between the several seeds.

Blue palo verde (*Cercidium floridum* syn. *C. torreyanum*) is one of the most lovely trees of the deserts of the southwestern United States and Mexico. Short-trunked, and up to 30 feet tall, but often lower, in

Cercidiphyllum japonicum, in winter   *Cercidiphyllum japonicum*, in summer

spring it produces an abundance of bright yellow ¾-inch-wide flowers. Its branches and foliage, the latter not long persisting, are slightly bluish-green, which explains the vernacular name. Each of the two primary divisions of leaves of the blue palo verde has one, two, or occasionally three pairs of ¼-inch-long, narrowly-ovate leaflets. The flowers are succeeded by flat, hairless seed pods up to 3½ inches long by about ½ inch wide. These were used by the Indians as food. Blue palo verde favors places where its roots reach underground supplies of moisture. Differing from it chiefly in that each of the primary divisions of the leaves have four to eight pairs of pubescent leaflets, and the seed pods are cylindrical, *C. microphyllum* is a native of the same general geographical region. It does not exceed 20 feet in height.

Garden and Landscape Uses and Cultivation. Only in desert and semidesert places closely similar to those where they grow as natives can palo verdes be expected to flourish. They can be raised from seeds and should be grown in cans or other containers until large enough to plant in their permanent locations.

CERCIS (Cér-cis) — Redbud, Judas Tree. Redbuds are well known to most American gardeners. They are esteemed for their pretty spring displays of dainty bloom and for their yellow fall foliage. There are six or seven species, members of the pea family LEGUMINOSAE, natives to North America, southern Europe, and Asia. Their generic name is a modification of *kerkis*, which the ancient Greeks used for some kind of tree, possibly *Cercis siliquastrum.* In the United States the designation Judas tree is sometimes quite wrongly used as a common name for native species. Legend has it that following his betrayal of Christ, Judas Iscariot hanged himself on a redbud. If he did, it was surely not an American species, but the local *C. siliquastrum,* and for that the appellation Judas tree should be reserved.

Redbuds are deciduous trees or shrubs with alternate, undivided, heart-shaped to kidney-shaped, toothless leaves with five to nine conspicuous veins radiating from their bases. Except for *C. racemosa*, which has its blooms in racemes, the flowers are borne in clusters along shoots one year old and older. Very unusual for temperate-region trees, they sometimes are borne on the major branches and trunk. The flowers are not quite pea-like (redbuds belong to a different section of the LEGUMINOSAE than peas), but have much the aspect of pea flowers. They have an irregular, five-toothed calyx, five petals of which the uppermost is smallest, ten separate stamens, and one style. The fruits are several-seeded, thin pods with thickened upper margins.

The eastern North American redbud (*C. canadensis*) has a natural range that extends from New Jersey to Missouri, Flor-

Cercis canadensis, in winter

Cercis canadensis (flowers)

ida, New Mexico, and Texas. A graceful, wide-branching tree up to 40 feet tall, this kind favors moist woodlands. It is hardy to a little north of New York City. Usually broader than their 2 to 4½ inch lengths, the leaves are heart-shaped, generally with a short-pointed apex. They are hairless above, on their undersides hairy or not. The ½-inch-long, purplish-pink flowers come just before the leaves and provide an outstanding display. Variety *C. c. alba* has pure white blooms, those of *C. c. plena* are semidouble. The blooms of *C. c.* 'Flame', a variety of more erect growth than usual, are also double. Soft pink rather than purple-pink blooms are borne by varieties 'Wither's Pink Charm' and 'Pinkbud'.

Differing from eastern North American redbud chiefly in having thicker leaves, glaucous on their uppersides and rounded or notched at their apexes *C. reniformis* (syn. *C. canadensis reniformis*) is native of Texas and New Mexico.

California or western redbud (*C. occidentalis*), a rounded shrub or small tree up to 15 feet tall, differs quite markedly from its eastern relative. Its roundish, hairless, kidney- to heart-shaped leaves, 2 to 4 inches across and broader than long, with seven to nine chief veins, are notched or rounded at their ends. They resemble those of the Judas tree, but are brighter green. In the wild spontaneous from California to Utah and Arizona, this sort has purplish-pink blooms averaging slightly larger than those of *C. canadensis*. It is not hardy in the north.

Cercis chinensis (flowers)

Cercis occidentalis

Tallest of redbuds, but in cultivation rarely attaining its maximum height of about 50 feet, *C. chinensis* is often of shrub dimensions. Native of China and Japan, and hardy in southern New England, in bloom it is one of the handsomest species. It has lustrous, roundish, hairless leaves, short-pointed at their apexes, and with deeply-heart-shaped bases. Its bright purplish-pink blooms are up to ¾ inch long. The narrow seed pods are 3 to 4½ inches long. Chinese *C. racemosa,* a tree up to 30 feet tall, differs from all other redbuds in

Cercis chinensis (foliage)

its rosy-pink flowers being in pendulous racemes 1¾ to 4 inches long. The somewhat heart-shaped leaves, pubescent beneath, are up to 4 inches in length, as are the seed pods. This, not hardy in the north, is an especially lovely kind that can with confidence be recommended for planting in mild regions.

The Judas tree (*C. siliquastrum*), little known in America, is a flattish-topped tree up to 40 feet high, but usually much lower. Native of southern Europe and adjacent Asia, it has glaucous-green, hairless, roundish leaves 3 to 5 inches wide, with heart-shaped bases and usually rounded, less often pointed apexes. They are scarcely as long as wide. The multitude of bright purplish-pink blooms, ½ to ¾ inch long, make a splendid spring display. A white-flowered variety is *C. s. alba*. The Judas tree is not hardy in the north.

Garden and Landscape Uses. Redbuds are elegant when planted informally in more or less naturalistic landscapes, and for formal use in more manicured ones. They are lovely at the fringes of woodlands, the eastern North American kind especially lending itself to interplanting with flowering dogwoods to produce beautiful effects similar to those so frequent in the wild. Grown as a tall shrub, *C. chinensis* is very effective in clumps or beds alone or grouped with other shrubs. The white-flowered varieties of redbuds are especially lovely, but are less robust and persistent than the typical pink-flowered species.

Cultivation. Redbuds resent transplanting. Best results are had by setting out small specimens, and pruning them fairly drastically at planting time. Preserve as many roots as possible, and do not allow them to dry. Failure usually follows moving redbuds from the wild. Nursery specimens are far more likely to survive. Redbuds adjust to various soils, preferring deep, fertile, well-drained ones. The eastern North American species does well in part-day or light shade, but if the soil is not excessively dry, it will grow in full sun; the others thrive best in sun. Routine care is minimal. No regular annual pruning is needed, but any desirable to improve the shapes of the specimens may be done in late winter or spring. This may be as severe as necessary because redbuds produce new shoots freely from old wood. If *C. chinensis*, grown as a shrub, becomes too tall and lanky it can be restored to size and shape, at the sacrifice of a year or two's bloom, but cutting it down to within a foot or so of the ground just before new growth begins in spring, then fertilizing and mulching and watering so that the ground does not become excessively dry during the summer. Pruning may also be required to remove limbs affected by cankers, die-back, and wilt diseases, which sometimes affect these trees. The species

are best increased by seeds. These may be sown as soon as ripe in a cold frame or in an outdoor bed protected from animals and other disturbing factors. Alternatively, they can be stored, and later, after immersing them in water at 190°F for a few hours and stratifying them at 40°F for three months, be sown in a greenhouse or a cold frame or outdoors. Varieties, and species of which seeds are not available, can be propagated by grafting onto seedlings and by summer cuttings under mist or in a greenhouse propagating bench.

CERCOCARPUS (Cerco-cárpus) — Mountain-Mahogany. Eight to ten closely related and often intergrading species of evergreen or nearly evergreen shrubs or low trees of mostly arid, mountain parts of western North America constitute this genus of the rose family ROSACEAE. The name comes from the Greek *kerkos*, a tail, and *karpos*, fruit, and refers to the fruits. They are planted to some extent in regions where they are native, but are little used elsewhere. Their wood is very hard and heavy and makes good fuel. The young shoots are eaten by grazing animals.

Mountain-mahoganies have alternate, undivided leaves on short, spurlike twigs. Their insignificant greenish or reddish axillary flowers, on terminal or short branches, are without petals and have five sepals, ten to forty-five stamens arranged in two or three rows, and a solitary style. The blooms are solitary or are in groups of up to five. The fruits (achenes) are dry, one-seeded, and have attached, as tails up to 3 or 4 inches long, the persistent, silky, feathery styles.

A variable species that includes a few botanical varieties, **Cercocarpus betuloides** is a loose shrub or small tree 6 to 20 feet

Cercocarpus betuloides

tall that occurs in the wild from Oregon to Baja California. It has erect or spreading branches and short-stalked, obovate to

broadly-elliptic leaves mostly up to 1 inch long. They are more or less toothed, but are without inrolled margins and are not resinous. They are dark green and hairless on their upper sides, somewhat hairy beneath. The flowers, usually two or three together, are ¼ inch wide or slightly wider. A variety native in southern California, with leaves up to 2 inches long and flowers in groups of five to fifteen, has been designated *C. b. multiflorus*. Another variety, with leaves up to 2 inches long or even slightly longer, *C. b. traskiae* inhabits Santa Catalina Island. The veins are clearly impressed on the upper sides of the leaves. Beneath, the leaves are white-tomentose.

From the above, **C. ledifolius** differs in having toothless, lanceolate to oblanceolate leaves, resinous and with revolute margins. They are ⅓ to 1 inch or slightly more in length and short-stalked. Their undersides are typically tan or pale green and more or less furnished with short hairs. The upper sides are slightly hairy to nearly hairless and green. This species, which has flowers up to ¼ inch wide, solitary or in twos or threes, is a shrub or tree 6 to nearly 40 feet in height. It is indigenous from Washington to Baja California, Montana, Colorado, and Arizona. Native from Utah to Arizona and California, *C. intricatus* is, as its name implies, intricately branched. Up to 10 feet tall, it has linear to narrowly-oblong leaves up to ½ inch long with usually rolled-back margins.

Cercocarpus intricatus

Garden and Landscape Uses and Cultivation. These natives of dry soils and fairly mild climates succeed under similar conditions under cultivation and provide quite attractive shrubbery, useful for screening and espaliering and as hedges. Their flowers are inconspicuous, but their long-tailed fruits make quite pretty displays. Under favorable conditions mountain-mahoganies grow rapidly. They respond well to pruning and are easily shaped and restricted to size. They are resistant to salt spray and find clayey soils agreeable.

Propagation is easily effected by seeds and by cuttings.

CERDANIA. See Cordia.

CEREUS (Cè-reus). This name has been applied to a very great number of cactuses many of which, including some commonly called night-blooming cereuses, belong in other genera. The modern limitation of the genus *Cereus* varies considerably depending upon the interpretations of individual botanists. Here it is accepted as comprising about twenty-five species of the West Indies, northern South America, and eastern South America to Argentina. Some authorities include, with considerable reasonableness, kinds that have for long been segregated as separate genera, such as *Carnegiea*. Cereuses belong in the cactus family CACTACEAE. The name the Latin *cereus*, a wax taper, alludes to the forms of some species. For plants called night-blooming-cereuses see *Epiphyllum, Hylocereus, Nyctocereus, Selenicereus,* and Night-Blooming-Cereus. Desert night-blooming-cereus is *Peniocereus greggii*. Moon-cereus is *Selenicereus*.

Cereuses are treelike, shrubby, or sometimes more or less sprawling with erect, spreading, or prostrate, strongly-ribbed stems furnished with spiny areoles (specialized cushion-like areas on the stems of cactuses). In *Cereus* areoles that bear flowers and those that do not are similar. The generally large, usually white, more rarely red, blooms, which open at night, have greenish outer petals and numerous stamens. They are funnel-shaped. Their long perianth tubes, more or less naked near their bases, have scattered, small scales above. Upon withering the perianth drops, but the long style usually is persistent and remains. The ovoid to oblong, red or less commonly yellow fruits are without scales or spines. When ripe they split down one side.

Tall, treelike kinds with short trunks and massive thick-jointed stems include **C. hexagonus.** This fairly commonly cultivated native of northern South America and the West Indies, usually branched from the base, attains heights of approximately 50 feet. Its jointed stems, erect or in old specimens somewhat spreading, are deeply four-, five-, more commonly six-, or more rarely seven-ribbed. The edges of their thin angles are undulated. The small areoles are ¾ inch apart. Those on old branches have clusters of up to ten or more unequal spines over 2 inches long. Young branches are spineless or nearly so. From 8 to 10 inches long, the slender-tubed, many-stamened blooms, white tinged with purple and 5 to 6 inches wide, are developed freely along the stems. Very variable, sometimes nearly spineless **C. jamacaru,** of Brazil, has glaucous-blue younger parts usually with spines. This massive species,

Cereus hexagonus

up to about 35 feet high, has a short trunk and usually a large, dense head of erect, four- or five-ribbed branches, the ribs on younger stems thin and undulated. The areoles are large, ¾ inch to 1¼ inches apart. The spines, up to 8 inches long or perhaps longer, are not yellow even when young. The blooms, white with green outer petals and up to 1 foot long, are succeeded by bright red fruits sometimes 4½ inches long by 3½ inches wide that con-

tains edible white pulp. Slow-growing C. **monstrosus** has nearly spineless, irregularly-knobby, rather evenly-winged stems.

Treelike and up to 20 feet tall, Brazilian **C. glaucus,** in cultivation sometimes misidentified as *C. argentinensis*, which name belongs to another species, is bluish and has branches with usually seven, sometimes six or eight slightly scalloped ribs. Its clusters of yellow spines spaced 1 inch to 2 inches apart on all but old stems are 1 inch to 2 inches long and five to fifteen in a cluster. Longer spines with more in a cluster are likely on old stems. Almost 1 foot long, the flowers are white. The white-fleshed, red fruits are 3 to 4 inches long or sometimes longer.

Cereus jamacaru

Cereus glaucus

Cereus peruvianus

Cereus alacriportanus

red-based spines that are bright yellow when young, and gray later, in clusters ¾ to 1 inch apart. Six to nine, all spreading, compose each cluster. Its stems have usually five ribs. The flowers, nearly 1 foot long, are white tinged with pink, the inner petals fringed or not, the outer ones narrow.

A bluish-green plant often cultivated as *C. peruvianus* may be a hybrid. The true species is green or grayish-green. Native of southeastern South America, not of Peru as its name implies, in the wild it sometimes attains a height of 40 feet but in cultivation is usually considerably lower. It has a much branched head of many massive, erect branches with generally eight or nine ribs, but sometimes not more than four. A little over 1 inch long, the brown to black spines are in clusters of five to ten, ¾ inch apart. The white blooms, about 6 inches long, are succeeded by subspherical, orange-yellow, black-seeded fruits about 1½ inches in diameter. Often cultivated *C. p. monstrosus* differs in the ribs of the more slender, erect stem being curiously molded in irregular lumpy tubercles. It grows slowly. In contrast to the last, *C. p. monstrosus-minor* has thicker stems, remains dwarf, and is green. It branches freely. Similar to *C. peruvianus* and sometimes considered a variant of it, *C. alacriportanus*, of Uruguay, Paraguay, and southern Brazil, differs chiefly in having

Its stems up to 60 feet long or longer, in the wild erect or leaning against trees or rocks, *C. dayamii* is native to forest lands in Argentina. Branching freely, the stems,

Cereus dayamii

4 to 8 inches thick and dull green, have five to six notched ribs with clusters of usually not more than four short spines. Up to 10 inches long, the flowers are white inside, greenish toward their outsides. The red fruits, up to 3½ inches long, have white flesh and black seeds. Similar to *C. peruvianus*, but without spines, *C. gonianthus* is a hybrid of *C. dayamii*. Up to about 15 feet tall and branched from the base, this has short-jointed, deeply-five- to six-angled stems. The inner petals of the flowers are white, the outer ones red. The fruits are edible.

Erect, freely-branched, and up to 6 feet or more in height, Brazilian *C. tetragonus* has a narrow, compact head of closely

Cereus peruvianus monstrosus

Cereus peruvianus monstrosus, as a pot plant

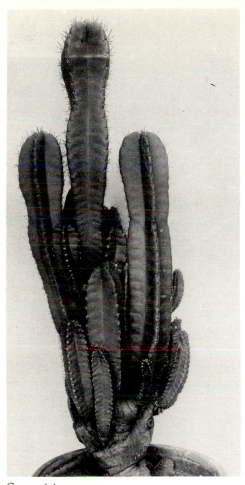

Cereus tetragonus

placed branches, green even when young. Usually they have four, seldom five deep ribs closely set with clusters of brown to almost black spines from white-felted areoles. In each cluster there are one to several centrals and five or six slightly more slender radials. They are 2 to 3 inches long. The reddish funnel-shaped flowers are nearly 6 inches long. From 5 to 10 feet tall and erect, the stems of *C. azureus*, of southern Brazil and northern Argentina, are up to 1½ inches thick. They are bluish-green to dark green with something of a metallic sheen and have six or seven blunt, deep ribs. The clusters of eight to sixteen short, black spines are closely spaced. Open by day, the white flowers are 9 inches to 1 foot long. The fruits, elliptic to ovoid, are about 1¼ inches long.

Bushy, massive, up to 12 feet high and broader than high, *C. huntingtonianus* has many erect stems with usually seven, sometimes six or eight ribs with spine clusters about ¾ inch apart. In each cluster there are one or more or no central spines, gray to black, 1½ to 6 inches long, and three to four radials about ½ inch long. The light pink blooms are about 1½ inches in diameter, their inner petals somewhat fringed. The long-ovate fruits, about 3 inches long, have red pulp. The nativity of this sort is not known. It is probably South American. Brazilian *C. aethiops* is bushy, has bluish to purplish, usually much-

branched stems 3 to 6 feet tall, with seven or eight ribs. The spines are black, the radials number nine or more. There is generally only one central spine. The flowers are 7 to 9 inches long, 4 to 5 inches wide, and white with pink outer petals. The brownish fruits are ovoid-oblong, a little more than 2 inches long. Native of Argentina, *C. forbesii* has erect, grayish, five- to seven-ribbed stems 8 to 10 feet tall. The stout, needle-shaped spines are in clusters of five or six radials about 1½ inches long and three or four 2½-inch-long centrals. About 7 inches long the flowers are white with the outer petals tipped with pink. The red-fleshed fruits, about 2½ inches long, have purple skins. Venezuelan *C. horridus* is shrubby, has five- to nine-ribbed, green stems with spine clusters approximately 1½ inches apart, each of about five radials and three centrals ½ to ¾ inch long, or on old stems more and longer spines. The flowers are white and up to 9 inches long. The whitish-fleshed fruits are about 3 inches long. Related to *C. jamacaru*, Brazilian *C. validus* (syn. *C. caesius*) attains heights of 6 feet or more and branches somewhat. Its young stems glaucous and all its joints spiny, but the spines not yellow, this kind has four- to eight-ribbed branches that are erect. The stout spines, up to ¾ inch long, are in clusters of five radials and solitary or sometimes two or three stouter centrals, the latter occasionally 6 inches in length. The funnel-shaped blooms are white with reddish outer petals. From *C. jamacaru* this is distinguished by the outer petals of its blooms being reddish, not green.

Erect to sprawling or semiprostrate, *C. obtusus* inhabits coastal Brazil. It has dull, glaucous-green stems branched from their bases, deeply-ribbed when young, but later with only three to five blunt, shallow ribs or angles. The irregularly-spaced clusters of yellowish spines consist of one central and five to seven radials up to 2 inches long. The blooms, up to 1 foot in length, are white with very narrow, greenish outer petals. Related to the last, highly variable, and hence well named, *C. variabilis* is native to Brazil and Uruguay. Up to 12 feet tall, it has stems 2½ to 3½ inches in diameter with seven or eight deep, notched ribs. The clusters of yellow to brownish spines are of five to seven radials, a little more than ½ inch long, and one or two slightly longer, straight central spines. From 8 inches to more rarely 1 foot in length, the white flowers have conspicuously-toothed inner petals and brownish-green outer ones. Possibly only a variety of the last, *C. pernambucensis* has more or less prostrate stems that spread to form wide colonies. They are pale bluish-green to whitish-glaucous stems with three to five strongly-scalloped ribs. The spine clusters, about ¾ inch apart, sprout from brown-woolly areoles. Each is of four to ten needle-like, brownish spines up to ¾ inch long. The flowers are 4½ to 6 inches long. A crested variety is *C. f. monstrosus*.

Garden and Landscape Uses and Cultivation. The impressive, stately, treelike species of *Cereus* are frequently grown for ornament in warm, dryish parts of the Americas and elsewhere. They, as well as

Cereus huntingtonianus

shrubby kinds, are favorites for inclusion in outdoor and indoor collections of succulents. Most become sizeable specimens in a relatively few years. Of vigorous growth and considerable adaptability, they respond readily to conditions suitable for most cactuses. For more information see Cactuses.

CEREZA is *Cordia nitida*.

CERIMAN is *Monstera deliciosa*.

CERINTHE (Cerín-the)—Honeywort. Three annual species of this group of ten Old World annual and perennial herbaceous plants are occasionally cultivated in flower gardens. The genus belongs in the borage family BORAGINACEAE. Its name is from the Greek *keros*, wax, and *anthos*, a flower, in allusion to an ancient belief that bees visited the flowers to obtain wax.

Honeyworts have alternate, undivided, usually glaucous leaves and drooping, prevailingly yellow flowers in very leafy-bracted racemes or clusters. The best species is perhaps *C. retorta,* a native of Greece, 1½ to 2 feet tall, with spoon-shaped or oval, glaucous leaves, which on the upper parts of the stems, successively change into colorful purple bracts. The bracts, among which are displayed the purple-tipped tubular yellow blooms, provide the chief show. The leaves usually have white warts on both surfaces.

A quite delightful species from the Mediterranean region is *C. major.* It is much branched, attains a height of 1 foot to 2 feet, and has broad-oval, grayish-green leaves, which have hairs fringing their edges. Its tubular yellow blooms are banded or edged with maroon or reddish-purple; the bracts are purple. This is considered to be a good bee plant. Slenderer than the last is *C. minor,* a native of southern Europe. Its leaves are comparatively narrow oval or spoon-shaped and pale green, often with grayish-white warty markings, and small yellow tubular flowers that sometimes are marked with fine brownish spots.

Garden Uses and Cultivation. Except for *C. minor,* which prefers light shade, these plants succeed best in sunny locations and in any ordinary, well-drained, garden soil. They are pleasant subjects for inclusion in beds containing a mixture of flowers and are easy to grow. Seeds may be sown in early spring and covered to a depth of not more than ¼ inch outdoors where the plants are to remain, or they may be started about eight weeks earlier indoors, be grown on in flats, and be planted outside about the time that snapdragons, China-asters, and stocks are set out. A distance of about 6 inches is sufficient between individuals. Blooming begins in eleven to thirteen weeks from seed sowing.

CEROCHLAMYS (Ceroch-lámys). The only species of this *Mesembryanthemum* relative, of the carpetweed family AIZOACEAE, is a low succulent of South Africa. Botanically it is closely allied to *Astridia* and in appearance resembles *Rhombophyllum nelii.* Unlike the latter, the ends of its leaves are not two-lobed. From *Astridia* it is segregated on technical differences of the flowers (the nectary is composed of separate glands), and more obviously by its leaves being conspicuously coated with wax instead of velvety pubescent. This accounts for the name, from the Greek *keros*, wax, and *chlamys*, a mantle.

Nearly stemless, *Cerochlamys pachyphylla* (syn. *C. trigona*) has usually two pairs of leaves set at right angles to each other and with the bases of each pair slightly united. They are very fleshy, three-angled, and up to about 2 inches long by ½ to ¾ inch wide. Narrow toward their bases, they have flat to slightly rounded upper surfaces, roundish keels, and chin-like ends. They are firm and, beneath the coating of wax, gray-green tinged with red or brown. The *Mesembryanthemum*-type flowers, 1½ to 2 inches in diameter, are purplish-pink with the bases of their many petals almost white. The stamens have white stalks and yellow anthers. There are five stigmas. The flower stalks, about 1¼ inches in length, arise from between a pair of small bracts. Variety *C. p. albiflora* has white blooms.

Garden Uses and Cultivation. Gems for collectors of choice, nonhardy succulents, this species and its variety are easy to cultivate and bloom with fair freedom. They require the same treatment as *Bergeranthus* and may be multiplied by seeds and cuttings. For additional information see Succulents.

CEROPEGIA (Cero-pègia)—Rosary Vine or String-of-Hearts. Nonhardy, perennial herbaceous plants to the number of about 160 species constitute *Ceropegia* of the milkweed family ASCLEPIADACEAE. Natives of Africa, the Canary Islands, Madagascar, warm parts of Asia, the Mascarene Islands, and Australia, they have a name alluding to the waxy aspect of the flowers, derived from the Greek *keros*, wax, and *pege*, a fountain.

Ceropegias mostly have tubers or clusters of fleshy roots, less frequently, fibrous ones. Their stems are erect, prostrate, pendulous, or vining. The leaves are opposite, or rarely wanting. Small to fairly large, the flowers are solitary, in pairs, umbel-like clusters, or less often racemes, lateral from the nodes, more rarely terminal. The blooms have a small, five-lobed calyx, a tubular corolla more or less swollen at its base and with five lobes (petals), separate and erect, spreading, or reflexed, or with their apexes joined to form a kind of cage or canopy. The corona or crown at the center of the bloom is double and intricately and beautifully formed. The five stamens are united as a column around the short styles. The fruits are paired, slender, spindle-shaped, or cylindrical, podlike follicles. The flowers

Cerochlamys pachyphylla

trap small flies that, attracted by odor and color, enter the corolla tube. The down-pointing hairs that line the tube temporarily prevent the insects' return. Not until they have withered can the creature escape, which it then does with pollen clinging to it. The pollen is deposited on the next bloom visited.

Rosary vine or string-of-hearts (*C. woodii*) is by far the most commonly grown kind. Native of South Africa, this is a neat, hairless trailer with fairly large, beadlike tubers strung at intervals along its slender stems. Roots are produced from the nodes (joints). From ¼ to over ½ inch long, the rather distantly spaced, fleshy leaves have heart-shaped bases. They are dark green netted with whitish veins. Usually in pairs, the long-stalked flowers are pinkish to light purple. Their petals are united by their tips. The bottoms of the curved corolla tubes are swollen.

Ceropegia woodii

These less frequently cultivated kinds find favor with collectors of succulents: *C. africana*, of South Africa, has tuberous roots, hairless stems, and stalked, lanceolate, ¾-inch-long leaves, often with recurved tips. Its short-stalked flowers, spherically swollen at their bases and a little over 1 inch long, are green, with brownish corolla tubes. The hair-fringed petals, joined at their tips, are deep violet on their insides. *C. ampliata* is a thickish-stemmed vine with small, early-deciduous leaves. Its attractive flowers, 2 inches long or slightly longer and ¾ to over 1 inch across, have corolla tubes much inflated at their bases and purple, united petals. The inside of the corolla tube is white veined with green. This is a native of South West Africa. *C. barklyi*, of South Africa, is a slender-stemmed, somewhat twining vine with a half-subterranean tuber and stalkless or very short-stalked, tapering, ovate-lanceolate, fleshy, white-veined, light green leaves. The short-stalked, slender-tubed blooms are in umbel-like clusters. The base

of the corolla tube is considerably swollen. The petals, attached at their apexes, are greenish outside. Inside they are netted with purple. *C. cimiciodora*, native to South Africa, is fleshy-stemmed and rather similar to *C. stapeliaeformis*, from which it differs most noticeably in its flower buds being flattish rather than extended in beak-like fashion. The leaves are small and scalelike. The blooms, about 2 inches long and at their star-shaped tops ¾ inch wide, are mottled gray with purple specks at their apexes. The petals, their tips not joined, spread widely. *C. debilis* is a tropical African. Tuberous-rooted, it has thin,

Ceropegia debilis

twining or drooping stems and very slender, linear leaves up to 1¼ inches long, grooved along their upper sides. The slender, 1-inch-long flowers, spherically swollen at their bases, are solitary or in twos or threes. They are greenish marked with reddish-purple and have dark purple interiors furnished with long, brown hairs. The slender petals join at their tips to form a tall canopy. *C. dichotoma*, endemic to the Canary Islands, has erect, forking, jointed, gray-white to white or sometimes violet, cylindrical stems, finger-thick and up to 3 feet tall. The slender, soon-deciduous leaves, pointed-narrow-linear, are about 1½ inches long. Lemon-yellow, the blooms, about ¾ inch long, come from near the tops of the stems. They have petals united at their apexes. *C. distincta* is a native of Zanzibar. A twining vine, it has long-ovate to broad-elliptic-ovate, stalked leaves with slightly heart-shaped bases. They are 1¾ to 2½ inches long. The stalked flowers, ¾ to 1 inch long, solitary or in pairs, have sharply bent corolla tubes swollen at their bases, broadened in funnel-fashion above. The petals, united at their tips, arch to form a five-angled lid over the mouth of the funnel. *C. elegans*, of India, Ceylon, and the Celebes Islands, is a trailing twiner with distantly-spaced, pointed-lanceolate

leaves 2 inches long or slightly longer, fringed with minute hairs. In pairs, its purple-spotted, white flowers are funnel-shaped and about 2½ inches long. *C. fusca*, of the Canary Islands, has erect, jointed, branched or branchless, cylindrical stems, up to 6 feet tall, tapering toward their apexes, at first nearly black, later chalky-white. Its linear, soon-deciduous leaves are 1½ inches long. The flowers, in tufts from stems formed the previous year, are brown with yellow insides. *C. haygarthii* is a vigorous trailer from South Africa. Its long-heart-shaped, stalked leaves have blades about 1½ inches long by nearly 1 inch wide. The beautiful flowers, their purple-spotted, pink corolla tubes with somewhat swollen bases, are funnel-shaped and are covered with a lid formed of the five corolla lobes from the center of which projects a slender, dark purple, pistil-like column tipped with a small knob and a brush of long hairs. *C. linearis* (syn. *C. caffrorum*) is a wiry-stemmed, South African vine with tapered, ovate-lanceolate to linear, red-veined leaves up to 1¼ inches long. The flowers, much like those of *C. barklyi*, in clusters of up to five, are green lined with purple outside and darker purple inside. *C. nilotica* (syn. *C. mozambicensis*), of East Africa and Ethiopia, is a tuberous-rooted climber with four-angled, twining stems thickened at the nodes, and short-stalked, ovate-lanceolate leaves ¾ to a little over 1 inch long. In groups of five or six, the dark brown flowers have club-shaped corollas swollen at their bases, yellow-spotted on their inside. They are widened above, 1¼ inches long or a little longer. The triangular lobes of the corolla are united at their tips. *C. oculata* is a tropical Asian twiner with ovate-heart-shaped, hair-fringed, slightly hairy leaves with small, fleshy glands at the bottoms of their blades. About 2 inches long and much swollen at their bases, the corollas have yellow-green tubes purplish-spotted above and dark green-spotted petals joined at their tips. *C. radicans* is a South African. A charming creeper with rooting stems, it has erect, thick, ovate to nearly round, short-stalked leaves ½ inch to nearly 2 inches long. Singly from the leaf axils, the stalked, emerald-green flowers banded with purple and white are held erectly. They are 3 inches long and have a slender, cylindrical corolla tube, swollen at its base, widened toward its apex. The erect, long-lanceolate corolla lobes have their tips united, their margins recurved, and their inner surfaces somewhat hairy. *C. rendallii*, of South Africa, is a climber. It has pointed-ovate to long-linear, blunt to pointed leaves ½ inch to 1½ inches long, ½ inch wide or much narrower, with a tiny spine at the apex. The short-stalked flowers, slightly more than ½ inch wide, have somewhat curved, greenish-white corolla tubes with purple, swollen bases. The tubes widen

Ceropegia radicans

above. The clawlike, heart-shaped, green corolla lobes have their tips united. *C. robynsiana* is a West African. It has long, climbing stems. Its stalked, fleshy, ovoid leaves are up to 3½ inches long by rather more than one-half as wide. The curious, whitish-green, red-brown-spotted blooms, about 2 inches long, are spherically-inflated at their bases, above broadened into a funnel-shaped tube with the connected corolla lobes protruding like a long beak. *C. sandersonii*, of South Africa, is a climber with distantly-spaced, short-stalked, heart-shaped-ovate leaves up to 2 inches long by about 1⅓ inches wide. Its beautiful blooms, solitary or up to four together from the leaf axils, are short-stalked. They are about 3 inches long by 2 inches wide across the parachute-like canopy formed by the united lobes of the corolla. The lobes are much narrowed in their lower parts, their margins fringed with hairs. The corolla tube, slender below, is trumpet-shaped above. The blooms are green, the parachute with darker green mottlings. *C. stapeliaeformis*, of South Africa, is a trailer with gray-spotted, dull green, slightly knobby, thick stems suggesting those of a stapelia. The upper parts of the stems are thin, trailing, and up to 4 feet or more in length. The leaves are reduced to tiny scales. In groups of four or more, the upturned flowers, 2 to 2½ inches long, are on their outsides white spotted with brown, on their insides white. The corolla tube, a slender cylinder with a swollen base, widens above and has wide-spreading lobes not joined at their tips.

Garden and Landscape Uses and Cultivation. Ceropegias are interesting, easily-grown plants for outdoors in warm, dry climates, for greenhouses, and for growing in sunny windows. Outdoors they may be used as low vines by providing them with wires or other slender supports about which they can twine their stems, or they may be allowed to trail on banks and in rock gardens and similar places. Indoors they are well suited for pots and hanging baskets. They adapt to almost any well-drained soil and are very easily increased by division, cuttings, and seeds. They are satisfied with a night temperature in winter of 50 to 55°F increased during the day by from five to fifteen degrees depending upon the brightness of the weather. The greenhouse should be well ventilated on all favorable occasions. Watering must be done carefully to keep the soil just moist, never wet.

CEROPTERIS. See Pityrogramma.

CEROXYLON (Ceróx-ylon)—Wax Palm. Little known in cultivation, this northern Andean genus of the palm family PALMAE is nevertheless of considerable interest. It consists of about twenty species of bisexual, feather-leaved palms. The name is derived from the Greek *keros*, wax, and *xylon*, wood, in allusion to the waxy coating that covers the trunks and leaves. The wax of the Quindio wax palm, exploited commercially, is similar to that of the carnauba palm (*Copernicia prunifera*) and is used for the same purposes. That of other kinds is also used, but less extensively than the product of the Quindio wax palm.

The genus *Ceroxylon* has the distinction of including the world's tallest palms and also of growing at higher altitudes than other members of the palm family. On the Colombian-Ecuadorian frontier not far from the equator, *C. utile* exists at 13,450 feet in a region where the timberline for other trees is 11,000 feet and other palms do not ascend above 4,000 feet. Until the discovery of the gigantic redwoods (*Sequoia sempervirens*) and eucalypts (*Eucalyptus regnans*), species of *Ceroxylon* were believed to be the tallest plants on earth. They sometimes exceed 200 feet in height.

The wax palm (*C. alpinum* syn. *C. andicola*), rarely 190 feet, more often up to 160 feet tall, has a slender trunk swollen at its middle and a crown of leaves up to 20 feet long with numerous slender leaflets notched at their ends and dark green above and silvery below. The flowers are comparatively large. The stamens number nine to fifteen. The purplish fruits are about 1 inch in diameter.

Garden and Landscape Uses and Cultivation. Trials of these palms in Florida and southern California have produced indifferent results. They are plants for collectors, but unfortunately insufficient experience with their cultivation is available to make firm recommendations. In their native habitats they are rarely or never exposed to freezing, yet the maximum day temperature does not rise above 63 or 70°F. This wax palm has been successfully grown for many years in a greenhouse at the Royal Botanic Gardens, Kew, England, but there it is not subjected to the high summer temperatures common in most parts of North America. Comparatively low maximum temperatures are most probably a requisite for the successful cultivation of these palms. For additional information see Palms.

CESTRUM (Cés-trum)—Jessamine. Of rather different aspect from most cultivated members of the nightshade family SOLANACEAE to which it belongs, the genus *Cestrum* comprises 150 species of shrubs and small trees native to the warmer parts of the Americas and West Indies. A few are cultivated. The name is an ancient Greek one for some other plant.

Cestrums have alternate, lobeless, toothless leaves, and tubular, white, greenish, yellow, or red, sometimes fragrant flowers in terminal or axillary clusters. The blooms have five-toothed, bell-shaped or tubular calyxes. The corollas, often enlarged in the upper parts of their tubes, have five lobes (petals). Generally the stamens number five. The fruits are whitish, red, or black, scarcely fleshy berries.

The hardiest species is the willow-leaved jessamine (*C. parqui*), a native of Chile. This favorite is an evergreen shrub, about

Cestrum parqui

Cestrum aurantiacum

Believed to be a hybrid between *C. elegans* and *C. fasciculatum*, an attractive plant named **C. newellii** has the brightest-colored blooms of any cultivated *Cestrum*. They are crimson and in short clusters. The leaves are hairy and have red veins.

Cestrum newellii

6 feet tall, with stalked, long-pointed, lanceolate to oblong leaves up to about 6 inches long, and greenish-yellow flowers about 1 inch long, with erect or spreading petals. Although it is commonly reported that the flowers are fragrant at night, this certainly is not always true. When bruised the foliage has a disagreeable odor. This species is less showy in bloom than most cultivated kinds. The night-flowering jessamine (**C. nocturnum**), a native of the West Indies, is less hardy to cold than the preceding one. A slender-branched shrub, up to 12 feet tall, with evergreen, short-pointed, elliptic to oblong-ovate leaves up to 8 inches long, it has greenish-white or creamy blooms, about ¾ inch long, which are intensely fragrant at night. They are in axillary clusters and have spreading or erect petals. It is not always easy to distinguish between *C. nocturnum* and *C. parqui*.

The day-flowering jessamine (**C. diurnum**) differs from the last two in having flowers fragrant by day and with petals that bend backward when the blooms are fully mature. The flowers are ½ to 1 inch long, white, and in short clusters terminating long stalks from the leaf axils. This species attains a height of 15 feet and has bluntish, oblong to elliptic, evergreen leaves 2 to 3½ inches long by about 1 inch wide, paler beneath than on their upper sides. Also with petals that bend backward when the flowers are fully mature, **C. aurantiacum** is a semiclimbing, evergreen shrub native of Guatemala. Its ovate to broadly-elliptic, somewhat pointed leaves are up to 4 inches long and up to 2¾ inches wide. Its stalkless blooms are in clusters of two to five, grouped in terminal panicles. They are ¾ to 1 inch long, orange-yellow, and fragrant at night.

With reddish-purple flowers in loose, more or less nodding, terminal clusters, **C. elegans** (syns. *C. purpureum, Habrothamnus elegans*) is an old-time favorite. It is a somewhat climbing, evergreen shrub, native to Mexico. Its branches are hairy, its leaves narrowly-ovate to ovate-lanceolate and 2½ to 5 inches long by 1 inch to 1½ inches

wide. From the kinds described above this species differs not only in the color of its blooms, but in the corolla tubes being conspicuously narrowed at their mouths. They are ¾ to 1 inch long, swollen from the base upward to the mouths, and hairless. The pointed petals bend backward when the blooms are mature. The fruits are spherical, red, and ⅓ inch in diameter. Variety *C. e. smithii* has rose-pink flowers. Another purplish-red-flowered species, with blooms rather larger than the last, is the Mexican **C. fasciculatum.** From *C. elegans* and its variety this differs in having the outsides of its flowers hairy and its rather spherical clusters of blooms more compact and usually nestling against a collar of small leaves. The leaves are ovate and up to 2½ inches long.

Garden and Landscape Uses. Very beautiful for outdoor planting in warm climates, and for greenhouse cultivation, cestrums give little trouble to the cultivator. The hardier kinds, in addition to *C. parqui*, are those indigenous to Mexico. They are useful in gardens in the deep south and California and are esteemed for their forms and foliage as well as for their free-blooming propensities and the attractiveness of their flowers. They bloom chiefly in winter and spring.

Cestrum elegans

Cultivation. A sunny location or one in part-day shade suits cestrums. They are satisfied with ordinary garden soil that does not become too dry. In greenhouses they may be accommodated in ground beds or containers and are attractive when trained against a wall or a pillar. The hardier kinds are satisfied in a greenhouse where the winter night temperature is 50°F, but those more tropical in origin require temperature five to ten degrees higher. Day temperatures may exceed night ones by five to fifteen degrees, depending upon the weather. After blooming, the plants are partially rested by keeping the temperature on the low side and the soil dryish for four to six weeks, then they are pruned back hard and, if in containers, taken out, shaken free of as much soil as possible, and after the roots are trimmed back, repotted in fertile, porous soil, watered, and started into growth again. During the summer they may be buried to the rims of the containers in a bed of sand, peat moss, or similar material, outdoors. To encourage bushiness the tips of the shoots are pinched occasionally until mid-July. Well before fall frost the plants must be transferred to a greenhouse. An alternative method is to plant directly in outdoor beds after the weather is quite warm and settled and to lift the plants carefully and pot them in early fall. After this potting they must be kept in a shaded, humid greenhouse for a week or two to encourage reestablishment of the roots to prevent wilting and consequent loss of foliage. During their season of active growth sufficient water should be given to keep the soil evenly and moderately moist. After the containers are filled with roots regular applications of dilute liquid fertilizer are beneficial. Propagation is easy by means of cuttings, usually taken in spring, in a warm greenhouse propagating bench.

CETERACH (Céter-ach). This name is pronounced as though the final ch were k. That of three quite similar species of ferns of Europe, Asia, Africa, and islands of the Atlantic, it is a form of the Arabic name of *Ceterach officinarum*. Belonging to the spleenwort family ASPLENIACEAE, ceterachs grow in the ground and in fissures of rocks. They are small plants with short, erect rhizomes, and thick, lanceolate, pinnately-lobed fronds (leaves), densely-scaly on their undersides. Their spore clusters, long, narrow, and scarcely with an indusium (covering), angle outward from the middle veins of the leaf lobes.

Typical of the group, *C. officinarum* often inhabits crevices in old walls, especially those containing lime mortar. Its fronds, in dense tufts, are 4 to 6 inches long and have stalks up to 3 inches long. The blades are cut almost to the midrib into broad, blunt, alternate lobes. This is a variable species, but the variants are

Ceterach officinarum

mostly unstable and tend to revert to the typical kind. Similar *C. aureum,* of the Canary Islands and Madeira, is larger.

Garden Uses and Cultivation. The hardiness of the fern described above is not precisely known. It prospers in gardens in the Pacific Northwest and probably where winters are considerably harsher. It thrives in crevices between rocks, preferably more or less vertical ones, in gritty, peaty soil made agreeable by the addition of crushed limestone or gypsum. For the best results the location should be open and quite sunny. In too dense shade the fronds become floppy and less attractive. Water during dry periods. Propagation is by division and by spores. For more information see Ferns.

CEYLON-GOOSEBERRY is *Dovyalis hebecarpa.*

CEYLON-IRONWOOD. See Mesua.

CHAENACTIS (Chaen-áctis). About twenty-five species, natives of western North America, compose *Chaenactis* of the daisy family COMPOSITAE. Annuals, biennials, and herbaceous perennials are included. The name comes from the Greek *chaino,* to gape, and *aktis,* a ray, and alludes to the marginal florets of the flower heads of some species. The group is not commonly cultivated.

These plants have alternate, usually dissected leaves and solitary or loosely clus-

tered heads of yellow, white, or pink flowers. Technically all the florets are of the disk type, but the outer ones are often enlarged and raylike. All are bisexual.

A variable annual, *C. glabriuscula* is yellow-flowered and 4 inches to 1 foot tall. It branches above and has leaves up to 3 inches long, generally two or three times pinnately-lobed. The uppermost leaves are not divided. The flower stalks, 1½ to 4 inches long, carry solitary heads about ½ inch across. This species grows in well-drained soil in sun. It is suitable for adding variety to flower borders and, in its native region, for inclusion in collections of wild plants. It is raised from seeds sown outdoors in spring.

CHAENOMELES (Chaeno-mèles)—Flowering-Quince, Japanese-Quince. Old-time gardeners frequently called these shrubs japonicas and knew them also as burning bushes. The first designation came from the name under which they were usually cataloged, *Cydonia japonica,* the second from the fiery color of the flowers of popular kinds. Among reasons cited for keeping *Chaenomeles* separate from *Cydonia,* with which it was once botanically united, is that its three species produce fertile hybrids between themselves, but will not cross with quinces (*Cydonia*), apples (*Malus*), pears (*Pyrus*), or other near relatives in the rose family ROSACEAE to which they belong. The group, the name of which comes from the Greek *chainein,* to split, and *melea,* an apple, and was given on the mistaken assumption that the fruits split into five parts, has been cultivated in the Orient for more than four centuries, and for well over a century and a half in Western gardens. It has given rise to numerous horticultural varieties, some of which are among our finest flowering shrubs. An unusual characteristic of *Chaenomeles*, shared only with *Cydonia* in the section of the *Rosaceae* to which they belong, is that each compartment of the fruit contains many rather than one or two seeds. From *Cydonia* the genus *Chaenomeles* differs in its styles being fused for one-third to two-thirds of their lengths from their bases. It is native to eastern Asia.

Flowering-quinces are deciduous, or partially evergreen, densely-branched shrubs or rarely small trees, usually thorny, and with alternate, or on older branches clustered, stalked, undivided, toothed leaves, each tooth and indentation between teeth terminating in a gland. Leaves on young shoots, but not on older ones, have at the bottoms of their stalks a pair of kidney-shaped, leafy stipules (basal appendages). Sometimes the young, unfolding foliage is bronzy. Older leaves are commonly dark green and lustrous. They do not color conspicuously in fall. The numerous flowers come chiefly in spring, but their appearance is slightly erratic, and it is not unusual for a few to open in fall or, in mild climates, in winter. They may be single, semidouble, or double, and range from 1 inch to 2 inches in diameter. They have short stalks and are one alone to several in a cluster or sometimes in leafy racemes and panicles. The spring crop of blooms usually expands before the leaves, but the latter begin their development before the flowers fall. There are both bisexual and unisexual blooms. The flowers have five sepals and, except in semidouble and double varieties, mostly five rounded petals, but the number of petals may vary considerably between flowers on the same plant, and their colors are affected to some extent by seasonal weather conditions. The petals fall before fading. There are forty to sixty stamens arranged approximately in two rows. Not infrequently some are to a greater or lesser extent petal-like. The normally five, but sometimes more styles are partially joined into a column longer than the stamens. Flowering-quince fruits are large, short-stalked, and apple-like in general appearance, but they vary considerably in shape and size, sometimes being pear-shaped. Sometimes they are ribbed. Their skins are thin, not downy, but in some kinds are sticky. The fruits, fragrant when mature, drop soon after they ripen. They make good jelly.

The first flowering-quince introduced to Western gardens was the Japanese-quince (*C. speciosa* syn. *C. lagenaria*), which was brought to Europe in 1796. A spiny shrub

up to about 6 feet tall or sometimes taller, it has dark green, often glossy, ovate to oblong, sharply-toothed leaves 1¾ to 4 inches long by ¾ inch to 1½ inches wide, usually hairy on their midribs. The red, pink, or white, cupped blooms are 1½ to 2 inches across. The yellow or yellowish-green, apple-, pear-, or egg-shaped fruits are up to 3 inches in length. This and its varieties are the most commonly cultivated kinds. Despite its common name it is not native to Japan, but to China, Tibet, and Burma. Brought to Japan in the middle of the sixteenth century it has since been widely cultivated and has become naturalized. It is frequently depicted in Japanese

Chaenomeles speciosa

art. Numerous horticultural varieties have been raised in America as well as abroad. Among them are *C. s.* 'Apple Blossom', with single to semidouble blooms tinted with pink and yellow. *C. s. candida*, with single pure white flowers. *C. s. cardinalis*, which has double bright red flowers. *C. s. contorta*, with twisted branches and pink-lined white flowers. *C. s. gaujardii*, the single flowers of which are pink. *C. s. grandiflora*, with white flowers tinted with yellow. *C. s. kermesina semiplena*, with semidouble pink to red blooms. *C. s. macrocarpa*, a spineless red-flowered variety. *C. s. marmorata*, a tall kind with large, marbled, single pink and white flowers. *C. s. nivalis*, a rather low grower, the pure white flowers of which are single. *C. s.* 'Phylis Moore', a kind with semidouble pink blooms. *C. s. rosea-plena*, with partially double pink blooms. *C. s. rubra grandiflora*, with deep red double flowers. *C. s. sanguinea-plena*, the double blooms of which are scarlet. *C. s. simonii*, with double red blooms. *C. s.* 'Snow', with single, white blooms, and *C. s. umbilicata*, tall and one of the best, with rose-pink single flowers.

Dwarf Japanese-quince (*C. japonica*) has spreading branches and short, slender spines. Ranging in height from 1½ to 4 feet, it has ovate to spatula-shaped, short-stalked leaves up to 2 inches long and ¾ inch to slightly more than 1 inch wide. They have coarse, rounded teeth and are

Chaenomeles speciosa (flowers)

Chaenomeles japonica (flowers)

Chaenomeles japonica (fruits)

without hairs. The salmon-pink to orange-red, cupped or flat blooms are 1¼ to 1¾ inches wide and have forty to sixty stamens. The yellow, often red-blotched, irregular fruits, resembling gnarled apples, are slightly sticky and about 1¾ inches in diameter. This species is native to Japan. Variety *C. j. alpina*, which has been known as *C. j. sargentii*, is lower, more branched, and smaller in all its parts than typical *C. japonica*, but in cultivation it has not maintained these distinctive characteristics. It has single salmon-pink to orange-colored blooms. Variety *C. j. tricolor* has leaves variegated with pink and white. Other varieties of *C. japonica* include *C. j.* 'Arthur Hill', with single salmon-pink flowers. *C. j. aurea*, the blooms of which are single and orange flushed with deep rose. *C. j.* 'Dorothy Rowe', with white, single flowers tinted with pink and yellow. *C. j. maulei*, with single, salmon-pink to orange flowers.

Sometimes 20 feet tall, although usually lower in cultivation, **C. cathayensis** (syn. *C. speciosa cathayensis*) is the least hardy species. Gaunt, with comparatively few erect branches, and short lateral branches terminating in spurs, this kind has elliptic to lanceolate leaves 2 to 3 inches long or occasionally slightly longer, usually with sharp, bristle-tipped, marginal teeth, and when young and sometimes later, covered on their undersides with rusty hairs. Produced on older shoots, the cupped white to pink blooms, usually margined with deeper pink, are 1¾ inches in diameter. The ovoid fruits, up to 6 or even 8 inches long by about one-half as wide, are at first green, but become yellow and sometimes reddish as they ripen. This, the least attractive species, is native to China, Tibet, Bhutan, and Burma.

Hybrid flowering-quinces are numerous. Those between *C. japonica* and *C. speciosa* are classed as *C. superba*. Results of hybridizing *C. superba* with *C. cathayensis* have been given the group name *C. californica*. Since one of their parents is a hybrid, it follows that these represent the mingling of three species. The name *C. vilmoriniana* is reserved for the hybrid prog-

eny of *C. cathayensis* and *C. speciosa*. To the results of mating *C. cathayensis* and *C. japonica* the designation *C. clarkiana* is given.

In general hybrid flowering-quinces are intermediate between their parents. Of **C. superba** there are very many excellent varieties. In spring they bloom freely on their old wood. The flat to cup-shaped flowers are in clusters of two to six. They come in white, pinks, reds, and especially noteworthy, in reddish-oranges. These hybrids are more like *C. japonica* than *C. speciosa*. They have mostly round-toothed leaves and apple-shaped fruits. Among *C. superba* varieties are *C. s.* 'Cameo', with yellowish-pink double blooms. *C. s.* 'Charming', which has single reddish-orange flowers. *C. s.* 'Coral Beauty', also with single reddish-orange flowers. *C. s.* 'Crimson and Gold', a rather low variety having single dark red flowers with conspicuous golden stamens. *C. s.* 'Crimson Beauty', which has red single blooms. *C. s.* 'Glowing Ember', with reddish-orange single flowers. *C. s.* 'Knap Hill Scarlet', low and branching more or less horizontally and with yellowish-pink to scarlet single blooms. *C. s.* 'Rowallane', with single flowers of brilliant red.

The **C. californica** hybrids resemble *C. cathayensis* in their erect growth, but their branches are more numerous. They have lanceolate, saw-toothed leaves. Their flowers, 1½ to 2¼ inches across, are usually blends of or are self-colored pinks and rosy-reds. Named varieties include *C. c.* 'Cardinal', with single red blooms. *C. c.* 'Clark's Giant Red', a nearly spineless variety with large single red flowers. *C. c.* 'Dawn', with pink and carmine blooms. *C. c.* 'Enchantress', the single flowers of which are light and dark pink. *C. c.* 'Nasturtium', with large nasturtium-red blooms. *C. c.* 'Rosy Morn', with flowers of soft pink. *C. c.* 'Sunset Glow', with single rosy-pink to rosy-red flowers.

Among the best white-bloomed flowering-quinces in the double-flowered **C. vilmoriniana** group are *C. v.* 'Afterglow' and *C. v.* 'Mount Everest'. In both the blooms become pink as they age. The blooms of *C. v. vedrariensis*, are single, white tinted with pink. Unfortunately *C. vilmoriniana* varieties are too tender for regions of harsh winters.

Garden and Landscape Uses. Flowering-quinces are colorful spring-blooming shrubs, handsome in flower and foliage, and in fall displaying decorative fruits. Well-satisfied with any fairly good soil provided it is well drained, they need full sun and, in northern gardens, because their flower buds are formed in fall and are liable to damage by severe cold or drying, shelter from winter wind. The hardiest, reliable throughout most of New England, are *C. japonica* and its varieties. Almost as hardy, although with flower buds more susceptible to damage by cold, are *C. spe-*

ciosa and its varieties. The species *C. ca-thayensis* and its hybrid progeny, *C. californica*, *C. vilmoriniana*, and *C. clarkiana*, and their varieties, are less hardy and should not be relied upon much north of Philadelphia, and even there they may suffer some winter damage.

They are displayed to excellent advantage against backgrounds of evergreens and are useful as single specimens, in groups, either alone or mixed with other shrubbery, and as components in foundation plantings. They stand shearing well and at one time they were greatly favored for hedges. Low kinds are very suitable for plantings on banks. In Europe flowering-quinces are quite extensively used for espaliering against walls. Branches cut in late winter and stood in water in a warm place indoors soon open their flowers and are pleasing decorations.

Cultivation. Early fall or spring are the best times to plant flowering-quinces. It is usually advisable to prune away about one-third of their tops at planting time, and this is especially true if they have lost many roots in the digging operation. Established specimens need some pruning from time to time to remove old, worn-out branches and encourage their replacement with more vigorous ones. Such pruning is done as soon as flowering is through. Propagation is by cuttings 4 to 6 inches long taken with a heel (sliver) of older shoot attached to their bases, and planted in a cold frame in early fall, by layering, and by budding onto seedlings in summer. Some kinds can be increased by removing rooted suckers in spring or fall. Seeds, sown in a bed protected from disturbance by birds and animals or in a cold frame, in fall, germinate with facility, as they do if stratified through the winter and sown under similar conditions in spring. Seeds of hybrids and selected varieties do not, of course, give plants true to parent types. The offspring are likely to vary widely.

CHAENORHINUM (Chaenorhín-um). This genus differs from nearly related toadflax (*Linaria*) in the plants being glandular-pubescent, in the flowers having open throats, and in technical characteristics of the fruits. Its twenty species are natives of Europe, especially the Mediterranean region, and Asia. They include annuals and herbaceous perennials with undivided, opposite or alternate leaves and asymmetrical two-lipped flowers in the axils of the upper leaves, which often form leafy racemes. *Chaenorhinum* belongs in the figwort family SCROPHULARIACEAE. The name is from the Greek *chaino*, to gape, and *rhis*, a nose or snout. It refers to the open throats of the flowers.

Perennial *C. glareosum* (syn. *Linaria glareosa*), of Spain, is naturalized in North America. From 6 inches to 1 foot tall, it has numerous stems, the nonflowering ones

slender stolons with tiny scalelike leaves. The regular leaves are oblong to linear-lanceolate and glandular-pubescent. The long-stalked, lilac flowers about ¼ inch long are in loose leafy racemes. From the last, southern European *C. origanifolium* (syn. *Linaria originifolia*) differs in not having stolons. Up to 10 inches tall but often lower, this has oblong to obovate, slightly sticky-hairy, fattish leaves ¼ to ½ inch long and rose-purple to white, tiny snapdragon-like flowers ½ inch long each with a short spur. Another southern European lacking stolons, *C. villosum* (syn. *Linaria villosa*) is a sticky-hairy perennial up to 1 foot tall or rather taller. It has thickish, obovate to nearly round leaves ½ to 1 inch long and violet-striped, lilac or yellowish flowers from a little less to a little more than ½ inch long. Annual *C. minus* (syn. *Linaria minor*), of Europe, is freely-branched and about 1 foot high. It has stalkless, linear-lanceolate leaves and in loose racemes long-stalked, lilac blooms ¼ inch or so long. This is naturalized in North America.

Garden Uses and Cultivation. The species discussed here are interesting as rock garden plants and may be used at the fronts of mixed borders and beds of flowers. They are rather pretty, but not very showy. The annual species must be, and the perennial one may be, raised from seeds. This presents no difficulty; those of the annual are sown in early spring where the plants are to bloom and are covered to a depth of up to ¼ inch. The resulting plants are thinned to 4 inches apart. The flowering period, which begins ten to twelve weeks from seed sowing, is of short duration, ordinarily up to two weeks. Seeds of the perennials may be started indoors in late winter or early spring by sowing in well-drained pots or pans of porous soil or by sowing in cold frames or in a well prepared seedbed outdoors in May. The young plants are transplanted to flats or to nursery beds to be grown on until they are planted in their permanent locations at a spacing of 6 to 8 inches between plants. The perennial sorts are also easily increased by cuttings inserted in early summer in a propagating bed in a shaded cold frame and by division in spring or early fall. The perennials are not very hardy in climates harsher than that of New York City and are likely to be winter-killed in damp or clayey soils. It is well to carry young plants over in a cold frame to provide for possible replacements. Chaenorhinums grow well in sun or part-shade in any ordinary garden soil that is well drained.

CHAENOSTOMA. See Sutera.

CHAEROPHYLLUM (Chaero-phýllum)—Turnip-Rooted Chervil. Three of the nearly forty species of *Chaerophyllum* of the carrot family UMBELLIFERAE are natives of North

America, two European species are naturalized there, one, the turnip-rooted chervil, which occurs spontaneously near Washington, D.C. This is quite distinct from salad chervil (*Anthriscus cerefolium*). The name is a modification of the ancient Greek one *chaerophyllon*, for the salad chervil, and is derived from the Greek *chairo*, to be pleased, and *phyllon*, a leaf. It alludes to the attractive foliage.

Native in north temperate regions around the world, chaerophyllums are annuals and biennials, with thrice-pinnately-divided, ferny leaves, and compound or solitary umbels of small white flowers. They differ from *Anthriscus* in their fruits (often called seeds) being without beaks. The native American species are annuals, *C. procumbens* is up to 2 feet tall, *C. tainturieri* and *C. texanum* up to about 2½ feet tall.

Turnip-rooted chervil (*C. bulbosum*) is a biennial 3 to 6 feet tall, cultivated for its edible roots, which are used as a vegetable. Other kinds of *Chaerophyllum* scarcely have horticultural interest, although they are pretty enough to be admitted to semi-wild places and some to native plant gardens.

Cultivation. Seeds of turnip-rooted chervil should be sown in early fall as soon as they are ripe or stratified in slightly moist peat moss or similar material under cool conditions and sown in spring. If they are stored dry and sown in spring they may take a full year to germinate. Ordinary, well-cultivated vegetable garden soil is satisfactory and the rows may be spaced 1 foot to 1½ feet apart. The young plants are thinned to stand 1½ to 2 inches apart and are cared for in the same manner as carrots. The crop, ready for harvesting in late summer and fall, consists of small, carrot-like gray or blackish edible roots. Seeds of annual kinds may be sown in spring in sunny places where the ground is not excessively dry. The seedlings should be thinned to about 6 inches apart.

CHAFFSEED is *Schwalbea americana*.

CHAIN FERN. See Woodwardia.

CHAIN ORCHID. See Dendrochilum.

CHALCAS PANICULATA is *Murraya paniculata*.

CHALICE VINE. See Solandra.

CHALK. This is a comparatively soft form of limestone composed largely of fossilized shells. White, grayish, or slightly yellowish, it is easily pulverized. In England the famous white cliffs of Dover are composed of chalk, and it is the dominant underlying rock in some other regions there.

In English gardening literature reference is often made to chalk gardens. These are simply gardens in areas where the soil contains much chalk and so is highly alkaline. Plants that prosper in such places are those that also favor or tolerate limestone. Acid-soil plants will not succeed in chalk soils.

Chalk may be used in the same way as limestone to correct excessive soil acidity. For this purpose bulk for bulk it is about one-half as effective as limestone.

CHAMAEBATIA (Chamae-bàtia). Two species of evergreen or semievergreen shrubs compose this group of the rose family RO-SACEAE. Closely allied to *Purshia*, the genus *Chamaebatia*, endemic to California and Baja California, is not of prime horticultural importance. Its name derives from the Greek *chamai*, low, and *batos*, a bramble, and alludes to the appearance of the flowers. Neither species is hardy in the north.

Chamaebatias are glandular-pubescent, heavily aromatic shrubs with leaves two or three times pinnately-divided into numerous tiny segments. The white flowers, each with five sepals, five petals, numerous stamens, and a solitary pistil, are in terminal clusters. The fruits, small, dry, and single-seeded, are enclosed in the persistent calyx. From 8 inches to 2 feet tall, *C. foliolosa* is freely-branched. Its clammy, nearly stalkless, obovate leaves are less than twice as long as wide, and 1 inch to 3 inches long. The flowers, ¾ inch in diameter, are in clusters of four to eight. Differing in having elliptic leaves about three times as long as they are wide, *C. australis*

Chamaebatia australis

Chamaebatia australis (flowers)

is from 2 to more than 6 feet high and has smaller flowers than *C. foliolosa*.

Garden and Landscape Uses and Cultivation. In warm, dryish climates these plants are adapted for rock gardens and shrub borders. They need full sun and well-drained soil. Propagation is by seeds sown in spring and by cuttings made of firm, but not hard shoots in summer.

CHAMAEBATIARIA (Chamae-batiària). The only species of this genus of the rose family ROSACEAE inhabits dryish soils from Idaho and Nevada to Arizona and California. It is nearly related to *Spiraea*. Its name alludes to its likeness to *Chamaebatia*. Up to 6 feet tall, *Chamaebatiaria millefolium* is an aromatic, deciduous, erect, densely-branched, pubescent shrub with alternate, twice-pinnately-divided, short-stalked leaves, ovate-oblong in outline, 1 inch to 3 inches long, and divided into numerous tiny segments. Its white flowers, in terminal, leafy panicles about 6 inches long, are about ½ inch across. They have five rounded, erect petals and numerous stamens. There are five pistils. The fruits are dry and technically follicles.

Of minor horticultural importance, this shrub is hardy in southern New England. It is most likely to be cultivated in botanical collections and, in its native range, in collections of wild plants. For its successful growth it needs full sun and well-drained soil. It is increased by seeds sown in spring and by cuttings of firm leafy shoots in summer.